CONTRACTS: CASES AND THEORY OF CONTRACTUAL OBLIGATION

Preface

1. This book is designed for a 5-6 credit class. Those teaching a Contracts course with fewer than 5 credits should contact one of the authors for suggestions on what materials to omit. Two syllabi are to be found following the Table of Contents.

Syllabus A is laid out for a 6 credit Contracts course meeting 50 minutes 3 times a week for both semesters of the first year. A 5 credit course would require minor changes, including the probable omission of Chapter 10. (Few instructors manage to cover the materials on third party beneficiaries and assignment.) The syllabus assumes a thirteen week semester of teaching, leaving one additional week for review, practice exams, etc.

Syllabus B is laid out for a 6 credit Contracts course meeting 1 hour and 15 minutes 2 times a week for both semesters of the first year. A 5 credit course would require similar minor changes. Again, this syllabus assumes a thirteen week semester of teaching, leaving one additional week for review, practice exams, etc.

2. Pedagogical approach used. This book focuses on teaching analytical and reasoning skills while covering the rules of contract law. To free classroom discussion from overly doctrinal lecturing and to facilitate a more intensive analytical and critical approach, this book introduces students to the social development of the common law generally and to particular issues specifically. Each casebook section is introduced with heavily researched contract theory drawn from both the First and Second Restatements, legal history, and debate as developed through the scholarly literature. This background material is designed to "tee up" the issues then dealt with by the opinion(s) in the case that follows. Instead of "hiding the ball," this technique "identifies the ball" before proceeding with how the game is played. The numerous notes and questions following each case are designed to further exercise and develop the student's analytical skills and critical understanding of the reasoning of the case, both explicit and implicit. They are also designed to develop related doctrine. In general, unlike many casebooks, the notes are not used to annotate other case decisions dealing with the same or similar issues. In teaching with these materials, we always have two questions in the background: how might this litigation have been avoided; and how might this case have been better presented and argued.

3. Coverage. This book covers the topics conventionally included in a Contracts casebook. The coverage includes basic UCC Article 2 issues and facilitates a comparison and contrast with common law outcomes. We alert students that we do not attempt to provide the detailed UCC coverage they will get in a second or third year Sales course. We include new issues brought about by the Internet and related technologies. We also include materials introducing students to the Convention on the International Sale of Goods, emphasizing those situations in which the CISG may trump UCC Article 2 in United States courts.

4. **These materials are classroom tested.** We have tested this casebook approach for years in our respective classrooms and find that it produces more effective student learning outcomes than the traditional approach.

5. **Aids useful for professors adopting this book.** The casebook itself, reviewing and positioning the breadth of sometimes divergent scholarship, provides a summary reading background for the professor as well as the student. The **Teachers Manual** that is available for the professor is designed to greatly reduce the time and effort required to prepare for and teach the course. It includes:

- Briefs of every case included in the book;
- Answers to every question posed in the Notes following the cases;
- An "Interesting Discussion Issues" section following most cases and suggesting ways of opening up class discussion of the case.

A digital set of PowerPoint Slides providing focus questions for each segment of the book is obtainable on request from the authors. These questions are designed to help direct student reading and analysis of the case, as well as opening up class discussion. The digital format will facilitate posting these PowerPoint slides on TWEN or BLACKBOARD.

6. **A Supplement specially designed to mesh with citations in the Casebook and Teachers Manual.** This Supplement is unique in including a number of sections of the Restatement (First) of Contracts, as well as the Restatement (Second) of Contracts. It also includes relevant provisions of the UCC Articles 1 and 2, the Convention on the International Sale of Goods, the Federal Arbitration Act, and the civil law-based 1999 Chinese contracts code.

7. **The first chapter of the Casebook.** The Chapter 1 material is designed to facilitate a number of pedagogical approaches to the first contracts class session. This material covers: (1) a basic exploration of the debate over appropriate levels of private autonomy versus state intervention in ostensibly private orderings, (2) an overview of several major schools of American jurisprudence and their relationship to contract law, and (3) a survey of the principal sources of contract law covered in this course. Approaches to this material vary widely --- one of the authors spends between one and two class sessions on the first two topics alone, while others find it useful to assign this material for reading before the semester begins. Regardless of the approach adopted, the material in this chapter is straightforward and self explanatory, and the detailed Teachers Manual explication begins with Chapter 2.

TEACHER'S MANUAL
to accompany
CONTRACTS
CASES AND THEORY OF CONTRACTUAL OBLIGATION

By

James F. Hogg
Professor of Law
William Mitchell College of Law

Carter G. Bishop
Professor of Law
Suffolk University Law School

Daniel D. Barnhizer
Associate Professor of Law
Michigan State University College of Law

AMERICAN CASEBOOK SERIES®

THOMSON
™
WEST

Mat #40498046

610 Opperman Drive
St. Paul, MN 55123
1–800–313–9378

Printed in the United States of America

ISBN: 978–0–314–16933–4

TEXT IS PRINTED ON 10% POST CONSUMER RECYCLED PAPER

CONTRACTS: CASES AND THEORY OF CONTRACTUAL OBLIGATION

Table of Contents

CHAPTER 4 – THE SCOPE OF CONTRACTUAL OBLIGATIONS

CHAPTER 7 – CONTRACTS UNENFORCEABLE BY LATER EVENTS: DISCHARGE OF FUTURE DUTIES ABSENT A BREACH

CHAPTER 8 – WHEN AN ENFORCEABLE PROMISE BECOMES DUE: BREACH OF PROMISE AND CONDITIONS

CHAPTER 9 – REMEDIES FOR BREACH OF CONTRACT

CHAPTER 10 – RIGHTS AND DUTIES OF PERSONS NOT ACTUAL PARTIES TO THE CONTRACT

SUGGESTED SYLLABUS A

NOTE:

This syllabus is laid out for a 6 credit Contracts course meeting 50 minutes 3 times a week for both semesters of the first year. A 5 credit course would require minor change including the probable omission of Chapter 10 (few instructors manage to cover the materials on third party beneficiaries and assignment). The syllabus assumes a 13 week semester of teaching leaving 1 additional week for review, practice exams, etc.

Class 1

Reading: Chapter 1

Topics:

Introduction to contract law with a focus on the tension between private autonomy and freedom of contract.

Introduction to contract jurisprudence.

Classes 2 & 3

Reading: Chapter 2A

Topics:

The nature of promising—commitments.

King v. Trustees of Boston University (distinguishing promises from other statements of intent or opinion)

Class 4

Reading: Chapter 2B.

Topics:

Understanding contractual intent—the objective theory of contracts.

Lucy v. Zehmer (joke promises and the objective theory of contract)

Class 5

Reading: Chapter 2C(1)(a)

Topics:

Enforcing promises—legal theories of obligation.

Dougherty v. Salt (consideration and the unenforceability of donative promises)

Class 6

Reading: Chapter 2C(1)(b)

Topics:

Enforcing promises—legal theories of obligation.

Consideration.

Hamer v. Sidway (bargain theory of consideration)

Batsakis v. Demotsis (bargain theory of consideration—inadequacy versus failure of consideration)

Classes 7 & 8

Reading: Chapter 2C(1)(c) & (d) & 2C(2)(a)

Topics:

Enforcing promises—legal theories of obligation.

Consideration.

Hayes v. Plantation Steel Company (past consideration)

Kirksey v. Kirksey (gratuitous conditional promises)

Obligation by reason of reliance—the promissory estoppel doctrine.

Ricketts v. Scothorn (detrimental reliance on non-commercial promises)

Introduction to Hohfeldian jural relations.

Class 9

Reading: Chapter 2(C)(2)(a) & (b)

Topics:

Obligation by reason of reliance—the promissory estoppel doctrine.

Wright v. Newman (detrimental reliance on non-commercial promises)

Contract and family law—detrimental reliance in the family context.

Class 10

Reading: Chapter 2(C)(2) (c) & (d)

Topics:

Charitable subscriptions.

Allegheny College v. National Chautauqua County Bank (enforceability of charitable subscriptions under promissory estoppel)

Obligation by reason of reliance—the promissory estoppel doctrine.

Barker v. CTC Sales Corporation (promissory estoppel in the context of commercial promises)

Class 11

Reading: Chapter 2(C)(2)(d) & 2(C)(3)

Topics:

Obligation by reason of reliance—the promissory estoppel doctrine.

Cohen (promissory estoppel in the context of commercial promises)

Obligation by reason of unjust enrichment—the restitution doctrine.

Bloomgarden (requirement that party seeking restitution not be a volunteer or officious intermeddler)

Class 12

Reading: Chapter 2C(4)

Topics:

Obligation by reason of a promise for benefit received – the promissory restitution doctrine.

Mills v. Wyman (promissory restitution)

Webb v. McGowin (promissory restitution)

Class 13

Reading: Chapter 3A

Topics:

Reaching agreement through offer and acceptance—mutual misunderstanding and objectification.

Raffles v. Wichelhaus (offer and acceptance, mutual failure to agree, misunderstanding)

Class 14

Reading: Chapter 3B(1) & (2)

Topics:

Reaching agreement through offer and acceptance—the theory of offer and acceptance.

Owen v. Tunison (requirement of a definite offer)

International Filter Co. v. Conroe Gin, Ice & Light Co. (exercising the power of acceptance, acceptance as a condition on formation of the contract)

Class 15

Reading: Chapter 3B(3)

Topics:

The mailbox rule.

Acceptance by silence.

Day v. Caton (acceptance by silence)

Class 16

Reading: Chapter 3B(4)

Topics:

Contracts of adhesion.

Carnival Cruise Lines v. Shute (enforceability of adhesion contracts)

Classes 17 & 18

Reading: Chapter 3C(1) and (2)

Topics:

Termination of the power of acceptance—termination by offeror's revocation.

Dickinson v. Dodds (effect of notice of revocation of offer prior to acceptance)

Termination of the power of acceptance—termination by offeree rejection or counteroffer.

Step-Saver Data Systems v. Wyse (battle of the forms / UCC § 2-207)

Filanto, S.P.A. v. Chilewich Int'l (conflicting forms under the Convention on Contracts for the International Sale of Goods)

Class 19

Reading: Chapter 3C(3) & 3D(1)

Topics:

Termination of the power of acceptance—termination by death or incapacity.

Effect of pre-acceptance reliance.

Unilateral contracts.

Petterson v. Pattberg (full performance as a condition of acceptance, effect of revocation of offer in the context of imperfect performance)

Davis v. Jacoby (distinguishing unilateral and bilateral contracts, effects of express acceptance versus effects of acts constituting acceptance)

Class 20

Reading: Chapter 3D(2)

Topics:

Effect of pre-acceptance reliance.

Bilateral contracts.

James Baird Co. v. Gimbel Bros. (pre-acceptance reliance in the context of commercial bids)

Drennan v. Star Paving Co. (pre-acceptance reliance in the context of commercial bids)

Class 21

Reading: Chapter 3D(2) & (3)

Topics:

Bilateral contracts continued.

Berryman v. Kmoch (requirement of definiteness of detrimental reliance)

Effect of pre-offer reliance on negotiations.

Pop's Cones, Inc. v. Resorts Int'l Hotel, Inc. (detrimental reliance on promises and representations made during negotiations)

Class 22

Reading: Chapter 3D(4)

Topics:

Pre-contractual agreements.

Empro Mfg. Co., Inc. v. Bal-Co Mfg., Inc. (enforceability of letters of intent)

Classes 23 & 24

Reading: Chapter 3E

Topics:

Electronic contracting.

Hill v. Gateway2000, Inc. (enforceability of shrink-wrap & click-wrap contract terms)

Klocek v. Gateway, Inc. (enforc eability of shrink-wrap & click-wrap contract terms)

Class 25

Reading: Chapter 4A(1)

Topics:

Identifying the terms of a written agreement—the parol evidence rule.

Integration and collateral agreements.

Thompson v. Libby (collateral agreements)

Mitchell v. Lath (collateral agreements)

Class 26

Reading: Chapter 4A(1)

Topics:

Identifying the terms of a written agreement—the parol evidence rule.

Integration and collateral agreements.

Masterson v. Sine (modern test for integration and enforceability of collateral agreements)

MCC-Marble Ceramic Center, Inc. v. Ceramica Nuova D'Agostino, S.P.A. (parol evidence in transnational contracting)

Class 27

Reading: Chapter 4A(2)

Topics:

Effect of a merger and integration clause.

Lee v. Joseph E. Seagram & Sons, Inc. (admission of parol evidence in the face of parties' failure to include merger clause in agreement)

The parol evidence rule and the valid contract requirement.

Danann Realty Corp. v. Harris (use of merger clause to bar admission of evidence of fraud)

Class 28

Reading: Chapter 4B

Topics:

Interpreting the terms of the agreement.

Pacific Gas & Electric Co. v. G.W. Thomas Drayage & Rigging Co. (admission of parol evidence provisionally to determine existence of ambiguity versus admission of parol evidence to interpret meaning of ambiguous document)

Frigaliment Importing Co. v. B.N.S. Int'l Sales Corp. (sources of meaning and methods of interpreting ambiguous terms)

Class 29

Reading: Chapter 4C(1)

Topics:

Supplementing the agreement with implied terms—terms implied under the common law.

Wood v. Lucy, Lady Duff-Gordon (implication of best or reasonable efforts term)

City of Yonkers v. Otis Elevator Co. (implication of best or reasonable efforts terms)

Classes 30 & 31

Reading: Chapter 4C(2)

Topics:

Supplementing the agreement with implied terms—caveat emptor and warranties.

Keith v. Buchannan (express and implied warranties in sale of goods)

Consolidated Data Terminals v. Applied Digital Data Sys., Inc. (warranty disclaimers)

Class 32
Reading: Chapter 4D
Topics:
Insurance contracts—reasonable expectations doctrine and contra proferentem.
Wilkie v. Auto-Owners Ins. Co. (reasonable expectations & interpretation under neoformalist principles)

Class 33
Reading: Chapter 4E
Topics:
Implied obligation of good faith.
Locke v. Warner Bros., Inc. (implied duty of good faith and fair dealing)

Class 34
Reading: Chapter 4F
Topics:
Course of dealing, trade usage, course of performance.
Nanakuli Paving and Rock Co. v. Shell Oil Co. (establishing trade usage, interpretation through course of dealing and course of performance)

Class 35
Reading: Chapter 4G
Topics:
Employment contracts.
Dufner v. American College of Physicians (at-will employment)

Class 36
Reading: Chapter 5A & B(1)
Topics:
Distinction between void and voidable contracts.
Buckeye Check Cashing, Inc. v. Cardegna (distinction between void and voidable contracts in context of arbitration clause)
Public policy doctrine—illegal contracts.
Anheuser-Busch Brewing Ass'n v. Mason (public policy doctrine in context of contracts used in illegal business)

Class 37
Reading: Chapter 5B(2)
Topics:
Public policy doctrine—contracts in contravention of public policy.
Hewitt v. Hewitt (common law marriage, implied contracts of support)

Class 38
Reading: Chapter 5B(3)
Topics:
Public policy doctrine—covenants not to compete in employment contracts.
American Broadcasting Cos. v. Wolf (interpretation of covenant not to compete, public policy in employment contracts)

Class 39
Reading: Chapter 5B(3)
Topics:
Public policy doctrine—covenants not to compete in employment contracts.
White v. Fletcher/Mayo/Assocs. (interpretation of covenant not to compete, public policy in employment contracts)

Class 40
Reading: Chapter 5C(1,)
Topics:
Unconscionability.
Williams v. Walker-Thomas Furniture Co. (development of doctrine of unconscionability)

Class 41
Reading: Chapter 5C(2)
Topics:
Elements of unconscionability.
Stirlen v. Supercuts, Inc. (procedural and substantive elements of unconscionability)

Classes 42 & 43

Reading: Chapter 5D(1) & (2)

Topics:

Statute of Frauds—is the contract within the statute?

Coan v. Orsinger (contract not to be performed within one year of the making thereof)

Statute of Frauds—satisfying the writing requirement.

Crabtree v. Elizabeth Arden Sales Corp. (multiple memoranda offered in satisfaction of statute of frauds)

Class 44

Reading: Chapter 5D(3) & (4)

Topics:

Excusing noncompliance with the Statute of Frauds.

McIntosh v. Murphy (enforceability of oral agreement upon which promisee detrimentally relied)

Merchant's exception to the Statute of Frauds.

Bazak Intern. Corp. v. Mast Indus., Inc. (UCC § 2-201(2))

Class 45

Reading: Chapter 6A, B & C

Topics:

Contracts unenforceable by election—regulating the agreement process.

Election of remedies—preclusion by affirmation of a voidable contract.

Election of remedies—preclusion by election of remedies.

Lack of legal capacity of one of the parties.

Contracts with minors.

Halbman v. Lemke (restitution for damage to goods sold through contract with minor)

Lack of legal capacity of one of the parties.

Mental incapacity.

Ortelere v. Teachers' Retirement Bd. (incapacity as inability to comprehend versus inability to act in reasonable manner)

Contracts affected by relationship of trust and confidence.

Classes 46 & 47

Reading: Chapter 6C(1)

Topics:

Abuse of the bargaining process by one of the parties to the contract.

Intentional and negligent misrepresentation.

Hill v. Jones (misrepresentation and the duty to disclose)

Enhance-It, LLC v. American Access Technologies, Inc. (misrepresentation and duty to disclose, economic loss rule, election of remedies)

Class 48

Reading: Chapter 6C(2) & (3)

Topics:

Abuse of the bargaining process by one of the parties to the contract.

Duress.

Totem Marine Tug & Barge, Inc. v. Alyeska Pipeline Service Co. (economic duress)

Abuse of the bargaining process by one of the parties to the contract.

Undue influence.

Odorizzi v. Bloomfield School Dist. (undue influence)

Classes 49 & 50

Reading: Chapter 6D(1) & (2)

Topics:

Failure of the bargaining process.

Mutual mistake.

Sherwood v. Walker (essence of the bargain test for mutual mistake)

Lenaweee County Board of Health v. Messerly (mistaken belief relating to a basic assumption of the parties test for mutual mistake)

Unilateral mistake.

Cummings v. Dusenbury (unilateral mistake and the requirement that the mistaken party have exercised reasonable care)

Classes 51 & 52
Reading: Chapter 7A & B
Topics:
Contracts unenforceable by later events—history of impossibility doctrine.
Contracts unenforceable by later events—modern impossibility, impracticability, and frustration of purpose.
Transatlantic Financing Corp. (impossibility versus increased difficulty of performance)
Mel Frank Tool & Supply, Inc. v. Di-Chem Co. (impossibility and frustration of purpose by reason of supervening legislative act)

Class 53
Reading: Chapter 7C(1)
Topics:
Contracts unenforceable by later events—discharge of duties by assent or modification.
Pre-existing legal duty rule.
Angel v. Murray (attempted modifications for increased costs of performance in context of service contract)

Class 54
Reading: Chapter 7C(1)
Topics:
Agreed resolution of disputes—accord and satisfaction.
Clark v. Elza (oral settlement agreement as defense against reopening original cause of action)
Dispute resolution under duress.
Kelsey-Hayes Co. v. Galtaco Redlaw Castings Corp. (economic duress in context of contract modifications)

Class 55
Reading: Chapter 7C(2)
Topics:
Effect of writing restricting oral modification—"No Oral Modification" clauses.
Wisconsin Knife Works v. National Metal Crafters (enforceability of no-oral-modification clause)

Class 56
Reading: Chapter 8A
Topics:
Breach of promise and non-satisfaction of conditions.
Anticipatory repudiation.
Truman L. Flatt & Sons Co. v. Schupf (requirement of definiteness for anticipatory repudiation)

Class 57

Reading: Chapter 8B(1)

Topics:

Conditional promises—express conditions.

Oppenheimer & Co. v. Oppenheim, Appel, Dixon & Co. (interpretation and application of express conditions)

Class 58

Reading: Chapter 8B(2)

Topics:

Conditional promises—ordering of performances.

El Dorado Hotel Properties, Ltd. v. Mortensen (use of conditions to render parties' performances dependent, independent, or simultaneous)

Classes 59 & 60

Reading: Chapter 8B(3) & (4)

Topics:

Conditional promises—constructive conditions.

Jacob & Youngs v. Kent (constructive condition of substantial performance)

Conditional promises—relief from conditions.

Holiday Inns of America, Inc. v. Knight (excuse, waiver, and other relief from conditions)

Class 61

Reading: Chapter 9A & B

Topics:

Remedies for breach of contract.

Introduction to damages interest.

Election of remedies for breach.

Election to seek rescission and restitution off the contract.

United States v. Algernon Blair, Inc. (recoverability of restitution damages in excess of contract price in context of total breach of contract)

Class 62

Reading: Chapter 9C(1) & (2)

Topics:

Election to seek damages on the contract—expectancy damages.

Hawkins v. McGee (difference in value measure)

Class 63
Reading: Chapter 9C(2)
Topics:
Election to seek damages on the contract—expectancy damages.
American Standard, Inc. v. Schectman (cost of repair or completion measure)

Class 64
Reading: Chapter 9C(3)
Topics:
Election to seek damages on the contract—reliance damages.
Walser v. Toyota Motor Sales, U.S.A., Inc. (availability of reliance measure as alternative to expectancy damages)

Classes 65 & 66
Reading: Chapter 9C(3)
Topics:
Limitations on expectancy and reliance interests—foreseeability.
Hadley v. Baxendale (foreseeability of general and special damages)
Florafax Int'l, Inc. v. GTE Market Resources, Inc. (foreseeability of general and special damages)

Classes 67 & 68
Reading: Chapter 9C(3)
Topics:
Limitation on expectancy and reliance interests—mitigation.
Rockingham County v. Luten Bridge Co. (avoidability of losses after notice of breach)
Parker v. Twentieth Century Fox-Film Corp. (mitigation in the context of employment contracts)

Class 69
Reading: Chapter 9C(3)
Topics:
Limitation on expectancy and reliance interests—certainty.
A-S Development, Inc. (certainty and expert models for assessing damages)

Class 70
Reading: Chapter 9D
Topics:
Equitable remedies—requirement of no adequate remedy at law.
Sedmak v. Charlie's Chevrolet, Inc. (propriety of specific performance in sale of goods contract)
Equitable remedies—personal services contracts.
Lumley v. Wagner (negative injunctions to enforce personal services contracts)

Class 71
Reading: Chapter 9E(1) & (2)
Topics:
Remedies specified by contract.
Adams Co. v. City of Denver (enforceability of liquidated damages clause)
Modification or restriction of remedies by contract.
Schrier v. Beltway Alarm Co. (enforceability of exculpation clause)

Class 72
Reading: Chapter 9E(2)
Topics:
Remedies specified or modified by contract—failure of essential purpose.
Cayuga Harvester, Inc. v. Allis-Chalmers Corp. (UCC § 2-719 and failure of essential purpose of remedy provisions)

Class 73
Reading: Chapter 9F(1)
Topics:
UCC buyer and seller remedies—buyer remedies.
Perfect tender rule.
Monetary damages for breach.
Dangerfield v. Markel (determining damages when buyer covers through multiple market purchases over significant period)

Class 74
Reading: Chapter 9F(2)
Topics:
UCC buyer and seller remedies—seller remedies.
UCC § 2-708 and the lost volume seller rule.
R.E. Davis Chem. Corp. v. Diasonics, Inc. (seller's damages for breach by the buyer, lost volume seller rule)

SUGGESTED SYLLABUS B

NOTE:

This syllabus is laid out for a 6 credit Contracts course meeting 1 hour and 15 minutes 2 times a week for both semesters of the first year. A 5 credit course would require minor change including the probable omission of Chapter 10 (few instructors manage to cover the materials on third party beneficiaries and assignment). The syllabus assumes a 13 week semester of teaching leaving 1additional week for review, practice exams etc.

Class 1

Reading: Chapter 1

Topics:

Introduction to contract law with a focus on the tension between private autonomy and freedom of contract.

Introduction to contract jurisprudence.

Class 2

Reading: Chapter 2A

Topics:

The nature of promising—commitments.

King v. Trustees of Boston University (distinguishing promises from other statements of intent or opinion)

Class 3

Reading: Chapter 2B & C(1)

Topics:

Understanding contractual intent—the objective theory of contracts.

Lucy v. Zehmer (joke promises and the objective theory of contract)

Enforcing promises—legal theories of obligation.

Dougherty v. Salt (consideration and the unenforceability of donative promises)

Class 4

Reading: Chapter 2C(1)

Topics:

Enforcing promises—legal theories of obligation.

Consideration.

Hamer v. Sidway (bargain theory of consideration)

Batsakis v. Demotsis (bargain theory of consideration—inadequacy versus failure of consideration)

Class 5

Reading: Chapter 2C(1) & C(2)

Topics:

Enforcing promises—legal theories of obligation.

Consideration.

Hayes v. Plantation Steel Company (past consideration)

Kirksey v. Kirksey (gratuitous conditional promises)

Obligation by reason of reliance—the promissory estoppel doctrine.

Ricketts v. Scothorn (detrimental reliance on non-commercial promises)

Introduction to Hohfeldian jural relations.

Class 6

Reading: Chapter 2C(2)

Topics:

Obligation by reason of reliance – the promissory estoppel doctrine.

Wright v. Newman (detrimental reliance on non-commercial promises)

Contract and family law—detrimental reliance in the family context.

Charitable subscriptions.

Allegheny College v. National Chautauqua County Bank (enforceability of charitable subscriptions under promissory estoppel)

Class 7

Reading: Chapter 2C(2) & C(3)

Topics:

Obligation by reason of reliance – the promissory estoppel doctrine.

Barker v. CTC Sales Corporation (promissory estoppel in the context of commercial promises)

Cohen (promissory estoppel in the context of commercial promises)

Obligation by reason of unjust enrichment – the restitution doctrine.

Bloomgarden (requirement that party seeking restitution not be a volunteer or officious intermeddler)

Class 8

Reading: Chapter 2C(4) & Chapter 3A

Topics:

Obligation by reason of a promise for benefit received – the promissory restitution doctrine.

Mills v. Wyman (promissory restitution)

Webb v. McGowin (promissory restitution)

Reaching agreement through offer and acceptance—mutual misunderstanding and objectification.

Raffles v. Wichelhaus (offer and acceptance, mutual failure to agree, misunderstanding)

Note:

Many instructors require a full class to analyze the promissory restitution materials and a full class to cover *Raffles*. Despite the brevity of the readings for these cases, it may be necessary to split these readings.

Class 9

Reading: Chapter 3B(1), B(2) & B(3)

Topics:

Reaching agreement through offer and acceptance—the theory of offer and acceptance.

Owen v. Tunison (requirement of a definite offer)

International Filter Co. v. Conroe Gin, Ice & Light Co. (exercising the power of acceptance, acceptance as a condition on formation of the contract)

The mailbox rule.

Class 10
Reading: Chapter 3B(4) & B(5)
Topics:
Acceptance by silence.
Day v. Caton (acceptance by silence)
Contracts of adhesion
Carnival Cruise Lines v. Shute (enforceability of adhesion contracts)

Classes 11 & 12
Reading: Chapter 3C(1) & C(2)
Topics:
Termination of the power of acceptance—termination by offeror's revocation.
Dickinson v. Dodds (effect of notice of revocation of offer prior to acceptance)
Termination of the power of acceptance—termination by offeree rejection or counteroffer.
Step-Saver Data Systems v. Wyse (battle of the forms / UCC § 2-207)
Filanto, S.P.A. v. Chilewich Int'l (conflicting forms under the Convention on Contracts for the International Sale of Goods)
Note:
This is a lengthy reading, but difficult to split up because of the long *Step-Saver* case. The instructor may wish to have students begin with *Filanto*, which provides a nice comparative study for the American battle of the forms discussion in *Step-Saver*. Alternatively, it is possible to cover *Dickinson* relatively quickly and combine it in a class with *Step-Saver* and then carry the *Step-Saver* discussion over, followed by a brief discussion of the international rule. Alternatively, the instructor may wish to not assign *Filanto* and treat *Dickinson* and *Step-Saver* in separate classes, with additional practice problems, or catch-up taking the remainder of the time.

Class 13

Reading: Chapter 3C(3) & D(1)

Topics:

Termination of the power of acceptance—termination by death or incapacity.

Effect of pre-acceptance reliance.

Unilateral contracts.

Petterson v. Pattberg (full performance as a condition of acceptance, effect of revocation of offer in the context of imperfect performance)

Davis v. Jacoby (distinguishing unilateral and bilateral contracts, effects of express acceptance versus effects of acts constituting acceptance)

Class 14

Reading: Chapter 3D(2)

Topics:

Effect of pre-acceptance reliance.

Bilateral contracts.

James Baird Co. v. Gimbel Bros. (pre-acceptance reliance in the context of commercial bids)

Drennan v. Star Paving Co. (pre-acceptance reliance in the context of commercial bids)

Berryman v. Kmoch (requirement of definiteness of detrimental reliance)

Class 15

Reading: Chapter 3D(3)

Topics:

Effect of pre-offer reliance on negotiations.

Pop's Cones, Inc. v. Resorts Int'l Hotel, Inc. (detrimental reliance on promises and representations made during negotiations)

Empro Mfg. Co., Inc. v. Bal-Co Mfg., Inc. (enforceability of letters of intent)

Class 16

Reading: Chapter 3E

Topics:

Electronic contracting.

Hill v. Gateway2000, Inc. (enforceability of shrink-wrap & click-wrap contract terms)

Klocek v. Gateway, Inc. (enforc eability of shrink-wrap & click-wrap contract terms)

Class 17
Reading: Chapter 4A(1)
Topics:
Identifying the terms of a written agreement—the parol evidence rule.
Integration and collateral agreements.
Thompson v. Libby (collateral agreements)
Mitchell v. Lath (collateral agreements)

Class 18
Reading: Chapter 4A(1)
Topics:
Identifying the terms of a written agreement—the parol evidence rule.
Integration and collateral agreements.
Masterson v. Sine (modern test for integration and enforceability of collateral agreements)
MCC-Marble Ceramic Center, Inc. v. Ceramica Nuova D'Agostino, S.p.A. (parol evidence in transnational contracting)

Class 19
Reading: Chapter 4A(2)
Topics:
Effect of a merger and integration clause.
Lee v. Joseph E. Seagram & Sons, Inc. (admission of parol evidence in the face of parties' failure to include merger clause in agreement)
The parol evidence rule and the valid contract requirement.
Danann Realty Corp. v. Harris (use of merger clause to bar admission of evidence of fraud)

Class 20
Reading: Chapter 4B
Topics:
Interpreting the terms of the agreement.
Pacific Gas & Electric Co. v. G.W. Thomas Drayage & Rigging Co. (admission of parol evidence provisionally to determine existence of ambiguity versus admission of parol evidence to interpret meaning of ambiguous document)
Frigaliment Importing Co. v. B.N.S. Int'l Sales Corp. (sources of meaning and methods of interpreting ambiguous terms)

Class 30
Reading: Chapter 5C(1) & C(2)
Topics:
Unconscionability
Williams v. Walker-Thomas Furniture Co. (development of doctrine of unconscionability)
Stirlen v. Supercuts, Inc. (procedural and substantive elements of unconscionability)

Class 31
Reading: Chapter 5D(1) & D(2)
Topics:
Statute of Frauds—is the contract within the statute?
Coan v. Orsinger (contract not to be performed within one year of the making thereof)
Statute of Frauds—satisfying the writing requirement.
Crabtree v. Elizabeth Arden Sales Corp. (multiple memoranda offered in satisfaction of statute of frauds)

Class 32
Reading: Chapter 5D(3) & D(4)
Topics:
Excusing noncompliance with the Statute of Frauds.
McIntosh v. Murphy (enforceability of oral agreement upon which promisee detrimentally relied)
Merchant's exception to the Statute of Frauds.
Bazak Intern. Corp. v. Mast Indus., Inc. (UCC § 2-201(2))

Class 33
Reading: Chapter 6A & B(1)
Topics:
Contracts unenforceable by election—regulating the agreement process.
Election of remedies—preclusion by affirmation of a voidable contract.
Election of remedies—preclusion by election of remedies.
Lack of legal capacity of one of the parties.
Contracts with minors.
Halbman v. Lemke (restitution for damage to goods sold through contract with minor)

Class 34
Reading: Chapter 6B(2) & B(3)
Topics:
Lack of legal capacity of one of the parties.
Mental incapacity.
Ortelere v. Teachers' Retirement Bd. (incapacity as inability to comprehend versus inability to act in reasonable manner)
Contracts affected by relationship of trust and confidence.

Class 35
Reading: Chapter 6C(1)
Topics:
Abuse of the bargaining process by one of the parties to the contract.
Intentional and negligent misrepresentation.
Hill v. Jones (misrepresentation and the duty to disclose)
Enhance-It, LLC v. American Access Technologies, Inc. (misrepresentation and duty to disclose, economic loss rule, election of remedies)

Class 36
Reading: Chapter 6C(2)
Topics:
Abuse of the bargaining process by one of the parties to the contract.
Duress.
Totem Marine Tug & Barge, Inc. v. Alyeska Pipeline Service Co. (economic duress)

Class 37
Reading: Chapter 6C(3) & D(1)
Topics:
Abuse of the bargaining process by one of the parties to the contract.
Undue influence.
Odorizzi v. Bloomfield School Dist. (undue influence)
Failure of the bargaining process.
Mutual mistake.
Sherwood v. Walker (essence of the bargain test for mutual mistake)

Class 38
Reading: Chapter 6D(1) & D(2)
Topics:
Failure of the bargaining process.
Mutual mistake.
Lenaweee County Board of Health v. Messerly (mistaken belief relating to a basic assumption of the parties test for mutual mistake)
Unilateral mistake.
Cummings v. Dusenbury (unilateral mistake and the requirement that the mistaken party have exercised reasonable care)

Class 39
Reading: Chapter 7A & B
Topics:
Contracts unenforceable by later events—history of impossibility doctrine.
Contracts unenforceable by later events—modern impossibility, impracticability, and frustration of purpose.
Transatlantic Financing Corp. (impossibility versus increased difficulty of performance)
Mel Frank Tool & Supply, Inc. v. Di-Chem Co. (impossibility and frustration of purpose by reason of supervening legislative act)

Class 40
Reading: Chapter 7C(1)
Topics:
Contracts unenforceable by later events—discharge of duties by assent or modification.
Pre-existing legal duty rule.
Angel v. Murray (attempted modifications for increased costs of performance in context of service contract)

Class 41
Reading: Chapter 7C(1)
Topics:
Agreed resolution of disputes—accord and satisfaction.
Clark v. Elza (oral settlement agreement as defense against reopening original cause of action)
Dispute resolution under duress.
Kelsey-Hayes Co. v. Galtaco Redlaw Castings Corp. (economic duress in context of contract modifications)

Class 42
Reading: Chapter 7C(2)
Topics:
Effect of writing restricting oral modification—"No Oral Modification" clauses.
Wisconsin Knife Works v. National Metal Crafters (enforceability of no-oral-modification clause)

Class 43
Reading: Chapter 8A
Topics:
Breach of promise and non-satisfaction of conditions.
Anticipatory repudiation.
Truman L. Flatt & Sons Co. v. Schupf (requirement of definiteness for anticipatory repudiation)

Class 44
Reading: Chapter 8B(1) & B(2)
Topics:
Conditional promises—express conditions.
Oppenheimer & Co. v. Oppenheim, Appel, Dixon & Co. (interpretation and application of express conditions)
Conditional promises—ordering of performances.
El Dorado Hotel Properties, Ltd. v. Mortensen (use of conditions to render parties' performances dependent, independent, or simultaneous)

Class 45
Reading: Chapter 8B(3), B(4) & 9A
Topics:
Conditional promises—constructive conditions.
Jacob & Youngs v. Kent (constructive condition of substantial performance)
Conditional promises—relief from conditions.
Holiday Inns of America, Inc. v. Knight (excuse, waiver, and other relief from conditions)
Remedies for breach of contract.
Introduction to damages interest.
Election of remedies for breach.

Class 46

Reading: Chapter 9B & 9C(1)

Topics:

Remedies for breach of contract.

Election to seek rescission and restitution off the contract.

United States v. Algernon Blair, Inc. (recoverability of restitution damages in excess of contract price in context of total breach of contract)

Election to seek damages on the contract—expectancy damages.

Hawkins v. McGee (difference in value measure)

Class 47

Reading: Chapter 9C(1) & C(2)

Topics:

Election to seek damages on the contract—expectancy damages.

American Standard, Inc. v. Schectman (cost of repair or completion measure)

Election to seek damages on the contract—reliance damages.

Walser v. Toyota Motor Sales, U.S.A., Inc. (availability of reliance measure as alternative to expectancy damages)

Class 48

Reading: Chapter 9C(3)

Topics:

Limitations on expectancy and reliance interests—foreseeability.

Hadley v. Baxendale (foreseeability of general and special damages)

Florafax Int'l, Inc. v. GTE Market Resources, Inc. (foreseeability of general and special damages)

Class 49

Reading: Chapter 9C(3)

Topics:

Limitation on expectancy and reliance interests—mitigation.

Rockingham County v. Luten Bridge Co. (avoidability of losses after notice of breach)

Parker v. Twentieth Century Fox-Film Corp. (mitigation in the context of employment contracts)

Limitation on expectancy and reliance interests—certainty.

A-S Development, Inc. (certainty and expert models for assessing damages)

Class 50
Reading: Chapter 9D
Topics:
Equitable remedies—requirement of no adequate remedy at law.
Sedmak v. Charlie's Chevrolet, Inc. (propriety of specific performance in sale of goods contract)
Equitable remedies—personal services contracts.
Lumley v. Wagner (negative injunctions to enforce personal services contracts)

Class 51
Reading: Chapter 9E(1) & E(2)
Topics:
Remedies specified by contract.
Adams Co. v. City of Denver (enforceability of liquidated damages clause)
Modification or restriction of remedies by contract.
Schrier v. Beltway Alarm Co. (enforceability of exculpation clause)

Class 52
Reading: Chapter 9E(2)
Topics:
Remedies specified or modified by contract—failure of essential purpose.
Cayuga Harvester, Inc. v. Allis-Chalmers Corp. (UCC § 2-719 and failure of essential purpose of remedy provisions)

Class 53
Reading: Chapter 9F(1) & F(2)
Topics:
UCC buyer and seller remedies—buyer remedies.
Perfect tender rule.
Monetary damages for breach.
Dangerfield v. Markel (determining damages when buyer covers through multiple market purchases over significant period)
UCC buyer and seller remedies—seller remedies.
UCC § 2-708 and the lost volume seller rule.
R.E. Davis Chem. Corp. v. Diasonics, Inc. (seller's damages for breach by the buyer, lost volume seller rule)

Class 54

Reading: Chapter 10A

Topics:

Rights and duties of third parties to the contract—third party beneficiaries.

Martinez v. Socoma Cos. (third party beneficiaries and government contracts)

Class 55

Reading: Chapter 10B

Topics:

Assignment and delegation.

Herzog v. Irace (validity of assignments)

Delegation of contract duties.

Assignment of entire contracts.

Sally Beauty Co. v. Nexxus Prods. Co. (assignments of contracts following corporate acquisitions)

CHAPTER 1

INTRODUCTION TO CONTRACT LAW STUDY AND JURISPRUDENCE

Table of Contents

NOTE

For Teaching Manual support for Chapter 1, see **Preface, Paragraph 7.**

CHAPTER 2

ENFORCEABILITY OF PROMISES: THE NATURE OF LEGAL DUTY & OBLIGATION

Table of Contents

Introduction to Chapter 2 Coverage

A promise is defined as the words or conduct of the maker so communicated to another person to cause that other person to reasonably believe that the maker has stated a firm commitment. Several important ideas are suggested by this definition. A promise need not be communicated expressly by words or even in written form. A promise may be communicated merely by the conduct of the maker. Second, the definition suggests that the recipient is the referent and not the maker. It is often said that a contract involves the "meeting of the minds" of the parties. While this is normally true it is certainly not required and a promise may be made even though the maker subjectively does not intend the communication to state a commitment. This idea is captured in the objective theory of contracts.

The fact that a promise is made does not mean that the law will enforce the promise. Something more is needed and is referred to as a theory of legal obligation. The term obligation implies that the maker of a promise has a legal duty to perform the promise and the recipient has a legal right to that same performance. Of course, the law provides many theories of legal obligation arising from different legal doctrines such as tort law. But this course is concerned with obligation arising from a contractual relationship. The primary theory of contractual obligation is the bargain theory promoted by Oliver Wendell Holmes at the turn of the nineteenth century. The bargain theory provides that a promise is enforceable when supported by bargained for consideration. The bargain means that the maker of the promise must seek an exchange with another person who provides either a counter promise or requested performance. The bargain theory of consideration has weaknesses primarily found in exchanges not involving a bargain but nonetheless triggering detrimental reliance by the recipient of the promise. For example, the maker might intend a promise to make a gift in the future without seeking anything in return but the promise triggers reliance by the recipient. In such cases, the law provides other theories of obligation including promissory estoppel, restitution and promissory restitution. Restitution theory can be particularly confusing because the law grants restitution even when no promise has been made (often referred to as quasi contract law or *quantum meruit* law). The chapter materials will help the student sort out these theories so that the student can understand them better. The point here is that, like consideration, these alternative theories of obligation offer the law to protect the reasonable expectations of the injured party.

The Teachers Manual materials for this chapter are organized on the assumption that the professor has simply assigned Chapter 1 to be read by the students and not discussed those materials in class. Alternatively, some of the introductory material in that chapter can be handled through limited discussion in class.

Because of the contrast between undergraduate reading and law school reading, we like to start with the question: What is a "casebook" and why do we use it instead of a comprehensive text? The answer to this question addresses a common erroneous belief of beginning students that the Contracts class is presented for the purpose of teaching the legal rules relating to the formation, interpretation and enforcement of contracts. While this is a substantial part of the purpose of the course, an equally important purpose is coverage of the various ways in which the reported decision of a case becomes a tool in the hands of the lawyer. These uses include drafting contracts, counseling clients on the meaning of and performance requirements of a contract previously entered into, and litigating issues raised with respect to the formation, meaning, validity and available remedies for breach of a contract.

Further commentary on these uses begins with our analysis of the decision in *Lucy v. Zehmer*, the second case in this chapter.

Chapter 2 begins with a focus on the nature of a "promise," the first essential building block in the formation of an enforceable contract. We explore what constitutes a "promise," and the various legal theories that may support the enforceability of such a promise. The plain barter transaction, goods for goods, or goods for services, or services for goods is the most basic "contract" tr ansaction with the "promise," if any, frequently implied rather than express. As the business environment becomes increasingly complex, a future promised action becomes the item of exchange on one side of the transaction, and then on both sides. *Slade's Case* in 1602 was a watershed decision in moving English common law to recognize the enforceability of the contract in situations where the actions of both sides were promises as to conduct in the future.

Contracts are the essential element of many familiar transactions—buying or leasing a car, buying or renting a home, obtaining a loan, insurance required by the lender to support a loan, hiring an employee or being hired as an employee, for instance. They represent a fundamental exercise of free will and private autonomy. Normally, no one questions the existence of promises inherent in the transaction—their presence is obvious. The situations that present challenging problems with respect to promises are usually at the periphery of our daily affairs, but it is these peripheral situations that trouble or elucidate the legal theories involved. At issue is whether there is a duty to perform the promise and a corresponding right to such performance.'

What constitutes a promise? According to Restatement (Second) of Contracts § 2:

(1) A promise is a manifestation of intention to act or refrain from acting in a specified way, so made as to justify a promisee in understanding that a commitment has been made.

A. THE NATURE OF PROMISE—A COMMITMENT

King v. Trustees of Boston University
CASE BRIEF

This 1995 decision of the Massachusetts Supreme Court involved an appeal from a jury determination that Dr. Martin Luther King, Jr. had made a "charitable pledge" (enforceable promise) to Boston University ("BU") of certain papers he had deposited with BU. The plaintiff, wife, and administratrix of the estate of her late husband, sued BU claiming that the papers previously deposited belonged to the estate and not to BU. In response to special questions, the jury determined that Dr. King had made a promise to give the papers in a letter signed by him and dated July 16, 1964, and that this promise was enforceable as a charitable pledge "supported by consideration or reliance." The jury also determined that the letter was not a contract (Supreme Court opinion).

By way of background, in 1963 BU commenced plans to expand its special collections and construct a library to hold new additions. Thereafter BU began its efforts to obtain Dr. King's papers. In a letter dated July 16, 1964, Dr. King named BU as the repository of his correspondence, manuscripts and other papers, and certain awards. The key paragraphs in the letter recited:

> "... I name the Boston University Library the Repository of my correspondence, manuscripts and other papers, along with a few of my awards and other materials which may come to be of interest in historical or other research.
>
> ... It is my intention that after the end of each calendar year, similar files of materials for an additional year should be sent to Boston University.
>
> All papers and other objects that thus pass into the custody of Boston University remain my legal property until otherwise indicated, according to the statements below. ...
>
> I intend each year to indicate a portion of the materials deposited with Boston University to become the absolute property of Boston University as an outright gift from me, until all shall have been thus given to the University. In the event of my death, all such materials deposited with the University shall become from that date the absolute property of Boston University."

The jury did not reach BU's defenses based on statute of limitations or laches claims. The usual contract claim limitations period is six years from the date of breach but the date and fact of such breach (refusal to return following demand by Mrs. King after her husband's death?) are not discussed in the opinion. "Laches" (Norman French word) is an equitable defense usually based on unreasonable delay in making a demand or taking action together with detrimental reliance by the other party. The supreme court affirmed the decision of the trial court entry of judgment based on the jury's verdict, thus dispensing with the need to address these other issues.

Since the plaintiff appellant had moved for judgment notwithstanding the verdict, and then appealed the refusal of the trial court to grant such a motion, the supreme court reviewed the facts of record in a light favorable to the BU's claim (whether there was a basis for support of the jury verdict to be found in the record).

BU claimed that the facts of record were sufficient to raise a question of fact for the jury as to whether there was a promise by Dr. King to transfer title to his papers to BU and whether any such promise was supported by consideration or reliance by BU. The plaintiff disputed BU's arguments but the supreme court found them sufficiently supported in the record.

In light of the jury's finding that there was not a contract, but rather a "charitable pledge," the court reviewed the case on the basis of "charitable pledge" law. Existing Massachusetts law provided that for there to be an enforceable charitable pledge there had to have been a promise supported by consideration or reliance. Thus the court's search was two-fold: first for evidence of a promise and then for consideration or reliance.

The court found the words of the letter quoted above sufficient to establish gift intent—promise. In so finding the court attached considerable weight to the fact that Dr. King had transferred possession of some of the materials at the time of the letter and possession of others at a later date. Mrs. King had argued that the letter was merely a non-binding statement of future intent and not a promise. The court concluded that there was adequate evidence in the record to support the jury's finding of a promise.

The second primary issue in the case was whether, as required by Massachusetts case law, BU had established that the promise was supported by consideration OR reliance. Since the jury found that the letter was not a "contract," it appears that the jury based its finding of enforceability on BU's reliance. The opinion does not clearly come down on a finding of reliance rather than of consideration. The opinion is somewhat ambiguous on this point—once again relying on the evidentiary showing required to overrule a jury verdict, a showing not found in the record.

INTERESTING DISCUSSION ISSUES

1. *Distinction between completed versus incomplete gift.* It may be useful to compare with the class the difference between a completed gift (which normally cannot be undone) and a gift that is incomplete. While Dr. King had possession of some of his materials transferred to BU, concurrently with the letter, the record established that Dr. King added additional materials subsequently. The letter was explicit in indicating that no completed gift transfer was intended at the time of the letter and that the transfer of possession, at that time, created only a bailment, title then being retained by Dr. King. The jury had to find, therefore, that Dr. King promised to complete the gift at a later time.

2. *Why did delivery of possession make a difference to the court?* The court did not expand on just how the delivery of possession helped to establish the existence of a promise as contrasted with a mere statement of future intent. Students may have difficulty with the court's reasoning on this point. The court may have thought that, because possession had been transferred, all that was required to find that the gift had been completed was evidence of completed gift intent. The letter provided such evidence of completed intent as of the date of Dr. King's death.

3. *The case turns on a procedural point.* The case turns on the important procedural point about the strength of the evidence required to overrule the jury's findings of fact, a showing the court found to be absent.

4. *Difference between a testamentary gift, a contract to make a will, and a contract or enforceable promise made during the promisor's lifetime.* The court found it important to distinguish between a "testamentary gift," a contract to make a will including particular terms or dispositions, and a contract or enforceable promise made during the promisor's lifetime but to take effect as of the death of the promisor. By statute, a will is required, at the least, to be in writing, signed by the testator in the presence of two witnesses who, in turn must sign as witnesses to the testator's signature. These requirements are designed to protect against fraudulent claims of oral, or written but unattested, testamentary disposition. The court found these requirements were not applicable because Dr. King made the enforceable promise during his lifetime and the gift was complete during his lifetime or at the latest at the time of his death. It was thus not a "testamentary" gift, a gift that takes effect after the death of the donor—a fine point of distinction.

The court was also concerned about the specific statutory requirement (part of the Statute of Frauds) relating to the form of an enforceable promise to make a will with particular terms. The court held Dr. King did not make a promise to leave a will with particular terms but made a binding promise effective during his lifetime or at the latest at the time of his death. In any case, said the court, the requirements of the Statute of Frauds had been met.

For comparison purposes, suppose that Dr. King's letter had said either of the following:

(a) "I intend to leave these materials to BU after my death;" or
(b) "I promise to make a will leaving these materials to BU after my death."

5. *Standard required for a finding of consideration.* It would be helpful to tell the students that for a finding of consideration to support the promise the court would have had to find sufficient evidence of a two way bargained for exchange entered into by the parties. Clearly, there was no such evidence in the record. It is also useful to note for the students at this point that many cases in this book contain discussions of material that will be explored in greater detail in later classes. While a full discussion of consideration and detrimental reliance is probably not useful at this point, the *King* case will provide a useful starting point for discussions of later consideration and promissory estoppel cases such as *Dougherty* and *Allegheny College*.

6. *Differentiating the roles of judge and jury.* This opinion invites student discussion of the difference in the roles and functions of the trial judge on the one hand, and the jury on the other. Given the 7th Amendment to our Constitution, what kind of showing should be required to overrule the verdict of the jury? Why such a requirement? The answer lies in the language of the Amendment and in our common law history:

Amendment VII. Civil Trials

> **In suits at common law, where the value in controversy shall exceed twenty** dollars, **the right of trial by jury shall be preserved, and no fact tried by a jury, shall be otherwise reexamined in any Court of the United States, than according to the rules of the common law.**

The United States "inherited" the English common law as it stood in 1791—which is why, for instance, no jury is required with respect to issues heard at that time in a court of Chancery (equity).

7. *Reliance as a basis for enforcement of a promise.* The route for a court to find a promise enforceable by reason of detrimental reliance rather than bargained for consideration has most of its roots in 20th century state case law. Much of that history relates to promises of gifts,

pledges or contributions to a charity. Under earlier English common law, an unexecuted promise to make a gift was a "nudum pactum" or unenforceable promise as a matter of judge-made policy. See *Dickinson v. Dodds,* set out in Chapter 3. Around the time of the turn of the 20th century a number of cases began to appear holding that gifts to a charity should be treated differently and enforced if reasonable detrimental reliance on the promise of the gift could be shown. Charities apart, the courts had established that it was not reasonable for the promisee to rely on a promise that could not be, or had not been, converted into a contract by bargained for acceptance of that promise. Out of empathy for the needs of charitable organizations, and appreciation of their social function, courts began to find detrimental reliance in one of two ways. The first involved a charitable fund drive where the signed pledge typically recited that it was given in consideration of the pledges of others. The detriment thus posed was detriment to a third party and not the charity itself. The second involved the charity itself offering proof of a detrimental change of position in reliance on the making of the pledge, by for instance beginning performance of the purpose for which the charitable solicitation had been made. Numerous courts over the next several decades suggested that while courts were enforcing charitable pledges on such a basis, the search for such forms of reliance was mystical if not fanciful. Restatement (Second) of Contracts § 90 modified Restatement (First) of Contracts § 90 and added a new subsection (2) as follows:

> (2) A charitable subscription or a marriage settlement is binding under Subsection (1) without proof that the promise induced action or forbearance.

Thus Restatement (Second) of Contracts § 90(2) states, in effect, that neither consideration nor reliance is required to support a charitable "subscription" but the Massachusetts Supreme Court's opinion notes in Footnote #4 that Massachusetts has declined to apply and enforce this aspect of § 90. Instead Massachusetts has focused on the requirement of § 90(1) that consideration or reliance are relevant to whether the promise must be enforced to avoid injustice. Note also that the opinion recites that the Supreme Court of Maryland had similarly rejected the position taken by Restatement (Second) of Contracts § 90(2) in *Arrowsmith v. Mercantile-Safe Deposit and Trust Co.*, 313 Md. 334, 545 A.2d 674 (1988). Quoting from the Florida Court of Appeals decision in *Jordan* (276 So.2d 102, 1973, subsequently affirmed by the Florida Supreme Court), the Massachusetts Supreme Court said, "To ascribe consideration where there is none, or to adopt any other theory which affords charities a different legal rationale than other entities, is to approve fiction." See Footnote #4.

8. *The rationale for developing the Restatements.* This opinion provides an early and interesting opportunity to engage student discussion on the role, function and effect of the Restatements on judicial reasoning. What factors persuaded the ALI to adopt § 90(2) in 1981 and what factors persuaded the Supreme Courts of Massachusetts, Maryland and Florida to decline to adopt and follow that subsection?

Apparently, in adopting § 90(2) in 1981, the ALI thought there was some basis for presuming universal reliance by the charity on each such pledge or subscription. The commentary to § 90(2), explaining the basis for its inclusion in Restatement (Second) of Contracts says:

> Subsection (2) identifies two other classes of cases in which the promisee's claim is similarly reinforced. American courts have traditionally favored charitable subscriptions and marriage settlements, and have found consideration in many cases where the element of exchange was doubtful or nonexistent. Where recovery is rested on reliance in such cases, a probability of reliance is enough, and no effort is made to sort out mixed motives or to consider whether partial enforcement would be appropriate.

But as the text says, no "promise" no enforceable commitment!

Factors affecting the decision of these courts not to follow § 90(2) could have included the following: a long and continuous line of common law decisions holding that a "naked promise" is not enforceable—the importance of continuity of precedent; to enforce a "naked promise" would expose people to the risk of losing their property by reason of ill-considered and hasty "promises" such as a statement to a child "Of course I will give you the lake cottage"; absent a bargained for exchange there is a heightened risk of fraudulent testimony especially where the alleged gift promise is oral; the risk of undermining the policies behind the Statute of Wills and the Statute of Frauds; and the absence of a clear reason to enforce promises to charities and not other gift promises. Students will also wonder why the ALI included promises of "marriage settlements" along with promises to charities. There is no good explanation for the inclusion of marriage settlements in Subsection (2).

NOTES AND QUESTIONS

1. *Existence of a promise.* Dr. King did not make a completed gift at the time of the letter. No proof of promise is required to support the transfer of title accomplished by a completed gift. Absent a completed gift, the rules applied by this court required that there be proof of a promise to make a gift in the future, contrasted with a mere statement of intention to make a gift in the future. Finding such a promise was

crucial to BU's right to retain the materials. Clearly, Dr. King arranged for the transfer of possession of some of his materials at the time of the letter and arranged for the transfer of others later. This transfer of possession created a "bailment"—a legal concept that distinguishes between possession and ownership. For instance, leaving a car at a garage for repairs does not transfer ownership of the car and, subject to paying the bill for the work done, the owner retains the right to recover possession as one of the incidents of ownership. The garage becomes a "bailee" and the owner a "bailor." Bailment alone did not give BU any right to retain the materials as against Dr. King's estate. There had to be a "promise" to complete the gift at a later date, especially in light of the recital in the letter that the materials remained Dr. King's legal property. Next the letter stated "intent" but not "promise"—"I intend each year to indicate a portion ... to become the absolute property" of BU. Thus the words of promise had to be found in the words, "In the event of my death, all such materials deposited with the University shall become from that date the absolute property of Boston University." The court found that the wording of the letter constituted a sufficient record on the basis of which the jury could reasonably conclude that Dr. King intended a completed gift, at the latest, at the time of his death. Is the court's search for a promise a search for Dr. King's subjective intent or for a reasonable objective manifestation of such intent? Based on the wording of the letter, there can be no doubt about Dr. King's subjective intent. Why then, does the court struggle with whether there was adequate evidence of such intent? The answer lies in the court's search for a standard applicable not only in Dr. King's case, but in others generally. What factors should be considered in formulating such a standard? Is it the role of the court to formulate such a standard or of the state legislature? As much of the discussion in the opinion indicates, the state had enacted at least two different laws that could, arguably be applicable—the Statute of Wills and the Statute of Frauds. The opinion explains why the first is not implicated and why the second, although not implicated, would be satisfied by the signed letter.

Lurking behind the search for a promise is the need to protect and enforce the policy behind the Statute of Wills, requiring that a testamentary disposition be in a writing signed by the testator in the presence of two witnesses who also sign attesting that signature. The Statute of Frauds, on the other hand, requires a note or memorandum signed by a person promising to make a particular gift by will. The students may wonder whether a letter, such as that signed by Dr. King, constitutes sufficient protection against fraud and perjury after his death.

Why would the court look for the presence of a promise? Inherent (natural law?) respect for the right of private ownership of property suggests that a coherent legal system must provide a set of rules regulating the transfer or loss of such rights. These rules have traditionally distinguished between bartered for exchanges and transactions by way of gift. The donor of a completed gift, such as by delivery of property accompanied by a statement of gift intent, cannot thereafter retract the gift. The court classified Dr. King's transaction as a gift to take effect, not at the time of the letter, but at a later date to be not later than the date of his death. The letter indicated on its face that the gift intended was to take effect in the future. The court drew a close but bright line between a gift completed before or at the time of the donor's death and a "testamentary" disposition.

Was Dr. King's intention a question of fact or law? The answer is that it was a question of mixed fact and law. Initially, the issue was one of facts indicating intent, an issue for the jury. Thereafter, the question was one of interpretation, and thus law, whether there was sufficient evidence of intent and promise in the record to support the rationality of the jury's finding that a promise was made. The Supreme Court does NOT hold that Dr. King had the necessary intent. RATHER, it holds that there was sufficient evidence in the record to support a finding of intent and consideration or reliance by the jury. The implication is that if the jury had found for Mrs. King, the court would not have reversed that finding. This implication serves as a basis to remind students of the importance of the way in which the lawsuit comes out at the trial level even though it may thereafter be appealed. The scope of the appeal is limited and those limitations change depending upon the procedural posture of the case.

2. *Opinion or prediction of future events.* To illustrate the difference between a statement of future intent (not a promise) and a promise of action to be taken in the future, compare:

(a) "I intend to offer this farm for sale for $50,000"; and
(b) "I offer (promise) to sell you this farm for $50,000 if you accept my offer by agreeing to pay me that price."

The first formulation carries no present commitment, only a statement of the possibility of future commitment. As an example of the difference between a statement of opinion, a question and a promise, compare:

(a) "This farm is worth at least $50,000"; with
(b) "Would you sell this farm for $50,000"; with
(c) "I offer (promise) to sell you this farm for $50,000 if you accept my offer by agreeing to pay me that price."

The key to the distinction between an expression of future intent or a prediction or expression of opinion on the one hand, and an assurance of future action on the other, is the presence or absence of commitment (promise) on the part of the maker—often a fine line of interpretation.

3. *UCC & CISG approach to promise.* The UCC does not claim to be a complete code of law governing the sale of goods. Under UCC §1-103, as the note indicates, the principles of law and equity supplement all provisions of UCC Article 2, governing the sale of goods, as well as the other UCC Articles. Thus with respect to mistake, misrepresentation and fraud, for instance, the common law applies to sales of goods to the extent there are no specific sections of Article 2 on those subjects. As the text indicates, the terms "promise" and "contract" are most likely to be given the same meanings under the UCC as under the common law.

Similarly, the Convention on Contracts for the International Sale of Goods ("CISG") is limited in its scope and does not purport to supply all the legal requirements relating to the international sale of goods. First, the CISG only applies to contracts for the sale of goods between parties whose places of business are in different states, generally where both are signatories to the CISG. CISG Art. 1(1)(a). Second, the CISG, with minor exceptions, does not apply to "goods bought for personal, family or household use" nor to goods sold by auction, sales on execution, sales of securities, sales of ships or aircraft, and electricity. CISG Art. 2. Third, Article 4 provides that the CISG "governs only the formation of the contract of sale and the rights and obligations of the seller and the buyer arising from such a contract." CISG Art. 4. Article 4 explicitly exempts questions of contractual validity and property rights in the goods being sold. Id. Where the CISG is silent on an issue of law, such questions "are to be settled in conformity with the general principles on which [the CISG] is based or, in the absence of such principles, in conformity with the law applicable by virtue of the rules of private international law."

While Articles 14-24 deal explicitly with the requirements of contract formation—offer, acceptance, and revocation—the CISG does not deal explicitly with the promissory nature of contracts. Instead, the relevant inquiry is the parties' intent to be bound, without regard to the manner in which that intent is expressed. See, CISG Art. 14 ("A proposal for concluding a contract addressed to one or more specific persons constitutes an offer if it is sufficiently definite and indicates the intention of the offeror to be bound in case of acceptance."); Art. 11 ("A contract of sale need not be concluded in or evidenced by writing and is not subject to any requirement as to form."); cf. Art. 8(3) ("In determining the intent of a party or the understanding a reasonable person would have had, due consideration is to be given to all relevant circumstances of the case including the negotiations, any practices which the parties have established between themselves, usages and any subsequent conduct of the parties.").

4. *Jurisprudential analysis of Dr. King's teachings and contract law.* The note refers to the "stark" rules of contract law. A quick review by the student of a few of the sections in the Restatement (Second) of

Contracts suggests that rules therein stated can be appropriately described as "black letter" rules. As the materials in this chapter unfold, the student should be asking: Where did these rules come from? Who made them? Are the courts empowered to make them? Whose values do they reflect and represent? Are they universal in application? Can they be changed by legislation? Do they provide discretion for the individual judge to apply in accordance with the judge's own sense of fairness? To what extent are they explained and justified by notions of "freedom of contract" or "private autonomy" or to what extent are they applied and enforced by virtue of the state's sovereign power?

Dean Morant's article, cited in this paragraph, notes that, "On its face, the theory of contract is objective, eschewing any notion of societal inequities that girded Dr. King's beliefs. ... Justice, as a tacit force, results from strict adherence to stark rules of bargain formation. ... Dr. King's humanistic desire for universality, hope and love, interpreted within the contextual realities of pejorative human behavior, such as prejudices, discrimination, and bias, illustrates a theoretical weakness of contract law. ... This reality of bargaining behavior shatters contract law's illusion of objectivity. It also commensurately prompts discussion of methods to cure the transitional ills resulting from those problems. ... The law of contract also provides remedies for those who suffered some cognitive impairment at the time they entered the bargain. However, these correctional tools remain elusive, and only scratch the surface of transactional problems related to greed, prejudice and other forms of negative opportunism. These problems alter bargaining judgment and marginalize disadvantaged. ... But contextual realities demonstrate a need to construe and apply contract rules more flexibly, thereby allowing decision makers to take into account such transactional ills as bias, opportunism, and prejudice.... The contextual examination of his writings illustrates Dr. King's theoretical support for a more elastic application of the rules for contractual remedies such as unconscionability, duress, undue influence, and capacity." The full import of Dean Morant's comments will be better appreciated by students substantially later in their course on Contracts.

5. *Promises and morality.* This paragraph raises the profound question of whether, and if so why, a promise should be kept, and if not whether the promisor should be sanctioned. Many trees have been killed to provide the paper for hundreds of books and articles, in this country and around the world, devoted to one or more of the many aspects of this subject. In the world of business, the first and easiest answer is certainty and predictability in our business affairs. There is a common expectation in the marketplace that a contract, properly entered into, will be performed. Any impairment of that expectation produces some degree of loss for the promisee, a loss that should be compensated. Where one party to the exchange has suffered a loss in

reliance on the promise, the extent of that reliance suggests a further basis for relief or compensation. Unjust enrichment can provide a third justification for relief, as where one party, in performing her side of the bargain, has conferred a benefit (value) on the other party, a benefit that is not offset or counterbalanced by any return performance.

6. *Non-promissory theories of obligation.* See text. The point of this anthropological material is two-fold. First, students should understand that promise is not the only mechanism for making and receiving binding commitments. As the Malinowski and Mauss readings indicate, reciprocity and "informal" mechanisms for recognizing obligations may in some circumstances provide greater commitments than a mere promise. Second, this material permits the introduction of principles of comparative law and the relevance of anthropological principles to the study (and hopefully practice) of law.

B. UNDERSTANDING CONTRACTUAL INTENT: THE OBJECTIVE THEORY OF CONTRACTS

Unless read previously, we strongly recommend that the instructor read the Fuller and Kennedy articles cited in the introductory note.

Lucy v. Zehmer
CASE BRIEF

This is a 1954 decision of the Supreme Court of Appeals of Virginia. W.O. and J.C. Lucy sued for specific performance of the following contract: "We hereby agree to sell to W.O. Lucy the Ferguson farm complete for $50,000, title satisfactory to buyer." The contract was signed by A.H. Zehmer and his wife Ida S. Zehmer. J.C. Lucy sued as assignee of a one-half interest in the farm. W.O. Lucy had not signed the writing.

The Zehmers' defense was that the signed writing was a joke and not intended seriously. They denied delivery of the signed writing to Lucy. They alleged further, that Lucy had attempted to offer $5 "to bind the bargain," which they refused. They said that when A.H. Zehmer realized that Lucy thought the transaction was serious he assured Lucy that he had no intention of selling. Lucy left insisting that he had bought the farm.

The trial court refused to grant an injunction and dismissed the bill (complaint). The Virginia Supreme Court granted the Lucys' appeal, ordering specific performance. W.O. Lucy testified that: he had made a previous unsuccessful attempt to buy the farm; that he came to the Zehmers' restaurant and immediately began discussing the purchase of the farm; Zehmer said he would take $50,000; Lucy urged Zehmer to write out an agreement; Zehmer did so using the word "I"; Lucy said

Mrs. Zehmer would have to sign; Zehmer rewrote the agreement (as sued on); Zehmer asked Mrs. Zehmer to sign and she said that for $50,000 she would and did; Lucy offered $5 but Zehmer refused saying that the signed agreement was sufficient.

The discussion lasted 30-40 minutes. Although they both had several drinks Lucy said that he was not intoxicated and did not believe that Zehmer was either. Next day (Saturday) Lucy assigned a one-half interest in the farm to J.C. Lucy and on Monday engaged an attorney to examine title. That review was favorable. Lucy wrote that he was ready to close but Zehmer refused asserting that he had not agreed or intended to sell.

A.H. Zehmer testified that: "I was already high as a Georgia pine;" they argued for some time about whether Lucy had the $50,000; he wrote the agreement on the back of a restaurant guest check; his wife at first refused to sign but on his assuring her that it was all a joke she signed; Lucy said "Let me see it (the writing)" and put it in his pocket; Zehmer told him he was not going to sell the farm.

Ida Zehmer testified that: she signed after being told that it was all a joke; that she told her husband he should have taken Lucy home (presumably because she thought Lucy was drunk).

Lucy testified that at a social gathering on Sunday Zehmer said he did not want to "stick" him with the contract because Lucy was too drunk. A disinterested witness supported Lucy's account.

While the Zehmers insisted the writing was a "dare" or joke, the court allocated the burden of disproving the writing to them and then found that burden not satisfied. Lucy did not understand the transaction to be a joke—he considered it to be a serious business transaction. The evidence established that Lucy was entitled to so believe. The court stated the applicable rule in the following words: "In the field of contracts, as generally elsewhere, we must look to the outward expression of a person as manifesting his intention rather than to his secret and unexpressed intention. 'The law imputes to a person an intention corresponding to the reasonable meaning of his words and acts.'" The court added one caveat: "If the words or other acts of one of the parties have but one reasonable meaning, his undisclosed intention is immaterial except when an unreasonable meaning which he attaches to his manifestations is known to the other party. Restatement of the Law of Contracts, Vol. I, § 71, p. 74."

While the remedy of specific performance is equitable, and therefore discretionary, the supreme court, unlike the trial court, found no reason not to grant the injunction, especially since Zehmer had admitted that $50,000 was a fair price.

The court found no basis for a defense based on intoxication. The court stated the relevant standard for avoidance based on intoxication as, "The record is convincing that Zehmer was not intoxicated to the extent of being unable to comprehend the nature and consequences of the instrument he executed, and hence that instrument is not to be invalidated on that ground." The court found such a defense to be inconsistent with Zehmer's detailed testimony of the event and his wife's testimony that she suggested that Zehmer drive Lucy home. In any event, the Zehmers' counsel conceded during oral argument that Zehmer was not too drunk to make a binding commitment.

A SUGGESTED APPROACH TO TEACHING THIS CASE

It is often useful to ask the students why a particular case was included in the casebook. This case provides just such an excellent opportunity. The facts suggest a bewildering number of issues but the justification for inclusion is the stated doctrine that words or actions of one party directed to another are to be interpreted NOT by what the user subjectively intended but rather by what the recipient reasonably understood. The core of the case is the Lucys' argument that W.O. Lucy reasonably understood the written note signed by the Zehmers as the acknowledgment of a serious agreement to sell the Ferguson farm whereas the Zehmers' argument was that the whole thing was a joke. Finding that W.O. Lucy truly believed that agreement had been reached (offer and acceptance) and that such belief, induced by the Zehmers' words and actions, was reasonable, the court found an enforceable agreement in spite of the absence of a literal "meeting of the minds." Said the court:

> Not only did Lucy actually believe, but the evidence shows he was warranted in believing, that the contract represented a serious business transaction and a good faith sale and purchase of the farm.
>
> In the field of contracts, as generally elsewhere, we must look to the outward expression of a person as manifesting his intention rather than to his secret and unexpressed intention. The law imputes to a person an intention corresponding to the reasonable meaning of his words and acts. First Nat. Bank v. Roanoke Oil Co., 169 Va. 99, 114, 192 S.E. 764, 770.

As someone said a long time ago, "Devil alone knoweth the mind of man."

For the students, the case may raise a bewildering number of additional questions. It is useful to address those questions, and then afterwards focus on the key issue of the case. *Lucy v. Zehmer* provides students with a learning opportunity on how to brief a case, how to structure their notes, and why their notes need to be carefully focused. We let the students flounder in class and then, before the next class hour, suggest that they read the following 8 page note. It is designed to give them some guidance on their own "briefing," study and use of the case. Copies of this note can be obtained from the authors. Answers to the questions are found within square brackets below. This bracketed material is not included in the digital version which can be posted on TWEN for student reading.

HOW AND WHY TO READ A CASE[1]

The second case in the casebook is *Lucy v. Zehmer*. As you read this case you should be thinking of the following questions:

- What is this case about?
- What questions does this case raise for me?
- What principle (rule) or principles of law does it state?
- How might I use this case?

Case decisions are one (compare statutes, regulations) of the primary sources of our law. From reading the decision of a judge or judges in another case we can find statements of principles and see how those principles were applied by the judge(s) to the particular facts of that case. If we were representing a client in a lawsuit involving somewhat similar facts, or the potential application of somewhat similar principles, we might be able to use the other decision (and its reasoning) to persuade our judge to rule in our client's favor. The closer (more analogous) the case to our client's situation, the more persuasive our argument is likely to be. In other words, we look for the principles of law as stated in earlier cases as the source of principles applicable to our client's case.

We can also use decisions in earlier cases as a basis for predicting how a judge would rule on our client's facts or situation if those facts or situation were litigated (made the subject of a lawsuit), and we can thus use case decisions as an aid in helping our client plan or structure his or her business, or counsel our client on selecting a course of future action. Case decisions provide a basis for predicting how the law might be applied in the future to our client's situation, thus providing guidance for our client on how to avoid problems.

Much of our "common law" was developed through case by case decisions. Parts of that common law have been codified or revised by statute, with the usual result that the statutory statement of the applicable principles replaces the earlier common law web of decisions. The Uniform Commercial Code provides an illustration of this process. In time, a further web of case decisions arises around the text of the statute providing further insight into how that statute is to be read, understood and applied, and once again, the body of case law (decisions) gains in importance. Numerous illustrations of this process will be found as we proceed through the casebook.

If you were a judge, presiding over a trial, the facts in issue had been determined, and you decided that the facts before you, or the principles involved, were identical to, or essentially the same as, those presented in an earlier trial, would you apply the principle stated in the earlier case and follow that principle to the same conclusion on the facts before you? Would your reasons for adopting the earlier decision and applying it to the facts in the trial before you include any or all of the following?

- someone else thought carefully about this issue and their decision is probably a correct one;
- the earlier decision was reported and may have been relied on by others, so that I should not adopt a different rule or principle out of concern for raising new doubts about what the rule really is—certainty as to the applicable rule is important;
- I am a judge on the district court bench. As such, I am to apply those principles that have been established in earlier decisions of appellate courts in my jurisdiction by which I am bound. The facts of this case, or the principles involved, are indistinguishable from those ruled on by such an appellate court in an earlier case and therefore I am bound to follow that earlier decision.

Any one or all of the foregoing reasons may explain the willingness of a judge to follow the ruling of an earlier decision. In American jurisprudence, where that earlier decision was made by an appellate court in the judge's own jurisdiction, the earlier decision is said to be "binding" on the trial judge. Where it was made in an earlier case by a judge at the same level as the currently presiding judge, the earlier case may be persuasive but is generally regarded in this country as not binding. Earlier this century, English courts sometimes held that a trial judge could be "bound" by the earlier decision of a similar trial judge, or that a court of appeals could be "bound" by the earlier decision of that court of appeals. United States courts are not so wedded to "precedent," but they are bound to follow applicable rulings of higher level courts in their own jurisdiction. Thus a decision of the Minnesota Supreme Court, the highest state court in Minnesota, is said to be "binding" on both the Minnesota Court of Appeals and Minnesota district courts. State court decisions of courts in states other than that in which the trial is being held are never binding on the trial court—but for the reasons described above they may be strongly "persuasive." We will deal later with federal decisions which rule on matters of state law, and how those decisions may provide guidance as to applicable state law.

Earlier decisions are, then, a source of "principles" which may apply to the facts in the case which you are litigating. Your reading of those earlier cases must involve at least two steps if you are to argue effectively:

- The case you refer to ("cite") must set out and support the principle you are advocating as the "law";
- And you must convince your judge that the principle of the cited case is properly applicable to the solution of your case, including its particular facts.

Principles of law are usually relatively abstract propositions. To lead to a decision on a new set of facts or situation, the principle must be found applicable to the instant facts or situation in a way that is consistent with the way in which that principle was applied in the earlier case.

In reading a case, then, you must look for the "principles" involved, and you must also look for the critical facts to which that principle was applied, and how the court applied that principle to those critical facts.

What else must you focus on in reading a case? Consider the following:

- Who are the parties before the court? (Consider the clarity of "plaintiff" and "defendant" and the potential ambiguity of "appellant" and "appellee" (who received the favorable decision in the lower court and who "appealed"?)
- How were the facts established? Was there a trial to a jury and a verdict? Did the judge enter judgment based on that verdict? Was the lower court judgment based on the pleadings (without a trial) or on a motion for summary judgment (i.e. on the state of the record in the case prior to actual trial)? The "procedural" posture of the case may be critically important with respect to the version of facts used or relied upon by the appellate court. The numerous differences will be explored further in your Civil Procedure course, and from time to time in this course. You should always focus on the procedural "posture" of the case you are reading.
- What court wrote the decision? In *Lucy v. Zehmer* it was the Supreme Court of Virginia. Since the Supreme Court is the highest court in the state of Virginia, this decision would be "binding" on all appellate and district courts in Virginia. Beware the label "Supreme Court." In New York, for instance, the Supreme Court is of a lower level than the Court of Appeals which is the court of highest level in the state of New York.
- What year was the case decided? A case earlier in time may be superseded or "overruled" by a later decision of a court on the same level. The Minnesota Supreme Court, from time to time, expressly (or sometimes impliedly) overrules earlier decisions of the same court.
- Where can you find a report of the full decision? Casebook editors frequently edit (omit parts of) the full decision. You may want to see the whole case. Where do you find it? You will see in the heading of the case "196 Va. 493; 84 S.E.2d 516." These

are cites to two different places where you can find the decision. The first cite is to the Virginia state law reports. The second cite is to West's Southeastern Reporter which collects and publishes decisions from a group of states in the "south east." Minnesota's reported decisions are to be found, for instance, in West's Northwestern Reporter. The "2d" refers to a second sequence. When the spirit moved them, West ended their first sequence of reported cases and began a second sequence. The fact that a case is found in such a second sequence is indicated by the "2d." Reports of the federal courts of appeals are now into a third sequence, "3d" etc. When you cite a case to a judge as part of your argument you must include both the state and West Reporter system references ("citations") to where the case can be found.

As you read *Lucy v. Zehmer* you should think about answers to the following questions. The answers to some of these questions may not be found in the report of the case. Any time you have a question about a case you should note your question down and seek an answer. An excellent alternative is to post your question on one of the "discussion forums" contained in your TWEN program for this course.

- Who were the parties to this case? [W.O. and J.C. Lucy (plaintiffs), and A.H. and Ida S. Zehmer (defendants)]
- J.C. Lucy was not at the bar on Saturday night and did not participate in the negotiation of the agreement. How and why does he appear as one of the plaintiffs? [Assignment of beneficial interest in contract—assignment will be covered in Chapter 10.]
- The recital of facts in the case notes that Mr. Zehmer needed to have Mrs. Zehmer's signature on the written agreement. Why did he need Mrs. Zehmer's signature? [Dower or other statute based right of a spouse in real estate—compare community property]
- What was the relief sought? The normal relief sought by a plaintiff is an award of damages. What is "specific performance"? [Injunctive relief—tried to a judge alone because of the state of English common law in 1791 when such a proceeding was required to be brought in a court of Chancery (equitable)]
- Was the agreement in writing? Was it signed by all the parties? Only by the Zehmers? Is it binding even though not signed by W.O. Lucy? Why would an agreement between two parties signed by one, but not the other, be enforceable? [Distinguish oral or written from signed written agreements—Statute of Frauds, 1677 established the requirement of a "note or memorandum in writing signed by the party to be charged"—

the Zehmers here were the "party to be charged" and hence there was no requirement that Lucy sign. If the Zehmers had sought to enforce the contract against Lucy their action would have been barred by the Statute of Frauds since, as to Lucy, there was no such "note or memorandum". The students will wonder whether it is fair for a contract to be enforceable by Lucy but not by the Zehmers—no mutuality of obligation]

- Should an oral agreement (one not reduced to writing) be enforceable? [An oral agreement will be enforceable unless there is a statutory requirement that the particular form of contract be evidenced by a signed writing. The Statute of Frauds adopted by the English parliament in 1677 was reenacted by the legislature of every state in the United States. Further coverage of this statute and its detailed requirements and associated case law is found in Chapter 5. It is noteworthy that a Texas Court of Appeals found an oral contract for the sale of a $7 billion dollar business was enforceable despite the absence of a detailed signed written agreement—see *Texaco, Inc. v. Pennzoil, Co.*, 729 S.W.2d 768 (1987)]
- The agreement read as follows : "We hereby agree to sell to W.O. Lucy the Ferguson Farm complete for $50,000, title satisfactory to the buyer." Is this a complete agreement? If it was enforceable only if in written form, does this memorandum contain all the necessary and appropriate terms of the agreement? [The Statute of Frauds is usually interpreted to require that the note or memorandum contain all of the essential terms of the agreement. Commonly, an agreement for the sale and purchase of land will contain a full "legal description" of the property. "Ferguson Farm" is not such a legal description of the property to be sold but that description can be proven by evidence of "facts of independent significance". Compare: a contract to sell "my home in Minneapolis." City records can be used to establish that I own only one such home, and the street address of that property. From the street address a full legal description can then be established by evidence, sufficiently reliable since not dependent on the testimony of either of the parties.]
- What does "complete" mean? If Mr. Zehmer had a new tractor and a header harvester located on the Ferguson farm would they be included in the sale described in this agreement? How about furniture in the farmhouse on the property? [Problematic—machinery, animals and crops growing on the farm would likely be held included—non-fixture house furnishings would be arguable]
- What does $50,000 mean? Could W.O. Lucy show up at the "closing" with his personal check for $50,000? What if his check bounced when it was presented at his bank for payment? Does

it mean that he would bring $50,000 in cash? [An issue of interpretation that did not need to be decided in the case—appropriate drafting should describe specifically the method of payment such as by "certified check" or "banker's check" etc.]

- What does "title satisfactory to buyer" mean? Did this language give W.O. Lucy the opportunity after the agreement was entered into to cancel the deal? Without liability? If Lucy was dissatisfied, would his dissatisfaction have to relate reasonably to problems with the "title" (ownership) of the Ferguson farm? ["Title satisfactory to buyer" is given an objective interpretation satisfied by a legal opinion or title insurance policy in accordance with applicable state title standards—thus Lucy could have avoided legal commitment based on these words only if the Zehmers' title was not in accord with such title standards. This was an objectively conditioned "out." A brief comment on the difference between a promise and a condition may be appropriate. Conditions are covered in Chapter 8. Students can be given a useful example of a financing contingency, frequently inserted in the sale and purchase of homes.]
- What is a "closing"? Clearly the case speaks of two sets of events—the first (the bar on Saturday night) when the agreement was made; and second the "closing" (at a later date) when a deed to the farm would be exchanged for the money (purchase price). Do all agreements follow this form—where performance of the bargain occurs some time after the agreement is entered into? [It is useful to provide students with a brief description of this common two part transaction—the signing of the enforceable contract followed, frequently sixty days later, by the closing of the transaction. A brief comment on the business reasons for the separation of these two steps maybe helpful to students.]
- What was the plaintiff's theory as to why he and his brother should get an order of the court for specific performance? [That the parties had entered into a valid and legal agreement (contract) which the Zehmers later refused, without excuse, to perform.]
- What was the Zehmers' theory as to why they should not be ordered to specifically perform the contract? [That Zehmer never intended to sell the farm—it was just a joke.]
- Can a person who is intoxicated enter into a binding agreement (contract)? [The court's standard, "not intoxicated to the extent of being unable to comprehend the nature and consequences of the instrument."]
- Was Zehmer drunk at the time of the signing? Was W.O. Lucy drunk at that time? Who decided this issue? On the basis of what facts? Was Mrs. Zehmer drunk? If not, was it sufficient

that she was sober? [There was no suggestion that Mrs. Zehmer was drunk at the time. Based on the record evidence and the admission of the Zehmers' counsel at the hearing before the supreme court, that court found that A.H. Zehmer was not sufficiently drunk for intoxication to serve as a basis of avoidance of the contract. While he testified that he was "high as a Georgia pine" the court found this inconsistent with his detailed testimony of the events, Mrs. Zehmer's testimony that he should drive Lucy home, and counsel's "concession".]

- Does the court frame the applicable principle in this case this way? When A and B negotiate a deal, the words that A uses are to be interpreted (understood) in the way in which they would be understood by a reasonable person in B's shoes? [Yes.]
- Does the court indicate exceptions to any such rule or principle? What explains those exceptions? [" If the words or other acts of one of the parties have but one reasonable meaning, his undisclosed intention is immaterial except when an unreasonable meaning which he attaches to his manifestations is known to the other party."]
- What would happen if the reasonable person in B's shoes might understand the words used by A to have two or more different meanings? [Reliance by B on the meaning chosen by B should not be reasonable.]
- What would happen if A used the words, intending to use them with a special meaning, and B knew that A was using the words in that special way? Would it matter if the reasonable person in B's shoes might understand them in a different sense? [See the quote from the opinion above.]
- If the court's approach is called "objective interpretation," why is such an approach important? [The application of this doctrine is fundamentally important because it provides a level of certainty as to the enforceability of agreements and protects against subsequent claims of subjective intent by one of the parties.]

We have talked of the use of this decision in litigation involving different parties and different facts. The principle of this case embodies the concept of "objective interpretation," a concept that is basic to many, many other decisions by different courts. In fact, this case states a fundamental principle of contract law. But what might this case have to tell you about the drafting of a contract?

In this course there are always at least two pending questions:

- How might the case have been presented or argued better? What additional evidence might have been offered (consistent with the facts given in the case) which, if believed, would have affected or altered the outcome (decision)?

- How might the agreement (contract) between the parties have been drafted so as to avoid the problem presented by the situation reported in the case? We start with the assumption that litigation is always a less than optimal result. The best result is an agreement where both (or all) parties understand the deal in the same way (i.e. have the same expectations about performance of the agreement) and each side performs as expected. To win a disputed issue at trial is only second best to the outcome of performance by all sides as expected. There are almost always significant costs for both (or all) sides in litigation. To avoid a problem through good drafting of the agreement is therefore presumptively an optimal outcome.
- Suppose that you are drafting an agreement for a client. Suppose the agreement is for the sale of a house. Would you describe the property to be sold and transferred as the "house and contents" or the "complete" house? After reading the decision in *Lucy v. Zehmer*, how would you reword your draft? [Define specifically was is included and what is not included in the sale.]

Back to additional questions raised by the case:

- Why did Zehmer claim that he had never "delivered" the signed memorandum to Lucy? That Lucy had grabbed it from the table and put it in his pocket? [Where A makes an offer requiring B's acceptance in writing, the legal concept of "delivery" of the writing comes into play—the act of acceptance is not deemed effective and complete unless and until B "delivers," that is places beyond his further control, the writing evidencing acceptance. The record of the case is somewhat shaky on this point.]
- Why did Lucy offer Zehmer $5 after the agreement was made and signed? What does the judge do with this issue? [Lucy apparently knew enough to be dangerous about the law of contracts for the sale and purchase of real estate. He confused the requirements of an enforceable option to purchase the farm with an actual enforceable agreement for its sale and purchase. Is the fact that Lucy tried to get Zehmer to accept the $5 some evidence that Lucy did not think a firm commitment had been obtained from the Zehmers? The court appears to ignore the issue of the $5.]
- Was this case tried to a jury? If not, why not? [Trial before a judge alone because the injunctive relief sought was an equitable remedy.]
- What was the procedural posture of this case as it came up to the Virginia Supreme Court on appeal? What had the trial judge done with this case? [The trial judge declined to issue the

injunction and dismissed the plaintiffs' claim. This action was the basis of the appeal.]

- What did the Supreme Court do with the trial judge's decision? [They reversed the trial court decision].
- What persuaded the Supreme Court to reverse the trial judge? [They found that the written signed note created a presumption of enforceability of the agreement and that the presumption was not rebutted by the evidence of record.]
- Did they differ with the trial judge as to the facts? As to the applicable principles of law? How could they differ with the trial judge on matters of fact when they did not hear the witnesses? Had there been a jury verdict for the defendants below would the Supreme Court have found the facts to be different than those found by the jury? If so, on what basis? [The record of the case does not establish why the trial judge dismissed the plaintiffs' bill. The Supreme Court, there being no jury involved, reviewed the record de novo and substituted their own view of both the relevant law and facts.]
- In litigation, who has the "burden of proof"? What is "burden of proof"? If, at the conclusion of the trial, the facts as presented to the court are unclear, does the plaintiff win or does the defendant win? [The plaintiff has the initial burden of proof and, if after all the evidence is presented, that burden has not been shifted, the plaintiff loses for failure to prove his or her case. Once the burden is shifted to the defendant by evidence introduced, the defendant will lose unless the defendant in turn by further evidence shifts the burden back to the plaintiff. Burden of proof should be covered in the Civil Procedure course. The court in this case found that the signed writing shifted the burden of proof to the Zehmers and that they failed to rebut that burden.]
- Who, according to the Virginia Supreme Court, had the burden of proving that either an agreement had been made or that the parties had not intended to make an agreement? What of the words of the Supreme Court with respect to the "joke" defense, "Bizarre defense ... clear evidence is required to sustain it"? Of course, after putting the matter that way the Court then decided that the "bizarre" defense had not been established! [The court held that the introduction into evidence by the plaintiff of the signed note shifted the burden to the defendants. The defendants then failed to rebut that burden.]
- The Supreme Court added, "The record is convincing that Zehmer was not intoxicated to the extent of being unable to comprehend the nature and consequences of the instrument he executed, and hence that the instrument is not to be invalidated on that ground." Did the trial judge reach the same

conclusion on the facts? [The opinion in this case does not answer this question.]

- What shall be said of the Supreme Court's observation that Zehmer's counsel at the trial had "conceded" that Zehmer was not too drunk to make a valid contract? [This provides an opportunity for a comment in class about the significance of oral argument before the court, as contrasted with the written briefs submitted.]
- The Supreme Court makes much of the fact that Zehmer made two different drafts of the memorandum—the first began with "I," and the second with "We." Why would the court think that was significant? [The court found this part of the evidence of adequate thought and care put into the writing, supporting the conclusion that the writing was intended to have effect as a contractual commitment.]

Ultimately, the Supreme Court framed the key issue or assumed the key issue to be: whether W.O. Lucy could reasonably believe that Zehmer intended a serious bargain and a valid and binding offer to sell the Ferguson farm for $50,000, an offer which Lucy accepted, thus creating an "agreement" on those terms. The Court weighed the following factors in deciding (resolving) that issue:

- The proposed sale was under discussion for 40 minutes before the memorandum was signed
- W.O. Lucy objected to the first draft and Zehmer rewrote it to meet Lucy's objection
- Zehmer obtained Mrs. Zehmer's signature on the memorandum
- There was a contemporaneous discussion of what was intended to be included in the sale
- Provision was inserted in the agreement for a lawyer's examination of title and that examination proved satisfactory (Zehmer had good title to the Ferguson farm which he was capable of transferring to another by a valid agreement to that end)
- The memorandum was sufficiently complete
- W.O. Lucy took possession of the memorandum without objection or request by Zehmer that he give it back.

If you were arguing a case in your home state today based on a similar note or memorandum, would you expect to have to establish that your facts were the same, on all the above counts, as those in *Lucy v. Zehmer* before you could seek to persuade your judge to apply the law as established in *Lucy v. Zehmer*? Then what was the law established in that case? And why are the various fact sets that the Supreme Court found persuasive important to anyone seeking to persuade a court to adopt the ruling of *Lucy v. Zehmer*? How would you try to establish the fact that the "Lucy" in your case reasonably understood that your "Zehmer" had made an offer, seriously intended, which could be turned into an agreement by acceptance by your "Lucy"?

At the outset of this note you were asked three questions. The second was, "What questions does this case raise for me?" As you can see, a single reported case can raise a multitude of questions and suggest many different problems for either litigator or draftsperson. One of the objectives of this course in Contracts is to have you learn the basic principles of law applicable to the making and performance of contracts (agreements). It is of primary importance, therefore, that, as you read a case in the casebook, you extract from that case the principle or principles involved together with the reasoning behind the application of those principles. In several months you will be taking a mid-year exam in Contracts. For that exam you will be studying the materials you have read. The basis for your study will be the notes that you have prepared: notes of the cases in the book (and other materials including the Restatement and the UCC), notes of other reading you will have done, together with notes you derived from classroom sessions. You might well end up with 50 pages or more of such notes by the end of November. Were you to copy down too much of the case into your notes, you might end up with 200 pages of your notes, far too many notes for you to review shortly before the day of your exam. Were you to copy down too little of the case, you may miss something basic to the decision and something basic to the applicable principle, thus shortchanging yourself in preparing to take the exam. How much is too much, and how much is too little, is something that you will have to judge based on further experience in this course as well as your other first year courses.

At some point in your Contracts class I will call on you by name and ask you to tell the class what, in your view, a particular case was all about. I may ask you to brief a particular case and publish your brief for the benefit of the class in our TWEN program. I may pull your brief up and show it on the screen in class and invite other members of the class to comment. In these and other ways you will sharpen your judgment about what is important and what is unimportant in a case, and therefore, in your notes.

While one basic objective of this course is to have you learn the basic principles of Contract law, another basic objective is to train you in the reading, understanding and use of cases—cases are one of the primary tools of the lawyer both for litigation, drafting and counseling."

NOTES AND QUESTIONS

1. *Specific performance remedy.* See the discussion in the text, Par. (1). The remedy of specific performance, a form of injunction, owes its history to the Court of Exchequer as described in Chapter 1. This

remedy was and is equitable in nature, involving a trial to a judge and not to a jury. This explains the absence of any jury verdict in the court below. The decision to grant an equitable remedy or not lies completely in the discretion of the judge. The plaintiff has no "right" to such a remedy even if the terms of the contract provide expressly that injunctive relief is to be available for breach. The trial judge refused to grant the injunction but we are not told the reasons for that decision. The Virginia Supreme Court, based on its reading of the whole record, decided to grant the injunction, noting that A.H. Zehmer had admitted that $50,000 was a fair price.

2. *The joke defense.* This defense would be relevant if the court's rule or standard was a true "meeting of the minds." The standard applied by the court, objective interpretation, focuses not on what the subjective state of mind of the Zehmers was in fact, but rather on what Lucy could reasonably understand the Zehmers' intent to have been. Use of the objective standard raises a fascinating theoretical issue—see Professor Kennedy's article cited in the text—with respect to the rationale for enforcing or not enforcing contracts. Use of this objective standard is inconsistent with a pure "will" or "private autonomy" explanation. A more attractive rationale may be found in the social and business good that derives from fulfillment of the expectation that contracts, when entered into, will be performed. That expectation is basic to the effective functioning of our commercial world. A pure will theory would fundamentally undermine that expectation. The student might consider the extent to which there is a pure "meeting of the minds" on the terms of the policy when the student purchases automobile insurance. The choice by the court of the objective standard comes from a choice between competing alternatives and students may wish to consider the factors supporting the court's choice—such as relative certainty of outcome, relative predictability, relative administrative efficiency of outcomes, and comparative fairness (the Zehmers were charged with the responsibility of knowing that their actions could be interpreted by Lucy as indicating intent to contract—in effect, if there was a mistake, they caused that mistake). Will the students agree that a Zehmer-like person should know what the other party will reasonably understand? Does the word "reasonable" in the standard introduce an element of uncertainty and unpredictability, and create a substantial subjective power of choice in the judge?

See the remainder of text. What distinctions, if any, can be drawn between the joke promise in *Lucy v. Zehmer* and the joke promises above? The distinction, if any, turns on whether the joke offeree knew or should have known that the offer was intended only as a joke – objective interpretation. Assuming that all of the plaintiffs in the situations described above really did subjectively believe that the promised awards or payments were real, why shouldn't the alleged promisors be held liable for making those promises? The "objective" interpretation cuts both ways. The subjective belief of the offerees that the offer was genuine and not a joke should not trump the objective assessment of the offer – joke or no joke. If the test were the subjective belief of the offeree there could be no end to the lawsuits that could be brought under these circumstances, lawsuits not objectively justifiable.The distinctions, if any, must be based on the "reasonableness" of the promisee's reliance and/or on an interpretation of what the promissory words should actually be understood to mean.

3. *Ethical representation of a client.* The key issue was whether Lucy could reasonably understand that a binding commitment to sell the Ferguson Farm was intended. This is a question of fact which counsel for the Zehmers struggled unsuccessfully to challenge before the Supreme Court. They had, after all, prevailed at the trial level. Perhaps the weakest point in the opinion is the way in which the "delivery" of the note and the offer of the $5 are handled. Perhaps these two factors might have been exploited by counsel for the Zehmers more effectively, arguing that Lucy "snatched" the note and that there was no effective "delivery" of that note by A.H. Zehmer. The evidence with respect to Lucy's proffer of the $5 might have been exploited by suggesting that this constituted substantial evidence of Lucy's doubt as to whether a contract had been entered into.

On the civil side, a lawyer has no obligation to accept a case. When the lawyer does accept a case he or she assumes a duty to apply the talents and ability of an average lawyer in that community. Lawyers are sometimes sued for malpractice, i.e. failure to represent their client effectively. The legal standard normally applied in a legal malpractice case is the community standard of law practice in that locale. Nothing in the opinion suggests that the Zehmers' counsel failed to provide effective counsel. Students need to appreciate that, in most cases, there is room for a court to decide the issues either way—herein of the skill of counsel in (a) convincing the court to decide in his/her client's favor and (b) providing an acceptable logical and persuasive line of reasoning, consistent with applicable law, for the court to follow to reach that result.

Both Mr. and Mrs. Zehmer were clients. Under applicable rules of professional conduct, counsel was able to represent both of them since they shared a common cause. Representing both of them required, of course, the informed consent of each of them. The risk that the separate interests of the parties may diverge and that, when that happens, the lawyer must withdraw from the representation, is a risk the lawyer must weigh in undertaking a joint representation.

4. *Mrs. Zehmer's role.* The court does not deal expressly with Mrs. Zehmer's intent other than to conclude that Lucy could properly understand that, by reason of the course of negotiations and the production of the writing signed by both Mr. and Mrs. Zehmer, a

serious commitment to the sale and purchase was manifested by both Mr. and Mrs. Zehmer. Note that there is a significant difference in the testimony of Lucy, on the one hand, and the Zehmers, on the other, as to the circumstances of her signing. The court described Lucy's testimony on this point, "Mrs. Zehmer said she would for $50,000 and signed it." Zehmer testified, in the court's words, "Zehmer walked over to where she was and she at first refused to sign but did so after he told her that he 'was just needling him [Lucy], and didn't mean a thing in the world, that I was not selling the farm.'" The court does not deal expressly with this discrepancy, but the students may wonder whether it could be important. We do not know why the trial judge dismissed the complaint. It is possible that he found the Zehmers to be the more credible witnesses. But the supreme court, based on its reading of the full record of the trial below, found adequate evidence to support their ruling based on the objective standard.

5. *Role of assignment.* The text asks and answers the question as to how J.C. Lucy obtained the right to enforce the contract.

6. *Intoxication and voidable contracts.* Had one or other of the parties been "intoxicated" to the extent of the standard stated by the court, the contract would be voidable and not void. See, e.g., Restatement (Second) of Contracts § 16 ("A person incurs only voidable contractual duties by entering into a transaction if the other party has reason to know that by reason of intoxication (a) he is unable to understand in a reasonable manner the nature and consequences of the transaction, or (b) he is unable to act in a reasonable manner in relation to the transaction.").

The difference between "void" and "voidable" contracts is important. A contract which is void creates no rights and duties for either the parties or third parties. For example, a check signed by the payor under the threat of a pistol held to the head of the payor by the payee is void and not voidable. A contract that is voidable may be avoided by one of the parties or by both parties. Offer and acceptance have been manifested by the parties but the true intention manifested by either the offer or the acceptance may be questioned because of facts not apparent on the face of either the offer or the acceptance. To avoid the contract, and thus negate rights and duties arising under the shared manifestations of intent, appropriate affirmative action and notice are required. The party with the power to avoid may elect not to exercise that power and then the contract becomes conclusively binding. Generally, such a power must be exercised promptly, and the power may be lost by delay. Furthermore, bona fide purchasers for value without notice can acquire rights under a voidable contract that then cannot be defeated by attempted exercise of the power of avoidance. Thus, assuming that the contract for the sale and purchase of the Ferguson Farm was voidable, if Lucy had assigned the written contract to a bona fide purchaser for value without notice of the basis for avoidance, the purchaser's right to enforce the contract would not be defeated by any claimed avoidance based on "intoxication." In this situation, the intoxicated party is the appropriate and better burden bearer than the third party purchaser.

7. *Will theory and contract damages.* Expectancy damages are granted in order to place the party injured by the breach in the position that party would have been had the contract been performed. This is the basic remedy for breach of contract—see R2K §347. In situations such as *Zehmer,* the grant of a remedy enforcing "reasonable expectation" cannot be justified on a theory of "will"—that is that the Zehmers voluntarily accepted their exposure to such a remedy. Instead, the remedy is justified by commercial necessity. While there is appropriate theoretical support for expectancy damages, the facts of *Lucy v. Zehmer* raise an interesting question challenging the universality of the norm of expectancy damages for breaches of contract. The court apparently concluded that a binding commitment came into being when Lucy picked up the signed note. It should be noted that immediately thereafter Zehmer proclaimed that he had no intent to sell the farm and that, at this point, Lucy had suffered no reliance damage of any sort. The grant of injunctive relief in this case had to be based on "expectancy" rather than "reliance." The student may wonder whether such a drastic outcome, from the Zehmers' point of view, was justified by reliance, if any, that lasted only a matter of moments.

8. *Tort law alternative liability for careless misrepresentation.* Is the objective theory of contracts essential to protect the reasonable interests of a recipient from careless misleading statements? Where the injured party has truly relied on the contract, established objectively, expectancy damages or injunctive relief may be appropriate. As noted under Par. (7) above, Lucy's reliance was, at best, a matter of moments. Whether "justice" was rendered in this circumstance by granting the injunction can be debated. Let the student assume for the moment (but see Chapter 6 below) that a tort action based on negligent speech is available, what would such a remedy have produced on the *Zehmer* facts? Unlike the forwards looking contracts expectancy measure, the tort measure is backwards looking and designed to restore the plaintiff to the situation the plaintiff was in before commission of the tort. The application of such a tort measure would have produced no recovery—the plaintiff was no worse off after the moments of reliance than he was before.

C. ENFORCING PROMISES: LEGAL THEORIES OF OBLIGATION

1. Obligation by Reason of an Agreement Supported by Consideration

The Massachusetts Supreme Court in the *King* case required not only proof of a promise but also "consideration or reliance." We now explore the scope and extent of such reasons. The text provides a short history of the writ of assumpsit, *Slade's Case*, and the development of the doctrine of "consideration." The pending problems for students are: Should a promise alone be enforceable without more? If not, why not? If so, what more is or should be required and why?

a. The Donor-Promise Principle

Dougherty v. Salt
CASE BRIEF

This is a 1919 decision of the New York Court of Appeals. Here an aunt signed a printed form promissory note for $3,000 payable at her death or before, and delivered the note to her young nephew. After the aunt's death her executrix (manager of the estate and named in the will as such—compare administratrix, administrator appointed by the court but not named in the will) refused to pay the note and the boy's guardian brought suit. The defense was that the promissory note was not supported by consideration and thus unenforceable. The trial judge submitted the question of consideration or not to the jury and the jury found in the plaintiff's favor. The judge then set aside the verdict and dismissed the complaint, holding in effect that no cause of action had been proven. The intermediate appellate court reversed the dismissal and reinstated the jury verdict. The Court of Appeals reversed the decision of the intermediate appellate court and ordered a new trial, not dismissal of the action (truly a perplexing outcome). For there to be anything to retry there would have to be the possibility of a substantiated cause of action. Since the Court of Appeals found the note to be unenforceable by reason of lack of consideration, what issue was left upon which the plaintiff might be able to prevail? Directing trial of a claimed defense of forgery, as the court did, does not answer this question.

INTERESTING DISCUSSION ISSUES

The answer to the question, "Why is this case in the casebook?" is clear. Justice Cardozo made two important points: (a) the promissory note constituted a promise to do something in the future (and thus was not a gift completed by and at the time of delivery of the note) which was enforceable, if at all, only if the promise was supported by consideration; (b) the recital in the note that value (consideration) had been received could be challenged and contradicted by other testimony (here the guardian plaintiff's own admission). Note that the latter point will also be relevant in later discussions regarding the parol evidence rule.

The student should ask the following questions. Was the evidence of gift intent clear? Answer, only maybe—the aunt, if alive, might have paid the note, or might have changed her mind. Why were the words reciting consideration included in the form of note? Answer, they were included in the wording of the promissory note printed form. Was the delivery of the note, reciting consideration, intended to complete the gift transaction? Apparently this was the aunt's intent. Why was the gift not complete at that point? Presumably, the answer is that the gift was not complete because the note contained no more than a promise that payment would be made in the future. Why would the court require a showing of consideration if the recital of value received (consideration) were challenged? Answer, because for a number of reasons, mostly historical, promises to make a gift in the future were not enforceable without bargained for consideration, and lack of consideration could always be shown regardless of the wording of the writing.

Should this result remain good law today? What are the arguments involved in enforcing or not enforcing the note? In the absence of a bargained for exchange, why should a mere promise be enforceable and may not be withdrawn by the promisor during her lifetime or automatically by her death? The editorial notes before the case summarize various considerations, other than pure common law history and precedent, that may support the ruling in the case. Perhaps the most persuasive is that the maker of a gift-promise should retain the freedom to change her mind at any time before full performance. The gift-promisor should have a point of repentance, an opportunity to consider or reconsider. Another consideration can be derived from the evidentiary "formal" function of the bargain-exchange. Where such a bargain-exchange can be shown, there is substantially less risk that the alleged gift-promise is the product of false testimony. Yet a third consideration is that the recipient is not being deprived of anything, the gift never having been completed. This consideration loses its persuasiveness under circumstances where the gift-promisee has relied on the promise (reasonably) and changed position detrimentally.

It is this third consideration which can form a useful bridge between the result in this case and the result in *King*. The students should be aware, however, that the result in *King* is not universally recognized (just as R2K §90(2) has a number of unbelievers)—there still being diehard states that refuse to enforce a gift-promise whether or not relied upon, presumably concluding that there is no reasonable basis for reliance upon a promise of the making of a gift in the future. Hopefully, the student then asks what considerations these various conflicting state court decisions are taking into account in stating their own rule.

NOTES AND QUESTIONS

1. *Matter of law.* "Under the modern procedure of judgment notwithstanding the verdict, a judge may dismiss a case after a jury renders a verdict for the plaintiff. The standard for judgment notwithstanding the verdict is the same standard for dismissal by summary judgment or directed verdict. A judge determines whether a reasonable jury could find for the non-moving party. Under the motion, the sufficiency of the evidence is examined....." Suja A. Thomas, "The Seventh Amendment, Modern Procedure and the English Common Law," 82 Wash. U. L.Q. 687, 741 (2004).

2. *Testamentary transfers.* Emma Salt, the executrix, did not pay the note because she believed that payment was not required and her belief was sustained by the Court of Appeals decision. Clearly, Helena could have provided for an enforceable testamentary gift of the $3,000 in her will. The important point is that she did not do that. How might she have guaranteed that payment would be made? Most easily through the means of a bargained for exchange (something of value) with the boy's guardian. Without extending this Contracts course into a course on Trust Law, it would also have been possible for her to use a declaration of trust.

3. *The donative-promise principle.* The text lists some policy reasons for not enforcing a donative promise in the absence of a completed gift transaction or in the absence of detrimental reliance on the promise.

4. *False and nominal consideration.* More will be said on this subject following Berryman v. Kmoch in Chapter 3.

5. *An argument for enforcement.* It is easy to make a case for a state statute creating a form of gift-promise that is enforceable. Apparently some states still preserve the concept of the attachment of a seal to a writing as a sufficient formality to make the gift-promise enforceable. Acknowledgement of completed gift intent in a writing signed before a notary public could serve a similar function. That many states have not bothered to authorize and create such a formal process bespeaks a low level of social concern with these peripheral problems. See the description of a Model Promises Enforcement Act in Eric Mills

Holmes, "Stature and Status of a Promise Under Seal as a Legal Formality," 29 Willamette L. Rev. 617, 667 (1993).

Is there a reason to distinguish between intrafamilial and other types of donative promises? The family context may and does raise very difficult questions respecting property—see, for instance, the discussion of palimony cases later in Chapter 5.

6. *Promissory certainty.* Farnsworth's observation (echoed in Ian Ayres's and Gregory Klass' more recent work titled "Insincere Promises" (2005)) notes that promisors and promisees lack the ability to make a nuanced promise that conveys the degree of their intent to perform or not. Curtis Bridgeman, in "Misrepresented Intent in the Context of Unequal Bargaining Power," 2006 Mich. St. L. Rev. 993, notes, however, that contract law already permits parties to communicate the likelihood of their performance through mechanisms such as a reservation of a right not to perform the promise under certain conditions or even at the promisor's discretion. Thus, for example, airlines routinely include savings clauses in their contracts with passengers reserving the right not to comply with published schedules. See, id. Other contracts described by Bridgeman provide even greater degrees of commitment by the promisor while still communicating that there is a likelihood the promisor will not perform. See, id.

b. The Peppercorn Principle and the Equivalency Theory

Consideration analysis is usually confined to form and not the comparative value of the exchanges. The policing of the relative fairness of the transaction is left to the separate judgment of each party to the exchange. Is the "will" theory, and the doctrine of consideration with it, deficient to the extent that it presumes a "level playing field" for both parties, a presumption that is often not true?

Hamer v. Sidway
CASE BRIEF

This is an 1891 decision of the New York Court of Appeals. The offer by William E, Story was for a unilateral contract—a promise of $5,000 if William E. Story, 2d would "refrain from drinking, using tobacco, swearing, and playing cards or billiards for money until he became 21 years of age. ..." William, 2d complied and asked for his money. He was not paid during William, Sr.'s lifetime. William, 2d assigned his claim to his wife who in turn assigned it to the plaintiff (money lender?). William, Sr.'s executor (that darned estate administrator again!) refused to pay, defending on the basis that the promise of $5,000 was not supported by consideration and was therefore unenforceable. William, Sr., the defense claimed, was not benefited by anything that William, 2d did and therefore there had been no exchange of value. It was clear that a bargain had been struck—the defense was based on assessment of the benefit flowing to William, Sr. as without value. The court in direct terms dismissed the notion that measurement of value, if any, to William, Sr. had anything to do with the doctrine of consideration. An exchange was required, and where that exchange involved detriment to the promisee that detriment constituted sufficient consideration. The court provided this quote, "In general a waiver of any legal right at the request of another party is a sufficient consideration for a promise." This case announces the proposition, generally thereafter accepted, that so long as there is a bargained for exchange, and the exchange on either side is not illusory or valueless, the court will not find it either necessary or appropriate to place a value on that which is exchanged by either party. The doctrine of consideration deals with form and not the fair value of the exchange. Waiving any legal right, such as playing billiards for money, is enough to satisfy the requirements of form if that waiver was bargained for. "Nothing is consideration which is not bargained for as such."

INTERESTING DISCUSSION ISSUE

The facts of the *Shadwell* case, referred to in the opinion, extend the problem further. The only possible inferred exchange on those facts is Lancey's going through with the intended marriage to Ellen. They were already engaged and Lancey therefore had a legal obligation to marry Ellen according to then existing English law. If he was already so legally obligated, what legal right was he giving up so as to provide the necessary consideration? Herein of the "pre-existing duty" rule which generated too many consideration law disputes. Justice Cardozo dealt with precisely this issue in *DeCicco v. Schweitzer*, 221 N.Y. 431, 117 N.E. 807 (1917) where he found consideration to support a promise of a marriage settlement in the agreement of the two affianced to proceed with their marriage, they having the right to rescind their agreement to marry by mutual accord. The only difficulty with that opinion is that he had to manufacture an agreement between the affianced couple not to rescind.

NOTES AND QUESTIONS

1. *Origin of the "peppercorn doctrine."* The explanation, but not justification, for the difference in treatment under rules of contract and rules of trust law lies in the English distinction between the rules of the Kings (Queens) Bench and Chancery. Trust law was the creation of equity—Chancery. In assessment of the various considerations to be

taken into account in deciding whether or not a binding commitment should be found and enforced, this historical difference offers no solace.

2. *Restatement approach.* See text.

3. *The trust as an alternative to unenforceable donative promises.* See Note (1) comment above.

4. *Contract, trust and the statute of limitations.* The gift of the $5,000 having been found complete, William, Sr. owed the $5,000 as a debt to William, 2d. Suit on that debt could have been barred by the common six year statute of limitations. Finding William, Sr. to have created a trust over the money, the statute of limitations did not run—William, 2d was the beneficial owner of the money (holder of the equitable title) thus avoiding any issue as to the statute of limitations.

5. *Legality of the promisee detriment.* See text.

Batsakis v. Demotsis
CASE BRIEF

This is a 1949 decision of the Texas Court of Civil Appeals. Both Batsakis (creditor) and Demotsis (debtor) were residents of Greece on April 2, 1942. On that date Demotsis signed a letter acknowledging receipt from Batsakis of $2,000 to be repaid at the end of the war or before if possible and at 8% interest. When this note was not paid Batsakis sued for $2,000 plus accrued interest. Demotsis entered a general denial. The court sitting without a jury, entered judgment for the plaintiff in the amount of $750 plus interest. The plaintiff appealed. At issue was the admission by the trial judge of evidence that the true transaction involved the delivery of 500,000 drachmae ($25 in 1942) in exchange for the signed letter and promise to repay $2,000. The Texas Court of Appeals accepted the plaintiff's arguments, reformed the judgment to reflect an order to pay the full $2,000 plus accrued interest.

INTERESTING DISCUSSION ISSUES

That there was a bargained for exchange in 1942 was not in doubt. At issue was whether the court would look at the very severe value imbalance between what the plaintiff gave and what the defendant promised to pay. The decision was consistent with traditional doctrine that courts should not attempt to weigh and compare the relative value provided by each side in the exchange. The students should inquire why the courts adopted such a position and whether that decision should be perpetuated. The considerations involved include the inherent subjectivity of value—"value is in the eye of the beholder"—and the inappropriateness of a judge displacing the party's own assessment of value by the judge's personal subjective opinion. As another factor, judges have no special expertise or experience in valuing things—to do so suggests judicial "activism." Yet another, implicit in the development of the doctrine of consideration is that the role of the doctrine is to establish form and not content—proof of the bargained for exchange is proof that a binding transaction was intended, and that is all. This interpretation and application of the doctrine of consideration is once again at odds with the "will" theory since, taking the defendant's evidence of the transaction at face value, she could not have truly "intended" to promise to repay $2,000.

The doctrine, as applied, assumes that both parties were playing on a level playing field. Obviously, in 1942, they were not. The defendant could not get access to her own financing and needed funds desperately to get out of Greece with the Nazi army closing in behind. Was this transaction affected by unfairness, unconscionability, or coercion of some kind? The common law's remedies, if any, for such anomalies in the "meeting of the minds" were extremely limited. This case shows the unwillingness of this court to use the doctrine of consideration as a tool to limit possible serious "unjust enrichment" by the plaintiff. The opinion does not explain clearly why the trial court found liability for $750 but not $2,000.

The defendant failed to make any express argument based on unconscionability of the bargain. (The defense of unconscionability is addressed in detail in Chapter 5). It can be argued that, in fact, the bargain was not unconscionable. Given the then state of war, the plaintiff certainly ran a substantial risk that he would never get repaid. Should that aspect of the risk affect any consideration of relative "unconscionability"?

Suffice it to say that the case stands as a current example of a court's refusal to consider the relative equivalence between the value of performance on one side compared to that on the other.

The case also stands again for the proposition that evidence as to the presence or absence of consideration can always be introduced regardless of recitals to the contrary in signed written documents. Should courts be concerned about allowing relatively unreliable oral evidence to contradict the relatively more reliable evidence of the signed written document?

NOTES AND QUESTIONS

1. *Terminology - "Want" or "failure" of consideration.* The signed letter shows that the defendant got what she sought. There was no total failure of consideration. The problem was the apparent unfairness of the bargain. Should the doctrine of consideration function as a tool to deal with serious unfairness—through a finding of want or failure of

"adequate" consideration? The court said emphatically "No." The defendant apparently failed to plead "unconscionability" directly—see "Discussion Issues" above.

2. *Inadequacy of consideration.* Her concern was indeed with gross inadequacy. Why was this not argued? It may well have been argued since something must have moved the trial court to find liability for payment of $750, not $2,000. The question of whether the contract was entered into under duress is covered in the notes on the case above. The students might wonder about the following set of facts: a young and inexperienced buyer agrees in a signed writing to pay $2,500 for a new refrigerator that she could have purchased at another store for $1,000. Should liability depend on the doctrine of consideration and the relative value on each side of the exchange?

3. *Doctrine of fair exchange.* See text. Students should recognize that inadequacy of consideration, represented by a gross disparity of value exchanged between the parties, generally will not in itself cause the contract to be unenforceable. But such gross value disparities may indicate that the contract suffers from other defects, such as fraud, duress or unconscionability.

4. *International civil law doctrine of fair exchange.* See text.

5. *Policing inadequacy of consideration.* The apparent benefit will be a fair result in the particular case. The apparent cost can be found in the old saying, "Hard cases make bad law" - in other words, a case decision functions as a statement of a rule to be applied to other cases and not just the case specifically involved. "Bending" the law to suit a particularly hard set of facts suggests a precedent that may, in turn, produce an unfair or inappropriate result when applied in a subsequent case. If a student wants to argue that, because of this problem, we should abandon the concept of "stare decisis," the alternative is likely to be a very serious loss of certainty and predictability—one of the highest order concerns in the field of contract law.

6. *Contract interest.* Two of the authors would argue vigorously that the requirement that the sum be "definite" in order to recover prejudgment interest can work severe injustice in the world of liability insurance where the insurer can and frequently does defer payment for years through litigation about "how much" if any is involved—thus avoiding a claim by the insured for a "sum certain." Thi s issue is discussed at greater length in Chapter 9.

c. The Past Consideration Doctrine

Hayes v. Plantations Steel Company
CASE BRIEF

This is a 1982 decision of the Supreme Court of Rhode Island. After 25 years of continuous service, including serving as general manager at the end, Hayes announced his intention to retire. He retired six months later. One week before he retired, an officer of the defendant company promised that the company would "take care of him." The following year, and for each of the three more years thereafter, Hayes received a check in the amount of $5,000. Corporate management changed and the new management refused to make any further payments to Hayes. Hayes sued alleging an implied-in-fact contract as well as promissory estoppel and detrimental reliance. The trial court found for Hayes holding that an implied-in-fact contract had been entered into entitling Hayes to received $5,000 a year for life. It also held that Hayes had made out a case for enforcement based on promissory estoppel. Hayes testified that he would not have retired had he not expected to receive a pension. The officer of the company who had made the promise testified that it was his personal intention that the payments would continue "as long as I was around" and that Hayes stopped by each year after receiving the check to thank the officer and ask how long the payments would continue so that he could plan an orderly retirement. The trial court held specifically that Hayes' retirement was in response to the promise and that Hayes refrained from seeking other employment in further reliance on that promise. While the Supreme Court noted that the company board did not adopt any resolution approving these payments, students should be advised that the officer had the necessary authority to bind the company if the evidence supported a binding promise.

The Supreme Court recited the strong presumption that should follow the findings of the trial court sitting without a jury unless its conclusions were "clearly wrong" "or that the trial justice misconceived or overlooked material evidence."

Nevertheless, the Rhode Island Supreme Court reversed the trial court, holding both that there was no enforceable contract to support the payments and that there was no basis for promissory estoppel.

The court found there was no "promise"—the officer did not quantify the amount that would be paid. The only evidence of amount came from the checks as they were later written and delivered. But the basis of the court's opinion was that there was no "consideration" provided by Hayes to support the alleged contract. Valid consideration must be bargained for and it must induce the return act or promise. Hayes had announced his intention to retire six months earlier and his decision was arrived at without regard to any promise made on behalf of the company. The promise, if any, was made as a "token of appreciation" for Hayes' past service. Any payments were thus a gift. Hayes' argument that he continued working for a week after the making of the promise was found unpersuasive, and no covenant not to compete was negotiated.

While the court found that the doctrine of promissory estoppel had been adopted in Rhode Island, it was inapplicable on the facts of this case since there was no evidence that the promise induced Hayes' retirement. The court found that Hayes' annual inquiry about whether he could expect a check for the following year negated the existence of any detrimental reliance.

INTERESTING DISCUSSION ISSUES

This case involves the application of the traditional "consideration" doctrine that nothing can be consideration that is not bargained for as such and that there must be a bargained for exchange. The doctrine of promissory estoppel could not save Hayes because, in the eye of the Supreme Court, there was no reasonable detrimental reliance on his part. Should the court have focused on the trial court finding that Hayes refrained from seeking other employment in further reliance on that promise? Could the court have distinguished between a remedy based on the extent of Hayes' financial loss through such reliance versus enforcement of a bargain with benefit of the bargain damages? Compare the language of the Restatement (Second) of Contracts § 90, "The remedy granted for breach may be limited as justice requires."

The second universally pending question, "How could this dispute have been avoided by better drafting?" deserves a comment—tied to the court's observation about the absence of a covenant not to compete. Had Hayes been represented by counsel during that last week of service, counsel could have recommended that Hayes negotiate a pension in a specific amount for life based on a covenant not to work for a competitor of the company for a short stated period or, in the alternative, to hold himself available for a short period to serve as a consultant to the company. Since courts do not investigate the relative value of the exchange, either would clearly suffice to support an enforceable contract and both are commonly used in such agreements. Was the largest defect in Hayes' argument that no specific amount was stated as part of the promise?

NOTES AND QUESTIONS

1. *Searching for a theory of obligation.* The promisee's motivation for his decision to retire is important only if his decision was bargained for. Under classic consideration doctrine, nothing is consideration that is not bargained for as such. Motive is subjective with the promisee—bargained for consideration is objective, negotiated between the

parties. As noted above, should the supreme court have focused on the trial court finding that Hayes refrained from seeking other employment in further reliance on that promise? If that reliance was not based on a bargained for exchange, it does not meet the classic requirements of consideration. But it might meet the requirements of detrimental reliance under Restatement (Second) of Contracts § 90. The Supreme Court determined that the company did not seek Hayes' retirement as the underpinning for their conclusion that the retirement was not part of a bargained for exchange. The court did not confuse motivation with bargain, given the court's underlying findings of fact. The relevance of a covenant not to compete is discussed in the "Issues" section above. Again, the court's implied findings of fact include that Hayes' continuing to work for one more week was not bargained for.

The court's rejection of the trial judge's findings of fact supporting promissory estoppel is problematic. The court's reasoning is orthodox if, indeed, Hayes did not rely on a promise of a retirement benefit. But the trial court found as a fact that Hayes had detrimentally relied. The trial court's finding is, however, difficult to reconcile with the evidence in the record that Hayes visited the company each year to say thanks and at the same time inquire whether the payment would be continued. "He inquired each year about whether he could expect a check for the following year. Obviously, there was no absolute certainty on his part that the pension would continue." The difference then between the trial court and the supreme court depends upon a different conclusion as to the factual record. Since the trial judge observed the witnesses while the supreme court did not, the reader might expect the supreme court to explain in greater detail why it rejected the trial court's finding of fact.

It may be helpful during this discussion to explore the question of how the company could have made an enforceable promise to Hayes supported by a valid consideration. Students will often respond that it might have been enforceable if Hayes had done some additional work, stayed an additional day, or otherwise incurred an additional duty that would satisfy the bargained-for exchange requirement. All of these purported considerations from Hayes suffer from the fact that it is extremely unlikely that the parties would alter their promissory interaction in this manner. In other words, the company appears happy to have Hayes retire, and the possibility that Hayes might work for some additional period "in exchange" for a life pension seems akin to the sham consideration at issue in *Dougherty*. Another possibility might have the company promising to give Hayes a life pension if he gave up his right to change his mind about retiring in the final week of his retirement. This option seems more realistic and arguably creates a consideration without having to change what the parties actually did. It also emphasizes that a promise to refrain from acting (i.e., surrender a legal right) may supply a consideration just as well as an affirmative action or a promise to undertake such an action in the future.

The two theories of consideration and promissory estoppel are not inconsistent. They are based on and operate from different premises. The theory of consideration, as discussed earlier in the text notes, is a theory based on form. The theory of promissory estoppel is based on substantial and reasonably foreseeable reliance. As Restatement (Second) of Contracts § 90 points out, the remedy "may be limited as justice requires." Consideration theory addresses form, substantiating the fact that a bargained for exchange was achieved, not fairness in the sense of reasonable equivalence in the exchange. "Fairness," as related to bargained for exchanges, may be reviewable under other doctrines including unconscionability, fraud, duress, misrepresentation, undue influence, etc.

2. *Pernicious problem*. As pointed out above, the difference between the conclusions of the trial and the supreme courts is based on contrary findings of fact. The questions posed in this note/question raise interesting issues with respect to possible factual reliance that counsel for Hayes might have presented more effectively. One can speculate whether the outcome under both theories might have been different if Mainelli's promise had included a specific dollar amount to be paid each year and for life.

d. Gratuitous Conditional Promises

Kirksey v. Kirksey
CASE BRIEF

This is an 1845 decision of the Alabama Supreme Court. The students should note first that this is an old Alabama decision.

The plaintiff, "Sister Antillico," was the widow of the defendant's brother. At the time of the defendant's promise, she was living on public land, with her several children, under circumstances that could have led to her acquiring legal title to that land. In a letter addressed to her the defendant said: "If you will come down and see me, I will let you have a place to raise your family, and I have more land than I can tend; and on account of your situation, and that of your family, I feel like I want you and the children to do well." She responded by moving with her family and for two years the defendant put her in a comfortable house and gave her land to cultivate. The defendant thereafter gave her notice to leave. A jury found for the plaintiff and awarded her $200. The Alabama Supreme Court reversed, on the ground of lack of consideration to support the promise notwithstanding the suggestion of one of the justices that her "breaking up, and moving to the defendant's, a distance of sixty miles," constituted "sufficient consideration." The Supreme Court opinion turns on a finding of conditional gift-promise rather than bargained for exchange—Sister Antillico's moving was a condition of the gift but was not bargained for.

INTERESTING DISCUSSION ISSUES

This case was decided well before the doctrine of promissory estoppel evolved and provides an excellent illustration of the importance of the distinction between an award of reliance damages rather than an award of benefit of the bargain damages. Under classical "will" analysis, the terms, scope and extent of the defendant's promise were sufficiently vague that a court could have found it impossible to craft a specific remedy based on that promise. The extent of her "reliance" damages could have been determined with ease and the student may infer that this is precisely what the jury did in awarding her $200, the amount of her loss with respect to her inchoate title to the land she had been living on before she moved.

NOTES AND QUESTIONS

1. *The relevancy of motive.* The notes emphasize the difficulty of distinguishing between a bargained for promise and a conditional gift promise. A traditional example of the latter is, "If you will come by my shop on Tuesday, I will give you a new suit." There is no apparent benefit to the maker of the promise, there may be slight detriment to the promisee, but there is no true reasonable reliance in this hypothetical. In contrast, "Sister Antillico" changed her position substantially and to her detriment in relying on the defendant's promise.

2. *Gender bias.* Whether there was any gender bias in this case must lie in the eye of the beholder. The last question in the note, "What does your answer say about the legitimacy of contract law as an institution for creating enforceable obligations between and among individual members of differently situated social groups?" can be related back to Dean Morant's article cited above. The doctrine of consideration seems to be premised on a "level playing field" for both parties—a questionable premise in the family/social setting of this case. But if the playing field was not level, is the leveling to be adjusted through the revision of the form/theory of consideration or through another rubric—promissory estoppel plus detrimental reliance?

3. *The true story.* The true facts behind this case illustrate why a reliance measure of damages was apparently chosen by the jury and should have been affirmed on appeal.

4. *Another theory of obligation.* See the comment under Par. (3) above.

2. Obligation by Reason of Reliance: The Promissory Estoppel Doctrine

a. Noncommercial Promises

Ricketts v. Scothorn
CASE BRIEF

This is an 1898 decision of the Supreme Court of Nebraska. Grandfather Ricketts signed and delivered to Granddaughter Ricketts a promissory note for $2,000 payable on demand and at 6% interest. Grandfather died having paid one year's interest. Grandfather's administrator (the estate strikes again!) refused to pay the note. Granddaughter sued alleging both consideration supporting the note and detrimental reliance. The court dismissed the argument on consideration summarily—there was no bargained for consideration. The court upheld the claim, however, based on detrimental reliance on the promise.

INTERESTING DISCUSSION ISSUES

The analytic tool relied upon by the court was equitable estoppel or estoppel in pais. The use of this Norman French word suggests the relative antiquity of the concept. That doctrine, over centuries of usage, was a tool used as a shield and not as a sword. It was available as a defense to the claim of another, not as an affirmative cause of action involving the assertion of a right. In Hohfeldian terms, the concept was one of privilege/no right rather than right/duty. Nevertheless, the considerations underlying the long established doctrine were those of essential fairness—the plaintiff should not be allowed to "blow hot and cold" once there had been detrimental reliance on the "blowing."

This case illustrates one way in which legal concepts grow—by extension of previous doctrine. While the Nebraska Supreme Court did not acknowledge this fact, they were transforming an earlier doctrine and giving it a completely new application—moving from representations of past and present fact, to representations of future intent—and at the same time, moving from shield to sword. The considerations, however, were closely allied; a representation (in this case promise) together with reasonable detrimental reliance following precisely the reliance that the promisor did or should have foreseen. The court argued that the promisor (actually his estate) should be estopped from denying the promise that he had made. It should be noted that if this theory holds water, every gift promise would be enforceable. Why would that not be a good thing? Reasonable reliance was always a predicate of application of the doctrine of equitable estoppel.

This case illustrates further, the desire of a court for comfort found in allegedly supporting earlier decisions. The student should note the reasoning of the court by analogy to cases where gifts promised to charities had been enforced. Again, the student should note that the first impetus in the direction of a theory of promissory estoppel was found in these charitable gift decisions enforcing promises to make gifts where there had been detrimental reliance by the charity involved.

Again, this case invites comparison of the use of detrimental reliance to establish liability and the use of the same reliance to establish the measurement of the recovery. It is noteworthy that the court did not require investigation of the actual reliance costs of the granddaughter, but rather enforced the promise in the same way that a contract would have been enforced—awarding damages that placed the granddaughter where she would have been had the promise been performed and not where she would have been based solely on her reliance. If reliance had been used to calculate the amount of her recovery, presumably her ability to find a new job, at the same or better wage than she had previously received, would have been part of the test. Compare the jury's assessment of damage in *Kirksey* above.

NOTES AND QUESTIONS

1. *Estoppel in pais and promissory estoppel compared.* See discussion in "Issues" above. The court created a new doctrine of promissory estoppel—Katie relied on a promise of future action and not on a representation of past or present fact.

2. *Promissory estoppel, equitable estoppel and fundamental legal conceptions.* See text.

Wright v. Newman
CASE BRIEF

This is an 1996 decision of the Supreme Court of Georgia. Newman sued Wright to recover child support for her two children. While Wright was not the father of her son (DNA evidence) he had himself listed on the child's birth certificate and gave the child his surname. The majority of the court found he then paid support for 10 years before stopping.

The majority opinion stated that he would have been liable for child support if he were the true father or if he had adopted the child. Apart from these two situations he could only be liable based on a claim for breach of contract.

Did Wright make a promise of support? The majority found an implied-in-fact promise in the foregoing facts. The Georgia legislature had codified Restatement (Second) of Contracts § 90. It is noteworthy that the court treated the reliance as a complete substitute for consideration leading not only to enforceability of the promise but also to benefit of the bargain rather than reliance measured damages. The majority emphasized the extent of the reliance over a ten-year period. The sole dissent was based on an alleged complete failure on Newman's part to establish the measure of her loss due to reliance. In this decision §90 morphed from an alternative rationale for enforcing a promise to full equivalence with consideration notwithstanding the last sentence of subsection (1), "The remedy granted for breach may be limited as justice requires."

NOTES AND QUESTIONS

1. *Express and implied promises as bases for promissory estoppel.* A promise can be implied by or inferred from conduct. There is no reason not to apply promissory estoppel to an implied-in-fact promise.

2. *Codifying the common law.* Clearly, codification by statute does alter the role of the courts. But for this statute, the Georgia Supreme Court might, depending on prior precedent, have had to decide whether to adopt the concept of promissory estoppel at all, or if so, to what extent. The codification does not, however, lead to any automatic result. The Supreme Court played a specific role in deciding how the code section should be applied to the facts. As we will see in the next chapter, courts in different states are quite capable of reaching directly contrary results as to the meaning of a particular provision of the UCC Article 2.

b. Contract and Family Law

Professor Jacobs proposes a two year period after which the putative father can no longer seek to undo the previously presumed family relationship. The student should reflect again on the language of the majority opinion in *Wright v. Newman* above which bases the decision on implied promise but that argument is further buttressed by estoppel/reliance over the ten year period. "Moreover, he continued to do so for some ten years, holding himself out to others as the father of the child and allowing the child to consider him to be the natural father." In other words, the passage of time was a consideration, especially in the light of the interests of the child. Again, Justice Sears' concurring opinion emphasizes the time/reliance factor. Professor Jacob's proposal strikes a balance between the interests of the child and those of the putative father. Where paternity fraud leads to a "shotgun" marriage, should the marriage contract be voidable as a result of a fraudulent assertion of paternity?

NOTES AND QUESTIONS

1. *Detrimental reliance of children.* While the answer may lie in the eye of the beholder, the doctrine of promissory estoppel requires proof of both a promise and reasonable reliance thereon. Assuming that an implied promise could be found in the facts of the *Wright v. Newman* case, basing a remedy on reasonable detrimental reliance occurring over a sustained period of time is consistent with the basic theory.

2. *Classical contract consideration doctrine.* Classical consideration doctrine required a bargained for exchange. In some of these paternity cases the putative father may not have received any bargained for benefit. But the distinction between the classical doctrine and promissory estoppel simply emphasizes the different basis upon which promissory estoppel is founded—detrimental reliance and not bargained for benefit.

3. *Paternity fraud.* How can the mother's reliance be "reasonable" when inseparable from her fraudulent misrepresentation? If the primary concern, however, is the welfare of the child, sustained detrimental reliance should still apply for the benefit of the child. Perhaps this is the best illustration of the value of Professor Jacobs' proposed two year limitation period.

c. Charitable Subscriptions

Charitable pledge cards, used as part of a fundraising campaign, usually describe the purposes for the campaign and recite that the pledge is given in consideration of the pledges from others. If that recital is the only peg on which to hang a promissory estoppel argument, is the recital persuasive? Here the alleged reliance is by third parties and not the charity. Consideration, under classical theory, can be provided by a third party—see Restatement (Second) of Contracts § 71(4). But is reliance by a third party persuasive? Should the charity itself have to be the party reasonably relying? Recognizing that those from whom contributions are sought may have concerns based on the potential of financial reverses in their future, many charities include words in the pledge which excuse the pledgor in the event of such a financial reverse. Assuming a showing of reliance, should the pledgor or the pledgee be the judge of whether or not that condition has been triggered?

Allegheny College v. National Chautauqua County Bank
CASE BRIEF

This is a 1927 decision of the New York Court of Appeals. In 1921 Mary Yates signed an "estate pledge," "in consideration of others subscribing," for $5,000 payable to the Allegheny College, a charitable organization. The pledge recited a promise to pay 30 days after her death. An endorsement on the back stated that the gift was to be known as the "Mary Yates Johnston memorial fund." In 1923 she made a down payment of $1,000. In 1924 she repudiated the gift. She must have died shortly thereafter. The college then sued her executor. Students should note that this was not the case of a promise to leave the college a bequest under her will. It was a promise made in 1921, but to be paid 30 days after her death. Once a binding contract has been entered into, the death thereafter of a party does not ordinarily relieve that party's estate of the obligation to perform. Presumably, the doctrine of promissory estoppel operates in a similar fashion.

Students will note that she attached a condition to her pledge, namely that "This pledge shall be valid only on the condition that the provisions of my will, now extant, shall be first met." Instructors may need to explain the function and operation of a condition attached to a promise. A convenient example is found in the frequently used "financing contingency" incorporated in a contract for the sale and purchase of a house. Another example is "title satisfactory to buyer" in *Lucy v. Zehmer* above. The meaning of the condition she used is far from clear. Presumably her intent was that the pledge was not to be paid unless and until there were funds left over after satisfying all specific bequests ("I leave cousin John $10,000"). The opinion implies that the condition was not triggered.

Justice Cardozo started by stating that a promise is not enforceable without consideration—reliance is not enough. But then he referred to the "recent" theory of promissory estoppel. He declined to say whether that doctrine had become in its broad form a part of New York law. Although the case predates the Restatement (First) Contracts by five years, he was declining to commit to the broad principle later stated in Restatement (Second) of Contracts § 90. Nevertheless, he concluded that New York had adopted the doctrine as the equivalent of consideration in connection with the law of charitable subscriptions. That being said, the student will ask, "Why does he not end the opinion with one more sentence, "Her pledge is therefore enforceable as written"? Especially, since he noted the prior holding that the promise was enforceable without reference to proven detrimental reliance. There is no good answer to this question unless he wove his web of consideration in order to win a majority of the court.

His explanation of the reasons for the growth of this "exception" to the doctrine of consideration are interesting but not particularly persuasive. He cited "public policy," "breaches of faith towards the public," and the "unwarrantable disappointment of the reasonable expectations of those interested." Of greater weight might be the scope and extent of charitable giving and the value to the public at large of the good works performed by charities, perhaps relieving the public fisc to some extent.

He then proceeded to find the promise enforceable under the classical theory of consideration, an exercise not without "smoke and mirrors." He found bargained for consideration in an implied promise that he created that the college would name, declare and publish the fact of, the memorial fund created in her name. His arguments are somewhat belabored. He came close to acknowledging this when he said, "No doubt there are times and situations in which limitations laid upon a promisee in connection with the use of what is paid by a subscriber lack the quality of a consideration, and are to be classed merely as conditions." He did not have to find consideration in order to ensure that the college, having accepted money, would be required to apply that money in accordance with the terms of the promise. The student would never know from his opinion that principles of equity, dealing with the creation and enforcement of a "trust," had solved that problem long before. The acceptance of a gift subject to conditions makes the recipient a trustee of those funds which can only be spent as directed. See for instance the obligations of a law school which has accepted funds for a defined scholarship program. The state attorney general is the enforcer of such charitable trusts.

Note that, in dissent, Justice Kellogg found the recital of "in consideration of others subscribing" ineffective as consideration. Note also, his opinion that, "Therefore I can see no ground for the suggestion that the ancient rule which makes consideration necessary to the formation of every contract is in danger of effacement through any decisions of this court."

NOTES AND QUESTIONS

1. *Famous but controversial opinion.* The answer to the question, "Can you find the peppercorn?", is only in Justice Cardozo's mind—compare Justice Kellogg's dissent. Classic analysis would have found the pledge to be the promise of a gift subject to a condition. Students typically struggle with Cardozo's peppercorn and often use it as an excuse to see consideration everywhere, even in the clearest cases of conditioned gifts (which may be particularly problematic for future fundraising efforts at the professor's institution). Consequently, care should be taken to emphasize that this opinion is controversial as an analysis of consideration doctrine, and that students should always begin with an analysis of whether the parties intended a conditioned gift or a contract before proceeding to the consideration analysis.

2. *New York courts and promissory estoppel.* See text.

3. *Unilateral and bilateral contracts.* The danger of the Kellogg conceptualization is the risk that, as on the facts of this case, the offer was terminated before the specified act was performed. While full performance could have cemented the commitment, this was not the case. The problem of detrimental reliance raised in the context of a promise (offer) for the performance of an act is covered in the next chapter. As noted above, Cardozo's finding of a return promise by the college is tortured.

4. *Regretted decisions.* Mary Yates' promise was either enforceable as made or it was not. The doctrine of promissory estoppel apart, her pledge was a statement of future intent. Payment of the $1,000 produced a completed gift in that amount but did not provide "consideration" for the promise to pay the remaining $4,000. If the effective doctrinal reason for enforcing the promise was detrimental reliance by the college, then perhaps the payment of an installment added weight to reliance by the college on future receipt of the full amount.

5. *Role of case in prompting the adoption of promissory estoppel.* It is interesting that Cardozo's opinion was cited as the primary justification for Restatement (First) of Contracts § 90. While recognizing the doctrine of promissory estoppel as applied to charitable promises, he expressly refused to opine on whether the doctrine in a much broader form was any part of the law of New York.

6. *Assuming Restatement (Second) of Contracts § 90(2) applied.* Restatement (Second) of Contracts § 90 in the First Restatement format would have required both a promise and action or forbearance in reliance. The record in the case does not show specific reliance and therefore the college's claim might have failed. If, on the other hand, Restatement (Second) of Contracts § 90(2) as included in Restatement (Second) of Contracts had applied, no such reliance would have been necessary.

7. *Policy grounds for enforcement or non-enforcement of charitable subscriptions.* See text. "... If change is to be made it should be by legislative enactment, as in the matter of the tax status of charitable organizations. Do you agree? Is this a matter for the legislature or common law? History suggests that legislative action on this issue is unlikely. Change, if any, must therefore come through court decisions. To date, most courts except notably Iowa have not seen fit to follow the suggestion of Restatement (Second) of Contracts § 90(2).

8. *Is contract based upon promise or reliance?* How far a theory of "reliance" goes may depend on one's understanding of what may

constitute "reliance." In common parlance, where the plaintiff recovers "reliance" damages, the award compensates the plaintiff for out-of-pocket costs i.e. the plaintiff is restored to the position enjoyed before the breach of promise. Dominant case law establishes that loss of "expectancy" is the primary and basic measure of damages for breach of contract. See Restatement (Second) of Contracts § 347. "Expectancy" damages can be made to fit with "reliance" only if we stretch the common meaning of "reliance" to include reliance on the expectation that the promise would be fulfilled—a quite unusual meaning for "reliance." The "reliance" theory then, explains some damage recovery outcomes but not others. Again, the "will" theory does not provide a comfortable explanation for the award of "expectancy" damages. It may help explain the decision to find a binding commitment but not the resultant measure of damages. The societal need to depend upon the performance of contracts duly entered into provides a more persuasive explanation. The regular and reliable operation of our commercial world demands such an outcome. While, once again, the answer to the question posed may lie in the eye of the beholder, we prefer the Hillman view that, "Taken together, the parties' promises and a host of non-promissory principles govern the rights and duties of contracting parties...." In passing, it should be noted that the passage quoted from Professor Fried equates failing to keep a promise with lying. This equation is potentially dangerous, as will appear more clearly in Chapter 7 when we cover fraud and statements of future intent. The essence of fraud (lying) is the intention at the time of making the promise not to fulfill that promise contrasted with an intent at the time of the promise to fulfill it in the future but thereafter a change of heart (neither fraud nor lying).

Optional Problem 2-1

Happy Clothes, Inc. ("HCI") is the largest manufacturer of "environmentally conscious" clothing in the country. HCI specializes manufactures clothing made from "fair-trade" textiles that provide cotton, wool and hemp producers in developing countries an above-market price for their goods. With $40 million in annual sales, HCI has invested millions in maintaining a positive reputation in the image-sensitive market for "socially responsible" consumer products. Recently, however, HCI garnered a negative public reputation for socially and environmentally irresponsible development and business practices in developing nations. Last month, a segment on a popular television news magazine show reported that HCI subsidiaries were using prison and child labor in some countries to cut labor costs and dumping fabric dyes into rivers to avoid environmental expenses.Immediately following the report, HCI's competitors reported a 200% upsurge in sales of their products. HCI is losing market share as a result of its negative image. As part of a program to improve its image, HCI promises to give separate $400,000 contributions to the Clothes for Children Fund (a charity) and to Enviroaction (a non-charitable political action fund dedicated to promoting political candidates and environmental legislation). HCI's letter to each organization promises to make the contribution in four installments, "on condition (1) that the recipient use approximately $100,000 to purchase new HCI-manufactured clothing for their employees, and (2) that the recipient issue a press release upon receipt of each contribution stating that HCI is a responsible corporate global citizen." The internal policies of both institutions would have required some significant press release even if HCI had not requested one.HCI made an initial payment of $101,000, and each recipient purchased $100,000 worth of HCI clothing and issued the requested press release. Employees who received the clothing generally refused to wear it and derided HCI for making "such an obvious attempt to buy their way out of trouble." These statements were widely reported on Internet weblogs, and HCI later refused to pay the remaining $299,000 donations to each recipient.*Does HCI have an enforceable obligation to pay the remaining contributions?*

Answer:

HCI had no significant "charitable intent." What constitutes a "charitable gift" and why should such a gift be given special treatment? Should courts distinguish between a promise to a recognizable charity from one to a political action committee, clearly not a charity? HCI's requirement of the purchase of $100,000 in HCI clothing and the making of a press release should not be regarded as true bargained for consideration, but rather conditions attached to a gift promise. There is no showing of detrimental reliance on the promises of additional gifts by either organization. Thus § 90(1) does not appear to be triggered. Apart from the language of Restatement (Second) of Contracts § 90(2) there seems to be no sufficient reason to enforce either promise. There seems to be no good policy reason to save the promised gift to the charity while not saving the gift to the political action committee. The improper motives behind HCI's actions should not be a reason to enforce the promises.

d. Commercial Promises

Barker v. CTC Sales Corporation
CASE BRIEF

This is a 1991 decision of the Court of Appeals of Georgia. Barker, a former employee, sued CTC Sales alleging breach of an employment contract. The trial court dismissed the complaint as failing to state a cause of action. The Georgia Court of Appeals affirmed. The complaint alleged that the plaintiff had turned down a better job offer in reliance upon the CTC president's promise that plaintiff would remain employed until the company became insolvent.

An employment contract for an indefinite term is conventionally treated as terminable by either party on two weeks' notice. This common law concept had been codified in Georgia as had the concept of promissory estoppel. The Georgia statute stated that "[a]n indefinite hiring may be terminated at will by either party." The court of appeals held that the defendant's promise was one of employment for an indefinite period and therefore subject to termination. Since the contract could be terminated by the employer, there was no basis for a breach of contract action. The court likewise found no basis for recovery based on detrimental reliance. Given the statute (or common law) rule the court found no reason for an exception based on promissory reliance. By inference, the court found that any alleged reliance could not be reasonable.

NOTES AND QUESTIONS

1. *At-will employment relationships.* Of course, many employment contracts are negotiated subject to particular terms, such as employment for a three year term at a specific salary. The contracts are truly bilateral and enforceable, the employee suffering the necessary detriment by giving up the opportunity of employment elsewhere. Suits brought against the employee who leaves early and without excuse are nevertheless rare. Such suits are normally brought against the employer for improper early termination. These employment contracts often reserve the right of the employer to fire the employee for "cause"—frequently leading to factual and/or interpretational issues.

What makes the employer promise enforceable is usually the employee detriment described above. Another group of cases involve the pursuit of the necessary consideration where the employee is already employed and the employer makes some new promise—frequently via the wording of the employer's "handbook."

2. *Other "at-will" relationships.* The note makes the point that as the level of sophistication of the parties rises, the "reasonableness" of any reliance becomes harder to establish.

3. *Promissory estoppel and the UCC.* See text.

4. *Promissory estoppel as an alternate ground for enforcement of promises.* The note goes back to the *Hayes* case and asks what additional facts or argument might have supported recovery by Hayes based on " reliance" of the kind enforced in the *Feinberg* case. The expected answer is facts showing "substantial" and "continuing"

reliance based on the promise of a pension. The student should remember that no specific amount per year was included in the company "promise." Absent some monetary quantification, how could Hayes prove such detrimental reliance at the time he retired? That amount having been clarified by the annual payments of $5,000, could substantial and continuing reliance now be shown? Perhaps the most damaging evidence, tending to establish no such reliance, was Hayes' annual visit to the company and his question as to whether and for how long the payments would be continued. Again, it may be useful to remind the student that the calculation of damages under a reliance theory may be substantially different than under a consideration theory. If the retiree could obtain new employment at a comparable salary, even after several years of retirement and annual payments, would the detrimental reliance be cut off? If the retirement benefit were appropriately bargained for, the expectancy remedy would be applicable regardless of whether the employee could find new employment.

The student can be reminded that retirement benefits can be placed beyond dispute by a contract supported by appropriate consideration. Such support is frequently provided by an employee promise not to compete with or enter into employment with a competitor for a reasonable period of time, or a promise by the employee to make him/herself available as a consultant for a defined period of time.

Cohen v. Cowles Media Company
CASE BRIEF

This is a 1992 decision of the Minnesota Supreme Court. Cohen disclosed information to a reporter in return for a promise of source confidentiality. The newspaper editors decided to overrule the reporter's promise of source confidentiality and published Cohen's name as the source. Cohen was immediately fired by his employer, an advertising firm. Cohen sued for breach of contract and fraudulent misrepresentation. The court of appeals affirmed the jury's $200,000 award based on breach of contract but dismissed the fraud claim. The Minnesota Supreme Court affirmed the dismissal of the fraud claim but also dismissed the contract claim on the basis that the parties (reporter and Cohen) did not intend to enter into a contractually binding relationship. The court then considered the applicability of promissory estoppel but found enforcement on that basis would be inconsistent with the newspaper's First Amendment right of free speech (Cohen I). The United States Supreme Court reversed the holding on free speech and remanded the case to the Minnesota Supreme Court (Cohen II).

Following the remand the court found four issues to be addressed. Cohen had not pleaded or raised at trial the theory of promissory estoppel. Normally, an appellate court will not allow the raising of new issues for the first time on appeal. Here the court found breach of contract and promissory estoppel to be sufficiently close that the defendant was not prejudiced. The estoppel claim was thus preserved and available. The court declined to attribute a wider meaning to free speech under the state constitution and thus disposed of the second issue. The court declined to find a public policy basis for refusing to provide Cohen a remedy, thus disposing of the third issue. Discussion of the court's function and power with respect to issues of "public policy" is reserved until Chapter 6. The fourth issue involved the availability of the promissory estoppel doctrine and, if so, the appropriate damages remedy. Should the jury verdict of $200,000 be reinstated or the case remanded for a new trial? The court found the underlying jury instruction adequate and reinstated the $200,000 award. The wording of the instruction was:

> A party is entitled to recover for a breach of contract only those damages which: (a) arise directly and naturally in the usual course of things from the breach itself; or (b) are the consequences of special circumstances known to or reasonably supposed to have been contemplated by the parties when the contract was made.

The court adopted the language of Restatement (Second) of Contracts § 90(1) as applicable. The court found that four elements had to be satisfied: the promise must be clear and definite; the promisor must have intended to induce the promisee's reliance; such reliance must have occurred; and the reliance must have caused detriment. The court found all four elements to be satisfied.

Next, the court dealt with the question whether the promise must be enforced "to prevent an injustice." This issue, said the court, was one of law for the court since the answer involved a policy question. Justice Simonett noted that the question was "not whether the promise should be enforced to do justice, but whether enforcement is required to prevent an injustice." The court then held that it would be unjust to deny Cohen any remedy since he had relied on a long-standing journalistic tradition of respecting such promises. Noting the language of the Restatement that the "remedy granted for breach may be limited as justice requires," the court found the jury instruction quoted above to be adequate under this standard.

NOTES AND QUESTIONS

1. *Remedy limited as justice requires.* The note asks about the effect of shifting the standard from one of "doing justice" to "preventing injustice." The first standard may well address the Aristotelian

objective of "commutative justice" discussed in the Par. (2) note. "Preventing injustice" does shift the focus from any relative balance of interests between the two parties to a focus on the extent of the loss caused by the one party's actions to the other, independent of any gain or benefit to the first party.

2. *What is "justice?"* Here the note asks what conceptions of justice other than "commutative justice" could be used in the context of promissory estoppel. In the *Cohen* case there was no correlation of benefit and loss to be adjusted. Rather, the situation was one of loss to Cohen caused by actions of the paper that the paper knew or should have known would or could cause serious loss. That loss indeed did happen, and immediately. The history of the common law was one of applying a concept that loss should lie where it falls unless there is a good reason to shift that loss to another. Knowingly causing loss to another, in this case, was found to be a sufficient "injustice" requiring a remedy even though there had been no counterbalancing benefit to the newspaper.

Optional Problem 2-2

Until last year, Paul's Party Stores ("PPS") was one of fourteen distributors for four of the five major alcohol manufacturing companies, Teagrams Distillers, Inc., United Distilleries, Inc., Northeastern Wine and Spirits, Inc., and Johnnie Balker, Inc. PPS had been in discussions to execute a distributorship agreement with the fifth manufacturer, Dacardi Spirits Co. Every manufacturer distributes its booze to retail consumers through distributors like PPS under distributorship agreements that are subject to termination at the will of either party, without prior notice. Beginning in 2000, each of these manufacturers independently adopted internal policies limiting the number of distributors to no more than two or three. Although many other distributors lost all their accounts and went out of business, it initially appeared that PPS would survive the industry consolidation.

Three months ago, however, PPS lost the accounts for United, Northeastern and Johnnie Balker. Paul Smith (owner of PPS) contacted Teagrams to enquire whether they intended to retain PPS as their distributor. Teagrams was non-committal but upbeat about growing its business. Bill Matheson (executive vice-president in charge of marketing at Dacardi) informed Paul that "Dacardi is planning on making PPS a Dacardi distributor within the next two months."

One week later, Trish Jennings (owner of one of PPS's two remaining competitors) called Paul and offered to purchase PPS for $14.5 million. Paul talked to his financial manager and learned that he could profitably remain in business as long as PPS retained the Teagrams account or obtained a distributorship contract with Dacardi. Agonizing over whether to retire or to continue in business, Paul immediately called Bill at Dacardi. "Bill," Paul said, "I've got this great offer from Trish, and I'm thinking of taking it. I've got to know whether Dacardi is going to give PPS a distributorship." Bill responded, "I don't know how to put this promise more clearly - Dacardi has no intention of giving its line to any other distributor."

The next day, Paul entered negotiations with Trish in earnest to reach a price for the purchase of PPS's assets. One week ago, Trish made a final and best offer of $16.9 million to Paul, giving him 24 hours to consider. Paul again sought assurances from Bill, who unequivocally reconfirmed Dacardi's "intent to give PPS a contract." At the close of the 24 hour period, on the basis of Bill's repeated representations, Paul decided to stay in business and called Trish to reject her offer. A week later, Teagrams terminated its distributorship agreement with PPS, and Dacardi informed Paul that, (1) given the loss of the Teagrams contract, it did not believe Paul could remain in business, and (2) Dacardi had decided to award the distributorship contract to Trish Jennings. As a result of these developments, PPS will be bankrupt within a month.

Did Bill make an enforceable promise to award a distributorship to Paul?

Answer:

PPS has no "right" to a distributorship relationship with any of the five major manufacturing companies. It had an expectation of one with Dacardi, an "advantageous" relationship. Bill's (Dacardi) positive assertions that PPS had been selected as its distributor were made with knowledge of the offer to buy PPS that had been made. Thus Bill's continued assurances led PPS to incur a severe loss through not taking the purchase offer. If PPS' reliance was "reasonable," Bill can be said to have caused that loss thus creating an "injustice" requiring a remedy. The key lies in the answer to the question, was the PPS reliance "reasonable" given the relative sophistication of the parties? The second question is the appropriate measure of damages, if any. An "expectation" measure might give PPS the difference between the offered sale price and "0" (bankruptcy). This remedy, however, could cause a severe imbalance of cost/benefit for Dacardi. Is the creation of such a severe imbalance for Dacardi justified? Did Bill have any intention of incurring such a risk for his company? Did PPS have any basis for thinking that Bill was assuming any such risk? A "reliance" measure would seem to produce the same results. This could be characterized as the willful infliction of loss on PPS. Should such behavior be characterized as tortious? What is "justice" in this circumstance may depend upon the eye of the beholder.

3. Obligation by Reason of Unjust Enrichment: The Restitution Doctrine

Bloomgarden v. Coyer
CASE BRIEF

This is a 1973 decision of the United States Court of Appeals, District of Columbia Circuit. The plaintiff introduced a group of developers to each other and thus facilitated the ultimate formation of a new entity which was profitable. The plaintiff demanded that he be paid for his services, claiming (1) an implied-in-fact contract based on custom and convention, and (2) restitution based on unjust enrichment. The district court granted summary judgment to the defendants, holding: (1) that he did not have the requisite real estate developer's license required under D.C. law; and (2) that he had no personal expectation of reward. The D.C. Circuit affirmed on the second ground and thus did not rule on the first.

The D.C. Circuit court distinguished clearly between the showings required to establish either cause of action. The implied-in-fact contract theory required: (1) that the services be understood by the recipient to be performed for the recipient; (2) were not performed gratuitously, but rather with the expectation of compensation; and (3) that the services were beneficial to the recipient. The plaintiff failed to make any showing that the services were performed with, to the knowledge of the recipient, an expectation of compensation. Thus there was no basis for recovery on an implied-in-fact contract theory.

The Circuit court then ruled that where, as here, the facts were not in dispute, the question whether they raised a claim for unjust enrichment was one of law, properly disposable on a motion for summary judgment. It was not enough for the plaintiff to allege that he had conferred a benefit on the defendant. "Because quasi-contractual obligations rest upon equitable considerations, they do not arise when it would not be unfair for the recipient to keep the benefit without having to pay for it. Thus, to make out his case, it is not enough for the plaintiff to prove merely that he has conferred an advantage upon the defendant, but he must demonstrate that retention of the benefit without compensating the one who conferred it is unjustified." The court then stated that, "a duty to pay will not be recognized where it is clear that the benefit was conferred gratuitously or officiously, or that the question of payment was left to the unfettered discretion of the recipient." Thus the second cause of action failed for essentially the same reason—the absence in the defendants of any knowledge of the plaintiff's expectation of compensation.

NOTES AND QUESTIONS

1. *Intermeddler classification.* Bloomgarden was a gratuitous intermeddler. The defendants were enriched by his efforts, but were under no duty to compensate since they had no notice of Bloomgarden's intent that he be compensated. Clearly, the defendants held the high ground.

A fairly common problem can arise in the business world. Suppose that a company is doing business in a technology field. An unknown party makes an appointment to see the chief executive officer and, after being announced, describes a new product or process that may be of value to the company. The caller proposes a contract giving the caller a small percentage as a royalty on subsequent sales. The chief executive officer refuses to enter into such a contract. Subsequently, the company introduces and uses profitably a product or service similar to that described by the caller. The caller sues, and then the company claims that the new product or service was developed by the company and not because of the caller's information. What advice should legal counsel give the chief executive officer about how to deal with such situations?

2. *Unjust enrichment.* If Mary constructs a building on her lot that increases the value of John's adjacent lot, is it clear why Mary has no claim against John for the value increase created by her efforts? Mary's actions were not requested by John nor were they provided, objectively measured, with any expectation of payment by or contribution from John.

4. Obligation by Reason of Promise for Benefit Received: The Promissory Restitution Doctrine

See introductory text which outlines three categories of restitution-based recovery.

Mills v. Wyman
CASE BRIEF

This is an 1825 decision of the Supreme Judicial Court of Massachusetts. Levi Wyman was 25 years old, poor and sick, when the plaintiff provided him with food and shelter. Thereafter, Levi's father (the defendant) wrote a letter to the plaintiff interpreted by the court as containing a promise to reimburse the plaintiff for those expenses. When the father did not pay as promised, Mills sued. There being no consideration to support the promise (the case was decided in 1825), the trial court granted what today would be called summary judgment. The Massachusetts Supreme Court affirmed. The father may have had a moral obligation to pay in accordance with his promise, but there being no bargained for consideration and the services having been performed before the making of the promise, it was unenforceable. This is a classic "past consideration" case. Could a case of "promissory restitution" be made out? See Restatement (Second) of Contracts § 86 referred to in the notes following this case. The student should note that Restatement (Second) of Contracts § 86 requires that the promise be made "in recognition of a benefit previously received by the promisor." Here the benefit was received by the adult son and not the father. In any event, whether a case of "preventing injustice" could be made out on these facts is questionable, given that the services and goods were provided to the son as a gift.

INTERESTING DISCUSSION ISSUES

The student should ask again, "Why is the father's promise not enforced simply because it was made with appropriate intent?" The student should focus on the facts as recited by the court and not on those recounted in the notes based on further historical research. The court's explanation is not revealing, "Without doubt there are great interests of society which justify withholding the coercive arm of the law from these duties of imperfect obligation, as they are called; imperfect, not because they are less binding upon the conscience than those which are called perfect, but because the wisdom of the social law does not impose sanctions upon them." What is the "wisdom of the social law"? Suffice it to say that the common law position was clear and unbending—a "naked promise" was not enforceable. The notoriety of this principle, and the assumed public reliance thereon, should be sufficient justification?

The case is equally famous for the exceptions recited covering promises to pay debts barred by a statute of limitations, debts incurred by an infant, and debts barred by bankruptcy proceedings. These "exceptions" are covered in the notes following the case. Whether these "exceptions" are justified by the court's explanation is questionable as a matter of logic—"The general position, that moral obligation is a sufficient consideration for an express promise, is to be limited in its application, to cases where at some time or other a good or valuable consideration has existed." But logic aside, as the notes state in detail, these "exceptions" have for a substantial period of time enjoyed special though limited recognition.

NOTES AND QUESTIONS

1. *Restitution claim.* As noted above, Mills conferred a benefit on the adult son, not the father, and the benefit was conferred gratuitously. The possible applicability of Restatement (Second) of Contracts § 86 is discussed above. Could it possibly be argued that the father's promise should estopp him from pleading that the

consideration was past? By making this promise did the father acknowledge that the father, as well as the son, was actually benefited by Mills' actions? Could these arguments justify an application of § 86? Probably not.

2. *Antecedent consideration doctrine.* See text.

3. *Commentary.* See text.

Webb v. McGowin
CASE BRIEF

This is an 1935 decision of the Court of Appeal of Alabama. In this celebrated case, frequently matched with *Wills v. Wyman* above, the Georgia Court of Appeals found a promise based on moral consideration to be enforceable against the promisor's administrator. Webb, the plaintiff, saved McGowin from serious injury or death at the cost of himself suffering injuries that produced lifelong disability. In gratitude for saving his life McGowin promised to pay Webb $15 every two weeks for Webb's life. McGowin had fulfilled that promise faithfully for more than eight years when he died. His administrator (once again that estate!) refused to continue the payments and Webb sued. The lower court dismissed the complaint but the court of appeals reversed and remanded the case for trial.

The court's empathy was with the plaintiff all the way. The opinion shows an interesting effort on the part of the court to find precedents or analogies that would support its decision in Webb's favor. It pointed out that if a doctor had saved McGowin, the doctor's bill would be paid even if no prior request had been made. If McGowin's property had been preserved or improved, said the court, the bill would have been paid. This second statement is both interesting and untrue in the absence of knowledge and actual or implied consent on the part of the property owner (compare "officious intermeddler"). Then the court referenced the case of goods received followed by a subsequent promise to pay (one of the classic "common counts"). This is an interesting attempt to establish an analogy—an attempt that fails because the two sets of critical facts do not mesh. As the notes following the case indicate, Restatement (Second) of Contracts § 86 might be applied to justify the result—or this case might be the predicate for Restatement (Second) of Contracts § 86. The exceptions set out in Restatement (Second) of Contracts § 86(2) would not preclude the application of the rule stated in Restatement (Second) of Contracts § 86(1). Webb's services were neither gratuitous nor "officiously meddling."

The upshot of this case may well be that hard facts can make good law so long as the precedent is carefully confined to analogous hard facts.

NOTES AND QUESTIONS

1. *Restitution claim.* Webb clearly conferred a very substantial benefit on McGowin and this benefit was conferred neither gratuitously nor officiously. As discussed above, the decision in this case is most likely the basis for Restatement (Second) of Contracts § 86.

2. *History of Restatement (Second) Contracts § 86.* There is no clear answer to the question posed. Perhaps he was thinking that the promise carried with it an acknowledgement of actual benefit received, an acknowledgment that could or should remove the obstacle to a claim in restitution.

3. *Part performance.* The stream of payments made continuously over a period of more than eight years shows that the promisor had every intention of fulfilling the promise as long as he was able. The stream of payments removes any doubt about the sincerity of, and intent behind, the promise. It also serves as a substantial basis for finding detrimental reliance on Webb's part—or would that be better described as "grateful reliance" since Webb was described as totally disabled by the accident. The problem with executors and administrators, and the reason why they always appear as the "bad guy," is that by law they are required to pay the "debts" of the deceased. They are not authorized to make "gifts" at the expense of those entitled to inherit the estate assets. In cases of doubt as to the enforceability of the obligation, they are in effect required to refuse to pay in order to test the enforceability of the alleged obligation.

4. *Modern rule.* Mills suggests that moral consideration does not support enforceability of a promise. Webb suggests that moral consideration, at least in accord with the facts of that case, does support enforceability. Restatement (Second) of Contracts § 86 supports enforceability under certain circumstances. Arguably, they do not state three different rules. The qualification about the "purposes" of the Restatement is important. Where the drafters find significant conflict between reported decisions, clearly they feel free to choose that branch of the conflict which they find preferable, and not just that branch supported by a greater weight of decisions.

5. *Promise "is binding to the extent necessary to prevent injustice."* Restatement (Second) of Contracts § 86 says: "... to the extent necessary to prevent injustice." Restatement (Second) of Contracts § 90 says: "... if injustice can be avoided only by enforcement of the promise." Whether there is any intended difference must rest in the eye of the beholder.

6. *Remedy*. There is no good reason explaining the different approach. Questionable proofreading or comparison of the two sections? The question following the citation to the *Maglica* case is more difficult. The available remedy in that case was restitution based on unjust enrichment. The man owned the business. The woman provided a variety of services beneficial to the business. She sued for a fraction of the increase in the total value of the business attributable to her efforts. The court awarded her the cost the man would have incurred had he hired another person to do the work she had done. Since she had not been paid for that work, she was entitled to the reasonable value of her services, i.e. market value or the cost of obtaining the same services from someone else. While he may have been benefited by a much larger amount, in the absence of an enforceable agreement between the two, is not the objective value of the services conferred and received the better measure? Would not the "value" approach more closely resemble an "expectancy" measure under circumstances where it was clear there was no underlying enforceable contract?

Optional Problem 2-3

Mary Gonzales is the CEO of Health Risk Management, Inc., a publicly-traded health care management firm. Health Risk has supplemented the compensation of its senior executives with stock options. The company has been extremely successful under Mary's management. The value of Health Risk has sky-rocketed and along with it the value of Mary's unexercised stock options. To date, she has $10 million in value appreciation which will be realized when she exercises her options and sells the stock. She does not wish to sell the stock until she is no longer the CEO. She expects to retire in three years.

The College of Business at High-Tech University is very proud of Mary, one of its star graduates. High-Tech would like to add an addition to its building to be named after the Mary Gonzales Graduate Business Wing. To do so, Mary must pledge $1 million. She is willing to do so, but only if her stock appreciates further and she sells at the appreciated level. Thus, she would have to sell the stock for at least $11 million to lock-in her current appreciation and honor her pledge to the university.

Given the growth history of Health Risk, High-Tech is certain the stock will appreciate to at least $11 million. As a result, it decides to borrow to finance the new wing and begins construction. Throughout construction, High-Tech widely publicizes Mary's gift, incidentally promoting Mary's reputation in the business community and indirectly assisting Mary in closing several lucrative business deals for Health Risk.

The new wing is completed just as Mary is retiring three years later. Exceeding all predictions, her stock options are now worth slightly over $14 million. While Mary is driving home from her retirement party, a drunk driver runs a stop light and crashes into Mary's car. She is dead on arrival at the hospital.

As the heirs of her entire estate, Mary's children sell her stock but refuse to honor her pledge to High-Tech. The university consults you seeking advice regarding their legal options to enforce Mary's promise.

What do you advise and why?

Answer:

Mary signed a pledge of $1 million to High-Tech (presumably payable to a tax-exempt foundation established by High-Tech). The pledge was conditioned on: (1) her stock options appreciating in value to $11 million or more; and (2) her selling the options at $11 million or more. She died when the stock options were worth $14 million thus meeting the first condition but she did not sell them prior to her death putting in issue whether the second condition to her pledge was met. Does sale by her estate meet that condition? If it does not, the pledge is unenforceable. Assuming that it does, is the pledge enforceable? According to Restatement (Second) of Contracts § 90(2) it is enforceable without proof of reliance, but only Iowa has followed that subsection. Is proof of detrimental reliance then a requirement of recovery by High-Tech? Their argument would be that in borrowing to construct the new wing they relied detrimentally on the promise. The flaw in such an argument is that such claimed reliance may be unreasonable. When they borrowed they knew that the pledge would not be enforceable if the value of the stock options declined. There was a clear market risk that their value could decline, thus in borrowing the money High-Tech decided to assume the risk rather than rely on the pledge. The alleged reliance may be found, in these circumstances, not to meet the standard of "reasonableness."

Can an argument for High-Tech be made on the basis that the pledge was "morally binding"? In light of the authorities, probably not.

Can a successful argument be made based on "unjust enrichment"? Again, probably not. High-Tech may have conferred several benefits on Mary during her lifetime but it did so voluntarily (gratuitously) since it knew there would be no "pay day" if the value of the options sank below $10 million. While Mary knew that High-Tech was expecting that the pledge would be paid, that expectation was subject to two conditions, one of which was not met.

CHAPTER 3

REACHING AGREEMENT THROUGH THE PROCESS OF OFFER AND ACCEPTANCE

Table of Contents

Introduction to Chapter 3 Coverage

The meaning of promissory conduct is essential to understanding the legal commitments or duties of the maker of a promise. In the commercial world, a maker communicates promises by way of an offer that seeks and is conditioned upon acceptance by the recipient. The promises may also be subject to other conditions but the one that is important at the moment is the condition of acceptance. That doctrine provides that the maker of a promise intends the court to enforce that promise only if the recipient (1) agrees with the promise, (2) makes the requested counter promises or performances, and (3) notifies the maker accordingly. For example, Sarah might promise to sell her Honda car to Bill if he promises to pay $10,000. Sarah has sought a promise from Bill in return for hers and her promise will only become enforceable if Bill satisfies the condition by accepting. When this occurs, both promises become legally enforceable.

A. MUTUAL MISUNDERSTANDING AND OBJECTIFICATION

Raffles v. Wichelhaus
CASE BRIEF

This is an 1864 decision of the English Court of Exchequer. Raffles, the seller, entered into a contract with Wichelhaus, the buyer, covering 125 bales of Surat cotton, guaranteed "middling fair" "to arrive ex 'Peerless' from Bombay." Raffles sued because Wichelhaus refused to accept or pay for cotton from a "Peerless" that sailed from Bombay in December. Wichelhaus pleaded that he meant cotton from a ship of that name that sailed from Bombay in October. Raffles "demurred" i.e. pleaded that Wichelhaus' understanding was irrelevant and of no legal effect. The issue thus raised was whether Wichelhaus' answer stated a defense as a matter of law.

Black's Law Dictionary defines "demurrer" as follows: "demurrer (di-m <<schwa>>r-<<schwa>>r) [Law French *demorer* "to wait or stay"] A pleading stating that although the facts alleged in a complaint may be true, they are insufficient for the plaintiff to state a claim for relief and for the defendant to frame an answer. In most jurisdictions, such a pleading is now termed a *motion to dismiss*, but the demurrer is still used in a few states, including California, Nebraska, and Pennsylvania."

During the argument in the Court of Exchequer it was established that there were two ships named "Peerless," one of which left Bombay in October and the other in December. Wichelhaus claimed he meant the "Peerless" that left in October and Raffles, by the terms of his complaint, pleaded that he meant the "Peerless" that left Bombay in December.

The court held that, since each party intended a different ship, there was no "consensus ad idem" i.e. agreement on the same thing or shared mutual intent. Thus no enforceable contract was formed and Raffles lost.

Raffles was a cotton broker and Wichelhaus was a speculator on the cotton market in Liverpool. Cotton was scarce in late 1862 due to the Civil War and price fluctuations encouraged speculative contracts. Wichelhaus apparently entered into this contract in the expectation that cotton prices would continue to rise. Had he demanded and paid for the cotton ex the "October Peerless" he would have lost substantially. Had he accepted and paid for cotton from the "December Peerless" he would still have lost money but a lesser amount. It was to Wichelhaus' advantage to be able to escape from the commitment to purchase.

INTERESTING DISCUSSION ISSUES

Writers have asserted that this decision was a triumph for the "will" theorists. Others have asserted the contrary, that it was explained by "objective" theory. Thus, as stated in the notes following the case, the Restatement (Second) of Contracts rationalizes the case on the basis that neither Raffles nor Wichelhaus was at fault in failing to understand the other party's interpretation (compare Lucy v. Zehmer). As a consequence of the demurrer, Raffles admitted for purposes of his motion the truth of Wichelhaus' statement that Wichelhaus intended to buy cotton out of the "October Peerless." The record of the case fails to explore whether Raffles knew of the "October Peerless." Simpson provides a fascinating account of the market conditions and practices at the time—see Simpson, "Contracts for Cotton to Arrive: The Case of the Two Ships Peerless," 11 Cardozo L. Rev. 287 (1989). He suggests that it is quite likely that the only "Peerless" in the mind and knowledge of Raffles at the time of entering into the contract was the "October Peerless." Were this true then application of an objective standard would have fixed the "October Peerless" as the relevant ship. Had Raffles tendered delivery of the cotton from the "October Peerless" Wichelhaus would have suffered a greater loss. This probably explains why Wichelhaus made no demand for delivery of cotton out of the "October Peerless" but the lawyers and judges both failed to explore why Wichelhaus made no such demand and the possibility of the inferences that might have been drawn from that failure. By the time the suit in point commenced, it was too late for Raffles to make any such tender, assuming that Raffles had any cotton aboard the "October Peerless." If Wichelhaus had known of the "December Peerless" he could have been the party at fault under an objective standard.

The "will" and the "objectivist" positions overlap. The objectivist view controls where, as in Lucy, one party reasonably understands the words or conduct of another in a manner not intended by that other. The "will" position controls where the one party knows or should know the intent of the other—regardless of any objective "reasonable" understanding. As Farnsworth said in his treatise at § 7.9, "According to Corbin, 'it is certain that the purpose of the court is in all cases the ascertainment of the 'intention of the parties' if they had one in common.'" This may be a good point to compare the position of Article 8(1) of the CISG, which provides that "...statements made by and other conduct of a party are to be interpreted according to his intent where the other party knew or could not have been unaware what that intent was."

The instructor may wish to point out that the *Raffles* case has proven to be essentially a one of a kind—without significant comparables.

NOTES AND QUESTIONS

1. *Stopped by the Court.* Why would Milward, counsel for Raffles, think Wichelhaus' plea was irrelevant? Because Raffles had a written contract specifying a duty on Wichelhaus' part to buy the stated amount of cotton on the terms provided when the "Peerless" arrived. How and why does the court make or assume that the "identity" of the ship was then fundamentally important to the contract? As Simpson points out in his article cited above, the "ex ship" form of contract was a form of "arrival" contract. If the parties knew when the ship left Bombay they could make a reasonably accurate guess as to when it would arrive in Liverpool and draw their own conclusions as to prices likely to be applicable at time of arrival. The court would know that cotton prices had varied substantially over the period and that the relative timing of arrival of the ship in port and availability of its cargo for delivery could have a substantial bearing on profitability of the deal for both parties. Was Milward's puzzled and desperate shift to parol (oral) evidence a factor? Pollock C.B.'s interjection, "It would be a question for the jury whether both parties meant the same ship called the 'Peerless' rattled his cage because by bringing the demurrer Milward had admitted the truth of Wichelhaus' statement that Wichelhaus believed he was buying cotton ex the "October Peerless." He had thus lost any opportunity to challenge the truth of Wichelhaus' assertion. Pollock's next statement, "here it does not appear that the plaintiff had any goods on board the other [October] 'Peerless'" suggests that Raffles had no plausible case for arguing that there was a contract based on delivery ex the "October Peerless"—particularly since Raffles had made no tender of delivery from that vessel and the time to do so had long since expired. Milward next attempted to argue that parol evidence of the existence of two ships "Peerless" should be excluded because it contradicted the written word. [See Chapter 4 coverage of the parol evidence rule]. In response, Mellish cited the then-established

rule that in the event of latent ambiguity in the written words parol evidence was admissible to explain the ambiguity. With the admission of the parol evidence showing the existence of two ships Peerless, and the legal presumption that accepted all well-pleaded facts as true for purposes of the demurrer, Milward was trapped by his own procedural maneuver.

2. *Holmes' famous lectures.* Holmes' explanation is not convincing. The Restatement (Second) of Contracts explanation is more persuasive—see the discussion above.

3. *Fair-to-middling.* See text.

4. *Economic analysis.* The notion that "the ambiguity is resolved against the party who seeks to rely on it" is important in the context of interpretation and application of insurance policies where, in most situations, the insurer drafted the policy language and the insured had no opportunity to negotiate those terms. Was the concept of "contra proferentem" applicable or useful in *Lucy v. Zehmer*? Can it be applied in the context of "objective" interpretation? The issue in this latter case was not ambiguity of terms—they were plain and clear. The ambiguity, if any, related to Zehmer's conduct and intent. The court there applied its famous assignment of the burden of rebuttal, thus arguably following the suggestion in this note. The basic economic concept, embodied in objective interpretation, is the importance of contracts being binding and enforceable and not exposed to subjective, post hoc assertions that "that is not what I meant."

5. *The good ship Peerless.* See text.

6. *Modern restatement approach.* The key recitation from the Restatement (Second) of Contracts is "and neither party is at fault for failing to understand the other party's interpretation." Assuming a supportive fact finding consistent with this quotation, presumably *Raffles* would be decided the same way under the Restatement (Second) of Contracts. But we need to remember the trap self-inflicted by Milward in choosing the demurrer route. Why does (or should) the law prefer a "no contract" solution? The case does not deal with or dispose of this question because of its procedural posture. Would Wichelhaus have been bound to perform if Raffles had sued based on Wichelhaus' failure to accept delivery and pay for cotton ex the "October Peerless" (assuming Raffles had any cotton aboard that ship)? We will never know because Raffles let the opportunity to assert a contract based on delivery from the "October Peerless" go by irretrievably. The "no contract" decision certainly allowed Wichelhaus to escape a bad bargain—worse if he had had to perform under the "October Peerless" theory. In other words, there was no detrimental

reliance by Wichelhaus on a contract ex the "October Peerless" compared to the "December Peerless."

7. *CISG and objective theory*. See text.

8. *Practice Note—Arguing Before a Court*. See text.

B. THE THEORY OF OFFER AND ACCEPTANCE

While the divergent theories can be trying, fortunately in practice the differences in outcome between a "will" theory analysis and an "objective" one are in many cases not important. The requisite "mutual assent" (actual or objectively implied) is frequently clear. The Restatement (Second) of Contracts builds the structure of a contract on the basis of an offer followed by acceptance of that offer. This process is easily illustrated in the context of a familiar transaction—the sale and purchase of a home. Generally, the buyer will make a signed written offer which the seller is then privileged to accept—thus creating a right/duty relationship. Illustrating the concept of the offeror as the "master of the offer," the buyer will frequently require that the seller's acceptance take the form of the seller's written signature on the buyer's offer form plus delivery of that signed acceptance to the buyer on or before a specified date and time. Many commercial contracts do not fall conveniently into the Restatement (Second) of Contracts' binary form. Even where there are only two parties to the transaction, development of the negotiated terms may take a long and fairly tortuous path where neither buyer nor seller is the "author" of the final text. What is important is that the parties come up with an agreed upon written text, both sign that text and (often) exchange duplicate signed copies.

1. The Promissory Nature of an Offer

In almost all common situations, an offer includes a promise. Professor Goble's articulation of "non-promissory offers" is interesting, challenged as a matter of interpretation, but well outside the mainstream. To take one of his illustrations, "A hands B $100 and says, 'Pay me back in a year.' B takes the money and says, 'All right.'" Where there is no promise, in most cases there can be nothing to turn into a binding contract. The instructor might invite the student to compare again (see discussion under the *King* case in Chapter 2):

(a) "This farm is worth at least $50,000"; with
(b) "Would you buy this farm for $50,000?"; with
(c) "I offer (promise) to sell you this farm for $50,000 if you accept my offer by agreeing to pay me that price."

Alternatively, the instructor might suggest to the class the situation of a client who wants to invite offers without making one herself. For example, the *International Filter Co.* case, discussed later in this chapter, provides a good example of a vendor managing its interaction with the buyer so that the vendor remains the offeree. With such an objective in mind, how might the owner of land invite potential buyers to make offers without herself making a promissory offer to sell? This drafting exercise involves the express negation of any promise by the owner, express or implied.

Owen v. Tunison
CASE BRIEF

This is a 1932 decision of the Supreme Judicial Court of Maine. Owen (would-be buyer) wrote Tunison saying, "Will you sell [the property] for $6,000?" Tunison responded, "... it would not be possible for me to sell it unless I was to receive $16,000.00 cash." Owen replied, "Accept your offer ..." and sued when Tunison refused to go forward. The court held that Tunison's words did not amount to an offer to sell. The student should note that the reason for the holding is that Tunison made no express or implied promise to sell (and thus made no offer) that could be converted into a binding contract. It is important to distinguish preliminary negotiations from a promissory offer.

NOTES AND QUESTIONS

1. *Classifying the parties.* See text.

2. *Theory of obligation.* The other potentially available theory, detrimental reliance on a promise, likewise requires a promissory offer as the predicate of any potential liability.

3. *Failure of a promissory offer.* Whether the student agrees or not with the court's decision depends upon the interpretation placed on the words Tunison used. In a different factual surrounding context his words might be susceptible to interpretation as a promissory offer of sale at $16,000. The importance of this case is the lesson that words must be used carefully in such a context. Each party should use language that is unequivocally clear with respect to both offer and acceptance. Tunison's words were sufficiently ambiguous that they caused a law suit that went to the Maine Supreme Court. The student should heed the cost to both parties involved—cost that could have been avoided by clearer language from Tunison expressly negating any intent to make an offer.

4. *Magic words not required.* If Tunison's words were interpreted as an offer, did Owen make a promise to purchase on the terms of the offer? Owen used the magical words "Accept your offer... sixteen thousand cash" but added "send deed to Eastern Trust ... Please acknowledge." The student will learn the "mirror image" requirement of acceptance of an offer under the common law. It is not too early for the instructor to inquire whether the offer defined the required form of acceptance here and whether that requirement was met. The logic of the power of acceptance relates to the second step involved in mutual assent. Where the terms of the offer are "A + B" and the acceptance is of "A" but not "B" the requisite mutuality of assent is missing. Thus an interpretational issue is raised of whether Owen introduced conditions not found in the offer, namely that the deed be sent to Eastern Trust and that Tunison acknowledge. Were both of these forms of request or requirements in effect conditioning the effectiveness of the acceptance?

5. Advertisements versus offers. See text. Consider the last time you responded to an advertisement – did you believe that the advertisement was offering to sell you a good or service on specified terms or that the advertiser was merely inviting you to come and make an offer? The usual advertising copy should not raise the expectation in the reader that it is intended as an offer. Where, however, the advertisement contains more specific terms, an intent to offer may be inferred. Words such as "five at each store" or "one to a customer" may found such an inference. Even if Professor Eisenberg is correct about common consumer understanding, the presumption against intent to offer should be preserved. Very little harm is done to the consumer by reason of such a presumption and substantial harm can befall the seller if an advertisement is found to have created, measured objectively, an offer to sell on specific terms.

6. *Context, offers and the probability of performance.* The closing sentence is significant: "Should contract law account for parties' needs to communicate greater or lesser probabilities of performance or leave it to the parties themselves to arrange for their own security (or lack of security) for performance?" Where the owner of land makes an offer to sell that land when, subjectively, never intending to perform that promise, has the owner committed the tort of fraud? If so, is there need of any contractual remedy for nonperformance of the offer once accepted? The student may be reminded that the damages remedy in tort is usually designed to restore the victim to her position before commission of the tort whereas the contract measure is designed to put the victim in the position she would have been in had the promise been performed. The difference between the tort and the contract remedies is very important—and discussed in detail in Chapter 9. The potential of punitive damages for the tort of fraud adds a different dimension. But the great difficulty in bringing a tort action against a

nonperforming offeror is the necessity of proving the subjective intent of the offeror not to perform at the very time the offer was made. Proof of a later change of mind will not suffice. There is always a substantial risk that the terms of the offer will not be performed by the offeror and vice versa. The question asked is whether there is or may be value in the offeree asking the offeror about just how seriously the offeror intends to perform. This question is easily put in context by inviting the student to consider the familiar agreement for the sale of a home. Assume the buyer promises to pay $400,000 for the home. Suppose the buyer changes her mind and refuses to close. Has the seller been damaged? The answer is yes, because the seller, relying on the conclusion of an enforceable sales contract, has had to take her property off the market and thus may have lost the opportunity to sell to another buyer perhaps at an even higher price. Should the seller ask for security with respect to the buyer's performance? The market place answer is "Yes, indeed." This is precisely the function that the down payment, which is usually required—perhaps 5% of the purchase price—is designed to perform. That down payment is intended to serve as security for the buyer's promise to perform. Then why do we not conventionally require the seller to post a bond, in say the amount of 5% of the purchase price, to be payable to the buyer in the event the seller defaults? If the conventional answer to the question is the availability of injunctive relief, why is that not sufficient as security for the protection of the seller? The issue of whether, and if so when, to negotiate for security concerning performance by either offeror or offeree is an important issue to be considered in the context of many contract negotiations.

2. The Condition of Acceptance

Herein of the important statement that the offeror is the "master of the offer."

International Filter Co. v. Conroe Gin, Ice & Light Co.
CASE BRIEF

This is a 1925 decision of the Commission of Appeals of Texas. International Filter sent its traveling salesman, Waterman, to call on Conroe Gin in Texas. Waterman proposed the sale of a designated water purifier by International to Conroe. He presented a form document prepared by International to be signed by Conroe. Conroe signed that form and, presumably, gave it back to Waterman who then sent it to International's headquarters in Chicago. The document provided: "This proposal is made in duplicate and becomes a contract when accepted by the purchaser and approved by an executive officer of the International Filter Company, at its office in Chicago." The document later provided: "This proposal is submitted for prompt acceptance, and unless so accepted is subject to change without notice." Following receipt of the order in Chicago, International's "president and vice president" [sic] wrote "O.K." on the document and next day wrote a letter to Conroe acknowledging and thanking Conroe for the order. By letter sent two weeks later Conroe purported to cancel the contract. International rejected this attempt at cancellation and, when Conroe failed to perform, sued in Texas.

The case was tried without a jury and the judge found for the defendant on all issues. This decision was affirmed by the Court of Civil Appeals. International again appealed, this time to the "Commission of Appeals," which reversed and remanded holding (1) that the contract was complete upon approval in Chicago and (2) that no notice of such approval was required to be communicated by International to Conroe. In any case, the Commission found that the letter acknowledging the order was sufficient "notice" if notice had been required.

INTERESTING DISCUSSION ISSUES

The instructor may wish to comment upon the nature and jurisdiction of the "Commission of Appeals," the court which reviewed and reversed the prior decision of the "Civil Court of Appeals." Texas has a history of presenting an unusual hierarchy of courts. Its Court of Criminal Appeals is the court of final jurisdiction with respect to criminal cases. The Texas Supreme Court has no jurisdiction over these cases. On the civil side, Texas has, for a long period, had a Court of Civil Appeals from which the appeal is to the Supreme Court. As Robert W. Higgason observed in "A History of Texas Appellate Courts: Preserving Rights of Appeal Through Adaptations to Growth, Part 1 of 2: Courts of Last Resort," 39-Apr Hous. Law. 21 (2002):

> At several times throughout Texas history, when the high court's caseloads were especially substantial, the legislature would authorize an ad hoc tribunal to alleviate those docket pressures. Those tribunals were known as the Commissions of Appeals, and they were established as theoretically nonpermanent bodies that would assist during times of heavy backlogs on the courts' dockets. ... Another Commission of Appeals was established in 1918 to aid the Supreme Court with its docket. (The Supreme Court at that time was several years behind.)

The Student may find the terminology of the case confusing. What is a "plaintiff in error"? International was the "plaintiff in error"—having lost below, International appealed (brought a writ of error?).

Anyway, this case is always confusing to students. To them it seems natural that the salesman for International would make the offer which Conroe would then accept. International's form was cleverly designed to change the process by turning Conroe's signature of the form into an "offer" which was then to be "approved" (accepted) by an executive officer of International. The form, however, presented a threatened ambiguity in the last sentence, "This proposal is submitted for prompt acceptance, and unless so accepted is subject to change without notice." The court treated the "acceptance" so called for by the form as acceptance by International in Chicago. A careful reading of the form, however, indicates that International's action was described not as an "acceptance" but as an "approval." This could suggest that the form treated Conroe as "accepting" International's proposal subject to a condition subsequent that the contract be approved by an International executive in Chicago.

Such a fine parsing of the facts of the case is rarely offered. Traditional teaching has the instructor identify that the form placed Conroe in the position of "offeror" and International in the position of "offeree." As the notes after the case point out, Restatement (Second) of Contracts § 56 requires that notification by the offeree of acceptance of the offer must be provided unless the terms of the offer "manifests a contrary intention." This court, in interpreting the form drafted by International, found that notification of acceptance was dispensed with and that hence the contract became binding when the "president and vice president" wrote "O.K." on the form previously signed by Conroe. This case highlights the power of the offeror, as "master of the offer," to control precisely what constitutes acceptance and if and how that acceptance must be communicated.

We introduce a hypothetical to illustrate. Suppose B, a proposed buyer of a home, wants to submit an offer to buy A's home. If he signs a written offer failing to provide for form and manner of acceptance, how and when will B know for sure (i.e. whether he can safely make an offer on a different property) whether he has become bound to purchase B's property? An offer can be accepted within a reasonable time. What, in such circumstances, may be a "reasonable time"? To use a form of offer which permits such uncertainty is poor drafting. Hence the offer letter should specify precisely how long the offeree has to accept and also that the acceptance, if any, will be effective if and only if delivered to the offeror within the time limit stated in the offer letter.

NOTES AND QUESTIONS

1. *Home office control.* According to the clear terms of the proposal who had the power of acceptance, International Filter or Conroe Gin? Although the form spoke of the need for "prompt acceptance" it used the word "approval" to indicate the actual acceptance by International. The last sentence of the proposal form indicated that International

wanted a clear answer—binding contract or no—promptly. The form can be argued to use the word "acceptance" as signature by Conroe. This illustrates the power of word usage to confuse. Analytically, the form was drafted to position Conroe as offeror and International as offeree. The court agreed with such an analysis by referring to the Conroe "offer."

Given that International hired Waterman as its sale agent, why would it make a proposal to sell rather than an offer to sell? The answer to this question involves an understanding of sophisticated marketing control. A company selling products through traveling sales persons (c.f. selling a large and expensive computer system) has an endemic problem of sales persons who allow enthusiasm to book an order override common sense, home office instructions and restrictions. While companies spend much time in trying to train sales people that they have no power or authority to change or add to the terms of the company's printed form contract or the printed product specifications, and that no additional assurances beyond those specifications are to be given to the customer by the sales person, the inevitable often happens. In an attempt to control such potential excess "enthusiasm," companies frequently position the customer as the offeror and the company as the offeree—thus giving the company head office staff the last opportunity to review the written paper trail before accepting the offer solicited by the sales person.

2. *Notification requirement.* Does the February 14 letter, received in "due course," seem timely to you? If notification is required, then such notification must be "timely." This requirement minimizes the time period during which the offeror who fails to specify both time and manner of acceptance "twists slowly in the wind." "Timely" raises a factual issue—the solution of which can depend upon the surrounding circumstances. Conroe signed on February 10th. International's letter, treated as "notification of acceptance," was dated February 14th. The time is 1925—Given that Waterman had to transmit the offer signed by Conroe in Texas to International in Chicago, and that International needed to have some reasonable period to assess the offer and then respond, a letter dated February 14th appears to be clearly "timely." But the student needs to understand that the more issues such as this are left to subsequent interpretation rather than resolved expressly by clear drafting, the more problems and hence litigation can be expected. Winning the lawsuit is only second best to never having the lawsuit in the first place.

3. *"F.O.B." and other bill of lading terms.* See text.

3. The Mailbox Rule

Note the text's statement of the normative mutual assent rule that requires that both the offer and acceptance must be communicated or brought to the notice of the relevant party.

Problems arising from the use of asynchronous communication of offer and acceptance, such as by mail, fax, voicemail, email, are covered in the text. The common law "mail box" rule resolved this problem by making acceptance effective upon deposit in the mail. See Restatement (Second) § 63. Thus, if the offeror "invites" acceptance by mail – either implicitly by mailing the offer to the offeree or expressly – the offeree accepts the offer by placing the acceptance in the mail. This rule does not apply to acceptances of option contracts. Thus, an offeree who mails an acceptance may attempt to make an "overtaking" rejection, such as by telephoning or emailing a rejection to the offeror. This attempted revocation is ineffective.

Alternatively, the offeree may mail a rejection and then later attempt to overtake the rejection with an acceptance. A mailed rejection is effective only upon receipt and does not terminate the offeree's power of acceptance until it is actually received by the offeror. In that case, whether the contract is formed or not depends on which communication, the rejection or acceptance, reaches the offeror first. The revocation of an offer is only effective upon receipt. Consequently, a mailed acceptance immediately extinguishes the offeror's power of revocation, even if the offeror communicates that revocation to the offeree while the acceptance is still in transit.

Electronic communications raise significant complications for application of the mailbox rule. Some argue the mailbox rule should have no application to electronic transmissions.

Many statutes abrogate the common law mailbox rule in specific contexts. The CISG provides that acceptance of an offer is only effective upon receipt. Unlike the mailbox rule, the CISG places the risk of loss of the acceptance on the offeree, not the offeror.

4. Acceptance by Silence

Day v. Caton
CASE BRIEF

This is an 1876 decision of the Supreme Judicial Court of Massachusetts. Plaintiff alleged an express contractual agreement with defendant providing that plaintiff would construct a party wall along the parties' shared property line if defendant would pay for one-half the cost of construction in the event that defendant used the party wall in his own future construction. Defendant denied that the existence of such an express agreement. The trial judge instructed the jury that defendant's promise to pay for half of the wall could be inferred from the conduct of the parties if, "the plaintiff undertook and completed the building of the wall with the expectation that the defendant would pay him for it, and the defendant had reason to know that the plaintiff was so acting with the expectation and allowed him so to act without objection. . . ." Defendant appealed this instruction as erroneous.

The Massachusetts SJC determined that defendant's assent to the agreement to pay for half of the party wall could be inferred in situations where a party "voluntarily accepts and avails himself of valuable services rendered for his benefit, when he has the option whether to accept or reject them, even if there is no distinct proof that they were rendered by his authority or request. . . ." This rule is not absolute, but rather depends upon the surrounding facts and circumstances, and the court appears to adopt a sliding scale for determining when a party's silence may be deemed consent to pay for services or goods rendered. Where a party has a significant degree of notice that another is providing valuable services or benefits for which the other party expects payment, and the cost of notifying the provider is minimal, the recipient's silence may be interpreted to imply consent to pay. On the other hand, where the recipient receives only incidental notice, had little opportunity to reject the services or benefits, or could only notify the provider at great expense, consent cannot be inferred from the recipient's silence.

INTERESTING DISCUSSION ISSUES

Acceptance by silence regularly seems to intrigue students, possibly because many of them are familiar with the business model used by many book, music, and movie subscription clubs. These clubs often send subscribers monthly newsletters featuring selections that the subscriber must explicitly reject by return postcard to avoid having those featured selections shipped to the subscriber (along with a bill). Additionally, students seem to react to the apparent unfairness of a doctrine that permits a party apparently to impose a duty to reject an offer—a conception that flies directly in the face of the "normal" rules of offer and acceptance that they have just spent several classes learning. Class discussion on these issues is often vigorous.

The instructor may wish to begin with an overview of the common law rules regarding acceptance by silence, which are discussed in detail in the text preceding this case. In general, an offeror may not deem silence to be an acceptance. This may be a good opportunity to review the objective theory of assent and ask the students how a reasonable person standing in the shoes of the offeror could understand silence by an offeree even in the face of an offer indicating that silence would be deemed an assent. The possible meanings of the offeree's silence in such situations include (1) the offeree took the offer at face value and intends to accept (by silence); or (2) the offeree either did not receive or feels no need to respond to the offer. The follow-up question—how would that same reasonable person likely interpret the offeree's silence?—should cause the students either to admit that normally it is not reasonable for anyone to expect silence to indicate assent, or ideally that the consensual nature of silence depends heavily upon the surrounding facts and circumstances of the individual case.

Thus, while the maker of an impersonal, mass solicitation from a credit card company, mortgage brokerage service, or even book club could not reasonably interpret an offeree's silence as consent, other situations may make it reasonable for the offeror to deem silence to be consent. In the book, music, or movie club subscription example, for instance, the vendor may require an initial acceptance after which monthly offerings are sent requiring specific rejection of the next offering. In this context the vendor can reasonably interpret the subscriber's failure to return a postcard rejecting the monthly offering as consent to buy that offering because the underlying contract between the parties typically provides expressly for that relationship. A useful exercise might have students craft narratives that include an offer purportedly acceptable by silence followed by class discussion regarding whether the purported acceptance by silence would be effective, not effective, or a question of fact for the jury.

An additional point for discussion lies in the possibility that the offeror may be bound by the offeree's detrimental reliance upon the offer's promise to deem silence an expression of consent. Students should grasp that in some cases purporting to make the offer acceptable by silence leaves the offeror uncertain regarding its legal liability to the offeree.

NOTES AND QUESTIONS

1. *Question of law versus question of fact*: This question intends to focus the students on the ad hoc nature of the inquiry. In most cases in which the parties deal at arms' length, with no pre-existing relationship, a court likely could decide the acceptance by silence question as a matter of law. On the other hand, given that cases like *Day* suggest that courts should balance multiple factors such as the degree of notice to the offeree, the opportunity for the offeree to notify the offeror of rejection, and the cost for the offeree to notify the offeror of the rejection, it is possible that even at arms' length the parties may create the conditions necessary to indicate acceptance by silence.

The instructor may also want to focus the students on another law/fact issue, namely the problems of proof of an oral agreement. By this time, the students should be familiar with the proposition that the parties may form an enforceable contract by exchange of oral promises, without any additional requirement to evidence the bargain. But as this case indicates, when one of the parties seeks to enforce that oral agreement it may be difficult to prove the existence of an oral agreement. Thus, while an oral contract may exist legally, it may be difficult for a plaintiff to carry its burden of proving that contract if the defendant is willing to commit perjury and deny the contract's existence.

2. *Inferring acceptance by silence or inaction from previous relations and dealings.* See text.

5. Contracts of Adhesion

Carnival Cruise Lines, Inc. v. Shute
CASE BRIEF

This is a 1991 decision of the United States Supreme Court. The students will note that this is a decision of the United States Supreme Court. Straightforward contracts issues rarely get up to that court.

This was a suit in admiralty. The Shutes, residing in the State of Washington, paid a travel agent for two tickets for a week long cruise on the SS. Tropicale from Los Angeles to Puerto Vallarta and back to Los Angeles. The fare was forwarded to the Carnival company in Miami, Florida. Two tickets were issued and sent back to the Shutes with a notation on the face of the tickets that they were subject to the contract terms "on last pages." Section 8 of the contract terms read as follows:

> "It is agreed by and between the passenger and the Carrier that all disputes and matters whatsoever arising under, in connection with or incident to this Contract shall be litigated, if at all, in and before a Court located in the State of Florida, U.S.A., to the exclusion of the Courts of any other state or country."

During the trip Mrs. Shute was injured. The Shutes brought suit in federal district court in the State of Washington alleging her injury was caused by the defendant's negligence. Carnival moved for summary judgment based on the above clause—known as a "forum selection" clause. The federal district court dismissed the action on the ground that the court lacked personal jurisdiction over the defendant since Carnival's contacts with the State of Washington were insubstantial. The Shutes appealed and the Circuit Court of Appeals reversed, holding first, that the court had personal jurisdiction, and second, that the forum selection clause should not be enforced because it was not freely bargained for and that, since the Shutes were "physically and financially incapable of pursing this litigation in Florida," enforcement would deprive them of their day in court.

The Supreme Court reversed the Court of Appeals, holding that the forum selection clause was enforceable. Having so held, the court found it unnecessary to address the constitutional issue of adequate personal jurisdiction. Justice Blackmun wrote the majority opinion. Justice Stevens dissented with Justice Marshall joining in that dissent.

Justice Blackmun began by noting that since this was a case in admiralty, federal law governed the enforceability of the forum selection clause. He avoided consideration of an argument that the Shutes had never assented to (accepted) this clause on the basis that counsel for the Shutes in their written brief had conceded that the clause was reasonably communicated to them.

Both sides argued that a 1972 decision in *The Bremen* was dispositive of this case. *The Bremen* involved a contract to tow an oceangoing drilling rig from Louisiana to the Adriatic Sea. The contract provided that any dispute arising under the contract was to be resolved in the "London Court of Justice." The contract was entered into between two large (sophisticated) corporations. Following severe damage to the tow due to a storm in the Gulf of Mexico, the rig was towed to Tampa. The owner of the rig then sued in admiralty in federal court at Tampa. The defendant moved to dismiss based on the forum selection clause. The district court denied this motion and the denial was affirmed in the Circuit Court of Appeals. The Supreme Court reversed, holding the clause to be enforceable. "We conclude that the forum clause should control absent a strong showing that it should be set aside." Justice Blackmun observed that the opinion did not define precisely the circumstances that would make it unreasonable to enforce such a clause, but did state that "the party claiming [unfairness] should bear a heavy burden of proof."

The Court of Appeals had held that, unlike the parties in *The Bremen*, the Shutes were not business persons and did not negotiate the terms of the clause. Furthermore, enforcement of the clause would deprive the Shutes of an opportunity to litigate their claim.

Justice Blackmun observed that the Shutes' passage contract was "purely routine and doubtless nearly identical to every commercial passage contract issued by petitioner and most other cruise lines." He then set out three reasons for finding the clause enforceable. First, the cruise line has a special interest in limiting the fora (forums) in which it could be sued—an accident could affect a number of different passengers, each living in a different state—thus the company could be exposed to suit in a number of different states based on the same accident. Second, the clause had the "salutary effect of dispelling any confusion about where suits ... must be brought and defended...." Third, the Shutes had the benefit of reduced fares based on the inclusion of this clause in their contract.

Justice Blackmun rejected the Court of Appeals' conclusion that the Shutes were physically and financially unable to sue in Florida as not supported in the record. "The Court of Appeals' conclusory reference to the record provides no basis for this Court to validate the finding of inconvenience." There was nothing about the claim suggesting that it was inherently better suited to resolution in the State of Washington rather than in Florida. Such clauses were subject to judicial scrutiny for "fundamental fairness." But here there was no suggestion that Florida was chosen as the forum to discourage passengers from pursuing legitimate claims nor was there any suggestion of bad faith.

The Shutes had also claimed that the clause violated a federal statute, the Limitation of Vessel Owners Liability Act. Justice Blackmun found that that statute precluded attempts to escape liability for negligence. The clause here had no such effect since the Shutes were, by the express terms of the contract, entitled to sue in Florida. He cited the legislative history of that statute in support of his view.

Justice Stevens, writing the dissent, concluded that the clause should be unenforceable. He observed that the Shutes had no opportunity to read the terms of the contract until after they had paid their fares. He concluded that the clause was unenforceable both under traditional principles of admiralty law and under the federal statute. Exculpatory clauses were typically the product of disparate bargaining power and undermined the strong public interest in deterring negligent conduct. He inferred that there was a question of the reality of any consent to the forum selection clause. He quoted from an interesting 1902 decision of the Supreme Court stating that provisions limiting the liability of carriers for negligence "are both unjust and unreasonable, and will be deemed as wanting in the element of voluntary assent; and, besides, that such conditions are in conflict with public policy." With a neat turn of phrase he observed that such clauses "are all similarly designed to put a thumb on the carrier's side of the scale of justice." He observed that courts "have reviewed with heightened scrutiny the terms of contracts of adhesion, form contracts offered on a take-or-leave basis by a party with stronger bargaining power to a party with weaker power." Referring to domestic common law considerations, he noted that contracts of adhesion were subjected to scrutiny for reasonableness. He cited a leading UCC "unconscionability" decision (the *Williams* case from the District of Columbia) in support, "...the court should consider whether the terms of the contract are so unfair that enforcement should be withheld." He concluded that "the prevailing rule is still that forum-selection clauses are not enforceable if they were not freely bargained for, create additional expense for one party, or deny one party a remedy."

He pointed out that *The Bremen* was not an authority for this case since it involved a contract freely negotiated between parties of equal bargaining power.

INTERESTING DISCUSSION ISSUES

The first question a student is likely to ask about this case is "what is an admiralty case?" The short answer to this question is that the U.S. Constitution, Article III, § 2 provides, "The judicial Power shall extend ... to all Cases of admiralty and maritime Jurisdiction." The current basis for federal court exercise of admiralty jurisdiction is found in 28 U.S.C. § 1333. Thus the federal courts have exclusive jurisdiction of matters affecting navigable waters. Federal jurisdiction over this contract dispute depends on the subject matter—here a matter of travel on the high seas. See Thomas J. Schoenbaum, "Admiralty and Maritime Law," 3rd edition.

A student is then likely to ask, "What is the precedential value of this case in a state contract lawsuit?" The student may be tempted to think that, since this is a decision of the highest court in the land, it is or should be authoritative for courts in other jurisdictions. The answer to that question is that the case is persuasive, but not binding, authority in other jurisdictions. The extent of the persuasive effect is dependent on the case's reasoning and the analogy, if any, between the facts of this case and those of other cases. United States admiralty law is a mixture of statute and judge made law. Like state common law, admiralty law principles were drawn from the English common law.

It is interesting that both sides in the Supreme Court argued that the outcome for the Shutes was governed by the Supreme Court's earlier decision in *The Bremen*. Both the Court of Appeals, and the Supreme Court which reversed the Court of Appeals decision, found the answer to their conclusions in *The Bremen*. In the Supreme Court, Justice Blackmun found *The Bremen* to set out the principles to be applied in the Shutes' situation, while Justice Stevens in dissent found the case wholly distinguishable. This case provides an excellent exercise for students—requiring that they trace with precision how and why each side found support or total absence of support in the same case. It provides an interesting insight for students into the use of a prior precedent to either support or undermine an argument and a consequent decision. The instructor may find it worthwhile to explore in some detail how the majority opinion used *The Bremen* decision and how the dissent distinguished it as flatly irrelevant to the Shutes' case.

Justice Blackmun found the answer starting with the quotation from *The Bremen* that forum selection clauses were "not historically ... favored" but were "prima facie valid." While he conceded that factual differences between the two cases precluded automatic and simple application of *The Bremen* result, he did not develop those differences in a way that would have been helpful to the Shutes. Instead, he started from the statement of burden of proof in that case, namely that the clause should control "absent a strong showing that it should be set aside." He found such a showing missing. He summarily dismissed the Court of Appeals' basis that the clause was not dickered—the

Shutes' contract was purely routine, common in the industry, and it was unreasonable to assume that there could be negotiation over such a term. That was not an available alternative. He then stated his three reasons why the presence of such a clause made sense—there was a justifiable business reason (explanation) for its use. He rejected the Court of Appeals' other argument that the Shutes were unable to litigate in Florida as unsupported in the record. While such clauses were subject to judicial scrutiny for unfairness, he concluded (on what basis?) that there was no indication that the clause had been inserted in order to discourage litigation nor was there any suggestion of bad faith on Carnival's part After all, the forum selected was its home port and principal business office. In short, he found the presumption of enforceability stated in *The Bremen* had not been overcome. He found the statute inapplicable because the clause did not relieve Carnival of liability for negligence nor did it deprive the Shutes of an opportunity to litigate.

Justice Stevens began by mocking the notion that Carnival's ticket and attached contract gave any real notice of this forum selection clause. He observed that these terms were read by the passenger some time after the money (and hence the moment of mutual assent?) had been paid. He found economic efficiency and saving of Carnival's litigation expense to be poor reasons for supporting validity of the clause. He asserted that "exculpatory" clauses (the assumption that an exculpatory clause—relieving the benefited party of liability for negligence—is the same thing as a forum selection clause is interesting) were the product of disparate bargaining power and undermine public interest in deterring negligent conduct. He quoted from a 1902 Supreme Court decision suggesting that there was no real "assent" to such clauses and that they were contrary to public policy. In a footnote he derided Justice Blackmun's reason based on the Shutes' receiving a financial benefit because of the inclusion of such a clause. In what should be an interesting form of argument for students, he pointed out that such a reason goes too far in that it would justify an outright exemption of any liability at all. He then referred to traditional common law and cited Llewellyn, as well as the *Williams* decision (District of Columbia law)—there was no consent or manifestation of consent where the terms were so unfair that they ought not to be enforced. He concluded that the traditional common law required that such clauses be bargained for, must not create additional expense for one party, or deny anyone a remedy. Because *The Bremen* enforced a forum selection clause in a contract that had been freely negotiated between two large corporations, it had no application to the Shutes' case.

Students should find it interesting that the primary difference between the majority opinion and the dissent is the selection of a starting point—the allocation of the burden of proof.

While there may not be sufficient time for the instructor to explore the issue of statutory interpretation raised in the case, that issue is significant. Justice Blackmun read the statute as focusing on exculpation from liability for negligence. He gave a very thin reading to the words of the statute voiding any limitation "purporting ... to lessen, weaken or avoid the right of any claimant to a trial by a court of competent jurisdiction...." Reading that provision literally, he concluded that a Florida court was a "court of competent jurisdiction," and that therefore there was no violation of the statute. It would not have been difficult to reach the opposite conclusion, namely that the forum selection clause had the effect of lessening and weakening the claimant's opportunity to litigate.

A second point of interest is found in the decision at the Court of Appeals level—that the terms of the clause were not negotiated (dickered). The students should deal with the question, "Were this the law, what is the impact of such a rule on ALL form contracts?" Justice Stevens quotes from the 1902 Supreme Court decision suggesting that there is no true "assent" where unfair clauses are introduced into a take-it-or-leave-it form contract. The answer to this question goes back to Llewellyn's analysis covered in the text. The Court of Appeals' approach "proves far too much."

A third point comes out of Justice Blackmun's finessing of the "notice" issue. How could the forum selection clause have become a term of the contract under an offer and acceptance analysis? Where did the Shutes' acceptance (assent to) of that clause come from? Justice Blackmun avoids this issue by finding a conclusive admission by counsel for the Shutes that they had adequate notice of the clause. Recognizing that the opinion in the case would cover many different fact patterns than that raised in this case, Justice Stevens found any "notice" of the term to be highly questionable. After all, the Shutes had made their commitment when they paid their money—and at that time they had no notice of the clause. From the student's perspective, can the necessary mutuality ("meeting of the minds") be found here? If so, how? Does not Justice Blackmun's approach involve adding new terms (changing the contract) to the offer after that offer was made by payment of the fares? At what point in time was the contract entered into? Justice Blackmun's opinion assumes (concludes?) that the true contract was entered into only after the Shutes received their tickets together with the printed terms. This question will come back in an even stronger context when we get to "shrinkwrap" and "clickwrap" licenses.

Assuming the instructor has time, she may ask the question, "What was Carnival's motive in drafting this clause?" While Justice Blackmun presumes there was no evil motive behind insertion of the clause—after all, all such businesses use a similar approach—is that clear? Do students suppose that such a forum selection clause does not have a dampening effect on the bringing of negligence suits by passengers?

Justice Stevens says, "The fact that the cruise line can reduce its litigation costs, and therefore its liability insurance premiums, by forcing this choice on its passengers does not, in my opinion, suffice to render the provision reasonable." Is the consumer being treated very unfairly by the use of such a clause? Is not such unfair treatment the precise focus of the federal statute involved?

NOTES AND QUESTIONS

1. *Subsequent statutory amendment.* See text.

2. *Llewellyn's analysis.* The only truly negotiated terms of the contract were the fare, the ship, and the trip. The pages of contract terms attached to the ticket were basic "boiler-plate." The forum selection clause was clearly not negotiated. In a sense, both the majority and the dissent adopted Llewellyn's analysis. Both agreed that such clauses were subject to judicial scrutiny. Both addressed the question of whether the clause was fair. The two sides reached an opposite conclusion on this issue. The student may wonder what resources both sides drew on to find "fairness" or "unfairness." Justice Blackmun was impressed by the universality of the use of such a clause by all cruise lines. He was equally impressed by the practical impossibility of such a clause ever being seriously "dickered." His three "practical" reasons assigned to support his conclusion of fairness are somewhat thin. His choice results from his allocation of the burden of proof/persuasion.

3. *Duty to read doctrine; objective theory of contracts; and adhesion contracts.* Is it fair to apply a "duty to read" in cases such as this? Llewellyn says yes, to a point—that point being unreasonable or indecent terms. Specifically, how does the signature on a contract of adhesion relate to Llewellyn's argument that boilerplate terms and clauses are seldom read and cannot be changed in any event? What about important clauses buried in a long form designed to be hidden or with such an effect? The Shutes' ticket/contract was a routine relatively every day event. We can take "judicial notice" of the truth of Llewellyn's statement. If there is any doubt about this, the instructor can ask a student about when that student first studied the terms of her automobile insurance contract (which typically arrives weeks or months after the purchaser has "bought" the insurance coverage and which comes in perhaps 25 pages of printed form). What does the average student know or understand about the doctrine of "subrogation" and whether or not her health insurer, who has paid medical expenses arising from an accident, has a claim to part of any recovery from a tortfeasor? There are many reasons why consumers rarely read, and almost never try to dicker, terms in a printed form contract. Time constraints and lack of relevant knowledge or

understanding of the terms used are two among a number of the reasons for such common conduct. Many reasonable and necessary terms are included in such boilerplate and a different and very serious problem would be created if boiler-plate were to be thrown out in its entirety. In Carnival, the court held that receipt of the ticket without objection constituted effective acceptance of the terms of the attached contract—the equivalent of signing without reading.

Calamari does support Llewellyn's theory. If so, how do you reconcile the early will theory or subjective intent "meeting of the minds" theory with the later nineteenth century objective theory? The two cannot be reconciled—the objective theory is based on a reasonable need and expectation in our world of commerce. Is there yet another pendulum swing in contracts back to subjective intent? The probable answer is "No." Stated another way, do you think that objectivists like Holmes and Williston would agree with realists like Llewellyn? The answer to this question lies in the eye of the beholder but our answer would be "No."

A serious difficulty with the "duty to read" concept is the built-in assumption that the playing field is level for all players. Everyone must be able to read and understand, and the consequences of signing without reading or understanding follow from this assumption. As Dean Morant pointed out in his article, "The Teachings of Dr. Martin Luther King, Jr., and Contract Theory: An Intriguing Comparison," 50 Ala. L. Rev. 63 (1998), this assumption is basically flawed. Llewellyn's theory provides a means of correcting serious miscarriages of justice caused by such flaw.

4. *Restatement approach*. The text notes that, "Restatement (Second) of Contracts § 211(3) regarding standardized agreements provides that a term is not part of an agreement where 'the other party has reason to believe that the party manifesting such assent would not do so if he knew that the writing contained a particular term.'" The student should get acquainted quickly with the way in which trials are conducted and evidence introduced. How would the consumer prove that the form provider "had [such] reason to believe ..."? The text asks, "Where does this leave the doctrine of the duty to read, at least in form contracts?" Does it adopt Llewellyn's no true assent to unreasonable boiler plate? If so, is there any difference between the UCC and common law on this point?" Our answer would be that the Restatement incorporates Llewellyn's theory and, through UCC § 1-103, so does the UCC, at least subject to a possible difference where the parties are merchants (covered later).

5. *UCC duty to read*. See text.

6. *Disclosure timing*. See discussion above under "Interesting Discussion Issues."

7. *Adhesion contracts and socio-economic context.* Do you accept Pound's implicit proposition that, while contract law grounded in the notion that individuals were generally capable of protecting their own interests in dealing with others "worked" at some point in the past, it no longer works under current social and economic conditions? We reject that implicit proposition believing that the playing field has never been level for all parties to contracts. See comments under Note (3) above.

8. *Contract as thing and contract as product.* Are these arguments for regulating the "quality" of terms in consumer adhesion contracts through legislation rather than common law contract rules compelling? Why or why not?

The following examples can be provided of Leff's three strategies: (a) Regulating the parties with respect to who can enter particular types of transactions—for example, the Securities and Exchange Commission's regulations limiting those to whom offers can be extended in a "private offering;" (b) Regulating the deal making process, such as by requiring greater disclosure or waiting periods—federal banking regulation of consumer loans. Another example of this methodology can be found in UCC § 316 requiring that warranty disclaimers be "conspicuous"; (c) Regulating the contract terms as part of the product being sold—this approach is used less often, but see the effect of UCC § 2-207(3) and the "gap-fillers" (including implied warranties relating to the quality of the goods under UCC §§ 2-314 & 2-315). One of the authors vaguely recalls a proposal within the Federal Trade Commission staff in the early 1970's—the high point in that agency's efforts to become the protector of the consumer. That proposal would have involved the FTC issuing by regulation forms for a number of basic consumer contracts, such as the purchase of a car. Sellers of cars would have been required to use the prescribed form, unaltered, and no other. The proposal never advanced and there has been no public outcry for any such approach. In the world of insurance policies, the Commissioner of Insurance (or comparable officer) in most states has limited authority to approve or deny the use of particular forms of insurance policy within the state. The efficacy of this authority is sometimes called into question. The form of the so-called "Standard Fire Insurance Policy" was mandated by legislation and continues to be so mandated in some states. Similarly, the substantive terms of flood insurance policies, which are almost universally obtainable only under the National Flood Insurance Program operated by the Federal Emergency Management Agency ("FEMA"), are described by federal statutes and regulations. While the precise language may not be regulated, the content of a number of the provisions found in an automobile insurance policy are commonly required to be included in the policy by statute.

9. *Adhesion contracts, and "sticky" terms.* Does Korobkin's inertia theory explain why consumers sometimes fail to attempt to dicker over contracts that appear to be offered on a take-it-or-leave-it basis but would really be open to negotiation if consumers just asked? Are there any other reasons consumers might not attempt to negotiate in such situations? There are many reasons why consumers fail to even attempt to "dicker" the terms of form contracts. Some of those reasons include the following: the assumption that the terms cannot be negotiated and/or that the sales person has no authority to negotiate such terms; embarrassment; the desire to get the transaction concluded quickly and without hassle—the customer waiting in line to rent a car; focus on the thing, not the terms and the possible long delay in response to a request for modification of terms; and lack of knowledge as to both the meaning and function of the terms used in the form and the ways in which those terms might be modified. To a certain extent Korobkin's inertia theory is consistent with some of these common reasons for failing to dicker.

One of the authors attempts to clarify the distinction between contracts that actually are adhesive and contracts that only appear adhesive by making the following homework assignment either in connection with this set of readings or in connection with a separate discussion on negotiation: "HOMEWORK: Within the next two weeks, attempt to negotiate different terms in at least three situations traditionally presented by producers to consumers as standard form contracts offered on a take-it-or-leave-it basis. Two of these negotiations may involve attempts to change the price term on a retail consumer product or service. At least one attempt at negotiation must involve a non-price term. Draft a one-paragraph description of each negotiation attempt, including the original term, your alternative offer, and the outcome of the negotiation." This exercise offers several benefits beyond making clear that while many standard terms are offered on a take-it-or-leave-it basis, that does not mean the terms really are adhesive. First, 1L students often feel like they are not receiving any practical or "real" legal training during their first year. This exercise, in which the majority of students report at least one successful negotiation away from standard terms, provides a taste of the real-world effectiveness of what we are attempting to teach. Second, the exercise may enhance the instructor's credibility at a point in the semester when many students feel that they will never be able to understand law or get anything useful from study. Third, since many students will have never attempted to negotiate even a price discount at a retail establishment, it has a high potential to produce an "a-ha!!" learning moment. Fourth, the exercise forces students to realize that they can obtain substantial benefits for themselves (and incidentally their clients) just by asking for them.

10. *Social context and adhesion contracting.* What social and psychological pressures are at work on consumers in such situations that would tend to prevent bargaining? See comments under Note (8) above. Do you think that producers intentionally establish high-pressure situations to impair consumer willingness to bargain, or have those situations developed naturally as a result of the fast pace of the modern American economy? Both questions can be answered "yes" in certain circumstances.

C. TERMINATION OF THE POWER OF ACCEPTANCE

1. Termination by Offeror Revocation

Dickinson v. Dodds

CASE BRIEF

This is an 1876 decision of the English Court of Appeal, Chancery Division. On Wednesday Dodds agreed to sell his property to Dickinson for L. 800 in a signed written letter together with a signed postscript: "This offer to be left over until Friday, 9 o'clock, A.M. ..." On Thursday morning Dickinson decided to buy the property but thought that he had until Friday morning to conclude the deal. On Thursday afternoon Dickinson was told by his agent that Dodds was offering or had agreed to sell the property to a third party, Thomas Allan. Promptly (Thursday evening) Dickinson left a signed formal written acceptance of the offer at the house where Dodds was staying (his mother-in-law's). The evidence suggested that Dodds never knew of this "acceptance." At 7:00am on Friday, Dickinson's agent found Dodds and handed him a duplicate copy of the signed acceptance. Despite this purported acceptance, Dodds informed the agent that the agent was too late because Dodds had sold the property. A short time later, Dickinson himself found Dodds and handed him a third copy of the signed acceptance, but Dodds declined to receive it.

Dickinson sued for specific performance, joining Allan as well as Dodds. Counsel for Dickinson argued that the letter was a formal and complete agreement of sale and purchase, emphasizing the words in the letter, "I hereby agree to sell to Mr. George Dickinson ..." In the alternative, assuming that the letter was only an offer to sell, that offer was effectively accepted before it was withdrawn and therefore became a binding contract. Counsel argued *Adams v. Lindsell* was applicable by analogy, and that the acceptance was complete when delivered to Dodds' house. For a retraction to be effective it had to be communicated to the offeree, and no such notification occurred. Counsel for Dodds argued that the letter was no more than an offer—one which was withdrawn when Dodds sold the property to Allan. In any case, the postscript was "merely voluntary, without consideration, ... a nudum pactum ..." Finding that the letter was an agreement of sale, and not just an offer (despite the wording of the postscript "This offer ...") Vice Chancellor Bacon granted specific performance. It was a contract subject to a condition that "Plaintiff shall not be called upon to accept, or to testify his acceptance, until 9 o'clock ...." Moreover, if only an offer, withdrawal to be effective had to be communicated to the offeree.

Dodds appealed to the Court of Appeal, Chancery Division. Lord Justice James concluded that the letter was only an offer, as shown by the very words of the letter. It was settled law, he said, that "this promise, being a mere nudum pactum, was not binding" and could be withdrawn before acceptance. He found this conclusion to be based on the requirement of a mutual agreement occurring at the same moment of time. He then concluded that, based on the plaintiff's own pleadings, that Dickinson knew that the offer had been withdrawn before making any attempt to accept the offer. "It is to my mind quite clear that before there was any attempt at acceptance by the Plaintiff, he was perfectly well aware that Dodds had changed his mind ...." Lord Justice Mellish said he was "of the same opinion." The letter was only an offer to sell. He, however, added a touch of mystery to the decision by saying, "If an offer has been made for the sale of property, and before that offer is accepted, ... the person to whom the offer was first made receives notice in some way that the property has been sold to another person ..." the offer can no longer be accepted. He followed this conclusion with an example of an offer to sell a horse followed by a sale to a third person. His example could be interpreted as suggesting that the sale to a third person revoked the offer without reference to notice of the sale to the offeree. He then analogized to an offer followed by the death of the offeror before acceptance by the offeree. Here, he said, the law was clear that the offer could no longer be accepted following the death of the offeror. The third member of the court concurred.

INTERESTING DISCUSSION ISSUES

It is trite black letter law that effective revocation or withdrawal of an offer requires notice of the revocation or withdrawal to the offeree. When did Dickinson "accept" the offer? By leaving a copy of a signed acceptance at Dodd's house. Assuming *Adams v. Lindsell* (the mailbox rule) to be good law, surely leaving the letter at the house, in the same way that the postman would have left the letter had it been mailed, was effective as an act of acceptance unless the offer had been withdrawn prior to that time—Thursday evening. The mystery of this case lies in the wording of the trial court opinion that the information coming to Dickinson on Thursday afternoon was that "Dodds had been offering or agreeing to sell the property to Thomas Allan." Dodds did not give Dickinson notice of any withdrawal. Should third party word of conduct by Dodds, inconsistent with the offer remaining open, be sufficient notice? First year students have been tormented first, by a truncated version of this case in their materials, and next by a hypothetical withdrawal based on receipt of a "rumor." Lord Justice James buried that hypothetical by finding that, beyond peradventure, Dickinson knew of the sale to Allan before he left the "acceptance" at Dodds' house on Thursday evening. The student torture was always compounded by the fact that the mother-in-law failed to give the written acceptance to Dodds.

The result in this case is enshrined in the following words of the Restatement (Second) of Contracts § 43:

> "An offeree's power of acceptance is terminated when the offeror takes definite action inconsistent with an intention to enter into the proposed contract and the offeree acquires reliable information to that effect."

The student will wonder why Dodds' promise to keep the offer open until Friday morning should not be enforced. Perhaps the most persuasive reason is that to do so would hold Dodds bound to a contract at a time prior to Dickinson being bound, not yet having accepted. It is worth reminding the student of the facts set out in the introductory text, namely that, in the context of a sale of goods, an offer by a merchant, stating that the offer is irrevocable, is enforceable if in writing, signed by the merchant, and stated to be irrevocable for a period not to exceed three months. See UCC § 2-205. The CISG states that the offer is irrevocable in accordance with its terms, but this convention applies only to certain transnational contracts and does not apply to consumer goods.

There are clear overtones of the "will" theory in this case, especially in the opinion of Lord Justice Mellish when he provided two analogies. The first was the offer to sell a horse withdrawn by sale of the horse to a third person. The second was the death of the offeror after making the offer but before acceptance of that offer. While it is reasonably clear that the Lord Justice's hypothetical of the horse was based on knowledge of the sale to the offeree, it is crystal clear that revocation of the offer by the supervening death of the offeror was not tied in any way to notice of or knowledge of that death by the offeree. Thus, in the case of this analogy the "will" theory seems to trump the "objective" theory. The apparent basis of this analogy is that there cannot logically be a "meeting of the minds" where the offeror dies before the offeree accepts—both offeror and offeree must be alive (and competent) at the time the circle of commitment is completed. The unfairness of such a rule is easily illustrated. Suppose the offeror mails a signed written offer to sell 100 shares of stock for $1,000 a share to the offeree. The offeree has other opportunities to buy such stock but promptly mails a signed written acceptance to the offeror. A week later, when the offeree finds out that the offeror had died before he mailed his acceptance and that he has no enforceable contract, the stock price has increased to

$1,500 a share. Swift & Co. v. Smigel, 115 N.J.Super. 391, 279 A.2d 895 (1971), illustrates the same difficulty where the offeror becomes mentally incompetent after having made the offer but the offeree accepts without notice of the fact of the supervening incompetence. In that case the court found the continuing offer to be effectively accepted notwithstanding the supervening loss of competence by the offeror. Surprisingly, the Restatement (Second) of Contracts § 36 clings to the position stated by Lord Justice Mellish:

> "Methods of Termination of the Power of Acceptance
> (1) An offeree's power of acceptance may be terminated by ...
> (d) death or incapacity of the offeror or offeree."

See also Restatement (Second) of Contracts § 48.

The student may be interested in the process by which decisions of a three judge court of appeals were handed down in England at the time of this case. The judges sat in open court with copy of the printed case decisions behind them and available for inspection. Following argument by both counsel, the judges delivered their opinions orally, one by one. This practice led to a memorable experience in one court of appeals where the first judge delivered his opinion, the second said, "I have nothing useful to add" and the third said, "I concur," apparently leading to some very bad feelings on the bench.

NOTES AND QUESTIONS

1. *Mellish appointed.* See text.

2. *Intervening Allan purchase.* Having been informed of the sale by his broker Berry, Dickinson nonetheless attempted to exercise the power of acceptance created in the written offer. How does the court view Dickinson's behavior? Notice the lower trial court held for Dickinson. Why? The lower court held for Dickinson based on a strained interpretation of the letter—that it was an agreement to sell that took effect subject to a condition subsequent that Dickinson signify his acceptance before Friday at 9:00am. It may be useful to compare this theory of contract formation to the arguably ambiguous process used in International Filter Co., discussed above. In the latter case, the terms of the parties' communications could have been interpreted as (1) a proposal by International Filter specifying the terms on which they would entertain offers, an offer by Conroe Gin, Ice & Light in the form requested by International Filter, and an acceptance by International Filter at its offices in Chicago; or (2) an offer by International Filter conditioned on a final "approval" in Chicago, an acceptance by Conroe Gin, Ice & Light, and a final approval in Chicago. Students should be able to see that the designation of communications

as offers and acceptances is not always determined by the language used in those communications. Additionally, while it may not always be clear when the offer and acceptance were made, that determination may nonetheless have a significant impact on the outcome. This latter issue will be discussed in detail again in the Hill v. Gateway2000, Inc. and Klocek v. Gateway, Inc. cases later in this chapter.

In Dickinson, the trial judge gave no weight to the use of the word "offer" in the postscript. While Dodds gave no direct notice of withdrawal of the offer to Dickinson, Dickinson's behavior on both Thursday and Friday was instinct with his knowledge of Dodds' inconsistent behavior. He made, or caused to be made, three separate attempts to accept the offer—this conduct strongly suggests that he knew Dodds had sold (or was selling) the property to another. Lord Justice James says that Dickinson's pleadings established conclusively his knowledge that Dodds had sold to another.

Note (2) asks further, "Did Dodds make such an expression to Dickinson?" The answer is "No." If Berry told Dickinson that Dodds was "negotiating" to sell the property to Allan, and that if he wanted the property he should hurry his acceptance, would the case be resolved differently? Probably yes, assuming that the court found delivery of the signed written acceptance to Dodds' house effective as an acceptance (c.f. mailbox rule). If so, would it make any difference to you that Dodds had sold the property to Allan but that Dickinson had only learned of the negotiations? If not, do you think it provident that contract law should base enforcement upon whether Dodds utters "revoke" immediately before or after Dickinson utters "accept"? If Dickinson had only learned of negotiations (and not sale of the property) objective theory would base the answer on what Dickinson reasonably knew at the time he accepted (by leaving the acceptance at Dodds' house on Thursday evening). The effectiveness of acceptance should not depend on whether Dickinson or his agent said "accept" before Dodds uttered "revoke." There would be no substantial reliance by Dickinson in such a situation, and while reliance is not the key to completion of the circle of binding commitment in this situation, it certainly could have some impact on the court's decision on this assumed version of the facts. A court might well find that the exchange was essentially simultaneous—thus no effective acceptance. See Restatement (Second) of Contracts § 42.

3. *Evolution of the restatement rules.* See text.

4. *Revocation versus withdrawal.* Is there a difference between withdrawal and revocation? The answer is no. If an offer is mailed but the offeror telephones the prospective offeree to negate the offer prior to when it was received or otherwise communicated, has the offer been withdrawn or revoked? The answer is yes. The offer is not effective (capable of being converted into a binding commitment) until it is

received by the offeree—thus the oral notice of revocation, if received before the offer arrives, is timely. Does an offeratory communication create a power of acceptance prior to or before it reaches the offeree? The answer is no. Does this difference explain the distinction between withdrawal and revocation? Again, the answer is no—the two are one and the same thing, or at least have identical effect.

5. *Option contracts.* See text.

6. *In abrogation of the common law rule.* Would Dodds' offer have been legally irrevocable under Professor Eisenberg's theory? Yes. If you were the reporter for the Restatement (Third) Contracts, would you articulate a common law firm offer rule? While Professor Llewellyn was able to make such a change in UCC Article 2, that change was ultimately legislated. The reporter would be well advised not to "legislate" through the Restatement on a matter that has long and consistently been enshrined in state court opinions.

7. *UCC and CISG firm offer rules.* In the language of UCC § 2-205, did Dodds make an "assurance" that the offer would be held open? Yes. In the language of CISG art. 16(2), did Dodds "state" the offer was irrevocable or would be held open for acceptance? Yes. To understand the difference, if the offer merely stated it would expire after three days, would the offer be irrevocable under either or both authorities? Such an offer would not be a "firm" offer under the UCC because of the lack of the necessary "assurance." Such an offer would be irrevocable under the CISG because the convention contains no comparable requirement of "assurance."

8. *Role of detrimental reliance.* Do you think UCC § 2-205 displaces reliance? Yes, because a reasonable interpretation of the language of that section suggests that it "occupies the whole field" of what is or is not an enforceable "firm" offer. Did Dickinson incur the detrimental reliance necessary to invoke these reliance doctrines? Do we know about his reliance? If not, why not? The date of this case substantially precedes the evolution of a doctrine of promissory estoppel and detrimental reliance in this country. The extent to which that doctrine has been adopted in England even now is not clear. We do not know about Dickinson's reliance other than for the costs he may have incurred in delivering a copy of the acceptance to Dodds' home and the possible costs of having the agent, as well as himself, chase Dodds down at the railway station. Costs of this sort would not qualify as "reliance." Why do we not know? Because the doctrine of promissory estoppel had not yet developed and thus the value of evidence of reliance would not have occurred to counsel for Dickinson.

9. *Government contracts.* See text.

10. *Offer deposits.* See text.

11. *Lapse of time and late acceptance.* See text.

2. Termination by Offeree Rejection or Counteroffer

Step-Saver Data Systems, Inc. v. WYSE Technology
CASE BRIEF

This is a 1991 decision of the United States Court of Appeals, Third Circuit. Step-Saver ("SS") was in the business of buying both hardware and software components from other manufacturers, assembling them into packages, and selling those packages to buyers interested in obtaining a network system linking various terminals to a central processing computer. In the 1986-87 timeframe SS sold 142 such systems, incorporating packages purchased from both TSL and WYSE. Following receipt of numerous complaints from customers, SS requested technical assistance from both TSL and WYSE in solving the problems. Disputes developed and the problems were never solved. At least twelve lawsuits were commenced by customers against SS.

SS then sought a declaratory judgment that either TSL or WYSE or both of them were responsible to indemnify SS. This lawsuit was dismissed as "not ripe" for adjudication. SS then sued both TSL and WYSE for breach of warranties and TSL for fraud.

It is useful to focus on the suit against TSL. The process by which the purchases from TSL were made was as follows. SS would place orders for TSL software by telephone, usually for 20 packages at a time. TSL would accept those orders over the phone. SS would follow up with a purchase order specifying the items to be purchased, their price, and shipping and payment terms. TSL would ship the order together with an invoice containing terms essentially identical with those found in SS's purchase order. No reference in either the telephone call, purchase order or invoice was made to disclaimer of any warranties. Each software package had printed on the outside a "box-top license" setting out five terms relevant to the lawsuit: the transaction was a software license and not a sale of the underlying software, and this license was personal and nontransferable; all express and implied warranties were disclaimed except that the disk was free from defects; the sole remedy was return and replacement and both direct and consequential damages were excluded; an integration clause provided that the license terms were a final and complete expression of the terms of the parties' agreement; and a statement that, "Opening this package indicates your acceptance of these terms and conditions. . . ." together with an offer of refund if the package was returned unopened within 15 days.

TSL argued that the contract came into existence when the package was opened and that the terms of the box-top license were controlling. Since those terms included a statement that they were the final and complete agreement of the parties, UCC § 2-202 (parol evidence rule) precluded the introduction of any extrinsic evidence to add to or contradict the terms of the license. The district court held as a matter of law that the box-top license was the parties' final and complete expression. It thus granted TSL's motion in limine to exclude all extrinsic evidence of earlier oral or written express warranties. It also rejected SS's charge of fraud as unsupported. It then directed a verdict for TSL on all express and implied warranty claims and dismissed TSL from the case.

As regards TSL, SS raised two issues on appeal: that SS and TSL did not intend the box-top license to be a complete and final expression of their agreement (and thus extrinsic evidence as to warranties should have been admitted); and that there was sufficient evidence of fraud. The Third Circuit Court of Appeals reviewed the TSL case de novo since the district court had ruled on the contract issues as a matter of law. The circuit court reversed the district court on the first issue and remanded the case for trial on the warranty issues. It sustained the district court decision on the fraud issue.

Both sides argued that UCC Article 2 provided the governing law, thus providing common ground that the transactions in question involved the sale of "goods." A key difference between them was how and when the contract was entered into. SS argued that the contract was complete upon the conclusion of the telephone conversation accompanied by the confirming purchase order and invoice. TSL argued that contract was not complete until the purchaser opened the package, thus confirming agreement on the terms of the box-top license. UCC § 2-202 (parol evidence rule) thus precluded the introduction of any extrinsic evidence to add to or contradict the terms of the license. TSL argued that UCC § 2-207 was not applicable.

Contrary to TSL's argument the court found that UCC § 2-207 ("battle of the forms") was applicable. The court explained what had usually happened under the common law "mirror image" doctrine. The buyer would place a written order, containing the buyer's terms including warranties. The seller would respond with its written response containing the seller's terms and excluding warranties. The goods would be shipped and paid for and later a dispute would arise between the parties turning on the question of whose terms applied. Under the common law "last shot" concept, the seller's response was not an acceptance because it contained terms different than the offeror's. Instead it was a counteroffer the terms of which were accepted by the following performance. Thus the seller's terms usually prevailed. The court noted that the authors of the UCC considered this result to be unfair and designed UCC § 2-207 to undo that unfairness. "The insight behind the rejection of the last shot rule is that it would be unfair to bind the buyer of goods to the standard terms of the seller, when neither party cared sufficiently to establish expressly the terms of their agreement, simply because the seller sent the last form. Thus, UCC § 2-207 establishes a legal rule that proceeding with a contract after receiving a writing that purports to define the terms of the parties' contract is not sufficient to establish the party's consent to the terms of the writing to the extent that the terms of the writing either add to, or differ from, the terms detailed in the parties' earlier writings or discussions."

Applying UCC § 2-207 to the present facts, the court concluded that it was not necessary to decide precisely when the contract was entered into, but clearly held that a contract had been established when the products were shipped and paid for. The only remaining question was what the terms of that contract were. The essential terms were all agreed on by means of the telephone calls and the confirming memoranda. Thus the box-top license attempted to introduce terms additional to or different from the original terms. The license was therefore a proposal for additional terms which would take effect only if accepted by SS. Such acceptance never occurred (TSL attempted twice unsuccessfully to get SS to agree to a written set of terms to cover the transactions, and SS's president, Greebel, specifically objected to application of the box-top license terms against SS). Thus the parties had a contract but not agreement on the applicable terms. In this case, said the court, the UCC solution was to apply those terms which were agreed to by the parties together with the UCC gap-fillers (such as express and implied warranties—UCC § 2-313, -314) under UCC § 2-207(3). In any case, said the court, it was clear from the record that the box-top license was not a complete integrated statement. Whereas the box-top terms described the license granted as personal and non-transferable, the parties clearly intended, contradicting that provision, that SS was to be authorized to transfer the license to the ultimate purchaser. The court remanded the case for trial on the issues of warranties.

TSL had also argued that no completed contract could result from the telephone calls and exchange of memoranda because essential terms had not been agreed upon and included in those exchanges. In particular, the fact that the contract was one for a license and not for a sale of the underlying software had not been established. Thus, said TSL, there could be no enforceable contract while essential terms were still to be decided on. In rejecting this argument the court found that standard copyright law applied and that under that law all that SS could receive was a license and not title to the underlying software. Thus all the essential terms had been established—the nature of the transaction, together with the specific goods involved, the quantity and price.

TSL had argued, in the alternative, that the box-top license terms amounted to a "conditional acceptance" under the last phrase of paragraph § 2-207(1). TSL's theory was that because of this, the box-top terms were a counteroffer which was accepted by subsequent performance. The court stated its uncertainty whether a conditional analysis applied where the contract had been established by performance, but, for purposes of this case, assumed that such an analysis did apply. It found that the party seeking to enforce its form had the burden of proof and that the burden of establishing expressly conditional language had not been met. TSL's acceptance was thus not "conditional." In Footnote 34 the court observed that even in true "conditional acceptance" cases courts usually avoided finding the terms of the counteroffer controlling by requiring the counterofferor to establish that the offeror assented to those terms. In the absence of such proof the result was to be found in § 2-207(3). The court found the refund offer in the box-top terms failed to meet the requisite standard of proof that TSL was prepared to forgo its sale unless SS consented to its terms.

TSL advanced yet another argument that because of the successive purchases, SS was fixed with knowledge of TSL's terms. The court rejected all of TSL's arguments. TSL had suggested that failure to enforce the box-top license would "inevitably destroy" the software industry. The court was not concerned—conspicuous disclosure of warranty disclaimers was required and to be made available before the contract was formed.

In SS's suit against WYSE the jury had found for the defendant WYSE. The circuit court let that decision stand.

INTERESTING DISCUSSION ISSUES

1. *Is the granting of a software license a "sale of goods" under the UCC?* Some students may pick up on the fact that this transaction was, one way or another, the sale of a license and not a sale of goods. They may ask, "Why did the parties stipulate that the UCC Article 2 provided the applicable law?" For nearly twenty years it was uncertain whether a software license would be treated as a sale of goods under the UCC or not. A number of courts found it convenient to assume that the UCC does apply to such transactions. The definitive opinion in favor of UCC coverage is found in *Advent Systems Ltd. V. Unisys Corp.*, 925 F.2d 670 (3rd Cir. 1991). Some commentators have argued that the provisions of the CISG are ambiguous on this issue of inclusion or exclusion. Writers anticipate that the convention will be interpreted to include such license sales, unless of course, the contract expressly excludes application of the CISG.

2. *Step-Saver buries the common law "last shot" and "mirror image" doctrines as applied to the sale of goods.* Step-Saver provides an interesting application of the rules of offer and acceptance. Central to the court's analysis is the fact that both parties agreed over the

telephone to the purchase and sale of the described quantities of packages of the TSL software. Applying classical contracts concepts, there was an offer, based on quantity, price and delivery terms, together with a mirror image acceptance (with or without reference to the confirmatory memos). The "after-the-fact" injection of the terms of the box-top license was an attempt to add to or contradict terms of the existing agreement and thus, again under classical contract law principles, was a proposal to amend the original contract. Since the proposed amending terms were never accepted by the buyer, the original contract, together with other applicable legal rules, were the source of rights and duties for both sides. TSL failed in its argument that no contract was entered into until the box-top package was opened.

3. Avoiding the problem of the "gap-fillers"—UCC § 2-207 application to "shrinkwrap" and "clickwrap" licenses. The court pointed out that the decision was not the end of the world for hardware and software sales. All the seller had to do was give advance notice of restrictive contract terms. Between merchants, trouble could be prevented by appropriate instructions to the seller's order processing department. No signed written contract, no shipment of order. While *Step-Saver* involved a dispute between two businesses (merchants), the disturbing potential (and actuality) of the decision was its possible application to consumer transactions. What would the impact be on hardware and software sales if the "shrinkwrap" and "clickwrap" procedures were ineffective to protect the seller against a UCC § 2-207(3) exposure? If the contract was entered into at the time the consumer purchased the software package from the retail seller, and not when the consumer opened the package and read the terms, including the right of return, how could the manufacturer protect against buyer-oriented UCC "gap-filler" terms?

The eclipse of the *Step-Saver* threat began with the decision in *ProCD, Inc. v. Zeidenberg*, 86 F.3d 1447 (7th Cir. 1996). Judge Easterbrook explained the basically significant business reasons for recognizing the binding effect of terms accessed only after money had been paid and the product delivered. He also catalogued a number of familiar contract examples where the terms were communicated long after the basic commitment had been entered into. The most commonly recognized such situation was the automobile insurance policy where the consumer was protected by a telephone call followed by an invoice and payment of the premium. The formal policy was usually delivered later and separately. Judge Easterbrook found the answer in UCC § 2-204—"A contract for sale of goods may be made in any manner sufficient to show agreement ...." On the facts, he found the contract concluded only when the license terms were read and accepted. UCC § 2-207, he said, was inapplicable.

Importantly, Judge Easterbrook's reasoning has been strongly critiqued by some courts and commentators. As discussed in *Klocek v. Gateway, Inc., 104 F.Supp.2d 1332 (D. Kan. 2000)*, the rule developed in *ProCD* suffers from two major flaws. First, the *Klocek* court disputed Judge Easterbrook's unsupported assertion that UCC § 2-207 is irrelevant where there is only one form. As *Klocek* notes, nothing in § 2-207 requires that there be an actual exchange of forms between the parties. Second, *ProCD* also asserts that a vendor makes an offer by placing its items on a store shelf, that the customer then accepts by taking the package to a cashier and paying. The *Klocek* court notes that while this form would make the vendor the master of the offer who could then specify the permissible nature of the acceptance, such an interpretation is contrary to the general understanding that offering goods for sale is usually interpreted as an invitation to receive offers and that the consumer is traditionally deemed the offeror in consumer transactions. As a consequence, the *Klocek* court holds that UCC § 2-207 applies, and that the consumer is the offeror—meaning that any additional terms contained in the vendor's definite and seasonable expression of acceptance are mere proposals for inclusion in the parties' contract unless the vendor provides adequate notice that it is willing to do business only on its own terms.

4. *Step-Saver as a classic "battle of the forms" case. Step-Saver* is a classical UCC § 2-207 "battle of the forms" case. In many commercial contexts a buyer of goods will submit an order to the seller, the seller will process that order and ship the goods, and the buyer will pay the bill. The transaction may be initiated orally, and indeed the only agreement may be the oral exchange. Or the agreement may be oral, with no special terms discussed, followed by a "confirmation" from the seller setting out as the terms of the deal the seller's printed form terms. Or the order may be written on the buyer's printed form and terms, followed by the seller's confirmation containing very different terms, followed again by shipment and payment. Under UCC Article 2, the objective theory ("last shot" doctrine"), found in the seller's version of the terms together with shipment and payment as acceptance of the seller's terms, was found to operate "unfairly." Where the parties fail to deal with terms other than quantity, price and delivery, UCC Article 2 provides "standard" terms that are then implied as additions to the terms expressly agreed upon. The UCC "standard" terms, including express and implied warranties, and recoverable damages (especially consequential damages) are much more favorable to the buyer than to the seller.

UCC § 2-207 was designed to reverse the "last shot" doctrine of the common law, but this section (at least as it existed before the substantial redrafting in the 2003 revisions to Article 2) is a marvel of ambiguity. Subsection (1) begins, "A definite and seasonable expression of acceptance or a written confirmation ... operates as an acceptance even though it states terms additional to or different from those offered or agreed upon ...." The apparent intent of the drafters was that where the buyer submits an offer on the buyer's terms and the seller "accepts" while adding "additional" or "different" terms, that acceptance can nevertheless establish there and then a binding contract or commitment even though the parties had not yet agreed upon all of the terms. If the offeror acquiesces in the offeree's terms, then the problem is solved.

Under the first sentence of UCC § 2-207(2), additional terms in the expression of acceptance are deemed proposals if the transaction is between non-merchants (or between a merchant and a non-merchant). In that case, the additional terms remain proposals and are unenforceable in the absence of further agreement. Under the second sentence of subsection (2), if the transaction is between merchants, the provisions of subsection (2) come into play. If subsection (2) does not solve the non-matching of the terms, then the terms of the contract were established in accordance with subsection (3), namely those on which the parties agreed plus the UCC "gap-fillers." But not every seller response is a "definite and seasonable expression of acceptance." For instance, if the seller's response varies key terms of the offer such as price and quantity, courts have held that the response was not an acceptance at all.

Subsection (2) provided that "additional terms" (whether through accident or design, "different" terms are not covered by this subsection) function as "proposals." That is, such proposals become terms of the contract only when accepted by the other party—but where those "additional" terms are never accepted, the parties have a binding contract, reversing the common law "mirror image" rule. Between merchants, however, under subsection (2) such proposals become terms of the contract subject to three exceptions where: (1) the offer limited acceptance to the terms of the offer; (2) the proposed terms "materially alter" the offer; or (3) notification of objection was given before or within a reasonable time after receipt of the proposals.

5. *The history of lawyers reading UCC § 2-207 as a drafting challenge.* For more than twenty years, the effect of this legislative reversal of the common law "last shot" doctrine was to inspire lawyers to draft forms (both buyers and sellers) attempting to steer through and around UCC § 2-207 so as to leave their client with the controlling set of terms. Buyer-offeror forms would provide that their terms, and their terms only, would control the deal. Seller-offeree terms would provide that, on the contrary, their terms, and their terms only, would control the deal.

For the seller, the application of subsection (3) was ominous because the "gap-fillers" favor buyers over sellers. Subsection (2) suggested that offerors (buyers) might be able to escape the reach of the section if the offer indicated expressly that it was subject to acceptance only on its terms and no others. "Acceptors" had to find possible escape in the last phrase of subsection (1) "... unless acceptance is made expressly conditional on assent to the additional or different terms." Lawyers drafting forms for merchants attempted, in several different ways, to give their form the winning edge. Purchase order ("offer") forms became worded with the assumed magical incantation, "The terms of this offer are not negotiable or changeable and these are the only terms on which the offer will be recognized." This incantation prevented the seller's "acceptance" (see subsection (2)(a)) from introducing additional or different terms. Seller "acceptance" forms invoked the incantation of the last phrase of subsection (1), "This acceptance is expressly made conditional on assent to the terms in this acceptance," intending that UCC § 2-207 not apply. Buyer and seller forms passed like ships in the night. If an issue arose prior to shipment and payment, the damage was minimal—no contract had been concluded. If, however, sellers and buyers failed to police for signed contracts with appropriate terms, subsection (3) came into play and the terms of the agreement were those the parties concurred in plus the "gap fillers."

Step-Saver left open the possibility that "conditioned acceptance" would not lead directly to subsection (3) if and when the goods were shipped, delivered and accepted. Subsequent case law (majority) swept these situations into subsection (3).

6. *"Additional" versus "different" terms.* The other issue to be dealt with was caused by the failure of subsection (2) to deal with "different" terms. A few courts concluded that "additional," as used in subsection (2) should be interpreted to include "different," notwithstanding the clear meaning of "different" as involving contradictory, not just additional, terms. Holding that assent to additional or different terms must be express (thus avoiding the last shot consequence of subsequent performance), the majority of courts have swept acceptances with different terms into subsection (3).

NOTES AND QUESTIONS

1. *Renewal of terminated offer.* See text.

2. *Option contract.* See text.

3. *The common law last shot rule versus UCC § 2-207.* See text.

4. *Purposes of § 2-207.* See text.

5. *Definite and seasonable expression of acceptance.* See text.

6. *Sales of goods contracts between merchants versus non-merchants.*

7. *"Additional or different" versus "additional" terms—interpreting Subsections (1) and (2).* What possible problems can you foresee from a literal application of this statutory language? This section has been described by one critic as the worst example of legislative drafting available. While subsection (1) speaks of two sets of circumstances—"additional" terms and "different" terms, subsection (2) deals only with "additional" terms leaving the treatment of "different" terms hanging. Should "additional" in subsection (2) be interpreted to include both "additional" and "different"? See the discussion under the "Issues" section above.

8. *Proposals not included in the contract under § 2-207(2)(a)-(c).* In light of these exceptions, what drafting advice would you give to a client regarding the content of its form contract terms? The student should first distinguish between a contract between two merchants and a contract between a merchant and a customer (consumer). In *Step-Saver*, the contract was between two merchants. As discussed under the "Issues" section above, the "battle of the forms" is most likely going to be resolved under UCC § 2-207(3) regardless of efforts by either buyer or seller (or, more accurately, <u>because of</u> the efforts of both buyer and seller) to write into its paperwork that its terms shall control. Since the "gap-filler" provisions of the UCC on both warranties and consequential damages favor buyer over seller, this is not a desirable outcome for the seller. The only sure way for the seller to protect against such risks and be sure that its provisions will control is to refuse to sell unless and until a written contract, signed by both parties, covering all such transactions is concluded. Where numerous sales are contemplated between the parties, such agreements are typically referred to as "master agreements." When in place, such agreements allow individual transactions thereafter to proceed without a detailed signed agreement for each individual transaction. The student should note that TSL attempted twice, but unsuccessfully, to get SS to enter into such a contract. In the absence of a signed mutual agreement establishing the terms of the deal, the seller-shipper acts at its peril in fulfilling an order from a customer where the buyer's order form contains terms inconsistent with seller's.

If the underlying transaction contemplated by the seller is a sale to a consumer, the negotiation of a detailed agreement is impossible. Can the seller escape the trap of the "gap fillers" in such a situation, or is there a way out? The answer is "yes" but not based on the reasoning of *Step-Saver*. While there is a court decision to be found supporting almost any argument under UCC § 2-207, the "weight" of opinion has now shifted to the position taken by Judge Easterbrook in *ProCD, Inc.*

v. Zeidenberg, 86 F.3d 1447 (7th Cir. 1996). Under the principle of that decision (set out later in this chapter) shrinkwrap and clickwrap license agreements are enforceable even though the consumer pays and later finds out the terms of the sale by opening the box or clicking "accept" on the license terms, provided the consumer is given an opportunity after learning the seller's terms to return the product and receive a refund. See Terry J. Ilardi, "Mass Licensing—Part I: Shrinkwarps, Clickwraps and Browsewraps," 831 PLI/Pat 251, 2005. Were this not the case, most current form contract sales of both hardware and software, whether conducted over the Internet or not, would leave the seller exposed to "gap-filler" terms. The difference between a "clickwrap" and a "browsewrap" format is that in the former, the consumer cannot open the program without first being confronted by the terms of the transaction and then being forced to "agree" or "accept." With the "browsewrap," the consumer is given the opportunity to look at the terms of the deal but is not required to do so—the consumer may be required to "agree" or "accept" those terms seen or unseen. Given the state of the decisions, the "browsewrap" route must still be regarded as risky for the seller. Compare *Specht v. Netscape Communications Corp.*, 306 F.3d 17 (2d Cir.2002) (browsewrap contract not enforceable where, inter alia, purported contract terms were accessible only by website user's affirmative determination to seek out such terms and access same through a separate hyperlink) with *Register.com, Inc. v. Verio, Inc.*, 356 F.3d 393 (2d Cir. 2004) (browsewrap contract terms enforceable where website visitor informed of contract terms every time it accessed provider's web services).

9. *Acceptance expressly made conditional on assent to the additional or different terms and contracting by performance.* See text.

10. *Contracting by performance under Subsection (3).* How does § 2-207(3) determine the terms of the parties' contract? Does this process comport with the objective theory of contracts as described in previous cases, or have the UCC drafters created a new source of contractual liability? To the extent that UCC § 2-207(3) enforces those terms to which both parties have agreed, it comports with the objective theory. To the extent that it overrides terms asserted by one party but not consented to by the other, it is not consistent with that theory. Instead, this subsection establishes a rule of law applicable to the parties and fixing as the terms of their contract the "gap-fillers" of UCC Article 2. This rule of law was found necessary because of the relative unfairness of the "last shot" doctrine which did follow objective theory.

11. *Amendments to UCC § 2-207.* What problems do you think prompted this change? Would this new approach change the results of *Step-Saver*, *Roto-Lith*, or *Ionics*? The problems promoting this change were the multiple ambiguities in and divergent court interpretations of

subsections (1) and (2) of UCC § 2-207. The "conditional acceptance" language was interpreted by some courts as making the acceptance and its terms into a counteroffer, accepted by the buyer's performance, thus continuing to apply the "last shot" doctrine. The words of subsection (1), "additional to or different from," caused further divergent interpretation because subsection (2) applied expressly only to "additional" terms and not to "different" terms. Supposedly, if the parties cared enough each to insist on their own terms they would not enter into a contract by subsequent delivery and payment. If they did not have that requisite degree of care, then it was unfair to give the advantage to one set of terms rather than the other. Hence, in such a situation, reliance on the "gap-fillers" was fair. What the authors of the 2003 revision of UCC § 2-207 failed to revisit is the relative fairness, as between buyer and seller, of the UCC "gap-fillers." The 2003 changes give the former subsection (3) effect in any case where the parties have agreed, and then after such agreement, divergent terms appear. Such divergent terms from both sides are treated as "proposals" which then fail because of absence of agreement to such proposed terms.

For some time the ALI and NCCUSL worked on a proposed UCC Article 2B to govern computer information transactions. Subsequently it was decided that NCCUSL would promulgate such rules as a separate statute, called the Uniform Computer Information Transactions Act (UCITA). This draft statute was approved by NCCUSL but has met with little favor in state legislatures.

12. *The Uniform Computer Information Transactions Act ("UCITA") and application of U.C.C. Article 2 to software license contracts*. As the note indicates, as a matter of definition, it is far from clear that the sale of a software license is a "sale of goods." Court opinions, however, have tended to solidify around the holding of *ProCD* that the UCC does control. NCCUSL's attempt to generate a new UCC Article 2B have not been successful as described in the note.

Filanto, S.P.A. v. Chilewich International Corp.
CASE BRIEF

This is a 1992 decision of the United States District Court, Southern District of New York. Chilewich was an import-export firm based in New York. Filanto ("Fila") was a boot and shoe manufacturer based in Italy. Chilewich entered into a contract with Raznoexport ("Raz"), a Russian based entity, to supply it with a large order of boots. The terms of that contract required arbitration of disputes and differences under the contract in Moscow. Chilewich negotiated with Fila to supply the boots to be delivered under the Raz contract. Chilewich prepared, signed and sent to Fila in July, 1989 a contract providing that it was governed by the same terms as in its contract with Raz. A copy of the Raz contract was attached. In September Fila returned the contract signed, but with a letter attached recording Fila's understanding that only some of the terms of the Raz contract, not including the arbitration provision, were applicable to this contract. Chilewich claimed it never received this letter. In March, 1990, Chilewich prepared a memorandum agreement providing for delivery of 100,000 pairs of boots in September and the balance of 150,000 pairs in November. This memorandum provided explicitly that the terms of the Russian contract, including arbitration, were incorporated. Fila did not sign or return this agreement at that time but nevertheless Chilewich arranged payment (letter of credit) for, presumably, the first shipment. In August Fila returned the signed memorandum agreement, again purporting to exclude a number of the terms of the Russian contract including the arbitration provision. At the end of August Chilewich's agent faxed Fila requesting confirmation that all terms of the Russian contract were incorporated. Conflicting evidence was presented, each side claiming that the other had orally acquiesced in its position. In September Fila complained that Chilewich had not opened a second letter of credit for the second delivery. Chilewich's response noted problems with the Russian buyer. Chilewich failed to pay for 90,000 pairs of boots to have been purchased under the second installment.

Fila sued in federal district court in New York. Chilewich moved to stay the action pending arbitration in Moscow. Fila moved to enjoin arbitration or to order arbitration in the federal district in New York. After filing the complaint, Fila sent a letter to Chilewich purporting to rely on a provision found in the terms of the Russian contract that Fila had consistently claimed was not part of the contract. The court found this to be an "admission in law" (estoppel?) that terms of the Russian contract were applicable.

The court found jurisdiction under Chapter 2 of the Federal Arbitration Act, consisting of the Convention on the Recognition and Enforcement of Foreign Arbitral Awards, codified at 9 U.S.C. §201 et seq. The United States, Italy and the USSR were all signatories to this Convention and it was therefore applicable to this suit. The Convention required courts to recognize any "agreement in writing under which the parties undertake to submit to arbitration ...." The term "agreement in writing" was defined as "an arbitral clause in a contract or an arbitration agreement, signed by the parties or contained in an exchange of letters or telegrams." On this basis the court held that federal law governed issues relating to the arbitrability of a dispute, the Convention being a treaty, displacing other federal and state law under the Supremacy clause of the Constitution. The threshold question then, was whether the parties had actually agreed to arbitrate—did their correspondence constitute an "agreement in writing?"

The court then held that the CISG, and not the UCC, provided the applicable federal law. Said the court, "... absent a choice-of-law provision, and with certain exclusions not here relevant, the Convention governs *all* contracts between parties with places of business in different nations, so long as both nations are signatories to the Convention." Both Italy and the United States are parties to that Convention.

The arguments of the two parties followed the classic lines of a "battle of the forms." Chilewich argued that the March memorandum agreement was an offer which was accepted by subsequent performance (c.f. UCC §2-207(3)). Said the court, "While defendant contends that under Uniform Commercial Code § 2-207 this action would be viewed as an acceptance with a proposal for a material modification, the Uniform Commercial Code, as previously noted does not apply to this case, because the State Department undertook to fix something that was not broken by helping to create the Sale of Goods Convention which varies from the Uniform Commercial Code in many significant ways." The court's dig at the State Department is memorable. Fila argued that the March memorandum agreement was an offer, that its August response was a counter-offer and that the terms of the counter-offer were confirmed by the subsequent performance (c.f. "last shot").

The court found that the CISG takes the opposite view to that of the UCC §2-207, and adopts the common law "last shot" concept, except for "non-material terms" but an arbitration clause is defined to be a material term. The court then opened the somewhat mystical issue of whether a distinction is to be drawn between the existence of a contractual obligation (for the arbitrators to decide) as opposed to the existence of an arbitration clause (for the court to decide). The court concluded that it would "... direct its analysis to whether there was objective conduct evidencing an intent to be bound with respect to the arbitration provision. . ..." The court then concluded that the parties had agreed to arbitrate. It interpreted Fila's silence following the transmission of the March memorandum as acceptance of its terms. Said the court:

> "An offeree who, knowing that the offeror has commenced performance, fails to notify the offeror of its objection to the terms of the contract within a reasonable time will, under certain circumstances, be deemed to have assented to those terms. Restatement (Second) of Contracts § 69 (1981). . . . The Sale of Goods Convention itself recognizes this rule: Article 18(1), provides that "A statement made by or other conduct of the offeree indicating assent to an offer is an acceptance". Although mere "silence or inactivity" does not constitute acceptance, Sale of Goods Convention Article 18(1), the Court may consider previous relations

between the parties in assessing whether a party's conduct constituted acceptance, Sale of Goods Convention Article 8(3)."

The court concluded that Fila had a duty to respond and failed to do so. The court concluded that this view was buttressed by Fila's admission against interest in the letter written after the suit was commenced. Fila's "characterization of this action as a rejection and a counteroffer is almost frivolous." Arbitration in Moscow was ordered.

INTERESTING DISCUSSION ISSUES

The inclusion of this case in the casebook provides two separate opportunities. The first is to alert students to the existence and potential applicability of the Convention to contracts between a U.S. business and a foreign one (subject to the jurisdictional requirements of the Convention). The second is to note the significant differences between the legal rules established under the Convention and those applicable under either U.S. state common law or the UCC. Professors will find Professor Dodge's article, cited at the end of Note (1) particularly useful reading.

Professors may wish to outline the key elements of the Convention. As summarized by Professor Dodge, those key elements include:

- When and to whom the Convention applies—the federal district court decision notes that, ". . . absent a choice-of-law provision, and with certain exclusions not here relevant, the Convention governs *all* contracts between parties with places of business in different nations, so long as both nations are signatories to the Convention."
- This same quotation indicates that the parties may contract out of the Convention via a "choice of law" clause.
- The Convention does not apply to consumer goods contracts.
- The Convention has no "statute of frauds."
- The Convention has no "parol evidence" rule—parol evidence may be used to explain, supplement, vary, or contradict the terms of a written agreement.
- The Convention "deals only with contract formation and the rights and obligations of the parties. It is expressly not concerned with questions of validity ... such ... as incapacity, fraud, duress, mistake and unconscionability."
- The Convention allows "firm offers" without the limitations of UCC § 2-205, and does not require the offeror to be a merchant.
- The Convention reverses the "mailbox" rule, making acceptance effective upon receipt.
- As described in the case, the Convention adopts the common law "mirror image" and "last shot" concepts.

- The Convention establishes significantly different rules regarding remedies for breach.

To the extent the instructor has time, it may be useful to explore with students the various rationales underlying the above differences.

NOTES AND QUESTIONS

1. CISG counter-offer rule. What characteristics of transnational commercial contracting could justify such a broad materiality standard? As quoted in the note, CISG art. 19(3) makes all "additional or different" terms material—"Additional or different terms relating, among other things, to the price, payment, quality and quantity of the goods, place and time of delivery, extent of one party's liability to the other or the settlement of disputes are considered to alter the terms of the offer materially." The Convention thus departs substantially from the concept and approach of UCC § 2-207(1) and (2). Notice that the judge criticized the State Department's allowance of the various departures from the UCC. The State Department's reason, doubtless, was that, since an international convention was proposed, the striking of a balance between conflicting legal system norms and concepts would be required, and that the provisions of the Convention reflected a number of such compromises. The reason for the broad materiality standard is thus probably found in differing foreign systems rather than differences between transnational and national contracts. The major point, however, is that the Convention adopts the common law "last shot" rule and rejects the Llewellyn UCC approach. In the light of this result under the Convention, the students may be asked, once again, to review the respective advantages of the common law (and Convention) versus the UCC outcome.

Of course, the basic reason for inclusion of this case in the Casebook is to awake student awareness of the CISG and the way in which it can dictate the result in a case with a U.S. party directly contrary to generally applicable U.S. state law as found in the UCC.

2. *Accuracy of the case.* Given the CISG adopted a common law mirror image rule and not the UCC § 2-207 counteroffer approach, does *Filanto* apply the correct law and reach the correct outcome? Was this an acceptance or counteroffer under the mirror image rule? Was it an acceptance or a counteroffer under the theory of UCC § 2-207? Which rule did the court purport to apply? Did the court decide the case correctly? William S. Dodge, in the article cited at the end of this note, suggests that, as to offer and acceptance under the Convention, this case was wrongly decided. The March memorandum agreement was an offer. The August returned signed agreement together with the attached letter was a counteroffer. The terms of that counteroffer, applying the "last shot" analysis, were accepted by subsequent

performance and not the other way around. Dodge suggests however, that the court had another available possible justification for its decision, Fila's admission against interest.

3. *U.S. case law under the CISG.* Although recent years have seen an increase in judicial decisions grappling with the CISG, what factors could explain this relative paucity of decisions? Perhaps the most attractive reason is that carefully negotiated and drafted contracts (international contracts are more likely to fit this description) are usually performed as written. Allegations of nonperformance are relatively rare. The Dodge article could be read to suggest another reason—the complete lack of knowledge within the practicing bar of the applicability and terms of the CISG, a problem that, as Dodge suggests, demands correction.

3. Termination by Death or Incapacity

See text.

D. EFFECT OF PRE-ACCEPTANCE RELIANCE

1. Unilateral Contracts

Questions in the text: Do you agree with Professor Wormser? Is the early common law rule of unilateral contract "just, equitable and logical" merely because the offeree has an equal opportunity with the offeror to withdraw? Can you see cases of opportunistic behavior of the offeror capitalizing on an unsuspecting offeree by revoking an offer prior to the completion of the performance necessary to make a unilateral contract? Wormser completely overlooked the serious risks of detrimental reliance. Taking the house painting hypothetical in the text, suppose that B has painted 90% of the house when A purports to withdraw the offer. B had suffered the detriment of both time and materials expended. A is enriched by the difference in value of A's house before painting and after it is 90% painted. To leave B without a remedy appears to be very unfair. Hence the Restatement (Second) of Contracts § 45 provides:

> "Option Contract Created By Part Performance Or Tender
> (1) Where an offer invites an offeree to accept by rendering a performance and does not invite a promissory acceptance, an option contract is created when the offeree tenders or begins the invited performance or tenders a beginning of it.
> (2) The offeror's duty of performance under any option contract so created is conditional on completion or tender of the invited performance in accordance with the terms of the offer."

While this section is intended to protect the reliance interest of the offeree, it is to be noted that the protection only starts when performance begins or is tendered. Reliance involving preparation for performance is not protected.

Petterson v. Pattberg
CASE BRIEF

This is a 1928 decision of the New York Court of Appeals. Pattberg had loaned money to Petterson secured by a mortgage. On April 4, 1924 Pattberg wrote to Petterson agreeing to accept payment of the outstanding balance less a discount of $780 conditioned on the mortgage being paid on or before May 31, and the regular quarterly payment, due April 25, being paid when due. Petterson paid the quarterly payment as required and, prior to May 31, called at Pattberg's house. When Petterson knocked on the door, Pattberg wanted to know who was there. Petterson responded with his name and the statement, "I have come to pay off the mortgage." Pattberg responded that he had sold the mortgage (and that therefore he was no longer entitled to receive payment). Pattberg then opened the door, and Petterson exhibited the cash he had brought with him. Pattberg refused to take the money.

Petterson had contracted to sell the mortgaged property free and clear of the mortgage and, to make good on his promise, had to repay the full mortgage balance due. He sued to recover his $780 loss, and was successful below. On appeal to the New York Court of Appeals he lost. Justice Kellogg, writing for the majority (including Cardozo!) held that Pattberg's letter was an offer for a unilateral contract. Acceptance of a unilateral contract required performance of the act called for. The act called for by the letter was "payment" and Pattberg withdrew the offer before payment was effected. While noting that a decision on the issue was not required, Kellogg observed that he would reach the same result even if Petterson had tendered (translate physically offered the money to Pattberg) the money before Pattberg withdrew the offer. Only full performance of the stipulated act (payment) would close the contractual circle. Kellogg did not discuss the possibility of detrimental reliance by Petterson on the promise to accept less than the full principal. His analysis was simply based on formal offer and acceptance rules. Acceptance in the context of an offer for a unilateral contract could only be made by completion of the act specified in the offer.

Justice Lehman dissented with Justice Andrews concurring in the dissent. While, like Kellogg, he did not review Petterson's detrimental reliance, the clear implication of the dissent was that Lehman considered Pattberg's conduct to be unfair. Pattberg had, by his conduct, frustrated Petterson's good faith attempt to perform the act specified. The basis of his analysis for enforcing the promise was to investigate exactly what act the letter promise called for Petterson to do. "The plaintiff offered to pay, with the present intention and ability to make that payment." That, he concluded, was what the letter had called for and thus Petterson had "performed" as required to close the contract circle.

INTERESTING DISCUSSION ISSUES

1. *Fairness.* Most students find the result in this case unfair if not bizarre. They see Petterson's detrimental reliance clearly. (Although, it may be interesting to note that this case occurs at an early stage of development in promissory estoppel doctrine and, as related in the notes following *Allegheny College v. National Chautauqua County Bank*, 246 N.Y. 369, 159 N.E. 173 (N.Y. 1927), New York law has not yet adopted the theory of promissory estoppel). How could a court ignore the injustice of the result? What was the basis of the majority's conclusion? What could the basis be for a rule requiring full and complete performance before the promissory offer became irrevocable? The majority opinion provides little if any discussion of the "considerations" that might underlie the rule as applied. The case illustrates, then, the relatively late growth of any concept of detrimental reliance as a reason for enforcing a promise. The "logical" requirements of the doctrine of consideration dictated the result.

2. *Mutuality.* As pointed out in the notes introducing the case, the court might have tried to find a justification for its unilateral contract rule in a requirement of mutual obligation. One party could not be bound if the other was not similarly bound. In the context of a unilateral contract (A's promise to pay B for walking across the bridge) B is under no obligation to walk the walk, and this does not change even when B has walked most of the distance across the bridge. B is always free to change his mind. If so, is it fair to hold A bound even when B starts to walk across the bridge, a time when he can still change his mind? As Note (4) following the case points out, mutuality is a slim reed upon which to clutch. A reference to *Lucy v. Zehmer* will suffice. On the other hand, the bargained for exchange concept of the doctrine of consideration involves some version of a mutual obligation. The illusory promise cases illustrate the point. In the famous *Lucy, Lady Duff Gordon* case (222 N.Y. 88, 118 N.E. 214 (1917), Justice Cardozo was compelled to find implied in Woods' contract a promise to use reasonable efforts to market her wares in order to find her responsible for breach of her promise to make Woods her exclusive agent in the United States. Absent such an implied promise, Woods (who drafted the contract!) gave nothing in return for her promise. The challenge of trying to make the rules for unilateral contracts match the

rules for bilateral contracts lies at the root of the efforts under § 45 of both Restatements, as pointed out in Notes (2) and (3) following the case.

3. *Preparation for performance distinguished from actual commencement of performance.* As the facts of the case point out clearly, Pattberg's promise caused serious detrimental reliance and loss by Petterson. And yet Restatement (Second) of Contracts § 45 limits the point of protection to commencement of performance and excludes protection for acts that are only preparatory to performance. The Note (3) following the case references the possible application of Restatement (Second) of Contracts § 87(2) in such a situation:

> "(2) An offer which the offeror should reasonably expect to induce action or forbearance of a substantial character on the part of the offeree before acceptance and which does induce such action or forbearance is binding as an option contract to the extent necessary to avoid injustice."

Suppose B, living far from the Brooklyn Bridge, hired a taxi to get him to the bridge at a cost of $50. Should B be able to recover the $50 from A when A revokes the offer before B can walk the walk?

NOTES AND QUESTIONS

1. *Willistonian view.* See text.

2. *Implied subsidiary promise paradigm of first Restatement.* Did Petterson make a qualifying "tender of performance" before Pattberg revoked the offer? The answer depends upon what the reader reads into the language used by the Restatements. The innocent reasonable person on the sidewalk might well think that "tender" means "offer" in this context. Petterson certainly indicated that he was at the door to offer performance. Given that the offeree has not made a promise to perform, may quit at any time, and has incurred minimal or no reliance, does the rule go too far? This question may go too far—from the case it is clear that Petterson had indeed incurred substantial and reasonable detrimental reliance on the promise. Is it fair to bind the offeror in such circumstances? This becomes a factual issue—in the circumstances of the case, it would certainly have been fair in the minds of students. How do you evaluate Petterson's preparations to perform? He was at the door ready, willing and able to perform. He had relied to his detriment—but would that detriment be recoverable under Restatement (Second) of Contracts § 45 if the court were to find that he had only prepared to perform, not commenced performance?

In the end, this case arguably can be presented as a factual dispute between the majority and dissent over whether Petterson's polite statement, "It is Mr. Petterson. I have come to pay off the mortgage" was an act of part performance. The majority's opinion can be presented as an example of when formalism and abstract conceptualism is taken to absurd extremes—impliedly, it seems as if the majority would require Petterson to thrust the money through the half-open door to satisfy the conditions for acceptance and terminate Pattberg's power of revocation. In contrast, the dissent adopts a much more Realist stance and appears to accept that Petterson's courteous announcement of his intent should be deemed the equivalent of actual tender, even if it does not satisfy the formal requirements.

3. *Option contract paradigm of second Restatement.* Compared to the first Restatement, does the second Restatement alter the nature or increase the degree of reliance necessary to make the subsidiary promise or option contract enforceable? No, Restatement (Second) of Contracts continues the same "bright" (?) line between preparation for performance and actual performance or tender thereof. Would your answer to the question of whether Petterson tendered performance before Pattberg revoked change from the first to the second Restatement? The second Restatement adds the phrase "tenders a beginning of performance." What is intended by this phrase? The answer depends on the eye of the beholder. We think the answer should be the same under both the first and second versions. What is the relevance of the majority determination that: "Before a tender of the necessary moneys had been made, the defendant informed Petterson that he had sold the mortgage." The majority, in effect, holds that the act called for by the Pattberg letter was the act of actual payment. A precursor of actual payment would be the physical offering of the money ("tender") by Petterson to Pattberg. In the absence of such an offer, there could not have been an act of actual payment. How then does the majority opinion conceptualize the tender of performance when it is the payment of money? The majority's view is to equate "tender of performance" with actual payment. What is the effect of the continuing language: "It is unnecessary to determine, therefore, what the legal situation might have been had tender been made before withdrawal. It is the individual view of the writer that the same result would follow. This would be so, for the act requested to be performed was the completed act of payment, a thing incapable of performance, unless assented to by the person to be paid." Is this remark what is referred to as *obiter dictum*? Yes—a gratuitous statement by the court not required to move from the holdings of fact and the conclusions of applicable law to the finding or ruling.

4. *Mutuality of obligation.* Reconsider the facts of *Lucy v. Zehmer.* If Lucy had refused to perform could Zehmer have sued successfully for specific performance? The answer is "No," because of the peculiar and specific requirements of the Statute of Frauds. The requirement of a

writing is stated as "a note or memorandum in writing *signed by the party to be charged.*" In this case, the writing was signed by the Zehmers who were the "party to be charged." If the Zehmers had sued to enforce the contract, W.O. Lucy would have been the party to be charged and, since he did not sign the contract, it could not be enforced against him.

5. *Williston's jurisprudence.* See text.

Davis v. Jacoby
CASE BRIEF

This is a 1934 decision of the California Supreme Court. Caro Davis, the niece of Blanche Whitehead, married Frank Davis in 1913. Prior to that time she had lived with Blanche and her husband, Rupert Whitehead, at their home in California. Both Caro and Frank had a close relationship with Blanche and Rupert for the nearly twenty-year period when, in 1930, Blanche became seriously ill, and in early 1931 Rupert suffered severe financial losses and himself was in poor health. In correspondence, Rupert indicated how much it would help if Caro and Frank would come to California, Frank to help him with his business affairs and Caro to take care of Blanche. In a letter dated March 30, 1931, Rupert told them that under his will all of the property was to go to Blanche, and that he believed that under her will practically everything was to go to Caro. On April 12, 1931 Rupert wrote a letter to Frank and Caro saying, "So if you can come, Caro will inherit everything and you will make our lives happier and see Blanche is provided for to the end. . . . Will you let me hear from you as soon as possible, . . ." Frank immediately wrote saying that they would come but could not leave until April 25. In the meantime Frank and Caro began preparations to wind up their business in Windsor, Ontario so that they could leave for California. On April 22, before they had left Windsor, Rupert committed suicide. They went to California immediately and Caro took care of Blanche until she died on May 30.

After Blanche died, they discovered that the wills were not as previously represented. Blanche's will left everything to Rupert and Rupert's left a life estate to Blanche and a remainder to two nephews who were not close to Blanche and Rupert.

Caro and Frank brought an action for specific performance of a promise by Rupert to leave a will bequeathing everything to Caro. The district court dismissed the action, finding that Rupert's letter of April 12 containing the promise was an offer for a unilateral contract and he died before performance of the act specified was complete. His death thus automatically revoked the offer for a unilateral contract. On appeal, Frank and Caro argued that the offer was for a bilateral contract and that this offer had been accepted by Frank's letter two days later "accepting" Rupert's proposal, announcing their plans to leave Windsor in April 25 (3 days after Rupert committed suicide).

The court found the key question to be whether Rupert's letter of April 12 called for acceptance only by an act or by a return promise. Citing both the Restatement (First) of Contracts § 31 and Williston's treatise, the California Supreme Court held that, in case of ambiguity as to whether the offer was for a unilateral or a bilateral contract, there was a presumption that a bilateral contract was contemplated. Applying that presumption to the present facts, they found the April 12 letter to be an offer for a bilateral contract, an offer that was accepted on April 14 prior to Rupert's suicide. They found this presumption reinforced by the words of Rupert's letter, "Will you let me hear from you as soon as possible. . . ." Since it was clear to the court that an award of damages would be insufficient to render justice, they ordered specific performance as requested.

NOTES AND QUESTIONS

1. *Interpretative solution.* See text.

2. *Necessity of bilateral interpretation.* If the offer was one to enter into a unilateral contract, when would acceptance have occurred? The answer depends upon what act the offer called for as the form of acceptance. The trial court apparently interpreted the letter as specifying the act as caring for Blanche for the rest of her life. What is the effect of the offeror's intervening death on an unaccepted offer? As noted earlier, the death of the offeror, according to the Restatement, automatically terminates the offer and that offer cannot be converted into a binding contract by an acceptance occurring after the death of the offeror.

3. *Promissory nature of the offer.* Examine the quoted portion of that letter again and determine whether the letter alone constituted a promise. "Caro will inherit everything" was properly interpreted by the court (as well as by the district court below) as a promise. From whose vantage point must the letter be examined? Under objective interpretation, the reasonable understanding of Caro and Frank Davis would control. Given the context of the letter, do you think an offer was made? Yes.

4. *Risk-sharing analysis.* Brietzke's (1996) article suggests that as the federal government pares back welfare-state entitlement programs, courts appear to be responding by adopting complex theories of tort liability that "split" responsibility for injuries suffered by individuals for which the defendant is only partially responsible. Although contract law has not been subjected to obvious liability splitting mechanisms comparable to enterprise liability or statistical causation theories in

tort law, Brietzke argues that judges have engaged in selective manipulation of contract doctrines to split risks of contract losses between the parties. As Brietzke argues:

> What accounts for these kinds of changes? Judge Calabresi concludes that the splitting of liabilities in tort is based on "not merely fault, but a more complex and hybrid complex we call 'responsibility.'" This apt term could also be used in contracts—as a supplement to the older "will" theory, which has a court merely tease out the parties' intentions—and it reflects judgments about where the judge and jury "would rather put the loss," regardless of fault on occasion. . . . [M]any or most of these judgments presumably aim to socialize the relevant risks and the compensation for them. This process is frequently trivialized as a search for the "deep pocket": the legal person best able to pay compensation, at least in part, and especially when this person can lay part of the costs of compensation off onto others in society. Insurance companies and large corporations with a "market power" are favorite deep pockets because they can pass on part of the costs of compensation in the form of higher insurance premiums (or hidden exemptions from coverage) and higher product prices.

Paul H. Brietzke, Commentary, *Interpretations of Calabresi*, 30 Val. U. L. Rev. 885, 889 (1996). Arguably, *Davis v. Jacoby* is best interpreted as just such a manipulation of doctrine and facts—deeming the April 12 letter to be an offer to enter a bilateral, rather than a unilateral, contract—to spread the responsibility for injury from the Davises to the estate which was arguably better able to bear the loss.

2. Bilateral Contracts

The introductory notes raise an important question. Where the contract involves both goods and services, should the common law apply or should the UCC apply or should both apply? Because of the significant differences between the two systems, application of both would create serious problems, and this result is not followed. Courts decide that one or other of the two systems applies and applies to both services and goods. Thus there is only one "law" of the contract. Most courts select the one or the other based on whether the dominant factor in the contract is goods or services.

James Baird Co. v. Gimbel Bros., Inc.
CASE BRIEF

This is a 1933 decision of the United States Court of Appeals, Second Circuit. Knowing that a large public building was to be constructed in Pennsylvania, Gimbel sent a letter to some twenty to thirty contractors who were likely to bid on the complete construction job. This letter offered to supply all the linoleum required by the contract specifications. The letter concluded, "If successful in being awarded this contract, it will be absolutely guaranteed, . . . and . . . we are offering these prices for reasonable" (sic), "prompt acceptance after the general contract has been awarded." Baird received one of these letters, and relied on this linoleum pricing when it submitted its complete contract bid. After Baird's bid was submitted but before the contract was awarded, Gimbel telegraphed all recipients of the letter stating that the price in the letter had been based on a mistake, withdrawing that pricing, and substituting new pricing about twice as much as the original. When Baird was awarded the contract, it formally accepted the Gimbel offer. When Gimbel refused to recognize the existence of a contract for the linoleum, Baird sued.

Said Judge Learned Hand, writing for the Second Circuit, "Unless there are circumstances to take it out of the ordinary doctrine, since the offer was withdrawn before it was accepted, the acceptance was too late. Restatement of Contracts, § 35." Plaintiff argued that the Gimbel offer was irrevocable once Baird used the pricing in making its bid. At the time of receiving the purported revocation of the original offer, Baird could have withdrawn its construction bid but would have been unable to file another bid and could have forfeited its deposit. Use of the pricing was argued to be the act of acceptance of the offer. Since Baird's action on the offer letter did not bind it to any contract with Gimbel, the court concluded there was no enforceable contract (lack of mutual obligation). This conclusion was buttressed by the words of the letter, "... we are offering these prices for . . . prompt acceptance after the general contract has been awarded," indicating the only way in which Gimbel's offer could be accepted. Then, rubbing salt in the wound, the court said, "and in commercial transactions it does not in the end promote justice to seek strained interpretations in aid of those who do not protect themselves."

Judge Learned Hand then considered Baird's argument based on promissory estoppel. "We may arguendo accept it [Restatement (First) of Contracts § 90] as it there reads, for it does not apply to the case at bar." He then concluded, "In the case at bar the defendant offered to deliver the linoleum in exchange for the plaintiff's acceptance, not for its bid, which was a matter of indifference to it." In effect he concluded that there was no basis for any reliance by Baird. He likewise rejected the argument that the letter could create an irrevocable option because the result would be completely one-sided, binding Gimbel but not Baird.

INTERESTING DISCUSSION ISSUES

Judge Learned Hand noted that the origin of the promissory estoppel doctrine was in the charitable gift cases. He recognized that Restatement (First) of Contracts § 90, published in final form just one year before the writing of this opinion, broadened the concept considerably. His acceptance of the Restatement position was somewhat cautious or even grudging—see his words "We may arguendo accept it as it there reads...." The importance of this opinion lies in the fact that he did recognize the apparent extension of that doctrine, albeit grudgingly. Clearly, that section requires that any reliance be "reasonable" and, given his interpretation of the Gimbel letter, there was no basis for any such reasonable reliance by Baird. His position, however, may give too literal a reading to the words of the Gimbel letter—a letter which was not written for lawyers to read but for "ordinary" business people. Can the students see any reason why Gimbel should have sent out such a letter short of encouraging contractors bidding on the whole project to price their linoleum component based on the letter pricing? Should Judge Learned Hand have taken a broader view of that letter and the context in which it was sent? Should he have given the letter a more "objective" interpretation? Or was he somewhat unenthusiastic about broadening the concept of promissory estoppel?

His sentence, rubbing salt in the wound, may stretch beyond the scope of reasonable "judicial notice" of general/sub contracting practices. It is highly doubtful that contractors at that time (or now) did protect themselves against withdrawal of such quotes by means of negotiating an option contract with each subcontractor. The very short time intervals involved and the multiplicity of subcontracts suggested by the words of the opinion make the practice the court seems to recommend unrealistic.

On the other hand, this case may provide an opportunity for discussing extra-legal mechanisms for enforcing such promises, or at least punishing promise-breakers. In the absence of a legal response, reputational effects should punish promise-breakers to some extent, depending on communications within the local general contractor community and the size of that community.

The students should be referred to UCC § 2-205 which provides for irrevocable offers under the conditions stated therein. The CISG, as previously mentioned, also makes irrevocable offers enforceable.

NOTES AND QUESTIONS

1. *No Party Bound Model.* Assuming the general contractor acted reasonably and fairly, was it fair for Judge Hand to allocate the risk of subcontractor bid mistake to the general contractor? Yes, based on the

language Gimbel used, the cost numbers were offered "for reasonable" (sic), "prompt acceptance after the general contract has been awarded." If the prices could not be accepted until after the general contractor had been awarded the main contract, then a careful reading of the wording would preclude any reasonable reliance on those numbers prior to acceptance. The situation in the case is analogous to that where A makes a promise offer requiring acceptance and the offeree claims to rely without having "accepted." But, given that this was an every day transaction between business people and not lawyers, is such a reading slicing the salami too fine? It seems clear that Gimbel made the mistake, Baird acted in good faith in incorporating the Gimbel numbers and then Baird lost because of Gimbel's mistake. Students will argue that the mistake was Gimbel's and that liability should thus go to them. What policy justified allocating the risk of error away from the party committing the error, especially when another party justifiably relied on the bid? Judge Learned Hand's answer was based on the express language of Gimbel's offer—which said that it could not be accepted until after the award of the main contract—a very literal application of the concept of "master of the offer." Who is in the best position to prevent the error—the person who made it or another? The author of the mistake—should the rule applied encourage careful rather than careless quotations? Could Baird have sustained an action in tort for negligent speech? No.

2. *Option contract analysis.* At the time *James Baird Co.* was released in 1933, the 1932 Restatement (First) of Contracts § 45 was released. That section provided that an offer to enter into a unilateral contract stated an implied-in-law subsidiary promise not to revoke the offer after the offeree tendered or began the requested performance. Why did Judge Hand not apply this rule to the case? The Gimbel letter did not invite acceptance by using the letter prices. Instead, it stipulated an acceptance that could only occur after Baird's bid was accepted. Judge Hand rejects promissory estoppel as found in Restatement (First) of Contracts § 90. Why? Does he think that promissory estoppel simply does not apply to an offer? If so, is this because he thinks an offer is not a promise or because he interprets the offer in this case as demanding consideration? Stated another way, if the offer had not been qualified by specific acceptance language, do you think that Judge Hand would have applied promissory estoppel to make the offer irrevocable once used? He did not reject promissory estoppel—he accepted it "arguendo." He might have considered relief based on Baird's detrimental reliance, but such reliance was not reasonable where the terms of the offer precluded such reliance and required acceptance after award of the contract. Judge Hand acknowledged that if the subcontractor had made an express promise to keep its offer open, the general contractor's reliance "might" have made the promise enforceable under promissory estoppel. Does this

suggest that Judge Hand thought no express promise was made and none could be implied? Yes. Even if such a promise was implied, do you think Judge Hand would have applied promissory estoppel? He might have done so, but we will never know. What do you think Judge Hand meant by the following language: "The contractors had a ready escape from their difficulty by insisting upon a contract before they used the figures: and in commercial transactions it does not in the end promote justice to seek strained interpretations in aid of those who do not protect themselves. . . ." He meant that Baird could have entered into a bilateral contract for consideration providing Baird with an option to call for the linoleum at the prices quoted. While Baird *could* have done so, the practical time, effort and cost considerations would probably preclude such a course of action measured by any cost/benefit analysis for Baird.

3. *Offer not a promise.* Does Judge Hand confuse the definition of a "promise" with a "contract"? Yes.

4. *Fear of contract.* Liability for breach of contract is strict—excuses for nonperformance are generally irrelevant. Liability based on promissory estoppel is, as Restatement (Second) of Contracts § 90 points out, not strict but rather, "The remedy granted for breach may be limited as justice requires." Says the comment in Note (4), "Thus, some formalist scholars, according to Kreitner, oppose creation of contractual liability on the basis promissory estoppel because that doctrine imposes an unassented-to contract on the basis of an essentially tort-like theory of liability (detrimental reliance)." Their opposition merely draws attention to the substantial differences in remedy for breach of contract compared to detrimental reliance (promissory estoppel). Consent is not the only basis for providing a fair result. Which of these visions is more compelling as an organizing or justifying force for enforcement of contract promises? Both contract and promissory estoppel have their place. What is the purpose of contract law for individuals? For society in general? To provide a basis for reliance and predictability in commercial transactions and relationships. When, if ever, should the interests of the polity justify judicial imposition of terms into ostensibly private contracts to which the parties themselves never agreed? When fairness suggests the appropriateness of so doing—compare UCC § 2-207, etc. (See Carnival Note (8) discussion.)

Drennan v. Star Paving Company
CASE BRIEF

This is a 1958 decision of the Supreme Court of California (in bank). Drennan was preparing a bid as general contractor on a school job. An estimator for Star Paving telephoned to Drennan a bid of $7,131.60 for the paving work. Drennan relied on this bid, included it in calculating his total bid and listed Star Paving as the sub for this work. Drennan was awarded the contract. Next morning, he visited the Star Paving office and was immediately told that the bid had been provided in error and that Star Paving would not do the job for less than $15,000. Drennan tried for several months to find another sub for this work and eventually had to pay $10,948.60 to get the paving work done. Drennan then sued for the difference between Star Paving's bid and the ultimate price of getting the work done. Drennan won at the trial level, and Justice Traynor, writing for the California Supreme Court affirmed.

Traynor pointed out at the beginning that:

> "There is no evidence that defendant offered to make its bid irrevocable in exchange for plaintiff's use of its figures in computing his bid. Nor is there evidence that would warrant interpreting plaintiff's use of defendant's bid as the acceptance thereof, binding plaintiff, on condition he received the main contract, to award the subcontract to defendant."

The sole available theory to support the trial outcome was Restatement (Second) of Contracts § 90 promissory estoppel. Traynor pointed out that rule applied in California. Star Paving's bid constituted a promise to perform, and it had reason to expect that, if theirs was the lowest bid for that portion of the work, it would be used, and it induced "action ... of a definite and substantial character."

Traynor continued:

> "Had defendant's bid expressly stated or clearly implied that it was revocable at any time before acceptance we would treat it accordingly. It was silent on revocation, however, and we must therefore determine whether there are conditions to the right of revocation imposed by law or reasonably inferable in fact."

Citing Restatement (First) of Contracts § 45, he noted that reasonable reliance afforded a compelling basis for implying a subsidiary promise not to revoke an offer for a bilateral contract. Consideration was not necessary. His string cite ended with, "cf. James Baird Co. v. Gimbel Bros., 2 Cir., 64 F. 2d 344."

Referring to the issue that the sub would be bound while the general was not, he said:

> "It bears noting that a general contractor is not free to delay acceptance after he has been awarded the general contract in the hope of getting a better price. Nor can he reopen bargaining with

> the subcontractor and at the same time claim a continuing right to accept the original offer."

But here, Drennan had acted promptly to accept Star Paving's sub bid. Star Paving acted by mistake but that mistake was not one of which Drennan knew or should have known. The price in the bid was within a predictable range. Then came an interesting obiter dicta comment: "Even had it been clearly understood that defendant's offer was revocable until accepted, it would not necessarily follow that defendant had no duty to exercise reasonable care in preparing its bid." In any event, the loss should fall on the party that caused it. Drennan acted reasonably to mitigate damages.

INTERESTING DISCUSSION ISSUES

Perhaps the thorniest issue underlying Traynor's opinion is the lack of any mutuality of obligation. As he held, the sub bidder was bound to perform at the bid price while Drennan was not bound, assuming it won the award, to use Star Paving rather than someone else. After the award, Drennan was free to either or both "bid chop" or "bid shop." Traynor does point out that any attempt to do either would release Star Paving from any further obligation to perform. Questions relating to construction industry practices are discussed under *Baird* above.

The next issue is Traynor's discussion of the case where the bid is made expressly subject to withdrawal prior to acceptance. First, he suggested that such reservation of right to revoke would, in that circumstance, be respected. Later, he suggested that, even so, Drennan's reliance could be reasonable.

The opinion reference to "mistake" by Star Paving may prompt questions about whether, and if so when, mistake may affect the enforceability of a contract. We suggest telling the students that the subject of mistake will be covered in depth in Chapter 6. In the alternative, they can be referred to Restatement (Second) of Contracts §§ 151-158.

The opinion also raises the issue of mitigation. We prefer to avoid discussion of the doctrine at this point but, if necessary, students can be told that the subject is covered as part of the materials on damages in Chapter 9.

As an exercise in understanding the jurisprudence of an individual judge, the instructor may wish to have the students attempt to describe general principles about Justice Traynor's jurisprudence. Chapter 4 includes two additional key opinions by Justice Traynor—*Masterson v. Sine* and *Pacific Gas and Electric Company. v. G. W. Thomas Drayage & Rigging Company*—and between these three opinions the students should be able to predict how Justice Traynor would deal with other legal issues.

NOTES AND QUESTIONS

1. *Comparing Baird and Drennan.* Do you think state law accounts for the different outcomes? No. The two courts applied different contract law concepts, tied to the distinguishing facts of the two cases. In *Baird,* the court applied an apparently formalist jurisprudence to find that the Gimbel offer was expressly subject to acceptance only after the construction contract award had been made. The offer was withdrawn to Baird's knowledge before that happened. Thus, any claim of reliance would be unreasonable since the language of the offer indicated expressly the only way in which it could be relied on—acceptance after the award. In *Drennan,* Justice Traynor appears to adopt a more Realist position to conclude that the bid was provided over the telephone in a situation in which the bidder foresaw or should have foreseen that the bid would be relied upon and it was so relied upon. If the two cases apply the same law, do you think the different language or terms of the offer accounts for the different outcomes? Yes, based on a literal reading and understanding of the facts in *Baird.* The two cases did not apply the same law. *Baird* applied basic offer and acceptance rules finding no room for reasonable detrimental reliance. *Drennan* applied Restatement § 90 detrimental reliance principles. If not, do you think the two judges simply had different views about the same law? Not necessarily. Learned Hand did not apply promissory estoppel because he found that any alleged reliance would not be reasonable. He was not prepared, however, to commit to the law as stated in Restatement § 90—"We may arguendo accept it as it there reads, for it does not apply to the case at bar." It may well be, however, that Learned Hand took too "literalist" an approach to the facts in *Baird.* The Gimbel letter was not written for lawyers (although it was construed by a lawyer-judge)—the reasonable person on the sidewalk could well have understood the letter as making a then-present offer that could in fact be relied upon by the contractor. If Gimbel did not intend reliance by bidders, why would it send the letter out? Given the *Drennan* case reference to *Baird,* is it possible that Justice Traynor intended to rebuke the earlier approach and set the law on a different course? Justice Traynor's reference was merely a citation to *Baird* preceded by "c.f."—compare. We do not know whether Traynor meant by "compare" that the facts were different or the law being applied was different, or just that the result appeared to be different.

2. *Effect on second Restatement.* See text.

3. *Implied subsidiary promise.* Justice Traynor implies a subcontractor promise to keep its bid open or irrevocable until the general contractor has an opportunity to be awarded the bid contract and notify the subcontractor of acceptance. Is the promise implied-in-

law or implied-in-fact? It is implied-in-fact because, as Traynor points out, "Had defendant's bid expressly stated or clearly implied that it was revocable at any time before acceptance we would treat it accordingly." Does Justice Traynor use a theory of consideration or a theory of reliance in the form of promissory estoppel? Clearly, the latter. Does it make a difference? Yes indeed, since there was no showing of bargained for consideration. Judge Hand would not imply such a subsidiary promise in *Baird,* because he found the conditions of acceptance clearly defined in the Gimbel letter. If Star Paving had made clear that its bid was revocable, would Justice Traynor respect that intent? Yes, but .... "Even had it been clearly understood that defendant's offer was revocable until accepted, it would not necessarily follow that defendant had no duty to exercise reasonable care in preparing its bid." How would you compare the language of Judge Hand: "The contractors had a ready escape from their difficulty by insisting upon a contract before they used the figures: and in commercial transactions it does not in the end promote justice to seek strained interpretations in aid of those who do not protect themselves. . . ."? Perhaps he made too large an assumption about the state of the playing field and whether it was truly level. The reader has to doubt that, in the world of construction and subcontract bidding, it is at all practical to expect that a contractor would or could protect itself against withdrawal of a sub bid by means of an executed bilateral contract. His notion that there was no need for the court to protect the plaintiff where there was an available means for the plaintiff to protect itself and the plaintiff failed to use that opportunity may be based on a questionable premise.

Which default rule do you favor? A presumption that favors the general contractor unless the subcontractor states otherwise (*Drennan*) or one that favors the subcontractor unless the general contractor specifies otherwise (*Baird*)? Traynor's position appears to produce a fair result based on foreseeability of the reliance. But the fairness of that result is not quite so clear when we look at the full picture. Suppose that Drennan won the award and then went back to Star Paving saying, "You can have the subcontract if you reduce your price by a further $1,000" ("bid chopping")? Drennan would have no obligation to use Star Paving as its subcontractor and so would be privileged to seek an after-the-award reduction in Star Paving's bid. Admittedly, doing so would release Star Paving from any obligation—but the question remains, is it fair to hold the sub potentially bound when the general is not similarly committed? As between a general contractor and a subcontractor who do you expect might be better equipped to understand the rules of the bidding game and negate the default rule? No generalization is possible—the level of knowledge and experience on either side is directly dependent upon the particular facts involved. The student should not overlook the commercial context of contracting and subcontracting. Reputation in the trade has to be important. The general who "bid shops" or "bid chops" is likely, in the future, to find difficulty in interesting subs in bidding at all. Likewise, the sub which refuses to back its bid may substantially lessen the likelihood of its being taken seriously in the future.

4. Damages. The *Drennan* case awarded the general contractor damages in the amount of $3,817, the difference between the Star Paving bid of $7,131 and L & H Paving bid of $10,948. Is this damage award necessary to compensate the general contractor for a reliance loss, an expectancy loss, or both? Students can be reminded of the qualification on the extent of relief to be provided under Restatement § 90. While the measure of damages can, and frequently will be, different under reliance and expectancy tests, in this particular fact situation, they are the same.

5. *Drennan limitations.* See text. Note also Justice Traynor's qualification where the general knows or should know that the sub's bid was mistaken.

6. *Irrevocable by statute.* See text.

Berryman v. Kmoch
CASE BRIEF

This is a 1977 decision of the Supreme Court of Kansas. Berryman, the owner of a parcel of land, brought an action to have a written signed option agreement that he had signed in June, 1973, declared null and void. Kmoch, the optionee, counterclaimed for damages for breach of the option contract. The critical words in the option contract were:

> "For $10.00 and other valuable consideration, I hereby grant unto you or your assigns an option for 120 days after date to purchase the following described real estate …."

The trial court granted summary judgment for Berryman, holding that the option contract had been granted without consideration. Although the agreement recited that the option was granted "for $10 and other valuable consideration," the $10 had not been paid.

Kmoch was a real estate broker and the drafter of the option agreement. In July Berryman called Kmoch and purported to revoke the option. In October, having been told that the land in question had been sold, Kmoch purported to exercise the option. Berryman responded by bringing the present action. Kmoch acknowledged that the $10 had not been paid, but asserted on appeal that he should have been permitted to introduce evidence at the trial of time spent and expenses incurred by him as a result of the option. The Kansas Supreme Court held that an option, granted without consideration, was a mere offer that could be withdrawn before acceptance. Kmoch argued the parol evidence rule precluded the introduction of evidence to contradict the writing but the court held, consistent with established doctrine, that the rule does not preclude the introduction of evidence to show absence of consideration.

The court then considered Kmoch's argument based on promissory estoppel, which Kansas had espoused, but in perhaps a narrow fashion requiring a showing that "a refusal by the court to enforce the promise must be virtually to sanction the perpetration of fraud or must result in other injustice." The court found that the requirements for application of this doctrine had not been met. Kmoch drafted the agreement and knew that the $10 consideration had not been paid. His acts alleged as acceptance conferred no benefit on Berryman. He did not assume any duty as a result of the agreement and said the court:

> "The evidence which appellant desires to introduce in support of promissory estoppel does not relate to acts which could reasonably be expected as a result of extending the option promise. It relates to time, effort, and expense incurred in an attempt to interest other investors in this particular land. The appellant chose the form of the contract."

In other words, the court found no reasonable detrimental reliance. Reverting to the issue of consideration, the court said that Kmoch's argument that his acts in investigating financing of the land purchase confused motive with consideration. Kmoch's activities with respect to financing were not bargained for, and he was under no duty to undertake any such actions. Rubbing salt into the wound, the court noted that Kmoch did not tender the $10 in his counterclaim. His ability to accept the offer in the option agreement was terminated by Berryman's revocation by telephone in July.

INTERESTING DISCUSSION ISSUES

The Notes deal with the key issues in this case of false recital of consideration (Note 3) and nominal consideration (Note 4).

The court poses, but does not answer, the possible problem of the option agreement being assigned to a good faith purchaser for value without notice of the falsity of the recited consideration. We do not pick up on this possibility in class, but if students raise the question, the answer is to be found in the bona fide purchaser for value rule of equity.

The court discusses the difference between "motive" and "consideration." Nothing is "consideration" that is not bargained for as such and the court finds that Berryman did not bargain for Kmoch's efforts to find financing, nor was Kmoch obligated to undertake any such efforts.

Kmoch argued that the agreement, if only an offer, was one which called for acceptance by Kmoch performing the acts he undertook in investigating financing and find others to join him in purchasing the property. In other words, he argued that the offer was for a unilateral and not a bilateral contract. The court, in effect, found that the agreement called for a formal acceptance of the option offer and not for the performance of any such acts. This issue was resolved by interpretation of the document that Kmoch had drafted.

NOTES AND QUESTIONS

1. *Express option contract.* In the June 19th "contract," Berryman appears to clearly grant Kmoch an option for 120 days to purchase the land. Is a promise of irrevocability expressly or impliedly made for the 120 day period? Yes. If so, does the option contract meet the "requirements for the formation of a contract?" How is this determined? Those requirements include an objective manifestation of mutual assent and a bargained-for consideration. Since Kmoch admitted that the $10 had in fact not been paid, he could not argue persuasively that the $10 was the exchange that he had in fact bargained for. Did Berryman bargain for $10 or for "other valuable consideration?" If we shift from the $10 to "other valuable consideration," we deal with a conventional recital intended, when used frequently in printed forms, to express the formal intent of the parties to be bound. The recital is intended to operate in the same way that, historically, the affixing of a seal to a written document operated. The court dealt with the question whether there was any such "other valuable consideration" in this case but found any absence of evidence that any such other evidence was in fact bargained for. In so acting, the court denied the intended formal effect of such a recital. In the world of commerce, there is a need for an acceptable evidentiary form. Many believe that the recital of $1 paid meets such a requirement of form and makes the contract enforceable. Whether this court would support such a belief is not clear since the court did not address what the result would have been had the $10 in fact been paid. What form might that other consideration take?

Kmoch argued that it took the form of his expending time and effort to find others to join him in the purchase and, in effect, find the requisite financing. The option agreement could have been drafted to make such efforts required in good faith and, in that event, the option would have been enforceable. The court reminds us that Kmoch was an experienced real estate broker and he was the person who drafted the agreement that Berryman signed. Is it possible that Berryman would grant the option with little monetary consideration for the purpose of encouraging Kmoch to make investigation and complete the purchase?

That Berryman had such a purpose at the time of signing the option agreement is highly likely. If so, it was reasonable for Berryman to foresee that Kmoch would take such actions as a result of the signing of the option agreement. The court found, however, that while such actions may have explained Berryman's *motive,* they constituted neither acceptance by performance nor acts in reasonable reliance on the option agreement. This court's reading of the option agreement is comparable to that of Judge Learned Hand in *Baird*—the offer was to be accepted if at all by formal exercise of the option and not by reliance of some sort.

2. *Restatement (Second) of Contracts rule for reliance on offer.* This Note draws attention to Restatement (Second) of Contracts § 87(2), a provision which was not found in Restatement (First) of Contracts. Should Berryman have expected Kmoch to incur substantial reliance on the option contract? The court held that Kmoch was under no duty to do anything as a result of the option agreement but this does not answer the question of whether there was reasonable reliance which should have been foreseen by Berryman. The whole purpose of granting the option was probably the encouragement of Kmoch to figure out a way of buying the property on the terms stated in the option agreement. Would this amount to "action or forbearance of a substantial character"? Comment (b) to that section, addressing situations like that in Kmoch, suggests that granting relief would be appropriate:

> "The fact that the option is an appropriate preliminary step in the conclusion of a socially useful transaction provides a sufficient substantive basis for enforcement, and a signed writing taking a form appropriate to a bargain satisfies the desiderata of form. ..."

Should Restatement (Second) of Contracts § 87(2) be limited to construction bid cases? Examples of its application beyond these cases are rare.

3. *False recital of nominal consideration in option contract.* This Note emphasizes the stark difference in the treatment in Restatement (Second) of Contracts between an option contract including nominal consideration (enforceable) and other contracts including nominal consideration (unenforceable). The Restatement rationale, as spelled out in the quoted comment, is not clearly, or persuasively, stated. But, with no market study to support us, we think the widespread public belief that an option contract supported by nominal consideration is enforceable provides a possible rationale.

The theory and result in the Restatement (Second) of Contracts has not been universally adopted and indeed may constitute a minority rule. Does this help explain the result in *Berryman* since the option contract recited the payment of "$10 and other valuable consideration" which Berryman testified was never paid? This case does not reach the question of nominal consideration because of the finding that the $10 was not paid. The court does not address the probable result if the $10 had in fact been paid. How should the courts determine whether the signed document is correct and that the consideration was paid or whether it was not paid? If we need a substitute for the writing under seal, and that need is particularly urgent in the context of options, then the recital of consideration, no matter how nominal ($1?) should satisfy the need for form, rendering the promise enforceable. This appears to be the justification for the Restatement's differentiation between options and all other situations. If we think that the doctrine of consideration is one of the high points of contracts jurisprudence, then we follow substance over form and reject nominal consideration as being effective. How did the court decide in *Berryman*? The parties both agreed that the $10 had not been paid or received. Did Kmoch acknowledge that the $10 had not been paid? Yes. If you represented Kmoch, what meaning would you attach to the language "For . . . other valuable consideration. . . .?" We would interpret these words as Kmoch's counsel did, arguing that Kmoch's acts subsequent to the grant of the option constituted precisely such "other valuable consideration," an argument the court rejected. Do you agree with the approach of the restatement? Should the courts enforce the writing or evaluate testimony as to whether $1 was paid? We think there is a need for a vehicle to make an offer "firm." Compare UCC § 2-205, applicable however only to offers by merchants and subject to the further conditions provided in that section. The widely shared belief that the exchange of $1 is effective supports a finding of enforceability in such circumstances. If the justification for enforcement is the need for such a form, then the use of the form should control and the courts should reject any attempt to introduce contradicting evidence. If this purpose is accepted, it should make no difference whether, in fact, the $1 changes hands.

4. *Reliance on a purported transfer of an interest in real property for nominal consideration.* What legitimate business considerations could drive contracting parties to execute an option contract granting an option to purchase real property at a specified price while reciting a mere nominal consideration? There are many possible such interests. The first and foremost is the desire of both parties to create a relatively short option period to assure irrevocability. Consider the potential renter who wants to have a week in which to discuss the rental with her spouse while being sure that the rental opportunity remains open for that period. The value of the short time interval may be inconsequential. The value of the underlying lease is supported by its own bargained for consideration. Can these cases be explained by the parties' ignorance of the legal effects of their purported nominal

considerations? No. On the contrary, we believe that many lay as well a business people believe such short term options supported by the consideration of a recited payment of $1 are enforceable. If it is true that many parties are generally unaware of these legal effects, how should courts respond to the possibilities of opportunistic behavior by a party who is aware of the legal rule applicable in her jurisdiction? Perhaps the better result would be to follow the general market assumption of enforceability if someone could cite a supporting analysis of market practice.

5. *Mailbox rule and option contracts.* See text. Another possible explanation of the result in option contracts is that the wording of the option is usually interpreted to call for exercise of the option by providing actual notice to the offeror—another example of the "master of the offer" concept.

3. Pre-Offer Reliance on Negotiations

As the text notes, one or both parties may detrimentally rely upon assurances, promises, or representations made in the course of negotiations before the parties conclude an express agreement describing their respective rights and duties. But absent such an express agreement, contract law generally does not favor contractual liability based on negotiations because the terms of the deal at the negotiation stage are simply too vague and uncertain. In these circumstances, should the law provide a remedy for a person who relies on an indefinite or vague assurance made during the course of negotiations? The answer should be, generally speaking, no. Common sense would suggest that negotiations are precisely that, and not binding commitments. But the opportunities for confusion between the end of negotiation and the beginning of commitment are many. If so, what theory supports the obligation and what is the nature of the obligation? Most courts will follow the logic of *Baird* that if the parties understand commitment to depend upon the making of a formal acceptance by the offeree, nothing short of the stipulated formal acceptance will close the contract circle. Theories vary on these important matters with general consensus only upon the single idea that at some point precontractual liability is appropriate. Where this is the case, the theory of liability is most likely to be found in detrimental reliance—the common question being, was any reliance during the negotiating process "reasonable"? The case below explores the application of promissory estoppel. Is this theory the same as liability based on a contract? No—see the potential difference in remedy available. Compare Restatement (Second) of Contracts § 90 with Restatement (Second) of Contracts § 347.

§ 90. Promise Reasonably Inducing Action Or Forbearance

(1) A promise which the promisor should reasonably expect to induce action or forbearance on the part of the promisee or a third person and which does induce such action or forbearance is binding if injustice can be avoided only by enforcement of the promise. The remedy granted for breach may be limited as justice requires.

(2) A charitable subscription or a marriage settlement is binding under Subsection (1) without proof that the promise induced action or forbearance.

§ 347. Measure Of Damages In General

Subject to the limitations stated in §§ 350-53, the injured party has a right to damages based on his expectation interest as measured by

(a) the loss in the value to him of the other party's performance caused by its failure or deficiency, plus

(b) any other loss, including incidental or consequential loss, caused by the breach, less

(c) any cost or other loss that he has avoided by not having to perform.

Pop's Cones, Inc. v. Resorts International Hotel, Inc.
CASE BRIEF

This is a 1998 decision of the Superior Court of New Jersey. Pop's Cones was a retail franchisee of TCBY, a national franchisor of frozen yogurt products, operating in Margate, New Jersey. Resorts was a casino hotel in Atlantic City leasing retail space along prime boardwalk frontage. Taube, president of Pop's, had discussions with Resorts in the May-June, 1994 timeframe about relocating to Resorts' property. Taube alleged discussion of a specific boardwalk location. Resorts' agent told Taube that they were very anxious to have Pop's as a tenant and that financial issues could easily be resolved. In the summer of 1994 Resorts allowed Pop's to operate a vending cart at no cost in order to test the market. Pop's got initial approval from the franchisor, TCBY, to move the location of their outlet. Based on the summer test, in August Taube drafted and mailed to Resorts a written proposal covering the boardwalk site providing for a rental of 7% gross and a term consisting of the remainder of the lease existing on the boardwalk property plus two six year option extensions. In mid-September Taube pushed for a response from Resorts, noting that Pop's lease at the Margate site was due to expire October 1, unless renewed before then. In a conversation in later September, a Resorts agent (Phoenix) assured Taube that "we are 95% there" and needed only a senior officer's signature. Phoenix also assured Taube that that officer would follow Phoenix's recommendation and approve the lease contract. Taube spoke of the Margate lease, and Phoenix advised her to "pack up" and "plan on moving." In reliance on that advice she told the Margate landlord that Pop's would not be renewing its lease there. She then moved the store property into storage and proceeded to incur other costs related to moving to the boardwalk property. By letter dated December 1, Resorts forwarded a written offer on substantially less favorable terms than previously discussed. The offer letter also contained a paragraph saying that the letter was not a binding commitment—such commitment would abide the execution of a definitive lease agreement. Further discussions were held in December and then adjourned. A January 30 letter from Resorts advised that Resorts was withdrawing its offer to lease the boardwalk property to Pop's. Subsequently, Resorts leased the property to a different TCBY franchisee.

Pop's sued for promissory estoppel damages. The trial court granted summary judgment to Resorts on the ground that no "clear and definite promise" had been made by Resorts. Pop's appealed. The appellate court opinion pointed out that the trial judge erred in treating the case as one to enforce a promise to enter into a specific lease. Rather, this was a complaint seeking damages caused by reliance on Resorts' assurances. The court outlined the four requirements, under New Jersey law, for a recovery based on promissory estoppel: (1) a clear and definite promise; (2) made with the expectation that the promise will be relied upon; (3) the promisee must in fact rely on the promise; and (4) detriment of a definite and substantial nature must be incurred in reliance on the promise. The court noted that both Restatement (Second) of Contracts § 90 and recent cases were "seemingly" relaxing the strict requirement of "a clear and definite promise." The trial court had based its judgment on the absence of agreement on key basic terms of any lease transaction covering the boardwalk property such as rent and term of the lease.

The appellate court had also to deal with a Statute of Frauds problem. A lease is a contract with respect to an interest in land. Leases for a year or less are frequently exempt from the reach of the statute but the proposed lease here was a multi-year lease caught not only by the "land" clause of the Statute of Frauds but also by the "contract not to be performed within the space of one year" clause. The court noted the disposition of New Jersey courts to give considerable weight to the provisions of the restatements. Under § 90 the court found that strict adherence to the "clear and definite promise" requirement was being eroded. Restatement (Second) of Contracts § 139(1) provided an exception to the application of the Statute of Frauds in point on the present facts. Reviewing the course of the discussions, the notice by Taube to Resorts of the need to act on the Margate lease, and the specific assurances received, the court found that Pop's had made out a prima facie case sufficient to prevent summary judgment and present issues of fact for a jury. In closing, the court pointed out that Pop's complaint sought neither enforcement of a lease nor speculative lost profits that it might have earned had the lease for the boardwalk property been executed.

INTERESTING DISCUSSION ISSUES

It may be necessary to explain to students the business reasons for franchising and the relationship created between franchisor and franchisee. No detail may be required. It may be sufficient to explain the financing reasons behind the practice. The McDonalds company, as franchisor, owns the trademark and trade name and licenses, subject to strict conditions, licensees to operate under that name and logo. In return for granting such a license, McDonalds is paid a percentage of the profits of the retail outlet and requires that outlet to buy its supplies from McDonalds. Thus McDonalds "gets a piece of the action" at each retail outlet without incurring the capital and operating expense of building and operating each retail outlet. The franchising business is regulated in considerable detail by both the Federal Trade Commission and individual state law. The practice illustrates the old bon mot of "using other people's money."

This case is redolent with bad faith by Resorts, but traditionally, bad faith was not an independent cause of action. As the notes introducing this case point out, the key question is whether a court should provide a remedy for reliance on indefinite or vague assurances under a theory of promissory estoppel. Cardinal to that theory is the requirement of a promise coupled with reasonable foreseeable and actual detrimental reliance. The issue most in focus is the reasonableness of a party to negotiations relying on the state of those negotiations when that party knows or should know that the point of commitment for both parties is the signing of a concluded written contract. Normally, the negotiations environment will preclude any such reasonable reliance. But, as in the facts in Pop's, certain kinds of behavior are sufficiently clearly unfair that some remedy should be available. In the context of different agents representing a principal, the actions and knowledge of both or all agents can be tacked together in determining whether fraud was committed. Here, Pop's did not allege fraud and, had it done so, would most likely have lost on that issue. To sustain a charge of fraud, Pop's would have to have proved that Phoenix, the agent who gave the assurances, knew at the time the assurances were made that there was no intention of fulfilling them. The defense of subsequent change of mind would almost certainly have defeated any such claim of fraud.

The other intriguing issue of the case is the types of damage sought to be recovered by Pop's compared to the types of damage that would be recovered under a successful suit to enforce a contract to enter into a specific lease. The court emphasized that Pop's was not claiming benefit of the bargain damages for failure of Resorts to grant the lease. Rather, Pop's was claiming damages that it incurred as a result of reliance on the Resorts' assurances. Pop's was apparently seeking the loss of profits that it would have made at the Margate location up to the time, eighteen months later, that it was able to reopen at another site. Presumably, it was also claiming the incidental costs associated with moving and storing the business property and costs incurred in the course of negotiation with Resorts. Could it have recovered the costs of seeking and finding a new location?

A student may refer to Restatement (Second) of Contracts § 139 and ask how a court can create by decision an explicit exception to the language of the Statute of Frauds. The answer (somewhat debatable) is that the court is merely interpreting and applying the statute in accordance with its basic purposes. The statute, for instance, is never applied in a way that would protect fraudulent behavior regardless of the express language of the statute. Gregory Maggs, in the article cited in this Note, asks and answers the following question:

> "So the question arises: How might judges who purport to adhere to textualism justify their use of estoppel to affect the application of statutes that say nothing about estoppel? Are they creating policy based exceptions to legislation? Or is the proper characterization of what they are doing more complicated than that?"

The professor may ask whether the reasonableness of Pop's reliance related to an implied lack of sophistication. Would the result have been different if Pop's had been a major corporation with a significant volume of franchise business? This question, in turn, suggests another—do we have one set of rules for the competent and a somewhat different set of rules for unsophisticates?

NOTES AND QUESTIONS

1. *Indefinite promise and Hoffman v. Red Owl.* What requirements, if any, does the Restatement (Second) of Contracts § 90 provide with respect to the clarity and definiteness of the promise? The black letter text simply says "promise" without further elaboration, but § 2 defines a "promise" as "a manifestation of intention to act or refrain from acting in a specified way, so made as to justify a promisee in understanding that a commitment has been made." One of the illustrations provided under § 90 summarizes the facts of the Hoffman case and says, "The assurances from B to A are promises on which B reasonably should have expected A to rely, ..." Thus the illustration shows the intent of the Restatement to treat the kinds of assurances give in Pop's to be treated as promises. What requirements, if any, does the Restatement (Second) of Contracts § 90 provide with respect to the

clarity and definiteness of the promise? The Restatement does not spell out any such requirements expressly. However comment (b) suggests that to be a basis for recovery the reliance must be "definite and substantial." Since reasonable foreseeability of detrimental reliance by the promisee is the first predicate of recovery under § 90, the "definite and substantial reliance" must be clear to the promisor as well. If § 90 is interpreted to contain no such requirements, does that imply that an indefinite or illusory promise will suffice? Yes, but only where the promise can serve as the predicate of definite and substantial reliance. What the section requires is a "promise," which has been interpreted to include "assurances" of a relatively general nature—such promises need not be specific enough to become terms of a contract. The content of the "promise" must be sufficiently specific to constitute a basis for reasonable reliance. An "illusory" promise is generally understood as a promise "giving the sleeve of one's vest"—that is, the maker of the promise gives nothing that could be enforced. To ask whether the assurances in Pop's case were "illusory promises" does not advance the ball. They could not have been advanced as terms of a contract because of their lack of sufficient specificity. The assurances that ". . . we would have little difficulty in concluding an agreement," and to "pack up" were sufficiently specific, however, to give Taube the understanding that Resorts would proceed in good faith to negotiate and conclude the deal. They were not sufficiently specific to stipulate the terms of an enforceable lease. The court drew a clear distinction between the standard for enforcing a lease contract and the standard required under § 90. Does the court state or imply that an indefinite or illusory promise is adequate? No, not in any such words. What the court does do is treat the assurances given to Taube as sufficiently specific to constitute a "promise." Metzger and Phillips, in their article cited in this Note, suggest that reliance was the basis and reason for enforcement in early English contract cases. Nineteenth century judges and writers, focusing on the laissez-faire premise, forgot this historical truth. Recovery for reliance based on promissory estoppel only started to come back into the common law at the end of the Nineteenth and the beginning of the Twentieth centuries. The extent and degree of this return is still in the making and shaping. These two authors describe two cases which, they say, involved the application of § 90 to reliance on an "illusory" promise. Both cases involved employees who quit their current job based on a promise of employment by another. Reliance on the promise of employment was found reasonable notwithstanding the acknowledged legal standard that employment under such a promise would be "at will" and that therefore the relying employee could claim to have lost no more than two weeks' wages. Some courts have seen this situation otherwise and granted reliance damages based on the employee's reasonable belief that she would be given an opportunity to perform not limited by the "at will" standard. Arguing that there is no reason to exclude reliance on illusory promises under § 90, the two authors say:

> "Reliance on illusory promises, some argue, is unreasonable and therefore undeserving of protection. There are two main thrusts to this contention. The first and more general of the two is that the reasonableness of relying on a promise depends heavily on that promise's legal enforceability. The second and more specific contention is that there is something particularly unreasonable about relying on an illusory promise. Both lines of argument are unpersuasive for a number of reasons."

Normally, estoppel bars a person from asserting claims and defenses, from seeking remedies, from presenting testimony or from making certain arguments. Hoffman on the other hand did not use the doctrine defensively but rather offensively as a cause of action in which the defense of indefiniteness was not easily available because of the flexibility of reasonable reliance (versus contractual assent). How would Hohfeld rationalize this conceptualization? Pop's (and Hoffman) would create a right/duty relationship by successfully arguing the availability of a § 90 claim. Does Restatement (Second) of Contracts § 90 contemplate the use of the doctrine affirmatively in the form of an action to recover damages?

2. *Contract and duty to negotiate.* The actionable promise in *Pop's Cones* was an assurance that the deal was certain and therefore Pop's Cones should not extend its Margate property lease. Is there a special quality to such an assurance made in the context of negotiations? The answer is yes. The assurance relates not to a specific term under negotiation or yet to be negotiated, but rather to the fact that the negotiations will be pursued in good faith until either a successful end is accomplished or the parties, after a good faith effort, are unable to reach agreement. Is it clear that negotiations had terminated and the deal was completed? At the time when the assurances were given the deal had not been completed—both sides knew that a written signature from a superior Resorts agent was still required. Was there a contract? No. If so, was there a contract to complete negotiations or a contract on the specified lease terms? No—Resorts had made no enforceable promise to accept a particular lease with specific terms. Again, the court emphasized the difference between a suit to compel the execution of a lease in accordance with agreed terms and the instant suit which was based not on a completed enforceable contract but on reliance on the assurances that a deal would be concluded.

3. *Damages.* Why did Pop's not seek the lost profits it anticipated from the Resorts lease from the date of the anticipated lease until July 5, 1996? Are such damages recoverable under promissory estoppel? The

court makes an express point that Pop's did not seek these damages and implies that they would not be recoverable under a promissory estoppel claim. Any such claim would have to be predicated on the express terms of a lease governing the specific boardwalk property including rental and other costs. Such a claim necessarily involves enforcement of a specific set of lease terms—something that the parties had not yet agreed upon. Restatement (Second) of Contracts § 90 limits damages to reliance—the "action or forbearance" on the part of the promisee. And then, damages are available only if "injustice can be avoided only by enforcement of the promise" and may be "limited as justice requires."

4. *International precontractual liability and CISG.* See text.

5. *Contracting without consent.* Some of us, who have substantial practice experience and exposure in the drafting, negotiation and conclusion of substantial commercial transactions, do not find Ben-Shahar's proposal attractive. The give and take of such negotiations often involves compromise on both sides. Thus one side may agree on issue X but, subjectively, balance agreement on that specific issue against future to-be-sought-for agreement by the other side on a different issue. Ben-Shahar's proposal would introduce commitments ignoring the potential quid pro quo for such commitments, and distort the negotiating process. How would the outcome of *Pop's Cones* change, if at all, under Ben-Shahar's proposal? There would be no change since the Resorts agent with authority to commit to the transaction had not at that time indicated the necessary agreement. What are the benefits or harms of such an approach to negotiation and contract formation? See the observation above. Do current negotiation ethics and standards provide any support for this proposal? We, or at least some of us, believe the answer to this question is no. Consider a negotiation for a car with a $25,000 sticker price—what would happen if the prospective buyer offered $21,000 and the seller responded with a counteroffer of $27,500? Is the sticker price an offer or merely an invitation to the buyer to make an offer? When a particular model car is in scarce supply and the model is popular, dealers are known to tack on to the sticker price a substantial additional premium. Under Ben-Shahar's proposal the buyer would not be able to reduce his offer price and neither would the dealer be able to increase his price beyond the $27,500 counteroffer, but there would still be no commitment to a contract and each side would be free to stop bargaining.

4. Precontractual Agreements

Sophisticated business people and business lawyers often use precontractual agreements or exchanges of letters. Sometimes these are intended to and do create initial contracts the terms of which are conclusive but of limited application. Consider, for instance, the case of the seller of a business who wants to encourage a thorough "look-see" by a potential buyer but also wants to preserve the confidentiality of documents disclosed by the seller to the buyer as well as to limit the damage to the seller's workforce that could be caused by widespread gossip within the business that it was about to be sold. Such gossip could undermine employee confidence and encourage widespread transfers to other employment. Providing such a "look-see" opportunity involves significant time and expense to both the seller and the buyer. The seller wants to be as sure as possible that the buyer is a serious prospect. Thus the first step in the negotiation process may be the execution by both parties of a written "letter of intent." Such a letter could, for instance, reference the buyer's interest in a purchase, indicate the nature of the proposed deal as an "assets" or "stock purchase," and the proposed method of payment (cash, assumption of debt, stock etc.). Because of the important tax consequences attached to such choices, neither buyer nor seller may be serious about negotiation unless at least these fundamentals are viewed in the same way by both parties. Such letters of intent usually indicate nothing more than good faith intent to pursue negotiations along those defined lines. Rarely are they designed to establish any kind of binding commitment to the choices indicated in such a letter. The parties will not regard a subsequent change by either party with respect to one or more of the fundamentals as an occasion for possible liability in damages. Some courts and authors have found such letters to set up a subcontract involving a duty to negotiate in good faith.

But such letters may also include specific terms that are agreed to and intended to give rise to a binding and enforceable commitment. The most obvious common example of such a fixed commitment involves the buyer's promise to maintain the confidentiality of all papers and information provided by seller to buyer together with a duty to return all such materials (including all copies) in the event no final agreement is reached. The drafting of such a letter requires both care and skill. There are too many cases reported where the disappointed party sues alleging that the "letter of intent" was sufficiently specific about the basic terms of the deal that a court should enforce it notwithstanding the failure of the parties to subsequently reduce the agreement to a detailed formal document signed by both parties. As suggested in the Notes following the *Quake Construction* case, this common situation poses a most important drafting exercise.

If the words "letter of intent" can be dangerously ambiguous, the words "agreement in principle" can be even more so. The notorious *Texaco* case, referred to in the introductory note, is a classic example. The students can be reminded that in that case the court found there to be an enforceable contract for the sale and purchase of a $7 billion business notwithstanding the absence of any formal signed written detailed agreement and the reference in parallel press releases to the achievement of an "agreement in principle .... subject to execution of a definitive merger agreement ...." Even more poignant is the contrast described in the note between the Delaware Chancery Court decision and the Texas court decision. The trial of that case was held in the auditorium of the South Texas Law School. Lead counsel for Pennzoil is said to have closed his argument to the jury with the words, "In Texas we keep our word!"

The introductory note points out the relevance of Restatement (Second) of Contracts §§ 27 and 26—whether a precontractual agreement is binding depends upon the objective interpretation of the words and acts of the parties. Did they intend an enforceable commitment or did they merely "agree to agree" thus incur no binding commitment?

Empro Mfg. Co., Inc. v. Ball-Co Mfg., Inc.
CASE BRIEF

This is an 1989 decision of the United States Court of Appeals for the Seventh Circuit. This case involved a dispute about the enforceability of a "letter of intent." Empro sent Ball-Co a three page "letter of intent" to purchase the assets of Ball-Co. The letter of intent covered proposed price, downpayment and a ten year promissory note for the remainder, the note to be secured by the "inventory and equipment of Ballco." The letter stated: "[t]he general terms and conditions of such proposal (which will be subject to and incorporated in a formal, definitive Asset Purchase Agreement signed by both parties)." The letter also provided that "Empro's purchase shall be subject to the satisfaction of certain conditions precedent to closing including, but not limited to" the definitive Asset Purchase Agreement and, among five other conditions, "[t]he approval of the shareholders and board of directors of Empro." But Ball-Co, and not Empro, balked. Ball-Co wanted a security interest in the land under the plant; Empro refused to yield.

Learning that Ball-Co was negotiating with someone else, it filed a diversity suit contending that the letter of intent obliged Ball-Co to sell only to it, and sought a restraining order. The trial court dismissed the complaint based on the wording of the letter of intent. On appeal, Empro argued that the case could not be dismissed for failure to state a claim since the issue was one of intent of the parties.

Judge Easterbrook opined that such "intent" must be determined objectively. Under the parol evidence rule, the "subject to" language showed an objectively manifested definitive intent not to be bound. The words "letter of intent" can be used carelessly, and if the full agreement showed that the formal contract was to be nothing but a memorial of an agreement already reached, the letter of intent would be enforceable. From the beginning Ball-Co assumed that it could negotiate terms in addition to, or different from, those in the letter of intent. Ball-Co's lawyer returned the signed letter of intent stating that the "terms and conditions are generally acceptable" but that "some clarifications are needed in Paragraph 3(c) (last sentence)," the provision concerning Ball-Co's security interest. "Letters of intent and agreements in principle often, and here, do no more than set the stage for negotiations on details." Empro claimed unsuccessfully that it was entitled to recover its "reliance expenditures."

NOTES AND QUESTIONS

1. *Promises, consideration, and the one-sided nature of the letter of intent.* What was the consideration given by each side in this transaction in exchange for the other side's consideration? There being no binding agreement established, there was no such bargained for exchange. Did each side take on real obligations, or did one make only illusory promises? There were no promises – the letter was merely an indication of future intent to try to work out a final agreement. What would have happened if Ball-Co, rather than Empro, had attempted to enforce the letter of intent? The same result would have happened – no enforceable contract. Would this have made a difference with respect to the enforceability of the purported promises? No.

2. *Reliance and the one-sided nature of the letter of intent.* To what extent could either party reasonably have relied upon this letter of intent? There could be no reasonable reliance on the letter. Would actual reliance by either party be sufficient to render the letter of intent enforceable? No – because any such reliance would have been unreasonable, given the language of the letter. If a letter of intent does not generally provide sufficient consideration, indicate a sufficiently definite mutual intent to contract, nor provide a basis for reasonable reliance on its terms, what good is it? Such a letter provides a basis for the parties to focus on in their subsequent negotiations, tending to channel those negotiations effectively. Such letters are commonly used but must be drafted with particular care if no binding commitment is intended.

3. *Parol evidence rule.* See text. What would be the effect of such merger clauses upon letters of intent and similar writings? They could suggest that the parties to the letter intended it to be a binding commitment in its own right. Could such writings be introduced as evidence of the integration, terms, or meaning of a contract between the parties? Yes.

4. *The famous Texaco "agreement in principle" case.* See text.

5. *Punitive damage in contract cases.* See text.

6. *Agreement to agree and open terms.* See text. The message here is important for the students to understand and is only tangentially related to the case. The terms of a contract must be sufficiently definite to provide a reasonable basis for determining the existence of a breach and an appropriate remedy. When the parties leave one or more specific terms for later agreement, the intent is usually to postpone bargaining until subsequent events become more clear or certain. If they fail to agree, the issue becomes whether they intended no enforceable agreement or intended the court to supply the missing term. Stated another way, what is the intended legal consequence of their failure to later agree? If they intend for a court to supply the term, the court must nonetheless decide whether the agreement is sufficiently definite to be enforceable or merely an unenforceable "agreement to agree."

7. *Negotiations as a relationship-building device.* How can precontractual agreements such as letters of intent and agreements to agree further the development of trust and rapport between negotiating parties? They help establish reciprocal understood common goals that will shape further negotiation and drafting. Sometimes, a letter of intent can also include a specific separate agreement of its own, such as agreement to keep information provided confidential. To what extent does the *Quake Construction* majority opinion affect this relationship-building process? It affects that process only from the perspective of suggesting that the parties establish with maximum clarity what they are agreeing on (which can be relied on) and what they are merely describing as a proposed (but unenforceable) road map.

Optional Problem 3-1

Magnus owned 40 acres in Arlington Heights. He lived in a private residence on the property that also included a separate private nursing home structure. He intended to construct a retirement housing complex on the property. To carry out that intent, he formed a partnership with Hillman, and together they obtained $30 million in tax-exempt revenue bonds issued by the Village of Arlington Heights. Before construction, Magnus and Hillman entered extensive negotiations with the Lutheran Hospital to purchase the project, financing, and all interests therein. On October 17, the Magnus/Hillman Partnership and Lutheran Hospital signed a written "Letter of Intent" stating agreement on all required terms but stating that each party's obligations were subject to and contingent on the execution of a formal purchase agreement on or before November 17. If the purchase agreement was not executed within that time period, the Letter of Intent was to terminate and the parties would be released from any and all obligations. For various reasons, the parties did not timely execute the purchase agreement. Lutheran Hospital seeks to enforce the letter of intent and either purchase according to its terms or be awarded damages for breach.

Was the letter of intent a valid contract under the Quake Construction case?

Answer:

The crux of this problem is that the parties agreed on all of the applicable terms of the deal in their "Letter of Intent." Thus, but for the stated contingency, the court would have no difficulty in determining the bargain they had made and enforcing it. The difficulty derives from (1) the express contingency recited in the letter of intent that the obligations of both parties were to be contingent on the execution of a formal purchase agreement on or before November 17, and (2) their failure to execute any such "formal agreement." If the student applies the teaching of *Empro* to this problem, then step one is to decide whether the letter of intent was unambiguous or ambiguous. Lutheran Hospital is almost inevitably going to want to be able to introduce extrinsic evidence to explain or excuse the failure to execute on or before November 17. Lutheran Hospital may want to be able to explore through expert testimony the purpose and reasoning behind the formulation of the contingency. Magnus/Hillman is going to try to persuade the court that the words of the letter and the contingency are clear and unambiguous and therefore no extrinsic evidence should be admissible and the contingency should be enforced as written. If we were the judge we would be interested in finding out why the contingency was written into the letter of intent in that fashion. We can hypothesize a number of different reasons or explanations, the most simple being that the parties were not yet ready to reach an enforceable commitment – each wanted the time provided to reassess the deal with a failsafe provision that if they failed to agree by November 17 the deal was off the table. Hopefully, the students will then think carefully about the merits of the common law condition precedent to the introduction of extrinsic evidence to explain or interpret words used in a document – the necessary finding of law by the judge of ambiguity.

E. ELECTRONIC CONTRACTING

See the text summary of the effects of the Internet on methods of contracting, pricing and terms. The questions at the end of the introduction should be taken up at the end of the section on electronic contracting.

Hill v. Gateway 2000, Inc.
CASE BRIEF

This is a 1997 decision of the United States Court of Appeals, Seventh Circuit. This case is the second in a pair of opinions by Judge Easterbrook of the Seventh Circuit (the first being *ProCD, Inc. v. Zeidenberg*, 86 F.3d 1447 (7th Cir. 1996) which is heavily referenced in this opinion) addressing the validity of the "money now, terms later" paradigm for contract formation. Here, the Hills, plaintiffs, ordered a Gateway computer over the phone and paid at that time by credit card. The computer arrived in a box that gave no warning of contract terms. Upon opening the box the Hills saw that contract terms were enclosed but they failed to read those terms with care. One of those terms was a requirement that disputes be resolved by arbitration. Another term offered a refund if the computer was returned within 30 days. The Hills, disappointed with the computer and the service provided, sued in federal district court, having allowed the 30 days to go by without returning the computer. Gateway moved to enforce arbitration but the district court refused their request. The appeal to the 7th Circuit followed.

The Hills alleged that they did not see the arbitration clause and that it was not conspicuous. While the court opinion does not say so, it appears their argument was that the arbitration clause never became an effective term of their contract with Gateway. Judge Easterbrook, holding UCC Article 2 to be applicable, found no requirement that an arbitration clause be given special prominence (compare requirement of "conspicuousness" with respect to limitation of warranties in UCC § 2-316). Said he, "A contract need not be read to be effective; people who accept take the risk that the unread terms may in retrospect prove unwelcome." Referring to *ProCD*, he said that the vendor is the master of the offer and, as in *ProCD*, the contract was concluded, not when the telephone conversation ended, but when the Hills opened the box, found the contract terms and failed to return the computer and box within the 30 day period. Gateway argued that *ProCD* was not applicable for several different reasons. As in *ProCD*, Judge Easterbrook emphasized the practical marketing considerations that require that the terms in the box be effective. He found *ProCD* to be applicable. In so doing, he denied that *ProCD* was limited to a transaction between "merchants" under UCC § 2-207 (the Hills were consumers) and that the failure in this case of the box to warn that there were terms inside was of any significance. He concluded, "By keeping the computer beyond 30 days, the Hills accepted Gateway's offer, including the arbitration clause."

Klocek v. Gateway, Inc.
CASE BRIEF

This is a 2000 decision of the United States District Court, District of Kansas. This case provides a useful counterpoint for a provocative discussion regarding contract formation in the retail consumer context. In *Klocek,* the plaintiffs apparently purchased their Gateway computer from a retail store and later sought to bring individual and class action suits for breach of warranties, false promises of technical support, and false representations regarding compatibility of peripheral devices and internet services. Gateway attempted to compel arbitration (where the class action device would not be available) under a provision similar to that in *Hill.* Gateway's Standard Terms were included in the box of power cables and instruction manuals (although it doesn't appear that Gateway employed any device, such as a shrink-wrap seal that had to be broken before operating the computer, to warn purchasers of the importance of Standard Terms. The Standard Terms purportedly became binding under the following notice at the top of the first page:

> NOTE TO THE CUSTOMER:
> This document contains Gateway 2000's Standard Terms and Conditions. By keeping your Gateway 2000 computer system beyond five (5) days after the date of delivery, you accept these terms and conditions.

The Dispute Resolution term mandated arbitration in terms substantially similar to those in *Hill.*

After outlining the Congressional policy under the Federal Arbitration Act favoring arbitration where the parties have agreed in writing to arbitrate, the court turned to the question of whether Kansas and Missouri state law deemed terms packaged with a product to become part of the parties' agreement.

The district court judge in *Klocek* case disagreed with Judge Easterbrook and held that UCC § 2-207 does apply. The terms in the box were additional terms which, this being a consumer case, became terms of the contract only if agreed to by the purchaser. There being no such agreement in this case, the gap-filler terms were imported under UCC § 2-207(3). UCC § 2-207 applied to an acceptance or written confirmation and to an oral agreement.

This court also chastised Judge Easterbrook for finding that the vendor was the master of the offer and providing no authority in support of that assertion. (In *ProCD,* Judge Easterbrook did provide a single citation to *Peeters v. State,* 142 N.W. 181 (1913), for the proposition that the vendor makes an offer by placing software on the shelf, and the customer accepts the offer by paying and leaving with the goods. Inexplicably, *Peeters* concerns a criminal prosecution for improperly measuring strawberries for sale and does not at all deal with the identity of offeror and offeree in the retail context.) In contrast, *Klocek* observed that, "[i]n typical consumer transactions, the purchaser is the offeror, and the vendor is the offeree." Because Gateway failed to present any evidence rebutting this traditional understanding of retail sales, the court deemed Gateway's additional terms to be a non-conditional expression of acceptance.

In *Klocek*, applying either Kansas or Missouri law, the district court concluded that the vendor entered into the contract by agreeing to ship goods or, at the latest, shipping the goods. Since Gateway's terms were an expression of acceptance, and there was no indication by Gateway that the transaction was conditioned on the Hills' acceptance of the standard terms, the additional or different terms were no more than proposals which were not accepted. This court therefore refused to enforce that arbitration clause in Gateway's terms.

INTERESTING DISCUSSION ISSUES

These two cases are in direct opposition and provide substantial opportunities for stimulating student discussions. While Judge Easterbrook virtually ignores UCC § 2-207 with his unsupported statement that the section is irrelevant because there is only one form, the *Klocek* judge engages in a reasoned analysis that dismantles Judge Easterbrook's reasoning. First, the cases permit an analysis of traditional reasons for treating the customer as the offeror, rather than the vendor. The *Klocek* judge based this rule by analogizing the consumer purchase to price quotation cases under Restatement (Second) of Contracts § 26. As discussed previously in this chapter, an offer is the "manifestation of willingness to enter into a bargain, so made as to justify another person in understanding that his assent to that bargain is invited and will conclude it." Restatement (Second) of Contracts § 24. In retail consumer transactions, the vendor makes a price quotation to consumers by placing products for sale on store shelves or advertising them in circulars and other advertisements. Cf. Restatement (Second) of Contracts § 26, cmt. b ("*Advertising.* Business enterprises commonly secure general publicity for the goods or services they supply or purchase. Advertisements of goods by <u>display</u>, sign, handbill, newspaper, radio or television are not ordinarily intended or understood as offers to sell.") (emphasis added).

Second, *Klocek* attacks Judge Easterbrook's unsupported assumption in both *ProCD* and *Hill* that UCC § 2-207 does not apply to these consumer transactions because there is only one form. The professor may take the opportunity to discuss again § 2-207 and explore the question of whether *Klocek* or *Hill* best comports with a literal reading of that provision.

Third, both cases also deal with the type and degree of notice that the vendor must provide to the consumer in order for the vendor's later-following terms to control. In *Hill*, Judge Easterbrook implied that the Hills had sufficient notice of the following terms (including the arbitration clause) because "the Hills knew before they ordered the computer that the carton would include some important terms, and they did not seek to discover these in advance. Gateway's ads state that their products come with limited warranties and lifetime support." According to Judge Easterbrook, the Hills could have discovered these limits by making a request under the Magnuson-Moss Warranty Act, consulting public sources that "may contain this information," or reading the documents included with their purchase. While Judge Easterbrook conveniently fails to explain how the bare notice in the ads that there might be limits on the warranty should also serve to notify the consumer that the contract contained an onerous arbitration clause, such a conclusion must be inferred from his analysis.

The notice issue in *Klocek* arises in the context of whether Gateway adequately notified Klocek that its acceptance of his offer to purchase the computer was conditioned on Klocek's "assent to the additional or different terms. '[T]he conditional nature of the acceptance must be clearly expressed in a manner sufficient to notify the offeror that the offeree is unwilling to proceed with the transaction unless the additional or different terms are included in the contract.'" Because Gateway could not show any evidence that it informed Klocek at the time of the sales transaction that Gateway's acceptance was expressly conditioned on Klocek's acceptance of the additional terms, under § 2-207 those additional or different terms were deemed mere proposals. The mere facts that Gateway enclosed its standard terms inside the product box or that Klocek kept the computer for more than five days were insufficient to show that Klocek demonstrated acceptance of the additional or different terms.

Fourth, as a minor issue of persuasive writing and candor before a tribunal, Judge Easterbrook's citation to the completely irrelevant *Peeters* case may provide some interesting practice and ethics discussions. The opinion, as cited by Judge Easterbrook, appears to provide support (actually the sole support offered) for his characterization of the vendor as offeror and the customer as the offeree (a key point of law supporting his later analysis). The sole question at issue in *Peeters*, however, concerned whether a grocery store had made a "sale" as an element of an ordinance prohibiting the sale of goods in a container purporting to be one quart in volume, but "the interior capacity of which was less than one quart and more than one pint, dry measure, and not stamped on the outside thereof at the time of sale." *Peeters v. State*, 142 N.W. 181, 181 (Wis. 1913). The case did not address whether the customer, who entered the store, selected an allegedly under-capacity box of strawberries, placed 12 cents on the counter before the cashier, and walked out, was the offeror or offeree. As a matter of persuasive writing, if an attorney arguing the case had relied upon *Peeters* in the same manner as the *Hill* opinion does, the disconnect between the authority cited and the proposition would likely damage the credibility of the attorney's brief and the court's perception of the attorney's candor.

NOTES AND QUESTIONS

1. *"Money now, terms later" versus offer and acceptance.* Judge Easterbrook's opinion in *Hill v. Gateway, Inc.* and the earlier case of *ProCD, Inc. v. Zeidenberg,* 86 F.3d 1447 (7th Cir. 1996), arguably establish a new paradigm for contract formation. In contrast to the classical model of an offer followed by an acceptance, Judge Easterbrook's "money now, terms later" process permits a vendor to propose a contract for sale, the terms of which will be communicated to the consumer only after the consumer has paid the purchase price for the product. The contract formed under this new process becomes enforceable only after the consumer has had an opportunity to discover the additional terms and indicate acceptance by retaining the product or indicate rejection by returning the product for a refund. See *ProCD, Inc.,* 86 F.3d at 1451 ("Notice on the outside, terms on the inside, and a right to return the software for a refund if the term are unacceptable (a right that the license expressly extends) may be a means of doing business valuable to buyers and sellers alike.") Is it possible to fit this new paradigm into the rules of offer and acceptance developed in the previous cases dealing with non-electronic contracts? Yes, by determining that the time of acceptance of the offer of sale is not delivery of the product in the store but later upon opening the box and deciding not to return the product. Is it necessary to try to fit this new paradigm into the old? The rules of offer and acceptance were developed in the context of growing commercial experience. With the rapid technological revolution of the late 20th ce ntury, perhaps the better question is should we create new rules adapted to the new environment? The answer to this question may be yes. Given the default provisions of the UCC (implied warranties of merchantability and damages rules), sellers of goods need to be able to market their products with the degree of warranty (price point) that they choose. Given the detailed verbiage required to accomplish the seller's need and purpose, it is impossible to print that verbiage on the side of a box. Necessarily, such lengthy information is going to have to be included with (inside) the box. In the interest of serving reasonable commercial needs (together with reasonable customer opportunity to reject the goods after reading the terms) the "inside the box" rule seems appropriate to current business needs. Which opinion—*Klocek* or *Hill*—best represents the probable objective and subjective intentions of the parties? Why? See the discussion under "Interesting Discussion Issues" above.

2. *U.C.C. § 2-204(1) and shrink-wrap contracts.* U.C.C. § 2-204(1) provides that "A contract for sale of goods may be made in any manner

sufficient to show agreement, including conduct by both parties which recognizes the existence of such a contract." Based on your reading of the *Hill* and *Klocek* opinions, does the action sufficient to show agreement to the formation of a contract also have to be sufficient to show agreement to specific terms proposed by one or both of the parties? Yes, but the "duty to read" comes into play as soon as there is adequate notice provided of detailed terms and conditions. How did the Hills' conduct show agreement to the license restrictions? On opening the box they discovered that specific terms were enclosed and they then had a duty to read those terms. What could Gateway have done differently to make sure its preferred contract terms were enforceable against Klocek? It could have required that before Klocek could get the computer to run Klocek must read and agree to all the terms of the contract including the right to return—a "click wrap" technique.

3. *Consumer or vendor as offeror.* Why is it crucial for Judge Easterbrook's conclusion in *Hill* that Gateway is the offeror? How does the *Klocek* court respond to the proposition that the offer is made by the vendor when it displays the product for sale? As discussed above, the answer to this question depends in part on whether UCC § 2-207 governs the transaction. Under the *Klocek* analysis, the consumer makes an offer by placing an order with the vendor or otherwise offering to buy the vendor's goods. The vendor's acceptance at the time of sale operates as a definite and seasonable expression of acceptance under § 2-207(1), unless the vendor specifically notifies the consumer that the vendor is unwilling to contract unless the vendor's additional terms to follow later control. Without such notice of conditional acceptance, under the first sentence of § 2-207(2), the vendor's additional following terms would be treated as mere proposals for inclusion in the parties' contract that the consumer could accept or ignore at will.

In contrast, Judge Easterbrook's analysis in *Hill* (and the earlier *ProCD* case) depends largely upon the proposition that the vendor, as offeror, is entitled to determine the form of the consumer's acceptance, including whether the transaction will proceed under the money now, terms later contract formation process. Since consumers rarely—if ever—will have an incentive to submit their own forms in a retail transaction, the *Hill* rule will (at least under Judge Easterbrook's analysis) rarely invoke application of § 2-207.

4. *Applicability of UCC § 2-207.* Asks the Note, do you agree or disagree with the *Klocek* court's analysis of U.C.C. § 2-207? The application of this section to the facts depends upon two issues. The first is the timing of when a contract was entered into. If Judge Easterbrook's analysis is correct, the terms assented to by *Klocek* were the terms in the box and the time of conclusion of the contract was the opening of the box, discovering the terms, and failing to return the

computer and box. If the *Klocek* analysis is correct, the contract was complete upon shipment of the computer and the terms in the box were just proposals. The *Klocek* court treats Gateway's terms as an expression of acceptance and in any case the shipment of the computer did not communicate to the purchaser Gateway's unwillingness to do business other than on its terms. If, and only if, the student agrees with the *Klocek* analysis on the correct timing of the conclusion of the contract, the analysis is sound. Which opinion—*Klocek* or *Hill*—best represents the probable objective and subjective intentions of the parties? Why? The nub of the problem, and the key difference between these two cases, is the gap-filler provisions of the UCC dealing with express and implied warranties and the presumed availability of consequential as well as direct damages. These gap-fillers are strongly pro-buyer and anti-seller. No seller would intentionally enter into a sales contract without modification of those gap-fillers. Thus the real tension between the two cases is whether sellers should be given reasonable (their terms) protection against the gap-fillers or whether the consumer should be protected by enforcing the gap-fillers (allegedly "reasonable" terms). Thus there can be no question that *Klocek* fails to meet the subjective intention of Gateway. How about Gateway's *objective* intentions? It is difficult not to conclude that in today's market environment a consumer knows that important terms, including description of available warranties, accompany the purchase of any machine or software package. It is possible therefore to find objective intent based on this market awareness. Judge Easterbrook's two decisions, however, take the higher ground and depend upon his factual findings of practicality and market need—or as he puts it in *Hill*, the best interests of the consumer.

5. *Notice of additional terms.* The "money now, terms later" paradigm for contract formation established in *Hill* (and *ProCD*) still requires that the vendor notify the customer of the existence of the additional terms (and provide an opportunity to reject them). What degree of notice will satisfy this requirement? Under *Hill*, the notice required seems at best ephemeral. Although he does not squarely address the issue, Judge Easterbrook suggests that Gateway's notice in its ads that its warranty was "limited" gave sufficient notice to the consumers that additional terms would follow in the computer box describing their warranty and that this notice of additional warranty terms was sufficient notice of the existence of the arbitration clause. Given that the vast majority of consumers will fail to read or understand such terms, should the opportunity to read and reject the additional terms be legally relevant to whether those terms are included in the parties' contract? This question is intended to invoke discussion on the usefulness of formal default rules. The volitional choices of both parties to exercise or withhold consent to a proposed agreement lies at the foundation of contract. While few consumers read

or understand the terms of their standard form contract, the possibility that they might do so and choose to reject those terms arguably preserves the fiction that standard form agreements actually are contracts. If that fiction ever completely erodes, such that vendors become legally entitled to impose additional terms upon consumers without consumer consent, the rationale for restraint from state regulation of the terms of those transactions is tremendously, if not fatally, weakened.

6. *Facts "on the ground" versus facts in the courtroom.* See text.

7. *Using transaction costs as a weapon.* The Note emphasizes the way in which consumer transaction costs were severely exaggerated by the Gateway contract terms, including the arbitration clause. Buyers were precluded from finding out about Gateway's terms, and thus were unable to comparison shop. They had no way of knowing about the arbitration rules and potential costs for the consumer under the designated International Chamber of Commerce rules including arbitration in Chicago, an advance payment of $4,000 (half of which is not recoverable), and "loser pays." Thus the answer to the Note's question "Given that the difference in value between Gateway's advertised system and the system actually delivered was approximately only $1000, would any rational dissatisfied consumer seek recovery through the arbitral forum?" is a resounding "No."

8. *The hidden benefits of arbitration clauses in consumer contracts.* How would Ware respond to the arguments raised by the Hills? Which is a more important goal of contract law—protecting the rights of individuals to enter bargains they believe will maximize their own interests, fairness, or economic efficiency? This question takes us back to the question asked and discussed earlier about form contracts. Again, Karl Llewellyn's view, that form contracts should be enforced unless they are unconscionable, is applicable. Can an arbitration clause be unconscionable? It is arguable that Gateway's clause was over that edge in effectively preventing arbitration over a dispute about the computer because of cost built in to the specified arbitration process. If Gateway's objective in requiring arbitration was to make claim review simple and inexpensive, their clause dramatically failed to achieve any such objective. If, instead, their purpose was to frustrate and inhibit any customer litigation, it succeeded. The latter purpose could easily be found to be unconscionable under the Llewellyn test. Part of the purpose of sellers seeking arbitration is the lack of publicity accompanying an arbitral decision as compared with a court decision where, usually, the record is open to the public.

9. *Behavioral decision theory, complexity, and heuristics.* Even assuming that producers do not intentionally increase the complexity

of their offerings to take advantage of boundedly rational consumers, how can consumers respond effectively to the complexity of transacting consumer goods and services? There are a diverse number of sources available to the consumer which evaluate and compare competing products and services. The confused consumer is well advised to take advantage of such resources.

10. *Law of contract versus law of software.* Based on your readings in contract law so far, is Judge Easterbrook's refusal to consider developing a separate body of doctrines tailored to software or intellectual property in cyberspace justified? Doctrines tend to be relatively abstract concepts—such as that the terms of the contract are governed by the principle of offer and acceptance. That can be described as a doctrine. But the important question in *ProCD* and *Hill* was what was the offer and what was the acceptance and when did that acceptance occur? Just as the facts of a particular problem are always critical, so the steps taken in applying doctrine to those facts are also critical. We do not know what new doctrine Judge Easterbrook might have created for the solution of problems in the cyberworld. We do know that he applied standard contract principles, hundreds of years old and time tested for fairness to a new and fast evolving fact pattern. His application of the doctrine to that fact pattern could well be described as "new." What is particularly important is to appreciate the critical importance he attached to the practicalities of everyday life in the cyberworld market. His total focus on marketing considerations was new. What is old, as shown by Karl Llewellyn's thoughts about form contracts, is the boundaries of the unconscionable.

Says Note 6, "And what about the Uniform Commercial Code? As you have already seen in the cases dealing with sales of goods, Article 2 differs from the common law of contract in many important respects. What advantages and drawbacks are there in maintaining a single law to regulate voluntary agreements versus different sets of doctrines for specific types of transactions?" Our supposition is that Karl Llewellyn and his associates who drafted UCC Article 2 took the opportunity to introduce changes from the common law where they thought such changes were desirable. It was not so much that they thought such changes specially appropriate to contracts involving the sale of goods, but rather that they had a specific opportunity to make such changes in the context of UCC Article 2 where they had no such mandate with respect to the more general law of contracts. Simply put, we think they took advantage of the opportunities presented. It is noteworthy that courts have, by analogy, applied a number of those changes to common law situations such as the "lost volume seller."

If some agency were to try to write a new law of contracts specifically applicable to cyberware, what sources would they find to draw upon? Where would they find the basis of a fair balance between sellers and buyers, merchants and consumers? Borrowing from history, the answer would likely be by drawing analogies from past principles. Is not that exactly what Judge Easterbrook did?

11. *Acceptance by silence.* The Gateway standard terms in both *Hill* and *Klocek* purportedly were deemed accepted when the customers failed to reject the terms and return the computers before a deadline set by those same terms (30 days in *Hill,* 5 in *Klocek*). How can this result be distinguished from the rules regarding acceptance by silence discussed in *Day v. Caton* and Restatement (Second) of Contracts § 69? The easy answer, of course, is that *Klocek* and *Hill* both arise under the UCC, which is generally more lenient than traditional common law rules regarding contract formation. See, e.g., UCC § 2-204(1) ("A contract for the sale of goods may be made in any manner sufficient to show agreement, including conduct by both parties which recognizes the existence of such a contract."). This answer, however, is not wholly satisfactory given that these cases could have arisen easily in a non-sale-of-goods transaction.

The *Klocek* court held that Gateway's contract term deeming the consumer to assent to the additional terms after keeping the computer for more than five days was unenforceable because Klocek did not expressly agree to that additional term. *Klocek v. Gateway, Inc.*, 104 F.Supp.2d 1332, 1341 (D.Kan. 2000) ("The Court finds that the act of keeping the computer past five days was not sufficient to demonstrate that plaintiff expressly agreed to the Standard Terms) Accord *Brown Mach.,[Div. of John Brown, Inc. v. Herculese, Inc.*, 770 S.W.2d 416, 421 (Mo.App. 1989)] (express assent cannot be presumed by silence or mere failure to object)." It is likely that this conclusion would apply equally in the common law context.

Hill's justification for permitting the contract to base acceptance upon keeping the computer longer than 30 days is more problematic, but is likely reconcilable with the R2K § 69(1) rule on the basis that: (a) the consumer has taken and retained the benefit with a reasonable opportunity to reject and notice of the expectation of compensation; or (b) the offeror's notice of additional following terms would likely be deemed to give the offeree notice of the acceptance terms and the offeree intends to accept. Moreover, under Restatement (Second0 of Contracts § 69(2), "[a]n offeree who does any act inconsistent with the offeror's ownership of offered property is bound in accordance with the offered terms unless they are manifestly unreasonable." Arguably, breaking the seal on a box-top or shrink-wrap license, keeping and using the product for a lengthy period of time, or other acts of dominion would also act as an acceptance.

Optional Problem 3-2

On July 1, Lee Davis, a professional author, purchased a copy of a popular word processing program—WordSmith 2.0 by DataMine, Inc.—

at a local retail store for $159.95. The software packaging claimed that WordSmith 2.0 had been "developed especially for authors of large, book-length documents." At home, and before opening the box, he noticed the following statement printed on the top of the box: "Additional Terms and Conditions are listed in the User's Manual inside this box. Opening this box constitutes acceptance of these additional Terms and Conditions." Piqued, Davis drafted the following form:

> **Consumer Purchase Form**
>
> Dear DataMine, Inc.:
>
> I have recently purchased a copy of your WordSmith 2.0 software package. Pursuant to U.C.C. § 2-207, you are hereby on notice that all terms contained in any click-wrap, shrink wrap, browse-wrap, or any other agreement the terms of which were not immediately available at the point and time of purchase are REJECTED. In particular, I do not consent to any arbitration of disputes—any and all disputes arising from the purchase and sale of this copy of WordSmith 2.0 are subject to litigation before a court of competent jurisdiction in Illinois and shall be governed by Illinois law. If you do not agree to these terms, you may take possession of the aforementioned software, FOB my house, at your convenience.
>
> Sincerely,
>
> Lee Davis

Davis logged onto DataMine's website, obtained email and postal mail addresses for DataMine's customer service department and general counsel's office, and sent separate copies of the form to both offices by email. He immediately received an autoreply email back from DataMine acknowledging receipt of his separate emails to customer service and the general counsel. Each autoreply email concluded with the statement: "DataMine has consistently been ranked in the top ten software companies for customer service and responsiveness. It is our policy to respond to all customer emails no more than 48 hours after receipt."

Ten days later, Davis still had not received any response from DataMine. He opened the box and installed the software without examining the additional Terms and Conditions inside the User's Manual. During the installation process, the software presented Davis with a click-wrap agreement providing, inter alia, for arbitration of all disputes in Hawaii where DataMine's headquarters is located. Davis clicked the "I Accept" button as required to complete the installation. Following installation, he sent another copy of his original email to DataMine's customer service and general counsel's office. Other than an autoreply message acknowledging receipt, DataMine never responded to these later emails.

The WordSmith 2.0 software functioned poorly, and proved entirely incapable of handling even a medium-length book chapter. Davis sent an email demand for a full refund to DataMine's customer service department. Beyond the now-familiar autoreply message, DataMine never responded to this demand, and Davis filed suit for breach of contract in the Chicago, Ill. small claims court. How would a court respond to DataMine's motion to compel arbitration in Hawaii?

Answer:

The key facts here are: software purchase (license), box top warning of additional terms, "opening constitutes acceptance," customer writing letter rejecting terms before opening box, customer offer to return placing pick-up duty and cost on seller, acknowledged receipt of customer letter, later opening of box by customer, "click-wrap" assent required and given, repeat customer letter of no assent, arbitration clause requiring arbitration in Hawaii (home of software producer), suit by customer and motion by software producer to compel arbitration in Hawaii. Question: "How would a court respond to DataMine's motion to compel arbitration in Hawaii?"

In the light of the previous cases, the first key question would be "When was the contract completed?" The legend "opening constitutes acceptance" is unreasonable because it requires assent before the buyer has any opportunity to see the terms. It is highly unlikely that a court would enforce such a requirement, particularly when it is not accompanied by Judge Easterbrook's key requirement that there be a reasonable opportunity to return the product and get a refund. Next, the buyer's letter rejected any such terms so that, if UCC §2-207 were found to be applicable, the terms would be merely proposals that were not accepted and the gap-fillers would apply, and the arbitration clause would not be part of the contract. Then, the buyer's letter purports to "return" the product to the seller but requires the seller to have it picked up and pay the costs of such return. Judge Easterbrook makes it clear that a right to return and obtain a refund is required in order to cement the contract terms into the deal. He does not expressly deal with the intriguing question of whether the costs of such return must be borne by the seller. He does, by implication, require that the buyer take the step of arranging the return. Whether he would find that the seller must reimburse the buyer for all return costs has yet to be decided. Practicality suggests that the buyer should have to initiate the return and, if necessary, pay the return shipping costs but the seller would be most unwise to refuse to reimburse the buyer promptly for such costs. Such a duty seems to flow naturally from Judge Easterbrook's analysis. This issue can be posed to students as a seller client counseling situation—as counsel to a seller in such a situation, what would you advise with respect to the terms on arranging for return and reimbursement? But then the buyer, ten days later, proceeds to open the box, install the software and is confronted with a "click-wrap" "I agree." He clicks on "I agree" but then resends another copy of his letter. Now he has a real problem since the logic of the cases suggests that he is now stuck with the terms of the agreement whether he read them, accepted them or not—see *Ticketmaster*. His conduct in clicking is irreversible. This then leaves the last question, is the requirement of arbitration in Hawaii fair? Our answer, going back to Llewellyn's response to form contracts is that by clicking on the "I agree" button, the buyer consents to all the terms that he read or could have read, provided that they are not unconscionable. We think this particular arbitration clause should be unconscionable—see the statutory provision discussed in *Carnival* earlier in the chapter. But note that the venue is conciliation court. Would a judge in such a court rule that she has authority to declare such a provision to be unconscionable? Would such a court have the power to order (grant injunctive relief) arbitration? We doubt it and expect that the buyer would have to appeal to a district court in order to get adequate relief. The professor may also wish to note the issue of the legal costs involved in attempting to challenge the seller successfully.

CHAPTER 4

THE SCOPE OF CONTRACTUAL OBLIGATIONS

Table of Contents

Introduction to Chapter 4 Coverage

Chapter 4 assumes that an agreement has been achieved between the parties and now goes on to consider issues involving the scope of the terms agreed upon or otherwise implied and the meaning (interpretation) of those terms. The chapter covers five different subject areas—the parol evidence rule, interpretation of the agreement, the unprovided or omitted case, good faith and other obligations implied by law.

Students inevitably have difficulty in differentiating between the rules dealing with the question of what terms were agreed upon contrasted with the question of giving meaning to the terms that were agreed upon or implied. Where the parties have reached agreement orally, and have not reduced that agreement to writing, there are no special problems involved in proving and enforcing the content of their oral agreement, assuming that an oral agreement covering such subject matter is enforceable. See Chapter 6 for a discussion of agreements which are enforceable only when authenticated by a signed writing. Where, however, the parties have reduced their agreement to a writing (usually signed by the parties), a new set of problems is implicated. Traditional wisdom says that where the parties have reduced their agreement to such a writing, logic suggests that the writing was intended by the parties as the definitive expression of the full scope and extent of their agreement—otherwise, why would they have produced the writing? Thus extrinsic evidence, outside the writing itself, should not be admitted to either contradict or add to the terms found in the writing. Given the focus of contract law on the shared intention of the parties, placing their written document on an evidentiary pedestal (protected against extrinsic evidence that would try to contradict or add to the written terms) should depend upon a showing that indeed the parties did intend the writing to be the exclusive source of their agreement. That they shared such an intent is basic to the function of the parol evidence rule. Where that was their intent, no extrinsic evidence, either oral or written, should be admissible to add terms to their agreement as evidenced in the writing. And the parol evidence rule says that. The first problem with the rule, however, is what evidence a court should consider in evaluating whether or not the parties did truly intend the writing to be the exclusive evidence of their agreement. The historical development of the rule has moved from the pursuit of such intent by looking only within the "four corners" of the writing for the answer, to a broader but not universally accepted approach involving a judge's evaluation of the impact of such extrinsic evidence before ruling on the issue of intent to integrate.

The contrasting roles of judge and jury are immediately implicated. Why, a student will ask, should the judge be deciding an issue which is essentially factual, namely the shared intent of the parties? This question can be answered in at least two ways. The first, and less satisfactory, answer could be the simple statement that the case law (including the restatements) defines the deciding of this particular issue of intent of the parties as one of law, not of fact. The second, possibly a little more satisfactory, answer involves reminding students of the history of the judicial struggle to place some restraints on unfettered jury decisional power. For several centuries the resolution of assumpsit-based cases was left pretty much to juries without specific judicial guidance or instruction. In the 19th century, both in England and the United States, judges began creating and enforcing rules limiting the scope of open decision making for juries. It is possible that the evolution of the parol evidence rule, imported from England, was part of this process. But, whatever the explanation, the decision on this issue of intent belongs to the judge and not the jury. If the judge decides that the parties did not intend the writing to be the exclusive source of the terms of their agreement, she will then allow the jury to hear the extrinsic evidence and resolve issues of credibility. If she decides the other way, the jury will never hear the extrinsic evidence and will decide any other issues in the case based on the writing. As a bootstrap argument, we can say that if the law were otherwise and the jury could always hear the extrinsic evidence before deciding issues of credibility, the extrinsic evidence would often contaminate the jury's decision of those other issues.

Students often have a difficult time appreciating that the function of the rule is limited to selecting the terms of the agreement to be implemented. It plays no part in a decision as to the meaning of those terms (interpretation).

The rule, however, has an additional element of complexity. The writing may be intended by the parties to be a record not of all of its terms but only of some of its terms. Here the apparent logic is that since the parties reduced some of the terms to writing, that writing was intended to be the authentic statement of those terms but not of other terms not covered in the writing. If the intent of the parties was one of "partial integration" rather than "complete integration" then that logic would preclude evidence to contradict the written terms but not evidence to establish the additional terms. Again, the same issue comes to the fore—what evidence should a court consider in resolving the question of law—was the intent of the parties a partial or a complete integration. Again we see the progression from the four corners approach to the consideration of all the available evidence of intention to integrate by the judge prior to ruling.

If the judge rules that the parties intended the written document to be a full and complete integration there is still the possibility that the parties entered into two rather than just one agreement so that integration of the written document dealing with the first agreement does not lead to any particular logical conclusion as to the second agreement. Thus a landlord and tenant could enter into one lease agreement in writing, while entering into an oral lease agreement dealing with different property. Reducing the first agreement to writing does not necessarily disclose any particular intent with respect to the second agreement. But we come back quickly to the challenge of slicing the salami—the separation of the two agreements described above may become less clear as the connection between them becomes closer. The closer the two agreements become, the stronger the logical conclusion becomes that the reduction of the one to writing indicates an intention of the parties that the second was not intended to be "operative." Herein the students learn about asserted criteria for a judicial finding that the second agreement was sufficiently "collateral" to permit its proof by extrinsic evidence notwithstanding the wholly integrated written document. A measure of confusion may be found in some cases as to whether classification of the oral agreement as "collateral" and thus enforceable is accomplished by viewing proof of the collateral agreement as negating intent to wholly integrate or as operating wholly outside the sphere of the integrated written document. Clearly the oral "collateral" agreement must not contradict the writing (subject to agreement modification discussed in this chapter) and is much more likely to be enforced where supported by a separate and distinct consideration.

The process of interpretation takes us back to the theory of objective interpretation found in *Lucy v. Zehmer* in Chapter 2 and the exception to that case where one of the parties knew or ought to have known that the other party attached a special meaning to the words used. Again the student will find that the judge has the key to the door through which a party asserting special meaning must pass before getting her evidence to a jury. Whether words used in an agreement are "ambiguous" is often the controlling key in the hands of the judge. The determination that words are "ambiguous," that is capable of being reasonably understood in two or more different ways is for the judge and not the jury. As in the case of the parol evidence rule, a similar debate arises as to how and on the basis of what evidence the judge is to make her ruling as to ambiguity. The more recent tendency is to allow the judge to consider and assess the full offer of proof as to available extrinsic evidence before ruling on whether the language is or is not ambiguous. But there is a wide divergence of practice between courts in different states on this issue.

The unprovided case material raises the question of the power of the judge, and the circumstances under which that power should be exercised, to fill in gaps in the agreement of the parties. There is tension between two different approaches. The first involves a finding of the judge that the parties intended an effective contract and the drawing of a conclusion from such a finding that the intent of the parties can be understood to imply the inclusion of any additional consistent terms required to assure effectiveness of the agreement. The second involves doubt about the propriety of the judge introducing terms into the contract that the parties did not in fact themselves introduce. Varying from jurisdiction to jurisdiction, the rationale may be offered that such implication is giving direct effect to the intent of the parties to be presumed from their express terms or conduct—"implied in fact." Another approach can be found in some cases whereby the judge purports to imply additional terms on the basis that, had the parties thought about the situation, clearly they would have agreed upon the term to be implied. As a matter of theory, it is sometimes not clear whether the court regards any such process of implication as governed by or outside the reach of the parol evidence rule. This issue may assume greater importance where extrinsic evidence is offered to show that the parties actually contemplated the unprovided case but nevertheless failed to provide for it.

The process of implication of certain warranties, especially as to quality, has undergone a substantial transformation, especially as a result of the adoption of UCC Article 2 including the implied warranties of merchantability and fitness for a particular purpose. Under the English common law the Latin phrase "caveat emptor," or "buyer beware," was taken seriously and protection for the buyer as to the quality of the product or service provided, absent fraud or deceit, had to be found in the terms of the contract. Karl Llewellyn believed this approach to be flawed and not reflective of the understanding of the business and consumer community. Hence UCC §§ 2-314 and 315 set forth those two warranties to be implied as a matter of law unless excluded in accordance with the terms of § 2-316. Massive attention has been given by the drafters of both commercial and consumer contracts to the limitation or exclusion of these implied warranties and such efforts, in certain contexts, have raised serious problems of possible unconscionability under both UCC § 2-302 and § 2-719. A very much more limited modification of the English common law approach is to be found in Restatement, Second, of Contracts § 195, dealing with contracting out of liability for negligence but not willful or intentional injury. A more extended treatment of clauses designed to limit or exclude damages and other remedies is to be found in Chapter 9.

Insurance contracts have developed as a sui generis class with respect to doctrines of contract interpretation. Considering these contracts to have particular importance in both the commercial and consumer contract world, we have included two cases, or "bookends" illustrating contrasting approaches to insurance policy interpretation. The concept of interpreting a contract, where ambiguous, against the draftsperson (the doctrine of "contra proferentem") finds its primary, and indeed almost exclusive, impact in this context. Insurance policies are contracts which, in most situations, are non-negotiable contracts of adhesion. Professor (later Judge) Robert Keeton introduced a novel interpretational concept, applicable to insurance policies, of "reasonable expectations." Both the *C & J Fertilizer* and the *Wilkie* cases provide disparate appraisals of that contentious concept.

Both the Restatement (Second) of Contracts and the UCC Article 2 provide that a duty to act in good faith is implied in every contract. Students naturally then ask whether the plaintiff can sue successfully for a breach of that duty of good faith. The answer "No" can be somewhat puzzling to them but hopefully, they get to understand the role good faith can play in the question of whether or not the conduct of one of the parties involved the breach of a substantive contractual promise.

"Course of dealing" (or in the language of the International Court of Justice, "authentic interpretation") introduces yet another approach to interpretation of a contract. The approach looks to the post-contract conduct of the parties as evidence of their intended meaning of terms of the contract. "Conduct speaks louder than words." The *Nanakuli* case introduces and examines the value of such post-contract behavior while indicating the difficulty of distinguishing such evidence from unilateral waiver. This case is also instructive on the UCC usage of course of dealing and trade usage. Both are available for purposes of interpretation and construction without any precondition of a finding of ambiguity and, indeed, according to some writers, may even contradict the written word of the contract. The old common law limitations on the use of trade custom are dramatically changed by UCC Article 2.

A. IDENTIFYING THE TERMS OF A WRITTEN AGREEMENT: THE PAROL EVIDENCE RULE

The name of the rule is, to start with, confusing. The word "parol" comes from the Norman French meaning oral or spoken. In fact, the rule can function to exclude all extrinsic evidence both written and oral. It is not a rule of evidence but rather a rule of substantive law. To the regular confusion of students it functions to permit a judge and not a jury to decide a question of fact—the intention of the parties to integrate. Legal draftspersons take advantage of the intent-based nature of the rule by frequently including a so-called "merger" clause which recites expressly that the parties intend the writing to be the exclusive record of their agreement and their intention that all earlier understandings be discharged. Such clauses are usually "boilerplate" and not dickered terms. The respect accorded these clauses varies from court to court and can be expected to reflect the individual specific facts of the case.

Some writers criticize the rule claiming that it functions to exclude extrinsic but truthful evidence. Why, they say, should we not admit all evidence extrinsic or otherwise and leave the issue of credibility to the jury? Despite these criticisms, courts continue to adhere to and enforce some version of the rule. It is difficult to provide a current rationale of this distrust of the jury. But a court finding that the parties did agree during their negotiations to a specific term not found in the final written document together with a court refusal to enforce that term does not necessarily support such criticism. Anyone experienced in negotiating contracts understands that such agreements may be reached in the course of the negotiation but the choice of the final terms of the agreement frequently involves negotiating tradeoffs. Thus it is just as possible that the omission of the term from the final document was intentional as that it was unintentional or a matter of oversight. In this context, the presumption in favor of the written document, compared to the extrinsic evidence, is understandable.

As the text points out, the two primary pending questions for the student are: a) what evidence of intent to integrate or not integrate will the judge consider in order to decide the question of law that the document is wholly or partially integrated; b) what rules shape the outcome regardless of what evidence the judge considers.

1. Integration Test and Collateral Agreement Rule

Thompson v. Libby
CASE BRIEF

This is an 1885 decision of the Minnesota Supreme Court. Thompson sold a quantity of logs to Libby under a written agreement that specified the logs covered by the transaction, the price of the logs, and the payment method to be used (Libby signed the agreement via his agent). The contract as signed read:

> I have this day sold to R.C. Libby, of Hastings, Minn., all my logs marked 'H.C.A.,' cut in the winters of 1882 and 1883, for ten dollars a thousand feet, boom scale at Minneapolis, Minnesota. Payment, cash, as fast as scale bills are produced.

After transfer of the logs to Libby, Thompson brought an action against him for failure to deliver the purchase money. Libby pleaded as a defense that Thompson had breached an oral warranty of the quality of the logs that was made at the time of sale. Thompson objected to oral testimony to prove existence of the warranty because the contract of sale was complete in writing. Nevertheless, the trial court permitted the testimony to be presented to the jury. We are not told what the jury's verdict was but must presume that it was adversely affected by evidence of the oral warranty. Thompson appealed from an order of the district court denying his motion for a new trial based on the admission of that testimony.

Justice Mitchell said that the parol evidence rule holds that "parol contemporaneous evidence is inadmissible to contradict or vary the terms of a valid written instrument." The rule was established in order to prevent the inconvenience and injustice that would result if terms of a contract, written after consideration and deliberation, were liable to being controlled by "the uncertain testimony of slippery memory." Where parties have committed an agreement to writing, without uncertainty as to the object or extent of the agreement, it is presumed that the writing covers the whole agreement.

The remaining question is how to determine if the writing was intended to be the complete and final expression of the agreement. The only criterion of the completeness of the written contract as a full expression of the agreement of the parties is the writing itself. In this case, the written agreement purported to be a complete expression of the entirety of the parties' agreement. Parol evidence of extrinsic facts or evidence would be admissible to apply the contract or to better understand its language, but new terms cannot be added by parol evidence. In the case of a sale of personal property, a warranty of the item's quality is a term of the contract, and is not something to be found as a separate or independent collateral contract, and therefore may not be added to a written contract by oral testimony.

The court distinguished *Thompson* from *Healy v. Young*, which permitted the introduction of oral testimony. The writing in that case was a bill of sale executed by way of part performance of an oral agreement. Presumably, the bill of sale, on its face, did not state a complete and enforceable legal obligation. The court also found that the terms of the oral agreement were a distinct collateral matter from the written bill of sale. The court also stated that while many matters could generally be considered as "collateral"—e.g., in a lease, covenants for repairs or payment of taxes could be considered collateral—the parol evidence rule would nonetheless bar the addition of such terms to a written agreement. While title would pass in a sales contract regardless of the presence of the warranty, the warranty is a term of the sale, and not an independent contract. To justify the admission of a parol promise by a party to an agreement on the ground that it is collateral, the promise must relate to a subject distinct from that to which the writing relates.

Since the district court permitted parol evidence of a warranty on the logs, the court held that the order refusing a new trial must be reversed.

INTERESTING DISCUSSION ISSUES

1. *How Justice Mitchell decided that the parties intended the writing to be a wholly integrated document.* The fundamental logic of the parol evidence rule is premised on the intention of the parties that the writing serve as the complete and exclusive record of their agreement. The evidence of that intent by the parties is critical to the logic flow of the rule. Justice Mitchell referred to no evidence of that intent beyond the four corners of the writing. His yardstick for that

intent was whether or not the writing constituted a complete and enforceable contract. If it did, then the parties must have intended the writing as a complete integration. His illustration of a bill of sale not, by itself, constituting an enforceable agreement, is consistent with his yardstick. To be irreverent, his view can be translated as "smelling" the intent of the parties from the face of the document rather from any extrinsic evidence that could be offered to explain that intent or explain how, if an oral warranty of quality was given, that warranty was omitted from the writing. While the writing deserves appropriate dignity, his view runs the risk of ignoring persuasive extrinsic evidence as to the true intent of the parties.

2. *Why the intent of the parties, a question of fact, is decided as a matter of law by the judge and not by the jury.* This issue is covered in the introduction to the chapter.

3. *The significance of the word "collateral."* Justice Mitchell referred to other earlier cases that had held, apparently, that a warranty of quality could be a "collateral" agreement and, as such, be proven by parol testimony without violating the rule. While he disagreed expressly with those cases (overruled?), he did provide some recognition for the notion that under some circumstances a "collateral" agreement could be proven by parol. His example of lease terms indicates that his criterion for finding a wholly separate agreement, thus not subject to the logic of the rule, was that such an agreement must be separate from the agreement reflected in the writing. If the alleged "collateral" agreement was a term that might ordinarily be expected to be included in the writing, then it could not be a provable "collateral" agreement. Thus, the key for him on this issue was that, as a matter or ordinary experience, a warranty of quality is sufficiently related to the basic consideration of the sale and purchase of the logs that it could not qualify as a "collateral" agreement—essentially a second agreement possessing its own distinct subject matter and terms.

NOTES AND QUESTIONS

1. *Early parol evidence test.* What do you suppose the court means by the following statement: "To justify the admission of a parol promise by one of the parties to a written contract on the ground that it is collateral, the promise must relate to a subject distinct from that to which the writing relates."? The examples of lease terms, given by Justice Mitchell, that would be appropriate to a lease but not collateral including anything that would logically be pertinent to the lease agreement. Thus, for him, a promise that is collateral is one that relates to a distinctly different transaction. How does the court apply the distinctness test? It decided whether the warranty of quality would be an appropriate term in a written sale of logs, concludes that it would

be, and therefore cannot be a "collateral" term. What does the distinctness test presume? It presumes first, that the writing was intended to be a wholly integrated document setting forth an agreement for the sale and purchase of logs and thus any term that could reasonably relate to such a sale of logs could not be "collateral." Do you agree with that presumption? No, but the disagreement relates to the way in which the court determined that the parties intended the writing to be a wholly integrated document. If that was their intent, then evidence of the oral warranty should not be admitted. How did the court decide the question of intent to wholly integrate? Justice Mitchell opined that such intent must be determined from the face of the instrument itself (four corners rule) and if the instrument was effective in stating a legally binding agreement, then it was wholly integrated. His conclusion is not supported by any compelling logic.

2. *Role of judge and jury.* Since the Supreme Court reversed the trial judge's decision to admit the evidence of the oral warranty, what is the point of a new trial? The new trial is required because, presumably, the evidence of the oral warranty that was wrongly admitted was reflected in some way (we are not told how) in the jury's verdict. Since the jury's verdict was biased by that evidence, a new trial where that evidence would be excluded was required. Is it relevant to the parol evidence rule even if Thompson admits he made the warranty so that the truth of the statement is not in doubt? Yes, because the issue of discharging intent of the writing is still covered by the rule. Even if such a warranty was in fact made during the course of the negotiations and admitted, it was not included in the final writing and a reasonable explanation of the omission is that the parties changed their mind during the course of the negotiations. If such a discharging function had not been intended for the writing, presumably the warranty, as an important consideration, would have been included in the writing. Reliance on the writing, according to this court's statement of the rule, should be preferred to admission of oral testimony about why the oral warranty was not included in the writing.

3. *Express warranties and contract disclaimers.* If the contract had stated a written disclaimer of prior express warranties, how do you think the conflict should be resolved? See, UCC § 2-316(1). Whether the writing was intended by the parties as either a partial or a complete integration of their agreement, extrinsic oral evidence would not be admissible to contradict the writing and any testimony about a warranty of quality would contradict the "as is and without warranties" language. Absent fraud or deceit, the buyer would be charged with knowledge of the recital in the contract that the sale was "as is and without warranties." Justice Mitchell expressly distinguished any situation involving fraud or reformation of the contract. Stated another way, does the parol evidence rule in general grant greater dignity to

the writing or the prior oral negotiations? Yes—honoring the presumed purpose of the parties in reducing their agreement to a signed writing—making that writing the best evidence of their agreement. If the answer is that the later writing is more important, why would the written disclaimer not always discharge prior oral warranties? Absent fraud or deceit, or possible mistake (see Chapter 6) and presuming that the oral warranties are not part of a "collateral agreement," the written disclaimer should discharge prior oral warranties.

4. *Interpretation rules and other exceptions.* Justice Mitchell expressly opined that extrinsic oral evidence would be admissible in order to "apply" the terms of the contract to its subject matter (construe the contract) or to obtain "a more perfect understanding of its language (interpret)." Many students have profound difficulty in distinguishing the function of the parol evidence rule (deciding what terms are included in the contract) and the function of interpreting the terms of the contract (giving meaning to the words actually used). It is worth repeating several times that the parol evidence rule plays no part in the interpretation of the words used in the contract. A somewhat similar problem with extrinsic oral evidence frequently arises, however, with respect to interpretation but the key to the admission of such evidence is, once again, the ruling of the judge that the language in question is ambiguous.

Optional Problem 4-1

Libby agreed to purchase Thompson's farm for $150,000 but only if Thompson agreed to remove an unsightly icehouse located across the road on other land Thompson owned. Thompson agreed. The farm purchase agreement was written and signed by both parties and included all the terms related to the purchase of the farm but failed to mention Thompson's promise to remove the icehouse. Libby purchases the farm and later requests Thompson to remove the icehouse but he refuses. Libby sues to enforce the promise but when he attempts to introduce evidence of Thompson's oral promise, Thompson's attorney objects on the basis of the parol evidence rule but Thompson admits making the oral promise.

What is the outcome of case based solely on the basis of the collateral agreement as stated in Thompson v. Libby?

Answer:

A collateral agreement, according to Justice Mitchell, is an agreement separate and distinct from the one recorded in the writing. A student may argue that the purchase of the farm is one agreement while the removal of the icehouse is another. The primary difficulty with any such argument is that no separate consideration is stated applicable to the promise to remove the icehouse. The $150,000 price covers both the promise to sell the farm and the promise to remove the icehouse. Thus, Justice Mitchell would decline to hold the promise to remove the icehouse as a collateral agreement since everything relating to the $150,000 price would logically be included in the writing. He would find the intent to wholly integrate from the face of the writing which stated terms constituting an enforceable contract. Had a separate consideration been called for as the price of removing the icehouse, Justice Mitchell might have ruled that this was indeed a collateral (i.e. a distinct second and separable) contract. The fact that Thompson admits making the oral promise probably would not affect Justice Mitchell's ruling. The "discharging" effect of the writing would preclude enforcement of an oral agreement occurring during the negotiations but not included in the final writing. The logic of the rule is that if the parties had intended such an oral agreement to be part of the deal they would have included it in the writing—non-inclusion reflects a presumed mutual change of mind discharging the earlier promise.

Mitchill v. Lath
CASE BRIEF

This is a 1928 decision of the New York Court of Appeals. The Laths owned a farm that Mrs. Mitchill wanted to purchase. During sale negotiations, the Laths made an oral promise to Mrs. Mitchill that they would remove, from land across the road from the farm, an icehouse that Mrs. Mitchill found objectionable. Mrs. Mitchill relied upon this promise and her husband signed a written purchase contract to buy the Laths' farm—the written contract did not include the icehouse agreement. After completion of the transaction, the Laths refused to remove the icehouse. Mrs. Mitchill sued for specific performance to enforce the Laths' promise; both the trial and appellate courts found in her favor, concluding that the promise had been made. The Court of Appeals of New York reversed the lower courts' holdings and dismissed Mrs. Mitchill's complaint, finding that admission of the parol evidence with respect to the icehouse was precluded by the parol evidence rule.

While the parol evidence rule bars the admission of oral or written evidence to alter a written contract, the rule does not apply to an oral collateral contract that is distinct from and independent of the written agreement. Under New York case law, three conditions must exist before oral evidence will be admissible to add to the terms of the written agreement. The oral agreement must: (1) be an agreement collateral in form; (2) not contradict express or implied terms of the written contract; and (3) be one that the parties would not ordinarily be expected to embody in the written contract.

MAJORITY: The court held that Mrs. Mitchill did not satisfy the third requirement, and she may not have satisfied the second requirement (no contradiction—this second requirement was not examined). The court found that an inspection of the contract showed a full and complete agreement, such that one reading the agreement (objectively) would conclude that the parties' reciprocal obligations had been fully detailed. The court held that even the fact that Mrs. Mitchill found the icehouse objectionable did not suggest that there might be an independent agreement as to its removal.

In such cases as this, the decisive factor is how closely bound the collateral agreement is to the written agreement. In several cases similar to *Mitchell*, courts have held that an oral stipulation that was said to be the inducing cause for the subsequent execution of an agreement (leases, in these cases), concerning an act to be done by the inducing party, would not be admissible as evidence. The court found the authority cited by Mrs. Mitchill to be either unpersuasive or confined to the specific facts of those cases.

Finally, the court rejected Mrs. Mitchill's claim that she made the collateral agreement, while Mr. Mitchill, her husband, made the sales agreement, and that no assignment of the agreement to Mrs. Mitchill existed. In rejecting this argument, the court held that Mrs. Mitchill served as principal from the very start of the process, and thus the contract must be treated as though she had made it personally.

DISSENT: Justice Lehman, in dissent, accepted the rule as formulated by the majority, but disagreed with respect to the rule's application to the facts in this case. Justice Lehman agreed that the first condition of the majority's test—that the agreement must be collateral in nature—was met. Next, Judge Lehman stated that the second condition—the oral agreement must not contradict terms of the written agreement—was met because of the fact that the further obligation was in no way inconsistent with the written contract. But with respect to the third point, Justice Lehman found that this promise was not one that would ordinarily or naturally be expected to be included in the writing. This issue could not be resolved without a comparison of the writing with the oral agreement.

Given the evidence in the case, there is no doubt that the parties did make the oral agreement. And while inspection of the agreement shows it to be complete with respect to the land transaction, it is not clear whether it was intended to embody discussions as tangential to the actual purchase as those regarding the icehouse. "I do not think that in the written contract for the conveyance of land here under consideration we can find an intention to cover a field so broad as to include prior agreements, if any such were made, to do other acts on other property after the stipulated conveyance was made."

INTERESTING DISCUSSION ISSUES

1. *How the court decided the issue of intention to integrate.* The court in this case looked at the writing, determined that it constituted an enforceable agreement, contained a detailed list of terms and concluded on this basis that the parties had intended the writing to be a wholly integrated document. They considered the nature and content of the oral promise and the surrounding circumstances, but not any extrinsic oral or written evidence of the intention of the parties as to integration or not. Justice Lehman did not dissent on this point. This so-called "objective" approach does not consider the possibility of a mutual subjective, but not ordinary, intent to integrate or not integrate. What useful policy can be served by an interpretational approach that eschews proof of the true intent of the parties? The answer lies in the exposure of one party to the agreement to the jury listening to self-serving and possibly fraudulent oral testimony. The policy behind the Restatement (First) position, which this court implements, is that it is better to sacrifice the case where the oral evidence as to intention to integrate could be useful in order to protect against "slippery" extrinsic oral testimony.

2. *The "collateral agreement" test.* Does the admission of evidence involving a "collateral agreement" require a predicate finding of a mutual intention to integrate partially and not completely? The answer, as a matter of logic, should be "No." At one end of the scale, the collateral agreement can be a wholly separate agreement, with its own terms and its own separate bargained for consideration. In such a case the parol evidence should have no application to proof of the second oral "collateral" agreement. See Restatement (Second) of Contracts § 216(2)(a). But as the "collateral" agreement moves across the scale and becomes more nearly an additional (but not contradictory) term of the primary written contract, such a predicate finding becomes critical. Consider, for instance, the problem of Father Bussard in his suit against the College of St. Thomas—*Bussard v. College of St. Thomas,* 294 Minn. 215, 200 N.W.2d 155 (1972). He agreed to sell his publishing business to the College for an agreed price, the deal was negotiated and then enshrined in a signed written agreement containing all the terms appropriate to such an agreement. He claimed an extrinsic oral agreement or "understanding" that he would be retained as publisher for life. There was no additional or special consideration for such a promise but the extrinsic evidence in support of his assertion was powerfully persuasive. The Minnesota Supreme Court could not find a separate and distinct second agreement, different from the signed written one, but they did conclude that the evidence of the "collateral" agreement indicated that the parties did not intend the writing to be wholly integrated. It is worth noting that the writing in that case did not contain a "merger" clause.

NOTES AND QUESTIONS

1. *Natural omission test.* Is it possible to make a determination whether the farm purchase documents were completely integrated and intended to discharge the icehouse promise by examining the purchase documents alone? Justice Lehman, in dissent, stated clearly that such a comparison was essential. Justice Andrews equally clearly made such a comparison as a necessary predicate to deciding whether the latter could reasonable be expected to have been included in the writing. How can the natural omission test be applied without at least assuming the icehouse promise existed and then comparing the subject matter of the two agreements? It cannot be applied without such a comparison. Since both the majority and dissent apply the same natural omission tests, why do they reach opposite outcomes? Both apply an "objective" test to decide whether the reasonable person would expect the oral warranty to have been included in the writing if it was intended to be enforceable. They took conflicting positions as to what the reasonable person would expect. Is it the evidence the two sides are willing to consider or is it simply what each side makes of the same evidence? The latter.

2. *"Parol" evidence defined.* See text.

3. *Prior, contemporaneous, and subsequent parol evidence.* See text.

4. *Rule of evidence or substantive law.* See text.

5. *Four corners rule and the collateral agreement rule.* See text.

6. *Unique objective versus subjective integration intent.* The determination of whether the parties might "naturally" include or exclude the evidence requires a search for the intent of those parties. The note above discusses the evidence that may be considered. But is the judge searching for the intent of one of these parties or the intent of both? Neither—the judge is searching for a presumed hypothetical "reasonable person" intent. "Of course, in *Mitchill v. Lath* the court was faced with conflicting intent perspectives." This assumption is not necessarily so clear. Since Lath in fact promised to remove the icehouse did he not represent that he did not regard the writing as wholly integrated and exclusive of that promise? And did not Mrs. Mitchill share that intent so that here there was a shared mutual subjective intent which should have permitted enforcement of the "collateral" agreement? The difficulty with this argument is that it does not directly address or consider the possible discharging intent of the final writing—an intent that the earlier promise be dropped from the deal

and hence was not included in the writing. What is clear is that the rule as applied by this court does preclude the giving of effect to the proven mutual subjective intents of the parties with respect to integration or not. Williston, in the Restatement (First) of Contracts, deliberately excluded such evidence of subjective intent. Oral statements of the parties as to what they actually intended would not be considered. Did the majority in *Mitchill v. Lath* employ this test? Yes.

Carefully examine again the majority opinion in *Mitchill*. What is suggested by the language of the opinion set forth below?

> At least, however, an inspection of this contract shows a full and complete agreement, setting forth in detail the obligations of each party. On reading it, one would conclude that the reciprocal obligations of the parties were fully detailed. Nor would this opinion alter if he knew the surrounding circumstances. The presence of the icehouse, even the knowledge that Mrs. Mitchill thought it objectionable, would not lead to the belief that a separate agreement existed with regard to it. Were such an agreement made it would seem most natural that the inquirer should find it in the contract. Collateral in form it is found to be, but it is closely related to the subject dealt with in the written agreement—so closely that we hold it may not be proved.

The key words are "it would seem most natural that the inquirer should find it in the contract." The court compared the oral agreement with the writing and then provided an "objective" application of the test. While the court did not emphasize the fact that no separate consideration had been given for the promise to remove the icehouse, that factor is often significant in the decisions. There is a common sense (logical?) basis for concluding that if Mrs. Mitchell was bargaining for the removal of the icehouse as part of the return to her for the payment of the purchase price, she would have included the promise in the contract which covered the payment.

Did the court consider extrinsic evidence of integration or only the face of the document? The court relied on the face of the document (including the detailed list of terms) but also considered the oral promise. They also considered the surrounding circumstances but found them of no probative value as to intent to integrate. Was the decision in accord with the parol evidence rule stated in Restatement (First) of Contracts? Yes. In the final analysis, how does the court determine that the promise to remove the icehouse was not an agreement that "might naturally be made as a separate agreement?" The court concluded that if the removal of the icehouse was being purchased, the promise of its removal would have been included along with all of the other terms of the sale. By reference to the parties' actual intent or by reference to what a mythical person (like the judge) might think in similar circumstances? The latter—the court did not consider the possibility of the mutual subjective intent of the parties. Justice Lehman, in dissent, disagreed with this conclusion, drawing a distinction between those terms which were pertinent to the sale and purchase (conveyance) and the term as to the icehouse which, in his opinion, was not. Exactly whose intent is Restatement (First) of Contracts § 230 seeking? Certainly not that of the parties, but rather the objective opinion of a reasonable person (the judge) acquainted with the terms of the contract together with the oral term.

7. *Famous and poetic.* See text.

8. *No jury involved.* Was the majority concerned with the possibility that the admission of the parol evidence might mislead the jury? This was an action in equity seeking specific enforcement so a jury was not involved. So there could be no concern *in this case* that the extrinsic evidence might mislead a jury. If the doctrine developed out of a concern over the reliability of a jury, why would it have any application to this case and action? Part of the history of this rule may have related to the court's interest in establishing fences around freewheeling jury decisions. But part of the reasoning behind the rule relates to the "discharging" effect of reducing the agreement to writing. Experience suggests that that which is important to either party will be set down in the writing. Things agreed upon earlier in the negotiations may be traded away at or before the signing—hence the importance of the final writing.

9. *Truth or consequences?* The answer again is found in the assumption that earlier agreements are merged into and discharged by the final writing. Drafter beware! Why did Mrs. Mitchill's legal counsel allow this to happen?

10. Second restatement integration and collateral agreement rule. Restatement (Second) Contracts § 216(2)(b) adopts and employs a similar judge determined natural omission test for the collateral agreement rule and when applicable regards the written instrument as only partially integrated. The partial integration determination then allows the parol evidence to add its terms to the overall contract of the parties so as to include the terms of both the parol and written agreements. While a number of decisions in different states follow the parol evidence rule so applied, there is no logical compulsion to interpret the rule in this way. If there are in truth two separate and distinct agreements then there is no logical inconsistency in concluding that the writing is a conclusive and complete integration while at the same time concluding that there is a second separate and enforceable agreement wholly independent of and not dependent upon the integration of the writing. Where there is only one unallocated consideration for both the written agreement and the oral one, a court motivated to enforce the oral promise will find it easier to justify enforcement based on a holding of partial integration. The *Masterson* case which follows illustrates a basic shift in approach to the task of deciding intent to integrate or not, a shift flatly inconsistent with the Restatement (First). The *Masterson* court admits and considers testimonial evidence of the negotiations to prove integration or natural omission.

11. *Consistency test.* Since the majority ultimately determined that the parol agreement, if made, would normally be included in the agreement by the parties, the majority did not decide the "contradiction" issue. The majority nonetheless suggested that the parol agreement would require the seller to do more than what was required in the writing and thus might violate the contradiction test because the writing at least "implied" the seller was to do no more. Would this not always be the case? The majority focused on the price paid for the property and thus implied that the burden of removing the icehouse, if enforced, would add to and therefore conflict with the agreed price. If this standard is adopted, no parol agreement could ever be admitted because it will always require more than the writing. Do you agree with this standard? Perhaps and perhaps not—depending upon the specific facts of the particular case. The dissent devoted more time to this question than the majority. What was the dissenting view on consistency? Justice Lehman focused on the conveyance and its terms in contrast with the collateral promise of removal of the icehouse—a not particularly persuasive argument. The *Masterson v. Stine* case below states a more complete and modern version of the contradiction test.

Optional Problem 4-2

Libby agreed to purchase Thompson's farm for $150,000 but only if Thompson agreed to remove an unsightly icehouse located across the road on other land Thompson owned. Thompson agreed. The farm purchase agreement was written and signed by both parties and included all the terms related to the purchase of the farm but failed to mention Thompson's promise to remove the icehouse. Libby purchases the farm and later requests Thompson to remove the icehouse but he refuses. Libby sues to enforce the promise but when he attempts to introduce evidence of Thompson's oral promise, Thompson's attorney objects on the basis of the parol evidence rule but Thompson admits making the oral promise.

What is the outcome of case on the basis of the collateral agreement as stated in Restatement (First) Contracts?

Answer:

On the basis of the teaching of *Mitchill v. Lath,* the oral promise is considered alongside the signed written agreement and is then subjected to the three part "collateral agreement" test formulated in that decision. The fact that Thompson admitted making the statement, as in the main case, makes no difference. The truth of the making of the promise is not the issue under the *Mitchill v. Lath* doctrine—the question is the "discharging intent" of the final signed written instrument. Finding that the promise is one that might naturally be included in the writing, the court finds a conclusive presumption that any prior oral or written agreements are discharged if not set out in the final writing.

In the *Masterson* case that follows the court considered a broader range of evidence than the *Mitchill* court while seeking a more specific intent aimed at the parties' actual but objectively measured intent. Corbin disagreed with Williston's view as expressed in the Restatement (First). He argued that the search should be for the precise intent of the parties—thus placing a higher value on actual intent than on the risks of allowing "slippery" testimony.

Masterson v. Sine
CASE BRIEF

This is a 1968 decision of the California Supreme Court. Masterson and his wife Rebecca owned a ranch as tenants in common; they conveyed the ranch to the Sines (Mrs. Sine is Mr. Masterson's sister) by a grant deed that reserved to the grantors an option to purchase the property within the next ten years for essentially the same consideration paid by the Sines. At some point following the conveyance, Mr. Masterson was adjudged bankrupt; Mrs. Rebecca Masterson and the bankruptcy trustee brought a declaratory relief action to establish their right to enforce the option on the property. In a bench trial, the court admitted, over Sine's objection, extrinsic evidence regarding the consideration intended by the parties, as well as the definition of a clause involving the intended function of a depreciation of improvements to the property clause affecting the option price. The court also used the parol evidence rule to deny admission of extrinsic evidence by Sine to show that the parties had intended to keep the property within the Masterson family, and that the option was therefore personal to the Mastersons, and could not be exercised by the bankruptcy trustee. The court entered judgment for the plaintiffs, permitting them to exercise the option; the Sines appealed the decision, and the Supreme Court of California held that the trial court had erred in excluding the extrinsic evidence regarding the personal nature of the option.

Justice Traynor, writing for the majority, stated that the crucial issue in determining whether there is an integrated document is whether the parties intended their writing to serve as the exclusive embodiment of the agreement. An integration clause stating that there are no previous agreements that are not contained in the writing may help resolve the issue. But the collateral agreement in question must be examined to determine whether the parties would have included the subject of that collateral agreement in their written agreement. Circumstances at the time of the writing may also help. In a number of earlier cases, California's courts had repudiated the strict formulation of the rule that completeness of a document is to be determined on the face of the document, permitting parol evidence to prove the existence of a separate oral agreement that is not inconsistent with the terms of the written agreement, even though the written document appears to be complete. Even under the rule that the writing alone is to be consulted, courts had found it necessary to examine the alleged collateral agreement before concluding that proof of such agreement was precluded by the writing alone. That case law was inconsistent. As Wigmore (On Evidence) said, the conception that the writing is wholly and intrinsically self-determinative of intent is impossible.

The court stated that there are two important policies to be accommodated in formulating a rule governing parol evidence: (1) the assumption that written evidence is more accurate that human memory; and (2) the fear that fraud or unintentional misrepresentation by interested witnesses will mislead the finder of fact. The first can be respected by precluding contradiction of the writing. In his evidence treatise, Prof. McCormick argued that the parol evidence rule arose to help the court to control a jury's tendency to be swayed by either sympathy or other impassioned pleas regarding the existence of a collateral agreement. Respect for this rationale could be preserved by only excluding the extrinsic evidence when the fact finder is likely to be misled. The court supported this proposition with citations to § 240(1)(b) of the Restatement (First) of Contracts, which permitted parol evidence "to prove the existence of a separate oral agreement as to any matter on which the document is silent and which is not inconsistent with its terms" even in cases where the instrument appeared, on its face, to be complete, and UCC § 2-202, which only excludes parol evidence "if additional terms are such that, if agreed upon they would ***certainly*** have been included in the document."

Since the option clause in the deed of the present case did not explicitly provide that it contained the complete agreement, and since the deed was silent as to assignability, there was reason to examine parol evidence. Additionally, the difficulty of inserting a collateral agreement into the formalized structure of a deed made it less likely that all terms would have been included in the agreement. Finally, there was nothing in the record to indicate that the parties to the transaction [though advised by lawyers] had any warning of the disadvantages of failing to put the whole agreement in the deed document. As a result, this case was one in which it was reasonable to expect that the collateral agreement alleged "might naturally be made as a separate agreement." In a footnote, the court said that even where it would be natural for the collateral clause to be included, extrinsic evidence should be permitted to show that the unnatural actually happened. The notion that integration could be determined solely from the writing was outmoded.

Despite the fact that an option agreement is generally presumed to be assignable, unless otherwise indicated, the existence of a written memorandum does not necessarily preclude parol evidence to rebut a term that the law would otherwise presume as part of the process of interpretation. Regardless of this presumption, where there is not a controlling statute, the parties are free to provide that a contract or duty is nontransferable. And even where there is no explicit agreement, either written or oral, that contractual duties shall be personal, courts will effectuate presumed intent to that effect if the circumstances indicate that performance by the substituted person would be different from the performance contracted for.

The court held that the trial court erred in excluding the Sines' evidence regarding the non-assignability of the option, which was intended to keep the property in the Masterson family. The trial court's judgment was reversed.

Justice Burke, in dissent, identified four shortcomings of the majority opinion: (1) it undermined the parol evidence rule based on an 1872 statute; (2) it rendered suspect instruments of conveyance that are absolute on their face; (3) it materially decreased the reliance that may be placed on written instruments affecting the title to real estate; and (4) it unintentionally opened the door to a new technique for defrauding creditors.

The trial court properly admitted parol evidence to explain the parties' intended meaning of "same consideration" and "depreciation value" in the deed because the meaning of those phrases was not clear. But since there was nothing unclear about the granting language of the option, the trial court properly excluded parol evidence on that matter. California statutes clearly state that an option is freely assignable; its assignability can only be restricted if written language indicates such an intent. Therefore, to seek to restrict the grant by parol evidence is to contradict the written document in violation of the parol evidence rule, especially where that evidence is the proffered testimony of the bankrupt optionee himself. While the trial court properly admitted extrinsic evidence to explain and apply the option pricing formula, there was nothing ambiguous about the option grant itself.

The option was, by ordinary interpretation, assignable and therefore to admit evidence of non-assignability was to contradict the writing.

The majority stated the rule that contradicting or varying terms of a writing by parol evidence is not permissible but then inexplicably proceeded to subvert it. The contract of sale in question was carried out through a title company upon written escrow instructions executed by the parties after various preliminary negotiations. In neither the escrow instructions nor the deed was there any language suggesting that the option was agreed or intended by the parties to be personal to the grantors. On three separate occasions, the trial judge correctly sustained objections to the presentation of testimony as to non-assignability by Mr. Masterson. But the majority opinion held that the testimony should have been allowed, thereby permitting the Sines to limit and contradict the plain terms of the written option in violation of the parol evidence rule.

He challenged the majority view that the earlier case law was inconsistent, just as he challenged the view that the writing could not and should not be the sole source of evidence of intent to integrate.

The statutes of California clearly manifested a policy in favor of free transferability of all types of property, including contract rights. Therefore, the right of an optionee to transfer his option to purchase property is one of the basic rules accompanying the option, unless it is limited under the language of the option itself. To permit the use of parol evidence to limit an option is to authorize the option grantor to attempt to limit or reclaim rights with which he has already parted. In nearly all cases that the majority cited to support its application of the parol evidence rule, the writing in question was obviously incomplete on its face, which was not the case in this instance. Though the majority cited Prof. Corbin's contracts treatise, they were unable to muster any California case law supporting the proposition that even under the rule that the writing alone is to be consulted, it was found necessary to examine the alleged collateral agreement before concluding that proof of it was precluded by the writing alone.

The majority, in holding that parol evidence "should only be excluded when the fact finder is likely to be misled" and that "the rule must therefore be based on the credibility of the evidence," promulgated a new test for parol evidence that was previously unknown, creating an approach that opened the door to uncertainty and confusion. As the majority attempted to justify use of its new rule by stating the difficulty in modifying the formalized structure of the deed, the dissent rejected such an argument, stating that the addition of a mere "this option is not assignable" phrase would have sufficed; such clauses are frequently included in deeds without problem. The dissent also demonstrated that the majority's claim of naïveté on the part of the parties was unsupported, as the terms of the transfer were composed by attorneys for the parties.

The dissent next disagreed with the majority's "fallacious assertion" that the right to transfer or assign an option, without provisions forbidding such transfer, is merely a disputable presumption. In the current case, there was no lack of terms to make the instrument whole and complete, and there was therefore no reason to restrict the right of free transferability of property and options, one of the most fundamental tenets of substantive law.

With respect to bankruptcy proceedings in general, this decision made it much easier for a bankrupt to defeat his creditors, as he could merely produce parol testimony that any options that he held were subject to an oral "collateral agreement" with another party, and thus the property was nontransferable. The existence of this case demonstrated that the bankruptcy trustee perceived significant value in this option, but the trustee's efforts had been trumped by an asserted oral collateral agreement.

In conclusion, he raised questions about the bankrupt's wife's right to exercise the option—an issue not covered in the majority opinion.

Justice Burke would have held that the trial court acted correctly in rejecting the admission of the parol evidence, and would have affirmed the judgment.

INTERESTING DISCUSSION ISSUES

1. *The dramatic difference between Mitchill and Masterson.* The key to the *Mitchill* decision was the court's use of the four corners approach, looking solely to the language of the writing in order to determine intention to integrate. The key to the *Masterson* decision was the admission and use of extrinsic evidence, including the personal testimony of Masterson, one of the option grantors. Does this approach increase the risk of a judge being influenced by both "slippery" and self-serving testimony of one of the parties? Opening the door to permit extrinsic evidence of mutual integration intent is not without risk, but the key decision remains with judge and not jury. As Justice Traynor put it, extrinsic evidence should be excluded "only when the fact finder is likely to misled."

2. *The significance of a "merger" clause.* The deed in question did not contain a merger clause and thus Justice Traynor's comment that such a clause may help resolve the issue of intent to integrate was obiter dicta.

3. *The "collateral agreement" test.* Justice Traynor started with looking at the collateral agreement itself and the surrounding circumstances, but concluded that extrinsic evidence should only be excluded when the fact finder would be misled.

4. *Was there a good explanation for omitting the collateral agreement from the deed?* While providing a good explanation for the failure to include the collateral agreement in the writing may not be described as part of the standard, it can be important. See the *Bussard* case discussed in "Interesting Discussion Issues" paragraph 2 following the *Mitchill* case. Father Bussard explained that the negotiations were between men of the cloth, and that his employment for life was instinct in the negotiations.

NOTES AND QUESTIONS

1. *Corbin embraced and Williston rejected?* Does the Restatement (Second) of Contracts adopt Corbin's approach or continue the Willistonian approach of the Restatement (First) Contracts? It follows Corbin's approach. See, Restatement (Second) of Contracts § 214(b) (agreements and negotiations prior to or contemporaneous with the adoption of a writing are admissible in evidence to establish that an integrated writing is partially or totally integrated). Compare, Restatement (Second) of Contracts § 214(b) with Restatement (First) of Contracts § 230 quoted in the text before the *Mitchill* case. Do they embrace the same evidence or has the evidence to be considered broadened to embrace Corbin's view? The Restatement (First) restricted analysis of intention to integrate to the meaning that would be attached to the integration by a "reasonably intelligent person acquainted with all operative usages and knowing all the circumstances prior to and contemporaneous with the making of the integration, other than oral statements by the parties of what they intended it to mean." In other words, the test was the four corners of the writing together with evidence of contemporaneous circumstances. By allowing admission of "agreements and negotiations prior to or contemporaneous with the adoption of the writing" to establish intention to integrate, completely or partially, the Restatement (Second) adopted Corbin's view.

2. *Whose discharging integration intent controls?* Restatement (First) of Contracts § 230 evaluated the evidence to determine the intent of a "reasonably intelligent person" but not the objective intent of the parties themselves. Thus, if the parties shared a common intent not to discharge, even though a reasonably intelligent person might have intended otherwise, the *Mitchill* court could actually reach a result not intended by either party. Restatement (Second) of Contracts § 201(1) provides that where the parties have the same meaning, that meaning controls. Does this make more sense to you? It does. The fear of listening to and then trusting "slippery" extrinsic evidence can be minimized by the court requiring a clear showing before allowing a jury to hear the evidence. The reach of Justice Traynor's standard that "Evidence of oral collateral agreements should be excluded only when

the fact finder is likely to be misled" preserves the role of the judge as gatekeeper. Should the parties to a contract be permitted to share a common but unreasonable intent? Yes, as Justice Traynor observed in Footnote 1. He also noted that "judges are not likely to be misled by their sympathies."

3. *Consistency test.* The trustee in *Masterson* argued that an option is transferable under California law unless the option itself states otherwise. Since the option was silent on its transfer to "someone outside the family circle," exactly how did the majority dismiss this argument? The majority said that what was involved was only a rebuttable presumption of intent and that admitting the extrinsic evidence to show a different intent was not contradicting the writing. What was the dissent's response? That the presumption gave meaning to the words used in the deed and that therefore the extrinsic evidence was contradicting the writing. Which view do you find most compelling? The majority view because first, the presumption serves merely as a guide to presumed intent absent other evidence, and the extrinsic evidence supplies such other evidence. Are there two rules for inconsistency analysis—one for inconsistency with the express terms of the writing only or also with terms implied by law? In the majority's view, no. If the term involved is one merely of a presumption as to intent, displacing the presumption is not contradiction, but rather interpretation. If the term implied by law was a statutory mandate, the result would be different, the court said. Was this an issue with the majority in *Mitchill v. Lath* when the majority noted that the promise to remove the icehouse "implied that the defendants are not to do anything unexpected in the writing?" In a sense, yes. While this view of the *Mitchill* court was not necessarily part of the holding, but rather addressed the possible question of whether the icehouse promise might contradict the writing, its view was an application of the old Latin tag "expressio unius est exclusio alterius"—loosely translated, a recital of express terms suggests that, by reason of the recital, additional terms were impliedly negated. As a canon of interpretation, this tag does not have great strength. Are the two implications referred to in these two cases the same kind of implied term? No. In *Mitchill*, the implication addressed the intention to permit or not permit additional terms based essentially on the "four corners" test. In *Masterson*, the issue was more a concern as to interpretation of the language of the option. If not, what is the difference? In fact, the two situations both address the challenge to find the true intent of the parties as to integration. But *Masterson* rejects the "four corners" approach stating it to be "outmoded," and overruling by implication a series of earlier decisions. The gist of *Masterson* is that the judge should consider and assess all of the available extrinsic evidence before ruling on whether any part of that evidence should go to the trier of fact, assuming that such trier will be a jury and not the judge herself.

4. *UCC parol evidence rule.* The UCC version of the collateral agreement rule is then reflected in UCC § 2-202(b), *comment 3:* "If the additional terms are such that, if agreed upon, they would certainly have been included in the document in the view of the court, then evidence of their alleged making must be kept from the trier of fact." Do you agree with the majority that this collateral agreement rule would exclude less evidence? Yes. The important new phrase in the UCC section and in the comment is "would *certainly* have been included." As the note points out, "trade usage" is an implied-in-law term and is not subject to the parol evidence rule—a change from the earlier Uniform Sales Act.

5. *UCC consistency rule.* See text.

6. *The parol evidence rule and standardized contracts.* The Restatement (Second) follows Llewellyn's lead in providing that terms in standardized contracts are enforceable unless bizarre or unusual from the point of the consumer. What about the effect of a merger clause declaring the writing to be complete? Such a clause, consistent with Llewellyn's thinking, should be enforceable unless to do so would produce a bizarre or unusual result.

Optional Problem 4-3

Libby agreed to purchase Thompson's farm for $150,000 but only if Thompson agreed to remove an unsightly icehouse located across the road on other land Thompson owned. Thompson agreed. The farm purchase agreement was written and signed by both parties and included all the terms related to the purchase of the farm but failed to mention Thompson's promise to remove the icehouse. Libby purchases the farm and later requests Thompson to remove the icehouse but he refuses. Libby sues to enforce the promise but when he attempts to introduce evidence of Thompson's oral promise, Thompson's attorney objects on the basis of the parol evidence rule but Thompson admits making the oral promise.

What is the outcome of case on the basis of the collateral agreement as stated in Restatement (Second) Contracts?

Answer:

The judge should consider the collateral agreement as alleged, the surrounding circumstances, and all other extrinsic evidence, before ruling on whether the agreement was wholly integrated. The judge would then make a decision as to the credibility and weight of the extrinsic evidence before ruling as a matter of law on the issue of intention to integrate.

The next case, dealing with the law of extrinsic evidence under the Convention on the International Sale of Goods, provides an interesting contrast with both *Mitchell* and *Masterson*, holding that the parol evidence rule does not apply to contracts falling under the CISG. Students should think about why the rule is inapplicable in such cases and whether the outcome under the CISG is to be preferred to that under our common law and the UCC.

MCC-Marble Ceramic Center, Inc. v. Ceramica Nuova D'Agostino, S.P.A.
CASE BRIEF

This is a 1999 decision of the United States Court of Appeals, 11th Circuit. Marble Ceramic Center (CCC) was a Florida corporation engaged in retail sales of ceramic tiles; Ceramica Nuova D'Agostino (CND) was an Italian corporation engaged in the manufacture of ceramic tiles. Representatives of the companies met in 1990 at a trade fair in Italy, where MCC negotiated an agreement to purchase tiles from CND based on samples at the fair. Though MCC's president spoke no Italian, he communicated with CND's commercial director through a translator who worked for CND. The parties came to an oral agreement as to the terms of price, quality, quantity, delivery, and payment, which they memorialized and signed on one of CND's pre-printed order forms. According to MCC, the parties also entered into a requirements contract in February 1991, subject to which CND agreed to supply MCC with tile at certain discounts, provided that MCC bought sufficient quantities of tile.

MCC brought suit against CND, claiming a breach of the 1991 requirements contract because CND failed to satisfy orders in April, May, and August of 1991. As one of its defenses, CND claimed that it was under no obligation to fulfill MCC's order because MCC had defaulted on payment for previous shipments. In support of this position, CND relied on the pre-printed terms on the order forms that MCC had signed. One of the terms, which were written in Italian, provided that default or delay of payment provided CND the right to suspend or cancel other pending contracts. CND also counterclaimed for MCC's nonpayment of previous orders. MCC responded that the tile it had received was of lower quality than had been agreed upon, and was therefore entitled, under the United Nations Convention on Contracts for the International Sale of Goods (CISG), to reduce payment in proportion to the defects. MCC sought to rely on multiple affidavits that tended to prove an oral agreement that the parties intended not to be bound by the pre-printed terms of the contract.

These affidavits included affidavits from CND agents indicating that CND was aware of this intent not to be bound by the pre-printed terms. But the magistrate judge held that the affidavits did not create an issue of material fact, and recommended that the district court grant summary judgment for CND, which it did. MCC appealed.

The primary issue in this case was whether a United States federal court must consider parol evidence in a contract dispute governed by the CISG. The court held that the CISG governed because both parties to the suit had their place of business in a country that is a signatory of the Convention. Article 8 of the CISG governs the interpretation of international sale of goods contracts and formed the basis for MCC's appeal. Article 8(1) of the CISG instructs courts to interpret the statements and other conduct of a party according to his intent as long as the other party knew or could not have been unaware of that intent—the plain language of the Convention thus requires an inquiry into a party's subjective intent so long as the other party to the contract was aware of that intent.

In this case, the affidavits stated that the oral agreement established the terms of quantity, quality, a description of goods, delivery, price, and payment. The affidavits also stated that the parties memorialized the agreement on a standard CND order form, but that all three affiants contended that the parties subjectively intended not to be bound by the terms on the reverse of that form, despite a term below the signature line that specifically incorporated those terms. Article 8(1) of the CISG requires a court to consider this evidence of the parties' subjective intent. The fact that the affiants acknowledged that MCC did not intend to agree to the pre-printed terms brought the case squarely within Article 8(1) of the CISG.

Given that the trial court should have examined the affidavits as evidence of the oral agreement, the question for the court was whether the parol evidence rule, which bars evidence of an earlier oral contract that contradicts or varies the terms of a subsequent or contemporaneous written contract, plays any role in cases involving the CISG. While the CISG contains no express statement on the role of parol evidence, it is clear that the drafters of the CISG were comfortable with the concept of permitting parties to rely on oral contracts because they eschewed any statutes of fraud provision and expressly provided for the enforcement of oral contracts. And Article 8(3) of the CISG expressly directs courts to give due consideration to all relevant circumstances of the case, including the negotiations to determine the parties' intent—a clear instruction to admit and consider parol evidence regarding the negotiations to the extent that they reveal the parties' subjective intent.

In looking for U.S. case law, the court found surprisingly little regarding the CISG. Only two such cases touched on the CISG's effect on parol evidence, one suggesting that the parol evidence rule is inapplicable in light of Article 8, and the other case unconvincingly finding that the parol evidence rule should apply, despite the fact that the court could identify no CISG provisions supporting its argument. While one court and a lone academic have attempted to harmonize the CISG and the parol evidence rule, the court held that these efforts were unpersuasive because of the fact that a large number of states who signed the CISG have rejected the rule in their domestic jurisdictions. And since the Convention was intended to provide parties with greater certainty as to applicable principles of contract law, the courts should not upset the CISG regime in order to insert familiar principles of domestic law. While U.S. courts will apply local rules of evidence, the parole evidence rule is one of substantive law and not evidence, and thus the law of Article 8(1) of the CISG must be applied.

The opinion implied a preference for U.S. law and the parol evidence rule as tending to support values of good faith and uniformity (reliance of written contracts). The court pointed out, however, that its interpretation did not suggest that parties under the CISG cannot rely on written contracts; rather, the interpretation only applies to instances where both parties acknowledge a subjective intent not to be bound by the pre-printed terms of a contract form. (The court should have referred to the "knew or could not have been unaware" standard of the CISG.) And the parties can eliminate even these possibilities by simply adding a merger clause to their agreement. (This too, may be an overstatement by the court).

While the affidavits were relatively conclusory and unsupported by facts that would objectively establish MCC's intent not to be bound by the pre-printed terms, Article 8(1) nonetheless required the court to consider the evidence and whether the other party was aware of it. The CISG precluded summary judgment because MCC had raised an issue of material fact concerning the parties' subjective intent to be bound by the form's pre-printed terms. The CISG also precluded the application of the parol evidence rule, which would otherwise bar the consideration of evidence concerning a prior or contemporaneously negotiated oral agreement.

INTERESTING DISCUSSION ISSUES

1. *Two basic points are made by this case.* The first is the CISG rejection of the parol evidence rule. The second is the desirability of U.S. courts continuing to apply the parol evidence rule, even as revised by Justice Traynor and the Restatement (Second). The court is impliedly critical of the CISG position, suggesting a preference for the U.S. parol evidence rule based on concepts of good faith and the preservation of the reliability of a writing. See the court's footnote 10, "We agree that such an approach 'would render terms of written contracts virtually meaningless and severely diminish the reliability of commercial contracts.'" The case poses the challenge—does the parole

evidence rule continue to serve a useful purpose? See the discussion of this issue in Note 2 below.

2. *The importance of mutual and not unilateral uncommunicated subjective intent under the CISG.* Article 8(2) (see the court's footnote 6) provides that where the "knew or could not have been unaware" standard is not applicable on the facts, an objectively reasonable standard is to be applied to statements and conduct of a party. But Article 8(3) preserves a role in the process of determination of intent for the relevant circumstances including negotiations, any practices established by the parties, usages (trade?) and any subsequent conduct of the parties.

3. *Signing a contract in a foreign language.* The court says, "Signer beware!" The duty to read and understand doctrine is alive and well. Even where a contract is translated into two or more languages, a problem can still arise as a result of translation problems and inconsistencies between the different versions.

4. *The CISG rule granting the buyer the right to reduce the price in the event of delivery of nonconforming goods.* No such remedy is available under the UCC. The student should note the Article 50 CISG requirement (see the court's footnotes 4 and 21), attached to the exercise of that remedy, that the buyer notify the seller of the specific defect in the goods within a reasonable time of delivery. This requirement is comparable to that of the duty of the buyer under the UCC to notify the seller of specific reasons for refusal to accept delivery.

NOTES AND QUESTIONS

1. *CISG parol evidence rule.* See text.

2. *Abolish the parol evidence rule.* What arguments can you make for eliminating the parol evidence rule in common law? Arguably, it enforces an "objectively" determined intention to integrate while refusing to consider a mutual subjective intent to the contrary. The court should be able to consider all extrinsic evidence before ruling on the issue of intent to integrate. The judge will not be swayed by empathy for the plaintiff, but continues to play an effective watchdog role through the required ruling on integration as a matter of law. The Restatement (Second) provides a way for a court to avoid the parol evidence rule trap, but a significant number of courts continue to apply the "four corners" rule. Note the court's quotation from *Honnold* indicating a "growing body of opinion" criticizing the rule. The court in the MCC case implied a preference for the parol evidence rule based on respect for good faith and certainty for the written contract. Does a

court have the power to simply abolish the rule? In those states where the rule is enforced on the basis of prior case law, the state's supreme court would have the power to overrule prior decisions, as Justice Traynor impliedly did in *Masterson*. A few states codified some of the basic contract law rules. In such a state a court might not have the power to overrule prior decisions applying the statute—see Justice Burke's argument to that effect in *Masterson*, and Justice Traynor's sidestep of that problem. Does a court have the power to abolish the UCC version of the parol evidence rule? No, since the UCC is statute law and not case law. But judges will still have room to interpret, especially given the UCC word "certainly." Do you think the parol evidence rule should be retained under common law? Yes. Despite the fact that the judge can consider all extrinsic evidence before ruling on intention to integrate, the rule is still given effect if the judge decides that the writing was intended to be wholly integrated. The rule also applies with respect to extrinsic evidence seeking to contradict the writing. It is noteworthy that the extrinsic evidence in *MCC* directly contradicted the writing.

3. *Add back parol evidence rule?* Assuming that *MCC-Marble* remains the final word and the CISG does not state a parol evidence rule, would that fact prevent the parties from adding a clause to their contract to adopt some form of a parol evidence rule? First, the parties by express language can always exclude the applicability of the convention. Second, according to the court in this case, the parties can finesse the rule by the inclusion of a "merger" clause. The court's opinion implies that there was no "merger" clause included in the writing in this case. Even if such a clause were included, the court's statement is still too strong. The extrinsic evidence might establish the requisite knew or should have known evidence, the "merger" clause notwithstanding. After all, the extrinsic evidence in the case directly contradicted the writing but was found admissible just the same.

Optional Problem 4-4

Libby agreed to purchase Thompson's farm for $150,000 but only if Thompson agreed to remove an unsightly icehouse located across the road on other land Thompson owned. Thompson agreed. The farm purchase agreement was written and signed by both parties and included all the terms related to the purchase of the farm but failed to mention Thompson's promise to remove the icehouse. Libby purchases the farm and later requests Thompson to remove the icehouse but he refuses. Libby sues to enforce the promise but when he attempts to introduce evidence of Thompson's oral promise, Thompson's attorney objects on the basis of the parol evidence rule but Thompson admits making the oral promise.

What is the outcome of case on the basis of the collateral agreement as stated in the CISG?

Answer:

Since Thompson admits making the collateral agreement, this proves mutual subjective intent which is then controlling even although it may contradict the writing.

"Merger" clauses are frequently used in lawyer drafted and negotiated agreements as well as in standardized form contracts. The court in MCC suggested, we think erroneously, that the use of such a clause may be conclusive evidence of intention to integrate. It certainly may be powerful evidence of such intent and, if dickered, conclusive. But the student should note the caveat included in Comment e to Restatement (Second) of Contracts § 216: "But such a clause does not control the question whether the writing was assented to as an integrated agreement, the scope of the writing if completely integrated, or the interpretation of the written terms." The effect given to "merger" clauses can vary significantly from state to state.

2. The Effect of a Merger or Integration Clause

Lee v. Joseph E. Seagram & Sons, Inc.
CASE BRIEF

This is a 1977 decision of the United States Court of Appeals, 2nd Circuit. Harold Lee (deceased at the time of the appeal) and his two sons owned a 50% interest in Capitol City Liquor Company, Inc. (Capitol City). Harold's brother, Henry Lee, and Henry's son, Arthur, owned the other 50%. Capitol City carried a number of products of distiller Joseph E. Seagram & Sons, Inc. (Seagram) and a large portion of its sales were generated by Seagram products. Harold Lee had worked for Seagram in various capacities for thirty-six years before acquiring his interest in Capitol City. During this time with Seagram, Harold "enjoyed the friendship and confidence of the principals of Seagram." In 1958, Harold bought Capitol City from Seagram's holdings in order to introduce his sons to the liquor distribution business, and to satisfy's Seagram's desire to have a friendly Seagram distributor in Washington, D.C.

In May 1970, the Lees wanted to sell their respective interests in Capitol City, so Harold contacted Jack Yogman, a senior Seagram executive, whom Harold had known for many years. Harold offered to sell Capitol City to Seagram, on the condition that Seagram would agree to relocate Harold and his sons to a new distributorship of their own in another city. After negotiations with another Seagram officer, the Lees executed a sale of their assets to a new distributor. The promise to relocate Harold and his sons was not included in this agreement, or in any other agreement.

Fifteen months later, the Lees sued Seagram for breach of the oral agreement to relocate Harold and his sons to another distributorship. The Lees alleged that Seagram had opportunities to obtain another distributorship for them, but had refused to do so. The Lees claimed that they had fulfilled their obligations under the contract by agreeing to sell Capitol City to Seagram, but that Seagram had failed to perform its obligations. The trial court permitted the jury to find, and the jury did find, "an oral agreement with defendant which provided that if they agreed to sell their interest in Capitol City, defendant in return, within a reasonable time, would provide the plaintiffs a Seagram distributorship whose price would require roughly an amount equal to the capital obtained by the plaintiffs for the sale of their interest in Capitol City, and which distributorship would be in a location acceptable to the plaintiffs." Seagram appealed, arguing that, as a matter of law, (1) plaintiffs' proof of the alleged oral agreement was barred by the parol evidence rule; and (2) the oral agreement was too vague and indefinite to be enforceable.

The Court of Appeals, applying New York law, agreed with the trial court's ruling that the parol evidence rule did not bar proof of the oral agreement. While the trial court rejected Seagram's pre-trial summary judgment motion because the ambiguity of the sales agreement required evidence to determine if the agreement was completely integrated, Seagram failed to introduce any evidence of integration intent at trial. Rather, Seagram argued that the oral agreement was either an inducing cause for the sale, or was part of the consideration for the sale (see *Mitchill v. Lath*); in either case, it should have been included in the written contract. But the Lees argued that the oral agreement was a collateral agreement, and since it was not contradictory to the terms of the sales agreement, proof of it was not barred by the parol evidence rule.

Since the case was appealed after a jury verdict, the Court of Appeals stated that it must assume that there actually was an oral contract as the jury had found. In a general sense, the court stated the issue as "whether, in the context of the particular setting, the oral agreement was one which the parties would ordinarily be expected to embody in the writing." More specifically, the court narrowed the issue to "whether the oral promise to the plaintiffs, as individuals, would be an expectable term of the contract for the sale of assets by a corporation in which plaintiffs have only a 50% interest, considering as well the history of their relationship to Seagram."

The court of appeals found several reasons why the oral agreement to provide Harold and his sons with a distributorship would not be expected to be included in the sales agreement. First, the sale of

Capitol City involved owners other than Harold and his sons; the transaction was primarily a sale of corporate assets. Collateral agreements that survive the closing of a corporate deal (e.g., consulting agreements, shareholder employment agreements) are often set forth in separate documents. Since all parties to the Capitol City sale were not going to be involved with the new distributorship agreement, it is reasonable that the agreement would have been set forth outside the sales agreement.

Second, Harold Lee and Yogman had a long, close relationship of confidence. As such, it would not be surprising that Harold would have considered a handshake sufficient to cement the deal. Also, since the negotiations concerning the sales agreement were not conducted by Yogman, it is very possible that the two deals were not integrated in the mind of the Seagram negotiator.

Third, the sales agreement did not contain an integration clause or any terms that contradicted the separate distributorship agreement. The written sales agreement dealt only with compensation for corporate assets; thus, the oral agreement did not vary the consideration in the sales agreement.

The second issue on which Seagram disputed the jury verdict was that the oral agreement was too vague and indefinite to be enforceable. Seagram argued that the failure to specify price, profitability, or sales volume of the distributorship under the oral agreement rendered the agreement unenforceably vague. Seagram also argued that since there were no limits on the Lees' discretion in rejecting a distributorship, the agreement was illusory (since the Lees undertook no bargained for burden in return for the promise).

The agreement as recognized by the jury discredited each of Seagram's arguments regarding the oral agreement. With respect to the essential terms, the jury gave credit to evidence that established, with reasonable specificity, the purchase price, profitability, and sales volume of the oral agreement distributorship. The evidence available to the jury included testimony from the Lees, industry valuation standards, and the Capitol City transaction itself. The court held that any remaining gap in the terms of the agreement could, if necessary, be filled by implication by the court. Such interpretation by the court would be more equitable than the court's refusal to enforce an agreement of the parties.

With regard to the discretion afforded the Lees, the court held that the discretion was not a fatal defect, as it was not "unbridled." In all cases, New York courts would impose an obligation of good faith on the exercise of discretion. Moreover, there was extrinsic evidence of what would constitute an "acceptable distributorship," the offering of which would discharge Seagram's duty. Seagram's tender of reasonable performance under the agreement would discharge its obligations regardless of whether the Lees chose to accept the distributorship. The court held that, "[s]ince the obligations of the parties under the contract therefore were ascertainable, it was not void for indefiniteness."

INTERESTING DISCUSSION ISSUES

1. *The search for a reasonable explanation of the omission.* This case highlights the importance of the explanation provided for omission of the oral agreement or term from the writing when searching for an indication that the hypothetical reasonable person would or would not expect the oral agreement to be included in the writing. The court hypothesizes several such explanations: the lack of identity of the parties to the two transactions, some of whom were not even parties to the sale and purchase, the close relationship of confidence between Lee and the senior Seagram officer, and the use of other Seagram officers to negotiate the sale and purchase. The court, however, fails to consider another possible explanation. Lee, who owned only 50% of the company, was negotiating for the sale of both halves while seeking a spiff out of the sale beneficial only to him (and his sons) and not to the owners of the other half—that could be a conflict of interest. He might well have been embarrassed if the other Lee and owners of the other half knew that he was negotiating, using the sale of both his and their business, in order to secure a special benefit for himself (and his sons) not extended to the owners of the other half! But, of course, this is speculation.

2. *Using an "objective" standard.* The statement of the court, "We assume that the District Court determined intention by objective standards," is truly puzzling.

3. *The contradiction standard.* The *Mitchill* court, finding but a single consideration for both the sale and purchase and the oral promise, found potential contradiction by the oral promise of the total price recited in the agreement. The same argument could be made in this case since, once again, there was a single consideration tying both the sale and the oral promise together. The court, obviously, even though applying New York law, was not persuaded by any such argument.

4. *The vagueness issue.* Did the court make a contract for the parties or simply interpret the understanding they had reached? This case is an interesting example of a court finding a basic intent to carry out the oral agreement and then fleshing out the actual or implied terms of that agreement by implication in fact and reference to industry practices regarding valuation of such businesses. Students can be reminded that the parol evidence rule has no application to the function of interpreting the agreement made by the parties.

NOTES AND QUESTIONS

1. *Promissory estoppel to avoid parol evidence rule.* See text.

2. *Strategic error or wise counsel.* Seagram's chose to argue the law and not the facts by asserting that regardless of the actual intent of the parties the parol evidence rule barred proof of the parol agreement. They failed to offer any evidence of intention to integrate at the trial. Was this folly or wise? Given the ruling of the trial court, their decision was unwise unless ... (see next question). Can you offer a reason why Seagram's lawyers might have adopted such a position? Yes. Their witness(es) might have confirmed the existence of the oral agreement.

3. *Absence of merger clause.* The *Lee* case did not involve a merger or integration clause. What inference did the court draw from the failure to include such a customary clause? It did not hold that the absence of a such a clause was conclusive evidence of no intention to integrate. Rather, it held that it did not have to deal with the evidentiary weight that the presence of such a clause might have introduced. It proceeded to consider the reasonableness of the omission of the oral agreement from the writing and the possible explanations of such omission. Have such clauses become so customary that an omission of the clause creates a presumption the writing is not integrated? No. What effect would this court have accorded the writing if a merger clause had been included? We will never know, but it is possible/probable that this court would not have treated the inclusion of such a clause as conclusive. See the authorities cited in the text.

4. *Subject matter relationship.* How does the court view the subject matter relationship between the parol agreement and the written agreement? The court makes a point of the fact that the oral agreement included parties who were not parties to the written sale agreement—this was noted as one of the explanations for why the oral agreement might have been omitted from the writing. Was the case decided under the first or second restatement? The opinion cited to the Restatement (First) but also cited Corbin extensively. Since the date of the decision was 1977 it is likely that drafts of the Restatement (Second) were in circulation. While the court found New York law applicable and cited the *Mitchill* decision, it cited other New York authority to soften the hard line of that case.

Optional Problem 4-5

Libby agreed to purchase Thompson's farm for $150,000 but only if Thompson agreed to remove an unsightly icehouse located across the road on other land Thompson owned. Thompson agreed. The farm purchase agreement was written and signed by both parties and included all the terms related to the purchase of the farm but failed to mention Thompson's promise to remove the icehouse. *The written agreement contains a merger clause that states the writing is the final and complete agreement of the parties.* Libby purchases the farm and later requests Thompson to remove the icehouse but he refuses. Libby sues to enforce the promise but when he attempts to introduce evidence of Thompson's oral promise, Thompson's attorney objects on the basis of the parol evidence rule but Thompson admits making the oral promise.

What is the outcome of case on the basis of the collateral agreement as stated in the Restatement (Second) of Contracts?

Answer:

§ 216(2) provides that an agreement is not completely integrated if the writing omits a consistent additional term that is either agreed to for a separate consideration or such a term as, in the circumstances, might naturally be omitted from the writing. We still wonder what complete integration has to do with the issue if there is a separate consideration—presumably establishing two separate and distinct agreements, the first found to be wholly integrated but the second a separate free standing agreement.

3. Parol Evidence Rule & Valid Contract Requirement

Danann Realty Corp. v. Harris
CASE BRIEF

This is a 1919 decision of the New York Court of Appeals. Plaintiff Harris claimed that defendant Danann Realty Corp. (Danann) induced him to enter into a contract of sale of a lease of a building owned by Danann because of false oral representations made to Harris regarding the expenses of the building and the profits to be derived from such an investment. The trial court dismissed the complaint, but the Appellate Division reversed the dismissal and granted leave to appeal, certifying the question of whether the complaint contained facts sufficient to constitute a cause of action.

Judge Burke wrote for a majority of the court, who found that Harris did not state a cause of action for failure to establish reliance on the alleged misrepresentations. In considering the trial court's dismissal, the court stated that it was required to assume as true Harris's statement that, during negotiations, Danann made material misrepresentations regarding operating costs and profits. But the court also noted that such allegations were in direct conflict with the written contract, which expressly stated that the seller (Dannan) made no representations, and that the buyer (Harris) acknowledged that the seller made no representations regarding the property.

The court stated that the parol evidence rule would not bar the showing of fraud in the inducement or execution despite a general statement that a written instrument embodies the whole agreement, or that no representations have been made. But the court also noted that the specific, plain language of the contract stipulated that Harris did not rely on any representations regarding the matter on which he now claimed fraud. The court held that this specific disclaimer vitiated Harris's claim of reliance on the oral representations. The court held that the specific disclaimer distinguished Harris's situation from previous cases that had not allowed the seller to use a general disclaimer to shield himself from fraud; in none of those cases did the plaintiff deny reliance on representations in the way that Harris did.

There was no allegation that Harris either did not read, or did not understand, the contract in question. In cases "where a person has read and understood the disclaimer of representation clause, he is bound by it." The court held that phrases from other opinions could not undercut the "fundamental precept" that reliance must be justifiable under all circumstances before a complaint can be found to state a cause of action in fraud. In fact, the court held that since Harris represented in the contract that he was not relying on representations by Danann, allowing him to thereafter claim that he had relied on representations would reward Harris's deliberate misrepresentation to Danann. If the language used in this contract were insufficient to estop a party from claiming that he entered a contract under fraudulent representations, no language would be able to accomplish such a purpose.

Judge Fuld's strong dissent stated that, if a party has actually induced another to enter a contract by fraudulent means, there should be no language capable of shielding him from the consequences of such fraud. Judge Fuld quoted a New York case that stated "a party who has perpetrated a fraud upon his neighbor may (not) contract with him, in the very instrument by means of which it was perpetrated, for immunity against those consequences, close his mouth from complaining of it, and bind him never to seek redress" (*Bridger v. Goldsmith*). Judge Fuld also recounted other New York cases to show that the specificity of the disclaimer had not before been recognized as a bar to proving fraud, and that the policy against allowing those inducing fraud to shield themselves should be the policy of primary importance in this case.

Judge Fuld also argued that, rather than being limited, the disclaimer in question was broad and all-encompassing, and was no more specific than a number of other New York cases that the majority cited. Moreover, he stated that if obtaining immunity from charges of fraud could be defeated with certain terms, drafters would simply become more inventive in order to satisfy the demand of fraudulent parties.

The rule that "fraud vitiates every agreement which it touches" has been expressed in the courts of New York, as well as throughout the United States and Great Britain. In none of those cases have the courts differentiated based on the form of the exculpatory clause inserted in the contract. Judge Fuld then followed with a very long string cite to other jurisdictions, an overview of numerous cases in which courts had stated that those acting fraudulently could not be permitted to protect themselves by agreement, and an illustration that the cases used by the majority were readily distinguished because they had been decided on other grounds or because they were narrowly applicable.

Finally, Judge Fuld held that estoppel could not be used in this case. An instrument that is essentially equitable in nature, estoppel should be used to prevent fraud, not to further it. "Surely the perpetrator of a fraud cannot close the lips of his victim and deny him the right to state the facts as they actually exist." Since the questions of whether Danann made certain material misrepresentations, and whether Harris relied upon those misrepresentations, are questions of fact, they are not capable of being determined on the pleadings alone.

INTERESTING DISCUSSION ISSUES

1. *The old Latin tag "omnia fraus corrumpit."* Literally translated, this phrase, borrowed from Roman Law, says that fraud corrupts everything. It can be used to support a rule that a litigant can always introduce extrinsic evidence to establish fraud. But a number of elements are required in order to prove fraud, one of which is that the false representation must have been "material," and another of which is that the defrauded party must have relied upon the false representation. In the case above, the plaintiff sued for fraud but the defendant claimed, based on an express recital in the writing, that the plaintiff had acknowledged in the writing that he was not relying on any representation made by the defendant—thus could not prove the element of "reliance" required to substantiate a claim for fraud. Six members of the New York Court of Appeals agreed that the plaintiff could not successfully allege and prove fraud in light of the "no reliance" provision in the writing. Only one member of the court dissented. Judge Burke, dissenting, argued, in effect, the Roman Law maxim—no skill in drafting should permit the draftsperson to avoid or evade a charge of fraud. A number of courts follow Judge Burke's dissenting view rather than that of the majority. Again, the tension is between the duty to read and understand and the duty of good faith, fairness and honesty.

NOTES AND QUESTIONS

1. *Character of fraud.* Was the alleged fraud characterized as execution fraud or inducement fraud? This was fraud in the

inducement. Should it make any difference? Yes, fraud in the execution indicates no valid contract and therefore any merger or waiver/release clause in the agreement would be inoperative. Do you suspect that if the alleged fraud had been characterized as execution fraud, the merger clause would have any effect regardless of specificity? No. What do you make of the majority opinion statement: "To put it another way, where the complaint states a cause of action for fraud, the parol evidence rule is not a bar to showing the fraud either in the inducement or in the execution despite an omnibus statement that the written instrument embodies the whole agreement, or that no representations have been made." Is the court conflating execution and inducement fraud? Yes. If so, do you think this is appropriate? No, as explained above.

2. *Problematic "specific" merger clause.* The majority opinion takes care to mention that a "general and vague merger clause" would be regarded differently than one which purports to specifically identify the misrepresentation sought to be disclaimed. What is the policy behind such a distinction? The general and vague clause would, in all likelihood, be a "boilerplate" and not a "dickered" clause. Not surprisingly, and based on the strength of the dissent, other states follow the dissenting opinion approach.

3. *Standard form contracts.* Do you think the effect of a merger clause should depend upon specific assent to that particular clause? Both sides of the question can be argued. There can be a difference between a general clause thrown in by the drafter and a clause negotiated by the parties. But showing that a detailed "no representation/no reliance" clause was "dickered" may run afoul of the duty to read and understand as pointed out by the majority. Recall that Karl N. Llewellyn argued that form contracts actually created two contracts: a contract on negotiated terms and a separate contract on boilerplate. The latter terms were significantly more suspect and only presumptively enforceable (from signature and "duty to read") unless the clause (i) impaired the meaning of the negotiated terms or (ii) was unfair. Under this now famous "circle of assent" analysis, should a general merger clause or even a specific merger clause be enforced if part of the boiler-plate terms? The answer should depend upon whether the outcome, as indicated by the clause, is found to be "unfair."

B. INTERPRETING THE TERMS OF THE AGREEMENT

It is important to remind students of the fundamental difference between deciding what terms the parties agreed upon and interpreting or giving meaning to the terms they did agree upon. We now shift from ascertaining the agreed terms to interpreting those terms. The logic behind the parol evidence rule does not extend to this second function and the parol evidence rule thus has no role to play in interpretation.

The meaning of the terms agreed upon can be unclear either because those terms are vague (unclear contextual meaning) or ambiguous (subject to at least two reasonable meanings). Both vagueness and ambiguity can give rise to "misunderstandings" between the parties at the time the contract is made. Vagueness can prevent the creation of an enforceable contract where the court is unable to discern the basic terms required to create an enforceable contract. Ambiguity rarely precludes the creation of a contract but raises the question of which meaning is to prevail.

Interpretation is a matter for the judge unless it depends on the credibility of extrinsic evidence. Evidence of non-ordinary meaning will usually be excluded by the judge unless and until she rules that the wording is ambiguous. Once again, the key issue is the scope and extent of the evidence that a judge should consider before ruling on the presence or absence of ambiguity. Not surprisingly, Williston and the earlier supporters of the "four corners" rule argued that the decision as to ambiguity or not should be made based on the facial content of the writing. Corbin, on the other hand, argued that the judge should not rule on the issue of ambiguity until she had heard and considered all the proffered extrinsic evidence. The UCC adopts this view. Moreover, evidence drawn from course of performance, a course of dealing, or a usage of the trade is admissible under the UCC without proof of ambiguity. Clearly, the doctrine of "objective" interpretation comes to the fore again, and a showing of non-ordinary meaning, to be effective, must indicate that one party's special meaning was either known to, or should have been known by, the other party.

The party asserting special meaning will, logically, have the burden of proof. Many arguments as to meaning may fail because the party with that burden is unable to discharge it. Resolution of interpretation arguments reflects the tension between objective and subjective meaning. Strict adherence to the objective theory leads to the application of the "plain meaning" rule, that is the meaning that the words used would carry to the objectively reasonable person. The plain meaning rule, though widely attacked, is still followed in a number of states. Its use can block evidence that both parties in fact agreed orally to a special meaning, and thus can defeat pursuit of the true intention of the parties.

From the text: "In the cases below determine two things. First, does the court apply the older or newer interpretation version. Second, is there a reasonable and broader objective meaning of the term in question and if so is the plaintiff attempting to prove a narrower subjective meaning?"

Pacific Gas and Electric Company. v. G. W. Thomas Drayage & Rigging Company *CASE BRIEF*

This is a 1968 decision of the California Supreme Court. Defendant G.W. Thomas Drayage & Rigging Co. (Thomas) contracted with Pacific Gas & Electric Co. (PGE) to remove and replace the upper cover of PGE's steam turbine. Thomas agreed to perform the work "at (its) own risk and expense" and to "indemnify" PGE "against all loss, damage, expense and liability resulting from ... injury to property, arising out of or in any way connected with the performance of this contract." Thomas also agreed to carry at least $50,000 insurance to cover liability for injury to property. During the work, the cover fell and caused over $25,000 of damage to the turbine rotor. PGE secured a judgment against Thomas on the theory that the indemnity provision covered injury to all property, regardless of ownership of the property. While the court stated that the language of the agreement was the classic language of a third-party indemnity provision (cover loss to third party property not PGE first party), it nonetheless held that the plain language of the contract required Thomas to indemnify PGE for injuries to PGE's property and refused to admit extrinsic evidence from Thomas that the parties' mutual intent was to cover injury to the property of third parties, and not PGE's property.

Said Justice Traynor, writing for the majority of the California Supreme Court, "The test of admissibility of extrinsic evidence to explain the meaning of a written instrument is not whether it appears to the court to be plain and unambiguous on its face, but whether the offered evidence is relevant to prove a meaning to which the language of the instrument is reasonably susceptible." The court used this test because it stated that a rule limiting the interpretation of a written instrument to its four corners would either deny the relevance of the intent of the parties or presuppose "a degree of verbal precision and stability our language has not attained."

Because the courts must ascertain and give effect to the intent of the parties as expressed in the contract, exclusion of relevant extrinsic evidence to explain the meaning of a written instrument can only be justified if it were feasible to determine the meaning of the parties' words from the instrument alone. Since words do not have "absolute and constant referents," the meaning of a writing can only be found by interpretation in light of all the circumstances that reveal the manner in which the drafter used the words.

The fact that terms appear clear to a judge does not preclude the possibility that the parties chose those terms to express a different meaning. In order to make a rational interpretation of the terms, a preliminary consideration of all credible evidence to prove the parties' intent is required. If, after reviewing extrinsic evidence, the court decides that the language is "fairly susceptible" of one of the interpretations argued for, extrinsic evidence relevant to prove such meanings is admissible.

In this case, the Supreme Court of California determined that the trial court had erroneously refused to consider extrinsic evidence in interpreting the agreement. Since the clause was reasonably susceptible to the meaning argued by Thomas, the evidence offered should have been admitted to prove that meaning (that injuries to PGE property were not covered).

Finally, the court addressed two other issues unrelated to interpretation. First, the court held that, in the event that the jury found that PGE's proffered meaning of the contract was correct, the jury could find that PGE was not entitled to recovery if PGE's own active negligence caused the harm; no four-factor test was required. Second, the court provided instruction on the use of invoices as admissible or hearsay evidence.

INTERESTING DISCUSSION ISSUES

1. *The significance of Justice Traynor's opinion.* Just like the "four corners" approach to applying the parol evidence rule, the old "plain meaning" rule sought to find the intended meaning of the parties within the writing itself and without resort to extrinsic evidence of subjective intent. As he pointed out, the old rule could frustrate the shared intention of the parties to use words with a special meaning attached. The novelty of his opinion was the ruling that the judge should listen to and consider all extrinsic evidence of intent, subjective and objective, before ruling, as a matter of law, that the extrinsic evidence was sufficiently persuasive to permit it to be admitted and shared with the jury, or on the contrary that it was not sufficiently persuasive and should be withheld from the jury. This concept is sometimes described as the power of the judge to declare the presence or absence of ambiguity as a matter of law.

2. *The meaning of the word "indemnify."* This is a technical word with a commonly understood technical meaning—which is to hold someone harmless against liability to a third person (neither the indemnitor nor the indemnitee). Under normal circumstances technical words are to be given their technical meaning. Given this meaning of the word, unless otherwise explained, PGE would not be able to recover for injury to their property. It should be noted, in this regard, that earlier on PGE had sued Thomas for negligence but later dismissed that count of the complaint. What is somewhat troublesome is the requirement of the agreement that Thomas was to "procure not less than $50,000 insurance to cover liability for injury to property." Did this language foresee that Thomas would take out insurance coverage to protect PGE against damage to its property? Justice Traynor found these words to be inconclusive as to the issue of intent involved. He

said in footnote 9, "Defendant's agreement to procure liability insurance to cover damages to plaintiff's property does not indicate whether the insurance was to cover all injuries or only injuries caused by defendant's negligence." Again the use of the word "liability" was troublesome to PGE's argument. If the insurance was to cover property damage not caused by the negligence of Thomas, the coverage would not properly be referred to as "liability" coverage.

3. *A note on drafting conventions.* Lawyers, in drafting a business document, will often include an article towards the beginning of the document dealing with "definitions." If a word is so defined, by custom that word is then given an initial capital letter wherever it occurs in the document. Such "definitions", if carefully prepared, should finesse arguments about meaning, at least with respect to the defined words.

NOTES AND QUESTIONS

1. *Plain meaning rule.* Does Justice Traynor suppose that words have a "plain meaning"? No. What is the intent of his language that "[a] word is a symbol of thought but has no arbitrary and fixed meaning like a symbol of algebra or chemistry"? The meaning of words used depends on the mutual intent of the parties. Where the words used have an ordinary or "plain" meaning, they will be given that meaning by a court unless the court is persuaded by appropriate evidence that either the parties mutually intended that special meaning or one party so intended and the other knew or should have known that the special meaning was intended by the other—true *Lucy v. Zehmer* objectivity. Justice Holmes once remarked that "[a] word is not a crystal, transparent and unchanged; it is the skin of a living thought and may vary greatly in color and content according to the circumstances and the time in which it is used." *Towne v. Eisner,* 245 U.S. 418, 425 (1918). Do you think Traynor and Holmes philosophically agree? No, based only on that extract. The difference between them lay in the kind of evidence each was prepared to consider with respect to proof of intent. David G. Garner, *"A Failed Coup on the Judicial Monarchy,"* 1999 B.Y.U. L. Rev. 887 (1999). Indeed, if a reasonable argument exists that a term requires interpretation, is the term already being interpreted? Yes, by the party making the argument but, like bringing suit, it takes only one to do so — bringing the suit does not assure a successful outcome.

2. *Knew or had reason to know analysis.* Has the Restatement (Second) of Contracts embraced or abandoned the "plain meaning rule"? Yes, in so far as excluding evidence of mutual intent is concerned. No, where one of the parties argues a special meaning which the other did not share and of which the other had no reason to know. What is the focus of language that in cases of misunderstanding

there must be an inquiry into the meaning attached to the words by each party and into what each party knew or had reason to know? Where the words have an ordinary or "plain" meaning, that is the meaning the court will enforce unless either: the mutual intent of the parties to use the special meaning is proven; or it is established that one of the parties intended the special meaning and the other knew or should have known that.

3. *Who decides what.* Is it reasonably clear that the judge decides whether a term is ambiguous and therefore that decision is reviewable *de novo* by an appellate court as in *Pacific Gas and Electric Co.*? Yes. If ambiguity is determined however, and the judge allows the jury to hear the extrinsic evidence, the jury determines the meaning of the ambiguity.

4. *Contrary lower court rulings on plain meaning.* See text.

5. *Old rules die hard.* See text.

6. *Two stages remain.* See text.

The previous case considers the admissibility of parol evidence in the form of prior negotiations. There are other types of interpretive evidence, such as prior usage and custom of the parties, trade usage and performance of the parties after concluding the agreement.

Frigaliment Importing Co. v. B.N.S. International Sales Corp.
CASE BRIEF

This is a 1960 decision of the United States District Court, Southern District of New York. On May 2, 1957, defendant B.N.S. International Sales Corp. (BNS), a New York corporation, contracted to sell 75,000 lbs. of 2½-3 lb. frozen chickens ($0.33/lb.) and 25,000 lbs. of 1½-2 lb. frozen chickens ($0.365/lb.) to Frigaliment Importing Co. (FIC), a Swiss corporation. On the same day, the parties signed a second contract that was nearly identical, except that only 50,000 lbs. of the heavier chickens were required, and the price for the smaller chickens was changed to $0.37/lb. New York law (pre-UCC) controlled both agreements. When the initial shipment arrived in Switzerland, FIC found that the larger chickens were not young chickens suitable for broiling and frying, but stewing chicken ("fowl"). FIC protested but apparently accepted the first shipment and did not stop the second shipment from being sent from New York. On inspecting the second shipment in transit, FIC refused to accept delivery and stopped transportation of this shipment at Rotterdam. FIC subsequently sued BNS for breaching the contract, arguing that the "chicken" under their agreement was to include only young chicken (for boiling or frying), not stewing chicken, while BNS argued that chicken merely means either of those types of the genus.

The court found the word "chicken" ambiguous as a matter of law, and turned to the agreement for aid in interpreting the term. The court immediately rejected FIC's argument that since only young birds come in the smaller size, all the birds must be broilers or fryers; the court held that a contract for goods could be filled with different kinds of that good even though only one kind came in both sizes. Next, the court rejected FIC's claim that, while most of the contract was written in German, it used the English word "chicken" because the parties understood that "chicken" meant young chicken, whereas the German word "Huhn" included both old and young chickens. During negotiations, FIC's agent had specifically answered that "Huhn" would be acceptable; FIC attacked this on the basis that the man who responded to the cable had no authority to interpret it. The court found this unpersuasive because FIC could not "at the same time rely on its cable to Stovicek (its agent) as its dictionary to the meanings of the contract and repudiate the interpretation given the dictionary by the man in whose hands it was put."

The court also rejected FIC's argument that there was a definite trade usage of "chicken" to mean "young chicken." Under then existing New York law, Since BNS was new to the trade in 1957, FIC had to show that either BNS had actual knowledge of such usage, or that the usage was so widely known that actual knowledge by BNS could be inferred. Since no actual knowledge could be shown, FIC had to show that the usage was so ubiquitous that "the presumption is violent that the parties contracted with reference to it, and made it part of their agreement." FIC produced as expert witnesses a New York chicken buyer, an officer of a company that sold chicken, and an employee of a company that produced a daily market report on the poultry trade to state that "chicken" meant young chicken, not stewing chicken. But the court noted that the buyer was careful in his own practice to specify "broiler" or "fowl", and the officer of the chicken-selling company also testified that he asked for clarification when he received orders for "chicken."

BNS produced the owner of a chicken processing plant, a food inspector, and another witness who testified that "chicken" was a word of broad meaning. BNS also showed that Dept. of Agriculture (USDA) specifications included young chickens and stewing chickens under the classification "chickens," and their price reports avoided the use of "chicken" without specification. The court also found persuasive BNS's argument that USDA regulations were referenced in the agreement, and thus should help to interpret the term "chicken."

The court also gave significant weight to BNS's argument that, given then prevailing market prices, it would have been impossible to procure young chickens at the price listed and make any sort of profit on the transaction. FIC was well aware of the prevailing prices in the market, and BNS would have been unlikely to enter into a deal in which it was impossible for them to make money.

Finally, the court referenced FIC's conduct after receiving the first shipment, which included stewing chicken. When FIC objected to the fact that stewing chicken was included in the shipment, BNS refused to recognize their objection and announced that they were about to send the next shipment, and asked whether FIC would accept a shipment of 50,000 lbs. chicken and 25,000 lbs. broilers. BNS argued that if FIC thought that it was entitled to young chickens only, it would not have accepted a shipment where BNS had clearly distinguished between broilers and chickens.

The court ruled that, after reviewing all of the evidence, it was clear that BNS believed that it could comply with the contracts by delivering stewing chicken in the larger size of birds. Since BNS's subjective intent coincided with an objective meaning of "chicken" (under the USDA regulations, trade usage, and market realities), FIC bore the burden of showing that "chicken" was used in the narrower rather than in the broader sense. FIC did not sustain this burden, and thus the broader definition of chicken prevailed.

INTERESTING DISCUSSION ISSUE

1. *"Ordinary" meaning.* It may help students if they understand the importance of Restatement (Second) of Contracts, § 202(3) which states, "Unless a different intention is manifested, (a) where language has a generally prevailing meaning, it is interpreted in accordance with that meaning." This "ordinary" meaning of the words used is frequently the starting point of any argument as to intended meaning. If such an ordinary meaning is proven, then that meaning will prevail unless and until that ordinary meaning is displaced by proof of shared mutual intent to use a special meaning or the "knew or should have known" alternative is in play. In this case BNS established, primarily through the Department of Agriculture regulations, incorporated by reference into the contract, that the word "chicken" could be used to include any one or more of six different types of chicken, including either or both fryers and stewers.

NOTES AND QUESTIONS

1. *The term "chicken."* Judge Friendly states that "the word 'chicken' standing alone is ambiguous." Do you agree? The term "chicken" does not appear ambiguous in the sense of having a double meaning. The author was drawing a distinction between vagueness

and ambiguity. At least one of the authors believes that Judge Friendly was correct in that the word could reference either fryers and broilers or stewers. The word was thus ambiguous as to which of the two categories of bird was intended. The parties intended two different types of chickens and so whose meaning controls? Restatement (Second) of Contracts § 201(2) appears to treat vagueness and ambiguity the same resolving the matter against the party most at fault for the misunderstanding upon proper proof and upon the lack of proof against the plaintiff who carries the burden of proof to win its case. One of the authors questions this statement and believes that Judge Friendly applied the "plain meaning" of the word "chicken" which could include either or both fryers (broilers) and stewers. There was insufficient evidence of mutual subjective intent to establish the word "chicken" as meaning only fryers and broilers. There was also insufficient evidence upon which to conclude that BNS knew nor should have known that FIC used the word "chicken" to include only fryers and broilers.

2. *Mere matter of failed proof.* In the actual case the buyer accepted the first shipment of chickens and sued alleging breach of contract. Given the state of the record, how would the case have been determined if the buyer had rejected the first shipment of chickens and left the seller to sue the buyer for non-acceptance? We think it would not have changed the outcome of the decision—BNS would still have prevailed. FIC's act of acceptance was only the last indicator of FIC intent considered by the court. Do you think the seller would have been more able to prove its meaning than the buyer? We think the seller did prove the plain meaning of the word "chicken" (Department of Agriculture regulations) and thus, there being no sufficient evidence of shared subjective intent, whether the suit was brought by the buyer or the seller the result would have been the same. If not, what does this tell about cases of misunderstanding in equipoise (where both parties offer a rational meaning of a vague term but neither was at fault in not knowing the other party's understanding)? At least one of us does not know the answer to this question since in this author's opinion the misunderstanding was not in equipoise.

3. *Preliminary determination of vagueness or ambiguity.* If New York is a plain meaning rule jurisdiction, the court must first find the term ambiguous before it can admit evidence to interpret. Even in California, the court must first find the term is "reasonably susceptible" to two meanings before it will admit evidence to interpret. Why do you think the plain meaning rule and its threshold "ambiguity" determination from the four corners of the document itself remains the dominant rule in the United States? Presumably, the same considerations are in play as they were with the "four corners" test and the parol evidence rule. The first consideration is the risk of fraudulent

or "slippery" testimony as to alleged shared subjective intent, and the second is the importance of the meaning of the document being certain and uniform to different readers (certainty). Some state courts, in applying the "plain meaning" rule will consider extrinsic evidence before concluding that the meaning is in fact "plain," or is in fact "ambiguous." Do you think the California rule substantially expands the plain meaning rule? The answer depends upon whose version of the "plain meaning" rule is in question. Certainly, Justice Traynor's opinion is inconsistent with the old version of the "plain meaning" rule where that meaning was to be derived from a reading of the four corners of the writing itself and nothing else. The point of Justice Traynor's approach is that the judge should not rule on admission or exclusion of the extrinsic evidence of intended meaning without first listening to and evaluating that evidence.

4. *Types of evidence considered to resolve the interpretation question.* See text.

5. *Interpretation versus construction.* See text.

6. *Law as literature.* See text.

C. SUPPLEMENTING THE AGREEMENT WITH IMPLIED TERMS

In the process of construing a contract a court may supply terms where the parties omitted them. The line between a clause included by construction from one included by interpretation of implied intent is often difficult to see. Restatement (Second) of Contracts § 204, comment d, suggests that a court, in construing a contract, may include a term that "comports with community standards of fairness and policy...." The explanation of the court's willingness to incorporate a term through the process of construction is frequently based on a finding that the parties intended to enter into an effective contract and that intent would be defeated unless the court included the term. The open encouragement found in the UCC for a court, by construction or interpretation, to fill in terms omitted by the parties, has had an impact on the Restatement (Second). Under the Restatement (First) it was somewhat likely that a court would find a contract unenforceable because of a missing but necessary term. Restatement (Second) of Contracts § 204 provides that:

> When the parties to a bargain sufficiently defined to be a contract have not agreed with respect to a term which is essential to a determination of their rights and duties, a term which is reasonable in the circumstances is supplied by the court.

One of the key phrases in this section is "bargain sufficiently defined to be a contract." Perhaps this phrase is intended to relate to the question "did the parties intend a binding commitment"? If so, the court should feel relatively free to fill in gaps. Compare UCC § 2-204(3):

> Even though one or more terms are left open a contract for sale does not fail for indefiniteness if the parties have intended to make a contract and there is a reasonably certain basis for giving an appropriate remedy.

1. Common Law Implications

Wood v. Lucy, Lady Duff-Gordon
CASE BRIEF

This is a 1917 decision (Justice Cardozo) of the New York Court of Appeals. Defendant Lady Duff-Gordon styled herself "a creator of fashions" (a yesteryear Martha Stewart of sorts). Her endorsement on fashion and home products tended to increase the value of the endorsed products in the mind of the public. Plaintiff Wood entered a contract (which he drafted) with Lady Duff-Gordon for the exclusive right, subject to her approval, to place her endorsement on other parties' products, and the exclusive right to sell and license the sale of her products in the United States. In exchange for these exclusive licensing rights for a one-year period, Lady Duff-Gordon was to receive from Mr. Wood half of "all profits and revenues" (notice that "profits" and "revenues" are different numbers) resulting from his efforts.

Mr. Wood sued Lady Duff-Gordon for damages after she endorsed products in the United States without his knowledge, and refused to account to him for the profits of such transactions. In her defense, Lady Duff-Gordon claimed that while the agreement contained recitals and numerous terms and was signed by both parties, Mr. Wood did not promise to do anything (make any reasonable effort to market her products and endorsements), and thus the alleged contract was illusory and thus unenforceable.

Justice Cardozo rejected Lady Duff-Gordon's claim, and held that an enforceable contract had been entered into. While there was no explicit promise that Mr. Wood would employ reasonable efforts to market Lady Duff-Gordon's products and endorsements, Justice Cardozo held that the law had advanced beyond the necessity for primitive formalism, and that such a promise was to be implied from the language of the contract. The fact that Mr. Wood accepted an exclusive agency was essentially an assumption of the duty to employ reasonable efforts to market and sell the products and endorsements. And the fact that Mr. Wood agreed to account monthly for all revenue received and to seek to protect all relevant intellectual property indicated his intent to perform the duties that would result in benefits to Lady Duff-Gordon. Therefore, the assumption of duty and intent to perform were sufficient to show the court that the parties had created a valid contractual agreement and that a promise to use reasonable efforts should be implied.

INTERESTING DISCUSSION ISSUES

1. *Bargain sufficiently defined to be a contract.* This case illustrates the policy view announced in Restatement (Second) of Contracts § 204, set out above. The two keys to Justice Cardozo's decision were first, that the parties had clearly indicated their intent to enter into a binding contract, and second, that for such a contract to be effective, it was necessary to imply a duty on Wood's part to use reasonable efforts to market Lady Duff Gordon's properties. Whether his ruling constituted implication in fact or implication in law resides in the eye of the beholder.

2. *Wood drafted the contract.* Should the fact that Wood drafted the contract make any difference? It did not to Justice Cardozo.

3. *Lady Duff Gordon's personal history.* She and her husband were passengers on the Titanic, but both lived to tell about it. For an account of her experiences in a lifeboat see the account under the name of "Lady Duff Gordon" in the Wikipedia Encyclopedia.

NOTES AND QUESTIONS

1. *The role of interpretation.* See text.

2. *Implied-in-fact and implied-in-law compared.* Did Justice Cardozo imply an obligation to use "reasonable efforts" from the other terms of the agreement or law in general? He found a mutual intention of the parties to enter into an enforceable business deal. Having done so, he concluded that the deal would not be enforceable absent a duty on Wood's part to use reasonable efforts to market Lady Duff Gordon's interests. Such a duty was therefore properly to be implied. Whether he was spinning this duty out of the intention of the parties as reflected in the terms of the contract (implied-in-fact) or as a term to be implied by law is not clear, and this absence of clarity illustrates the fine line between terms that are implied in fact compared with those that are implied in law. What do you think he meant when he stated: "We think, however, that such a promise is fairly to be implied. The law has outgrown its primitive stage of formalism when the precise word was the sovereign talisman, and every slip was fatal."? Like Justice Traynor in the PG&E case earlier, he was saying that language is often imprecise and needs to be understood, interpreted and applied in the

light of the purpose of the parties in entering into the contract. The intended "purpose of the parties" is a powerful tool for interpretation. Draftspersons, recognizing the power of purpose, frequently place near the beginning of their contract a "purpose" clause setting out in summary form the driving purpose behind the transaction.

3. *Default and immutable terms.* See text.

4. *UCC sources of default and immutable gap-filler rules.* Under UCC § 1-102(3), rules stated in the UCC are default rules and may be modified by agreement unless the UCC provides otherwise. The Uniform Commercial Code also states immutable rules including good faith. UCC §§ 1-201(19); 1-203; 2-103; and 1-102(3) (good faith may not be eliminated). In exclusive dealing contracts, the UCC implies an obligation to use "best efforts." UCC § 2-306(2). What is the difference between reasonable efforts and best efforts? The difference may well be in the eye of the beholder. Some may argue that a person can exercise "reasonable efforts" while still serving the person's own interests. Some may argue that a promise to use "best efforts" requires the person to place respect for that obligation ahead of any personal interest. Is best efforts a higher standard of obligation? It may be so understood.

5. *CISG gap-filler provisions.* See text.

In the case that follows, why did the court refuse to provide a "reasonable" term? Because one of the parties, to the knowledge of the other party, had established in the course of their negotiations that any such "reasonable" term was unacceptable. A term will not be implied where the parties were aware of the gap and affirmatively chose not to fill it.

City of Younkers v. Otis Elevator Company
CASE BRIEF

This is a 1988 decision of the United States Court of Appeals, Second Circuit. Otis Elevator Co. (Otis) was founded in Yonkers, N.Y. in 1853 and ran a manufacturing plant there. In 1968, Otis needed to modernize and expand its Yonkers plant in order to remain commercially viable. In an effort to retain a major employer, the City of Yonkers began negotiations with Otis to determine how Otis's plans could be executed at the Yonkers plant. Otis proposed a plan involving condemnation and urban renewal to allow for the necessary expansion, and Yonkers and the Yonkers Urban Renewal Agency entered into a letter of intent for the project in June 1972. After City Council approval in September 1972, Otis and the Agency began purchasing and clearing the land adjacent to the plant. In September 1974, the Agency conveyed the adjacent land to Otis by a disposition agreement. The plant construction was completed in November 1976, and in December 1976, Otis and the Agency executed a termination agreement, releasing each other from further liability with respect to the conveyance.

In the early 1980s, two of the three components produced at the Yonkers plant were rendered irrelevant by new electronic components. Due to this significant change in the technology of elevator manufacture, the Yonkers plant became economically unfeasible. Otis closed the plant in 1982. Upon closing of the plant, Yonkers sued Otis in federal district court, claiming fraud by Otis and also claiming that Otis had been obliged to continue operation in Yonkers for "a reasonable time to be set by law." The court granted a summary judgment motion by Otis, holding that the statute of frauds barred the contract claim; the court also imposed Rule 11 sanctions of $5,000 on Yonkers and its attorney for filing fraud claims that "lacked any colorable factual basis." Yonkers appealed.

With regard to the contract, Yonkers' primary argument was that Otis breached the contract by withdrawing from the city before "a reasonable time had passed" since the land transfer agreement; alternatively, Yonkers claimed that relief could be provided on the basis of quasi-contract or equitable estoppel. Yonkers conceded that there was never an express promise that Otis would remain for a reasonable time, but argued that the promise was implied in either fact or law.

Review of the record revealed that the parties bargained to keep Otis in Yonkers, but the only limit on Otis's right to leave was the "economic reality" attributable to the sizeable new investment Otis had made in the redevelopment there. Several Otis officers testified that the company would not have agreed to use the expanded plant for a fixed time period because of their economic concerns and the need for future flexibility. While both sides hoped that Otis would stay, even the Agency's director testified that Otis could have unilaterally determined the length of its stay. The June 1972 letter of intent further supported this view, as the letter clearly distinguished between use of the words "goal" and "commitment"—Otis's continuing presence in Yonkers was merely a goal. A private opinion of Yonkers' legal counsel was introduced into evidence to the effect that the letter of intent did not create any legal rights for failure to meet this goal.

The court concluded that the facts of this case did not justify the finding of an implied promise: "No rational trier of fact could conclude that this was the intention of the parties, which they inadvertently failed to express; or that the parties never considered the duration of Otis' commitment to Yonkers, but would have agreed upon the promise for which Yonkers contends had they done so." Rather, the court held that the fair and reasonable reading of the situation was that Yonkers relied on, and Otis was deterred from leaving by, the significant investment that Otis made in renovating its plant. It would therefore have been an imposition by the court to add to the contract an obligation that would be manifestly unreasonable in these circumstances.

The court also held that the quasi-contract claim was unavailable because an express contract covered the subject matter. And the court rejected Yonkers' equitable estoppel argument because such relief is only available where there has been a misrepresentation of fact, reasonable reliance upon that misrepresentation, and injury resulting from the reliance. Since there was neither a clear promise (promissory estoppel) nor a misrepresentation, the equitable estoppel (as well as a promissory estoppel) claim failed.

Finally, the court upheld the Rule 11 sanction on the ground that Yonkers refused to withdraw the fraud cause of action until Otis filed for summary judgment. While Yonkers argued that it was only after reasonable inquiry that it discovered the lack of basis for the fraud cause of action, the court held that the lack of basis for the cause of action at filing mandated the imposition of sanctions under Rule 11.

INTERESTING DISCUSSION ISSUES

1. *Basis of the decision.* Both parties said that Otis had made no express promise to remain in Yonkers for any length of time. Nothing in the evidence supported an implied-in-fact promise to remain. Unlike the *Wood* case, there was no need to imply any such promise in order to make the agreement between the parties effective. Again, there was no basis in fairness (public policy) to imply as a matter of law any such promise since both parties had, during the negotiations, understood the issue and failed to incorporate any such promise in their agreement. Thus there was no omission by "oversight" problem to resolve.

NOTES AND QUESTIONS

1. *How does the case differ from Lucy?* What does the court determine through interpretation that avoids a *Lucy*-like outcome? The parties had entered into a development agreement which constituted an enforceable contract. But a promise by Otis to remain in Yonkers was not necessary to assure effectiveness of that contract. On the contrary, both parties recognized during the negotiations that Otis had not and would not promise to remain in Yonkers for any period of time. Implication of a promise to remain would therefore be completely contradictory to the position taken by both parties during the negotiations. The evidence established that this was not the case of a provision omitted by oversight. A term will not be implied under such circumstances. Is the result based on the intent of the parties or public policy? The result is based on intent of the parties and on public policy.

The parties having both recognized the absence of a promise to remain, and having both failed to insert any responsive provision in their contract, their understanding of the gap and their decision (intention) not to fill the gap precluded any promise to remain by implication. Given this same understanding of intent, it would be unfair (contrary to public policy) for the court to include an implied-in-law promise.

2. *Statements of contractual purpose.* See text. From a drafting perspective, what function do such statements of purpose serve? The "purpose" of the parties is a primary tool for interpretation of the contract. By reciting that purpose clearly in the draft the parties maximize the court's understanding of that purpose and the likelihood of correct judicial interpretation. Based in part on your reading of *Otis Elevator Co.*, how can such contractual statements of purpose affect a court's interpretation of an ambiguity or a gap in the parties' contract? See above.

3. *Alternatives to contract recovery.* See text. Why should a court be more reluctant to imply a promise in the promissory estoppel context than in the case of an express contract? Because the focus of the promissory estoppel doctrine is the making of a clear promise and the reasonable detrimental reliance on that promise.

4. *"Integration" of promissory estoppel and quasi-contractual relief.* See text. Why should the fact that the parties have defined their relationship through an express contract prohibit the City of Yonkers from pursuing non-contractual relief through a restitution theory? Basic to the restitution theory is the concept that the retention of the benefit must amount to unjust enrichment. If the benefit is covered by the contract then the retention of the benefit cannot be "unjust." Would the same reasoning also apply to a promissory estoppel claim similarly made in the face of an express contract? Yes.

5. *Equitable estoppel and misrepresentation.* See text.

2. Caveat Emptor & Warranties

S sells a good to B and makes no representation or promise as to the quality of the good. Should we presume, as a matter of law, that if B wants any right to complain about the quality of the good B must include appropriate protective language in the contract? Failure to do so places the risk of quality on the buyer (who could have protected herself by requiring appropriate language of promise)? Or should the court imply a promise of at least average quality in the sale of a good without regard to whether the contract of sale contained any promissory language of quality? The English courts established the rule of caveat emptor requiring the buyer to obtain protection, if any, with respect to quality by means of a contractual promise. No promise of quality was implied.

Suppose that, instead, S agrees to build a house for B and the contract contains no express language covering the quality of the workmanship to be used. Is B at risk unless promissory language with respect to quality is included in the contract? U.S. courts have frequently implied a promise that the work would be done in a "good and workmanlike" manner. They have been less inclined to leave B without a remedy even though the contract was silent with respect to quality.

Can B sue for negligence? Where privity exists, many courts have held that B's protection if any must be found in the language of the contract and not in the tort of negligence (See discussion in Chapter 9 following the *Cayuga* case).

The text notes that the Uniform Sales Act (1906) provided that a sale of goods by description from a merchant, absent a defect obvious upon inspection, was subject to an implied warranty of merchantable quality. About 32 states adopted this uniform act.

a. Warranty Liability

The Uniform Commercial code, issued in 1951, contains § 2-314, the implied warranty of merchantability, and § 2-315, the implied warranty of fitness for a particular purpose. Contracting out of these implied warranties is covered in Chapter 9. While both these implied warranties are "default" rules, UCC § 2-316 creates specific requirements with respect to contracting out.

UCC § 2-313 deals with express warranties and defines an express warranty to include any affirmation, promise, description or sample relating to the goods that becomes part of the "basis of the bargain." The Uniform Sales Act required the buyer to prove actual reliance on the express warranty. The UCC has no comparable requirement except to the extent that the buyer must show that the warranty became part of the "basis of the bargain."

Has reliance been eliminated and, if not, how is the "basis of the bargain" test to be factually determined? Reliance has not been eliminated, but according to the case that follows, a seller's factual representation is presumed to become part of the basis of the bargain and the burden is then on the seller to prove that the representation was not a consideration inducing the bargain. Thus the proof of reliance has been shifted from the buyer to the seller together with a presumption that the seller's representation was an express warranty until the seller proves the representation was not a consideration inducing the bargain.

Keith v. Buchanan
CASE BRIEF

This is a 1985 decision of the California Court of Appeals. Keith purchased a sailboat from defendants in 1978 for $75,000. While he had substantial experience in sailing, he had not previously owned a sailboat. He attended a boat show and picked up a brochure about the boat he bought called an "Island Trader 41" and described as "seaworthy," indeed "a picture of sure-footed seaworthiness." Keith testified that he relied on the representations in the sales brochure. He and a sales representative of the defendant discussed Keith's desire for a boat that was ocean-going and would cruise long distances. Keith asked a friend to inspect the boat and the friend gave the boat a good report. After delivery of the boat a dispute arose as to its seaworthiness. Keith sued for breach of both an express and an implied warranty. The trial court dismissed the complaint following the close of plaintiff's case, holding that the statements were merely opinions or commendations and not express warranties. The court found no implied warranty of fitness for a particular purpose because Keith relied on his own expert in buying the boat.

The California Court of Appeals held that no particular form of words was required to create a warranty but that expressions of opinion or commendation (puffing?) did not. To establish an express warranty under the UCC there had to be an "affirmation of fact or promise" or "description of the goods." Next, that statement had to be "part of the basis of the bargain." The court ruled that "Statements made by a seller during the course of the negotiation over a contract are presumptively affirmations of fact." Statements made in a sales brochure can create express warranties, and the court found that the statements made in the brochure were warranties.

While, prior to the UCC, reliance had to be established, now such statements only had to become "part of the basis of the bargain." Some commentators had interpreted this provision as shifting the burden of proof to the seller while others thought the UCC eliminated reliance altogether. The court opined that the UCC had abandoned the concept of reliance. "A warranty statement made by the seller is presumptively part of the basis of the bargain, and the burden is on the seller to prove that the resulting bargain does not rest at all on the representation." Inspection before delivery may result in waiver of warranties—but not if the defect was not actually discovered and waived.

Keith's inspection by an agent did not waive the express warranty. That inspection would not have revealed whether or not the boat was seaworthy.

Keith also claimed breach of an implied warranty of fitness for a particular purpose. The predicates for such an implied warranty are: the seller had reason to know the particular purpose for which the goods were required, and that the buyer was relying on the seller's skill or judgment to select or furnish suitable goods fit for the purpose. Here the element of reliance was important. The trial judge ruled that Keith had not relied on the defendant's judgment and the Court of Appeals affirmed that holding.

The decision of the trial court regarding an express warranty was reversed and the case remanded.

NOTES AND QUESTIONS

1. *Statements of value, opinion or commendation or "puff."* The *Keith* Court noted that while formal words are not required in order to create an express warranty, statements of value, opinion, or commendation do not create a warranty. Why not? As covered in Chapter 2, liability for breach of contract must relate to a promise and the failure to fulfill that promise. Statements of opinion are not promises. "Commendations" are trickier. "The thing I am proposing to sell to you is a great thing." Should this statement be interpreted as a promise that the thing is "great" or a statement of opinion that it is "great"? Whether or not a commendation can be or should be interpreted as a promise is to be tested "objectively," that is to say by what the person to whom the comment was addressed could reasonably understand. The more specific the commendation the more likely it is that the statement will be interpreted objectively as a promise rather than a statement of opinion. The defendant in the case above argued that "seaworthy" was no more than a commendation or "puffing." More recent cases indicate that "puffing" is and should be a dangerous undertaking for a seller. What is the definition of the term "warranty"? Black, the bible, declines to offer a definition of warranty but does define "breach of warranty" a s " A breach of an express or implied warranty relating to the title, quality, content, or condition of goods sold." We would translate "warranty" as a "promise" usually relating to title, quality, content or condition of either goods or services. UCC § 2-313(2) states that "an affirmation merely of the value of the goods or a statement purporting to be merely the seller's opinion or commendation of the goods does not create a warranty." *Comment 8* further provides that "some statements or predictions cannot fairly be viewed as entering into the bargain." Does the comment suggest that justified reliance is relevant and that buyer reliance on such statements is not justified? The test is, or should be, whether the person to whom the statement was made could reasonably believe that the statement was intended as a promise and was sufficiently specific that a remedy could be based on failure to fulfill that promise. Do you think the statements should be evaluated according to the intent of the maker of the statement or the objective understanding of the purchaser? Clearly, the latter, but the purchaser's understanding must be objectively reasonable.

2. *"Seaworthiness" test to distinguish puffery and warranty.* The *Keith* Court adopts a "presumptive test" that statements made by a seller during the course of negotiation over a contract are "presumptively affirmations of fact" unless it can be demonstrated that the buyer could only have reasonably considered the statement as a statement of the seller's opinion. Under this approach what must the purchaser prove and how must the seller defend? The purchaser must prove that the seller made a statement of fact relating to the subject matter of the sale, and not one of opinion. This court then engaged a rebuttable presumption that the statement became part of the "basis of the bargain." The burden then shifted to the defendant seller to show that the statement was not an inducing factor in bringing about the sale and purchase. The dispute related to the "seaworthiness" of the vessel. What exactly would a reasonable person expect from a 41-foot seaworthy vessel? Transpacific travel? West coast port-to-port travel? Overnight cruising capability on the open seas? To be "seaworthy" a boat would presumably have to operate with safety on the "seas" which must mean "high seas." Many sailboats forty-one feet in length or even less compete regularly in ocean sailing competitions. Unfortunately, we are not told what properties of the boat Keith claimed made it unseaworthy, and so we can only guess. A good question for the class—as counsel for Keith, what evidence would you seek to introduce at trial to show that the boat was not in fact seaworthy?

3. *Basis of the bargain test.* Under UCC § 2-313(1)(a)(-(c), no form of express warranty is actionable unless it becomes part of the "basis of the bargain" for the purchase of the goods in question. *Comment 3* makes clear that the seller need not "intend" to make a warranty and thus the test is the objective understanding of the purchaser and further once a warranty statement is made it becomes presumptively part of the basis of the bargain. Indeed, under *comment 3,* once a warranty is made, the seller can only remove the warranty from the presumptive basis of the bargain by "clear affirmative proof." How does the *Keith* Court implement this test which involves relative buyer-seller proof of reliance? First, the court found that the seller had made a statement of fact relating to the subject matter of the sale, namely that the boat was "seaworthy." Having made this finding, the court applied a rebuttable presumption that this statement was part of the "basis of the bargain." The burden was then shifted to the seller to show that the statement was not an inducing factor in the sale. When the seller failed to discharge this burden of proof the seller lost. Does the Court require the buyer to prove that the purchase would not have occurred absent the warranty (specific reliance test) (No!) or that the warranty was a dominant factor in purchase decision (presumed reliance by significance of the warranty)? No. The seller was required to prove that the statement was not a consideration inducing the bargain. Presumably, this means that the seller had to show that the

statement was not a factor in the buyer's decision to buy. Here the evidence clearly established that "seaworthiness" was a factor that played some part in the buyer's decision. If the warranty was irrelevant to the purchase decision, can it still become part of the basis of the bargain (reliance irrelevant test)? No. If the statement was irrelevant, it could not be an inducing factor and thus could not become an express warranty. Or is there some middle ground? Yes, as explained above. The *Keith* Court adopts a two-prong middle ground approach requiring: (i) that a warranty is a factor or consideration inducing the buyer to enter into the bargain, and (ii) since once made the warranty is presumptively part of the basis of the bargain, the seller has the burden of proof to establish that the resulting bargain does not rest at all on the representation. What then is left for the plaintiff's proof and thus the major obstacle to recovery? The plaintiff must prove a statement of fact, which is neither a statement of opinion or "commendation," that relates to the subject matter of the purchase. If the plaintiff need only prove a warranty was made and the seller must then prove the warranty was not a factor at all in the decision to make the purchase, how successful do you think the seller will be? Once the relevant statement is proven, there is little chance for a seller to avoid responsibility. Even if a warranty exists, is the buyer's knowledge of that warranty at least an element of the case? Yes. How can something the buyer is not aware of become part of the basis of the bargain? Given the unlikely proof that the warranty was no part of the buyer's decision to make the purchase, what element of the case takes on a more important dimension? Proof that the seller made a relevant statement of fact and that the buyer was aware of that statement of fact. Thus statements of the seller, included in a brochure, would have no effect unless the buyer read the brochure before conclusion of the sale and purchase and then testified that he relied on a statement or statements in the brochure. Given the uncertainty associated with the distinction between warranty and puffery might this test assume more importance? A seller, having made a relevant statement of fact, is on thin ice in trying to defend on the basis of puffery. Such a defense can only be expected to succeed if the objective reasonable person in the buyer's shoes would not have taken the statement seriously and would not have relied upon it. If so, how do the notes above resolve this question in cases of doubt? Since the seller has been assigned the burden of proof, once a relevant statement of fact is proven, the seller will lose in cases of doubt because of failure to rebut the presumption. If again the buyer presumptively wins, how can a buyer ever lose an express warranty case when the product fails to comply with the terms of a marginal express warranty? Perhaps on the basis of a failure to show a causal relationship between the unfulfilled statement and the damage that occurred, or perhaps on the basis of an inspection that should have shown the defect—thus precluding the statement from becoming part of the basis of the bargain. Does the confluence of all these factors create seller strict liability for even marginal expressions considered an express warranty? Not necessarily.

4. *Waiver by inspection.* The *Keith* Court mentions that a buyer's actual knowledge of the true condition of the goods prior to purchase may make it plain that the seller's express warranty was not relied upon as an inducement for the purchase. When effective, it appears the *Keith* Court views physical inspection as a primary method for the seller to prove that the express warranty, even if made, did not become a "basis of the bargain." For example, if in this case, the buyer inspected the boat and knew it was not "seaworthy", the buyer would be precluded from suing for a breach of the admitted express warranty. Even though expert boat builders physically inspected the boat, why was that inspection ineffective as to the express warranty that the yacht was seaworthy? The court held that the "seaworthiness" of the boat could not be tested by inspection without putting the boat in the water and taking it out for a sea trial.

The Court also mentions that in such cases, the express warranty may be deemed "waived" by the purchaser. The term "waiver" is most often defined as a "voluntary and intentional relinquishment of a known right." Calamari and Perillo on Contracts §11.29(c) (Fifth Edition 2003). Do you think the use of the term "waiver" is accurate in this context? Yes, because if the buyer is aware of the defect before "accepting" the goods, the buyer is "waiving" the right to hold the seller responsible for that defect. Do you think that a buyer truly intends to relinquish the right to insist on strict compliance with an express warranty merely because the buyer inspects the goods? The buyer may not so intend, but the law says that the inspection gives the buyer a clear chance to find and do something about the nonconformity with the statement. As a matter of policy, the buyer should have some responsibility to inspect and, in the face of nonconformity, complain while refusing to accept. The buyer's duty to read and understand the contract could provide some parallel reasoning. If the inspection occurs "after" the contract is made but before delivery, would the inspection still be relevant to express warranties? The student will be tempted to say "yes", so long as the buyer still has the right to refuse to accept. Read footnote 3 in the case. But that footnote recites the following information from a comment to UCC § 2-316:

> [3] Evidence was presented of examination or inspection of the boat after the making of the contract of sale and prior to delivery and acceptance of the vessel. Such an inspection would be irrelevant to any issue of express warranty. Although it deals with implied warranties as opposed to express warranties, the Uniform Commercial Code comment 8 to section 2-316 (Cal. U. Com. Code, § 2-316) is instructive: "Under paragraph (b) of subdivision (3) warranties may be excluded or modified by the circumstances

> where the buyer examines the goods or a sample or model of them before entering into the contract. 'Examination' as used in this paragraph is not synonymous with inspection before acceptance or at any other time after the contract has been made. It goes rather to the nature of the responsibility assumed by the seller at the time of the making of the contract." (See U. Com. Code com. 8 to Cal. U. Com. Code, § 2-316, West's Ann. Com. Code (1964) p. 308, emphasis added.)

UCC § 2-316(3)(b) provides that the "implied" warranties of merchantability and fitness for a particular purpose are eliminated if the buyer examines or refuses to examine the goods and the defects would have been discoverable. The section does not mention express warranties and indeed under UCC § 2-316(1) express warranties may not be eliminated by the seller. What is the difference between the seller eliminating an express warranty and a buyer waiving an express warranty? The seller is not permitted to eliminate an express warranty, that is to say the seller cannot take the statement back. But the buyer can choose not to be concerned about the statement and thus may "waive" it. Does the distinction make sense to you? Yes—the difference involved is between conduct of the seller and conduct of the buyer.

5. *Marine insurance policies.* Most marine insurance policies contain express and implied warranties by the insured that the vessel is seaworthy. For this purpose, the term "seaworthy" is most often defined as a ship properly equipped and sufficiently strong and tight to resist the perils reasonably incident to the voyage for which the vessel is insured. Do you suppose that the yacht in this case was insured? Most likely yes. Would the insurance necessarily be ineffective by virtue of the holding of the case? Applying the warranty in the policy, the answer would appear to depend upon the "nature of the voyage for which the vessel was insured."

6. *Privity requirement.* See text.

7. *Implied warranty of fitness for a particular purpose.* UCC §2-315 creates an implied warranty of fitness for a particular purpose. In order for the warranty to be implied-in-law, the seller must know buyer's "particular purpose" for the goods, recommend a particular product to suit that purpose, and the buyer must rely on the seller's skill and judgment in the selection and recommendation. As a result, reliance on the seller's recommendation is critical. For this reason, UCC § 2-316(3)(b) negates the reliance requirement when the buyer actually inspected the goods prior to purchase, or refused to do so, and in either event the inspection would have made clear the goods were not appropriate. The *Keith* Court determined that inspection by the

buyer and his experts *after* the yacht was purchased was adequate to determine that the yacht was indeed not seaworthy (as defined by the buyer's needs). Ignoring for the moment that the inspection occurred after purchase, why would such an inspection eliminate an implied warranty of seaworthiness but not an express warranty of seaworthiness? The distinction is one of policy—the thought being that a seller who makes an express warranty should not be able to negate that promise by general words of denial later in the contract. The implied warranty is based on an assumed intent of the parties unless that assumed intent is rebutted. The inspection can serve as just such a rebuttal. Does the distinction make sense to you? Yes, since the policy purposes behind the treatment of the two situations are different.

What do you suppose that a purchaser's "particular purpose" might include? Any specific purpose provided that such purpose is brought to the attention of the seller clearly. In order to invoke this particular implied warranty, must the particular purpose be any purpose other than an ordinary purpose? Yes, said the Crane case, because function under the ordinary purpose is protected by the implied warranty of merchantability. If so, why do you suppose this requirement exists? See the preceding sentence. If the requirement were otherwise, how would the implied fitness warranty overlap with the implied merchantability warranty? See the same sentence.

8. *CISG and express warranties.* See text.

9. *Implied warranty of merchantability.* UCC § 2-314(1) provides that a warranty that goods are merchantable is implied in a sale of goods by a merchant of those types of goods. UCC § 2-314(2)((c) generally states that goods are merchantable if they are "fit for the ordinary purposes for which such goods are used." The *Keith* Court stated in note 4 that no claim was made for breach of the warranty of merchantability. Why do you think the buyer and counsel decided not to pursue this implied-in-law warranty? Probably because the seller could show that the boat involved was fit for ordinary sailing purposes. Keith had a special purpose in mind and communicated that purpose to the seller. While lack of merchantability clearly implies that the goods are defective for their generally intended use, does an express warranty or a warranty for a particular purpose require that the goods be defective? No, just that the goods be inappropriate for that particular purpose. Stated another way, could goods be perfectly merchantable and yet breach either an express warranty or the warranty of fitness for a particular purpose? Yes.

10. *Non-UCC implied warranty of quality.* The materials above are concerned with UCC statutory overrides of the common law doctrine of *caveat emptor* but only with respect to the sale of goods. Where does that leave the common law doctrine of *caveat emptor* with respect to a

transaction not involving the sale of goods? See the text that follows this question. Stated another way, does the Restatement (Second) of Contracts include any provisions regarding implied promises similar to merchantability and fitness for a particular purpose? It should not be a difficult task to imply a warranty that the work will be done in a good and workmanlike manner—comparable to the attorney's responsibility to exercise a level of skill comparable to that practiced in the particular area. Certainly, as with an express warranty, an express promise of quality would be enforceable just as any other promise. But absent such a promise, does the law imply a promise or warranty of quality? If it does not, it should, based on common expectation.

b. Warranty Disclaimers

The text describes the two important ways in which sellers can try to limit their liability. The first, the subject of this section, involves an attempt to exclude the warranty from the sale. Thus the used car sales person frequently sells "as is—without warranty." The second, covered in Chapter 9, involves an attempt to limit the liability flowing from a breach of warranty—consider, as one example, the clause familiar in burglar alarm service company contracts—"liability, if any, for breach shall be limited to $250." Under the UCC, warranty disclaimer requirements vary depending on whether the warranty involved is express, implied warranty of merchantability or implied warranty of fitness for a particular purpose. UCC § 2-317(c) provides that an express warranty (even though narrower than the implied warranty, displaces that implied warranty. The implied warranty of fitness for a particular purpose is not disclaimed by an inconsistent express warranty.

Implied Warranties. Any disclaimer must follow the paths specified in UCC § 2-316. The easiest way is use of the general disclaimer "as is—where is," "with all faults" or similar language. Both warranties can be eliminated or modified by course of dealing, trade usage and course of performance. To exclude the implied warranty of merchantability that word must be used and, if the contract is in writing, the exclusion must be "conspicuous." The disclaimer of the implied warranty of fitness must also be conspicuous and can only be disclaimed in writing. If and when the seller demands that the buyer inspect the goods, claims for defects that could have been discovered by inspection are also precluded. The examination must occur before the sale and not afterwards.

Express Warranties. The express warranty and the disclaimer will be read together, if possible, and if not, the express warranty will control and the disclaimer will have no effect. But if the express warranty was made during negotiations and the disclaimer is in the final writing, the parol evidence rule will preclude proof of the express oral warranty if the document is wholly integrated. A merger clause can affect this result.

Consolidated Data Terminals v. Applied Digital Systems, Inc.
CASE BRIEF

This is a 1983 decision of the United States Court of Appeals, Ninth Circuit. Applied Digital ("ADDS") manufactured computer terminals. Consolidated Data Terminals ("CDT") was a distributor pursuant to a detailed written master agreement. In 1977 CDT placed its first orders for a new Regent 100 series, represented to be fast (in accordance with a specified rate) and "inherently reliable." In fact, the terminals were highly unreliable and never functioned at anything like the advertised speed. CDT customers complained and returned terminals. ADDS tried but was unsuccessful in fixing the problems. ADDS and CDT both competed for Intel business. Initially CDT's bid to supply Regent 100's was accepted as the lowest priced bid but ADDS found out, lowered its price and was awarded the bulk of the Intel contract. CDT sued alleging breach of contract, interference with a prospective business advantage (tort) and fraud. During the trial CDT was allowed to amend its complaint to include new claims for fraud and negligence by ADDS in its design, manufacture and sale of the Redgent 100's. The trial judge found that ADDS had breached warranties in the sales contracts for the Regent 100's, had negligently designed and sold these terminals, had fraudulently represented them as "inherently reliable," and had tortiously interfered with CDT's relationship with Intel. CDT was awarded some $585,000 in damages.

By way of damages the trial court found CDT had incurred $15,000 in expenses in attempting to service the defective terminals, and that breaches of warranty caused the termination of what otherwise would have been a profitable distributorship arrangement for CDT. The court awarded damages based on projected profits from future sales in the amount of $11,800. The court awarded $28,700 as compensatory tort damages and $500,000 in punitive damages.

The Ninth Circuit Court of Appeals ruled that the applicable law was New York's. The statement about performance speed in the Regent 100 specifications was an express warranty. ADDS claimed that a disclaimer clause in the contract negated any such liability. Paragraph 6 of the terms and conditions provided that "ADDS makes no warranty, express or implied," other than a 90 day guarantee covering materials and workmanship. The court ruled that the disclaimer could not be permitted to override the "highly particularized warranty created by the specifications." Applying UCC § 2-316(1) the court ruled that the express warranty overrode the general disclaimer of warranty where the two provisions could not be reasonably reconciled.

NOTES AND QUESTIONS

1. *Express warranty and disclaimer.* The ADDS written specifications regarding the Regent 100 CRT terminals stated that the baud rate was 19,200 and separate promotional literature stated that the terminals were "inherently reliable." In fact, neither expression was in accord with the facts. Do either or both the expressions constitute an "express" warranty under UCC Section 2-313? Yes. If so, why? Because both were statements of fact (neither opinion nor commendation) related to the basis of the bargain and ADDS failed to disprove the applicable presumption of inducement. Each contract of sale for terminals stated that "ADDS makes no warranty, express or implied" with regard to the terminals. Were both the warranties and disclaimer contained in the same document? Presumably no, since the statements of fact were found in the product specifications, and most likely, these specifications were not included in the terms and conditions of the contract. Notice that the terms of the distributorship agreement were incorporated by reference into every sales contract. If so, why was the warranty disclaimer ineffective under UCC Section 2-316(1)? Because the statements and the disclaimer were inconsistent, could not be construed together, and thus the statement warranties prevailed. If not in the same document (expanded to include those incorporated by reference), should the Court have considered whether evidence of the warranties was admissible under the parol evidence rule? The terms and conditions of the basic contract were incorporated by reference into every order placed by CDT. These orders formed the paramount evidence of the contract and, doubtless likewise incorporated by reference the product specifications. If so, would CDT have likely prevailed under its breach of warranty claim? The court would most likely have read all the documents as tied together and thus would not have applied the parol evidence rule to exclude any evidence found in the specific contract or incorporated therein by reference. Did this contract reflect a merger clause? Yes. What should be the effect of such a clause under the parol evidence rules as applied to written disclaimers preceded by prior express oral warranties? The warranties here were in writing, not oral, and doubtless incorporated by reference directly into the specific sales agreement specifying the terminals to be ordered. The specifications cannot be separated from the product reference description contained in that agreement. The brochure reference to "inherently reliable" must have been treated in a similar fashion by the court. It would be scandalous for the court to find the basic contract either wholly or partially integrated so as to exclude evidence incorporated in the underlying agreement. In the absence of an express incorporation by reference clause, the court would have implied such a clause as necessary to give effect to the product specifications which must be understood to be basic to the

description of the articles covered by the specific sale and purchase agreement.

2. *Combined effect of warranty and disclaimer in same contract.* UCC Section 2-316(1) stating rules regarding the disclaimer of warranties obviously applies only when there is an express warranty. Should it be possible to read a contract as a whole, combine the effect of the warranty and disclaimer together and conclude that no warranty was made? Not if the process involves the contradiction of the express warranty. Did the Court consider this approach? Yes, but ruled that the two were contradictory and that therefore the express prevailed. The purpose of allowing the warranty to prevail over the disclaimer, assuming a warranty exists, is to protect a buyer from "unexpected and unbargained" language of an inconsistent disclaimer. UCC § 2-316, *cmt. 1.* If the buyer is aware of both the warranty and the disclaimer, would a reasonable buyer conclude that a warranty had been made? Presumably, a reasonable buyer would rely, above all, on the product's technical specifications. If not, is the purpose of the invalid disclaimer well served by eliminating the disclaimer? The "If not" is not applicable. Would a reasonable person simply conclude no warranty at all was made? No, in view of the specifications and the associated brochure.

3. *At-will contracts.* The distributorship was not for a specific duration but rather could be terminated at-will be either party. The contract also provided that such termination was to be triggered by 90-day notice. UCC Section 2-309(2) provides that a contract indefinite in duration is nonetheless valid for a "reasonable time" but nonetheless may be terminated by either party at any time. In such cases, reasonable notice must be provided and this rule is immutable. UCC § 2-309(3). The distributorship agreement in this case was supplemented by separate contracts involving the purchase of computer terminals. Since the terminals were clearly goods, the case was governed by the UCC. If the case had involved simply a distributorship agreement, would the relationship be governed by the UCC or common law? Although the subject matter of the agreement was goods, the actual dealership agreement was not. It is arguable that the basic ingredient of a dealership agreement is the relationship it creates between the parties including promises such as "best efforts" and covenants not to sell or promote a competitive product. If so, the common law principles and not the UCC should apply to the interpretation and enforceability of that contract. But specific sales orders entered into and accepted pursuant to the terms of the master agreement should be interpreted as sales of goods and therefore subject to the UCC rules.

D. INSURANCE CONTRACTS

As the text says, insurance contracts present special problems for contract law. They are usually, but not inevitably, contracts of adhesion and marketed on a take-it-or-leave-it basis. For larger corporate insureds, insurance companies sometimes write tailor made policies referred to as "manuscript" policies. Much of the case law however, deals with the adhesion policy version. The practice of interpreting a policy "contra proferentem" (against the draftsperson) finds its high point in this context. If the insurer failed to make the terms of the policy clear (unambiguous) then the fault is and should stay with it—giving the policy holder the benefit of the doubt in choosing the two or more competing meanings of the ambiguous word, phrase or clause. This approach can be even sharper in contexts where the insurer starts off with broad words of coverage and then, much later in the policy, proceeds to try to take back significant parts of that broad coverage through more specific "exclusion" clauses. Courts take a particularly sharp view at such exclusionary provisions. Following the Llewellyn thesis on interpretation of adhesion contracts, Restatement (Second) of Contracts § 201(2)(b) provides in essence that an insured's meaning will control over the insurance company meaning where the insured had no reason to know of the insurance company's meaning whereas the insurance company had reason to know of the insured reasonable objective understanding. Professor (later federal district judge) Robert E. Keeton is generally credited with creating the doctrine of "reasonable expectations", now reflected in a comment to Restatement (Second) of Contracts § 211(2) as well as in § 211(3). This doctrine has been controversial and has been roundly denounced recently by the Michigan Supreme Court. See *Rory v. Continental Ins. Co.*, 471 Mich. 904, 688 N.W.2d 93 (2004).

Wilkie v. Auto-Owners Insurance Company
CASE BRIEF

This is a 2003 decision of the Michigan Supreme Court. Janna Frank and Paul Wilkie were driving together when a car driven by Stephen Ward crossed the center line and collided with the car that Frank was driving (the insured owner was Mrs. Wilkie, the mother of Paul who was a passenger), injuring Frank and killing Wilkie and Ward. Ward's car was insured under a policy with a $50,000 limit; Frank split this amount with Wilkie's estate, $25,000 each. Wilkie's car was insured under an Auto-Owners Insurance Co. policy for "underinsured-motorist" coverage. This is a form of coverage, required by statute in some states but optional under Michigan law. It provides a fund against which a claim can be made in the event that the claim against the tortfeasor cannot be satisfied because of the tortfeasor's insufficient automobile insurance coverage. The coverage in this case had limits of $100,000 per person and $300,000 per incident. Auto-Owners' liability was limited to the amount by which these limits exceeded the underinsured motorist's own coverage. The policy clearly stated that the Auto-Owners limits of liability were not to be increased because of the number of persons injured, claims made, or cars involved in the accident.

Auto-Owners agreed that the accident was Ward's fault, and that Frank's and Wilkie's damages exceeded $100,000. But Auto-Owners disputed the amount owed to Frank and Wilkie, claiming that it only owed $50,000 each because the $100,000 limit for each of them was to be reduced by the $50,000 coverage of the Ward policy. Frank and Wilkie claimed that Auto-Owners owed them each $75,000 because each received only $25,000 from the Ward policy. Unable to come to a resolution, Frank and Wilkie sought a declaratory judgment against Auto-Owners, and were granted summary judgment by the trial court, which held that they should receive $75,000 each from Auto-Owners. On appeal, the court held that the language of the Auto-Owners policy was ambiguous in directing how to apply the underinsured policy limit (Ward's, the tortfeasor) as a setoff. As a result, the court construed the terms against the drafter ("contra proferentem") Auto-Owners, and upheld the trial court's ruling (the court also held that this result was consistent with the doctrine of reasonable expectations). Auto-Owners appealed to the Michigan Supreme Court.

The supreme court majority held that the interpretation of the contract was a matter of law, and would thus be reviewed de novo. In evaluating the clause, the court first highlighted the fact that the contract stated that the amount by which the $100,000 for each person exceeds the total limits *available* to the owner or operator of the underinsured vehicle will determine the amount to be paid. Further, the amounts available are not to be increased because of the number of persons injured. The court found the clarity of the language to be much greater than did the court of appeals, and found the language especially clear when the two clauses were read in conjunction with one another. Thus the court found the policy unambiguously required that the face amount of Ward's coverage be deducted in calculating both of the claims, thus limiting Frank' s and Wilkie's recovery to $50,000 each.

The court also attacked the rule of reasonable expectations as "contrary to a bedrock principle of American contract law that parties are free to contract as they see fit," with the court enforcing the agreement unless some highly unusual circumstances dictate otherwise. The court held that the rule of reasonable expectations, which is antagonistic to the parties' freedom of contract, is invalid as an approach of contract interpretation. The court next traced Michigan's history with the rule: its ostensible genesis in *Rombough*; the court's rejection of the rule in *Raska*; a plurality's expansion of the rule in *Powers*, where the plurality held that ambiguity was not a prerequisite to applying the rule; the court's approval of the rule in *Vanguard* (in spite of the fact that *Raska* was binding precedent, while *Powers* was not); and, finally, the court's repudiation of the rule in *Nikkel*.

In light of the twisting and inconsistent history of the rule, the majority felt that it was necessary that it "clearly articulate the status of the rule of reasonable expectations in this jurisdiction." As such, they held that the rule has no application to unambiguous contracts, as a policyholder could not reasonably expect something different from the clear language of the contract. The court found that the rule amounted to a mere "surrogate for the rule of construing against the drafter."

The majority reversed the court of appeals and found that the insurance policy between Auto-Owners and Wilkie unambiguously limited Auto-Owners' liability to $50,000 each for Wilkie and Frank.

CONCURRING IN PART, DISSENTING IN PART (Weaver, J.): Justice Weaver agreed that the rule of reasonable expectations had no application in interpreting an unambiguous contract, but disagreed that the underinsured-motorist provisions of the policy were unambiguous. Given the ambiguity, Justice Weaver chose to construe the language against the drafter, finding that Wilkie and Frank were entitled to $75,000 each.

DISSENTING (Cavanagh, J.): Justice Cavanagh argued that the rule of reasonable expectations was distinct from the rule of *contra preferentem*, was generally confined to the field of insurance contracts, and was not limited to cases of ambiguous language. Rather, the rule could be used to help in determining if the language in question was ambiguous. This assistance is especially important in insurance contracts, given their unique character as having "no meeting of the minds except regarding the broad outlines of the transaction." For such contracts of adhesion, it is appropriate to consider not just the text of the contract, but the insured party's reasonable expectations, given the circumstances of the transaction.

Justice Cavanagh proceeded to examine New York's special treatment of insurance contracts in *Steven*, where a court struck down unexpected and inconspicuous limitations in an insurance policy as against public policy, as well as the New Jersey Supreme Court's holding in *DiOrio* that a court cannot be indifferent to the fact that an insurance buyer "scarcely understands the detailed content of what he is buying." Based on the imbalance of power inherent in insurance contracts, and the requirement of a meeting of the minds, Justice Cavanagh stated that policies protecting the insured should guide the court's interpretation of such contracts.

Justice Kelly also dissented. The key language in the policy was the provision that underinsured coverage was limited to the lowest of: (1) the amount by which the underinsured Motorist Coverage limits stated in the Declarations exceed the total limits of all bodily injury liability bonds and policies *available* to the owner or operator of the underinsured automobile. ..." She found the word "available" to be ambiguous—capable of meaning either "actually" available or "potentially" available. Hence the "contra proferentem" rule should apply. She also rejected the majority's rewriting of the earlier case law and invalidation of the "reasonable expectations" doctrine.

INTERESTING DISCUSSION ISSUES

1. *The challenge of interpreting an insurance policy—a contract of adhesion.* The *C & J Fertilizer* and the *Wilkie* cases are at opposite ends of the insurance policy interpretation spectrum. But each provides valuable insights into the processes of judicial interpretation and the choices that can become available along the way. *C & J* bases the result on a mutual intention of the parties found, not in the buried fine print definition, but in the objectively ascertained general intention of people buying and selling "burglary" insurance. The *C & J* court, unlike the handling of unconscionability cases, is not striking the applicable "indecent" clause or provision, but finding that provision better understood in the light of a more general intention of the parties. The "contra proferentem" approach is more difficult to reconcile or explain in terms of shared intention of the parties. It stretches the imagination to suggest that the average insured, at the time of contracting or of receiving the printed policy, both recognized the ambiguity and relied on that version favorable to the insured's ultimate claim. Any such reliance after the fact is more likely to be attributable to the suggestions of the client's legal counsel. In truth and in fact, the "contra proferentem" rule penalizes the insurer by holding it to the version of the ambiguity more favorable to the insured—usually without respect to any claim of subjective intent allegedly held by the insured. It is a rule based on "fairness" to the insured, penalizing the insurer for its failure to express coverage intent more clearly. But the "contra proferentem" rule was probably so well entrenched in Michigan supreme court jurisprudence, as well as in treatises, law review articles and case law across the country, that the majority, was not prepared to invalidate it even though it was prepared to invalidate the "reasonable expectations" rule.

The challenge for students in this case is: were the applicable terms of the policy ambiguous? The "reasonable expectations" doctrine was not necessary to a decision of the case—see Justice Kelly's opinion based on interpretation of the word "available" as either "actual" or "potential." The majority seized on the opportunity presented by this case to invalidate the "reasonable expectations" doctrine in Michigan. The question of ambiguity can best be presented by asking the students why the policy provided a cap of $100,000 per person and a cap of $300,000 for the aggregate of claims arising from one incident. What function was performed by these two disparate caps? Moreover, as

Justice Kelly, again, pointed out, the key language seized on by the majority provided that the limits of coverage (not any particular claim) were not to be extended by the presence of multiple persons injured etc.

NOTES AND QUESTIONS

1. *Inequality of bargaining power.* The doctrine of reasonable expectations was founded upon the power imbalance created by an adhesion contract and the inequality of bargaining power between the insurance company and the insured. Does *Wilkie* truly promote freedom of contract between equals or regress to the less desirable status? The *Wilkie* majority ignores the adhesion and take-it-or-leave-it nature of the usual insurance contract. The very strong language of rejection of the "reasonable expectations" doctrine is problematic. The majority recognizes the vitality of the ambiguity doctrine—contra proferentem—a doctrine raising issues of objective interpretation. But the doctrine of "reasonable expectations" also raises an issue of objective interpretation—the gathering of meaning of intent from the general parameters of the agreement rather than the "obscure" detail of buried terms. Thus the doctrine of "reasonable expectations" can be distinguished from the doctrine of unconscionability (Llewellyn's "indecent" terms). The latter simply denies effect to the conscience shocking term or provision. The former finds a true intent based on the general shape and context of the insurance agreement rather then the minute details. The Michigan Supreme Court has staked out, by majority decisions, a position at the far extreme of states interpreting insurance policies solely on the basis of literal (although buried) meaning.

2. *The resurgence of formalism?* See text. Given the clear return to a formalist jurisprudence, what changes in contracting behavior would you expect to see between Michigan parties? A slew of cases following *Rory* show the rejection of interpretational techniques widely accepted elsewhere. How would your presentation of a contract case change if you were arguing before a Michigan court, as opposed to a California or Iowa court? See the answer immediately above. Are there any benefits to the Michigan approach? Yes, for insurance companies. As the minority judges on the Michigan Supreme Court pointed out, this line of recent decisions puts Michigan apart from the other states.

3. *Lack of ambiguity. Do you agree with the majority opinion that the underinsured motorist provisions were unambiguous?* No—we agree with the dissent. What rule of construction or interpretation would apply if the court found the provisions to be ambiguous? The minority would apply the (but for Michigan) universally applied rule of *contra proferentem.* Absent the availability of that presumption, presumably the usual evidence relating to ambiguity would be admissible but

without the controlling presumption of *contra proferentem*. Do you agree with the majority that the common law rules of interpretation provide sufficient guidance for interpretation of ambiguous insurance contract terms? NO! Insurance contracts are fundamentally contracts of adhesion, imposed as to terms without opportunity for negotiation. Many times, the terms of such contracts are provided to the insured long after the contract has been concluded and the premium has been paid. Students should consider their own experience with respect to the terms of their automobile insurance policy contract. Insurance policy forms are usually long, involved, and somewhere between difficult and impossible for the layman to understand. The basic fault of the Michigan Supreme Court holding is the implicit assumption that the contract takes place on an even playing field between players of equal knowledge, bargaining power and skills.

4. *Private autonomy and reasonable expectations.* Is the doctrine of reasonable expectations more threatening to the intent of the parties than the doctrine of *contra proferentem?* Yes, to the intention of the insurer, no, to the intention of the insured. Can you see why some courts might continue to insist on some ambiguity to construe language against the insurance company? Yes—given the insurance company's underwriting responsibility and interest in preserving the homogeneity of the pool of risks covered by the particular policy.

5. *Sources of the insured's expectations.* According to the dissent, what determines the "reasonable expectations" of the insured? First, the self-serving testimony of the insured, buttressed however by the court's taking judicial notice of the reasonableness of any such "expectation." Would the insured's knowledge (or lack thereof) in any of these situations have affected the outcome of the case? Yes! An "expectation" argument inconsistent with the insured's actual knowledge at the time would not work. If, at the time of the sale of the insurance policy in *Wilkie,* the insurance agent had explained the meaning of the policy asserted by the insurance company, would that explanation have been sufficient to obviate the insured's reasonable expectations to the contrary? Yes—those expectations would then be unreasonable. What if the issue of underinsured motorist coverage limits had never been discussed by the parties in any way at the time of contracting—could the insureds still assert that reasonable expectations formed after contract formation should control? Yes—but we recognize that the concept of "reasonable expectations" is usually based on a fictional intent derived from basic fairness and justice.

6. *The irony of emphasizing freedom of contract in the automobile insurance contract.* See text.

7. *The tort of bad faith in insurance contracts.* See text. If an insurance company deliberately uses an ambiguous term in order to argue later claim denial, should such behavior constitute an actionable tort? Perhaps. But much more surely, such knowledge should implicate the primary exception to the rule of objective interpretation—if one party knows or should know of a meaning attributed to words by the other party, then the other party's understanding prevails.

E. THE IMPLIED OBLIGATION OF GOOD FAITH

There is remarkable agreement that good faith is not an actionable independent duty but rather operates to help define the breach of a duty expressly stated in the contract. "The covenant may not, however, create rights and duties not otherwise provided for in the existing contractual relationship, as the purpose of the covenant is to guarantee that the parties remain faithful to the intended and agreed expectations of the parties in their performance."

So is contractual "good faith" a moral concept designed to punish the reason for the breach or rather a concept designed to clarify whether the duty is breached in the first place? The answer is the latter. If the latter, and the term is implied in law, does it not serve to expand the edges of the duty and if so by what measurable dimension? The answer to the first question is yes and the answer to the second question depends upon the facts of the particular case.

The New York 1933 Court of Appeals formulation of good faith performance is helpful:

> In every contract there is an implied covenant that neither party shall do anything which will have the effect of destroying or injuring the right of the other party to receive the "fruits of the contract," which means that in every contract there is an implied obligation of good faith and fair dealing.

Locke v. Warner Bros., Inc.
CASE BRIEF

This is a 1997 decision of the California Court of Appeals. In 1975, Sondra Locke and Clint Eastwood became personally and romantically involved while working on *The Outlaw Josey Wales.* For the next twelve years, they lived together in two of Eastwood's California homes and appeared in several films together. In 1989, Eastwood terminated the deteriorating relationship. In 1990, the parties reached a mutual settlement agreement under which Eastwood agreed to pay Locke $450,000 and convey certain land to her. Additionally, Eastwood secured a development deal for Locke with Warner Bros. Studios.

The first element of the Locke/Warner deal involved a three-year "non-exclusive first-look deal" that required Locke to submit to Warner any picture she was interested in developing before submitting it to any other studio; Warner would then have thirty days to accept or reject the submission. The second element of the deal was a $750,000 directing deal that allowed the studio to either use Locke as a director or pay her the fee without using her services. Though unknown to Locke, Eastwood had agreed to reimburse Warner for the cost of the contract if she failed to develop any projects. And while Warner fulfilled its requirements under the contract, Warner didn't develop any of Locke's projects or hire her to direct any other films.

In 1994, Locke sued Warner, claiming: (1) Warner denied her the benefit of the bargain because of her gender; (2) Warner breached the contract and deprived her of the benefit of the bargain by refusing to consider her proposed projects; (3) Warner's breach of the agreement was motivated by its discriminatory bias against women; and (4) Warner acted fraudulently in concealing and failing to disclose, at the time of entering into the agreement, the fact that it had no intention of honoring the agreement. Warner filed a motion for summary judgment and contended that it fulfilled all requirements of the agreement, and argued that the odds of having a film produced are generally low, and that many others had suffered fates similar to that of Locke. But Locke opposed summary judgment on the grounds that Warner had no intention of accepting any project, regardless of its merits, citing testimony of two Warner executives, one of whom was reported to have said "we're not going to work with her ... That's Clint's deal." Another said, "They are not going to make a movie with her here."

The trial court granted summary judgment for Warner, holding that Warner had no obligation to put into development any of Locke's projects, and that "[s]uch highly artistic and business decisions are not proper subjects for judicial review." The trial court found that: (1) the fraud claim was without merit; (2) there was no evidence of refusal to work with Locke at the inception of the deal; and (3) there was no evidence to support claims of gender discrimination. Locke appealed the judgment, and the Court of Appeals reversed the trial court's judgment with respect to the second claim (breach by refusal to consider) and the fourth claim (fraud), but upheld summary judgment of the first and third claims (gender discrimination).

With regard to claim 2 (refusal to consider Locke's projects), the court of appeals held that the trial court's ruling was incorrect because it failed to distinguish between Warner's right to make a subjective creative decision, which is not reviewable for reasonableness, and the requirement that Warner's dissatisfaction be bona fide. When a contract confers discretionary power on a party, that discretion must be exercised in accordance with principles of good faith and fair dealing. Here, the subjective standard of honest satisfaction was applicable, but the standard still required that the promisor who is the judge of his satisfaction must make his decision in good faith. Acting in bad faith and categorically rejecting Locke's work, regardless of the merits of her proposals, would be a violation of their contractual duty to review her proposals seriously.

Though Warner fulfilled its compensation requirements under the agreement, the deal's indirect benefits (opportunity to direct films and promote and enhance one's career) were also important aspects of the overall agreement. The statements of Warner executives Brassel and Wellnitz, indicating that the studio would not give serious consideration to Locke's projects, brought into question Warner's good faith performance, and created a triable issue for a fact finder. Warner argued that implied good faith could not create a duty that would vary the explicit terms of the contract, and pointed to California cases *Carma* and *Third Story Music* to support its free exercise of rejection discrimination. But the court distinguished Locke's situation from these cases, stating that the Locke/Warner agreement did not give Warner the express right to refrain from working with Locke, but only provided Warner with discretion in choosing whether to develop Locke's projects. Thus, Warner's alleged violation of the implied covenant of good faith and breach of the contract was a proper question for a trier of fact.

The court of appeals then moved to the count in Locke's complaint of fraud. The trial court had dismissed this claim based on the fact that Warner did not breach any obligations owed to Locke. The court of appeals found that the trial court's dismissal of this count was undermined by its findings regarding claim 2, above (failure to exercise discretion in good faith). Though Locke did not have direct evidence of fraudulent motivation behind Warner's actions, the court of appeals held that fraudulent intent must often be established by circumstantial evidence. Given the evidence regarding Warner's absolute unwillingness to work with Locke, the court found that a trier of fact could reasonably infer that, at the time of entering into the contract, Warner never intended to give Locke's proposals a good faith evaluation.

NOTES AND QUESTIONS

1. *Subjective dissatisfaction or something more?* Assuming that Warner Brothers Studios truly subjectively believed that Ms. Locke's proposals were not meritorious, would it be contractually entitled to reject them? The answer depends upon interpretation of the contract. A condition (requirement) of satisfaction can be worded either as requiring the exercise of an objectively reasonable decision or only a subjective decision. Conditions of approval involving artistic considerations, like those involved in this case, in the absence of language to the contrary, will be presumed to require only the

subjective and not the objective standard. Assuming a good faith exercise of the right of approval, Warner Brothers would have been entitled to reject Locke's proposals. Was there evidence questioning whether that was the case? No. The court of appeals held that Warner Brothers would be entitled to reject the Locke proposals provided it did so in good faith (i.e. after giving each of them appropriate consideration). If so, was the evidence credible? The court of appeals applied the normal presumption applicable to artistic judgment but that was not the issue. The court was prepared to recognize Warner Brothers' right to reject her proposals based on its subjective evaluations, but that right had to be exercised in good faith and Locke had, through deposition and affidavit testimony, raised an issue of fact as to whether Warner Brothers had acted in good faith. Such an issue was triable to a jury and could not be disposed of by summary judgment.

2. *Derivative or independent duty.* The contract gave Warner Brothers the right to exercise its own discretion but the obligation of good faith read into the contract an "honest dissatisfaction" duty. Do you think that was the reasonable expectation of Ms. Locke? Yes. Do you think Warner Brothers thought it was required to be dissatisfied with the proposals before rejecting them? No, but in so thinking, it was in error. If Warner Brothers truly thought the proposals meritorious and would make money, why would the Studio reject the proposals? Locke may well have been a "prickly personality" and they may have been forewarned about that. Dealing with Locke under those circumstances could cause many different kinds of problems all of which they would want to avoid. But if they were aware of her personality before they entered into the contract, promised to consider her proposals, but knew they would not do so because of her personality, their promise to consider was illusory and therefore fraudulent.

3. *UCC good faith.* See text.

4. *CISG and good faith.* See text.

5. *The tort of bad faith in insurance contracts contrasted.* See text.

6. *The tort of "bad faith" ambiguous drafting.* The answer to the question is perhaps, but the exception to "objective interpretation" is more likely to help.

F. COURSE OF DEALING, USAGE AND COURSE OF PERFORMANCE

Both the common law and the UCC regard "usage" evidence as relevant to the interpretation and meaning of an agreement and "ambiguity" is not required as a predicate of admission of such evidence. The three categories of usage, in ascending order of importance, are "trade usage", "course of dealing", and "course of performance. "Trade usage" or custom of the trade is, as the phrase suggests, based on conventions or understandings sufficiently common in the relevant trade, that a contract between parties in that trade may be presumed to be entered into against the background of that usage. "Course of dealing" draws not from custom of the trade but from customs, patterns and understandings of the parties themselves evidenced in their prior dealings. The presumption is that the parties intended to follow practices found in their previous dealings. "Course of performance" draws from the conduct of the parties, after their entry into the contract, tending to show the intention of both parties with respect the meaning or effect of their contract.

Since all three sources of usage are tied to presumptions about the meaning the parties must have intended, these presumptions are generally subordinated to the express language of the contract.

The presumption of intention of the parties drawn from trade usage is the most problematic of the three "usages" with respect to probative value. The implicit rationale for resorting to evidence of trade usage is that both parties were so familiar with such usage that it can be presumed that they contracted with that background in mind as part of the transaction. To justify such reliance, the trade usage must be commercially accepted by "regular observance." While historically trade usage was only a "gap-filler," it, as well as the other usages, are now part of the agreement with the rest of the terms.

Because of the parol evidence rule extrinsic evidence that contradicts a wholly or partially integrated document is not admissible. But, nevertheless, a completely integrated agreement may be supplemented or explained by any of these three usages. The extent to which such an "explanation" can approach contradiction but still be admissible is one of the subjects of the next case.

In a way, this understanding forces courts to resolve tensions between terms of an agreement which are themselves somewhat inconsistent. In a famous case, the Court determined that trade usage should be excluded whenever it cannot be reasonably construed as consistent with the terms of the contract. *Columbia Nitrogen Corp. v. Royster Co.*, 451 F.2d 3, 6-7 (4th Cir. 1971). This view excludes trade usage unless consistent with written terms. Another approach, recognizes that UCC § 1-205(4) is not a form of a parol evidence rule and therefore admits trade usage unless it is totally negated by the written term. Which approach is followed by the *Nanakuli* case below? The answer is the latter.

Nanakuli Paving and Rock Company v. Shell Oil Company, Inc.
CASE BRIEF

INTRODUCTION/OVERVIEW. This is a 1981 decision of the United States Court of Appeals, Ninth Circuit. Appellant Nanakuli Paving and Rock Company (Nanakuli) filed a breach of contract action against appellee Shell Oil Company (Shell) in February 1976. Nanakuli charged Shell with breach of a 1969 supply agreement under which Shell was to provide Nanakuli with asphalt. The contract provided that the price for asphalt was to be "Shell's Posted Price at time of delivery." Underlying the dispute as to pricing under this contract was the practice of government agencies in Hawaii, in inviting bids for construction projects, to refuse to permit bidders to include price escalation clauses based on future increases in product costs. Thus when Nanakuli submitted a bid for such a construction project, including asphalt work, it had to include, in its rolled up bid, asphalt priced as of the time of the bid submittal. Several months were likely to elapse between the date of bid submittal and the date of final contract award. Nanakuli claimed the benefit of a trade usage providing "price protection" for such bids so that when the bid was successful the price charged for asphalt would be that prevailing at the time of the bid and not that "at time of delivery" as provided literally in the contract. The comparative price differential between these two time points in 1973-74 was $44 versus $76 a ton. This huge and sudden price jump was caused by the 1973 Arab boycott of petroleum products.

At trial, the jury returned a verdict of $220,800 in favor of Nanakuli thus accepting its claim that Shell breached the 1969 contract when Shell refused to provide price protection on 7200 tons of asphalt in January 1974. But the judge set aside the verdict and granted Shell's motion for judgment notwithstanding the verdict.

Nanakuli had alleged that Shell failed to provide price protection under the contract, a practice that was routine in the industry, and that had become part of the course of performance under the parties' agreement. Nanakuli's first theory supporting price protection was that all material suppliers to the Hawaiian asphaltic trade followed the trade usage of price protection, so it should thus be assumed that the parties intended to incorporate the practice into their agreement. And beyond merely trade usage, Nanakuli also argued that, under the U.C.C., the actual performance of the agreement by the parties ("course of performance") should and did provide the best guide to the parties' intent. Under this 1969 contract Shell had allowed Nanakuli price protection in 1970 and 1971, and under a later but similar contract in

1977 and 1978. Nanakuli's second theory supporting price protection was that Shell was obliged to price protect Nanakuli because price protection was the commercially reasonable standard for fair dealing in the asphaltic trade in Hawaii in 1974. Thus, the U.C.C. would have required Shell to price protect in order to satisfy the requirement that Shell act in good faith.

Shell presented three arguments for upholding the district court's judgment notwithstanding the verdict, or in the alternative, claiming that the district court admitted improper evidence. First, Shell claimed that the court erred in failing to adopt Shell's definition of "trade" as the sale and purchase of asphalt in Hawaii, excluding from the definition other materials of the asphaltic trade such as aggregate ("crushed rock"). The Ninth Circuit Court of Appeals held that the district court did not abuse its discretion in defining "trade" to include both asphalt and aggregate but not cement, given the unique circumstances of the asphaltic trade on Oahu, and the close knowledge of the asphaltic business (both asphalt and aggregate) that Shell's Hawaiian representative possessed. Second, Shell claimed that prior instances in which it price-protected Nanakuli were only waivers, not a course of performance. The appellate court rejected this claim, finding that, given the available facts, the jury could have reasonably determined these instances to represent a course of performance. Third, Shell argued that price protection was inconsistent with the express terms of the contract, in which case the U.C.C. requires that the express terms control. The appellate court rejected this argument on the grounds that the jury could have reasonably construed price protection as consistent with the express terms, especially given the commercial context of the agreement and the fact that the practice does not totally negate the agreement.

I. Nanakuli was the smaller of two major paving contractors (Hawaiian Bitumuls (H.B) was the larger) on the island of Oahu. Until the mid-1960s, Nanakuli was not positioned to compete with H.B. for large government contracts such as major roads and airports. But in 1963, Nanakuli signed a long-term supply agreement with Shell Oil to supply its asphalt needs. The contract provided Nanakuli with an opportunity to expand its paving business to compete with H.B. for the largest jobs and provided Shell with a superior foothold in a market where they had very little volume. Both parties described their relationship as a partnership-like collaboration; the relationship included, among other acts, Nanakuli painting its trucks "Shell white" and Shell providing financial assistance toward Nanakuli's business expansion. On April 1, 1969, the parties agreed to a supply contract, a distributorship contract, and a volume discount letter, all of which were to last at least through July 1, 1976. Nanakuli contended that part of this agreement was a concession by Shell to provide price protection that would permit Nanakuli to compete with H.B. (a Chevron customer), and that the agreement provided, at a minimum, that Nanakuli would not be charged more than the price at the time of filing the bid for tonnage ultimately delivered and used at a later date. In addition to the close business relationship, Nanakuli testified that Shell representative Bohner was in Nankuli's offices at least twice weekly, and was very familiar with the company's business and competitive environment. The Ninth Circuit held that the jury could reasonably have inferred that Bohner knew much more about the industry than he testified at trial.

II. The importance of price protection to the Hawaiian paving industry stemmed from the fact that the largest contracts were government contracts, and neither local, state, nor federal agencies allowed escalation clauses for paving materials. As a result, aggregate suppliers routinely price protected paving contractors in the 1960s and 1970s, as did Chevron, the largest asphalt supplier on the island. At trial, two aggregate suppliers testified that, to their knowledge, price protection had always been practiced in that market, but that there was never an explicit statement of the practice; a Chevron representative testified similarly. Beyond this testimony, the trial court, over Shell's objections, permitted the admission of evidence concerning the continuation of the trade usage after 1969. The trial court permitted the admission of evidence to show that the parties could reasonably expect that the practice would be continued Under the U.C.C., the basis for incorporation of trade usage into a contract is the justifiable expectation of the parties that the usage will be observed. The admitted evidence showed that Chevron continued its price protection through 1979, and that Shell price-protected Nanakuli in both 1977 and 1978 on Oahu.

III. The U.C.C. considers actual performance ("course of performance") of an agreement to be the most relevant evidence of how the parties interpreted the terms of the contract. Between 1969 and 1974, Shell only raised its prices twice, in 1970 and 1971. In both cases, Shell price-protected Nanakuli, essentially allowing several months' notice of the price change before implementing the new price. Shell also price-protected Nanakuli for six months in 1976 and for three or four months in 1978. The court held that this evidence could have demonstrated to the jury the commercially reasonable standard of dealing that was in effect on Oahu in 1974, when Shell and Nanakuli came into conflict.

IV. Two important factors created Shell's 1974 price-protection refusal: (1) the Arab oil embargo; and (2) a change of senior leadership of Shell's asphalt management group. In 1973, the men at the top of Shell's asphalt sales group retired, including those who had negotiated the original 1969 agreement with Nanakuli. The incoming parties had no knowledge of the price-protection structure that had existed in practice, but was not included in the express terms of the Shell-Nanakuli agreement. While the grant of Shell's judgment notwithstanding the verdict was based on the fact that a 1970 letter had set out a specific procedure by which Nanakuli could retain price protection, the court found several problems with the trial court's reasoning. First, the mechanics of the 1970 letter proposal offered Nanakuli little real protection, and would have run counter to the justification for price protection. Second, if the practice of price protection had been incorporated into the parties' 1969 agreement, Shell could not unilaterally rescind this term after the contract had entered into effect. Finally, the letter had been addressed generally to Shell's Hawaii customers (and not specifically to Nanakuli), leading Nanakuli to believe that the letter was not relevant because of its preexisting agreement with Shell (the letter indicated that all previous agreements would be honored). Given the preexisting agreement, Nanakuli's understanding thereof, and the fact that Shell knew of Nanakuli's new projects almost immediately, the court found that the jury could have determined that Nanakuli was reasonable in believing that the letter did not apply to it.

When Nanakuli received Shell's December 1973 price increase notification, Nanakuli asked Bohner for price protection on 7200 pre-committed tons of asphalt. But when Bohner attempted to get approval for the price protection from Shell management—a group that had no knowledge of the parties' special relationship—management rejected his request, stating that "any past practice was inapplicable at the present time." The court held that this rejection of price protection was made without proper understanding of Shell's 1969 agreement with Nanakuli, or any knowledge of the parties' past pricing practices. And while Shell made its decision without regard to the commercial context that the U.C.C. holds necessary to an understanding of the written contract, Nanakuli officials acted in good faith reliance on their right to price protection.

V. The court held that the validity of the jury verdict depended on four legal questions. First, how broad was the trade to whose usages Shell was bound under the 1969 agreement with Nanakuli? Second, were the two instances of price protection of Nanakuli by Shell in 1970 and 1971 waivers of the 1969 contract or was the jury entitled to find that they constituted a course of performance? Third, could the jury have construed an express term of Shells' posted price at time of delivery consistent with a trade usage and Shell's course of performance of the 1969 agreement? Fourth, could the jury have found that the commercially reasonable standards of fair dealing in the trade in Hawaii in 1974 were to give some form of price protection?

The court approached question one by first stating that the Hawaii U.C.C. provided explicitly for liberal interpretation of commercial usages and practices. The reason that this flexibility was included was to permit the courts to develop the law under the U.C.C. in light of "unforeseen and new circumstances and practices . . . ." The U.C.C. defined usage of trade as "any practice or method of dealing having such regularity of observance in a place, vocation or trade as to justify an expectation that it will be observed with respect to the transaction in question." The court understood the use of the word "or" to mean that parties could be bound by a usage common to the place they are in business, even if it is not the usage of their particular trade. The court held that, in light of the wide reach intended by the U.C.C. drafters, Shell would be bound not only by the usages of other asphalt providers, but to the more general practices within the industry of which Shell should have been aware. Since Shell could not show ignorance regarding the practices, or an affirmative denial of them in the contract, Nanakuli was justified in relying upon these industry usages.

The court thus held that the trial judge had properly defined the scope of trade as the entire Oahu asphalt paving industry, and found that it was not unreasonable to expect Shell to have knowledge of so small a market. While Shell also claimed that the practice was insufficiently regular to constitute a trade usage, Nanakuli proved that price protection was a near-universal practice by suppliers to the asphaltic trade in 1969; Shell failed to show even one instance in which price protection was not granted. And though Shell argued that the usage was not specific enough to justify the jury award, the court held that the U.C.C. provided that remedies under the Code are to be "liberally administered" to return the injured parties to wholeness, and that the Code provided the jury with the task of determining the particular usage, and the amount of damages incurred.

VI. Waiver or Course of Performance? The court differentiated between course of performance (the manner in which the parties actually carried out the contract at issue) and course of dealing (relations between parties under previous transactions between them). While the U.C.C. provides that one instance is insufficient to constitute course of performance, there is no further delineation of the number of instances required to constitute course of performance. Given the fact that a Shell official, in 1970, used language to indicate that Nanakuli was likely entitled to some form of price protection, and the fact that the several acts of price protection were unambiguous, the court held that the jury had a reasonable basis upon which to determine that a course of performance had been established.

VII. Consistent with Express Terms? The court stated that, under the U.C.C., express terms do not constitute the whole of the agreement. Rather, evidence of usages, dealings, and performance of the contract are also pertinent to understanding the agreement. Performance, usages, and prior dealings are to be admitted in all cases, unless "they cannot be reasonably reconciled with the express terms of the contract." A finding of ambiguity is not required as a predicate to the consideration of such evidence. Performance of the contract is to be considered the most important evidence of the agreement because "[t]he parties themselves know best what they have meant by their words of agreement and their action under that agreement is the best indicator of what that meaning was."

In the cases of *Columbia Nitrogen*, *Schiavone & Sons*, *Amerine National*, *Chase Manhattan Bank*, *Brunswick Box*, and *Board of Trade of S.F.*, federal courts had been lenient in not finding consistent additional terms or usage to be inconsistent with express terms, and had not required ambiguity of terms to be necessary to admission of usage evidence. Each of the cases upheld the importance of usage evidence as demonstrating the true nature of the parties' agreement, and were liberal in their admission of such evidence. The Hawaiian courts had only addressed the issue once before *Nanakuli*, but in considering the question, the court in *Cosmopolitan Financial* held that the adoption of the U.C.C. had relaxed the "rigid adherence to the exclusionary effects of the parol evidence rule" and provided for opportunities for courts to gain a "wider insight" into the nature of the parties' agreement. Other state courts in Pennsylvania, Alaska, Texas, Georgia, and Colorado had also stressed the importance of admitting and considering trade usage evidence in evaluating an agreement. The two leading instances where usage evidence had been rejected were state cases from North Dakota—*Southern Concrete*—and New York—*Triple T*. The court found that neither case was persuasive because the courts in question had not given the proper attention to usage that the U.C.C. requires.

The court did recognize that usage must in fact be widespread in order to qualify as evidence. But the court also noted that usage evidence has the benefit of not requiring any protection against perjury because it is dependent upon the actions of others in the industry. In this case, the overwhelming evidence indicated that all suppliers to the asphaltic trade practiced price protection under the same circumstances. Since the U.C.C. allows usage a much greater role in varying the literal words of a contract, the court held that the jury could reasonably have found that price protection was incorporated into the 1969 agreement, and was reasonably consistent with the express terms regarding price at delivery.

VIII. Good Faith in Setting Price? For a merchant, good faith means "the observance of reasonable commercial standards of fair dealing in the trade." Chevron, in raising its price at the same time as Shell, provided six weeks notice to its customers, in keeping with the long-standing practices of the asphaltic industry on Oahu. But Shell provided absolutely no warning to Nanakuli, increasing its prices from $44 to $76 (per ton) in a matter of days. In light of this performance, the court held that the jury could have reasonably found that Shell violated the standards of fair dealing in springing its price increase on Nanakuli without comparable notice. Thus, either of Nanakuli's theories, course of performance or good faith, would have supported the jury's damages award.

INTERESTING DISCUSSION ISSUES

1. *Was the custom and usage of "price protection" used to interpret the "posted price at time of delivery" language of the agreement or was it used to "contradict" that language?* Evidence of any of the three "usages" i s admissible to interpret and give meaning to a contract without the requirement of any predicate finding of ambiguity. On the other hand, the intention of the parties, if clearly established by the terms of the contract, should be followed where the usage is directly contradictory to the express language of the contract. Was there a direct contradiction in this case and, of so, should the evidence of trade usage have been excluded? The "price protection" custom and usage did not deprive the pricing term in the contract of any and all effect. It merely served to postpone, for a reasonable period, the implementation of any new price. Once that notice period had expired, the "price at time of delivery" became effective and would be implemented. Beyond question, the New York Court of Appeals that decided Mitchell v. Lath would have found the custom and usage to be flatly contradictory of the language in the contract. Should the Ninth Circuit have ruled against admission of the trade usage evidence? The record in this case suggests strongly that Nanakuli believed "price protection" was impliedly included in the contract. Did Shell share that belief? There was substantial evidence in the record that senior Shell staff, prior to the 1973 company restructuring, shared that belief, or in the alternative, was charged with knowledge of Nanakuli's belief.

One pending question, not addressed by the court, was the explanation, if any, for the failure of the parties in 1969 to expressly include price protection as a term of the contract. Perhaps the rationale underlying use of the trade usage concept, is that the practice was so clearly applicable that the parties saw no need to include it expressly. The practice would be impliedly incorporated by reference. Was it possible to give meaning both to the price term of the contract and the trade usage? Yes, by understanding that the "posted price at time of delivery" was subject to a requirement of prior reasonable notice before implementation of a price change.

"Course of performance" evidence may raise additional questions not raised by trade usage or custom of the parties. If the "course of performance" evidence is directly contradictory to the language of the contract, such course of performance may, under some circumstances, be understood and treated as a modification of the original contract. The subject of contract modification or waiver is covered in Chapter 8.

NOTES AND QUESTIONS

1. *Trade usage and regular observance.* Nanakuli was able to admit evidence of the trade usage of price protection. Since a practice must be "regularly observed" in order to be admissible, how did

Nanakuli establish such a practice and its regular observance? By expert testimony as to the practice in both the asphalt and aggregate (crushed rock) trades. Nanakuli also obtained testimony from a senior employee of Nanakuli's only competitor on Oahu that the competitor received comparable price protection from its asphalt supplier, Chevron.

2. *Members and nonmembers of a trade.* Members of a trade are normally bound by their own trade usage even if not aware of the trade usage while nonmembers are normally bound by trade usage only if they should have been aware of the trade usage. How did the court define the "trade" in question? The trial court had defined "trade" to include not only asphalt but also aggregate (usually mixed with asphalt to create the pavement surface). The trial court refused to allow evidence of price protection in the cement trade, ruling that this was a separate and distinct trade. Had the evidence been limited to the asphalt industry only, the evidence would have shown only one other supplier and its practice. Once the aggregate trade was found sufficiently associated with the asphalt trade, there were numerous other witnesses available and able to testify to a uniform price protection practice. The Ninth Circuit concluded that the trial court had ruled correctly on this issue. Was Shell a member of the trade so defined? Shell was a member of the asphalt trade but not of the aggregate trade and hence protested the trial court's allowance of evidence as to price protection in the aggregate trade. But the Ninth Circuit held that the trial court had ruled correctly because of the clear record of the close ties between Nanakuli and Shell and the regular detailed knowledge of Nanakuli's business by a Shell representative. What was the trade usage in question? The trade usage was "price protection" as described in detail in the court's opinion and the brief above. Was this usage "regularly observed" in the defined trade? The evidence established that the practice was uniformly observed. Was Shell specifically aware of the trade and the trade usage and if not should it have been so aware? The evidence established that Shell was specifically aware of the trade usage.

3. *Failure of trade usage.* Even if Nanakuli had failed to establish the trade usage, and that Shell should have been aware of that usage, what other tiers of the trilogy could Nanakuli use to enforce price protection on Shell? The usage given the greatest weight in the trilogy, the course of performance of the parties. Common sense suggests that where, following the making of the agreement, the conduct or words of the parties indicated how they understood and interpreted terms of the agreement, such conduct or words should be used to establish the shared mutual intention of the parties as to the meaning of such terms. The use of "course of performance" evidence has been relied upon by

many courts, including the International Court of Justice in interpreting treaties.

4. *CISG treatment.* Like the UCC and the common law, CISG Art. 9 defines and uses the trilogy of usages for purposes of interpretation. However, the CISG does not rank the trilogy in a hierarchical form.

5. *Express exclusion of trade usage.* Given that Shell was the target of what it perceived as undesirable trade usage, could Shell have contracted out (excluded) such trade usage? The answer is yes. Such a provision would be designed to elevate the control of the specific language of the contract over local customs.

6. *Consistency rule.* How does the court resolve the question of the "consistency" between the price protection trade usage and the express written term requiring price to be determined at the time of delivery? See the "Interesting Discussion Issue" above. Is it possible that the contract could have included both written formulations? Yes. The parties could have defined price as "Shell's posted price at time of delivery" subject to advance notice for a defined reasonable period of time of any price increase so as to protect Nanakuli on bids made in good faith at the old price and accepted by the contracting agency. If so, how would the two provisions have been interpreted? Literally. What does this suggest about whether trade usage is an actual part of the agreement with equal dignity with other written terms? It suggests equal dignity subject to the hardest case where the custom is flatly inconsistent with and contradictory of the language of the contract.

G. EMPLOYMENT CONTRACTS

The pending question is whether an employment contract with no length of time of employment specified should be subject to an implied term of employment "for a reasonable period." The philosophy of the UCC with respect to the implication of reasonable terms would suggest just such an implied term. The American law result, however, is directly to the contrary. An employment contract lacking a specific term defining the length of the employment is commonly interpreted as an "employment at will" and, as such, is subject to termination on two weeks' notice. Employment law is the subject of standalone law school courses and it is not the purpose of this casebook to provide any effective coverage of this broad and important field of law. But it is the purpose of this chapter to cover, at least in outline, the subject of the implication of terms (both implied-in-fact and implied-in-law), such as the implied term of "employment at will", in contracts. Implied constructive conditions are covered later in association with breach of contract in Chapter 8.

As you study the following materials, form your own ideas regarding the importance of the at-will employment doctrine. Should it be retained or rejected and what arguments can you muster in favor of your arguments? The strongest argument in favor of retention is the more than 100 years of American case law applying this doctrine. Change would bring surprise to the world of business and such change should not be implemented without substantial reasons. Moreover, since the issue is one of important social policy, perhaps such a change should be made by legislators rather than courts. The next strongest argument in favor of retention of the current law is the classic difficulty of deciding where to slice the salami. Would the change involve switching to a presumption of indefinite continued employment unless dismissed for "cause"? Would we then need a compulsory retirement age in order to assure adequate opportunities for the young to get jobs? If not "working lifetime" then should we presume employment for not less that a year subject to earlier termination for cause? Lawyers who have litigated termination for cause cases will testify to the serious problems in and costs involved with attempted terminations for cause. Those familiar with some European country employment laws will recognize the very high cost in, for instance Belgium or Holland, of trying to terminate an employee there. The cost may be a year or years of salary. It is not clear that changing the "at will" presumption would work any particular improvement in the job market in this country. The strongest argument for change is the hardship that termination frequently inflicts not only on the employee but also on the employee's family. Again in today's world of high health care costs, a major cost of termination may be loss of health care benefits. While the health insurance carrier may be obligated to offer a continuation of those benefits for a relatively short period and at a market based fee, the loss of benefits can have severe consequences especially where the employee or a member of the family has a serious chronic medical condition which may affect cost or even availability of continuing health care insurance.

Dufner v. American College of Physicians
CASE BRIEF

This is a 2004 decision of the Court of Common Pleas, Pennsylvania. Dufner was hired by the American College of Physicians ("ACP") in 1998 and terminated in 2003. She alleged that her termination was retaliatory—attributable to complaints she made to management of a hostile work environment created by her co-workers. ACP countered that her termination was based on her violation of company policy, namely falsification of time sheet records. Dufner said she was wrongly accused of such falsification. Her complaint alleged: wrongful termination of an implied contract, defamation, contractual bad faith and wrongful discharge in violation of public policy. The trial court dismissed her complaint and she appealed.

The appellate court, addressing the breach of contract counts, ruled that she failed to attach a copy of any such contract to her complaint or otherwise verify the existence of any such contract. Absent any such contract, Dufner was an "at will" employee who could be "terminated for a good reason, bad reason, or no reason at all." To overcome the presumption of "at will" status the contract must be clear and definite. To overcome such a presumption she would have to prove: an agreement for a definite duration, providing for discharge only for cause, supported by additional consideration, or an applicable public policy exception. Dufner failed on each of these four requirements. She relied on statements in the company's employee handbook, but the court found no such clear intent as would be required. For a handbook to provide the necessary contractual commitment, it "must contain unequivocal provisions that the employer intended to be bound by it, and, in fact denounced the principle of at-will employment." The court also denied a claim based on promissory estoppel, saying that, "The Supreme Court of Pennsylvania has held that an at-will employee does not have a claim for promissory or equitable estoppel because of his alleged reliance on an employer's promise."

Addressing the retaliation charge, the court pointed out that she made her complaints to the company in the summer of 2002 but was not terminated until October, 2003. She would have a claim if her discharge was motivated by a specific intent to harm her, or the discharge violated a clear mandate of public policy. She failed to substantiate the existence of any such clear mandate of public policy. It would not be sufficient to establish that the employer's action towards her was unfair. Even if a public policy exception were available she could still be discharged if the employer had a "separate, plausible and legitimate reason for the discharge. The public policy exception has been defined very narrowly.

There was no basis for any finding based on violation of an implied contractual duty of good faith. Her count for libel and slander failed because of an absence of showing of publication to a third party. In any case an employer has an absolute privilege to publish defamatory matters in notices of employee terminations.

NOTES AND QUESTIONS

1. *Promissory estoppel exception.* Why was Alison Dufner's claim of promissory estoppel rejected? Impliedly, for lack of any specific promise. The court ruled that any such promise must be clear and definite. Specifically, what was the alleged source and nature of the employer's promise not to discharge her except for cause? We are not told other than by vague references to the employee handbook in question. Given this case, and this note, is promissory estoppel a likely

theory of obligation to overcome the "firmly entrenched presumption" enunciated by the *Dufner* decision? It is unlikely to provide any better vehicle than breach of contract. The two requisite ingredients, a clear promise and reasonable reliance were apparently missing in this case. The court may have intended to indicate that promissory estoppel cannot work because there can never be the necessary reasonable detrimental reliance where the employment contract is "at will."

2. *Additional consideration exception.* See text.

3. *Employee handbook implied-in-fact exception.* See text.

4. *Good faith and fair dealing.* It is also common to assert that the employer's discharge is in "bad faith" when not motivated by a reasonable cause. Citing, *Donahue v. Federal Express Corp.,* 753 A. 2d 238 (Pa. Super. 2000), the *Dufner* court determined that the claim was invalid "as a matter of law" when applied to directly rebut the presumption of at-will employment. What do you think the *Dufner* court meant by its statement that there is "no bad faith when an employer discharges an at-will employee for good reason, bad reason, or no reason at all, as long as no statute or public policy is implicated"? The court was apparently alluding to the clear legal principle that "bad faith" does not create a separate enforceable breach of contract. Bad faith can only interact with other facts tending to establish a breach of contract. Here, given the employer's right to terminate for good reason, bad reason or no reason negated the existence of any breach with which bad faith could interact. Building upon your understanding that good faith is not an independent duty but rather attaches to other obligations created by the contractual relationship between the parties or by statute, does this statement make sense? Yes. Is it consistent with your understanding of good faith after reviewing the *Locke* case? Perhaps not. The Locke court said that Warner Brothers could exercise their right to reject Locke's projects but could only do so in good faith, that is after a reasonable review of the substance of her proposal. Here the court found the employer had the absolute right to terminate and refused to look into the question of whether the employer had exercised that power after a reasonable review of Dufner's performance.

5. *Public policy exception.* Most states recognize a public policy exception to the at-will presumption. However, the "public policy" usually must be specifically enunciated in a statute, regulations or judicial decision. Alison Dufner made such a claim. Why was it rejected? Presumably, her argument was that any "retaliatory" termination should be reviewable as a matter of public policy. The court, in effect, held that the employer was free to terminate her even if such action was specifically retaliatory. According to the court, since no

reason for termination was required it did not matter whether the reason was in fact retaliatory.

6. *Federal law employment protections.* See text.

7. *Whistleblower exception.* See text.

8. *Employee demotions.* See text.

CHAPTER 5

CONTRACTS UNENFORCEABLE BY OPERATION OF LAW

Table of Contents

Introduction to Chapter 5 Coverage

This chapter addresses situations in which the state will refuse to lend its enforcement powers to private agreements and contracts by operation of law, even where the parties have apparently satisfied all of the requirements for formation (i.e., mutual assent) and enforceability (i.e., consideration). In many cases, such contracts are referred to as "void" contracts. The categories and subcategories of "void" contracts include:

- Illegal contracts or contracts that contravene public policy.
- Contracts required to be evidenced by a written memorialization pursuant to the Statute of Frauds.
- Contracts that are so grossly one-sided and unfair as to shock the conscience of the court.
- Contracts executed through fraud.
- Contracts executed under duress.

A. THE DISTINCTION BETWEEN VOID AND VOIDABLE CONTRACTS

It is important to distinguish between contracts that are void—i.e., that cannot be enforced at either party's election—and those that are merely voidable—i.e., contracts that the promisee may choose to enforce or avoid at the promisee's election. The category of "void" contracts includes those that are contrary to public policy, violate the Statute of Frauds, are unconscionable, or are procured by fraud in the execution or through physical coercion. Voidable contracts, such as agreements induced by fraudulent misrepresentations, contracts by infants, and other similar defenses, are the subject of Chapter 6.

Since the avoidance of all contracts requires that the moving party take some step or steps to assert invalidity the difference between 'void" and "voidable" may appear semantic. A number of authors have urged that both types be termed "unenforceable" contracts. But the distinction can still have important legal consequences. The words of a "void" contract have no legal effect, and by themselves create neither right nor duty, privilege nor power. The words of a voidable contract, in contrast, operate to create new legal relationships but such relationships can be extinguished at the election of one of the parties. A voidable contract can be ratified but a void contract cannot. A third party bona fide purchaser for value without notice can acquire rights under a voidable contract but not under a void one.

The distinction can create difficult conceptual problems in analyzing arbitration agreements under the Federal Arbitration Act or similar state statutes. The case that follows poses the question of whether an agreement that is void from its very inception should nevertheless bind both parties to arbitrate any disputes allegedly arising under that agreement.

Buckeye Check Cashing, Inc. v. Cardegna
CASE BRIEF

Justice Scalia delivered this 2006 opinion of the Supreme Court of the United States. Respondents brought a putative class action alleging that Buckeye had charged usurious interest rates in violation of various Florida lending and consumer-protection laws rendering the contract criminal on its face. The form of contract contained an arbitration clause providing that "Any claim, dispute, or controversy . . . arising from or relating to this Agreement . . . or the validity, enforceability, or scope of this Arbitration Provision or the entire Agreement (collectively 'Claim'), shall be resolved, upon the election of you or us or said third-parties, by binding arbitration. . . ." Buckeye moved to compel arbitration, but the trial court denied the motion, holding that a court rather than an arbitrator should resolve the claim that the contract was illegal and void ab initio. The Florida District Court of Appeals reversed but the Florida Supreme Court restored the district court ruling. The Supreme Court of the United States granted certiorari.

§ 2 of the Federal Arbitration Act provides:

> A written provision in . . . a contract . . . to settle by arbitration a controversy thereafter arising out of such contract . . . or an agreement in writing to submit to arbitration an existing controversy arising out of such a contract . . . shall be valid, irrevocable, and enforceable, save upon such grounds as exist at law or in equity for the revocation of any contract.

Justice Scalia said that challenges to the validity of arbitration agreements can be divided into two types. One type challenges specifically the validity of the agreement to arbitrate (claims not subject to arbitration under state law), and the other on a ground that affects the entire agreement. The current complaint was of this second type. In a footnote he said that the issue of validity is different from the issue of whether any agreement was ever concluded—this latter issue was not covered by the instant opinion.

He cited to the 1967 decision of the court in *Prima Paint Corporation* where the court held:

> [I]f the claim is fraud in the inducement of the arbitration clause itself—an issue which goes to the making of the agreement to arbitrate—the federal court may proceed to adjudicate it. But the

> statutory language does not permit the federal court to consider claims of fraud in the inducement of the contract generally.

This issue was one of federal and not state law. The court's prior opinions established three propositions. "First, as a matter of substantive federal arbitration law, an arbitration provision is severable from the remainder of the contract. Second, unless the challenge is to the arbitration clause itself, the issue of the contract's validity is considered by the arbitrator in the first instance. Third, this arbitration law applies in state as well as federal courts." He then concluded, "Applying them to this case, we conclude that because respondents challenge the Agreement, but not specifically its arbitration provisions, those provisions are enforceable apart from the remainder of the contract. The challenge should therefore be considered by an arbitrator, not a court."

He addressed the fact that the Florida Supreme Court had relied on the distinction between void and voidable contracts but concluded that *Prima Paint* makes this conclusion irrelevant. "[W]e cannot accept the Florida Supreme Court's conclusion that enforceability of the arbitration agreement should turn on 'Florida public policy and contract law.'"

He quoted respondents' argument as follows:

> Respondents point to the language of § 2, which renders "valid, irrevocable, and enforceable" "a written provision in" or "an agreement in writing to submit to arbitration an existing controversy arising out of" a "contract." Since, respondents argue, the only arbitration agreements to which § 2 applies are those involving a "contract," and since an agreement void *ab initio* under state law is not a "contract," there is no "written provision" in or "controversy arising out of" a "contract," to which § 2 can apply. Its last appearance is in the final clause, which allows a challenge to an arbitration provision "upon such grounds as exist at law or in equity for the revocation of any *contract*." (Emphasis added.) There can be no doubt that "contract" as used this last time must include contracts that later prove to be void. Otherwise, the grounds for revocation would be limited to those that rendered a contract voidable—which would mean (implausibly) that an arbitration agreement could be challenged as voidable but not as void. Because the sentence's final use of "contract" so obviously includes putative contracts, we will not read the same word earlier in the same sentence to have a more narrow meaning.

He concluded:

> It is true, as respondents assert, that the *Prima Paint* rule permits a court to enforce an arbitration agreement in a contract that the arbitrator later finds to be void. But it is equally true that respondents' approach permits a court to deny effect to an arbitration provision in a contract that the court later finds to be perfectly enforceable. *Prima Paint* resolved this conundrum—and resolved it in favor of the separate enforceability of arbitration provisions. We reaffirm today that, regardless of whether the challenge is brought in federal or state court, a challenge to the validity of the contract as a whole, and not specifically to the arbitration clause, must go to the arbitrator.

The decision of the Florida Supreme Court was reversed.

INTERESTING DISCUSSION ISSUES

1. *Whether it should make a difference that the underlying contract was illegal and void under state law.* Contract law has been, traditionally, state law and not federal law based. Do you think the enactment of the Federal Arbitration Act was intended to preempt state law applicable to void contracts? Was any such extensive preemption necessary to implement the basic purpose of the federal act, namely to recognize and enforce agreements to arbitrate?

2. *Whether the reasoning of the federal common law as applied is circular.* See "Notes and Questions" 1 below.

NOTES AND QUESTIONS

1. *Circular reasoning.* The circularity of Justice Scalia's reasoning in *Buckeye Check Cashing* is patent. *Buckeye Check Cashing* concerned a borrower's claims that the entire loan agreement was void as unconscionable, contrary to public policy, and illegal under Florida usury law. As the Florida Supreme Court noted, "[i]f the underlying contract is held entirely void as a matter of law, all of its provisions, including the arbitration clause, would be nullified as well." See *Cardegna v. Buckeye Check Cashing, Inc.*, 894 So.2d 860, 863 (Fla. 2005). While the U.S. Supreme Court held that the question of whether a contract that includes an arbitration clause is illegal or otherwise void must be determined by arbitration, if the contract is void ab initio then the parties technically never had an enforceable obligation to submit their disputes to arbitration. How does Justice Scalia's majority opinion in *Buckeye Check Cashing* purport to resolve this circularity (if at all)? He finds that as a matter of policy, and in accordance with earlier decisions of the court, the language of § 2 covers void and

voidable contracts equally. By so doing, he, in effect, ignores the circularity of reasoning involved. Reading between the lines, he may think that the federal statute encouraged the resolution of issues including validity by arbitration and to separate issues of voidness from issues of voidability would undermine the basic purpose of that statute. The unfortunate aspect of his opinion is that the statute is premised on an agreement of the parties to arbitrate and there is no such agreement where the whole agreement is void and unenforceable.

2. *Contractual validity versus contractual formation.* Footnote 1 of Justice Scalia's majority opinion purports to limit its holding to challenges to contractual validity and not to address situations in which a contract was never "concluded"—lack of a valid signature, an agent's lack of authority or capacity to bind its principal, and lack of mental capacity. Lack of a valid signature occurs in cases of forgery, fraud in the execution, or situations in which one of the parties has not actually expressed any form of consent to an agreement, all three of which would render the purported contract either void or non-existent. Similarly, a contract executed by an agent or purported agent who lacks authority to bind her principal cannot usually create any contractual duties on behalf of the principal, again a void or non-existent contract. But lack of mental capacity, as discussed in detail in Chapter 6, creates only contractual duties that are voidable at the option of the mentally incapacitated party or their guardian. How are these three situations different, if at all, from the facts of *Buckeye Check Cashing*? Logically, they are all similar but in Footnote 1 Justice Scalia simply says "Our opinion today addresses only the former . . . ." (i.e. issue of validity). The opinion, then, does not say that these other cases would be decided differently. Again, it seems that the court is impressed with the need to prevent taking away issues of validity from the arbitrator. This need is apparently found implied in the language of § 2.

3. *Privitization of public law.* Assume the contract at issue in *Buckeye Check Cashing* showed illegal usury on its face. The majority opinion in *Buckeye Check Cashing* holds that the determination of whether the contract violated consumer protection statutes, truth in lending statutes, or even the criminal law (to the extent it may be enforced by private actions) is a matter for private arbitrators, not for state courts. What are the dangers inherent in such a rule? Keep in mind that the traditional description of the benefits of arbitration is that arbitration is fast, cheap, and secret. If paycheck loan providers (or even truly criminal loan sharks) include an arbitration term in every contract, what does that mean for the ability of courts to continue developing the common law with respect to that type of transaction? If the decision of invalidity is made publicly by a court, and not privately by arbitration, the news media will publish the issue and its resolution

thus alerting readers to the invalidity of that kind of contract. The privacy of arbitration is likely to preclude any such media attention and thus prevent others similarly situated from learning that the contract in question is illegal. Forcing arbitration is likely to have a limiting effect on the number of plaintiff claims or defenses based on such illegality. It may also inhibit the bringing of class actions, a salutary remedy for such illegal practices.

4. *Arbitration clauses as privileged contract terms.* Does *Buckeye Checking Cashing* create a privileged status for arbitration terms, compared to other contract terms? Justice Bell of the Florida Supreme Court noted in his concurrence in *Cardegna v. Buckeye Check Cashing, Inc.* that, rather than complying with Congressional intent to treat arbitration clauses on an equal footing with other contract terms, the rule that would ultimately be adopted by the U.S. Supreme Court does privilege arbitration clauses over other contract terms.

> If, under Florida law, no contract ever existed here, then by definition no enforceable agreement to arbitrate ever existed. The dissenting opinion and the federal decisions on which it relies have elevated arbitration clauses to a more favored status, exempting them from the state's otherwise generally applicable contract law. The FAA, however, mandates only that arbitration clauses be given equal status. In this case, if a valid and enforceable contract exists, then a valid and enforceable arbitration clause exists. The problem is that we do not yet know if a valid and enforceable contract exists. 894 So.2d 860, 863 (Fla. 2005).

Do you agree or disagree with Justice Bell's assessment? The Supreme Court decision does indeed treat arbitration clauses differently by applying a newly created federal common law or interpretation of the Federal Arbitration Act. Whether such different treatment should be characterized as "privileged" or not may be a matter of personal opinion. What seems clear is that the Supreme Court wanted to accomplish the broadest possible scope for arbitral decision rather than limiting that scope by excluding contracts challenged as illegal and thus void. Other implications of this decision have been noted above.

B. THE PUBLIC POLICY DOCTRINE

The ability of private parties to create their own "private law" through entry into contracts is circumscribed by the doctrine of "public policy." "Freedom of contract" is trumped when the interests of the public clearly transcend the interests of the individual contracting parties. Contracts contrary to public policy are generally void. As stated in the Restatement (Second) of Contracts § 178, a promise or agreement is unenforceable on grounds of public policy in situations

(1) where the legislature has directly declared certain agreements or promises illegal, or (2) where judicial precedent has recognized the existence of a public policy against enforcement of such promises. But because of the way in which our case law evolves, the scope, extent and applicability of such "public policy" is not always clear. As Professor George Strong observed, "One of the reasons for the apparent confusion is the fact that illegality may appear in many forms and in varying degrees."

1. Illegal Contracts

Just as the Restatement (Second) of Contracts §§ 178(b) & 178(c) permit courts substantial leeway in balancing the interests of society and the public in determining whether to enforce an otherwise illegal contract, the dividing line between whether a contract actually violates or contributes to a violation of a statute, regulation or other rule is likewise blurred. As you read the following case, consider the reasons for avoiding a bright-line rule that would bar enforcement of all contracts that violate a provision of the law in themselves or that contribute to such a violation. Note that the parties may not be equally at fault—*in pari delicto.*

Anheuser-Busch Brewing Ass'n v. Mason
CASE BRIEF

This case is a decision of the Minnesota Supreme Court in 1890. The plaintiff sued to recover an unpaid debt for bottled beer sold to the defendant. The defendant answered alleging that, to the knowledge of the plaintiff, the defendant was a keeper of a house of prostitution and that the plaintiff sold the beer expressly for use and dispensation in and for carrying on and maintaining this house. Moreover, it was agreed that the beer was to be paid for out of the profits accruing from the defendant's unlawful occupation. For obvious reasons, the defendant put in no evidence in support of her answer but, rather, relied on admissions made by the plaintiff that, "when selling it to the defendant, he supposed she would sell or use it in her brothel."

The opinion of the court stressed that the illegality of the transaction under discussion occurred, if at all, in a matter collateral to the sale. It noted that, "The reports, both English and American, are replete with cases in which contracts of all descriptions have been held invalid on account of an illegality of consideration, illustrations of the acknowledged rule that contracts are unlawful and non-enforceable when founded on a consideration contra bonos mores, or against the principles of sound policy, or founded in fraud, or in contravention of positive provisions of a statute." The court also noted the complete lack of "harmony" in the many reported cases, but recited a rule distilled from two cases, one in New York and the other in New Hampshire, as follows:

> [M]ere knowledge by a vendor of the unlawful intent of a vendee will not bar a recovery upon a contract of sale, yet, if, in any way, the former aids the latter in his unlawful design to violate a law, such participation will prevent him from maintaining an action to recover. The participation must be active to some extent. The vendor must do something in furtherance of the purchaser's design to transgress, but positive acts in aid of the unlawful purpose are sufficient, though slight.

The court noted that there was no other evidence connecting the plaintiff or its agent with any violation of the law. The court, in rejecting the defense, stated:

> The burden was upon the defendant to show that an enforcement of the contract would be in violation of the settled policy of the state, or injurious to the morals of its people, and no court should declare a contract illegal on doubtful or uncertain grounds.

INTERESTING DISCUSSION ISSUES

1. *How and where to draw the line when the two parties to a contract are not equally at fault or equal participants in an illegal transaction.* The court here took a comparative approach to the comparability of fault or contribution to commission of a crime by the plaintiff and the defendant. By making the issue one of fact and not strictly law the court opinion invites litigation given the uncertainty of the standard applied. But the result has an element of reason to it given the fact that a contrary ruling (against the beer seller recovering) would do little if anything to advance the relevant public policy of suppressing prostitution.

NOTES AND QUESTIONS

1. *Source of the illegality.* On what basis did Mason argue that the contract with Anheuser-Busch was illegal? Mason alleged that the beer, to the agent's knowledge, would be consumed by those participating in the brothel, an illegal business, and would be paid for from the proceeds of that business. Mason's proof, however, established much less, only that the agent knew the nature of Mason's business and that "he supposed she would sell or use it in her brothel." What statute or public policy did the agreement allegedly violate or contravene? The operation of a brothel may well have been criminal as a matter of statute law. The issue, however, was one of public policy, namely whether the sale of the beer for consumption in the brothel

might be sufficiently closely associated with the illegal business and be tainted—the agent becoming an accomplice. The level of participation in that business was important—the court concluding in effect that the plaintiff merely sold the beer to the defendant without any actual participation in the illicit business. How would the court's analysis have differed, if at all, if the events of this case had occurred twenty years later, after passage of the eighteenth amendment to the United States Constitution? The sale of beer itself would have then been illegal and the suit to recover the price would have been dismissed. The sale would then have been the very thing the law was designed to preclude.

2. *A confederation of thieves.* Note that Mason appears to be attempting to avoid enforcement of a contract by claiming (s)he has engaged in illegal activity, of which Anheuser-Busch knew and in which the company allegedly participated. The case appears to turn on the issue of whether Anheuser-Busch's agent, who admitted knowing that the beer would be sold (or consumed) in Mason's house of prostitution, was a confederate of Mason and participated in the criminal activity. Is the court's distinction between contracts for an illegal activity versus contracts that take place in illegal or immoral circumstances or merely tend to promote illegality meaningful? While, as the court noted, the standards applicable are very vague, the plaintiff did not actually sell beer in the brothel or otherwise encourage or solicit the business of the brothel. From the plaintiff's point of view, there was no difference between the sale of the beer in this case and the sale of beer to anyone else. What the defendant chose to do with the beer was her business and not the plaintiff's. What actions by Anheuser-Busch would have been sufficient to make the company a confederate of Mason's and thereby render this contract unenforceable under the illegal contracts doctrine? The contract would have been unenforceable if the agent had actually carried the beer in to the brothel and sold it to those inside. It would also probably have been unenforceable if the defendant had proven what she alleged, namely that the agent agreed that he would be paid out of the proceeds of the business of the brothel.

3. *Law by other means.* Assume that the *Anheuser-Busch* court had held that the contract at issue was illegal because of the nature of the buyer's business (a house of prostitution). What would have been the reaction of other buyers who engaged in similar illegal businesses? They would have the beer delivered to an innocent address or buy it in the name of someone not associated with the business of the brothel. Would Anheuser-Busch be more or less likely to investigate the businesses of its customers before contracting with new businesses in the future? Anheuser-Busch would probably be less likely to investigate and claim simple ignorance. Thus denying the company's claim for the purchase price would not tend in any real sense to

diminish the business of brothels. The sanction of non-recovery of the price of the beer would therefore fail to relate to the advancement of the underlying public purpose, limiting or preventing the operation of brothels. If otherwise highly profitable but illegal contracts are unenforceable at law, what measures can the parties take to guard against the risk of nonperformance? Payment in advance could solve the problem, because the payor in such a situation would be precluded from seeking restitution by reason of the illegality involved. The following newswire story illustrates the risks involved in attempting to use public legal system tools to enforce warranty rights in illegal contracts:

> PALATKA, Fla., Dec. 19 (UPI)—A woman who tried to get her money back by complaining to police in Florida about the dealer who sold her poor quality crack cocaine ended up behind bars.
>
> Eloise Reaves of North Carolina lodged her complaint with a Putnam County deputy sheriff who was responding to a call to a convenience store, WJXT-TV in Jacksonville reported. Deputy Jeffrey Pedrick warned her that if the stuff tested positive for cocaine she would be arrested.
>
> Reaves, even after she was booked, told police they should find the drug seller and get her money back on the grounds that there was wax mixed in with the crack. She was later freed on bail. "Woman complains to cop about bad crack," UPI, Dec. 19, 2006.

Assuming the drug dealer is eventually captured and convicted under the criminal law for selling crack to Reaves, should Reaves be entitled to maintain a breach of contract action against the dealer? Clearly not—the parties were *in pari delicto,* that is to say each was a direct participant in the illegal sale of the drugs.

4. *Efficient deterrence and the superior risk bearer.* The issue of deterrence was discussed under Note 3 above: "The sanction of non-recovery of the price of the beer would therefore fail to relate to the advancement of the underlying public purpose, limiting or preventing the operation of brothels." Where one party gains as a result of a transaction and the other loses, courts seem to conclude that a stronger flavor of illegality should be required if that imbalance is not to be adjusted and the loss is to be left where it lies.

2. Contracts in Contravention of Public Policy

The text points out the risk involved of enabling an unelected judiciary to intervene in private contracts to effect vague standards such as public policy, "Although the doctrine is relatively easy to apply in cases where the legislature has declared certain types of promises and agreements to be illegal or unenforceable, it poses unsettling questions of vagueness, bias, and paternalism where the only source of public policy is the court's own determination." The text notes the extraordinary abuse under the Nazi regime of concepts of public policy applied to Jewish ownership. It also describes the facts and outcome of *In re Baby M* holding that the surrogacy contract involved violated New Jersey law. The text makes a particular point of the problem where a court creates a new category of public policy (violated by the contract in question) "out of the blue," i.e. without notice. Establishing such new categories challenges the ability of lawyers to predict and counsel clients. On the other hand, it could be argued that the categories of situation where courts have decided to protect uninformed consumers have been steadily growing over the last seventy-five years.

Hewitt v. Hewitt
CASE BRIEF

This case is a 1979 decision of the Illinois Supreme Court. The plaintiff, Victoria Hewitt, lived with Robert Hewitt for fifteen years and bore three children. She initially filed a complaint for divorce but admitted they had not obtained a marriage license. She then filed an amended complaint:

> (1) that because defendant promised he would "share his life, his future, his earnings and his property" with her and all of defendant's property resulted from the parties' joint endeavors, plaintiff is entitled in equity to a one-half share; (2) that the conduct of the parties evinced an implied contract entitling plaintiff to one-half the property accumulated during their "family relationship"; (3) that because defendant fraudulently assured plaintiff she was his wife in order to secure her services, although he knew they were not legally married, defendant's property should be impressed with a trust for plaintiff's benefit; (4) that because plaintiff has relied to her detriment on defendant's promises and devoted her entire life to him, defendant has been unjustly enriched.

The facts established that, while students, the plaintiff became pregnant and that thereafter the defendant told her that they were husband and wife and would live as such, and that he would "share his life, his future, his earnings and his property with her." Thereafter they held themselves out as husband and wife. She contributed to his professional education and obtained financial assistance for this purpose from her parents. Since the beginning of the relationship the defendant had accumulated "large amounts" of property and enjoyed a substantial current income.

The trial court dismissed the amended complaint holding that such claims had to be based on a valid marriage. The court of appeals found no substantial affront to public policy and reversed the trial court holding that the complaint stated a cause of action based on an express oral contract.

The supreme court reversed the court of appeals. It first described the bases for the lower court decision. The court of appeals had relied on the fact that the Illinois Marriage and Dissolution of Marriage Act, 1977, did not prohibit nonmarital cohabitation and that the Criminal Code made fornication an offense only if the behavior was open and notorious. As to the issue of an express oral contract, the lower court had adopted the reasoning of the much publicized California case, *Marvin v. Marvin,* described by the supreme court as follows:

> The courts should enforce express contracts between nonmarital partners except to the extent that the contract is explicitly founded on the consideration of "meretricious sexual services" and that "In the absence of an express contract, the courts should inquire into the conduct of the parties to determine whether that conduct demonstrates an implied contract, agreement of partnership or joint venture, or some other tacit understanding between the parties. The courts may also employ the doctrine of quantum meruit, or equitable remedies such as constructive or resulting trusts, when warranted by the facts of the case. . . ."

The court reached its conclusions because:

> In summary, we believe that the prevalence of nonmarital relationships in modern society and the social acceptance of them, marks this as a time when our courts should by no means apply the doctrine of the unlawfulness of the so-called meretricious relationship to the instant case. . . .
>
> The mores of the society have indeed changed so radically in regard to cohabitation that we cannot impose a standard based on alleged moral considerations that have apparently been so widely abandoned by so many. . . .

The supreme court rejected the *Marvin* reasoning, starting with the proposition that:

> The issue of whether property rights accrue to unmarried cohabitants can not, however, be regarded realistically as merely a problem in the law of express contracts. . . . There are major public policy questions involved in determining whether, under what circumstances, and to what extent it is desirable to accord some type of legal status to claims arising from such relationships. Of substantially greater importance than the rights of the immediate

> parties is the impact of such recognition upon our society and the institution of marriage. Will the fact that legal rights closely resembling those arising from conventional marriages can be acquired by those who deliberately choose to enter into what have heretofore been commonly referred to as "illicit" or "meretricious" relationships encourage formation of such relationships and weaken marriage as the foundation of our family-based society? In the event of death shall the survivor have the status of a surviving spouse for purposes of inheritance, wrongful death actions, workmen's compensation, etc.? And still more importantly: what of the children born of such relationships? What are their support and inheritance rights and by what standards are custody questions resolved? Does not the recognition of legally enforceable property and custody rights emanating from nonmarital cohabitation in practical effect equate with the legalization of common law marriage at least in the circumstances of this case? . . .

The court pointed out that this reasoning, if followed, would return Illinois law to something like common law marriage which had been outlawed in 1905. It quoted an 1882 decision to the effect that, "An agreement in consideration of future illicit cohabitation between the plaintiffs is void." The court acknowledged that "cohabitation by the parties may not prevent them from forming valid contracts about independent matters, for which it is said the sexual relations do not form part of the consideration"—citing Restatement (First) of Contracts §§ 589, 597. But this court resisted any such change based on changes in societal norms and attitudes, and suggested that it was naïve to believe that these relationships could be severed from or separated from the sexual activity. If the resolution of these issues was to depend on public policy that judgment should be exercised by the legislature and not the courts. "The issue, realistically, is whether it is appropriate for this court to grant a legal status to a private arrangement substituting for the institution of marriage sanctioned by the State."

The court then reached the reverse of the conclusion of the court of appeals with respect to the Illinois Marriage Act and concluded that the lower court decision contravened the act's policy of strengthening and preserving the integrity of marriage. Further that statute affirmed the 1905 abolition of common law marriage. The relationship established by the plaintiff would clearly have been a common law marriage. Unlike other states, including California, Illinois had rejected "no-fault" divorce, thus further manifesting a pro-marriage policy. The 1977 statute granted very limited recognition to a "putative" spouse (one who had gone through a marriage ceremony and co-habited in good faith) thus indicating opposition to any further expansion of cohabitation based claims. Moreover, the Illinois legislature had enacted the Marriage Act only two years earlier. The fault of the court of appeals was that, in effect, it had reinstated common law marriages.

The supreme court concluded that the plaintiff's claims were unenforceable since they contravened public policy.

INTERESTING DISCUSSION ISSUES

1. *Public policy as an "unruly horse."* The juxtaposition of the *Marvin* and similar decisions with the ruling in this case illustrates the extent to which application by a court of a judicially ascertained and determined "public policy" may be unpredictable. Says this court:

> The real thrust of plaintiff's argument here is that we should abandon the rule of illegality because of certain changes in societal norms and attitudes. It is urged that social mores have changed radically in recent years, rendering this principle of law archaic. It is said that because there are so many unmarried cohabitants today the courts must confer a legal status on such relationships.

And this court refused to abandon the "rule of illegality" as it found that rule to be. This court concluded that any such change should require action by the legislature and not the court. Why would the California Supreme Court and other courts be willing to change without legislative intervention? Or does the Illinois Supreme Court assume its conclusion by stating the preexisting "rule" rather than recognizing a new situation in need of a different solution?

2. *Conflating contracting for sexual favors with contracting for property rights.* This case provides an interesting comparison with the California *Marvin* decision. The heart of *Marvin* lies in that court's splitting off or separating the sexual content of the relationship from the property rights side. The Illinois Supreme Court said:

> It is true, of course, that cohabitation by the parties may not prevent them from forming valid contracts about independent matters, for which it is said the sexual relations do not form part of the consideration. (Restatement of Contracts secs. 589, 597 (1932); 6A Corbin, Contracts sec. 1476 (1962).) Those courts which allow recovery generally have relied on this principle to reduce the scope of the rule of illegality. Thus, California courts long prior to Marvin held that an express agreement to pool earnings is supported by independent consideration and is not invalidated by cohabitation of the parties, the agreements being regarded as simultaneous but separate.

It found that other courts that had followed *Marvin* applied a similar separation of consideration. The Illinois court's characterization of the relationship as one analogous to common law marriage ignores this separation of legal from illegal consideration.

NOTES AND QUESTIONS

1. *Sources of public policy.* Note the different sources of public policy analyzed by the *Hewitt* court to determine whether to enforce the contracts at issue. How did the court use statutes relating to family law, marriage (both statutory and common law), and probate law to develop a statement of public policy on an issue not explicitly addressed by the statutory law? The answer in the case is not dictated by the 1977 Illinois statute. The court's conclusion involved a two-step analogy process. First, it found that the 1977 statute emphasized and acted to protect the sanctity of marriage. Second, it found that the property arrangement disclosed by the complaint offended such sanctity. This second step deduction is not required by the assumption of the first. The second depends upon a separate conclusion, namely that enforcing such property right arrangements would interfere with such sanctity—a very different proposition and one not concurred in by the California, New Jersey, Michigan, Oregon and Minnesota courts cited in the opinion. The Illinois court also used a "parade of horribles" set of questions to support its conclusion—what would we do about issues of support, custody and inheritance etc. The court found a general public purpose (the strengthening and preservation of the institution of marriage) both explicit and implicit in the Illinois statute enacted only two years earlier. The court also relied on the 1905 statutory repudiation of the concept of common law marriage and the restatement of that repudiation in the recent statute. How does this treatment compare to the analysis by the *Anheuser-Busch* court? This court fails to explain how and in what manner enforcing the contractual commitments would actually weaken or impair the sanctity of marriage. The *Anheuser-Busch* court, on the other hand, seems to encourage an analysis based on whether the potential sanction of refusing enforcement would contribute to the important social and public policy to be protected. What other sources did the court address in determining the content of their respective jurisdictions' public policy on the enforcement of contracts between cohabiting parties? As noted above, the Illinois court decision pivots on its refusal to recognize a severable distinction between an agreement with respect to sexual conduct and one with respect to property rights. It also refused to recognize the significance of the alleged substantial shift in social mores and customs, stating that recognition of any such shift should come from the legislature and not from the court.

2. *Hierarchy of sources of public policy.* Of all the sources of public policy examined by the *Hewitt* court, are any more determinative of public policy than others? Clearly, a legislative declaration that a

particular class of contracts is contrary to public policy and unenforceable should be presumptively irrebuttable. But in *Hewitt,* for example, the court bases its determination that public policy barred enforcement of the contract for support partly on separate determinations that enforcement would be inconsistent with legislative pronouncements in other areas of the law and that the legislature had explicitly stated the elements necessary for recover by putative spouses. Is this latter source of public policy as determinative as an unambiguous legislative statement of policy? Clearly not. Nothing in the legislation required the court's refusal to look for separation of the meretricious consideration from the agreements on property rights. What about a court's reliance upon extrinsic reports of changing social mores and practices, or the impact of a new judicial determination of public policy on existing social and legal institutions? We do not know but may guess that the statements of change in social mores and practices were based on "judicial notice" rather than on evidence in the record. Should legal counsel be prepared to develop through appropriate testimony on the record the existence of such changes? Certainly, societal concepts change and, to the extent that judicially declared "public policy" depends upon such concepts, such public policy needs a measure of flexibility. One illustration of the importance of such change can be found in the twentieth century evolution of the doctrine of unconscionability now enshrined in both UCC § 302 and Restatement (Second) of Contracts § 208.

3. *Contract in the family sphere.* Many of the cases in this casebook address contracting problems arising out of complex intrafamilial relationships. See, e.g., *Dougherty v. Salt* (gift of promissory note by Aunt Tillie to nephew Charlie unsupported by consideration even though promissory note recited that consideration had been given); *Hamer v. Sidway* (promise by uncle to nephew of $5,000 if nephew refrained from drinking, smoking, and certain forms of gambling until age of 21 supported by consideration); *Kirksey v. Kirksey* (promise by landowner to provide living arrangements for poor relative held to be unenforceable promise of a gift); and *Wright v. Newman* (implied promise by defendant to support unrelated child held enforceable on grounds of promissory estoppel). Do these cases, as well as *Hewitt,* indicate that contract is particularly unsuited as a mechanism for resolving disputes between individuals engaged in family, conjugal, or similar relationships? Not necessarily. For one thing, *Hewitt* is now a minority position in a field dominated by the opposite result found in *Marvin.* But it may well be that the concepts and rules of contract law, hammered out in the context of commercial practice, are difficult to apply and extend to family and personal relationships. What potential alternatives are there for managing the promissory relationships between family members? We can remember that Fuller and Perdue, in their law review article in two parts, "The

Reliance Interest In Contract Damages," 46 Yale L.J. 52, 373, 1936-37, argued the importance of reliance and unjust enrichment rather than bargain as the preferable vehicles for determining damages in such relationships.

4. *Judicial competence and public policy*. The *Hewitt* court opined that the judiciary may be unsuited to make some determinations of public policy:

> In our view, however, the situation alleged here was not the kind of arm's length bargain envisioned by traditional contract principles, but an intimate arrangement of a fundamentally different kind. The issue, realistically, is whether it is appropriate for this court to grant a legal status to a private arrangement substituting for the institution of marriage sanctioned by the State. The question whether change is needed in the law governing the rights of parties in this delicate area of marriage-like relationships involves evaluations of sociological data and alternatives we believe best suited to the superior investigative and fact-finding facilities of the legislative branch in the exercise of its traditional authority to declare public policy in the domestic relations field.

Given that judicial declarations of public policy often occur in the context of an adversarial proceeding between two parties, or in some cases between one party and a representative of a class of individuals comprising the opposing party, are there any situations in which the *Hewitt* court would deem a court competent to make or change public policy in the absence of express legislation? Presumably, as the court did in this case, it would deduce public policy requirements from legislatively stated policies or historical common law categories.

5. *Public policy and the weight of precedent*. Compare the attitude of the *Hewitt* court toward the existing public policy against enforcement of contracts in consideration of a meretricious relationship. Does the court give deference to past, "settled" public policy? It purports to but, as pointed out above, the court's finding of consistent historical precedent may be the assumption of what it set out to demonstrate. Should the court give such deference, or should a court evaluate every claim that a contract contravenes public policy de novo? Broad based analyses of court decisions involving the application of such "public policy" suggest that courts are prone to find and apply public policy standards to recurring patterns of fact situation in a manner consistent with prior findings. These analyses suggest that courts are hesitant to create new categories or patterns of judicially determined "public policy." And, given the importance of predictability in our practice of law, both civil and criminal, such hesitancy may be wise. But the reader should remember that public policy has been and

continues to be an "unruly horse" and that there are wide divergences in its application from state to state, as is clear from the case law on enforceability of covenants not to compete covered in the next section.

6. *Bargaining power, marriage, and the enforceability of contracts for marital services.* Note that *Hewitt* involved substantial power imbalances between the parties. To one of our authors, it is not necessarily clear from the *Hewitt* decision that there was such a substantial power imbalance. At the beginning, when the relationship was first established, they were both students in college. True, it may be difficult to believe that plaintiff was sufficiently naïve to believe, as legal counsel apparently pleaded, that she did not know or realize that they were not truly "husband and wife." Later on in the relationship, it was clear that an economic imbalance had developed, one that could be difficult to explain in the absence of an element of dominance by the man over the woman in economic and business matters. Does this case illustrate potential bargaining power disparities that might exist between the parties in "negotiating" or "performing" a contract for marital services? Remember that it was the pregnancy that apparently initiated the relationship and its form. Much has been written about power disparities and the consequences of such disparities caused by such a development. Does gender play a role in the way either court addresses the potential for inequality of bargaining power between the parties? Not necessarily. The *Marvin* court seems to recognize the ability of the parties to bargain effectively about property rights and then enforce that bargain. There are traces of suggestion in the *Hewitt* decision that "he said, she said" claims about the nature of the bargain, if any, that was struck between the parties could be brought fraudulently. What about bargaining power disparities based upon informational advantages? Numerous cases involving claims like those in *Hewitt* suggest the advantage of one spouse over the other based on that spouse's actual conduct of the business, leaving the other spouse uninformed as to the facts. In *Hewitt*, it appears that the male defendant was responsible for convincing the female plaintiff that a formal marriage was unnecessary, suggesting that he may have known (or at least should bear the responsibility for the parties' mistake) that the law required otherwise to make his purported promise enforceable. How should courts address this apparent gross disparity of bargaining power, if at all? This claim, as pleaded by legal counsel, suggests a level of naivety on the part of the plaintiff, a former college student, that is difficult to comprehend.

7. *Remedies outside of contract law.* As discussed in Chapters 2 and 3, the doctrines of promissory estoppel and quantum meruit provide for the enforcement of promises "outside" of contract law. Specifically, in both *Hewitt*, the promisee provided substantial benefits to the promisor during the course of their relationship. If the public

policy doctrine prevents enforcement of the defendant's promises under contract law, why should the parties be denied recovery under non-contract principles and doctrines? In some circumstances, enforcement of a remedy by way of unjust enrichment would defeat the primary public policy just as any other remedy. One example will suffice. Suppose the owner of real property transfers that property to another in order to attempt to avoid the claims of creditors. If the transfer is based on an oral promise to reconvey at a later date, that oral promise is unenforceable on grounds of public policy, namely the need to discourage unlawful attempts to secretly hide owned assets from creditors. The transferee, having provided no consideration for the transfer, is benefited unjustly by the transfer but to remedy that injustice would contravene the underlying public policy—hence the transferee incurs a windfall but that windfall is not recoverable under a theory of unjust enrichment. This suggests that any consideration of the granting of a remedy based on unjust enrichment should depend upon whether the granting of such a remedy would be inconsistent with the public policy involved. In the thinking of the *Hewitt* court, a remedy based on unjust enrichment would undermine the values of marriage just as much as any other remedy would. In the thinking of the *Marvin* court, the property rights arrangement is separate and distinct from the meretricious aspect of the arrangement and thus should be enforced. Indeed, some courts have occasionally permitted quantum meruit recovery in such situations. See John W. Wade, "Benefits Obtained Under Illegal Transactions—Reasons For and Against Allowing Restitution," 25 Tex. L. Rev. 31, 31-33 (1946) (surveying judicial treatments of claims for restitution under contracts deemed void as contrary to public policy). What arguments can you make in favor of permitting the promisee to recover in restitution? As in *Anheuser-Busch,* the answer should depend upon whether the granting of any remedy is inconsistent with the applicable public policy. In that case, prohibiting recovery through denial of a remedy to the plaintiff would have contributed nothing to the enforcement of the applicable public policy against prostitution. Why might restitution not provide a particularly favorable recovery for the promisee? Because the remedy, if any, available under a restitution theory is limited to any increase in value actually benefiting the promise and is not measured by the bargain value of the promise.

3. Covenants Not to Compete in Employment Contracts

"Covenants not to compete" are used commonly in two different situations. The first such situation involves employees. Typically, the employer requires the employee to sign a covenant (promise) that the employee if terminated, or if she leaves the employment, will not work for a competitor of the employer for a stipulated period of time within a stipulated geographic area. "Competitor" will often be broadly defined.

The second such situation involves the seller of a business who, as part of the sale transaction, promises the buyer that the seller will not open a competing business or work for a competing business for a stipulated period of time within a stipulated geographic area. Both situations, while carrying the same label, pose different scopes of problem and, in some states, are reviewed under somewhat different standards.

The employee covenant is designed to protect the first employer against loss or transfer of important competitive information or important relationships to a competitor thus damaging the original employer's business. Consider, for instance, the case of a sales manager and vice president of a sizeable business. As an employee, the sales manager acquires knowledge of the employer's customer names, needs, and addresses, and also establishes important personal relationships with key employees of those customers. If the sales manager is free to leave the original employment and immediately go to work as sales manager for another company competing directly with the original employer, there is obviously some risk of competitive damage to the original employer. Suppose that the covenant she signed provides that she will not go to work for a competitor anywhere in the United States for a period of one year from the date of termination or resignation of the original employment. Next, suppose that the sales manager is fired or laid off. If the covenant is enforceable as written, the sales manager may well be unable to work anywhere else for a year, assuming that her skills are substantially limited to the industry or product set of the original employer. Such a barrier to work for a year can be a very serious deprivation to the employee, not only where the employee resigns and elects to work for another, but also where the employee is terminated or laid off. Because of the punitive effect of such a covenant, courts review them with some suspicion before ordering enforcement. First, the covenant must be reasonably necessary for the protection of the business of the employer. Second, the period of the prohibition of competition must also be reasonable in the circumstances relating to the employer's need for protection. Thirdly, the geographic area within which competition is prohibited must likewise be reasonably tailored to the real business needs of the employer.

As the text points out, these covenants are often obtained by employers with little or any notice or opportunity for the employee to object. Next, they have a certain "in terrorem" value to the employer since the employee may be unable to afford the cost of a legal challenge to the enforceability of the covenant or even knowledge of the fact that the covenant might be challenged and possibly be not enforceable. There is thus a substantial risk that such covenants will be obtained from people with respect to whom there is no real threat of competition if they leave the original employment but whose lives, nevertheless, may be restricted or hampered by the existence of such promises.

Thus at the most general level, as applied to employees, such clauses are enforceable only if they are reasonably required for the protection of the employer given the context and function of the particular employee, they are reasonable in scope and in geographic limitation. A covenant that flunks any one of these three requirements may be found unenforceable by a court and thus of no protective value to the employer and no restrictive effect on the employee.

Compare the case of a recently graduated accountant who accepts employment with an accounting firm and signs a covenant not to compete with any competitor for a period of one year anywhere in the United States. If she resigns or is terminated, and if that covenant is enforceable, she may be substantially deprived of any opportunity to work for a year in her area of expertise for which she was trained. By way of comparison, it is difficult to see how her employer could be damaged in any real way from her resigning or being terminated and going to work for another accounting firm.

Suppose she resigns and proposes to go to work for a competitor. Suppose further that her original employer starts a lawsuit to enforce the covenant she signed and to prevent the proposed new employer from employing her. The court has a clear choice between enforcing the covenant or finding it unenforceable. There is a third choice theoretically under which the court could rewrite the covenant cutting it down to reasonable limits with respect to different types of employment, length of time or geographic limits. This choice is often referred to as "blue penciling" by the court. In the context of employee covenants many courts refuse to consider any such third option. The reason for such a refusal lies in the reciprocal "in terrorem" effect that a court rejection of a covenant drawn in overly broad fashion would have. A court's refusal to "blue pencil" could be expected to make the drafters of such covenants tailor with much greater care the narrowness and specificity of application of the covenant. The threat of judicial denial could discourage the employer who is tempted to be overly and unnecessarily greedy in drafting the covenant. On the other hand, if a court were prepared to "blue pencil" a covenant under consideration, such an approach would encourage the drafters of such covenants to frame them over broadly thus increasing the risk of harm to ill-informed or financially challenged employees. If the court "blue penciled" the draft, then the employer would get the broadest protection the court was prepared to grant and would suffer no loss as a result of an excessively greedy draft.

Covenants not to compete entered into as part of the sale and purchase of a business pose a somewhat different problem. If the covenant is found by the court to be unenforceable, the buyer may lose the goodwill that she thought she was getting with the business she bought. The buyer's loss attributable to a finding that the covenant is unenforceable could be severe. As a result more courts are prepared to "blue pencil' a covenant not to compete signed in the context of the sale and purchase of a business.

American Broadcasting Companies, Inc. v. Wolf
CASE BRIEF

This is a 1981 opinion of the New York Court of Appeals, and involves a claimed non-compete agreement by a well known sportscaster for American Broadcasting Companies television in the New York area. Such personages attract a following and their presence can have a significant effect on listener ratings and hence on channel revenue. Their switch to a different network may cause a loss of revenue to the original employing channel or station.

Wolf had been employed by ABC since 1976. In February 1978 ABC and Wolf entered into an employment agreement which was to terminate on March 5, 1980. The elements of the non-compete provision contained in that agreement were synthesized by the court as follows:

> Under this provision, Wolf was bound to negotiate in good faith with ABC for the 90-day period from December 6, 1979 through March 4, 1980. For the first 45 days, December 6 through January 19, the negotiation with ABC was to be exclusive. Following expiration of the 90-day negotiating period and the contract on March 5, 1980, Wolf was required, before *accepting* any other offer, to afford ABC a right of first refusal; he could comply with this provision either by refraining from accepting another offer or by first tendering the offer to ABC. The first-refusal period expired on June 3, 1980 and on June 4 Wolf was free to accept any job opportunity, without obligation to ABC.

Renewal discussions began in September, 1979. While these discussions were continuing however, Wolf began talking with ABC's rival, CBS. On January 2nd, 1980, ABC expressed its willingness to meet substantially all of Wolf's demands but he rejected ABC's offer citing ABC's delay in communicating with him and his desire to explore his options in light of the impending expiration of the 45-day exclusive negotiation period (through January 19). On February 1st, 1980, Wolf orally agreed on terms of employment as a sportscaster for a CBS affiliate. His employment was covered by two agreements—the first covered his services as an on-the-air sportscaster and the second was an off-the-air production agreement for sports specials Wolf was to produce. This second agreement contained an exclusivity clause which barred Wolf from performing services of any nature for another entity without CBS' permission. Wolf signed the second production agreement on February 4 and at the same time CBS agreed in writing to hold the sportscaster offer open until June 4. In so doing Wolf breached his obligation not to accept other employment without giving ABC a right of first refusal. The next day Wolf resigned from ABC.

ABC made various offers on February 6 which Wolf rejected. He told ABC he had made a "gentlemen's agreement" and would leave ABC on March 5. Later in February, ABC and Wolf agreed that Wolf would continue to appear on the air during a portion of the first refusal period, from March 6 until May 28. As noted in the opinion:

> ABC commenced this action on May 6, 1980, by which time Wolf's move to CBS had become public knowledge. The complaint alleged that Wolf, induced by CBS, breached both the good-faith negotiation and first-refusal provisions of his contract with ABC. ABC sought specific enforcement of its right of first refusal and an injunction against Wolf's employment as a sportscaster with CBS.
>
> After a trial, the Supreme Court found no breach of the contract, and went on to note that, in any event, equitable relief would be inappropriate. A divided Appellate Division, while concluding that Wolf had breached both the good-faith negotiation and first-refusal provisions, nonetheless affirmed on the ground that equitable intervention was unwarranted.

The court of appeals affirmed the decision of the appellate division.

The court of appeals agreed that Wolf had breached his obligation to negotiate in good faith with ABC from December through March. Given the contract he had signed with CBS, any negotiations with ABC after February 4th were meaningless. But contrary to the decision of the appellate division, the court held he had not violated the first refusal provision. As the court explained:

> The first-refusal provision required Wolf, for a period of 90 days after termination of the ABC agreement, either to refrain from accepting an offer of employment or to first submit the offer to ABC for its consideration. By its own terms, the right of first refusal did not apply to offers accepted by Wolf prior to the March 5 termination of the ABC employment contract. It is apparent, therefore, that Wolf could not have breached the right of first refusal by accepting an offer during the term of his employment with ABC. Rather, his conduct violates only the good-faith negotiation clause of the contract.

This left as the pending question whether ABC was entitled to injunctive relief that would bar Wolf from continuing employment at CBS.

The court of appeals then reviewed the history of courts of equity refusing to order an individual to perform a contract for personal services, because of the inherent difficulties courts would encounter in supervising performance. It had also been suggested that any such attempted judicial compulsion would violate the 13th Amendment. "For practical, policy and constitutional reasons, therefore, courts continue to decline to affirmatively enforce employment contracts." But courts fashioned an alternate remedy, "Thus, where an employee refuses to render services to an employer in violation of an existing contract, and the services are unique or extraordinary, an injunction may issue to prevent the employee from furnishing those services to another person for the duration of the contract." An injunction was justified in such a situation because the employee "either expressly or by clear implication agreed not to work elsewhere for the period of his contract. And, since the services must be unique before negative enforcement will be granted, irreparable harm will befall the employer should the employee be permitted to labor for a competitor."

The court then noted that once a personal service contract has terminated it is impossible to decree affirmative or negative specific performance. "Only if the employee has expressly agreed not to compete with the employer following the term of the contract, or is threatening to disclose trade secrets or commit another tortious act, is injunctive relief generally available at the behest of the employer. . . . Even where there is an express anticompetitive covenant, however, it will be rigorously examined and specifically enforced only if it satisfies certain established requirements. . . . And, an otherwise valid covenant will not be enforced if it is unreasonable in time, space or scope or would operate in a harsh or oppressive manner. . . . The rules governing enforcement of anticompetitive covenants and the availability of equitable relief after termination of employment are designed to foster these interests of the employer without impairing the employee's ability to earn a living or the general competitive mold of society. . . ."

Since the contract ended in March, 1980, there was no existing employment agreement to support an injunction. Nor was there any express anti-competitive covenant that Wolf was violating. Breach of a duty to negotiate in good faith did not justify injunctive relief after the contract term was over. "Our public policy, which favors the free exchange of goods and services through established market mechanisms, dictates otherwise."

The court likewise refused to imply a covenant not to compete in the post-employment period. Wolf might, however, be responsible in damages.

Judge Fuchsberg dissented, finding the first refusal provision to be central. He disagreed with the majority's finding that Wolf had agreed with CBS before the time for application of the right of first refusal had arrived. "So precious a reading of the arrangement with ABC frustrates the very purpose for which it had to have been made. Such a classical exaltation of form over substance is hardly to be countenanced by equity."

INTERESTING DISCUSSION ISSUES

1. *The reasons for drafting covenants not to compete.* The notes at the start of this topic in the Teachers Manual illustrate reasons for inclusion of such clauses in both employment contracts and sales and purchases of businesses. Such clauses are particularly suspect in employment contracts for several different reasons. Employers tend to frame such clauses aggressively or "greedily" without careful regard to the shape and extent of an employer interest truly worthy of protection through the use of such a clause. Employees tend to sign such covenants either without careful thought or without true opportunity or means to challenge or bargain for their limitation or exclusion. The harm that such clauses can cause to the employee may not be apparent until after the employee is terminated or laid off. As the introductory notes suggest, there is usually a wide difference between the context and impact of a covenant in an employment contract compared with a covenant in a sale/purchase of a business. Thus many courts refuse to "blue pencil" employment covenants but will cut down and trim excessive clauses in sale/purchases.

2. *What explains the drafting of the ABC contract with Wolf and why was there no explicit covenant not to compete included? Had such a clause been included, would it have been enforced?* It seems that ABC was the victim of their own lawyer drafting. The contract focused on getting an opportunity for ABC to negotiate and then, that failing, to have a right of first refusal visavis any other offer from outside. The majority of the Court of Appeals read the lawyer drafting very closely with the result that ABC received no injunctive relief. The suggestion that they might recover damages in a different hearing probably just rubbed salt in the ABC wounds. The facts illustrate the value of quick injunctive relief where otherwise serious harm cannot be avoided. It is probable that the court would have granted injunctive relief had there been an express covenant not to compete of reasonable scope and extent.

NOTES AND QUESTIONS

1. *Purposes of noncompete clauses.* Why did ABC include the noncompete clause in Wolf's 1978 employment agreement? The fact is that the ABC contract did not contain an express noncompete clause. Instead of such a straight out noncompete clause, they fashioned a two-fold agreement: first, a promise to negotiate in good faith and for the first 45 days exclusively with ABC; second, *following the 90-day negotiation period,* he was obligated not to sign without giving ABC a right of first refusal. Careful and close reading of the contract led CBS to contract with Wolf *before* the period of first refusal took effect. ABC's contract was too clever and their attempt to get the court to *imply* a

covenant not to compete failed. A simple covenant not to compete would have better served ABC's interests. Given Wolf's prominence and the impact on his change of employment on ABC, it is highly probable that a simple straightforward covenant not to compete would have been enforced. Do those business justifications extend to more mundane employment agreements, such as sales staff or mid-level executives? The case law suggests that a positive finding of reasonable need on the part of the employer reflected carefully in the scope of duties prohibited as well as the time and geographic limits of that prohibition is a requirement for enforceability. To what extent do those justifications mirror the concerns surrounding injunctive relief for employment contracts discussed in Chapter 9? The New York Court of Appeals carefully reviewed the history of, and the reasons against, granting injunctive relief which would have the effect of compelling the employee to continue working for the complaining employer.

2. *Incentives to litigate noncompete clauses.* In *ABC v. Wolf,* which party had the greatest incentive and ability to challenge the validity of the noncompete clause—Wolf or CBS? Why? While both may have had that capability, CBS had the much deeper pocket and the ability to charge related legal costs as a business expense for tax purposes. What benefits might a competitor achieve by hiring a famous personality from ABC? The potential shifting of audience attention from the ABC television station to the CBS affiliate. What if Wolf, instead of being an on-air sportscaster with a distinct and marketable persona, had been a highly skilled cameraman or engineer at ABC? In this case, Wolf's livelihood would have depended on his work as a camera man. ABC, on the other hand, would not lose any good will or market share of audience attention because of his transfer of employment. The business need of ABC to be protected would be much less clear and would probably have been unprotectable. Would CBS have had the same incentives to litigate? Probably not—other skilled camera persons should have been available—no special expertise would have been involved. What if similarly skilled employees could be hired from non-competing sources? The market from which the employee is drawn should not be the issue—it should be the presence or absence of a reasonable business need on the part of the employer to be protected. If other skilled persons are available in the market then the employer does not have the requisite business need to protect against the camera person being hired away.

3. *Alternatives to noncompete clauses.* Are there any contractual mechanisms by which an employer might protect its legitimate business interests such as trade secrets and customer lists from exploitation by competitors who hire away the employer's employees that do not require a noncompete agreement? Yes. It can require an employee of appropriate responsibility and access to information to

promise not to remove or take away with her such trade secrets or customer lists. Breaches of such promises can be enjoined and other employers with notice of the wrongdoing of the employee can also be enjoined or sued for damages. Unlawful removal of documents from the employer can be stopped but it is difficult to prevent an employee from leaving with and using that which is committed to the employee's mind and which is part of his equipment used in the kind of work in which he engages.

4. *Assessing the reasonableness of the noncompete clause.* Timing can be critical for determining the reasonableness of noncompetition clauses. In *King v. Head Start*, 886 So.2d 769 (Ala.2004), the court rewrote a noncompete agreement between a hairdresser and her employer that prohibited her from working for any competing hair salon within a two-mile radius of any of her employer's locations for one year following termination. The court based its decision on factors such as the plaintiff's age, the difficulty of developing new skills, the hardships enforcement of the clause would pose to the plaintiff's family, and the fact that the employer's thirty locations effectively prevented plaintiff from any employment as a hairdresser. As Professor Rachel Arnow-Richman notes in an insightful analysis of the *King* decision, however, all of the factors relied upon by the court arose at the time of termination, or the "back end" of the contract. See Rachel Arnow-Richman, "Cubewrap Contracts and Worker Mobility: The Dilution of Employee Bargaining Power via Standard Form Noncompetes," 2006 Mich. St. L. Rev. 963. In contrast, if the court had examined the reasonableness of the noncompete clause at the "front end" of the parties' contractual relationship, when the plaintiff was just beginning her working career, had no family and many options, the clause might have been reasonable for both parties. To what extent, if any, did such timing issues play a role in *ABC, Inc. v. Wolf*? The length of any applicable time prohibition would have been critical. Had there been a straightforward covenant not to compete, a court might well have found, as Judge Fuchsberg found in dissent, that a 90-day prohibition would not have been unreasonable.

5. *The dangers of criminalizing breach of contract.* As footnote 5 of *ABC, Inc. v. Wolf* indicates, statutes imposing criminal penalties for nonperformance of a personal services contract are essentially indistinguishable from state enforced slavery or indentured servitude contracts. Likewise, as discussed further in Chapter 9, the same considerations prohibit courts from ordering specific performance of contracts for personal services.

White v. Fletcher/Mayo/Associates, Inc.
CASE BRIEF

This 1983 decision of the Georgia Supreme Court likewise involved the enforceability of a covenant not to compete. White was a former employee of the advertising company defendant. He became a corporate vice president of the employer in 1977 and a senior vice president in 1981. The employer corporation and its business were purchased by a third party which took the seller's name. Part of the purchase price of the business reflected the sale and transfer of client goodwill. White had no control over the decision to seek the sale and took no part in the negotiations. At the date of the sale (merger), White owned 4.62% of the total employer company stock transferred with a book value of about $85,000. The merger required the affirmative vote of a majority of the shareholders of the selling company and White voted his shares for the merger, thus receiving a profit over book value of about $60,000. He could have voted against the merger in which case he would have received the fair market value of his shares (a taxable event whereas the exchange of shares in the new entity was nontaxable).

The purchase (merger) was conditioned, among other things, on White signing a covenant not to compete. The court noted that:

> White testified that at the time FMA told him he should sign the agreements because they were necessary to guarantee his job and secure broader career opportunities for him. There was trial testimony for appellees that FMA's [the defendant's] biggest client was serviced out of the Atlanta office, that White supervised service of this and other accounts, and that he was asked to sign the covenants because, in light of his client contacts, he was considered a key employee.

Soon after the merger White was fired. He filed suit to determine whether he was bound by the noncompete covenants he had signed. The trial court found the covenants overly broad, but incidental to the sale and purchase of a business and thus subject to "blue penciling," and reduction in scope. Thus altered, the trial judge found the covenants enforceable. The Supreme Court reversed, concluding that employee covenants were not subject to "blue penciling," and having been found overly broad, were thus unenforceable. See the comments at the start of the notes to this section of the book. Had this been a covenant truly ancillary to the sale and purchase of a business the court would have permitted "blue penciling:"

> On the other hand, if a covenant not to compete has been made by a seller ancillary to the sale of a business, the seller "may be enjoined from competing to the extent that it is found essential, by

clear and convincing evidence, to protect the purchaser, despite the overbreadth of the covenant."

Thus the outcome of this case turned on whether the court classified the covenants not to compete as ancillary to the sale and purchase of a business or incidental to an employment contract. "In short, we do not blue pencil in employment contract cases, but do in sale of business cases." The court found that White's profit was strictly proportional to that of all the other shareholders, 94% of whom were not asked to make such covenants. He did not have the same unfettered bargaining power that the seller of a business would have and he had no control over management. If it appears that his bargaining capacity was not significantly greater than that of a mere employee, then the covenant should be treated like a covenant ancillary to an employment contract, and "[a]s such, it should be enforced as written or not at all."

INTERESTING DISCUSSION ISSUES

1. *A covenant in an employment contract compared to a covenant in a sale/purchase agreement.* The differences between these two types of covenant and the reasons for disparate treatment by the court are discussed in both the introductory notes and those that follow below.

NOTES AND QUESTIONS

1. *Different treatment of covenants not to compete in employment versus sale of business contracts.* The court in *White* approved different rules governing the validity of a noncompete clause in an employment contract as contrasted with a sale of business transaction. Do you agree with the court's decision on this point? Yes. Can you explain and justify this differential treatment? See the introductory comments to this section of the Teachers Manual. The court above explained the difference as follows:

> When a person sells a business and covenants not to compete in a certain territory, the buyer pays and the seller receives a part of the total purchase price as consideration for that covenant. The buyer frequently would not buy the business if the seller were free to begin competing immediately. By restricting the territory to an area less than that specified in the covenant, the court requires the seller to do that which the buyer and seller bargained for, yet in a smaller area than that agreed to by the seller. The reasons for rejecting severability in employee covenants, *Rita Personnel Services v. Kot,* supra, are not applicable to covenants not to compete made in conjunction with the sale of a business. Many courts in this country apply the 'blue pencil' to covenants not to compete.

Another way of explaining the difference is to focus on the punitive effect on the buyer of a business of holding the covenant either enforceable as written or wholly unenforceable. The rationale for such a covenant in the context of a sale and purchase of a business is also clear and tangible.

2. *The in terrorem effect of a noncompete clause in an employment contract.* The court in *White* explained its rationale for refusing to "blue pencil" noncompete covenants in employment contracts. Is the court's rationale persuasive? Yes. See the introductory comments to this section of the Teachers Manual.

C. UNCONSCIONABILITY—CONTRACTS VOID FOR UNFAIRNESS

1. History and Purpose of the Doctrine of Unconscionability

The discussion in the text describes the thin and murky history of the doctrine of unconscionability in the English courts, including the classic statement in *Earl of Chesterfield v. Janssen* (1751):

> [Unconscionability] may be apparent from the intrinsic nature and subject of the bargain itself; such as no man in his senses and not under delusion would make on the one hand, and as no honest and fair man would accept on the other; which are unequitable and unconscientious bargains: and of such even the common law has taken notice . . . .

This formulation of the standard is still sometimes repeated by modern courts. This topic should be linked with that of "adhesion" contracts in Chapter 3, and limitation of liability in Chapter 9. A number of claims of "unconscionability" are to be found in contracts limiting or excluding liability for negligence or containing indemnification clauses likewise seeking to protect the indemnitee from her own negligence. It is somewhat puzzling to find this aspect of unconscionability dealt with in Restatement (Second) of Contracts § 195 while general unconscionability is dealt with in a different section, § 208, essentially copying the language of UCC §302. As a matter of history, it is clear that nearly 500 years ago it was established that an innkeeper could not contract out of liability for negligence. A century or more later, a similar position was taken with attempts of carriers to contract out of liability for negligence. § 195 states that a party cannot contract out of liability for willful intent or gross negligence, or out of simple negligence in certain specified situations.

Karl Llewellyn's formulation of UCC § 302 and its broader influence were discussed earlier. The *Williams* case which follows is one of the often quoted modern cases on unconscionability. It can be described as an attempt at creating a concept of consumer protection and, as such, should be linked to the many parallel regulatory efforts to be found under the aegis of the Federal Trade Commission and the various banking agencies both federal and state.

Williams v. Walker-Thomas Furniture Co.
CASE BRIEF

This is a 1965 decision of the United States Court of Appeals District of Columbia Circuit. The issue involved in the cases consolidated under this heading was whether the seller of goods could replevy under the terms of the contracts of sale to the consumers. Each consumer (appellant) had purchased a series of pieces of furniture or other equipment at different times. These consumers made periodic payments in reduction of the aggregated purchase prices of the various pieces. The problem arose out of a term in these contracts under which the seller treated each installment payment as a fractional payment on each piece. Thus, so long as any unpaid balance remained, none of the aggregate of pieces had been paid for in full and, upon default, the seller moved to replevy all articles in spite of the fact that if the payments had been allocated in accordance with date of purchase many of these pieces would have been paid for in full. The effect of this contractual language was described by the court as follows:

> The effect of this rather obscure provision was to keep a balance due on every item purchased until the balance due on all items, whenever purchased, was liquidated. As a result, the debt incurred at the time of purchase of each item was secured by the right to repossess all the items previously purchased by the same purchaser, and each new item purchased automatically became subject to a security interest arising out of the previous dealings.

The appellants had been unsuccessful below in arguing that these contracts were unconscionable but the Circuit Court sustained their argument. The reasoning of the court was also based on the conduct of the seller in selling items of substantial cost to customers with known limited capability to ultimate pay the full price:

> Appellant's second argument presents a more serious question. The record reveals that prior to the last purchase appellant had reduced the balance in her account to $164. The last purchase, a stereo set, raised the balance due to $678. Significantly, at the time of this

> and the preceding purchases, appellee was aware of appellant's financial position. The reverse side of the stereo contract listed the name of appellant's social worker and her $218 monthly stipend from the government. Nevertheless, with full knowledge that appellant had to feed, clothe and support both herself and seven children on this amount, appellee sold her a $514 stereo set.

The District of Columbia Court of Appeals, below, could find no ground upon which to declare such contracts to be contrary to public policy. Said the Circuit Court, "We do not agree that the court lacked the power to refuse enforcement to contracts found to be unconscionable. In other jurisdictions, it has been held as a matter of common law that unconscionable contracts are not enforceable." The UCC § 302 was not available since the statute had not become law in the District of Columbia at the time these contracts were entered into. Nevertheless the court found this section to be persuasive authority. "Accordingly, we hold that where the element of unconscionability is present at the time a contract is made, the contract should not be enforced." The court then defined "unconscionability" as follows:

> Unconscionability has generally been recognized to include an absence of meaningful choice on the part of one of the parties together with contract terms which are unreasonably favorable to the other party. Whether a meaningful choice is present in a particular case can only be determined by consideration of all the circumstances surrounding the transaction. In many cases the meaningfulness of the choice is negated by a gross inequality of bargaining power. The manner in which the contract was entered is also relevant to this consideration. Did each party to the contract, considering his obvious education or lack of it, have a reasonable opportunity to understand the terms of the contract, or were the important terms hidden in a maze of fine print and minimized by deceptive sales practices? Ordinarily, one who signs an agreement without full knowledge of its terms might be held to assume the risk that he has entered a one-sided bargain. But when a party of little bargaining power, and hence little real choice, signs a commercially unreasonable contract with little or no knowledge of its terms, it is hardly likely that his consent, or even an objective manifestation of his consent, was ever given to all the terms. In such a case the usual rule that the terms of the agreement are not to be questioned should be abandoned and the court should consider whether the terms of the contract are so unfair that enforcement should be withheld.

Unconscionability was to be determined in the light of the circumstances existing at the time the contract was made. Since no findings on possible unconscionability had been made below, the case was remanded for further proceedings. Judge Danaher dissented, joining in the opinion of the Court of Appeals below.

INTERESTING DISCUSSION ISSUES

1. *Does the opinion provide meaningful guidance on what is unconscionable?* The court does not apply UCC § 2-302 since that provision was enacted after the contracts involved in the case were made. But the court found that section persuasive. As the comments in the text note, § 2-302 itself provides little if any guidance as to what should be regarded as "unconscionable." The decision does not actually hold that the contracts in question were unconscionable. It remanded for further findings on the subject. But the opinion does spell out some criteria:

- Absence of meaningful choice on the part of one of the parties together with contract terms unreasonably favorable to the other party;
- The meaningfulness of the choice may be negated by a gross inequality of bargaining power;
- How the contract was entered into;
- The educational level of the party adversely affected;
- Providing a reasonable opportunity to understand the terms of the contract;
- Terms hidden in a maze of fine print;
- Terms minimized by deceptive practices;
- Real or objectively manifested consent may be absent where there was little bargaining power and hence little real choice;
- Ordinarily, "one who signs an agreement with full knowledge of its terms might be held to assume the risk that he has entered into a one-sided bargain;"
- But, per Footnote 7, "a one-sided bargain is itself evidence of the inequality of the bargaining parties;"
- Terms must be considered in the light of the circumstances existing when the contract was made;
  Approves Corbin's test, "whether the terms are so extreme as to appear unconscionable according to the mores and business practices of the time and place."

The dissent emphasized that the trial court made no finding of actual sharp practice and that the appellant (buyer) "seems to have known precisely where she stood." This comment points out one difference between the majority and the dissent—for the majority, proven knowledge and consent may not leave the contract enforceable—unfairness may trump despite such knowledge and consent (especially where there is an educational or knowledge imbalance).

The dissent was concerned about the effect the decision might have on future credit transactions in the District. As Note 3, following, points out, the practical effect of the decision was very limited.

2. *Were the contract terms "shocking"?* Note 1, following, points out that such "add-on" security clauses were apparently permitted by 36 states, including Maryland, at the time of the decision. This comparison tends to highlight the potential unpredictability of such rulings based on "public policy." But the opinion makes some point of the seller's knowledge of Ms. Williams' financial condition and other responsibilities. This makes it more difficult to find the basis of the decision limited to the terms of the contract alone.

NOTES AND QUESTIONS

1. *Add-on security clauses.* At the time of the *Williams* decision, thirty-six other jurisdictions—including Maryland, which borders the District of Columbia—explicitly regulated (and therefore implicitly permitted) by statute the use of add-on security clauses of substantially the same form as employed by the Walker-Thomas Furniture Co. See Arthur Allen Leff, "Unconscionablity and the Code—The Emperor's New Clause," 115 U. Pa. L. Rev. 485, 554-55 (1967). Assuming that the company was driven solely by commercial concerns (and there is no evidence to the contrary), what is the business purpose of such clauses? The most significant issue in the case is the difficulty of imagining a reasonable purpose for such a clause. The court impliedly takes notice of this. Why would a business that sold household goods on credit desire such an apparently stringent and onerous security provision in its credit installment sale contracts? As the dissenting judge points out, sellers to such customers must take on substantial risk of default—repossession of the specific goods may be cold comfort given the likelihood of damage to the goods. Perhaps this could be some sort of justification for the onerous provision. If the lower court on remand concluded that the Walker-Thomas Furniture Co. add-on clause was in fact unconscionable, what alternatives would the company have for retaining a comparable degree of security in its credit sales contracts? As Note 3 below points out, tougher credit standards were found to be appropriate. Thus, from one perspective, this decision made it harder for the poor in the District to buy such goods on credit. Given the risk of damage to the goods through use by the customer, requiring a substantial down payment at the time of purchase could also be anticipated.

2. *Expansion of UCC § 2-302 to the general law of contract.* See text.

3. *Aftermath of Williams.* Assume that you represent Walker-Thomas Furniture Co. Following *Williams,* what advice would you give to your client regarding how the company should respond to that decision? What would have been the appropriate response by the Walker-Thomas Furniture Company following the *Williams* decision? As the following content of Note 3 suggested, a likely response would be stricter credit standards and a larger down payment. The 2007 subprime mortgage problems may seem to have something in common with the facts of this case.

4. *The "accidental" inclusion of unconscionability in UCC § 2-302.* Professor Allen R. Kamp provides a fascinating history of the UCC drafting process in "Uptown Act: A History of the Uniform Commercial Code: 1940-49," 51 SMU L. Rev. 275 (1998). Section 1-C of Llewellyn's original drafts of the Revised Uniform Sales Act of 1941—the immediate predecessor to UCC § 2-302—dealt with the problem of oppressive standard form contracts. As originally drafted, § 1-C directed courts to regulate the terms of standard form contracts in accord with principles of fairness, equity, and trade practices, and the section did not address unconscionability. See id. at 306. Hiram Thomas, spokesperson and attorney for the New York Merchants Association during the initial UCC drafting process, was "notorious for speaking without thinking" (id. at 306) and this quality may have led to the inclusion of "unconscionability" within later drafts of § 2-302.

> Thomas saw the remedy limitations sections as manifesting "a desire to prevent what are essentially tricky and fraudulent practices." It was at the end of this discussion that Thomas suggested the alternative term "unconscionable." He was searching for some standard that would distinguish between permissible and impermissible limitations of remedies, stating:
>
> I would suggest "or oppressively," some word like that. If you are going to have some standard, let it not be pure reason. You might use "unconscionable" or something the court can look at and say, this is so arbitrary and oppressive and unconscionable that we won't stand for it.
>
> Llewellyn welcomed Thomas's suggestion: "[t]he line of thought raised by 'unconscionable' is exactly what one wants and also gives a draftsman guidance. You can tell when you are approaching the verge of the unconscionable." Id. at 307-08.

2. Elements of Unconscionability

The doctrine of unconscionability rapidly gained wide acceptance, particularly with respect to oppressive exoneration from liability or indemnification clauses. See, for instance, James F. Hogg, *"Consumer Beware: The Varied Application of Unconscionability Doctrine to*

Exculpation and Indemnification Clauses in Michigan, Minnesota, and Washington," 2006 Mich. St. L. Rev. 1011. Compare the scathing article by Arthur Allen Leff, commented on in the text. Leff's proposed distinction between procedural and substantive unconscionability was significant. As the text points out, many courts require a showing of both types of unconscionability.

Stirlen v. Supercuts, Inc.
CASE BRIEF

This was a 1997 California appellate court decision. Here, the trial court refused to enforce a compulsory arbitration clause in an employment contract as against public policy and unconscionable. The court also held the applicable California statute not preempted by the Federal Arbitration Act. The appellate court sustained the trial court opinion.

Supercuts was a national hair care franchise business. Stirlen was employed as the company's vice president and chief financial officer from January, 1993 until March, 1944 when he was terminated. He commenced a wrongful termination suit in 1994 containing seven causes of action including one that the arbitration clause in his contract was null and void and unenforceable. Supercuts moved to compel arbitration but the trial court held the clause unenforceable.

In 1993 and early 1994 Stirlen had informed management of "accounting irregularities" that might be in violation of state and federal law. His sustained position on these issues led to his termination. The applicable California statute required an order to arbitrate if the court found that "an agreement to arbitrate the controversy exists," and the appellate court found the trial court's decision to be subject to *de novo* review.

Stirlen's employment contract recited that he was an "at will" employee, contained provisions protective of confidential or proprietary information, and a covenant not to compete. The arbitration clause consisted of four paragraphs. Paragraph (a) described claims that need not be submitted to arbitration, covering all claims that Stirlen might have violated the confidentiality and noncompete provisions of the contract. The second paragraph provided that all other claims, including claims of discrimination, were to be submitted to arbitration. The third clause restricted any remedy under arbitration to monetary damages not to exceed actual damage for breach of contract, and precluded exemplary damages or injunctive relief. The final paragraph described selection of the arbitrator and other details. The trial court found the requirement to arbitrate unenforceable on the basis of the third paragraph limiting an award to actual damages. This finding was based on a California statute providing:

> [a]ll contracts which have for their object, directly or indirectly, to exempt anyone from responsibility for his own fraud, or willful injury to the person or property of another, or violation of law, whether willful or negligent, are against the policy of the law.

The appellate court ruled that it was not necessary to address the question of whether the restriction on employee remedies was against the law since the issue could be most efficaciously resolved on the basis of unconscionability.

The trial court's reasoning was that the clause was "so one-sided as to be unconscionable," protecting the company from "all fraud, willful injury or violation of law." The appellate court studied and applied an earlier 1981 decision of the California Supreme Court. The doctrine of that case required that a court first determine whether the agreement to arbitrate was a contract of adhesion. If so, the court was then to determine whether other factors operated to render it unenforceable:

> [A]n adhesive contract "would remain fully enforceable unless (1) all or part of the contract fell outside the reasonable expectations of the weaker party *or* (2) it was unduly oppressive or unconscionable under applicable principles of equity.

The appellate court noted that the California statute had adopted the concept of UCC § 2-302 but made it applicable to all contracts, not just contracts for the sale of goods. In a 1985 decision, following enactment of the new statute, the earlier California Supreme Court decision was found to lead to the same result as the new statute:

> Under the U.C.C. provision, "'[u]nconscionability has generally been recognized to include an absence of meaningful choice on the part of one of the parties together with contract terms which are unreasonably favorable to the other party.' . . . Phrased another way, unconscionability has both a 'procedural' and a 'substantive' element." . . .
>
> "The procedural element focuses on two factors: 'oppression' and 'surprise.' . . . 'Oppression' arises from an inequality of bargaining power which results in no real negotiation and 'an absence of meaningful choice.' . . . 'Surprise' involves the extent to which the supposedly agreed-upon terms of the bargain are hidden in the prolix printed form drafted by the party seeking to enforce the disputed terms. . . .
>
> Substantive unconscionability is less easily explained. . . . One commentator sums up the matter as follows: "'[p]rocedural unconscionability' has to do with matters relating to freedom of assent. 'Substantive unconscionability' involves the imposition of harsh or oppressive terms on one who has assented freely to them." (Hawkland UCC Series § 302:02 (Art. 2), p. 246.) The prevailing

> view is that these two elements must *both* be present in order for a court to exercise its discretion to refuse to enforce a contract or clause under the doctrine of unconscionability. (*Id.*, § 3-302:03 (Art. 2), p. 249, and cases cited at fn. 4, § 302:05 (Art. 2), p. 266.) This is consistent with the concept of unconscionability articulated in *Scissor-Tail*. . . . [the earlier California Supreme Court decision]
>
> In the present case, the threshold question is whether the subject arbitration clause is part of a contract of adhesion, thereby establishing the necessary element of procedural unconscionability.

The appellate court held that the arbitration clause was a contract of adhesion, giving the following definition of such a provision:

> The standard definition of a "contract of adhesion" is "'a standardized contract, which, imposed and drafted by the party of superior bargaining strength, relegates to the subscribing party only the opportunity to adhere to the contract or reject it.'"

The court concluded that Stirlen had no realistic ability to modify the terms of the employment contract. Its terms were presented to him after he had accepted employment and he was told the terms were nonnegotiable. The fact that other elements of the contract were in fact negotiated did not change this conclusion. Thus the requirement of procedural unconscionability was met.

Supercuts argued that the substantive provisions of the arbitration clause were reasonable and fair, but the court found no reasonable business need for the discrepant treatment between the employee's claims and those of the employer. Such reasonable business needs must either be explained in the contract or established factually. The court rejected Supercuts' argument that the differentiation was justified by the employer's need for quick action, concluding that the arbitration statute provided reasonable protection in urgent situations. The court summarized the disadvantages to an employee of arbitration as follows:

> [A]rbitral discovery is ordinarily much more limited than judicial discovery, which may seriously compromise an employee's ability to prove discrimination or unfair treatment. . . . Procedural protections available in arbitration are inferior in other ways to those employees may obtain in a judicial forum. As the Ninth Circuit noted in *Prudential Ins. Co. of America v. Lai* (9th Cir.1994) 42 F.3d 1299, in California "the privacy rights of victims of sexual harassment are protected by statutes limiting discovery and admissibility of plaintiff's sexual history in a judicial proceeding." (*Id.*, at p. 1305, fn. 4.) No such statutory protection is provided an employee compelled to arbitrate a claim of sexual harassment against an employer under an agreement of the sort presented

> here, in which the parties do not agree that the civil discovery statutes shall apply. (See Code Civ.Proc. §§ 1283.05, subd. (a); 1283.1.)
>
> Further, except in extraordinary circumstances, parties who submit a dispute to private arbitration also give up their right to review of an adverse decision. . . . Thus, unlike Supercuts, which can obtain judicial review of an adverse judicial determination of its claims, its employees must accept adverse rulings on their employment claims *even if an error of fact or law appears on the face of the arbitrator's ruling and causes substantial injustice.* . . .

Supercuts' arbitration clause not only deprived employees of exemplary damages and equitable relief available under applicable federal statutes but deprived them as well of a reasonable attorney's fee, including litigation expenses and costs. "This would amount to denial of the underlying cause of action, which would be preserved in name only." The court concluded that "provisions of arbitration agreements unduly advantageous to one party at the expense of the other will not be judicially enforced." The agreement contained not even a "modicum of bilaterality." The provision appeared "calculated to intimidate any employee who might otherwise have the temerity to resist Supercuts' claims."

Supercuts argued without success that the Federal Arbitration Act precluded a finding that the clause was unconscionable and as such unenforceable.

INTERESTING DISCUSSION ISSUES

1. *The standards employed by the court to determine whether the contract term was unconscionable.* This court applied a recent California statute which, in essence, incorporated the spirit of UCC § 2-302 and applied it to all contracts, not just sales of goods. The findings required for unconscionability were absence of meaningful choice plus contract terms which were unreasonably favorable to one party. The concept had both a procedural and a substantive element. The procedural element came from oppression and surprise. The substantive element involved the imposition of harsh or oppressive terms on one who had assented to them. Both elements had to be present in order to find unconscionability. Applying these standards, the appellate court found first that the arbitration provision was a contract of adhesion notwithstanding the fact that issues other than arbitration had been negotiated. The discrimination between the rights of the employer and those of the employee could only be justified based on a reasonable business need of the employer. In this case neither the contract itself nor the testimony at trial established any such reasonable business need. The court concluded that "provisions of arbitration agreements unduly advantageous to one party at the

expense of the other will not be judicially enforced." It is noteworthy that the opinion in the *Williams* case was cited as persuasive authority.

2. *Buckeye.* But see the 2006 U.S. Supreme Court ruling in *Buckeye* earlier in this chapter.

NOTES AND QUESTIONS

1. *Relationship between adhesion contracts and procedural unconscionability.* What is the basis of the *Stirlen* court's determination that the employment contract was procedurally unconscionable? The court characterized the arbitration portion of the contract as one of adhesion and thus procedurally suspect. The court found that Stirlen was confronted with a "take-it-or-leave-it" situation with respect to these provisions. If an adhesion contract is a standard form contract offered by the stronger party to the weaker party on a take-it-or-leave-it basis, how does the *Stirlen* court justify its characterization, given that Stirlen actually did negotiate several terms of his contract? The court found, based on the record, that while some provisions were negotiable and in fact were negotiated, the provisions relating to arbitration were not. Should the determination of adhesiveness depend upon the manner in which the contract was offered? The manner of presentation of the contract in this case was emphasized by the court—Stirlen was given no chance to negotiate the arbitration provisions. Did the court make any determination regarding any alternatives Stirlen may have had, or whether he could have negotiated better terms if he had asked? The court accepted the record finding that the arbitration provisions were presented to Stirlen as non-negotiable and thus had no reason to consider whether he might have negotiated better terms. Nevertheless, a reading of the opinion strongly suggests that the court was prepared to hold the arbitration provisions unconscionable based on their substantive unfairness alone.

2. *Standards for substantive unconscionability.* While typical elements of procedural unconscionability, such as the use of hard bargaining tactics, burying clauses in fine print, and a gross inequality of bargaining power, are at least arguably objectively cognizable, what standards can limit a court's discretion with respect to substantively unconscionable? Just as Karl Llewellyn and the UCC did not try to define "unconscionability" with precision, neither did the California legislature nor this appellate court. The result may be "we know it when we see it." Does the *Stirlen* court provide any meaningful guidance beyond the 18th century *Earl of Chesterfield v. Janssen* formula, "such as no man in his senses and not under delusion would make on the one hand, and as no honest and fair man would accept on the other"? Not really. In *Stirlen,* the court's substantive unconscionability determination seems to rest entirely on two

conclusions: (1) the arbitration term lacked mutuality of obligation, and (2) Supercuts could not provide any reasonable business justification for the arbitration term. Would a term requiring submission of non-compete claims by Supercuts resolve the mutuality of obligation problem and render the contract enforceable? It is doubtful such a change would have made a real difference. The court was incensed with the way in which the drafting eliminated the most meaningful of Stirlen's claims in the event he was wronged. Would Stirlen have been any better off if the mutuality problem were resolved? Perhaps not. We can only speculate as to the decision the court might have reached had the narrow and restrictive provisions relating to arbitration been applicable uniformly to both sides.

3. *Relationship between unconscionability and public policy*. What if Supercuts had provided Stirlen an additional $1,000 explicitly as consideration for permitting Supercuts to retain its right to judicial rather than arbitral resolution of disputes? It is unlikely this appellate court would have been persuaded by any such "cute" drafting tricks. If California courts refuse to permit parties to bargain for certain terms under any circumstances, does any difference remain between the doctrines of unconscionability and public policy? Unconscionability is merely one branch of "contrary to public policy" and thus the two are clearly distinct.

4. *Inequality of bargaining power*. A disparity of bargaining power between the bargaining parties is a near universal characteristic of successful unconscionability claims. See Daniel D. Barnhizer, "Inequality of Bargaining Power," 76 U. Colo. L. Rev. 139, 196 (2005) ("With respect to unconscionability, for instance, many jurisdictions observe that inequality of bargaining power alone is sufficient for a determination of procedural unconscionability."). How would you describe the bargaining power relationship between the parties in *Stirlen*? The court regarded the relationship as one of unequal power. The terms of the employment contract were presented to him "after he accepted employment and were described as standard provisions that were not negotiable." Does the court's analysis of their relative bargaining positions focus more on characteristics of the parties or characteristics of the transaction and its surrounding facts and circumstances? The latter rather than the former. What if Stirlen, a successful, well-educated executive with substantial business sophistication and experience, rather than Williams and Thorne, had been the plaintiff in *Williams v. Walker-Thomas Furniture Co.*? Would that court have been more or less likely to grant relief? The court in Williams stressed Williams' comparative lack of education and knowledge. What are the difficulties in attempting to classify such an ambiguous and dynamic concept as "bargaining power"? Whatever the difficulties, they are better than allowing a grossly overreaching

exculpation or indemnification clause. Should the availability of relief under the unconscionability doctrine depend upon the court's perception of the parties' relative bargaining strength, or upon other, more objectively discernable factors? To some extent, the use of "relative bargaining strength" is a stalking horse for a different concept of unfairness—"we know it when we see it."

5. *Remedy for unconscionability*. What was the remedy for the *Stirlen* court's conclusion that the arbitration agreement in that case was unconscionable? The remedy was the striking of the motion to compel arbitration. Does that determination affect any other part of the parties' contract, or is the impact of the unconscionability finding limited solely to the arbitration clause? The determination affected only the arbitration clause but that clause covered a great deal more than the simple question of arbitrate or litigate. The clause purported to redefine the basic rights of the employee by numerous specific restrictions on the scope of any remedy available in arbitration.

6. *Arbitration and unconscionability*. Compare the *Stirlen* court's reasoning on the unconscionability of the arbitration agreement with the majority opinion in *Buckeye Check Cashing*. Following the latter case, is *Stirlen's* approach to analyzing the enforceability of the arbitration clause still good law? Perhaps. The answer may depend upon whether the issue gets into federal court or remains in the state (California) system. What if, rather than addressing the arbitration clause, Stirlen had been challenging the enforceability of the non-competition clause, arguing that the contract itself was unconscionable because (1) it was presented to him in a procedurally unconscionable manner, and (2) the prohibition on working for a competitor within the United States or Canada for two years following termination of employment was grossly overbroad. Who would decide these claims—an arbitrator or a court? Under the court's analysis the clause was either good or bad in its entirety—not good for some purposes and bad for others. The court's decision in the instant case would mean that issues involving the covenant not to compete would be decided by a court and not an arbitrator.

7. *"One-sided" arbitration terms and unconscionability*. See text.

D. THE STATUTE OF FRAUDS—CONTRACTS UNENFORCEABLE FOR WANT OF A SIGNED WRITING

The text notes that the general rule, unless altered by statute, is that oral contracts are enforceable despite the absence of a writing signed or otherwise. The *Texaco* case, cited in the introductory note, was in 1987 and still is a *cause celebre*. While the issue was not enforcement of an oral contract but rather tortious interference with an alleged oral contract, it is still an excellent cite for the proposition that oral agreements, even those involving more than 7 billion dollars, can give rise to enforceable rights.

The history of the English Statute of Frauds is important. Following the decision in *Slade's Case* in 1602, bilateral executory contracts became enforceable. In the next seventy years a number of suits alleging bilateral oral promises to be performed in the future were strongly criticized by reason of suspicion of widespread fraud and the then prevailing restrictions on testimony in court. At that time neither plaintiff nor defendant were competent to testify as to the matters in litigation and thus evidence depended on others who testified they overheard what one or other party had said. The dangers of fraud and perjury under such rules were clear and prompted the enactment by the English parliament in 1677 of the Act for prevention of Fraud and Perjuries. Section 4 of that act provided that five kinds of contract would be enforceable only in the event of a "note or memorandum signed by the party to be charged." Two of these five kinds of contract continue to be of particular importance in the United States—contracts for the sale of land and contracts "not to be performed within the space of one year." In 1954 England repealed the statute except for contracts for the sale of land and promises to answer for the debt, default or miscarriage of another (guarantees). The statute was reenacted at earlier dates, almost verbatim, in almost all states in this country. Suggestions for repeal have fallen on deaf ears but courts have created some interesting exceptions.

The text notes that Karl Llewellyn was an advocate of the statute and the purposes it served and incorporated his own watered down version in UCC § 2-201. A signed note or memorandum is required for all sales of goods for a price of $500 or more. The writing does not need to include any material terms other than the quantity of goods sold. The UCC version also includes several "savings clauses" which can save a contract which would otherwise fail under the general rule. One of the important such exceptions is the so-called "merchants exception" illustrated and discussed later in this chapter. Three other exceptions include the case where the seller has begun the manufacture of goods unsuitable for sale to others, admission of the contract in court by the party to be charged, and acceptance of payment or delivery in whole or in part (part performance).

The statute has been roundly criticized and has often been accused of protecting fraud rather than suppressing it. Some of this criticism is reviewed in the introductory text note material to this section. But the statute does arguably serve two purposes—the psychological, providing a legal formality marking intention to be bound, and the evidentiary, setting out the terms of the transaction.

We pose at the end of the chapter the questions of whether or not the statute should be preserved and whether, and if so how, it tends to prevent fraud.

Outside the question of its usefulness, problems under the statute can be broken into three categories: (1) does the subject matter of the transaction fall within the types enumerated in the statute; (2) if within the statute, is it evidenced by the requisite note or memorandum signed by the party to be charged; and (3) can compliance with the statute be excused?

1. Is the Contract Within the Statute of Frauds?

The five original types of transaction caught by section 4 of the original statute are described in the text. The UCC covers the sixth type, the sale of goods which in 1677 was covered by section 17. The text notes that many other types of transaction are enforceable only if recorded in a signed writing by reason of specific state and federal statutes to that effect. The three types of covered transaction, of importance to this first year course, are contracts for the sale of land (including interests in land), contracts not to be performed within the space of one year, and contracts for the sale of goods. A lease for less than one year is, under individual state laws, usually outside the statute but a lease for a year or more may be caught by the "one year" provision, or by the express language of the particular state statute. As the text notes, the "one year" provision is both the more controversial and the more troublesome in its application.

Coan v. Orsinger
CASE BRIEF

This is a 1959 decision of the United States Appellate Court for the District of Columbia. Coan sued Orsinger for breach of an oral personal services contract. He alleged that he was to be employed as resident manager of an apartment development in return for which he was to receive $75 per week in addition to a rent-free apartment for the duration of the contract. "This proposed agreement was to continue 'until the plaintiff (appellant) completed his law studies as a student duly matriculated in Georgetown University Law Center, Washington, D.C. or was obliged to discontinue these studies.'" A month after he assumed his duties he received a letter terminating the contract and this termination was later confirmed orally. Orsinger, in his answer, denied having entered into any contract on his own but admitted the making of an oral contract with the corporation of which he was the agent. "He denied, however, that the contract was to last for any definite period alleging that it was terminable at the will of either party." The defendants pleaded the Statute of Frauds and filed a motion for summary judgment which the lower court granted.

On appeal the court agreed that the complaint was barred by the statute's "one year" clause. Coan argued that the statute was not applicable because it could be performed within the space of one year. "This would result, it is contended, if appellant were obliged to discontinue his law studies because of 'deficient scholarship or for some similar reason,' a contingency which could occur within a year."

The gist of the majority's reasoning is found in the following paragraph:

> That contingency contemplates an annulment of the terms of the contract and would operate as a defeasance, thereby terminating and discharging the contract. Further performance under the contract would be impossible by either party. This annulment or defeasance provision does not contemplate the performance of the contract but only its termination and cancellation. Although it could be annulled within a year, it was none the less a personal service contract to last for more than a year, e.g., until appellant completed his studies at Georgetown University Law School. Although this annulment or defeasance provision relieves the parties from further performance of the contract, it is not the type of performance that is necessary to take the case out of the operation of the statute.

The majority quoted an earlier decision of the federal Eighth Circuit stating that:

> The statute looks to the performance and not the defeat of the contract, and a defeasance within a year would not constitute a performance according to the express intent of the parties, that performance should continue longer than a year.
>
> It is generally held that a contract for a definite period extending over a year is not taken out of the statute by an option allowing either party to terminate it within a year. The performance contemplated by the statute is a full and complete performance, and a cancellation is not such a performance.
>
> Much of the confusion in considering the applicability of the statute apparently arises from failing to keep in mind the distinction between a contingency of such a nature as fulfills the obligation and one that defeats or prevents it from being performed. The one that depends upon the defeasance or matter of avoidance is within the statute, while the other is not.

The majority then followed up with a statement that has proven baffling to many students:

> The courts thus recognize a distinct difference between a contingency which fulfills the terms of a contract and one which prevents fulfillment. If the contingency which fulfills and completes the terms of the contract happens or could possibly happen within

> a year, the contract is not within the statute. On the other hand, if the contingency prevents or discharges the parties from performing their obligations under the contract within a year, then the contract is within the statute.

Holding that, on the instant facts, the contingency involved would serve to defeat rather than further performance, the court sustained the defense based on the Statute of Frauds and the absence of note or memorandum signed by the party to be charged (the defendant).

Judge Danaher dissented. His opinion was based on the assumption (justified by the posture of the case—appeal from summary judgment) that the defendant had agreed orally to a three year contract. He noted that Coan had relied on Orsigner's promise by giving up his prospective employment with a real estate company, getting out of his then existing lease of an apartment by the payment of two months' rent, and incurring moving costs. In his view the contract consisted of two parts, the second being separate and distinct from the first. That first part looked to a three year term. The second looked to performance completed when and if Coan was obliged to discontinue his law studies. This could clearly have happened within a year.

> Had it so developed, the contract would have been fully performed on both sides, exactly in accordance with its provision, precisely as the parties had agreed. Thus, if performance follows the terms, if it accomplishes what the parties specified, and if that result could have occurred within the year, the requirements of the statute are met. . . .
>
> In other words we should examine the contract not in terms of nonliability for its breach but with respect to what was required for its performance. Thus viewed, we see that the parties agreed upon an alternative clause which admitted of performance within the year. Hence the contract was not within the statute.

Raising still further difficulty for students, he quoted from an earlier United States Supreme Court opinion to the effect that:

> It is difficult to understand how the duration of the patent and the duration of the boat differed from one another in their relation to the performance or the determination of the contract; or how a contract to use an aid to navigation upon a boat, so long as she shall last can be distinguished in principle from a contract to support a man, so long as he shall live, which has often been decided, and is generally admitted, not to be within the statute of frauds.

Judge Danaher continued:

> Suppose the questioned allegation had read that the contract was to continue in full force and effect 'until the plaintiff might be obliged to discontinue his studies, or until he shall have completed his law studies at Georgetown University Law Center.' Can it be doubted that the parties thus would be seen to have agreed that performance would be deemed complete if continued until the appellant should have been obliged to discontinue his studies? Or can it be doubted that such an eventuality might occur within the year? As the Supreme Court said, such a contract clearly is 'generally admitted not to be within the statute of frauds.' The performance being thus complete, we see the parties achieving precisely what they themselves said would constitute performance. There is no element of defeasance in it, I submit.

INTERESTING DISCUSSION ISSUES

1. *What was the purpose sought to be served by the "one year" provision of the statute?* We can suppose that the problem to be dealt with was the effect of passage of time on memory of witnesses to recall accurately events that occurred and words that were spoken more than a year earlier. That problem is real, although a confirming summary to the file is usually admissible or at least usable to refresh the writer's memory. We don't know whether there was such a thing as a statute of limitations in 1677. But we do know that in most states today the limitations period for breach of contract is six years. Thus suit can be brought six years after the breach of an oral contract that was to be performed within the space of one week. If we assume the purpose stated above, there is no consistency (in terms of inherent reliability of testimony or the opposite) of principle between the effect, today, of the Statute's "one year" clause and the six year statute of limitations covering oral as well as written and signed contracts.

2. *Is there a rational and persuasive difference between a condition the happening of which completes performance and a condition the happening of which defeats or cuts short performance?* An oral contract of employment for life is not caught by the statute but an oral contract of employment for five years is caught. Surely, both may be fully performed within the space of one year by reason of the death of the employee. Students are apt to disbelieve that the first oral contract is enforceable while the second is not. Part of the problem is that any difference between a condition defeasant and a condition that marks the completion of performance does not seem to relate in any rational way to any purpose behind the Statute of Frauds. This "angels dancing on the head of a pin" construction supplies much of the academic

pressure for abolition of the "one year" clause as England did in 1954. But the academics have not yet persuaded legislators.

3. *The judicial tendency to restrict the applicability of the statute by narrow reading of its terms.* Note 3 below discusses the prevailing judicial view of giving the statute a narrow reading. But strangely enough, and contrary to any such tendency, the instant case turns on a high level of contextual technicality as Judge Danaher points out in his dissent. The other applications of and exceptions to the "one year" rule, discussed in the Notes that follow, form the basis of the consistent academic opposition to this provision.

NOTES AND QUESTIONS

1. *Did the Statute of Frauds one year provision produce a just result in this case?* Do you think the "one year" clause served a useful social purpose in this case? No. The issue of whether to believe Coan's or Orsinger's version of the alleged oral agreement should have been left to the jury as a matter of finding of fact. Coan alleged that the contract was to continue "until the plaintiff (appellant) completed his law studies as a student duly matriculated in Georgetown University Law Center . . . or was obliged to discontinue these studies." Apparently, Coan's complaint was dismissed on summary judgment. Hence, his assertion of the facts was to be taken as accepted. Orsinger and Tyler Gardens both alleged that the contract was terminable at will (at the will of either party). If their claim was correct, was the contract capable of full performance within the space of one year? Yes, but the test of the applicability of the Statute had to be based on Coan's version of the facts. If we accept Orsinger's version, there would have been no basis for the lawsuit. The majority opinion proceeds upon the assumption that the contract was for a three year period, consistent with Coan's complaint. That opinion turns on the distinction between "full performance" and "performance cut short by reason of a condition or contingency." Does the majority's distinction between full performance on the one hand, and performance (complete upon its face) cut down by the falling in of a condition make sense to you? No—see "dancing on the head of a pin" comments in the "Interesting Discussion Issues" above. See Restatement (Second) of Contracts § 130 Comment *b*. Is this a distinction that individuals not trained in the law would be likely to be aware of and understand? Since law students have such consistent difficult with the distinction, the answer to this question is patently "No." This being the case, the "one year" rule may well operate to frustrate good faith common belief among non-lawyers that oral contracts are and should be enforceable. Much ink has been spilled to argue the proposition that "merchants" tend to believe that oral contracts are and should be enforceable.

2. *Judge Danaher's dissent.* Do you find his analysis persuasive? No. It is a bit too contrived. Rather than trying to weave a difficult verbal distinction, he should have attacked directly the implausibility of the "condition defeasant" concept. Were there two distinct ways in which the contract could have been performed, one of those ways possibly happening within the space of one year? Not really. As the majority viewed the facts, the employment was to be as long as he was in law school. He provided a hypothetical—suppose the contract had provided that it would continue until Coan might be obliged to discontinue his studies. He suggested that if that had been the contract all would agree that it would not be within the reach of the Statute. Do you agree with this assertion? No. If so, does the decision of the majority applying the Statute make any sense? Yes, based on the majority's statement of applicable law, but the logic of the "condition defeasant" is hard to accept.

3. *Judicial inclination to restrict the reach of the Statute to the narrowest possible basis.* See text.

4. *Applicability of the Statute of Frauds appearing from the agreement itself.* What do courts mean when they say that, to be caught, performance beyond a period of one year must be found in the express language of the agreement? Does this rule limit the court's analysis solely to the "four corners" of the agreement? In an "Alice in Wonderland" sense, yes. Since by hypothesis there is no writing, the "four corners" represent the terms of the oral contract such as the court finds them to be. Remember that, in contrast to questions of integration under the parol evidence rule, a Statute of Frauds question typically arises where there is only an oral agreement or an incomplete written memorialization of the parties' oral agreement. Consequently, unlike the court's analysis in *Thompson v. Libby*, there really are not any definite corners to which a court can refer. What types of evidence, then, would a court consider in determining whether the terms of the parties' agreement prohibited performance within one year? Any testimony of probative value addressed to the terms of the alleged oral agreement. This could include testimony of the parties themselves, testimony of others present at the time of the agreement, and different forms of writing not constituting a "signed memorandum." Does the court's consideration of such evidence make the argument circular? Not really, since the "four corners" are whatever the court decides, in the particular case, or in the particular posture of the case, the terms of the contract were. Does the use of evidence as to the substance of the oral agreement open up the same possibilities of fraud that the Statute was designed to prevent? Of course. The instant case turns on the slippery testimony of the "he said, she said." If Coan had pled and testified that the agreement was for one year, renewable by agreement for two more

years, would he have won (though his damages would have been limited to the one year expectancy)?

5. *Creating a "patchwork" of exceptions.* Many courts have held that a contract of employment for life is not caught by the statute since the employee might die within the first year and thus fully perform within that time period. In contrast, an employment contract for two years is clearly caught by the statute. Do you think that such a distinction makes sense? No—hence one of the bases for the academic opposition to the "one year" clause. Do you think that a statutory provision giving rise to such distinctions should be preserved? No, in the fairly consistent view of academics in opposition, Karl Llewellyn noteably on the other side. See Matthew R. Chapman, "Who Can Afford Common Sense? The Illinois Supreme Court Rejects Time-Honored Exception to Statute of Frauds One Year Rule in *McInerney v. Charter Golf, Inc.*," 43 St. Louis U. L.J. 137, 137-38 (1999) (describing death exception and noting possible trend in some jurisdictions—notably Illinois—toward reversing the exception). But while this patchwork of narrow interpretations and judicially-created exceptions may permit enforcement of contracts in individual cases, is that approach a proper function of the court given the Statute of Fraud's relatively explicit mandate? The explicit mandate was established in 1677 when neither plaintiff nor defendant could testify and there were few if any limits on the role and function of a jury. Things are very different today. Would courts be more likely to achieve justice in individual cases by a broad reading of the statute that creates sufficient numbers of unenforceable contracts that legislatures are forced to reform or repeal the statute? Legislators are rarely forced to do anything by court opinions that do not come from a ruling on a constitutionality argument.

6. *"One life" but not "two."* The *C.R. Klewin* decision, referenced in Note 2 above, referred to an earlier Connecticut Supreme Court decision, *Burkle v. Superflow Mfg. Co.*, 137 Conn. 488, 78 A.2d 698 (Conn. 1950), wherein it was argued unsuccessfully that a multi-year partnership agreement was not caught since all of the partners might die within one year. The *Klewin* court quoted from Burkle as follows:

> We noted that "[n]o case has come to our attention where the rule that the possibility of death within a year removes a contract from the statute has been extended to apply to the possibility of the death of more than one individual." *Id.,* at 494, 78 A.2d 698.

The *Klewin* court did not overrule this holding in *Buerkle*. Do you agree that the "death" exception makes sense when applied to one party to the contract but not to multiple deaths? No.

7. *Contracts where one side has fully performed.* Restatement (Second) of Contracts § 130(2) provides:

> When one party to a contract has completed his performance, the one-year provision of the Statute does not prevent enforcement of the promises of other parties.

8. *The possibility that the contract could be terminated within one year by mutual agreement of the parties.* Restatement (Second) of Contracts § 130, cmt. b states:

> Any contract may be discharged by a subsequent agreement of the parties, and performance of many contracts may be excused by supervening events or by the exercise of a power to cancel granted by the contract. The possibility that such a discharge or excuse may occur within a year is not a possibility that the contract will be "performed" within a year. This is so even though the excuse is articulated in the agreement. This distinction between performance and excuse for nonperformance is sometimes tenuous; it depends on the terms and the circumstances, particularly on whether the essential purposes of the parties will be attained. Discharge by death of the promisor may be the equivalent of performance in case of a promise to forbear, such as a contract not to compete.

The argument, popular with students, is that any contract can be completely performed within one year as a result of the mutual agreement of the parties to cancel or limit the time of its performance. The problem with this argument is that it proves too much—if successful, the "one year" provision would catch absolutely no contract at all.

9. *In order to be protected under the Statute of Frauds, must the defendant swear under oath that he did not enter into the oral contract alleged by the plaintiff?* Notice that the defendant in this case admitted that the parties had reached an oral agreement but asserted that this contract was not for a period of three years but at will. Thus no problem of false swearing arose in this case and others of a similar fact pattern. The same was true in the *McIntosh* case included later in this chapter. The plaintiff there alleged a one year contract and the defendant, while admitting that an oral agreement had been reached, asserted that it was for employment at will and not for one year. But suppose that you represent the defendant who tells you that he did enter into the oral contract as alleged by the plaintiff. Can you as counsel then assert the Statute as a defense? Some will argue that counsel can assert the statute but not enable the client to testify falsely. The counter argument is that the statute provides a protection to which the client is entitled and is to be protected from the "he said,

she said" risk if the issue becomes one of fact for the jury. Such an argument may have to depend upon the defendant refusing to answer that direct question and the court sustaining the right of the witness to so object.

Sometimes this difficult problem can be avoided by filing a motion to dismiss based on the plaintiff's pleading of a multi-year contract and yet failure to plead the requisite signed note or memorandum. Once the case goes into discovery, can counsel deny the making of the contract (knowing this to be untrue) or continue to represent the defendant if the defendant answers falsely to the pertinent question during a deposition? No. Counsel may not assist or participate in a false pleading or the giving of false testimony. Counsel's role as an officer of the court, reinforced by the professional responsibility rules, says no. Note that the UCC § 2-201 provides a "judicial admission" exception to the requirement of a signed note or memorandum. Under this section, the success of an assertion of the statute will probably depend upon whether or not the defendant can succeed in getting the case dismissed on the pleadings, and prior to the taking the defendant's deposition. For a discussion of these ethical problems and applicable professional conduct rules, see Carl A. Pierce, "Client Misconduct In The 21st Century," 35 UMPSLR 731 (2005), and Daniel J. Pope, "Client Perjury: Should A Lawyer Defend The System Or The Client?", 64 Def. Couns. J. 447 (1997).

2. Satisfying the Writing Requirement

The text emphasizes that the function of the parol evidence rule and the function of the Statute of Frauds are separate and address very different concerns. The issue under the parol evidence rule is whether the written memorial before the court represents a complete and unambiguous statement of the parties' bargain. Under the Statute of Frauds, the court must shift to the sufficiency of the written memorialization. The writing required by the statute must be signed "by the party to be charged." Students can be reminded that in the second case in the book, *Lucy v. Zehmer,* the memorandum was signed by the Zehmers but not by Lucy. Had the lawsuit been reversed, Lucy, by pleading the St atute, could have defeated a Zehmer attempt to enforce the contract.

Students need to appreciate that the "note or memorandum" need not be signed at the time the oral contract was entered into. It can be created at any time, usually after the oral agreement, and will be given effect by the court. It can be comprised of different pieces of paper prepared at different times. It can be an internal memorandum, prepared for the maker's own internal purposes, and never transmitted to the plaintiff. The note or memorandum must have existed at some point in time but, if lost, its contents can be attested to by appropriate testimony.

There are important differences between what the note or memorandum must contain to satisfy common law requirements and what it must contain to satisfy UCC § 2-201. It is commonly said that the writing "must state with reasonable certainty the essential terms of the contract. See Restatement (Second) of Contracts § 131(c). As the text points out, to satisfy this section the writing must:

> be 'sufficient to indicate that a contract for sale has been made between the parties and signed by the party against whom enforcement is sought. . . .' and (2) indicate the quantity of goods sold. See UCC § 2-201(1). Importantly, while § 2-201 specifically notes that non-quantity terms that are omitted or incorrectly stated will not render a contract unenforceable, 'the contract is not enforceable . . . beyond the quantity of goods shown in such writing.'

The writing must be signed by the "party to be charged," that is to say the person against whom the contract is to be enforced. "Signature," in this context, has taken on a special meaning. As the text points out, "The signature requirement may be satisfied by any mark that may be reasonably understood by the other party to the contract as indicating the signer's intent to authenticate the written document and to adopt or assent to that document." Such authentication transmitted electronically is usually sufficient.

Crabtree v. Elizabeth Arden Sales Corp.
CASE BRIEF

This is a 1953 decision of the New York Court of Appeals. Crabtree negotiated for a position with the defendant company. He wanted a three year contract because he would be giving up a secure well-paying job. The court noted:

> When Miss Arden finally indicated that she was prepared to offer a two-year contract, based on an annual salary of $20,000 for the first six months, $25,000 for the second six months and $30,000 for the second year, plus expenses of $5,000 a year for each of those years, Crabtree replied that that offer was "interesting." Miss Arden thereupon had her personal secretary make this memorandum on a telephone order blank that happened to be at hand:

EMPLOYMENT AGREEMENT WITH NATE CRABTREE

Date Sept. 26-1947 6: PM
At 681-5th Ave * * *
Begin 20000.
6 months 25000.
6 months 30000.
5000. per year Expense money
(2 years to make good)

Arrangement with Mr. Crabtree By Miss Arden Present Miss Arden Mr. John Crabtree Miss O'Leary

Crabtree accepted Ms. Arden's invitation and she wired back "welcome." A payroll charge card was written and initialed by the company general manager. It specified:

> . . . the names of the parties, Crabtree's "Job Classification" and, in addition, contained the notation that "This employee is to be paid as follows:
>
> First six months of employment
> $20,000. per annum
> Next six months of employment
> 25,000. per annum
> After one year of employment
> 30,000. per annum
> Approved by RPJ (initialed)

After the first six months Crabtree received the scheduled increase from $20,000 to $25,000, but the further specified increase at the end of the year was not paid. The comptroller prepared another pay-roll change card indicating that there was to be a "salary increase" from $25,000 to $30,000 "per contractual arrangements with Miss Arden." She refused to approve the increase and Crabtree left the employment and brought suit.

The defendant denied the existence of any agreement to employ Crabtree for two years, "and further contended that, even if one had been made, the statute of frauds barred its enforcement." The trial court found for the plaintiff on both issues and awarded damages of about $14,000. The appellate division affirmed. Since this was a contract not to be performed within one year the issue was whether there was a sufficient note or memorandum in writing.

The court began by holding that both payroll cards (signed after the oral agreement) were qualifying memoranda under the statute:

> That they were not prepared or signed with the intention of evidencing the contract, or that they came into existence subsequent to its execution, is of no consequence . . . it is enough, to meet the statute's demands, that they were signed with intent to authenticate the information contained therein and that such information does evidence the terms of the contract.

The only element of the agreement not substantiated by those writings was the length of Crabtree's employment contract. "Accordingly, we must consider whether that item, the length of the contract, may be supplied by reference to the earlier unsigned office memorandum, and, if so, whether its notation, '2 years to make good', sufficiently designates a period of employment."

The court noted that the statute does not require that the memorandum be in one document. "It may be pieced together out of separate writings, connected with one another either expressly or by the internal evidence of subject-matter and occasion." The court then explained the requirements for such a connection and the two differing sets of decisions thereon as follows:

> Where, however, some writings have been signed, and others have not as in the case before us there is basic disagreement as to what constitutes a sufficient connection permitting the unsigned papers to be considered as part of the statutory memorandum. The courts of some jurisdictions insist that there be a reference, of varying degrees of specificity, in the signed writing to that unsigned, and, if there is no such reference, they refuse to permit consideration of the latter in determining whether the memorandum satisfies the statute. . . . That conclusion is based upon a construction of the statute which requires that the connection between the writings and defendant's acknowledgment of the one not subscribed, appear from examination of the papers alone, without the aid of parol evidence. The other position which has gained increasing support over the years is that a sufficient connection between the papers is established simply by a reference in them to the same subject matter or transaction. . . . and oral testimony is admitted to show the connection between the documents and to establish the acquiescence, of the party to be charged, to the contents of the one unsigned.

The court adopted the second (more liberal) rule in the following words:

> [T]his court has on a number of occasions approved the rule, and we now definitively adopt it, permitting the signed and unsigned writings to be read together, provided that they clearly refer to the same subject matter or transaction.

It was not necessary that the signed acknowledgement of the contract appear from the writings alone, unaided by oral testimony. The threat of fraud and perjury in this situation was at a minimum. None of the terms of the contract were supplied by parol testimony. "If that testimony does not convincingly connect the papers, or does not show assent to the unsigned paper, it is within the province of the judge to conclude, as a matter of law, that the statute has not been satisfied."

The court concluded that the office memo, and the payroll change forms referred on their face to the same transaction. The defendant's assent to the contents of the unsigned office memorandum was also convincing. There was no doubt that the various pieces together contained all the essential terms of the contract. The term "2 years to make good" obviously indicated an employment contract of a two year duration.

INTERESTING DISCUSSION ISSUES

1. *Does the Statute of Frauds Memorandum Requirement serve a useful function, or cause the parties and the court to focus unnecessarily on the sufficiency of the memorandum rather than the existence and terms of the contract?* As mentioned in the Notes earlier, the Statute fulfils two functions: first, the requirement of a signed writing serves as a psychological warning to the signing party that she is entering into a binding commitment; second, the signed writing presumably serves as the best evidence of the terms agreed to by the signing party. *Crabtree* stretches to the limit the use of extrinsic evidence to establish that a binding commitment was intended. Both these purposes are worthy of respect and exceptions or extensions by interpretation should be undertaken with awareness of the risks of fraud and perjury involved on the particular facts. The focus on the sufficiency of the "memorandum" in this case was anything but unnecessary. Any other approach would result in the court unilaterally changing or repealing an existing statute adopted by the particular legislature. The creation of exceptions to the Statute involves tension between the judicial and the legislative functions.

2. *Choosing between requiring that the pieces be connected by internal reference one to the other and allowing the connection to be established by parol evidence.* The making of this choice lies at the heart of this lawsuit. The two choices available with respect to the evidence to be required to establish effective linking between different pieces of paper, some signed and others not, is covered in detail in Note 3 below.

NOTES AND QUESTIONS

1. *Essential terms and the written memorandum.* To satisfy the Statute of Frauds, the memorandum must contain the essential terms of the parties' agreement. What makes a term essential? Was the term regarding the length of Crabtree's contract a "promissory" term? Yes—a promise essential to Crabtree's suit for benefit of the bargain damages. Courts have said that any "promissory" term is essential and must be found in the writing. See e.g. Justice Cardozo writing for the court in *Marks v. Cowdin,* 123 N.E. 139 (NY 1919). What evidence would a court use to determine whether there was an "essential" term which had been omitted from the writing? Testimony of the parties or other competent testimony, or perhaps "judicial notice" of what routinely are "essential" terms.—where for instance the employment agreement contains no specified salary the memo would obviously be inadequate.. Does this result in a non sequitur? If the purpose of the statute was to preclude the use of oral testimony to prove the agreement, does it make sense to allow comparable oral testimony in an effort to show that the memorandum was incomplete? Nevertheless, there are court decisions which did just that—held that the writing did not contain all the essential terms of the agreement.

2. *The Statute of Frauds and parol evidence.* Justice Cardozo observed in *Marks* that it is always necessary to relate the words of a contract or memorandum to their corresponding reality through parol evidence. "We are turning signs and symbols into their equivalent realities. This must always be done to some extent, no matter how many are the identifying tokens. 'In every case, the words must be translated into things and facts by parol evidence' . . . ." Compare that statement to Justice Traynor's reasoning in *Pacific Gas and Electric Co.* regarding the relationship between words and their contexts:

> If words had absolute and constant referents, it might be possible to discover contractual intention in the words themselves and in the manner in which they were arranged. Words, however, do not have absolute and constant referents. "A word is a symbol of thought but has no arbitrary and fixed meaning like a symbol of algebra or chemistry . . . ." The meaning of particular words or groups of words varies with the "... verbal context and surrounding circumstances and purposes in view of the linguistic education and experience of their users and their hearers or readers (not excluding judges). . . . A word has no meaning apart from these factors; much less does it have an objective meaning, one true meaning."

What do these two quotes suggest about the relationship between parol evidence, the Statute of Frauds, and a court's search for the meaning of a written agreement? Words alone may not communicate meaning effectively without the provision of context through other testimony. The major issue in the instant case was whether the linking of the various pieces of paper could be done only on the basis of express internal reference one to the others or by parol evidence showing that the various pieces all referred to the same transaction. See the discussion in Note 3 below.

3. *Incorporation by reference and acts of independent significance.* The concept of incorporation by reference is useful. Consider, for instance, the employment contract that provides:

> The terms and conditions of employment found in the current "Employees' Manual" are incorporated in this agreement as if set out fully in the text. In the event of any conflict between the express terms of this agreement and the terms in the "Employees' Manual," these express terms shall prevail.

Is there a problem of "he said, she said" slippery testimony involved when evidence of the content of the Employees' Manual is introduced at trial? No, because the Manual is a document in existence at the time of reference to it and identifiable by independent evidence. Said Judge Fuld:

> The courts of some jurisdictions insist that there be a reference, of varying degrees of specificity, in the signed writing to that unsigned, and, if there is no such reference, they refuse to permit consideration of the latter in determining whether the memorandum satisfies the statute. ... That conclusion is based upon a construction of the statute which requires that the connection between the writings and defendant's acknowledgment of the one not subscribed, appear from examination of the papers alone, without the aid of parol evidence. The other position which has gained increasing support over the years is that a sufficient connection between the papers is established simply by a reference in them to the same subject matter or transaction.

Clearly, the unsigned writing to be incorporated must have been in existence at the time of the signing of the note or memorandum. Do you see any potential opportunity for fraud if Judge Fuld's "other position" is implemented? Since the various papers do not expressly refer one to the other, the linkage can only be established by extrinsic evidence of a type that could possibly be fabricated.

Consider a contract for the sale and purchase of a house and associated property. Suppose that the note or memorandum signed by the seller says, "I agree to sell my house in Edina to John Jones . . . (with other necessary and appropriate terms)." Do the words "my house in Edina" constitute an adequate description of the property to be sold to permit enforcement of the contract? Remember *Lucy v. Zehmer* and the words "Ferguson farm." Is there a risk of slippery testimony being used to establish the identity of "my house in Edina"? The problem addressed by the Statute of Frauds is at its most acute when the issue is to be resolved on the basis of oral testimony of the parties or their "affiliates." Giving meaning to the words "my house in Edina" does not depend upon any such slippery testimony. A city official can testify, based on review of the city records (real estate tax rolls), that the seller owned only one house in Edina and that it was situated at 440 Browndale Avenue. The apparently ambiguous description of the property to be sold can be resolved and made clear and specific through the testimony of a third party who has records to substantiate and who has no interest in the lawsuit. We sometimes refer to such testimony as proof of "facts of independent significance." There is a great deal of difference between giving effect to the words "my house in Edina" and accepting oral testimony of one of the parties or other "bystanders" of a promissory term of the contract not found in the note or memorandum.

4. *Did Elizabeth Arden deny making the employment agreement for two years?* The court notes that she both denied agreeing to a two year term and, in addition, pleaded the Statute as an affirmative defense. Does the verdict of the jury suggest that she may have committed perjury? Yes. How do you suppose the secretary testified? That the various parties were present in the room at the same time, that the terms of the deal were discussed and agreed upon and that she wrote those terms down on the back of the phone message slip.

3. Excusing Compliance Failure

The text cites Michael Braunstein's explanation of why the courts have created numerous exceptions to the enforcement of the Statute of Frauds. He suggested that where the Statute was applied to defeat a claim based on an oral contract wasteful breach resulted. The text notes that judicially created exceptions generally fall into two categories. If the contract is unenforceable a remedy in unjust enrichment may be available. In other situations promissory estoppel, equitable estoppel and detrimental reliance may provide for some relief. Dramatic illustrations of such situations can include the following types of situation: One of the parties to the oral agreement calls the other and falsely tells the other that she has signed the written agreement and put it in the mail. Or one of the parties promises the other that she will signed the orally agreed to writing and the other relies to her detriment.

McIntosh v. Murphy
CASE BRIEF

This is a 1970 decision of the Supreme Court of Hawaii. Murphy, the owner of an automobile dealership in Hawaii, interviewed prospective management personnel in Southern California in March, 1964. He talked with McIntosh about a sales manager position but no contract was entered into. In April, 1964, McIntosh received a call from Murphy's general manager "informing him of possible employment within thirty days if he was still available." McIntosh indicated interest and sent a telegram to Murphy that he would arrive in Honolulu on Sunday, April 26, 1964. Murphy telephoned McIntosh on Saturday, April 25, "to notify him that the job of assistant sales manager was open and work would begin on the following Monday, April 27. Surprised at the change in title, McIntosh reconfirmed the fact that he would be arriving and began work on Monday, April 27. In reliance he moved some of his belongings to Hawaii, sold other possessions, leased an apartment in Honolulu and gave up any other employment opportunities. After working for two and one half months he was discharged. Alleging that Murphy had promised employment for a year, McIntosh sued. At the conclusion of the trial the defense moved for a directed verdict arguing that the oral contract was in violation of the one year clause of the Statute of Frauds. The trial court dismissed the motion reasoning that Murphy bargained for a unilateral contract, acceptance by commencement of performance and thus the contract was performable within one year from the commencement of that performance. Alternatively, the trial court ruled that if acceptance occurred by telephone on Saturday, April 25, then the balance of the weekend would not be counted in calculating the year. Murphy had argued that the one year employment started on the Monday and hence the oral agreement was for one year plus one day. Of the trial court's decision the Supreme Court said, "With commendable candor the trial judge gave as the motivating force for the decision his desire to avoid a mechanical and unjust application of the Statute." The jury found for the plaintiff, accepting his allegation of a one year agreement.

The Supreme Court found it unnecessary to consider what the law would be had the oral agreement been made on the Saturday. It ruled for McIntosh based on equitable estoppel, a ground that had not been argued before the trial court. The court acknowledged that this argument violated the strict interpretation of the statute. Reviewing the history of the statute at the time of its adoption, the court said:

> Certainly, there were compelling reasons in those days for such a law. At the time of enactment in England, the jury system was quite unreliable, rules of evidence were few, and the complaining party was disqualified as a witness so he could neither testify on

direct-examination nor, more importantly, be cross-examined. . . . The aforementioned structural and evidentiary limitations on our system of justice no longer exist.

The court then found that the statute had been drastically limited by judicial construction over the years in order to mitigate the harshness of a mechanical application, and also noted the criticism of the statute by writers. Hawaiian courts had recognized an equitable doctrine justifying the enforcement of an oral agreement for the conveyance of an interest in land where there had been substantial reliance by the party seeking to enforce the contract. The court reviewed several cases where the conduct of the parties had given rise to "an estoppel to assert the statute." The court found substantial support for such a position in § 217A [now § 139] of the Restatement (Second) of Contracts and approved that statement of applicable law. The Supreme Court affirmed "on the ground that the plaintiff's reliance was such that injustice could only be avoided by enforcement of the contract."

Justice Abe dissented. It was for the jury to decide when the contract was entered into and if the jury decided it was entered into on the Saturday then the statute would have barred enforcement. McIntosh claimed there was a one year contract of employment while Murphy denied that claim and introduced evidence that all his hiring was on a trial basis, and that he had hired McIntosh on that basis. He believed the statute was enacted to avoid the consequences imposed by the majority—the subjection of the defendant to the jury's choice based on conflicting oral testimony of the parties. Moreover, he could not agree that the role of the court was to circumvent the statute by the exercise of the court's equity powers. "[I]t is for the legislature to amend or repeal the statute and not for this court to legislate." Justice Kobayashi jointed in this dissent.

INTERESTING DISCUSSION ISSUES

1. *Does the judicial creation and application of exceptions to the Statute ameliorate potential injustice and economic inefficiency without going to either complete repeal or outright enforcement?* Some would say that "hard cases make bad law" with respect to judicially carved exceptions to the Statute. They would say that reform should be left to the legislature and not accomplished by relatively random court decisions. Others (a majority) are of the opinion that the Statute can do as much or more harm than it does good. At the heart of the dispute is the question whether, under modern rules of procedure, juries can and should be left the responsibility of deciding whether in fact an agreement was made and which side's oral testimony should be believed. Complicating this issue is the kind of evidence a court should consider in deciding whether the statute applies or an exception

applies. The New York Court of Appeals 4-3 majority in the "merchant's exception" case below (*Bazak*) purports to preclude the use of parol evidence to decide whether or not that exception applied. But the minority directly challenged the majority analysis on this point. The dissent in the *McIntosh* case makes the same point—that the majority, in recognizing an exception, exposed the defendant to precisely the "he said, she said" risk that the statute was designed to avoid. Reliance on the creation of exceptions rather than outright repeal (other than with respect to contracts for the sale of land) tends to redress the worst cases of abusive shelter behind the statute but provides an incentive for litigation with unclear applicable standards.

NOTES AND QUESTIONS

1. *Did the use of promissory estoppel in this case produce a superior result?* The answer turns on whether we believe McIntosh's testimony as to the contents of the phone call including a one year term contract or Murphy's testimony that the employment was to be at will. Apparently, the jury believed McIntosh and not Murphy, but the risk of a jury resolving such "he said, she said" conflicting testimony was the basic justification for the original Statute of Frauds. This is precisely the point of Justice Abe's dissent. Do you think that the majority's use of promissory estoppel produced a superior result? Yes, provided that we accept the argument that such questions of fact should be left to the jury under modern rules of procedure. The English parliament revoked the "one year" clause in 1954 believing that the jury is competent to decide such questions.

2. *The Restatement (Second) of Contracts § 139 rationale.* Can you explain and justify the inclusion of this section in the Restatement? Would not § 90 alone be sufficient? Are there differences between the application of § 90 and § 139? Comments *a* and *b* to § 139 include the following:

> *a. Relation to other rules.* This Section is complementary to § 90, which dispenses with the requirement of consideration if the same conditions are met, but it also applies to promises supported by consideration. Like § 90, this Section overlaps in some cases with rules based on estoppel or fraud; it states a basic principle which sometimes renders inquiry unnecessary as to the precise scope of other policies. . . .
> *b. Avoidance of injustice.* Like § 90 this Section states a flexible principle, but the requirement of consideration is more easily displaced than the requirement of a writing. The reliance must be foreseeable by the promisor, and enforcement must be necessary to avoid injustice. Subsection (2) lists some of the relevant factors in applying the latter requirement. Each factor relates either to the

extent to which reliance furnishes a compelling substantive basis for relief in addition to the expectations created by the promise or to the extent to which the circumstances satisfy the evidentiary purpose of the Statute and fulfill any cautionary, deterrent and channeling functions it may serve.

3. *The timing issue.* Do you agree with the court's counting of time here with respect to the "one year" rule? The trial court failed to count the time correctly out of a desire to be able to find for McIntosh.

Part performance. Said the majority:

> It is also clear that a contract of some kind did exist. The plaintiff performed the contract for two and one-half months receiving $3,484.60 for his services. The exact length of the contract, whether terminable at will as urged by the defendant, or for a year from the time when the plaintiff started working, was up to the jury to decide.

Is the majority seeking to invoke a "part performance" explanation of their decision? No. Do you think that McIntosh's traveling to Hawaii and working for some two and one half months was necessarily referable to a one year contract? No—it could have equally been referable to Murphy's version of the agreement, namely retention on a trial basis.

4. *Restitution-based theories of recovery under the Statute of Frauds.* Besides reliance-based justifications for contractual enforcement, restitution may also provide a basis for recovery by the non-breaching party in the face of a contract rendered unenforceable by the Statute of Frauds. As with the reliance-based theories, how can restitution justify an exception to the Statute of Frauds' clear command that oral contracts within the statute are unenforceable? Recovery based on restitution is not recovery based on agreement—in this situation the court is not enforcing the agreement in violation of the statute, it is adjusting the Aristotelian imbalance between the parties.

5. *Outright fraud.* See text.

6. *Exceptions to the writing requirement under UCC § 2-201.* See text.

4. Merchant's Exception

As the text notes:

Karl Llewellyn, as a principal author of the UCC, was of the view that the Statute of Frauds law was, to some extent, out of step with business practice. One of the results of this thinking was the addition of subsection (2) to the UCC Statute of Frauds § 2-201:

> Between merchants if within a reasonable time a writing in confirmation of the contract and sufficient against the sender is received and the party receiving it has reason to know its contents, it satisfies the requirements of subsection (1) against such party unless written notice of objection to its contents is given within ten days after it is received.

Prior to the enactment of this section, the party sending the notification would be bound (note or memo in writing) but the other party would not. Under this section the memo from the sender can become binding as the receiver's memo. Case law substantiates the requirement to trigger this section that the court find that an agreement had been entered into before the memorandum was sent. Since the CISG contains no Statute of Frauds provision there is no need for a comparable exception under the Convention's rules. The text notes the criticism of the case that follows by Janet L. Raimondo. "She thus focused on the question whether the receiving merchant should have some explicit warning that the message received was in fact such a "confirmation" as would lead to an enforceable contractual commitment unless objected to by the receiver on a timely basis." It also notes the criticism of Shawn Pompian quoted here in part:

> The analysis begins with the proposition that parties are better placed to prevent disputes over the existence of a contract at the time they form an agreement than courts are placed to resolve such disputes after they arise. Standing alone, the proposition supports the imposition of a writing requirement to ensure that parties take into account the added costs to the legal system of failing to produce sufficient evidence of their agreements. Of the two formulations of a writing requirement discussed (a strict rule and a rule with exceptions), the strict rule is more effective in this capacity. The use of exceptions only enhances welfare if the exceptions are predictable and if they only apply to cases where the intent of the parties to form a contract is obvious from the circumstances. Experience with the existing exceptions to the Statute of Frauds makes these preconditions seem highly unrealistic. Consequently, in practice, a writing requirement with exceptions is unlikely to be an efficient solution.

Bazak Intern. Corp. v. Mast Industries, Inc.
CASE BRIEF

This is a 1989 decision of the New York Court of Appeals:

> This dispute between textile merchants concerning an alleged oral agreement to sell fabric centers on the "merchant's exception" to the Statute of Frauds (UCC 2-201[2]). We conclude that annotated purchase order forms signed by the buyer, sent to the seller and retained without objection, fall within the merchant's exception, satisfying the statutory requirement of a writing even without the seller's signature. It was therefore error to dismiss the buyer's breach of contract action on Statute of Frauds grounds, and deny it any opportunity to prove that the alleged agreement had indeed been made.

Since the appeal came up from a motion to dismiss, the court accepted the buyer's version of the facts. Mast, the defendant, contended that the only writings alleged in the complaint, the purchase orders sent by Bazak to Mast and Mast's confirmation of receipt of the purchase orders, were insufficient under UCC § 2-201 to satisfy the Statute of Frauds. The trial court denied the motion but was reversed by the appellate division which held that the claim was barred by the statute. The Court of Appeals reversed, restoring the trial court's dismissal of the motion.

The pivotal issue was whether the writings alleged in the complaint qualified as confirmatory writings under the merchant's exception. The Court of Appeals held that they did. The dispute between the parties was described by the court as follows:

> At the heart of the dispute are two issues involving the telecopied purchase orders. First, the parties disagree as to the standard for determining whether the purchase orders are confirmatory documents: Mast asserts that there is a presumption against application of UCC 2-201(2)—if the memorandum on its face is such that a reasonable merchant could reasonably conclude that it was not a confirmation, then the claim is barred as a matter of law by the Statute of Frauds. Bazak, on the other hand, argues for a less restrictive standard—that is, a requirement only that the writings afford a belief that the alleged oral contract rests on a real transaction, a requirement Bazak contends that it has met. Second, the parties disagree as to the application of the governing standard to this complaint. Bazak contends that the purchase orders were sent in confirmation of the agreement already reached, and that there is sufficient support for that interpretation in the documents

> themselves; Mast argues that on their face, the purchase orders are no more than offers to enter into an agreement, and thus inadequate to satisfy the Statute of Frauds.

The court accepted Mast's argument on both of these issues.

As a preliminary issue, the court ruled on the evidence to be relied on in deciding these questions. It refused to take account of the plaintiff's affidavits as to what took place:

> Parol evidence, even in affidavit form, is immaterial to the threshold issue whether the documents are sufficient on their face to satisfy the Statute of Frauds. Consideration of parol evidence in assessing the adequacy of a writing for Statute of Frauds purposes would otherwise undermine the very reason for a Statute of Frauds in the first instance. That issue must be determined from the documents themselves, as a matter of law (see, Scheck v. Francis, 26 N.Y.2d 466, 472, 311 N.Y.S.2d 841, 260 N.E.2d 493). Accordingly, the trial court erred in ruling that the Statute of Frauds issue should be determined as a matter of fact at trial, and to the extent that plaintiff's arguments are based on parol evidence set forth in Bazak's affidavits, we disregard them.

The court then stated the central question: were explicit words of confirmation required in the writings. The defendant argued that confirmatory language was necessary and that "an exacting standard should be imposed." The court acknowledged that cases cited by the defendant did stand for the proposition that a writing offered as confirmatory must explicitly alert the recipient to the fact that it was intended as a confirmation of a previous agreement. The Court of Appeals disagreed even though there was no mention of any express confirmation in the invoices:

> UCC 2-201(1) requires that the writing be "sufficient to indicate" a contract, while UCC 2-201(2) calls for a writing "in confirmation of the contract." We see no reason for importing a more stringent requirement of explicitness to the latter section, and holding merchants engaged in business dealings to a higher standard of precision in their word choices. The official comment describes UCC 2-201(1) as simply requiring "that the writing afford a basis for believing that the offered oral evidence rests on a real transaction." As Karl Llewellyn, a principal drafter of UCC 2-201, explained to the New York Law Revision Commission: "What the section does * * * is to require some objective guaranty, other than word of mouth, that there really has been some deal." (1954 Report of N.Y.Law Rev.Commn., at 119.) We hold that the same standard applies under UCC 2-201(1) and 2-201(2), noting that this

> conclusion accords with the majority of courts and commentators that have considered the issue. . . .

The court noted that special merchant rules were sprinkled throughout UCC Article 2. The suggested motivation was to "state clear, sensible rules better adjusted to the reality of what commercial transactions were (or should be), thereby promoting predictable, dependable, decent business practices." The concern of those arguing for a higher standard of proof was that a merchant might unilaterally create a binding contract simply by dispatching unsolicited purchase orders, thus unfairly disadvantaging the recipient. Said the court, "This argument is not without merit. However, in our view it overlooks other protections provided by UCC 2-201." First, the writing had to be sufficient to bind the sender, and second, the writing must still be "sufficient to indicate that a contract for sale has been made." Requiring explicit confirmatory language could work "unnecessary injustice and be unresponsive to the realities of business practice." Finally, as additional protection against abuse and inequity, the consequence of failure to give timely notice of objection was only to remove the bar of the statute. The plaintiff still had the burden of proving that a contract was indeed made, and the defendant could still show that the contract made differed from the one claimed by the plaintiff.

The court then held that the documents in question were sufficient, on their face, to indicate the existence of a prior agreement.

Judge Alexander dissented:

> In my view, the purchase orders at issue here, which describe themselves as offers and do not otherwise indicate the existence of a completed agreement are not "sufficient against the sender" (UCC 2-201[2]) because they fail to "indicate that a contract for sale has been made between the parties" (UCC 2-201[1]). Consequently they are not confirmatory memoranda sufficient to satisfy the Statute of Frauds and plaintiff's contract cause of action was properly dismissed.

His interpretation of the purchase orders was that they were merely offers; "the majority's determination that they evidence a completed contract is nothing more than speculation. . . . [A]mbiguous writings do not satisfy the statute." He found that the majority's result unfairly burdened receiving merchants and effectively negated the very purpose and intent of UCC § 2-201(2), to put both the sending merchant and the receiving merchant on an equal footing.

The majority opinion was a 4-3 decision.

INTERESTING DISCUSSION ISSUES

1. *Does the court's application of the "merchant's exception" leave the defendant completely open to the risk of oral "he said, she said" testimony?* Said the court:

> Thus, UCC 2-201(2) neither binds the receiving merchant to an agreement it has not made nor delivers an undeserved triumph to the sending merchant. It does no more than permit the sender to proceed with an attempt to prove its allegations.

The student will have difficulty in relating this statement of the majority to their earlier statement that the fact of "confirmation" must appear from the writings and not other parol evidence. Once again, as in *McIntosh,* the student may conclude that the jury's decision on "he said, she said" evidence may displace any real protection thought to be afforded by the Statute of Frauds (Llewellyn style).

NOTES AND QUESTIONS

1. *Was the existence of a concluded oral agreement prior to the issuance of the "confirmation" established?* It is critical to the application of the "merchant's exception" that the conclusion of an oral agreement be established as a predicate for any written "confirmation." Did the plaintiffs meet this proof requirement? The majority purport to ignore parol evidence of the agreement and to find the evidence of it wholly within the writings. The dissent turns on the writings being ambiguous at best.

2. *Does proof of the preexisting oral agreement solve the issue of fair notice to the receiver?* The majority in this four to three decision seems to suggest that proof of the oral agreement does away with the need for "notice" by the receiving party. Do you agree? No—by so doing, the majority allows parol evidence to suffice where § 2-201(2) required that there be a written "confirmation."

3. *Should fair notice to the receiver of the fact that the writing constitutes a "confirmation" be required?* Several courts, contrary to the majority holding above (as noted in the materials prior to this case), have so held. Do you agree? Yes. See particularly, the comments of the authors quoted in the introductory material to this section.

4. *Was the "confirmation" ambiguous?* Given the consequence of the receipt of such a notice without timely objection, some courts have held that the nature of the writing as a "confirmation" should be clear and not ambiguous. Was the "confirmation" in the above case "ambiguous"? The answer to this question is a matter of "fact"

depending upon the eye of the beholder—in this case 4 pairs of eyes to 3.

5. *Why did the court exclude parol affidavit evidence in deciding whether the writing constituted a "confirmation"?* Said the majority:

> Parol evidence, even in affidavit form, is immaterial to the threshold issue whether the documents are sufficient on their face to satisfy the Statute of Frauds. Consideration of parol evidence in assessing the adequacy of a writing for Statute of Frauds purposes would otherwise undermine the very reason for a Statute of Frauds in the first instance.

Do you agree? See the comment under the heading "Interesting Discussion Issues" above. The preceding cases illustrate a fundamental disagreement—should the "he said, she said" issues in the case be decided by a jury given the modern rules of procedure, or should the statutory requirement of a "note or memorandum in writing signed by the party to be charged" continue to be respected and not undermined by exceptions based on equitable grounds?

6. *Is it appropriate for the "merchant's exception" to distinguish transactions between merchants from other transactions?* Do you agree with the majority that "The Statute of Frauds remains a vital part of the law of this [and other] State[s]"? The statute continues to provide a degree of protection but the scope of that protection has been significantly narrowed by the various exceptions now recognized under the common law as well as under the UCC. Was the adoption of subsection (2) an appropriate response to reasonable business needs? The answer to this question depends upon assertions rather than documented sociological research. Do you agree with the majority's quotation suggesting that they agreed that this provision promoted "predictable, dependable, decent business practices"? The answer to this question is debatable, as indicated by the criticisms of the authors noted in the materials introductory to this section.

CHAPTER 6

CONTRACTS UNENFORCEABLE BY ELECTION: REGULATING THE AGREEMENT PROCESS

Table of Contents

Introduction to Chapter 6 Coverage

Unlike the situations covered in Chapter 5, this chapter deals with those where one or both of the parties may have the power to avoid the contract and thus render it unenforceable against them. See Restatement (Second) of Contracts § 7 ("A voidable contract is one where one or more parties have the power, by a manifestation of election to do so, to avoid the legal relations created by the contract, or by ratification of the contract to extinguish the power of avoidance.") The power of one of the parties to avoid the contract subjects the other to a correlative liability (Hohfeld). In most cases the person with the power of avoidance also has the power to affirm or ratify. The exercise of this latter power extinguishes any future power to avoid. As the text notes in detail, the power of avoidance implicates the final set of Hohfeldian correlatives: immunity and disability.

The central concerns of this chapter are the grounds that create the power of avoidance and the consequences associated with a proper exercise of that power. Absent ratification, the power of avoidance may be exercised either before or after performance by either or both parties. When exercised before performance, avoidance is normally asserted as a defense or "shield" against enforcement. Usually, restoration of the status quo is a requirement of effective avoidance. Following an effective exercise of the power to avoid, restitution may be the only available remedy to adjust the relations of the parties. But as the text notes, the relative restitution obligations remain in flux in many states. Ratification, on the other hand, leaves the contract intact with all appropriate remedies for breach.

Where the contract has been partly or fully performed, the exercise of the power to avoid or rescind the contract, again requiring restoration of the status quo, is exercised as a "sword" in the form of specific action triggering the trailing restitution obligation. Interestingly and as further explored in Chapter 9, the material uncured breach of the other party also creates an independent ground for rescinding the contract. As will be explored in Chapter 9, a material and uncured breach (usually referred to as a "total breach") presents the injured party with a choice quite similar to the one existing in favor of the holder of a power of avoidance. The total breach entitles the injured party to bring either (i) an equitable action to terminate or cancel the contract (Restatement (Second) of Contracts § 373) and seek the quasi-contractual restitution remedy for any benefit conferred on the other party or (ii) a legal action to enforce the contract itself either through an action for damages on the contract (Restatement (Second) of Contracts § 346) or specific performance of the contract where money damages are inadequate (Restatement (Second) of Contracts § 357). The second alternative actions on the contract are explored in Chapter 9, whereas the first alternative actions to rescind the contract are discussed in this chapter.

In both cases, the presence of the power of avoidance and the other party's total breach present the holder with an elective choice or "election of remedies." Historically, remedies to "enforce the contract" by seeking monetary damages have been regarded as inconsistent with, and an alternative to, remedies to "rescind the contract" by seeking restitution as if the contract did not exist. The choice of one of the remedies might, therefore, preclude the other on the ground that only one of the remedies was elected. Likewise, a party holding the power of avoidance might be precluded from exercising that power by some action or inaction constituting ratification or affirmance. Accordingly, before exploring the grounds creating the power of avoidance, this chapter begins with a consideration of preclusion by election and affirmance. Importantly, however, the law continues to evolve in this area largely because of the consequences resulting from the merger of law and equity.

A. PRECLUSION BY AFFIRMATION OR ELECTION OF REMEDIES

While affirmation and election of remedies are doctrinally distinct, they remain consequentially linked. Thus, while the "election" to pursue a particular remedy "on the contract" may constitute affirmation of a voidable contract, that same conduct may also constitute an election to preclude pursuit of an inconsistent remedy relating to a contract that is not voidable. Accordingly, affirmation and election of remedies are related by preclusive effects, but each applies in different contexts. For example, affirmation has no relevance for determining the expectancy, reliance, and restitution damages interests discussed in Chapter 9 as remedies for breach of contract. In situations involving mere breach of contract, the nonbreaching party generally only has a choice of which damages interest to pursue as a remedy for the breach. At that point, and without additional facts and circumstances giving rise to a power of avoidance, the nonbreaching party's remedies arise solely within the contract. Consequently, the breached contracts addressed in Chapter 9 do not give rise to any power of affirmation, only an election regarding which of several remedies the injured party will pursue.

1. Preclusion by Affirmation of a Voidable Contract

A voidable contract generally may not be avoided in part—the entire contract must be avoided including any part already performed. The only exception relates to divisible contracts. Where both parties have fully performed with regard to a "divisible portion," the power holder may avoid either the entire contract or the remaining divisible portions.

Most commonly, a party holding the power of avoidance may extinguish that power (thus creating a Hohfeldian immunity in the other party and a correlative disability in the power holder) by manifesting an intention to the other party to continue with the contract. Restatement (Second) of Contracts § 380(1). Such a manifestation constitutes an "affirmance" and has the effect of ratifying the contract. Accordingly, a promise to affirm an otherwise voidable duty is binding.

Even absent an express promise, a party holding a power of avoidance may affirm a voidable contract by undertaking any act with respect to anything received from the other party that is inconsistent with disaffirmance. The inconsistent dominion affirmance rule will often be triggered unless the power holder tenders a return of the consideration received in the exchange in connection with a declaration of disaffirmance.

In addition to affirmative acts, including a promise to affirm and exercising dominion and control over the consideration received, the power to avoid can be extinguished by mere delay. Accordingly, the party holding the power to avoid must exercise that power within a reasonable time of when the power is created and known to exist.

Once the power holder effectively exercises the power of avoidance, the election is normally irrevocable and the power holder cannot thereafter affirm, unless of course the other party consents to the new affirmance.

2. Preclusion by Election of Remedies

Generally, a party with the power of avoidance has no duty to perform while the power to avoid remains active. In some cases proper exercise of the power of avoidance requires that the power holder tender or attempt to return the consideration received from the other party. If such a tender of the original consideration is required, then the power holder may have to pay damages for nonperformance, unless that party tenders a return of the consideration before the power of avoidance is terminated. In this way, modern law attempts to override the ancient differences discussed below between law and equity where law required a tender as a condition of an action for rescission (avoidance) while equity did not. With the merger of law and equity, the tender condition is no longer important, at least in states that no longer follow the law rule. However, while this section concentrates on election of remedies—and thus differences between law and equity where the two have not merged—an important linkage to the avoidance section above remains. Even where a tender of consideration may no longer remain important as a condition to the exercise of a power of avoidance, recall that the mere retention of the consideration coupled with the exercise of the dominion and control resembling that of an owner may itself preclude avoidance.

However, beyond retention of consideration potentially constituting an affirmance of a voidable contract, the question remains whether, without more, the retention further constitutes some form of an implicit election to "waive" the right to sue for rescission to set aside the contract, thereby confining the party to an action to enforce the contract rather than set it aside. The remedies following each approach are quite different.

Modern contract law provides that if a party has more than one remedy (e.g., rescission and restitution or monetary damages), the choice to pursue one by suit or otherwise ordinarily does not bar a prayer in the alternative for the other relief. But where the remedies are "inconsistent" and the other party materially changes its position in reliance upon the power holder's choice of remedy, such pleadings in the alternative are not permitted. Importantly, the mere election of remedies is not binding even under modern law unless and until the other party has materially changed position in reliance on the remedy pursued. Of course, duplicate recovery is not allowed.

Assuming for the moment that an action to rescind is chosen, the restitution remedy to follow generally seeks to place the parties in their respective status quo remedies before the contract was formed. A party seeking rescission of the contract by exercising the power of avoidance will not be granted restitution unless either that party returns or offers to return, conditional on reciprocal restitution, any consideration received, or the court can assure such a balanced return when granting relief.

Historically, and particularly before the merger of law and equity, a suit for damages was deemed an action to enforce the contract. In contrast, courts deemed a suit for restitution an election to terminate or cancel the contract. However communicated, the notice of termination or cancellation was traditionally referred to as "rescission" (a party's unilateral avoidance or unmaking of a contract for a legally sufficient reason). This reinforced an "election" of remedies of sorts, requiring the plaintiff to seek either contract damages for breach of the contract or quasi-contractual relief for restitution, but not both. Also before the merger of law and equity, a rescission-related action could be brought either in law or equity.

Because of a degree of confusion between the rules of law and equity, the UCC dispensed with the term "rescission" and uses the term "cancellation." Thus, UCC §§ 2-106(3)-(4) use the term "cancellation" to refer to bringing an end to the contract because of the breach by the other party whereas "termination" refers to bringing an end to the contract for grounds other than breach.

The text then poses the following questions:

As you read and study these materials, you will learn that the approach of the Restatement (Second) Contracts, and largely common law, "restrict" the void category to relatively few categories such as fraud in the execution and physical duress. But is this "all or nothing approach" appealing? Whether or not it is "appealing" depends upon the discrepant consequences of labeling the transaction as "void" or "voidable." As between the parties, given the power to avoid, there seems to be no real difference. The importance of the distinction relates to the potential rights of third parties—bona fide purchasers for value without notice, whose interests will prevail in the context of a voidable contract but not in the context of one that is void. If not, what criteria might you suggest to replace the existing paradigm? Unless there is dissatisfaction with the recognition of potentially superior rights in a third party, there seems to be no reason to replace the existing paradigm. If a facts and circumstances test were preferred, what critical factors would you select to morph a voidable contract into a void contract? Assuming that any such change was preferred, the standard would have to balance in some way the conflicting interests of the party with the power of avoidance and the third party involved.

B. LACK OF LEGAL CAPACITY OF ONE OF THE PARTIES

Where the contract involves multiple parties in a special relationship such as a fiduciary relationship, modern law tends to characterize the resulting contract as "voidable" if the transaction is not on fair terms and each party knew all the material facts. Thus, a contract between a fiduciary and a beneficiary is voidable unless on fair terms and the beneficiary was aware of all relevant facts.

The text reviews the historical, but now extinguished, discrimination against women, blacks and others with respect to ownership and power to contract.

1. Contracts with Minors

Minors have long been limited in their capacity to enter binding contracts. Both Roman law and medieval law, for example, recognized that contracts made by minors were voidable at the option of the infant either when made or upon reaching the age of majority, albeit with some interspersed periods of uncertainty. Unless state law provides otherwise, an infant has the capacity to incur only voidable contractual duties until the beginning of the day before the person's eighteenth birthday, although in many states both men and women have full capacity upon marriage. The justification for the age restriction is that unsophisticated infants might enter into foolish contracts with unscrupulous adults. Under common law, the age of majority to contract was twenty-one, but states generally have lowered the age of majority for contract and for other purposes by statute.

While young adults have achieved many advances toward full enfranchisement of political, social, and economic rights, many injustices remain. In most states, the actual capacity of the minor is irrelevant, as is the fairness of the bargain or even misrepresentation of age. Some states recognize that intentional misrepresentation of age constitutes a tort or a form of estoppel that may vitiate the minor's power to disaffirm. Also, minors are often liable on contracts for necessaries such as food, shelter, and clothing, although sellers and lessors may only sue for restitution of the value of such necessaries, not the contract price.

Perhaps most controversial is the general rule that when infancy is asserted as a shield in a suit by the other party to enforce the contract, the infant's disaffirmance revests title to the property in the other party so long as the property still exists. But if the infant has dissipated the property, the other party has no further remedy. The risk of loss falls upon the other party. A few states have restricted this rule by statute or case law requiring the minor to restore the consideration. A contract with a minor is affirmed when the minor either expressly affirms or fails to disaffirm the contract within a reasonable time after reaching the age of majority.

As might be expected the dissipation rule is the most controversial. Upon proper disaffirmance, the majority rule—represented by the *Halbman* case below—places the risk of the dissipation upon the other party, regardless of whether the minor uses the infancy doctrine as a sword or a shield. Some jurisdictions, as discussed in the notes following *Halbman*, mitigate the harsh results of strict application of the dissipation rule when the minor brings suit using the infancy doctrine as a sword. This minority rule places extreme pressure upon whether the transaction itself was for credit or cash. In cash transactions, the minor would not be able to sue, retrieve the cash and return damaged or depreciated purchased assets. Of course, services can never be returned. In reading the cases, try to decide which view you prefer from a matter of fairness and if your decision has anything to do with your independent views as to whether the infancy rule itself is sensible.

Halbman v. Lemke
CASE BRIEF

This is a 1980 decision of the Wisconsin Supreme Court. Halbman, a minor, was an employee of a service station at which Lemke was the manager. In July 1973, Halbman entered into a contract with Lemke in which Lemke agreed to sell Halbman an Oldsmobile for $1,250. Halbman paid Lemke $1,000 cash, took possession of the car, and agreed to pay $25 per week until the balance was paid, at which point title would transfer. Five weeks after the purchase agreement, with $1,100 of the purchase price paid, a part within the car's engine broke. Halbman had the car repaired in September for $637.40 (Halbman did not pay for the repairs). In October, Lemke endorsed the title over to Lemke to avoid any liability for further use of the vehicle. On October 15, Halbman returned the title to Lemke via mail, disaffirmed the contract, and demanded the return of his money. Lemke refused.

In spring 1974, the repair bill still being unpaid, the car resided in the garage where the repairs were made. The garage, to satisfy its mechanic's lien, removed the engine and transmission, and towed the car to the home of Halbman's father. Lemke refused to remove the car from the home of Halbman's father, and the car was ultimately vandalized to the point of being unsalvageable. Halbman sued for return of the $1,100 that he had paid toward the car, and Lemke counterclaimed for the remaining $150 owed on the contract. The trial court granted judgment for Halbman, finding that a minor need only return the property in his hands in order to disaffirm a contract for purchase of an item (no need to make restitution for depreciation or damage). The appellate court appealed the court's finding regarding restitution, and Lemke appealed to the Supreme Court of Wisconsin.

The court framed the issue as "whether a minor, having disaffirmed a contract for the purchase of an item which is not a necessity and having tendered the property back to the vendor, must make restitution to the vendor for damage to the property prior to the disaffirmance." The court noted that neither party disputed the point of "settled law . . . that a contract of a minor for items which are not necessities is void or voidable at the minor's option." The challenge arose after disaffirmance, with regard to the rights and responsibilities of the parties "relative to the disposition of the consideration exchanged on the contract." While the court noted that a minor, upon disaffirmance, is expected to return as much of the consideration as remains in his possession, the court had never addressed the question of what happens when the property has been damaged to the point of being irrecoverable and the seller sues for depreciation costs.

Lemke argued that, under Olsen (another case from the Supreme Court of Wisconsin), different rules should be applied to a minor who disaffirms and seeks to recover his consideration than the case where the minor defends an action on the contract by the other party. Lemke argued in favor of an idea advanced in the dissent from the Olsen court of appeals opinion, that the minor's obligation to make restitution should turn on his ability to do so; since Lemke held $1,100 of Halbman's, there was no question about ability to repay. But the court held that Olsen merely said that restitution by a disaffirming minor included return of the property to the vendor. Here, full recovery of the depreciation of the car would amount to more than the minor possessed. Thus, absent an action in tort for damage to the property, the court held that "to require a disaffirming minor to make restitution for diminished value is, in effect, to bind the minor to a part of the obligation which by law he is privileged to avoid. The court declined to follow cases from other jurisdictions that placed a greater burden on the disaffirming minor because they forced the minor to bear the very burden from which the infancy doctrine should protect him; "modifications to the rules governing the capacity of minors to contract are best left to the legislature."

INTERESTING DISCUSSION ISSUES

1. *Should the parties be restored to their status quo before entering into the contract?* This case represents the strong majority of state court opinions. The fairness of allowing the minor to rescind thus canceling any further continuing obligation seems clear. In seeking such relief the minor is using the doctrine of minority as a shield against continuing liability. But if the contract is rescinded, then the benefits transferred by both sides to the other should be recovered as part of the process of rescission, putting the parties back where they were before they entered into the contract. It seems logical that if the minor has already paid money, she should be able to get that money back. It can be argued that this requirement does not involve the minor using the doctrine as a sword but rather, it simply fulfills what the minor has done by rescinding. Some writers, however, treat this as a "sword" and not a "shield" approach—see the discussion in various Notes that follow. Lastly, if the parties are to be restored to their original position, then the minor should have to give back what she received. Here comes the big problem, as in the instant case, where the property received by the minor has been damaged or lost and is not capable of being returned. Should the minor have to pay for the reasonable value of that property if she is unable to restore it? Some courts say "Yes" particularly if she is trying to recover moneys she paid to the other party. The strong majority says "No"—her only obligation is to return any of that property that she retains in whatever condition it happens to be in. She is not required to make good the difference in value. The rationale for this apparent exception to rescission accompanied by restoration of the status quo is that to grant such a remedy in effect leaves the minor subject to the disadvantages and costs of the agreement she entered into. In order to provide full protection for the minor against the greed and overreaching of the adult other party, she must be able to rescind and would not have a free choice to rescind if that choice was coupled with an obligation to pay money or doing something other than return whatever was in her possession at the time of rescission.

NOTES AND QUESTIONS

1. *Restoration of consideration. Halbman* appears to represent the majority view. However, the minority view is equally well reasoned, concluding that when the minor asserts infancy as a defensive shield, the minor is not liable for dissipation of the seller's consideration. But

when the minor uses the infancy doctrine to disaffirm and sues for the return of consideration, the minor is responsible for depreciation in the assets tendered back to the seller. See *Dodson v. Shrader,* 824 S. W. 2d 545 (TN 1992). Which view do you prefer and why? While there is an element of apparent fairness in holding the minor responsible for damage to the property caused by the minor, to so hold can completely subvert the purpose of the infancy rule, namely top shelter the infant from improvident bargains. Only the rule adopted in this case fully protects the infant against such improvidence. Does the offensive use of the infancy doctrine as a sword to permit the infant to retain any benefits dissipated during the performance of the contract make any sense? Yes. If so, under what rationale? The necessity of protecting the infant against improvident bargains, as noted immediately above.

2. *Recreational waivers involving negligent personal injury.* Should an infant be entitled to execute a legally binding waiver of liability for negligent infliction of personal injuries? The logic of protecting the infant suggests that the answer to this question should be "No." If not, should a parent's signature bind the infant so that the infant's disaffirmance before reaching majority and after injury is ineffective? Yes. In a number of important situations the infant's parent or guardian (duly appointed by a court) can bind the infant's estate as the infant's agent. Were this not the case, no infant would be allowed to participate in any activity where the provider of the activity required a reasonable waiver of liability. See *Sharon v. City of Newton,* 769 N. E. 2d 738 (Mass. 2002) (high school cheerleader's signature held not binding by itself, but father's additional signature was binding on the child). Consider the case of minors contracting with providers of organized sports activities such as fencing, horseback riding, archery, riflery, swimming, gymnastics, and the multitude of other childhood activities that involve some theoretical or real element of risk of injury. What would happen to the market for organized provision of such activities if there were no mechanism for waiver of liability for negligence? The availability of such activities would be dramatically reduced. Are there any alternative mechanisms by which organizers could protect themselves against such liability? Some try by forming a shell corporation with no real assets or insurance and conducting the activity through such a shell. Such a form of attempted evasion will usually leave the actual participant manager or provider of the service personally liable. One of the authors is reminded of the scene of bungee jumping near Queenstown in New Zealand. Some years ago, the only visible assets of those providing the jumping opportunity were the rubber ropes and towels to be wrapped around the jumper's ankles and the 1930's model broken down and ancient yellow school bus which served as the "office" for the undertaking. Do you think a parent should have the right to waive a third party liability to their child for negligent infliction of physical injury? Yes, for the same reasons noted

above—but for that ability, children would most likely be deprived of many opportunities to participate in many different sports. When injury results from gross negligence, the waiver is invalid on grounds of public policy. See Restatement (Second) of Contracts § 195, precluding the waiver of liability by contract of gross negligence or willful conduct.

3. *Why the switch from void to merely voidable?* As the introductory materials explained, early legal history treated infancy contracts as void, not voidable. Can you articulate the policy justifications for and against the switch? Those justifications are generally beneficial to the infant who, upon achieving adulthood, can affirm the contract. Were the contract void, it could not be affirmed. There may be disadvantages related to the possible acquisition of superior interests by bona fide purchasers for value. What other related doctrines are implicated by a switch from void to voidable contracts by infants? One in particular, a limited recognition of the infant's ability to own property. What policy questions relate to the possible solutions of those questions? The key issue is the rationale in favor of protecting an infant against improvident bargains. Some might argue in favor of a test of enforceability based upon the objective reasonableness of the bargain, or on the ability of the particular infant to exercise prudent judgment—compare an infant's liability in tort.

4. *Application of UCC. Halbman* involved the sale of goods (a car). Why does the court cite common law contract rules? Because the UCC is not a complete code and expressly incorporates the common law, unless inconsistent with the provisions of the UCC, under § 1-103. Could it be that the UCC itself assumes that most commercial transactions will not involve minors and in any event incorporates all common law not otherwise specifically displaced by a rule in the UCC? Yes. Specifically, what does UCC § 1-103 ("Unless displaced by the particular provisions of this Act, the principles of law and equity, including the . . . law relative to capacity to contract . . . shall supplement its provisions.") suggest about the capacity to contract? The common law with respect to infancy is thus expressly incorporated. But since this law can and does vary from state to state, this incorporation may derogate to this extent from the objective of uniform standards across state borders.

5. *Application of CISG.* See text.

6. *The necessaries exception.* The court begins with the statement that the car was not "a necessity." Should courts assess whether a given item is or is not a necessity from a subjective or objective perspective? The answer should first depend upon the common law rationale for this exception to the general rule of voidability. That rationale is, presumptively, the importance of the infant's need for

"necessaries" and the risk that the infant could be denied access to those "necessaries" were the rule otherwise. Given the validity of this assumption, then the test should be measured objectively, in terms of the reasonable understanding of the provider, rather than subjectively in terms of the understanding of the infant. If we are to be concerned about the availability of "necessities" to the infant, then we should value the objective judgment of the provider. Otherwise, we might further prejudice the availability of such necessaries to the infant. In other words, should "necessities" be limited in scope to the bare minimum necessary for sustenance in contemporary society, such as food, shelter, and clothing? Some courts have extended the list of "necessaries" to include education and medical attention. Or should the determination of whether a particular good is a necessity depend upon the individual needs, desires, and circumstances of the minor? The answer to this question should be "No," based on the reasoning provided above. Can you conceive of some circumstances where a car might be necessary to some minors but not to others? It could be necessary as a means of access to medical help or possibly to education. What about questions of degree? Degree should be relevant, but measured objectively as reasoned above. If transportation is deemed a necessity for a 16-year-old working minor, does that include a contracts for bus fare, a bicycle, a motorcycle, a 1978 Oldsmobile Cutlass Salon that "runs good," a new Dodge Neon, or a Cadillac? The answer should depend upon the reasonable objective judgment of the provider. If the court determines that the parties have contracted for a necessity, how should the court measure the minor's liability? Classic common law, as noted in the introductory materials, measured that liability by the value of the necessaries and not the promise. The two most obvious measures are expectancy damages measured by the contract itself or restitution damages measured by the value of the benefit conferred upon the minor. Given the capacity issues in question, is a market or restitution valuation more appropriate? Yes.

7. *Ratification after reaching the age of majority.* An infant need not take any action to disaffirm a contract until the age of majority. Restatement (Second) of Contracts § 14 cmt. c. Does this suggest that a minor's ratification of a contract while still a minor is not effective? Yes. If the contract itself is voidable because of infancy, should not also the ratification be voidable if made while a minor? Yes. The rules are clear that if the minor takes no action to disaffirm the contract within a "reasonable time" after reaching majority, the delay will constitute ratification by failure to exercise objection while retaining the fruits of the contract. A "reasonable time" will simply vary from case-to-case, depending in part on the sophistication of the minor.

2. Mental Capacity

The text notes that, unlike the Restatement (First), the Restatement (Second) lists separately identifiable categories of incapacity including guardianship, infancy, mental illness or defect, and intoxication. Like contracts with an infant, contracts with the mentally inform began in early legal history as void rather than voidable.

The traditional common law test for mental incapacity sufficient to avoid a contract considered only whether a person could understand the nature and consequences of the transaction—the so-called "cognitive test." Restatement (Second) of Contracts § 15 was particularly important because it purported to "expand" the voidable contract category to include a new category of voidable contracts where the incompetent party could understand the transaction but could not control their behavior with respect to the transaction. As the case below argues, this expanded "volitional test" encompassed those transactions where the person understood the nature and consequences of the transaction but nonetheless could not exercise personal control over their behavior, including entering a particular contract.

Ortelere v. Teacher's Retirement Board
CASE BRIEF

This is a 1969 decision of the New York Court of Appeals. As a New York City elementary teacher since 1924, Mrs. Ortelere was a member of the Teachers' Retirement System of the City of New York, which entitled her to certain pension and retirement benefits. In June 1958, she had executed a selection of benefits option that named her husband as beneficiary such that she would receive less by way of periodic retirement allowances, but if she died before receipt of her full reserve, the balance would be payable to her husband. In June 1960, she also named her husband as beneficiary of her service death benefits in the event of her death before retirement. In March 1964, Ortelere suffered a nervous breakdown and went on a leave of absence that expired in February 1965. Shortly thereafter, Ortelere became very depressed and was unable to care for herself. Her husband gave up his $222/week electrician job to care for her full-time. Due to their modest circumstances, retirement for both of the Orteleres (or the survivor of the two) would be provided almost entirely from Mrs. Ortelere's retirement benefits. In July 1964, Ortelere underwent psychiatric care for what was later determined to be involutional pyschosis and cerebral arteriosclerosis. On February 11, 1965, when Ortelere's leave of absence had expired and she was still under treatment, she executed—unbeknownst to her husband—the retirement application at issue, selecting the maximum retirement allowance payable during her lifetime with nothing payable on or after death and borrowed the maximum cash allowable from the Board. At that time, Ortelere included with her request a list of specific questions that appeared to indicate "great understanding of the retirement system, concerning the various options available." On March 28, 1965, she was hospitalized after an aneurysm, and died days later.

A physician for the Board of Education had examined Ortelere on February 2, 1965 and stated that she was rational and had apparently recovered from her depression. But Mrs. Ortelere's psychiatrist, Dr. D'Angelo, stated that Ortelere never improved enough to be able to return to teaching, and that at no time while she was in his care was she mentally competent or capable of making even small decisions. D'Angelo also described the effects of her psychosis as depriving those suffering from it from either the mental or physical strength to make any decisions. Contending that Mrs. Ortelere was not mentally competent to make the benefit election of February 11, 1965, her husband, as executor of her estate, filed suit to set aside her application for the above retirement benefits. The trial court held that Mrs. Ortelere was mentally incompetent at the time of her application, rendering it "null and void and of no legal effect." But the appellate court reversed, holding that, as a matter of law, there was insufficient proof of mental incompetency as to the transaction. Mr. Ortelere appealed.

The court stated that the "well-established rule is that contracts of a mentally incompetent person who has not been adjudicated insane are voidable." It also noted that the "traditional standards governing competency to contract," including the requirement that a party be able to make a rational judgment regarding the transaction, were formulated when "psychiatric knowledge was quite primitive" and fail to account for someone whose mental illness is unable to control her conduct, even though her cognitive abilities seem unimpaired. The court stated that, since policy considerations must be based on a sound understanding of mental illnesses, the Restatement (Second) test for evaluating competency would be a more desirable test, providing that a person only incurs voidable contractual duties by entering a contract by reason of mental illness where the other party has reason to know of the condition. The court felt that the test properly balanced the competing policy considerations of protecting parties with mental illnesses, while also protecting the expectations of parties bargaining in good faith by requiring that the opposite party have some reason to know of the mental condition of the first party, and that avoidance is limited to instances that are not inequitable.

The court finally settled on three facts that produced a decision in Ortelere's favor: (1) the Board had reason to know of Ortelere's condition by virtue of her leave of absence; (2) the Board had not undertaken any significant change of position; and (3) the goal of the benefit system was to protect its members and their dependents. As such, the court held that Ortelere entered the contract solely because of her psychosis, and held that a new trial should be held under more modern and proper standards of evaluating mental illness.

Judge Jasen, in dissent, argued that Mr. Ortelere had failed to bear the burden of proving mental incompetence to avoid the contract. Judging from the detail and specificity of her letter to the Board on February 8, Judge Jasen argued that Mrs. Ortelere had demonstrated "a mind fully in command of the salient features of the Teachers' Retirement System," and thus possessed the capacity to understand the answers. Since Mrs. Ortelere had no reason to think that she would be dying in the very near future, and since the additional income from her chosen benefit package would provide the means by which both she and her husband could live, the decision was not "so contrary to her best interests as to create an inference of her mental incompetence."

More generally, Judge Jasen disagreed with the majority's argument that then-current rules regarding mental competence were too restrictive. Rather, he argued that the rule represented a balance between protecting the above-mentioned interests in a way that had evolved over the course of many years. Also, the rule had proved workable in practice, thanks in part to the broad range of psychiatric testimony available, as well as the ability of jurors to evaluate abnormal conduct based on their own experience. As a result, he feared that the new test would prove unworkable, and would leave many contracts open to psychological challenge.

NOTES AND QUESTIONS

1. *Who may assert contract is avoidable?* See text.

2. *Proving incompetency.* Adjudication of incompetency is conclusive regarding incapacity at the time of the adjudication, although many jurisdictions treat adjudication as creating only a presumption of incompetency as to later transactions. See Henry Weihofen, "*Mental Incompetency to Contract or Convey,*" 39 S. Cal. L. Rev. 211, 211-213 (1966). While adjudication is not a pre-requisite under Restatement (Second) of Contracts, mere mental weakness is also inadequate. Indeed, in the absence of an incompetency adjudication, the party—or their representative or estate—may establish incompetency under either the "cognitive test" or the "volitional test." Compare Restatement (Second) of Contracts § 15(1)(a) (cognitive test) with Restatement (Second) of Contracts § 15(1)(b) (volitional test). Since the avoidance remedy is only available to the incompetent party, that party retains the burden to prove legal incapacity. Restatement (Second) of Contracts § 15 cmt c. Under the cognitive test, the party must prove he or she was unable to reasonably understand the nature and consequences of the transaction. While the test has been criticized as vague and ambiguous, it remains accepted in

most jurisdictions. See Milton D. Green, *"Judicial Tests of Mental Incompetency,"* 6 Mo. L. Rev. 141 (1941). When established, the cognitive test does not require that the innocent party was aware of the mental defect, but even a person otherwise failing the cognitive test might enter a valid contract if the contract was executed at a particularly lucid moment. Does the *Ortelere* majority determine that Grace Ortelere satisfied the cognitive test? No. Said the court:

> These traditional standards governing competency to contract were formulated when psychiatric knowledge was quite primitive. They fail to account for one who by reason of mental illness is unable to control his conduct even though his cognitive ability seems unimpaired.

Thus, by clear implication, the majority found it necessary, in order to reverse the appellate division, to add a volitional to the older cognitive test. If so, why? The majority held by implication that her competence met the cognitive standard.

Alternatively, as the *Ortelere* majority notes, some jurisdictions also embrace a broader volitional test. Unlike the cognitive test, the volitional test does not require that the party prove that he or she was unable to understand the nature and consequences of the transaction. Under the volitional test, a mentally infirm person might actually understand the nature and consequences of the transaction but nonetheless be unable to control their behavior. Accordingly, the volitional test only requires that the party is unable to act in a reasonable manner but unlike the cognitive test, the volitional test requires the other party must have reason to know of the condition. See Restatement (Second) of Contracts § 15(1)(b). In *Farber*, an earlier famous New York pre-Restatement (Second) of Contracts case cited by the *Ortelere* majority, a previously conservative businessman went on a spending spree after he passed from depression to manic-depression. In one transaction he contracted to purchase land, but two weeks later he was committed to a mental institution and later sued to avoid the contract. Even though the court concluded that manic-depression affected motivation rather than ability to understand, the contract was rescinded since this particular party would not have entered the transaction but for the manic-depression. See *Farber v. Sweet Style Mfg. Corp.,* 242 N.Y.S. 2d 763 (Sup. Ct. 1963). The Restatement (Second) of Contracts § 15(1)(b) does not entirely adopt the *Sweet* position because it requires that the innocent party be aware of the condition. Does the *Ortelere* majority follow the more conservative Restatement (Second) of Contracts version or the broader Sweet version? Yes. In other words, was the Teacher's Retirement Board aware or should they have been aware of Grace Ortelere's mental defect? Yes. The majority pointed to the Board's knowledge following Ortelere's mental breakdown. If so, did the court reject the broader view expressed in *Sweet* (not requiring awareness by the other party)? Not expressly. But the Restatement (Second) position is consistent with objective analysis. Balancing of the equities between an innocent party, on the one hand, and a delusional (but not overtly delusional to the knowledge of the other party) may well require awareness of the incapacity.

3. *Legal effect of performance.* Because the objective theory of contracts places the voidable determination on the knowledge of incompetency by the competent party, the power of avoidance terminates when the transaction is fully or partially performed such that avoidance would create injustice to either party. Accordingly, the clear majority rule is that the incompetent party may not avoid a contract in good faith, for fair consideration, and without notice of the incompetence by the competent party, at least unless the competent party can be restored to pre-contractual status quo. Restatement (Second) of Contracts § 15(2) and Restatement (Second) of Contracts § 15 cmt. f. Because of the lack of knowledge requirement, this section applies mostly to cognitive test incompetency transactions. What then should be the effect of legal performance and consideration restoration under the volitional test? The effect should be the same.

4. *Supervening incompetence.* See text.

5. *Restoration of consideration.* Since the cognitive test may be asserted to avoid a contract in the absence of knowledge of the other party regarding the mental infirmity and application of the cognitive test involves considerable uncertainty, the restoration of consideration rules are considerably more stringent than those involving minors. While a minor is ordinarily only required to restore what remains of the consideration, the mentally infirm must normally make full restoration even if the original consideration has dissipated. See, e.g., *Hauer v. Union State Bank,* 532 N. W. 2d 456 (Wis. App. 1995). Equitable exceptions normally exist where the competent party acted with knowledge of the other party's incompetency or where the incompetent received little actual benefit from the transaction. See Restatement (Second) of Contracts § 15(2) terminating power of avoidance entirely where the consideration was fair and the other party acted without knowledge of the infirmity. Given the nature of the volitional test, will the competent party be entitled to restoration? The same result should follow.

6. *Ratification and avoidability.* Absent an untimely death, all minors ultimately reach the age of majority at age 18 with full capacity to contract. This necessarily dictates that all minors must positively disaffirm their infancy contracts within a reasonable time of reaching the age of majority. The failure to do so constitutes a ratification by

failing to object to the contract's status while retaining the benefits of the contract. Should the same ratification rules apply to mental incompetents? It seems impossible to tie any particular period of time or regime to mental incompetency. The great danger with lapse of time is detrimental reliance by the other party who may have no knowledge or notice of the incompetency. Detrimental reliance under such circumstances should be available as protection for the other party. Indeed, how does a mental incompetent disaffirm a contract in the first place? Normally, through the action of a guardian. At least under the cognitive test, does not the fact of mental incompetency presume the person was generally not fully aware of the contract? Yes. Of course, unlike infancy, modern medicine can help cure or certainly mitigate the effects of mental illness. Upon reaching such competency status, do you think the same positive ratification rules should apply to the formerly mentally ill as to minors? No, but the other party needs to have the protection of detrimental reliance available. How would such a person recall a contract had been made when they were mentally ill? This seems like an impossible conundrum. Alternatively, given that individuals can control and treat many mental illnesses through medication, should those individuals be able to avoid contracts undertaken when they voluntarily stop taking those medications and thus render themselves incompetent? Yes, the nearest analogy being intoxication.

7. *Intoxication, drug addiction, and capacity to contract.* See text.

8. *Application of UCC.* See text.

9. *Application of CISG.* See text.

10. *Contracts Affected by a Relationship of Trust and Confidence.* Contract law is thus understandably suspicious of contracts between different parties when there is a pre-existing relationship between those parties that creates an expectation in one of the parties that the party with superior information will disclose all relevant facts known to that party. Accordingly, in such relationships of "trust and confidence," a person's non-disclosure of a known fact is equivalent to an affirmative assertion that the fact does not exist when the other person is entitled to know the fact. Similarly, a person is ordinarily not justified in relying on a statement of "opinion" rather than a statement of fact unless the recipient is in a relationship of trust and confidence with the maker of the opinion and the reliance on the opinion is reasonable. Undue influence depends in part on unfair persuasion of a party who, by virtue of the "relation between them," is justified in assuming that the other party will not act inconsistent with their welfare. The text distinguishes between a relationship of "trust and confidence" and a "fiduciary relationship." The point here is simple. In

analyzing various consequences of contract law, it is often important to also examine the relationship between the parties to the contract. The relationship might be created by the contract itself or might exist prior to the creation of the contract.

C. ABUSE OF THE BARGAINING PROCESS BY ONE OF THE PARTIES

Courts avoid assessing the fairness of the bargain from the perspective of the fairness of the exchanged considerations. In other words, as long as the parties abide by the accepted process for creation of enforceable bargains, courts will rarely overturn the resulting bargain even if it appears to be unfair to one of the parties. Of course, as suggested in the two-pronged procedural and substantive standard for unconscionability, deep flaws in the bargaining process often signal similar flaws in the substance of the bargain and vice versa.

Historically, the two most common categories of bargaining abuse involved deception and coercion by one of the parties in the formation of the contract. At the minimum, when applicable, these doctrines regulating misrepresentations and duress recognize a formative defect and therefore create a power of avoidance in the innocent party.

While both deceit and coercive conduct may create a power to avoid the contract, deceit in particular began as a tort doctrine. For that historical reason, ancient deceit and modern fraud actions most often implicate a choice between an action on the contract and an action to rescind the contract. The modern rules of election and preclusion are discussed at the beginning of this chapter. However, unlike most other avoidance grounds, fraud uniquely implicates both remedies because it operates both as an independent cause of action in tort (for which the plaintiff may recover both compensatory and punitive damages) and a defense to contract (giving rise to a power of avoidance in the victim). While fraud in tort requires proof of scienter, contractual avoidance for fraud does not.

1. Intentional and Negligent Misrepresentation.

Fraud with respect to the nature of documents signed (fraud in execution) prevents the formation of a contract. See Restatement (Second) of Contracts § 163 and discussion of "void" contracts in Chapter 5. As used in this section, fraud relative to the nature of the consideration itself (fraud in inducement) does not prevent the formation of the contract and thus creates an election of remedies in favor of the injured party.

Fraud in the inducement creates only a voidable contract. As such, the defrauded or injured party has a power to avoid the contract and obtain rescission and restitution for any consideration transferred to the fraudulent party. Alternatively, the injured party can affirm the contract and seek damages on the affirmed contract. While an action for damages on the contract alone might constitute an election to affirm or ratify the contract that extinguishes the power of rescission, the claims may be pleaded in the alternative with an ultimate election by the end of the trial to avoid double recovery.

Several factors influence an injured party's decision to pursue one or both remedies (rescission and restitution versus damages on the contract). First, contract law itself does not impose a damage remedy for misrepresentation. Rather, the injured party may recover damages only by pleading and proving the comparatively more stringent elements of a tort fraud cause of action, even though such damages are measured by the normative contract benefit-of-bargain rule. Of course, a tortious misrepresentation not made in connection with the formation of a contract would be based entirely in tort law and, if successful, damages would be measured in accordance with the normative tort out-of-pocket rule. But regardless of the measurement standard, damages on the contract for the tort of misrepresentation will only exist if the "tort requirements" for misrepresentation are first satisfied. Accordingly, to sue on the contract for damages related to a misrepresentation, the elements of the tort of misrepresentation must be proven.

The contractual conceptualization of misrepresentation is considerably broader than tort conceptualization and often does not even require scienter. While the tort damage claim (while measured in contractual terms) requires knowledge that the assertion was false, contract law may permit avoidance even where the deceitful party made a material but merely innocent misrepresentation. The tort damage claim would generally not be available in such cases. Accordingly, the provable state of mind of the maker of the assertion often plays a role in determining whether the injured party pursues the tort fraud action for benefit-of-the-bargain damages rather than the contractual action for rescission and restitution. For contract purposes, inducement of assent by either a fraudulent or material misrepresentation upon which the recipient is justified in relying renders a contract voidable.

Two separate sections of the Restatement (Second) describe when conduct is equivalent to an "assertion." First, "concealment" intended to keep another from learning true facts of which the party would otherwise have learned is equivalent to an assertion of a fact and is therefore a misrepresentation. Second, "non-disclosure" is also equivalent to an assertion and therefore a misrepresentation, but only where (i) the person knows disclosure is necessary to prevent a previous assertion from being fraudulent or material ("duty to correct"); (ii) the person knows disclosure would correct a material mistake of the other party, but only if non-disclosure amounts to a failure to act in good faith, (iii) the person knows that disclosure would correct a mistake regarding the contents of a writing evidencing the agreement, or (iv) when the other person is entitled to know the fact by reason of a relationship of trust and confidence between them. A misrepresentation is material if it is likely to induce a reasonable person to manifest assent. Again, unlike tort law, this form of misrepresentation does not state a scienter requirement and therefore is generally not actionable in tort damages. Nonetheless, it may be the basis of rescission. Rescission for either fraudulent or material misrepresentation will only occur if the other party to the contract is justified in relying on the misrepresentation.

Hill v. Jones
CASE BRIEF

This is a 1986 decision of the Court of Appeals of Arizona. In 1982, after several visits to the Jones' home, the Hills entered into a contract to purchase the Jones residence for $72,000. The purchase agreement provided that sellers were to pay for and place in escrow a termite inspection report stating that the property was free from evidence of termite infestation. Escrow would close two months later. A central feature of the home was a teak floor, in which Mr. Hill had noticed potential termite damage; Mrs. Jones assured him that the "ripple" in the floor was the result of water damage from a water heater leak. Mr. Hill was not totally satisfied with the explanation, but felt that the termite inspection report would reveal any termite damage. The report indicated no visible evidence of infestation, but failed to note the existence of any physical damage or evidence of previous treatment. Nonetheless, the realtor informed the parties that the home passed the termite inspection. Apparently, neither party ever saw the report. Upon moving in, the Hills found a brochure about termites in a drawer and learned, from a neighbor, of past termite infestation in the house. After the close of escrow, Mrs. Hill noticed crumbling wood in the steps leading to the living room, and an exterminator's inspection found damage to the floor, steps, and wood columns. Damage to the floor was estimated at over $5,000.

The Hills filed suit to rescind the purchase agreement, alleging that the sellers made misrepresentations concerning termite damage in the house and failed to disclose the existence of the damage and the house's history of termite infestation. Through discovery, the buyers learned that the sellers, upon purchasing the home in 1974, had received information from the previous owner about unrepaired termite damage, as well as guarantees by Truly Nolen regarding follow-up termite treatments. The buyers also learned that the neighbor had alerted the sellers twice about live termite evidence that had required termite booster treatments. The sellers did not disclose any of this information to the buyers before the close of escrow. The termite inspector, on second inspection, found two areas of termite damage that were obscured by the placement of boxes and a plant, respectively. He stated that the damage should have been found the first time, but argued that it is customary for the inspector to receive information about past termite history from the seller. The sellers showed that the buyers had ample opportunity to inspect the premises, and that the buyers knew what termite damage looked like. The trial court dismissed the misrepresentation claim because of an integration clause in the purchase agreement. The court also granted summary judgment on buyers' "concealment" claim, finding that there was no genuine disputed issue of material fact regarding the sellers' duty to disclose information about termite infestation. The buyers appealed.

With regard to the integration clause of the contract, the court of appeals overturned the dismissal of the misrepresentation claim. While the agreement indicated that the sellers would not be bound by any representation not contained in the agreement, the court found Mrs. Jones's assertion about the water damage—which was actually termite damage—could constitute fraud. As such, parol evidence is always available to show fraud, even if it varies the terms of the agreement. This rule is necessary in order to prevent the fraudulent actor from freeing himself of the consequences of his own fraud by agreement. Thus, the court held that the integration clause could not protect the sellers from liability if the buyers could show fraud.

With regard to the duty to disclose, the court framed the issue as "whether a seller has a duty to disclose to the buyer the existence of termite damage in a residential dwelling known to the seller, but not to the buyer, which materially affects the value of the property." The court held that such a duty does exist. Fir st, the court noted that vitality of the caveat emptor doctrine had waned during the latter half of the twentieth century. Instead, the modern view tends to hold that a vendor has an affirmative duty to disclose material facts where such disclosure would prevent the other party from holding a mistaken assumption or would correct such a mistake. Such failure to disclose could amount to an equivalent that the fact does not exist. The court stated that "[w]here a misrepresentation is fraudulent or where a negligent misrepresentation is one of material fact, the policy of finality rightly gives way to the policy of promoting honest dealings between the parties." As a result, the court held up the Florida disclosure rule ("Where the seller of a home knows of facts materially affecting the value of the property which are not readily observable and are not known to the buyer, the seller is under a duty to disclose them to the buyer.") as a model for future Arizona cases, noting its focus on the materiality of facts in dispute. Since termite infestation, both past and present, had been held to be a material issue in past cases, the court felt that the materiality of infestation in this case was one to be decided by a jury. Finally, the court noted that the sellers' argument that the nondisclosure did not influence the buyers' decision was undercut by the fact that Mr. Hill had stated that he intended to rely on the termite report in making his decision. The court reversed and remanded the case for full trial.

INTERESTING DISCUSSION ISSUES

1. *The historical context of caveat emptor and the rise of a duty to disclose in limited situations.* Historically, under the common law, the concept of caveat emptor or "buyer beware" protected a seller of goods or services from any duty to make a positive disclosure with respect to the subject matter of the contract. The seller could not make false statements but could say nothing. If questioned, the seller had a duty to respond truthfully and accurately. As the opinion in this case pointed out, the vitality of this concept "has waned during the later half of the 20th century." The old common law concept was apparently founded on the assumption that both parties were of equal bargaining power with equal access to all relevant facts. Given such an assumption, each party assumed the risk of her own exercise of judgment in proceeding with the transaction. Modern law, as evidenced in the Restatement (Second) of Contracts, recognizes the serious limitations of the old concept. One party may have information which the other does not have. Such information may not be readily obtained by inspection or even testing. The notion that each party should be responsible for its own inquiry and exercise of judgment often fails to correlate with the facts of a transaction as it failed in the instant case. Clearly there is such a failure where one side is misled by the statements of the other. Equally clearly, there is such a failure where one party deliberately takes affirmative steps to conceal facts (such as installing wallboard to conceal water leaks and water damage). The more difficult issues arise beyond these two clear situations, where there is no misrepresentation but one party has information which the other does not. Most commercial market transactions fall into this class and few would suggest that one party to a commercial transaction has to share motives and/or reasons for contracting to the other party. Where the line, set by the instant case, is to be drawn is not without difficulty. Restatement (Second) of Contracts § 161 (quoted in the case) suggests that the line be drawn as follows:

> A person's non-disclosure of a fact known to him is equivalent to an assertion that the fact does not exist in the following cases only:
> (a) where he knows that disclosure of the fact is necessary to prevent some previous assertion from being a misrepresentation or from being fraudulent or material.
> (b) where he knows that disclosure of the fact would correct a mistake of the other party as to a basic assumption on which that party is making the contract and if non-disclosure of the fact amounts to a failure to act in good faith and in accordance with reasonable standards of fair dealing.

(c) where he knows that disclosure of the fact would correct a mistake of the other party as to the contents or effect of a writing, evidencing or embodying an agreement in whole or in part.
(d) where the other person is entitled to know the fact because of a relation of trust and confidence between them.

Comment a to this section adds the following:

> Like concealment, non-disclosure of a fact may be equivalent to a misrepresentation. Concealment necessarily involves an element of non-disclosure, but it is the act of preventing another from learning of a fact that is significant and this act is always equivalent to a misrepresentation (§ 160). Non-disclosure without concealment is equivalent to a misrepresentation only in special situations. A party making a contract is not expected to tell all that he knows to the other party, even if he knows that the other party lacks knowledge on some aspects of the transaction. His non-disclosure, as such, has no legal effect except in the situations enumerated in this Section. He may not, of course, tell half-truths and his assertion of only some of the facts without the inclusion of such additional matters as he knows or believes to be necessary to prevent it from being misleading is itself a misrepresentation. See Comment a to § 159. In contrast to the rule applicable to liability in tort for misrepresentation, it is not enough, where disclosure is expected, merely to make reasonable efforts to disclose the relevant facts. Actual disclosure is required. Compare *Restatement, Second, Torts § 551*, Comment d.

Comment *c* deals with situations where there may be a duty to correct a prior statement. The question of where a duty to correct arises is an important topic under federal securities law.

One who has made an assertion that is neither a fraudulent nor a material misrepresentation may subsequently acquire knowledge that bears significantly on his earlier assertion. He is expected to speak up and correct the earlier assertion in three cases. First, if his assertion was not a misrepresentation because it was true, he may later learn that it is no longer true. See Illustration 1. Second, his assertion may have been a misrepresentation but may not have been fraudulent. If this was because he believed that it was true, he may later learn that it was not true. See Illustration 2. If this was because he did not intend that it be relied upon, he may later learn that the other is about to rely on it. See Illustration 3. Third, if his assertion was a misrepresentation but was not material because he had no reason to know of the other's special characteristics that made reliance likely, he may later learn of such characteristics. If a person fails to correct his earlier assertion in these situations, the result is the same as it would have been had he had his newly acquired knowledge at the time he made the assertion.

The rule stated in Clause (a), like that stated in Clause (d), extends to non-disclosure by persons who are not parties to the transaction.

UCC § 2-314 introduces an implied warranty of merchantable quality in a contract for the sale of goods if the seller is a merchant with respect to goods of that kind. This section may have the effect, in transactions to which it applies, of trumping any question of non-fraudulent failure to disclose. But the effect of § 2-316 may also have to be considered. This and other issues of implied warranty are discussed at greater length in Chapter 9.

NOTES AND QUESTIONS

1. *Avoidance or damages?* Buyers sought rescission of the purchase agreement rather than damages on the contract to purchase. Why? To prove the tort of fraud they would have had to prove scienter. To rescind for misrepresentation they only had to prove materiality and justifiable reliance. If the buyers had sought monetary damages, how would those damages have been measured? Traditionally, tort damages would have been measured by the cost of restoring the plaintiff to the position she was in before the tort. But more recently, many courts have used the contract benefit of the bargain measure in such a case. The trial court denied rescission and granted sellers' attorney fees. What explains the radically different outcome at the appellate level? The appellate court's finding of a duty to disclose the prior termite infection and treatment and a holding that this failure to disclose was the equivalent of a corresponding misrepresentation. The buyers asserted that the sellers made misrepresentations concerning termite damage in the home (but not the non-existence of termites) and failed to disclose the termite damage and termite history. Are these the same form of misrepresentation? No. One would be a misrepresentation of fact. The other would be a failure to disclose information that the seller should have known would be material to the buyer's decision to purchase. If not, what is the difference? One is a misrepresentation of fact, the other is a failure to disclose pertinent information. What was the basis of the misrepresentation claim? Failure to disclose under circumstances where such affirmative disclosure was required. Did the sellers voluntarily assert the home was termite free or in response to a direct question regarding the same? No. If not, can concealment alone be the basis of an assertion of a fact constituting a form of misrepresentation? Yes, but here the problem was not affirmative concealment but rather failure to disclose. If so, what is the legal basis for doing so? The duty to disclose, emphasizing the importance of exactly when such a duty arises.

2. *Attorney fees.* The American Rule on attorney fees provides that, absent contractual agreement to the contrary or other exceptional

circumstances or statute, each side must bear its own legal expenses. Why do you suppose the trial court awarded the sellers $1,000 for attorney fees? The trial court must have concluded that there was no reasonable basis for the plaintiff's suit given the then applicable Arizona law, including the law relating to merger ("integration") clauses. Why did the sellers appeal that aspect of the trial court decision? They must have wanted a substantially larger award of fees.

3. *Effect of integration clause.* The trial court dismissed the misrepresentation claim, however framed, on the basis of the integration clause. Did the trial court dismiss the concealment claim on the same basis? Apparently yes. Is concealment a form of misrepresentation? Yes. If so, and the integration clause effectively cured the misrepresentation claim, why was the clause not effective as to the concealment claim? The appellate court held that the integration clause could not block parol evidence of fraud, but it apparently conflated fraud and misrepresentation with respect to its treatment of the integration clause. Did the trial court utilize the integration clause to block admission of parol evidence to show misrepresentation? Apparently yes. Since the alleged misrepresentation occurred after the contract was executed, is evidence thereof subject to the parol evidence rule? The court assumed that the answer was yes. The logic behind the parol evidence rule suggests otherwise—that it bars only statements prior to finalization of the written agreement. If not, is the reason because of the timing of the misrepresentation or the fact that even parol evidence is admissible to prove fraud? The appellate court so held. Assuming that even parol evidence is admissible to show fraud in the absence of an integration clause, what does the presence of the integration clause add to the sellers' misrepresentation defense? In some states it will block a complaint based on misrepresentation. Does it seek to destroy "justified" reliance on a misrepresentation even if made? It can be so drafted. If so, do you think such a purpose should be sanctioned by the court? No. Most courts treat such clauses as "boilerplate" and evade them in the face of substantial evidence of misrepresentation. If not, and you represented the sellers in this case and prior to purchase, would you continue to recommend the inclusion of such a clause? Yes. If so, why? Depending upon the wording of the clause it can help establish absence of a basis for justifiable reliance. Does the clause have a broader purpose than eliminating responsibility for misrepresentations? Yes—it can preclude proof by parol evidence of alleged "additional" terms not found in the writing.

4. *Duty to disclose.* The duty to disclose identified in *Hill* is in tension with the general principle of contract law that parties dealing at arms' length typically do not have an affirmative duty to protect the other party's interests. The comments to Restatement (Second) of Contracts § 161 cmt. d illustrates and clarifies this tension:

> In many situations, if one party knows that the other is mistaken as to a basic assumption, he is expected to disclose the fact that would correct the mistake. A seller of real or personal property is, for example, ordinarily expected to disclose a known latent defect of quality or title that is of such a character as would probably prevent the buyer from buying at the contract price.... Nevertheless, a party need not correct all mistakes of the other and is expected only to act in good faith and in accordance with reasonable standards of fair dealing, as reflected in prevailing business ethics. A party may, therefore, reasonably expect the other to take normal steps to inform himself and to draw his own conclusions. If the other is indolent, inexperienced or ignorant, or if his judgment is bad or he lacks access to adequate information, his adversary is not generally expected to compensate for these deficiencies.

Which of these paradigms best reflects your actual expectations in dealing with others in your business affairs, including your contracts for housing, financial aid, real property, transportation, and with your law school? In the course of fifteen years of corporate law practice one of the authors always disclosed anything he thought material which the other side had apparently overlooked. Does the subject matter and context of the transaction alter your expectations regarding the other party's duty to disclose? Matters that are obvious upon inspection may not need to be disclosed where the other party has a full opportunity to inspect and that inspection would disclose the facts. Compare UCC § 2-316. It is worth noting that the scope of this duty to disclose has an ancient pedigree. Consider St. Thomas Aquinas's discussion of whether a seller is bound to state defects in the thing sold:

> Article 3. Whether the seller is bound to state the defects of the thing sold?
>
> * * * *
>
> I answer that, It is always unlawful to give anyone an occasion of danger or loss, although a man need not always give another the help or counsel which would be for his advantage in any way; but only in certain fixed cases, for instance when someone is subject to him, or when he is the only one who can assist him. Now the seller who offers goods for sale, gives the buyer an occasion of loss or danger, by the very fact that he offers him defective goods, if such defect may occasion loss or danger to the buyer—loss, if, by reason of this defect, the goods are of less value, and he takes nothing off the price on that account—danger, if this defect either hinder the use of the goods or render it hurtful, for instance, if a man sells a lame for a fleet horse, a tottering house for a safe one, rotten or poisonous food for wholesome. Wherefore if such like defects be

> hidden, and the seller does not make them *known*, the sale will be illicit and fraudulent, and the seller will be bound to compensation for the loss incurred.
>
> On the other hand, if the defect be manifest, for instance if a horse have but one eye, or if the goods though useless to the buyer, be useful to someone else, provided the seller take as much as he ought from the price, he is not bound to state the defect of the goods, since perhaps on account of that defect the buyer might want him to allow a greater rebate than he need. Wherefore the seller may look to his own indemnity, by withholding the defect of the goods. The Summa Theologica of St. Thomas Aquinas II-II, Q.77 (Fathers of the English Dominican Province trans. 1920) (Kevin Knight ed. 2006), available at http://www.newadvent.org/summa.

To what extent does this thirteenth century ethical analysis mirror modern ethical expectations and duties? Quite accurately.

Importantly, the restatement frames the duty to disclose in terms of the failure of a basic assumption. This mistake as to a basic assumption of the parties provides the basis for the unilateral mistake doctrine discussed later in this chapter. In general, a contract is voidable where one party at the time of contracting is mistaken as to a basic assumption and that mistake has a material effect on the agreed exchange of performances, provided that enforcement would be unconscionable or that the other party had reason to know of, or caused, the mistake. See Restatement (Second) of Contracts § 153. In the circumstances at issue in *Hill*, would the doctrine of unilateral mistake adequately protect the buyer? The answer would necessarily depend on whether the termite infestation was the subject of a basic assumption by the buyer. The standard of "basic assumption" is thought to require a greater degree of importance than one of "materiality." If so, what is the necessity of a separate duty to disclose a material fact if the lack of knowledge of that fact by the buyer provides an identical rescission remedy? It does not as noted immediately above. Doctrinally, what are the differences between these two concepts? Mistake relates to something basic but not considered by the parties, something outside the scope of the actual negotiations. Material misrepresentation relates to something part of those negotiations. In the latter case one party's mistake is caused by the other party, in the former it is not. This can and should make a substantial difference in the standard of proof required.

Enhance-It, LLC v. American Access Technologies, Inc.
CASE BRIEF

This is a 2006 decision of the United States District Court for South Carolina. Enhance-It (EI) purchased UV lighting equipment from American Access Technologies (AAT) and AAT's predecessor in interest. EI claimed that AAT shipped defective goods and asserted a host of claims, including claims of fraud and breach of contract accompanied by a fraudulent act, both of which were dismissed by the trial court. EI filed an amended complaint to correct the failings of these two counts. AAT argued that EI's amendments should be denied on futility grounds, as the allegedly false statement in question by AAT was only an opinion, and because the causes of action were barred under South Carolina law.

Regarding the claim for false statement, the court noted that in South Carolina the following elements were required to prove fraud: "(1) a representation; (2) its falsity; (3) its materiality; (4) either knowledge of its falsity or a reckless disregard of its truth or falsity; (5) intent that the representation be acted upon; (6) the hearer's ignorance of its falsity; (7) the hearer's reliance on its truth; (8) the hearer's right to rely thereon; and (9) the hearer's consequent and proximate injury." Here, the AAT representative claimed that the equipment in question had been tested for over a year with good results, and that the new equipment would perform better than the equipment it was to replace. The court noted that opinions as to future performance of new equipment may not properly be the subject of a finding of fraud. But EI's allegations that the equipment had not been tested for a year, and that good results had not been obtained, were matters of fact that could properly serve as the basis for a fraud action.

AAT also claimed that EI's complaint was futile because it requested a tort remedy for what was purely a breach of contract claim, something not permitted under state law. But the court noted that where contracts create special relationships between the parties, breach of such duties would justify an action in tort. Thus, rather than adopting AAT's view that EI was attempting to make a warranty claim into a fraud case, the court found that EI's allegations were that AAT had violated a duty imposed under tort law: the duty not to commit fraud. As a result, AAT could not take shelter under the economic loss rule, which protects only defendants in contract cases.

AAT next argued that EI's fraud claims failed to state facts separate from those of the contract bargain, and thus could only recover under the contract. But the court disagreed, stating that when a party is induced to enter a contract by fraud, he may elect to sue in either contract or tort, or both. Thus, EI would be permitted to advance both the contract and tort claims at trial, but would be forced to elect its remedies under one theory or the other after verdict but before entry of judgment. Since EI did not have to make such an election at the complaint stage, the court permitted both the tort and contract claims to move forward and granted EI's amendment.

INTERESTING DISCUSSION ISSUES

1. *Misrepresentation, if fraudulent, provides three different remedies.* As this case states, one who is induced to enter into a contract by fraudulent misrepresentation may elect to rescind the contract and recover on the basis of restitutionary remedies. Or in the alternative, may elect to affirm and not rescind and sue for damages based on breach of contract. Or in the alternative, may sue for the tort of fraud, usually claiming punitive as well as actual damages.

2. *What distinguishes a misrepresentation from a statement of opinion or a statement of future intent?* A misrepresentation, to be actionable, must be one of fact. Generally, a statement of opinion can be understood as if it carried the following qualification, "In my opinion, such as it is, and what there is of it. . . ." That is to say, the statement describes the state of mind of the maker and does not warrant the accuracy or correctness of the opinion. As the saying goes, "That is just one person's opinion!" As a result it is difficult to convert a statement of opinion into any kind of a promise. In the same way, generally a statement about the future necessarily has to be a form of statement of opinion. But a statement of opinion can be a statement of fact and thus the basis of a claim of misrepresentation. And that is when the person providing the opinion knows that the statement offered is not the true opinion of the maker or that the opinion offered has no reasonable basis in fact. . . . In the instant case, the seller represented that the tests were satisfactory and then argued that "satisfactory" reflected an opinion and not a statement of fact. The court did not agree.

3. *The "economic loss" rule—why negligent breach of contract gives rise to a remedy for breach of contract but not for a tort of negligent misrepresentation.* As discussed further in the introductory notes to this section and in Chapter 9 below, the so-called "economic loss" rule, as applied by a majority of courts, completely bars recovery of economic losses in tort. Some courts allow recovery in tort for such loss in limited situations. Thus, by way of illustration, in product liability cases the doctrine bars tort recovery when a defective product damages only itself. See Gennady A. Gorel, *"The Economic Loss Doctrine: Arguing For The Intermediate Rule And Taming The Tort-Eating Monster,"* 37 Rutgers L.J. 517 (2006). This author quoted the following definition of "economic loss," "the diminution in the value of the product because it is inferior in quality and does not work for the general purposes for which it was manufactured and sold." From this view, the author said,

personal injury and damage to other property are not such "economic losses."

The policy behind this doctrine was described as follows:

> The typical economic justification for strict liability is allocation of 'external' costs to the party best able to bear and prevent them. All liability schemes, of course, allocate losses among the parties. The question in this context is whether the parties are entitled to determine allocation for themselves. Strict liability enforces a loss allocation because the social interest in protecting consumers' health and safety justifies intervention in the system. The economic loss doctrine protects commercial parties' ability to determine their own allocation as a component of the terms of the deal.

The concept of 'freedom to contract' rarely arises in modern American legal opinions. However, it is a critical basis for not only the economic loss doctrine, but for the organization of this country's economy. The economic loss doctrine gives effect to the parties' arrangements for allocating risk of loss. Tort claims interfere with enforcement of the contract terms, and therefore ought to be disfavored in commercial disputes. Cortney G. Sylvester, *"Economic Loss: Commercial Contract Law Lives,"* 27 Wm. Mitchell L. Rev. 417, 423 (2000).

NOTES AND QUESTIONS

1. *Particularized pleading.* As noted by the court, a plaintiff alleging fraud must usually plead facts constituting a cause of action for fraud with "particularity," although state of mind elements such as scienter may be alleged generally. See, e.g., Federal Rule of Civil Procedure 9(b). This pleading standard often allows for dismissal of weak fraud claims at the pleadings stage rather than using trial to develop facts that might otherwise constitute fraud. Why would such a rule apply to fraud claims but not to other claims? Fraud, unlike many other causes of action, must be proved by clear and convincing evidence. Given this substantially higher required level of proof, it makes sense to require that acts of fraud be alleged with particularity. In the world of business and securities regulation, pleading with particularity is a standard used to pare down nuisance and "blackmail" suits that otherwise could be pleaded in generalities in the hope of settlement for something approaching estimated costs of defense. Christopher M. Fairman in *"An Invitation To The Rulemakers—Strike Rule 9(b),"* 38 U.C. Davis L. Rev. 281 (2004) argued that this differential pleading requirement should be abolished. He claimed that the origin of the requirement of pleading a fraud cause of action with particularity was to be found in the old split between law and equity. While this divided jurisdiction continued, a claim of fraud could only be brought in equity and in

the form of an action to set aside a judgment from the common law side. History aside, the requirement of pleading with particularity has an important current role to play, not only in fraud cases, but also in some corporate and securities law situations, strengthened by fairly recent Congressional legislation.

2. *Liberal pleading amendment.* State and federal rules of civil procedure generally permit liberal amendments to flawed pleadings. Indeed, this action arose out of a motion to amend the complaint to satisfy the heightened pleading standard after those claims were originally dismissed. Given that discovery may commence soon after the filing of the complaint and before dismissal, is the easy availability of amendments an invitation for parties to engage in fishing expeditions through their opponents' files in order to cobble together a workable claim? Yes indeed—and this is part of the current justification from the strict pleading requirements for fraud. Or, alternatively, do the amendment rules serve the interests of justice by preventing otherwise meritorious claims from being dismissed on a pleading technicality? Th e opinion in the instant quotes other case authority supporting liberal amendment rules, "Courts generally favor the 'resolution of cases on their merits' . . . [t]hus the substantive merits of a proposed claim [or defense] are typically best left for later resolution, e.g., motions to dismiss or for summary judgment, . . ., or for resolution at trial." Would you expect courts to be more or less generous in giving leave to amend an uncomplicated breach of contract action than in a fraud action? No. Why? This question is not applicable given the previous answer.

3. *Election of remedies.* The plaintiff does not need to make its election of remedies at any particular time in the action. Rather, the modern rule on election simply precludes a double recovery. Do you think this is a positive development in the law? Yes. Again it supports the reaching of the best substantive result rather than one apt to be distorted by technicalities of older forms of pleading and trial practice.

4. *Tortious breach or separate tort.* See text.

5. *Punitive damages under the UCC and the CISG.* See text.

6. *Promises as misrepresentations.* Many fraud claims involve situations in which the only statement at issue is a promise of future performance. Recall the definition of a promise from Chapter 2. Under what situations can a promise be equivalent to an affirmative misrepresentation? Where the promisor has no intention of fulfilling the promise at the time she makes the promise. Trying to prove this situation involves analyzing the subjective state of mind of the promisor at the time of making the promise. In some situations, where

the promisor makes a statement of opinion recklessly and without any reasonable basis for it, a court may infer fraudulent intent. The lead case is *Derry v. Peek*, 14 App. Cas. 337 (1889), a decision of the English House of Lords. Following the holding of the United States Supreme Court in *Ernst & Ernst v. Hochfelder*, 425 U.S. 185 (1976), a successful suit under section 10(b) of the Securities Exchange Act of 1934, and the rule thereunder, required proof of scienter (a subjective element embracing an intent to deceive, manipulate or defraud). Subsequent decisions found this requirement satisfied by reckless conduct. "Most federal circuits have approved some use of recklessness to satisfy the scienter requirement in 10b-5 actions." See Paul S. Milich, "*Securities Fraud Under Section 10(b) and Rule 10b-5: Scienter, Recklessness, And The Good Faith Defense*," 11 J. Corp. L. 179 (1986).

2. Duress

In the late 18th century, duress was actionable only if the resulting agreement was coerced by actual, not threatened imprisonment or fear of loss of life or serious physical injury. Under the Restatement (Second) of Contracts, other methods of overcoming free will have been recognized. But the free will of the particular person, not that of an objectively reasonable person, must be overcome to avoid the contract. Modern duress law normally renders a transaction voidable, but the contract will be void where the plaintiff had no intent to enter into the agreement and was coerced, for instance, at the point of a gun. Restatement (Second) of Contracts § 176, stating the modern and broader view of duress, provides:

(1) A threat is improper if
(a) what is threatened is a crime or a tort, or the threat itself would be a crime or a tort if it resulted in obtaining property,
(b) what is threatened is a criminal prosecution,
(c) what is threatened is the use of civil process and the threat is made in bad faith, or
(d) the threat is a breach of the duty of good faith and fair dealing under a contract with the recipient.
(2) A threat is improper if the resulting exchange is not on fair terms, and
(a) the threatened act would harm the recipient and would not significantly benefit the party making the threat,
(b) the effectiveness of the threat in inducing the manifestation of assent is significantly increased by prior unfair dealing by the party making the threat, or
(c) what is threatened is otherwise a use of power for illegitimate ends.

The greatest expansion in modern case law had been the extension of the doctrine to cover "economic duress." The uncertain parameters of this doctrine may encourage unsettling interference in the bargaining process.

Totem Marine Tug & Barge, Inc. v. Alyeska Pipeline Service Co. *CASE BRIEF*

This is a 1978 decision of the Supreme Court of Alaska. In June 1975, Totem entered a contact with Alyska Pipeline Service (APS) in which Totem was to transport pipeline construction materials from Houston to a port in southern Alaska. To fulfill the contract, Totem chartered a barge and an ocean-going tug, expenditures made possible by loans to totem from its president, Richard Stair, and Pacific, Inc., a stockholder of Totem. Under the contract, Totem was to complete performance by August 15, 1975. But Totem was delayed on numerous occasions by a variety of problems, including: (1) Totem had to load over three times the represented tonnage in Houston, during which time APS delayed in assuring Totem that it would cover extra expenses, causing a 27-day delay; (2) the additional tonnage slowed the barge's speed; (3) APS delayed in providing written confirmation that it would pay for an additional tug to speed the trip, causing a delay at the Panama Canal; and (4) the boats encountered a hurricane that delayed them for eight days. As the boats neared San Pedro, CA, where the crew was to be changed and the boats refueled, APS ordered the boats to dock in Long Beach, CA, where APS off-loaded the barge without Totem's consent. On September 14, 1975, APS terminated the contract without providing a reason. Totem submitted an invoice to APS for between $260,000 and $300,000, at which time an official from APS told Totem that payment would be made in perhaps a day, or perhaps in six to eight months. Totem had numerous obligations on payment schedules of 10–30 days and, according to Stair, would go bankrupt without immediate cash. Thus, Totem ordered its attorney to collect the funds, and to advise APS of Totem's financial straits. After negotiations, APS made a settlement offer of $97,500; Totem accepted.

In March 1976, Totem, Stair, and Pacific filed suit against APS seeking to rescind the settlement on the ground of economic duress, and to recover the balance originally due on the contract. APS moved for summary judgment on the ground that Totem had executed a binding release of all claims against APS, and that Totem thus could not prevail in its suit. The trial court granted APS's summary judgment motion; Totem appealed.

In determining whether there was a dispute as to a material issue of fact, the court examined the doctrine of avoidance of a release on the grounds of economic duress, which "has been broadened to include myriad forms of economic coercion which force a person to involuntarily enter into a particular transaction." The doctrine of avoidance by reason of economic duress was created in order to balance the competing interests of finality in dispute resolutions and equity regarding contracts created under coercion. The court stated that "one essential element of economic duress is that the plaintiff show that the other party, by wrongful acts or threats, intentionally caused him to involuntarily enter into a particular transaction." Additionally, "the victim must have no choice but to agree to the other party's terms or face serious financial hardship," i.e., no reasonable alternative existed. The court stated that, generally, whether a reasonable alternative existed was a fact-specific question, depending on a number of factors.

The court held that, in this case, Totem's allegations, if proved, would support a finding that it executed the release against APS under economic duress, as: (1) APS deliberately withheld payment of an acknowledged debt; (2) APS knew that Totem had no choice but to accept an inadequate sum to settle the debt; (3) Totem faced impending bankruptcy; and (4) Totem was unable to meet its pressing financial needs except by acquiescing to APS's settlement offer. While APS had made a proper initial showing of no genuine issues of material fact (by virtue of the release and settlement), the trial court had improperly stated Totem's burden. While the trial court held that Totem would not be able, on the evidence submitted, to sustain a burden of proof at trial, the proper analysis was whether Totem had raised evidence tending to dispute APS's evidence. The court held that it had, and that the case must be remanded for a new trial.

As a peripheral issue, the court rejected the claims of Stair and Pacific, who contended that even if Totem was bound under the settlement, that they were not bound by the agreement because they did not sign it. The court held these arguments without merit, finding that neither Stair nor Pacific was intended as a third-party beneficiary, and thus had no contractual claims against APS. Their fate in the lawsuit depended entirely on Totem's success or failure in pursuing its claims.

INTERESTING DISCUSSION ISSUES

1. *Was judicial intervention in this case on the basis of "duress" warranted?* This was the case of one of the parties to a settlement agreement, entered into while advised by legal counsel, seeking subsequently to have the settlement set aside. The public policy supporting an end to litigation and supporting the finality of a settlement agreement between the parties to a dispute has a high order of social importance. Settlement agreements negotiated with someone not represented by counsel may be, and frequently are, subject to scrutiny. But the student is entitled to think and believe that a settlement agreement reached with a party advised, during the negotiation process, by legal counsel is entitled to enforcement. The

student may think of the analogy from criminal law of the person convicted of murder arguing that she was not represented by competent counsel. Should Totem have had to allege in this case that the company was not competently represented in the negotiation? The Supreme Court may be pointing at this issue by saying in the proceedings to follow it would be necessary to hear from that lawyer. What might that lawyer testify to? Could the plaintiff have protected itself by legal action rather than execution of the settlement? The court here says "No." "An available alternative or remedy may not be adequate where the delay involved in pursuing that remedy would cause immediate and irreparable loss to one's economic or business interest." Could Totem have protected itself by electing to file for bankruptcy?

NOTES AND QUESTIONS

1. *Nature of wrongful threat.* What was the nature of the "wrongful" threat in the terms of Restatement (Second) of Contracts § 176? See §176(2)(b) and (c) quoted in this manual prior to the case:

> (2) A threat is improper if the resulting exchange is not on fair terms, and
> (a) the threatened act would harm the recipient and would not significantly benefit the party making the threat,
> (b) the effectiveness of the threat in inducing the manifestation of assent is significantly increased by prior unfair dealing by the party making the threat, or
> (c) what is threatened is otherwise a use of power for illegitimate ends.

Notice there are two standards. One applies to exchanges not on fair terms, while the other applies regardless of the fairness. Was the exchange in this case "fair"? According to the facts to be addressed by the court at this point, the answer to the question is "No." Do you have adequate information to properly evaluate the economic extent of Alyeska's damage claim? No. If not, then at this stage of the trial, which threat element is most likely involved? "What is threatened is otherwise a use of power for illegitimate needs."

2. *Cause of hardship.* While it is clear that duress is available when an improper threat induces a person with no reasonable alternative to form a contract, does this mean that duress embraces striking a hard bargain with someone in dire economic hardship? No. Most courts also require that the party exerting duress must cause the hardship itself. See Selmer Co. v. Blakeslee-Midwest Co., 704 F. 2d 924 (7th Cir. 1983). Thus, driving a hard bargain with a person already in difficulty is not economic duress. Note that Totem's urgent need for

cash arguably arose from the fact that the company overextended itself with its creditors and investors in order to get the Alyeska contract. Did Alyeska cause Totem's hardship or simply try to take advantage of Totem's hardship? If Alyeska refused to pay an acknowledged debt then due, they caused or at least contributed to the cause of Totem's hardship. Do you think this is a policy line worth drawing? Yes, because unless the line is so drawn, hardship (known or unknown to the other party) might be universally available to undo a prior settlement. If so, are there any other contractual protections for those in desperate economic circumstances? Filing a petition in bankruptcy would be the usual other choice.

3. *Settlement policy.* Parties are clearly encouraged to settle their own disputed obligations. In Totem, both parties had good faith, disputed claims, although Alyeska admittedly owed some amount. Does the application of the duress doctrine undermine the policy in favor of legitimate settlements? It has the potential to do so. See the comments under "Interesting Discussion Items" above. Parties often negotiate settlement agreements in situations where one of them suffers from a gross disparity of bargaining power arising from unequal financial resources. How do you suggest drawing a line between a settlement voidable for duress and a hard fought but legitimate settlement of a good faith, disputed claim? The line suggested above should be drawn—did the defendant cause or contribute to the cause of the plaintiff's hardship.

4. *UCC approach.* In the next chapter, parties to a contract often agree to settle disputes and then one party may later fail to comply with the terms of the settlement. A breach of the settlement agreement will require that the settlement promise is enforceable under some theory of legal obligation. When a party owes a fixed sum of money but refuses to pay unless the other party accepts less, what is the consideration for the promise to accept less? Does the UCC require consideration for modifications of existing agreements? No. See UCC §2-209(1). See also Robert A. Hillman, *"Policing Contract Modification Under the UCC: Good Faith and the Doctrine of Economic Duress,"* 64 Iowa L. Rev. 849 (1979) (arguing that the absence of specific statutory language on economic duress has led to ineffective applications and results).

5. *Unworkable standard?* See text.

6. *The blackmailer's fallacy.* To what extent is the proposition that duress denies the victim any reasonable alternatives merely a legal fiction? Alternatively, does the victim of duress really lack any bargaining power? Consider the problem of the blackmailer's fallacy:

A would-be blackmailer A once argued that as he was in a position to cause damage worth $1000 to a certain rich man B, he should be able to extract from B any ransom short of $1000, because after payment of r<$1000, B would still be better off than if he had to suffer the full $1000 damage.

But this argument is clearly fallacious. By similar reasoning, B could also have argued that A would accept any ransom r larger than nil, because after accepting a ransom r > $0, A would still be better off than if no agreement were reached and he did not receive anything at all. What both of these arguments really show is that in any bargaining between two rational bargainers, the outcome must fall between what may be called the two parties' concession limits, which are defined by each party's refusal to accept any agreement that would make him actually worse off than he would be in the conflict situation. But the two arguments in themselves say nothing about where the two parties' agreement point will actually lie between these two limits. They certainly do not allow the inference that this agreement point will actually coincide or nearly coincide with one party's concession limit. (Only if we know the two parties' attitudes towards risk-taking, and in particular towards risking a conflict rather than accepting unfavorable terms, can we make any predictions about where their agreement point will lie between the two concession limits.) John C. Harsanyi, "*Measurement of Social Power, Opportunity Costs, and the Theory of Two-person Bargaining Games,*" in Roderick Bell, et al., POLITICAL POWER: A Reader in Theory and Research at 226, 232-33 (1969).

Thus, although we would expect the dominant party in a duress or extortion situation to extract every available benefit from the weaker party, such an absolute disparity of bargaining power is unlikely. In reality, the victim of duress (or blackmail) still possesses substantial bargaining power, at least in the form of the ability to impose additional costs upon the stronger party:

> Even the most intuitively obvious case of an apparently "absolute" disparity of bargaining power—the hoary "your money or your life" demand by the highwayman or tax collector—never really removes all power from the victim of the duress. A victim of the most extreme coercion still possesses some power to choose between unpleasant alternatives. . . .
>
> The victim of the most egregious forms of duress still retains considerable power over the situation. He may comply, or he may resist. The power of confronting unjust opponents as a choice was made obvious by Gandhi's and Martin Luther King, Jr.'s use of passive disobedience as a tool to achieve their social aims. If the victim resists and fails—and thus concludes the encounter as a martyred corpse, an unconscious body or a part of the penal system such as Nobel Peace Prize winners Nelson Mandela of South Africa

> and Aung San Suu Kyi of Burma—the victim still retains the power to affect the outcome of the interaction with the stronger party. Unconscious victims require disposal or their evidence can increase the likelihood of apprehension; corpses create their own problems of concealment and disposal, and convicts impose substantial costs upon the penal system. All of these outcomes, however, have a real impact upon the ability of the criminal or tax collector to engage in their livelihood and thus demonstrate the power of the victim to affect the outcome of his or her interaction with the criminal or tax collector. Daniel D. Barnhizer, "*Inequality of Bargaining Power*," 76 U. Colo. L. Rev. 139, 163-64 (2005).

Given that the victim of duress likely always has the power to resist to some extent, should the standards for duress be changed to require the victim to attempt to resist before courts will permit avoidance on the basis of duress? Yes, unless any such attempt would be fruitless. Why or why not? The nature of "duress" suggests that there should be a required showing of "compelling" force. The absence of any attempt to resist could undermine the requisite showing of compulsion. We have to wonder how Totem's lawyer would have testified following return of this case to the trial court.

7. *The nature of consent under duress.* It is often said that the victim of duress does not truly consent to the proposed contract. But as John Dalzell notes, even—or perhaps particularly—in cases of physical duress there is little question that the victim desperately desires and in a sense truly consents to the contract rather than the threatened alternative:

> We have talked of contracts signed under duress as lacking "real consent." When I feel that I must choose between having a bullet lodged in my head and signing a contract, my desire to escape the bullet would hardly be described as unreal or merely apparent; and the signing of the contract is simply the expression of that fear of death. * * * Faced with the choice that was offered, the victim of duress gives a genuine consent rather than suffer the alternative consequences. John Dalzell, "*Duress by Economic Pressure,*" 20 N.C. L. Rev. 237, 238-39 (1941).

If Dalzell is correct, what exactly is the problem in the process of contract formation that the duress doctrine is supposed to police? The problem that the assent to the agreement, apparently given, is not a true bargained for consent but is rather an imposed consent. In contrast, consider misrepresentation doctrine which, among other things, addresses a failure of consideration in that the deceived party does not receive the consideration for which she bargained. In the case of duress, both parties must be aware of the threat and it is likely that both parties give genuine consent, even if one of the parties must choose between unpleasant alternatives. The problem of duress, then, appears only tangentially related to the process of contract formation. Is there any satisfactory way to explain duress doctrine as an abuse of the contracting process, or should it be conceived as a more tort-like response, similar to assault or wrongful imprisonment? It can be seen as an abuse of the contracting process because the terms which are the outcome of the "agreement" are not terms which have been freely negotiated.

Optional Problem 6-1

Call me Ishmael. I'm the owner of Pequod Towing, Inc., a specialty tug service. Last week, I had just finished towing an oil rig out of the Gulf of Mexico after it got smashed up a bit in Hurricane Lydia and was heading back to port when disaster struck. Without any warning, what was supposed to be a mild tropical depression developed into Hurricane Mairead, a Category 5 storm. I wasn't worried at all—my tug battens up real tight and, with 15,000 horsepower in her engines, I could ride out any storm. But then, wallowing out of the whitecaps and looking like she'd go under at any moment, an overladen oil carrier named the Exeter out of Nantucket nearly crashed into us. At that moment, the Exeter's captain radioed, explaining that she had a full cargo of 100,000 barrels of Texas light sweet crude oil aboard and that without a tow the ship would sink within the hour. I asked her what the Exeter's lifeboat situation was, and Captain Ahab informed me that she had more than sufficient lifeboats for her crew. Now, I wasn't born yesterday, so it didn't take but a moment to calculate that the cargo alone was worth $6,000,000. I radioed back and informed Captain Ahab that I was running a sale on rescue tows today and that I'd tow the Exeter to the nearest port for $3,000,000. I figured that was reasonable since, while it was 50 times more than a normal tow would cost, if they abandoned ship I could try to claim it as salvage and pocket at least that much from the salvage fees. Captain Ahab sounded like a beached whale being pecked to death by gulls for a moment, but then she said those magic words, "I accept."

I got her under tow but it was a near thing—I literally stared death right in the face a half-dozen times trying to get that ship under tow., Even with the tug's engine going full bore we almost lost both ships before getting to port. But the worst came the next day when Ahab's lawyers called to inform me that Ahab was suing to rescind the bargain we made because it was made under duress and was unconscionable.

Based on your readings, what is the likelihood Ahab will win on either argument? Can I collect anything?

Answer:

Unlike the case in the book, in this hypothetical Ishmael had no part in causing Ahab's hardship and hence, applying Restatement (Second) of Contracts § 176, the agreement would not be subject to attack on the basis of duress but might be subject to review for unconscionability. The story in this problem was, unfortunately, a not infrequent experience in the maritime world two hundred years ago. On this subject, see John Howard Thomas and Andrew W. Anderson, The Florida Bar, 2004, "*Maritime Law and Practice*," Chapter 8, Salvage, Section IX:

> Admiralty courts scrutinize salvage agreements closely for any sign of overreaching, improper coercion, or overcharging by salvors. Courts set aside contracts if they find that a salvor took advantage of a situation to impose unconscionable or inequitable contract terms on a vessel. Extortionate demands forced by a salvor on the master of a vessel not only will void a contract but often result in a salvage award that is less than it otherwise would be. If, however, the terms of the contract are reasonable and not oppressive, the contract will be upheld without regard to pressures created by the emergency faced by the vessel. The *Elfrida*, 172 U.S. 186, 19 S.Ct. 146, 43 L.Ed. 413 (1898); *Magnolia Petroleum Co. v. National Oil Transport Co.*, 286 F. 40 (5th Cir. 1923); The *Emulous*, 8 F.Cas. 704 (C.C. D. Mass. 1832).

3. Undue Influence

Virtually no case exists for a tort of undue influence and consequently relief, if any, may be found only in rescission of the contract. As with duress, undue influence has largely escaped the influence of the objective theory of contracts. Accordingly, the principal inquiry in undue influence is "unfair persuasion" rather than the coercion focus of duress. Indeed, undue influence continues a design to protect where duress cannot be shown. Today, undue influence can occur in two contexts: (i) unfair persuasion of a subservient party under the domination of another person or (ii) unfair persuasion of a person by another using a relationship of trust and confidence to deceive the other party. See Restatement (Second) of Contracts § 177(1). Undue influence is frequently argued by disappointed heirs. Particularly vulnerable to undue influence are business transactions between an attorney and client, where undue influence may be presumed from the fiduciary relationship and the contract set aside unless the contract is on fair terms and the client manifested assent with free will absent from the influence of the attorney.

Odorizzi v. Bloomfield School District
CASE BRIEF

This is a 1966 decision of a California court of appeals. Donald Odorizzi was employed as a teacher during the 1964 school year by the Bloomfield School District (District) and was under contract to teach during the next year. On June 10, 1964, Odorizzi was arrested on criminal charges of homosexual activity. The next day, after being arrested, questioned, and released by the police, and going for forty hours without sleep, Odorizzi was visited at his apartment by the superintendent of the District and his school's principal. The men told him that they had his best interests at heart, and that he ought to resign immediately from his teaching position. If he did not resign immediately, the District would suspend and dismiss him, publicize his arrest, and cause him "extreme embarrassment and humiliation"—but if he resigned at once, the incident would not be publicized and he would have a chance of being hired to teach elsewhere. Odorizzi claimed that during the meeting he was under severe mental and emotional stress, and that "because of his faith and confidence in their representations they were able to substitute their will and judgment in place of his own and thus obtain his signature to his purported resignation (on June 11)." The District accepted the resignation on June 13. In July, the criminal charges against Odorizzi were dismissed. In September, he sought to resume his employment with the District. Due to the District's refusal to reinstate him, Odorizzi filed suit to rescind his resignation because it was obtained through "duress, menace, fraud, undue influence, or mistake." The trial court sustained a demurrer to Odorizzi's complaint without leave to amend; Odorizzi appealed.

The court of appeals held that while the complaint did not state a cause of action for duress, menace, fraud, or mistake, it did state elements sufficient to justify rescission of consent because of undue influence. The court stated that duress consists in "unlawful confinement of another's person, or relatives, or property, which causes him to consent to a transaction through fear," and that menace, under California law, "is technically a threat of duress or a threat of injury to the person, property, or character of another." And since duress or menace requires unlawful action, and the threatened suspension and dismissal of Odorizzi did not meet this standard, as the superintendent and principal would have been within their legal rights to pursue such action in good faith.

The court also rejected a cause of action in actual fraud, which requires a pleading of "misrepresentation, knowledge of falsity, intent to induce reliance, justifiable reliance, and resulting damage." Odorizzi only pleaded misrepresentation. The court also rejected a cause of action in constructive fraud, which requires "a breach of duty by one in a confidential or fiduciary relationship to another which induces justifiable reliance by the latter to his prejudice." Here, Odorizzi failed to show that he had a confidential relationship with either the principal or the superintendent. The court noted that the absence of such a relationship was "especially apparent" in a case where the parties were negotiating for the termination of Odorizzi's employment. Thus, Odorizzi could not claim constructive fraud.

Finally, the court rejected any cause of action based on mistake, a doctrine that normally involves errors regarding the nature of the transaction or the identity of matters material to the contract. Here, the material facts were known to both parties, and neither party operated under any misunderstanding of law to his detriment. The mere fact that the parties' speculations about future events did not match with what actually happened was not sufficient to support a claim that the parties were acting under a mistake.

But the court did find that the complaint set out a proper claim that Odorizzi's consent to the agreement had been obtained through the use of undue influence, a term that the court described as "persuasion that tends to be coercive in nature, [and] that overcomes the will without convincing the judgment." California's statutory definition of undue influence included "taking an unfair advantage of another's weakness of mind; or . . . taking a grossly oppressive and unfair advantage of another's necessities or distress." While such cases often involve confidential relationships, the court held that such a relationship was not necessary when the undue influence involved taking unfair advantage of another's weakness. The court noted two elements that must be present in order to prove undue influence: (1) undue susceptibility; and (2) the application of excessive strength by a dominant subject against a subservient object. The undue susceptibility could range from a permanent condition because of which the person is entirely without understanding to a temporary condition whereby a person is merely weakened in spirit. The difficulty in balancing these two factors lies in "determining when the forces of persuasion have overflowed their normal banks and become oppressive flood waters." In suggesting examples of undue influence, the court suggested situations such as: "(1) discussion of a transaction at an unusual or inappropriate time, (2) consummation of a transaction in an unusual place, (3) insistent demand that the business be finished at once, (4) extreme emphasis on untoward consequences of delay, (5) the use of multiple persuaders by the dominant side against a single subservient party, (6) absence of third-party advisers to the subservient party, and (7) statements that there is no time to consult financial advisers or attorneys"—the presence of multiple elements at once may characterize the persuasion as excessive. Here, the representatives of the District used high-pressure negotiating tactics and threats about his future employment prospects, combined with assurances that they were only looking out for Odorizzi's best interests to get him to acquiesce to the resignation. While the court would not decide whether or not those actions rose to the level of undue influence over Odorizzi, it did hold that his pleading was sufficient to create a question of fact that would be appropriate for trial.

INTERESTING DISCUSSION ISSUES

1. *Was this really a case of duress and abuse of power rather than undue influence?* The court held that the facts as pleaded did not state a basis of relief based on "duress." This may be due to the quite narrow description of the "duress" cause of action—including "menace." This could be attributable to the fact that there is a Californian statutory definition of "duress." With the recent expansion of judicial thinking about "economic duress" the instant decision on this point might change.

2. *The threat of taking legal action.* The court noted that the threat of taking legal action is not (and should not) be by itself a basis for relief under a theory of undue influence. If the threat is based on bad faith, however, the situation is different. Students should notice the distinction drawn by the Restatement (Second) of Contracts § 176 between the threat of criminal prosecution and threat of the use of civil process. That section makes the threat of criminal prosecution improper whereas the threat of civil action is improper only if the threat is made in bad faith.

3. *Constructive fraud versus undue influence.* The court refers to "constructive fraud" as "a breach of duty by one in a confidential or fiduciary relationship to another which induces justifiable reliance by the later to his prejudice." The introductory note to this section suggests that the presence of a confidential relationship often supports one of the two common types of case of undue influence. The Restatement (Second) of Contracts does not include a provision on "constructive fraud," although a number of cases referring to the Restatement do.

NOTES AND QUESTIONS

1. *Factors implicating "unfair persuasion."* The *Odorizzi* court identified seven factors useful to determine whether a particular contract is the product of undue influence and include: (1) discussion of the transaction at an unusual or inappropriate time, (2) consummation of the transaction in an unusual place, (3) insistent demand that the business be finished at once, (4) extreme emphasis on untoward consequences of delay, (5) the use of multiple persuaders by the dominant side against a single servient party, (6) absence of third-party advisers to the servient party, and (7) statements that there is no time to consult financial advisers or attorneys. Does the court require

all factors to find undue influence? No. Said the court, "If a number of these elements are simultaneously present, the persuasion may be characterized as excessive." Were all factors satisfied in this case? Apparently, all seven factors were present in this case as pleaded. Students should note that the ruling was on the adequacy of the pleadings, not the facts ultimately determined at trial.

2. *Relationship between contract and rape law.* See text.

3. *Sexual orientation consequences.* The case notes that Odorizzi was arrested for criminal homosexual activity. Given the subjective nature of "unfair persuasion," is it possible to properly analyze this case absent some contextual understanding of the personalized effects of sexual orientation in California in 1964? No. See Curtis Nyquist, Patrick Ruiz & Frank Smith, *"Using Students as Discussion Leaders on Sexual Orientation and Gender Identity Issues in First-Year Courses,"* 49 J. Legal Ed. 535 (1999) (citing and discussing Odorizzi).

4. *Premarital agreements.* Do you think courts should attempt to police undue influence in contracts negotiated in the context of personal relationships? Yes. One of the most significant areas of undue influence law involves domination of elderly persons involving transmission of their assets and some forms of such domination involve the use of lifetime contracts. See Brian Bix, *"Bargaining in the Shadow of Love: The Enforcement of Premarital Agreements and How We Think About Marriage,"* 40 Wm. & Mary L. Rev. 145 (1998). How likely is it that a court will be able to unwind and accurately assess the complex interpersonal relationships and commitments that lead to such contracts? The issue may be difficult but it should be addressed on the facts and in accordance with the standards set out in the instant case. Should the court be more or less willing to find such contracts tainted by undue influence? There should be no particular presumption either way.

5. *Gender and undue influence.* Like the defenses of unconscionability, and to a lesser extent, duress, and in contrast to misrepresentation, undue influence depends upon personal characteristics of the party asserting the defense in addition to external factors. Specifically, successfully asserting one of these defenses requires the party claiming the defense to convince a court or jury that the party was particularly weak and susceptible to influence or pressure. Some commentators have observed the tendency of courts to adopt—unconsciously or otherwise—biased stereotypes of weakness in members of certain status groups, including women, the poor, minorities, and the uneducated. See, e.g., Arthur Allen Leff, "*Unconscionability and the Code—The Emperor's New Clause,*" 115 U. Pa. L. Rev. 485, 556-57 (1967) ("[I]t is arguable that sometimes

[judicial stereotypes of weakness] were wrong; not all old ladies . . . are without defenses. Put briefly, the typical has a tendency to become stereotypical, with what may be unpleasant results even for the beneficiaries of the judicial benevolence."); Brian Alan Ross, "*Undue Influence and Gender Inequity*," 19 Women's Rts. L. Rep. 97, 97-98 (1997) (noting in the context of will disputes "[I]t seems that the [undue influence] doctrine is largely a judicial vehicle for implementing social policy case by case through the use of such concepts as fairness, justice, and morality. Undue influence decisions often appear to be driven by oppressive, stereotypical assumptions about women and their 'proper' role in society, especially in a 'meretricious' relationship."). Moreover, as Richard Delgado suggests, enshrined judicial stereotypes may perpetuate negative self-images in the target status group:

> The dominant group creates its own stories, as well. The stories or narratives told by the ingroup remind it of its identity in relation to outgroups, and provide it with a form of shared reality in which its own superior position is seen as neutral. The stories of the outgroups aim to subvert that ingroup reality. In civil rights, for example, many in the majority hold that any inequality between blacks and whites is due either to cultural lag, or inadequate enforcement of currently existing beneficial laws—both of which are easily correctable. For many minority persons, the principle instrument of their subordination is neither of these. Rather, it is the prevailing mindset by means of which members of the dominant group justify the world as it is, that is, with whites on top and browns and blacks at the bottom.

See Richard Delgado, "*Storytelling for Oppositionists and Others: A Plea for Narrative*," 87 Mich. L. Rev. 2411, 2412-13 (1988). To what extent is it realistic to assume that members of a particular status group will define their self-identities by judicial stereotypes in contract defenses? There is a measure of realism in the will context (and similar) cases because the "victim" is most often an elderly woman—in part a function of the longer life expectancy of women than men. If such stereotypes exist, who is more to blame for their perpetuation—the judge who relies upon them, or the attorney who, in fulfilling her duty of zealous advocacy on behalf of her client, diligently exploits existing stereotypes to craft a compelling narrative for the court? Neither—the issue should be one of fact not clouded or loaded by any preconceived characteristic or relationship.

D. FAILURE OF THE BARGAINING PROCESS

The ancient concept of "*pacta sunt servanda*" serves to emphasize the importance of both keeping and enforcing agreements that have been made between the parties. The value of keeping and enforcing agreements is widely recognized throughout other legal systems in the world and has been frequently cited in opinions of the International Court of Justice as a foundational proposition of international law respecting the law of treaties. This section explores the effect on such agreements of erroneous assumptions by both or one of the parties with respect to facts as of the time of entry into the contract. In these cases, since the defect relates to the formation of the contract itself, serious errors create a power of avoidance in one or both of the parties. Chapter 8 includes treatment of the effect of erroneous expectations of the parties at the time of contracting with respect to future events. Some writers argue that such mistakes should be subject to the same rules whether the mistakes are as to present facts or to events that take place in the future. We believe that these categories are different when viewed from the perspective of appropriate remedies and thus are treated in different sections of this book.

We have already dealt with those situations where the mistake of one of the parties is caused by the act or conduct of the other. The law of mistake is separated from that of misrepresentation and fraud by reason of the absence of such a cause of the mistake.

The law of mistake is said to have developed over the last century. Earlier cases dealt with some of the same problem situations through a doctrine of "failure of consideration"—as a result of the mistake there was no true exchange involved. This approach could make difficult the separation of other "consideration" law under which courts refused to consider the relative adequacy or inadequacy of the exchange between the parties. See the discussion in Chapter 3 on the disinclination of courts to substitute their view of fairness of the exchange for that of the parties. But relevant imbalance of benefits to the parties crept in under the earlier English doctrine of "failure of consideration" and likewise has the capacity to creep back into judicial analysis of "mistake."

Mistake may be shared by both parties or only by one. Courts are less disposed to granting relief for unilateral mistake than for bilateral, as a comparison of the cases that follow indicates.

One special form of mistake needs to be noted—that kind of mistake which gives rise to the judicial remedy of "reformation." Technically, reformation is available for either party where there is adequate proof that the parties agreed on a set of terms but that set of terms was incorrectly or inaccurately reflected in the writing up of the agreement. The origin of the cause of action for "reformation" is to be found in the evolving law of the late middle ages. In the 15th century few could read or write and those that could do both were usually members of the clergy. Agreements were thus reached orally and then transcribed by a third person retained by the parties to perform that function. The old saying, "If it can happen, it will" proved true and mistakes occurred in the process of writing down the terms of the agreement accepted by the parties. In such situations relief was available in Chancery. The student should remember that the burden of proof there was the higher standard of "beyond reasonable doubt" and that other concerns of fairness were usually considered. The remedy of "reformation" survives today, despite the merger of law and equity, but the rules retain much of the flavor of the early equity approach. The parol evidence rule does not preclude the introduction of parol proof offered to establish a claim for reformation, just as it does not preclude parol testimony that the conclusion of the agreement was subject to an unfulfilled oral condition precedent.

1. Mutual Mistake

Eighteenth century thinking, emphasizing the need for a "meeting of the minds," tended to regard mutual mistake as vitiating the making of any true agreement thus leading to a conclusion that the agreement was void and not voidable. Modern law treats mistake, where operative, as a basis for avoiding the contract, not holding it void. To provide a basis for relief, the mistake must relate to a basic assumption which has a "material effect" on the agreed exchange or performances of the parties. This "materiality" element if often difficult to apply and creates a measure of unpredictability—undesirable where commercial certainty is a highly valued norm. Modern law of mistake defines the term "mistake" more narrowly. In this context, a mistake is an erroneous belief that is not in accord with the facts existing at the time of the making of the contract. Restatement (Second) of Contracts § 151. Thus, the term excludes common mistake elements, such as an improvident act or an erroneous prediction or judgment regarding future events. Restatement (Second) of Contracts § 151 cmt. a. However, the term "facts" does include the law. Accordingly, an erroneous belief with regard to the law as found in statutes, regulations or case law is included within the term "mistake." Restatement (Second) of Contracts § 151 cmt. b.

Risk allocation is an explicit part of modern mutual mistake law. But disputes about "mistake" usually arise where the parties failed to allocate relevant risk. Judicial risk allocation essentially results in an implied risk allocation term frequently seen to operate as if there were an implied condition in the agreement. This allocation frequently depends critically upon an assumed level of consciousness of the parties regarding the factual matter.

The UCC has no separate "mistake" provision—the common law is imported by virtue of § 1-103.

Sherwood v. Walker
CASE BRIEF

This is an 1887 decision of the Michigan Supreme Court and is one of a few cases that lawyers remember for the rest of their lives as "Rose of Aberlone." Plaintiff Sherwood was a banker who called on the defendants, Walkers, breeders of Angus cattle, to purchase some of their stock. Sherwood ultimately settled on a cow named "Rose 2d of Aberlone," who Sherwood was told was barren. Just six days after reaching an agreement on price and delivery and exchanging offer and acceptance via letter, Sherwood attempted to pick up the cow from the Walker farm. The man present at the farm refused to allow Sherwood to take the cow, and Hiram Walker refused to accept Sherwood's tender of payment for the cow. Sherwood then sued and secured the cow under a writ of replevin. At trial, the court refused the Walkers' motion to strike out, as irrelevant, testimony regarding the transaction. The Walkers then introduced evidence showing that at the time of the alleged sale, (1) both parties believed that the cow was barren; (2) the value of the cow if not barren would be $750 to $1,000; and (3) after the exchange of letters, the Walkers learned that the cow was likely with calf, at which time they refused to sell her to Sherwood. The cow gave birth to a calf five months after the Walkers refused to complete the sale agreement. At trial, the jury found for Sherwood, as did the county court of appeals. The Walkers appealed.

The first argument that the court discussed was the Walkers' claim that title to the cow never passed to Sherwood. [The ability to secure the cow under a writ of replevin was dependent upon title having passed to Sherwood previously.] The court began by noting that the memorandum of sale signed by the Walkers was sufficient to take the transaction out of the Michigan statute of frauds, and that the trial court had properly permitted the jury to determine the intent of the parties with regard to whether title was to have passed before delivery (the jury found that title was to pass before delivery).

After establishing the passing of title, the court moved on to determine whether the Walkers were entitled to rescind the transaction based on the parties' mutual mistake about the cow's inability to breed. The trial court had held that the fact was irrelevant and could not be used to avoid the sale. The Supreme Court of Michigan held that, while the issue was a close one, it was well settled that a party who has given consent to a contract of sale may refuse to execute it, or may avoid it after completion, if the assent or contract was made upon a mistake of material fact. "If there is a difference or misapprehension as to the substance of the thing bargained for; if the thing actually delivered or received is different in substance from the thing bargained for, and intended to be sold, then there is no contract; but if it be only a difference in some quality or accident, even though the mistake may have been the actuating motive to the purchaser or seller, or both of them, yet the contract remains binding."

The court held that this case was one in which the mistake "went to the whole substance of the agreement." The difference between the price of the cow as a breeder, versus her price as barren, was nearly tenfold, and thus the contract would not have been made except on the understanding that she was barren. As a result, there was a significant difference in the very nature of the cow, including the uses to which it could be put. Since the mistake affected the substance of the whole consideration, the court held that "it must be considered that there was no contract to sell or sale of the cow as she actually was." Thus, the court held that the trial court should have instructed the jury that if the cow was sold under a mutual mistake as to its breeding ability, the Walkers would have a right to rescind the contract. The court ordered a new trial.

Justice Sherwood (presumably not related to the plaintiff Sherwood), dissenting, agreed with the court's initial findings regarding the passing of title, but disputed that there was a mistake that should justify rescission. Much of the dissent was grounded in the assertion that the plaintiff believed, in spite of defendants' representations, that the cow might be made to breed, and that the plaintiff at no time stated that he was purchasing the cow solely for use as a beef cow. The dissent argued that when a mistaken fact is relied upon to rescind, that fact must exist at the time of the contract and be known to one parties. As such, the dissent compared the case at bar to the case in which one man buys a horse with the belief that it can run much faster than the current owner has been able to get it to run. In such a case, there would be no ground for rescission when the buyer is actually able to get the horse to run faster, making the horse much more valuable.

The dissent also argued that, whatever mistake was present was on the part of the defendants, acting on their own judgment—judgment that should have been much better informed that was the plaintiff's on this matter. In reviewing the authorities relied upon by the majority, the dissent concluded that there was no similarity between them and the current case, and that he could find "no adjudicated case going to the extent, either in law or in equity, that has been held in this case." Thus, where a seller represents to the buyer what he believes to be the qualities of the animal, and the buyer purchases relying on his own judgment, in the absence of any warranties or conditions, the contract should not be subject to rescission because the seller erred in his judgment of the qualities and value of the animal.

INTERESTING DISCUSSION ISSUES

1. *What were the facts?* The difference between the majority and the dissent in this case was not the legal principle or principles to be

applied, but rather as to the facts to which those principles were to be applied. Said the majority:

> It appears from the record that both parties supposed this cow was barren and would not breed, and she was sold by the pound for an insignificant sum as compared with her real value if a breeder. She was evidently sold and purchased on the relation of her value for beef, unless the plaintiff had learned of her true condition, and concealed such knowledge from the defendants.

Said the dissent:

> There is no pretense there was any fraud or concealment in the case. . . . In the spring of 1886 the plaintiff, learning that the defendants had some "polled Angus cattle" for sale, was desirous of purchasing some of that breed, and meeting the defendants, or some of them, at Walkerville, inquired about them, and was informed that they had none at Walkerville, "but had a few head left on their farm in Greenfield, and asked the plaintiff to go and see them, stating that in all probability they were sterile and would not breed." In accordance with said request, the plaintiff, on the fifth day of May, went out and looked at the defendants' cattle at Greenfield, and found one called "Rose, Second," which he wished to purchase, and the terms were finally agreed upon at five and a half cents per pound, live weight, 50 pounds to be deducted for shrinkage. . . . The record further shows that the defendants, when they sold the cow, believed the cow was not with calf, and barren; that from what the plaintiff had been told by defendants (for it does not appear he had any other knowledge or facts from which he could form an opinion) he believed the cow was farrow, but still thought she could be made to breed. . . . And the buyer purchased her believing her to be of the breed represented by the sellers, and possessing all the qualities stated, and even more. He believed she would breed. There is no pretense that the plaintiff bought the cow for beef, and there is nothing in the record indicating that he would have bought her at all only that he thought she might be made to breed. . . . The defendants say, or rather said, to the plaintiff, "they had a few head left on their farm in Greenfield, and asked plaintiff to go and see them, stating to plaintiff that in all probability they were sterile and would not breed." Plaintiff did go as requested, and found there these cows, including the one purchased, with a bull. The cow had been exposed, but neither knew she was with calf or whether she would breed.

According to the dissent, not only did the plaintiff not share the defendant's belief that Rose was barren, but in fact believed that she was fertile. Students will ask, "How could there be two such inconsistent versions of the applicable facts in the Michigan Supreme Court?" Some may be tempted to suggest that the important issue of fairness to the defendant was the price agreed upon. But, the instructor will respond, "Did we not agree chapters ago that a court will not review the relative value actually received by each party to the contract?" The instructor may be tempted to surmise that the majority's statement, "She was evidently sold and purchased on the relation of her value for beef, unless the plaintiff had learned of her true condition, and concealed such knowledge from the defendants," was "loaded" based on what the majority thought was a bargain that, in the circumstances, was unfair.

This case provides an excellent opportunity to point out that, in reading a case with a view to extracting the applicable legal principles, the reader should focus on the facts as found by the majority opinion. On dissenting Judge Sherwood's facts, he had the best of the argument. Due to the fact that the lawsuit was for replevin of the cow, the issue turning on whether title had passed, counsel for Sherwood may have thought it unnecessary to put his client on the stand and inquire as to his understanding and purpose at the time of negotiating the contract.

But these matters have little if anything to do with the law of the case—the majority's enunciation of the applicable principle of law with respect to mutual mistake:

> If there is a difference or misapprehension as to the substance of the thing bargained for; if the thing actually delivered or received is different in substance from the thing bargained for, and intended to be sold, then there is no contract; but if it be only a difference in some quality or accident, even though the mistake may have been the actuating motive to the purchaser or seller, or both of them, yet the contract remains binding.

Justice Sherwood, dissenting, concurred in this statement of principle, disagreeing only with the process of applying it to the facts. Thus a dilemma was created as to how to distinguish a mistake as to the substance of the thing from a mistake as to some quality or accident of the thing. Did the majority truly apply this standard to the facts before them? Was not the mistake as to Rose's capability one of quality?

NOTES AND QUESTIONS

1. *Allocating the risk of the mistake to Sherwood.* Focusing on the value of Rose alone provides certain inferences regarding what the parties had or should have had in mind about her qualities at the time of the contract. What other factors are important, and what do they suggest about the objective state of mind of each party? The Walkers had a number of cattle for sale but Sherwood decided to purchase Rose and only Rose. Must he not have had a substantial reason for picking

Rose rather than any of the others? For example, when Sherwood found no cattle to his liking at the first Walker farm, he was informed that Walker owned more cattle located at a second farm but those cattle "were probably barren, and would not breed." How would a reasonable observer understand that statement of Walker's opinion about the cattle on the second farm? These words, as stated by the majority, would convey a belief of probability but not certainty as to the state of the cows' including Rose's barrenness. The reasonable observer would infer that the Walkers were aware of the risk that Rose might or might not be barren and that, armed with such doubt, they should be found to take the risk as to whether or not she was barren. See Restatement (Second) of Contracts § 154:

> A party bears the risk of a mistake when
> (a) . . .
> (b) he is aware, at the time the contract is made, that he has only limited knowledge with respect to the facts to which the mistake relates but treats his limited knowledge as sufficient, or
> (c) . . . .

If the parties addressed the possibility that she was fertile, and yet failed to include a protective provision in the contract, how could the court, in effect, imply a condition precedent that the contract was to be binding only if she was barren? There is a cardinal rule of interpretation to the effect that a court should not imply a term contrary to the intention of the parties. After the contract was formed, why did Walker refuse delivery? He refused delivery because his agent had discovered (thought?) that Rose was with calf. The court stated that the "refusal to deliver the cow grew entirely out of the fact that, before the plaintiff called upon Graham for her, they discovered she was not barren, and therefore of greater value than they had sold her for." Does the sale plus the later refusal to deliver upon discovery that Rose was pregnant suggest anything about Walker's subjective state of mind? Yes, it suggests that at the time of the sale Walker believed Rose was barren. Walker was an experienced farmer, while Sherwood was a banker who also raised breeder cattle. Under the assumed risk standards of Restatement (Second) of Contracts § 154, who should bear the risk that Rose was not barren, given that Walker suggested to Sherwood that the cattle at the second farm are "probably barren," and Sherwood normally purchased cattle for breeding and not for beef value? Walker should bear the risk. Which theory of risk allocation do you think is most appropriate to allocate the risk to Sherwood in this case? The unfairness of the price agreed upon, as the comment to § 152 puts it, "He must show that the resulting imbalance in the agreed exchange is so severe that he cannot fairly be required to carry it out." The risk could well have been allocated to Walker on the basis that the parties were aware of the fact that Rose might or might not be fertile but Walker elected to go ahead with the sale without making any further effort to determine the facts.

2. *Materiality*. Was the mistake in this case "material" under Restatement (Second) of Contracts § 152(1)? The commentary to § 152 attempts to clarify the standards for materiality in the context of mistake:

> A party cannot avoid a contract merely because both parties were mistaken as to a basic assumption on which it was made. He must, in addition, show that the mistake has a material effect on the agreed exchange of performances. It is not enough for him to prove that he would not have made the contract had it not been for the mistake. He must show that the resulting imbalance in the agreed exchange is so severe that he cannot fairly be required to carry it out. Ordinarily he will be able to do this by showing that the exchange is not only less desirable to him but is also more advantageous to the other party. . . . In exceptional cases, the adversely affected party may be able to show that the effect on the agreed exchange has been material simply on the ground that the exchange has become less desirable for him, even though there has been no effect on the other party. Cases of hardship that result in no advantage to the other party are, however, ordinarily appropriately left to the rules on impracticability and frustration. Restatement (Second) of Contracts § 152 cmt. c.

How does the Restatement (Second) of Contracts commentary resolve the materiality question? The key sentence appears to be, "He must show that the resulting imbalance in the agreed exchange is so severe that he cannot fairly be required to carry it out." Does that circle back to the value of Rose depending upon whether she was barren or not? Yes. But the student needs to appreciate the change of language from the format enunciated in the instant case to the Restatement (Second) § 152 (1) describing the principle:

> (1) Where a mistake of both parties at the time a contract was made as to a basic assumption on which the contract was made has a material effect on the agreed exchange of performances, the contract is voidable by the adversely affected party unless he bears the risk of the mistake under the rule stated in § 154.

This new statement attempts to reduce the uncertainty that was implicit in the instant case's statement of the applicable principle:

> If there is a difference or misapprehension as to the substance of the thing bargained for; if the thing actually delivered or received is different in substance from the thing bargained for, and intended to

be sold, then there is no contract; but if it be only a difference in some quality or accident, even though the mistake may have been the actuating motive to the purchaser or seller, or both of them, yet the contract remains binding.

3. *Sherwood's reason for purchase.* Given that Sherwood is both a banker and a farmer who purchases and raises cattle for breeding purposes, do you think Sherwood purchased Rose for her beef value or her potential breeding value? We can only guess but there is a basis for an inference that he bought her for breeding. Otherwise, what lead him to select just this one cow from the number available at the Walker farm? If the latter, did Sherwood know that Walker was making a mistake? Said the majority, "She was evidently sold and purchased on the relation of her value for beef, unless the plaintiff had learned of her true condition, and concealed such knowledge from the defendants." The dissent disagreed, saying that there was no suggestion of fraud or concealment in the record. If so, would that make a difference in your analysis? Yes—this would bring the facts within those situations where one party has knowledge which should be shared with the other. See Restatement (Second) of Contracts § 161:

> A person's non-disclosure of a fact known to him is equivalent to an assertion that the fact does not exist in the following cases only: . . . (b) where he knows that disclosure of the fact would correct a mistake of the other party as to a basic assumption on which that party is making the contract and if non-disclosure of the fact amounts to a failure to act in good faith and in accordance with reasonable standards of fair dealing. . . .

It of course would suggest that at most there was a unilateral mistake made by Walker. Briefly review Restatement (Second) of Contracts § 153(b) and determine whether Walker should be able to rescind the contract if Sherwood "had reason to know" of Walker's mistake? That section would support Walker's right to rescind. Does the dissent suggest that both parties were aware of the possibility that Rose might not be barren? Yes. If so, should the parties be permitted to specifically negotiate a contract with such a risk inherent in the transaction? Yes. If there was a true "negotiation" over the risk of whether Rose was barren, what would you expect to happen to her price? The price fixed would be greater than the price per pound based on the extent of the risk involved. Would the bargained risk price be at either extreme (barren and low beef value or not barren and full breeder value) or somewhere in between? The latter. Since the contract price was set at full barren value, what possibilities exist with respect to Walker's assumptions? He was certain that she was barren and perhaps made the statement at the beginning of the discussion in order to avoid any latter claim of misrepresentation by Sherwood. See note 4 below.

4. *Express warranty negation.* Is it possible that Walker informed Sherwood that the cattle on the second farm were "probably barren" because he was aware that Sherwood was searching for breeding stock and he wanted to make certain that Sherwood could not later claim an express warranty of breeder status? Yes indeed. If so, why would an experienced farmer like Walker sell Rose purely as a beef cow? There is no rational explanation for the sale as a beef cow—Sherwood was not in that business from all we can tell.

5. *Distinguishing mistakes of fact from mistakes of value or quality.* The *Sherwood* cases purports to distinguish actionable mistakes of fact from non-actionable mistakes of value or quality. How convincing is this distinction? It is not convincing—see the discussion under Note 2 above. What major fact did the majority opinion use to justify the mistake of fact that Rose was sold as a mere beef cow rather than as a reproductive cow? The price. What does this tell you about the distinguishing mistakes of fact from mistakes as to value? The attempt is basically flawed and the Restatement (Second) of Contracts did its best to correct the flaw by revising the language of the applicable standard—see Note 2 above. See Kenneth L. Schneyer, *"The Culture of Risk: Deconstructing Mutual Mistake,"* 34 Am. Bus. L. J. 429 (1997) (arguing it is nearly impossible to make the distinction as well as to determine which party ought to bear the risk of mistake). For a comparative law view of the law of mistake in substance versus motive, see James Gordley, *"Mistake in Contract Formation,"* 52 Am. J. Comp. L. 433 (2004).

6. *Famous poems.* See text.

7. *Remedy a windfall or just right?* Notwithstanding the contract of sale, the seller was privileged to retain Rose of Aberlone, and the buyer was denied the right to complete the purchase. Considering that Rose was worth approximately $80 if barren and approximately $750 if not barren, there is approximately $670 awarded to the winner of the case. Should the "windfall" nature of the case become a factor in the outcome? Whether or not there was any "windfall" or not depends on whether there was a basic mistake involving an exchange of $80 for $750. Sherwood was no worse off after the rescission—he did not have to pay anything—his only disappointment was a lost future expectation. In every mutual mistake case, the party seeking to avoid the contract will seek to do so for economic advantage. That same advantage will be matched by a corresponding "loss" to the other party. Citing earlier mistake law, one scholar suggests that significant disparity in values is often the most compelling reason for the law to leave the parties in *status quo* and therefore deny rescission. See

Andrew Krull, "*Mistake, Frustration and the Windfall Principle of Contract Remedies*," 43 Hastings L. J. 1, 13-14 (1991).

8. *Rose was not the contract cow.* The principal controversy in the case may be stated as one of construction of a contract for the sale of a cow. Under one interpretation, Rose was that cow and under the other she was not. Why does the Court turn the decision on the buyer's imagined state of mind regarding whether the cow purchased was barren or not? The theory of mutual mistake requires that both parties share the same mistake. But for the majority's assumption as to Sherwood's state of mind at the time of the agreement, the theory would be inapplicable. See Robert L. Birmingham, "*A Rose By Any Other Word: Mutual Mistake in Sherwood v. Walker*," 21 U. C. Davis L. Rev. 197, 208-26 (1987) (analyzing the case through the use of Aristotelian categorical metaphysics to argue that the substance of a cow is a cow and not some quality such as whether barren). Is the case simply an exercise in historical "intertextual" str ategy whereby the Court does not rely upon prior legal precedents as much as texts across disciplines? No. Said the majority:

> But it must be considered as well settled that a party who has given an apparent consent to a contract of sale may refuse to execute it, or he may avoid it after it has been completed, if the assent was founded, or the contract made, upon the mistake of a material fact,—such as the subject-matter of the sale, the price, or some collateral fact materially inducing the agreement; and this can be done when the mistake is mutual. 1 Benj. Sales, §§ 605, 606; Leake, Cont. 339; Story, Sales, (4th Ed.) §§ 377, 148. See also, Cutts v. Guild, 57 N. Y. 229; Harvey v. Harris, 112 Mass. 32; Gardner v. Lane, 9 Allen, 492, 12 Allen, 44; Huthmacher v. Harris' Adm'rs, 38 Pa. St. 491; Byers v. Chapin, 28 Ohio St. 300; Gibson v. Pelkie, 37 Mich. 380, and cases cited; Allen v. Hammond, 11 Pet. 63-71.

If so, legal opinions may not be independent from their social, cultural and intellectual contexts. For such an argument, see Alani Golanski, "*Nascent Modernity In the Case of Sherwood v. Walker—An Intertextual Proposition*," 35 Willamette L. Rev. 315 (1999).

9. *Continuing vitality of case.* As discussed in the next case, Michigan has limited *Sherwood* to its facts, meaning that it arguably remains relevant to resolving mistakes in identical cattle purchase contracts, but the case is for all intents and purposes overruled. Instead, Michigan courts have shifted emphasis from whether a mutual mistake exists under Restatement (Second) of Contracts § 152 to which party bears the risk of loss of the mutual mistake under Restatement (Second) of Contracts § 154. Do you agree? This remains

to be seen, given the analysis of the next case in the book. Is the risk of loss analysis relevant unless and until a mutual mistake is established? It is relevant in evaluating the context of the mutual mistake. If *Sherwood* is limited to its facts in Michigan, when and how would a court apply the mutual mistake risk analysis? The court would follow the opinion of the next case adopting the language of Restatement (Second) of Contracts § 152.

10. *Personal injury releases.* See text.

Lenawee County Board of Health v. Messerly
CASE BRIEF

This is a 1982 decision of the Michigan Supreme Court which, in effect, reverses the holding of the prior case, *Sherwood v. Walker,* and substitutes the standard for mutual mistake found in Restatement (Second) of Contracts §§ 152, 154. In 1971, the Messerlys (co-defendants) purchased a 600-square-foot portion of land (and an additional one acre of land), on which was situated a three-unit apartment building. The previous owner of the property, Mr. Bloom, had installed a septic tank without permit and in violation of the health code. The Messerlys used the building as an income investment property until 1973, when they sold the property on a land contract to one Mr. Barnes. Barnes sold the one acre, but thereafter defaulted on the land contract, at which point the plaintiffs, Mr. and Mrs. Pickles (co-defendants) showed an interest in the property. Barnes (and his wife) executed a quitclaim deed to convey their interest in the land back to the Messerlys, who then sold the land to Pickles for $25,500. In the contract, a clause provided: "Purchaser has examined this property and agrees to accept same in its present condition. There are no other or additional written or oral understandings." Within the next week, the Pickleses went to introduce themselves to their tenants, and they discovered raw sewage seeping out of the ground. Tests showed that the sewage system was not sound, and the Lenawee County Board of Health (Board) condemned the property and initiated this action against the Messerlys as land contract vendors, and the Pickleses as vendees, to obtain a permanent injunction barring human habitation until the property was brought in compliance with the health code. The injunction was granted and the Board was permitted to withdraw from the lawsuit.

When no payments were made on the land contract, the Messerlys filed a cross-complaint against the Pickleses seeking foreclosure, sale of the property, and a deficiency judgment. The Pickleses then counterclaimed against the Messerlys and the Barneses for rescission of the contract, alleging (1) lack of consideration and (2) willful concealment and misrepresentation by the Barneses, a claim incorporated against the Messerlys. The trial court ruled that no action was available because there had been no fraud or misrepresentation; neither party knew of Mr. Bloom's previous actions, and the land was sold on an "as is" basis. Thus, the trial court ordered foreclosure against the Pickleses, together with a judgment against them for $25,943.09. The court of appeals upheld the trial court's ruling with respect to the Barneses, but reversed the finding of no cause of action on the Pickleses' claims against the Messerlys. The court of appeals held that the mutual mistake between the Messerlys and Pickleses went to a basic element of the contract (though the Pickleses did not plead mutual mistake, the trial court interpreted their "failure of consideration" claim to be a mutual mistake argument, an issue that is discussed in depth in footnote 5 of the casebook opinion), and that while the parties intended to transfer income-producing rental property, the Pickleses actually paid $25,500 for nothing. The Messerlys appealed.

To determine whether there was a mistaken belief held by one or both of the parties, the court stated that the "erroneous belief of one or both parties must relate to a fact in existence at the time the contract is executed." On this point, the court agreed with the court of appeals that both parties were mistaken as to the income-producing ability of the apartment building due to the sewage problems. And while the Messerlys contended that the defect was not discovered until after the contract was executed, the court noted that such information was irrelevant because of the fact that the actual defect predated formation of the contract. Having determined that a mutual mistake existed, the court shifted its focus to the legal significance of the mistake.

The court began its analysis of the significance of the mistake by noting that rescission due to mutual mistake is a remedy to be "granted only in the sound discretion of the court." Both parties attempted to convince the court that the current facts were in line with past decisions of the court, including the Pickleses arguing that *Sherwood v. Walker* (supra) should control. But the court felt that the "inexact and confusing distinction between contractual mistakes running to value and those touching the substance of the consideration [serve] only as an impediment to a clear and helpful analysis for the equitable resolution of cases in which mistake is alleged and proven"—thus, it confined the previous cases to their respective facts. Instead, the court felt that a better approach would be to grant rescission on a case-by-case basis where the "mistaken belief relates to a basic assumption of the parties upon which the contract is made, and which materially affects the agreed performances of the parties," citing Restatement (Second) of Contracts § 152. And while the court held that the mistake here did affect a basic assumption that materially affected the performance of the parties, it nonetheless denied the Pickleses' claim. Since both parties were unaware of the sewage system defect, they were both innocent; thus, the court had to decide which innocent party should bear the loss. While no express warranties were included in the contract, the fact that it included a clear "as is" clause was found sufficient by the court to justify that the Pickleses, as buyers, should bear the risk of loss. The court reversed the court of appeals decision and held that the Pickleses were not entitled to rescission of the contract.

INTERESTING DISCUSSION ISSUES

1. *The court's reversal of Sherwood v. Walker.* While this decision purports to limit the decision in *Sherwood v. Walker* to its facts, the effect is reversal of the basic holding of that case. The numerous questions in the Notes to the preceding case, *Sherwood v. Walker*, suggested the inadequacy of the test formulated by the Michigan Supreme Court in 1887. In the instant case, the distinction between essence and accidence was rejected. The new approved formula, taken from the Restatement, was:

> Often, a mistake relates to an underlying factual assumption which, when discovered, directly affects value, but simultaneously and materially affects the essence of the contractual consideration. . . . Instead [of the *Sherwood v. Walker* formulation], we think the better-reasoned approach is a case-by-case analysis whereby rescission is indicated when the mistaken belief relates to a basic assumption of the parties upon which the contract is made, and which materially affects the agreed performances of the parties.

The court applied this formula to the facts in the case as follows:

> Appellant and appellee both mistakenly believed that the property that was the subject of their land contract would generate income as rental property. The fact that it could not be used for human habitation deprived the property of its income-earning potential and rendered it less valuable. However, this mistake, while directly and dramatically affecting the property's value, cannot accurately be characterized as collateral because it also affects the very essence of the consideration.

But the court then considered "allocation of risk" under § 154 and concluded that the following provision in the contract, "Purchaser has examined this property and agrees to accept same in its present condition. There are no other or additional written or oral understandings," constituted an "as is, where is" clause effective to shift the risk of loss to the buyers.

NOTES AND QUESTIONS

1. *Nature of the mutual mistake?* The *Lenawee County* accepted the trial court's determination that the parties had been mutually mistaken regarding the income producing nature of the property. Specifically, both parties had assumed that the property was income producing, but that "fact" turned out to be untrue. For actionable mutual mistake to exist, the mutual mistake must relate to a fact in existence at the time the contract was formed. Restatement (Second) of Contracts § 152(1). Was the property income producing at the time of the contract? This should not matter. The question rather is whether the property was capable of producing income at the time of the agreement. At the time the contract was formed, the septic system was out of code, but the problem was not yet discoverable [had not yet been discovered]. This led the seller to argue this was not a fact in existence at the time the contract was formed, but a subsequent supervening event. As discussed in the next chapter, such supervening events usually do not excuse performance except in extraordinary circumstances. Moreover, even if a supervening event does excuse the future performance of one or both parties, the event will not justify rescission of the contract. If court had agreed with the seller's argument, do you think it likely the buyers would have obtained a return of the purchase price? If there was no mutual mistake of material fact it is highly unlikely that the buyers would have received their money back. Is mutual mistake the only arguable ground for rescission? No. Fraud, misrepresentation and concealment may all serve as a foundation for rescission but the trial court ruled that none of those had occurred in this case.

2. *Shift from essence or quality to risk allocation.* Unlike the cited *Sherwood* case, *Lenawee County* addresses the mistake doctrine as a question of which party should bear the risk of loss. For this purpose, the court focuses on Restatement (Second) of Contracts § 154. There was no counterpart to that section in Restatement (First) of Contracts, and hence the common law struggled with fine line distinctions between mere value or quality (which did not provide a basis for rescission) and those affecting (or destroying) the essence or nature of the consideration to one of the parties (which did provide a basis for rescission). The drafters of Restatement (Second) of Contracts § 154 attempted to eliminate such distinctions as artificial. See Restatement (Second) of Contracts § 154 cmt. *a* ("Stating these rules in terms of the allocation of risk avoids such artificial and specious distinctions as are sometimes drawn between 'intrinsic' and 'extrinsic' mistakes or between mistakes that go to the 'identity' or 'existence' of the subject matter and those that go merely to its 'attributes,' 'quality' or 'value.'"). Do you agree that such distinctions are artificial? "Artificial" is a difficult word—what is clearly to the point is the basic nature of the

mistake and the extent to which it changed the relative benefits to be received by both parties. While technically the modern risk allocation test shifts analysis from the existence of a mistake to whether the party seeking rescission assumed the risk of the mistake, is there really any dramatic difference in outcome absent an express allocation of risk clause in the contract? No. Assuming no express or implied allocation of risk, the decision to rescind or not turns on whether the shared mistake was basic and significantly affected the benefits received or performances required under the contract. Absent one party bearing the risk of a mutual mistake, what is the effect of (a qualifying) mutual mistake to the adversely affected party? Rescission of the contract, and loss of the bargain. See Restatement (Second) of Contracts § 152(a).

3. *Breach of promise?* If mutual mistake did not give rise to a power of avoidance (and hence a remedy of rescission and restitution), would the mistaken party have any basis for recovery of losses caused by the mistake? Only if a promise were implied by the court relating to the subject of the mistake. Is it possible for a mutual mistake to create a cause of action for breach of contract (and thus money damages)? Yes, in the limited circumstances just described. If the UCC governed this matter and the court could not determine any breach of an express promise, could the court imply any promises that the property was fit for its ordinary rental purposes? See UCC § 2-314(2)(c). No, because the seller was not a "merchant." But had the seller been a "merchant," an implied warranty of merchantability could have been implied unless the court found the so-called "as is" clause effective to exclude any such implied warranty. The implied warranty of merchantability can make a real difference. Consider one of the cases involving a sale of cows which, unknown to the seller, were infected at the time of the sale with a disease. Whether or not the parties shared a mutual mistake that the cows were healthy at the time of sale would not matter. The cows would be subject to an implied warranty of merchantable quality the breach of which would give rise to a claim for damages or rescission. What about the duty of good faith performance under both the common law and UCC § 1-102(3)? Since this case does not involve the sale of goods, and absent the discussed "as is" clause, would the buyer be foreclosed from arguing a warranty of habitability discussed in the last chapter, or would the doctrine of *caveat emptor* apply? The choice could be a "toss-up" in some courts.

4. *Effect of "as is" clause.* In the context of a sale of goods, an "as is" clause effectively negates all implied warranties, including the implied warranty that the goods are fit for their ordinary purposes. However, the "as is" language must make clear "in common understanding" that there is no implied warranty. See UCC § 2-316(3)(a). When the "as is" clause is effective, it simply removes a

promise and any trailing remedy that might otherwise accrue from a breach of that promise.

While the "as is" clause clearly negates implied warranties, does it necessarily follow that such a clause also positively allocates risk of loss to a party caused by a mistaken assumption by both parties to the contract? No. In fact, in footnote 15 of *Lenawee County*, the court cites to the effect of an "as is" clause to negate implied warranties under the UCC. Impliedly, the court also regarded the simple "as is" clause as a specific allocation of all unknown facts in existence at the time of the contract. Accordingly, the court treated the "as is" clause as an allocation of risk by the agreement of the parties. See Restatement (Second) of Contracts § 154(a). Do you agree? Not necessarily—the question should be whether the subject matter of the mistake was within the realm of risks considered by the parties. If the "as is" were final with respect to risk allocation the cases setting aside settlements would never be resolved based on mistake since the clauses in such cases routinely recite the settlement of claims "known or unknown." It is questionable whether the parties in the instant case really expected the risk of the property being unusable to be covered by the clause included, "Purchaser has examined this property and agrees to accept same in its present condition." In analyzing whether a particular contract clause allocates or assigns the risk of unknown facts at the time of contract, what should be the touchstone? The range of reasonable expectation based on facts known to the parties at the time of agreement. Would you expect the court to utilize the rules of interpretation to try to understand the meaning each party attached to such a clause? Yes. In this case, the court stated that to have "any meaning at all, it must be interpreted to refer to those defects which were unknown at the time that the contract was executed." Do you agree? Not necessarily—it can be argued that the mistake here was outside the range of contemplation of the parties at the time of the agreement. Is this an application of the plain meaning rule? Yes. Since the trial court did not rule on the meaning of the clause relative to the allocation of risk formulation, should the case have been remanded to determine the meaning of the "as is" clause in this case, or does the court infer that such clauses will always serve a similar risk allocation function as a matter of law? The decision in this case was a decision on the particular facts and should not be generalized to the extent suggested in this question. In other jurisdictions where more sympathy might exist for alternative meanings, can you suggest a reason that the clause in this case was ambiguous and thereafter reasonably susceptible to an alternative meaning? The words, "Purchaser has examined this property and agrees to accept same in its present condition" could have been interpreted as limited to risks discoverable by inspection" i.e. risks that an "examination" would have disclosed.

5. *Effect of inspection.* The "as is" clause in this case stated that the property had been "examined" by the buyer prior to purchase, and therefore the buyer "agrees to accept the same in its present condition." Given the court's enthusiasm for the effect of "as is" clauses under the UCC, is it surprising that the court did not also reference the effect of inspection of goods prior to purchase? Yes—see the comments under Note 4 above. See UCC § 2-316(3)(b). How does the UCC treat the effect of an inspection and why does the UCC have two separate sections referring to the effect of an "as is" clause and the effect of inspection? The UCC treats an inspection as barring things that an inspection would have disclosed. The UCC has two separate subsections because the "as is" subjection has a global effect eliminating all implied promises whereas the "inspection" subsection addresses situations where there would be an implied promise but for the inspection. The inspection clause eliminates liability and thus allocates the risk to the party for discoverable defects or those "defects which an examination ought in the circumstances to have revealed." Is this nearly as broad as the effect of an "as is" clause? No. The "as is" clause is designed to eliminate liability for things unknown as well as known. If not, does this raise a legitimate interpretative issue as to whether the parties intended Clause 17 as an "as is" clause or an inspection clause? Yes—see the comments above. If so, who decides such a question and does it require a remand of the case? The decision should be made by the decider of fact and hence it is arguable that the case should have been remanded to the trial court for such appropriate findings of fact.

6. *Effect of failure to discover on rescission.* Restatement (Second) of Contracts § 157 states that a mistaken party's failure to know or discover the facts before making the contract is not a bar to avoidance unless the failure amounts to not acting in good faith. Is there a difference between this provision and its application to avoidance and the UCC inspection clause that applies to negate an implied warranty? Yes. § 157 does not treat a failure to discover alone as an allocation of risk. The UCC treats such a failure as an allocation of the risk.

7. *Allocation of risk by reason of "conscious ignorance."* See text.

8. *Allocation of risk by court on other reasonable grounds.* See text.

9. *Distinguishing allocation of risks from other interpretive problems.* Every party, upon entering a contract, knows (or should know) that one or both parties lack complete information regarding the subject matter of the contract and that the contract may not be as good a deal as it first appeared. To a certain extent, then, a failure of the parties to allocate the risk of mistake expressly in their contract terms

is equivalent to any other ambiguity that the parties fail to resolve through express terms:

> In order to explain the mistake doctrines, then, we need to make additional assumptions. One possible assumption, which by now should be familiar, is that "transaction costs" prevent parties from designing optimal contracts. This is the implicit route taken by Rasmusen and Ayres in an article on the mistake doctrines. Before we turn to their argument, we should observe that using this assumption makes the analysis of the mistake doctrine the same as the analysis of any problem of contractual interpretation, where, as law and economics assumes, transaction costs prevent parties from defining a crucial term, like "chicken" in the *Frigaliment* case. The parties do not make a "mistake" in the ordinary sense of the term; they rationally choose to leave a contract incomplete in light of the costs of completing it. If one thinks that courts should use majoritarian defaults to determine such terms, then one should think that majoritarian defaults should also determine the parties' obligations if the cow is fertile or ill. On this view, the mistake doctrine should also have the same remedial implications as contract-interpretation disputes—namely, enforcement of the judicial interpretation rather than rescission and restitution—but of course it does not.

Eric A. Posner, "*Economic Analysis of Contract Law after Three Decades: Success or Failure?,*" 112 Yale L.J. 829, 846 (2003). In other words, a mere mutual mistake presents the court with a rational decision by the parties to submit to a judicial determination of where to place the losses, rather than bear the additional negotiation and transaction costs necessary to identify risks of mistake and agree upon an express allocation in the event those risks materialize. Do you agree or disagree with Professor Posner's analysis? No. Are there any good reasons for maintaining rescission and restitution as a remedy for mistake? Yes—the difference between undoing the transaction and restoring both parties to the original status quo compared to enforcing a loss on one party and a gain on the other.

10. *Mutual mistake and ante-nuptial contracts.* Consider the mistake and allocation of risk problems raised by prenuptial contracts. Many parties enter such contracts sharing a mutually mistaken belief as to the suitability of the other party as a marriage or spousal partner. See Ann Laquer Estin, "*Economics and the Problem of Divorce,*" 2 U. Chi. L. Sch. Roundtable 517, 578-582 (1995). Should courts provide such parties a grounds for avoiding the ante-nuptial contract (and obtaining rescission and restitution) in the face of such mutual mistakes? No—the risk of subsequent divorce is often the driving motive for entering into such agreements and thus the "mistake" is one

which the parties actually contemplated but nevertheless went ahead with their agreement. To what extent do other equitable and public policy factors weigh against such relief? Perhaps the concept of "pacta sunt servanda." Rather than weighing against relief however, it might be argued in some cases that such agreements preclude a court from making fair provision for one of the divorcing spouses. Alternatively, should courts merely assume that ante-nuptial contracts by definition allocate the risks of such mistakes between the parties? They generally do so, but in some situations the range of risks assumed at the time of contracting might be reconsidered by the court.

Optional Problem 6-2

Emma Anderson owns and operates a high-end music store that specializes in antique and collectible musical instruments. In 1996, John Miller asked Emma to assist him in acquiring a violin crafted by a well-known Dutch violin master, Carlos Ten Brink. Ten Brink violins, although not as famous as those crafted by Antonio Stradivari, are nonetheless highly sought-after in the music world and can fetch prices as high as $600,000 at private sale. Emma identified several individuals who were known to have purchased Ten Brink violins in the last decade and successfully solicited one owner to sell the violin to Emma for $400,000. John obtained an expert appraisal of the violin from a third-party appraiser, who identified the violin as a Ten Brink instrument from the maker's "golden period" and opined that the instrument was worth between $500,000 and $600,000. Emma and John entered into a contract to sell "one Ten Brink violin—$500,000 cash." In 2001, a radical musical historian published a very successful book in which she claimed that Ten Brink did not actually craft the violin purchased by John. Over the next six years, many collectors accepted this new theory and, when John attempted to sell his Ten Brink violin, several appraisers opined that the instrument was now only worth $250,000. In 2007, John sued Emma for rescission and restitution on the basis of mutual mistake.

How should a court decide this case?

Answer:

Emma's contract with John read "One Ten Brink violin—$500,000 cash." The violin was sold in 1996. Both parties intended to buy and sell a "Ten Brink" violin. John, the buyer, retained an expert third party appraiser who identified the violin as a "Ten Brink." A "radical" historian questioned the violin's authenticity leading collectors to lower substantially the market value of this instrument. John sued for rescission in 2007. The following issues are raised:

- Since the violin was a "good," the UCC applies;
- Was there a mutual mistake? Both Emma and John believed that the violin was a "Ten Brink"—the fact that a "radical" reviewer opined that the instrument was not a "Ten Brink" did not establish that opinion as "fact;"
- If the violin was not a "Ten Brink," then clearly the mistaken belief that it was constituted a mutual mistake;
- Was that mistake basic and did it change the substance of the agreement?
- Did the words used in the contract imply a warranty that the instrument was in fact a "Ten Brink" or were the words merely descriptive of and identifying the particular violin sold?
- If there was an implied warranty, did John rely on that term of the contract or did he rely on the advice of a third party appraiser?
- Could the origin of the violin be established by inspection?
- Since "mistake" is an equitable remedy, was relief sought within a reasonable time after the contract was entered into and performed?

The lapse of 11 years between date of contract and suit for relief suggests strongly that an equity court would not intervene to recognize a right of rescission. Cumulative arguments in the same direction would be: it is not clear, as a matter of fact, that the violin is not a "Ten Brink" as was believed and thus there may be no "mistake"; if there was a mistake the effect was a reduction in value which, under *Sherwood,* would have precluded recovery based on mistake, but if there was a mistake was it "basic"?; did the words of the contract imply an express warranty that the violin was a "Ten Brink"? this would be a difficult implication in the light of John's use of and reliance on a third party appraiser; the maker of the violin is not something that, necessarily, could have been discovered upon inspection.

2. Unilateral Mistake

Early law failed to recognize unilateral mistake as actionable at all. The early doctrine was clearly too severe, at least when the non-mistaken party was aware of the other party's mistake at the time of the contract. While modern contract law has come to recognize the equitable remedy of rescission on behalf of the unilaterally mistaken party, the remedy is narrowly tailored to protect the respective informational rights of the parties. Importantly, the contract is voidable only if one of two other conditions are present. Either enforcement of the contract must be unconscionable, or the other party had reason to know of the mistake (or caused the mistake). In this sense, unilateral mistake resembles misrepresentation doctrine. Recall that non-disclosure is equivalent to an affirmative misrepresentation where a party knows disclosure would correct a mistake of the other party and the failure to disclose fails to comply with standards of good faith. However, the duty to disclose is broader than unilateral mistake because it does not require a showing of a material effect on the agreed exchange and applies regardless of whether the mistaken party bears the risk of the mistake. Consequently, the law of unilateral mistake is sparingly applied and universally confusing. Law and economic scholars argue that requiring disclosure in such snap-up transactions induces more efficient behavior of the parties.

Cummings v. Dusenbury
CASE BRIEF

This is a 1984 decision of an Illinois Appellate Court. The defendants, the Dusenburys, sold a house to the plaintiffs, the Cummings. Shortly after moving into the home, the Cummings sued for fraud, rescission of the contract based on a unilateral mistake that the house was not suited to be a year-round dwelling, and for breach of an implied warranty of habitability. The Dusenburys built the house in the winter of 1973–74 as a kit log home; in 1977, they lived in the house for an entire year. Because of some leakage, the windows were replaced or reinstalled, which stopped the window leaks. Mr. Dusenbury testified at trial that the roof only leaked during an extremely cold winter with lots of snow, but it had not leaked during the year that they lived in the home. The house was leased by a number of different tenants, none of whom ever complained of leaks. In July of 1982, the Cummings viewed the property and asked their realtor to contact the Dusenburys with specific questions, several of which addressed the Cummings' concerns about being able to stay warm during the winter. In August 1982, the Cummings moved into the house. Soon thereafter, they found that the roof leaked when it rained, the windows leaked, flies were coming into the house, and the walls dripped with condensation during the winter. Experts testifying for the Cummings stated that the roof and walls did not meet minimum standards and were in need of significant repairs, and also that the house should not be classified as a year-round house. The trial court found for the Cummings and held that they were entitled to rescission; the Dusenburys appealed.

The Dusenburys contended that the doctrine of unilateral mistake was improperly applied by the trial court to grant rescission; only mutual mistake should justify such a remedy. But the court used the very case cited by the Dusenburys to set forth the rule regarding unilateral mistake: "If there is apparently a valid contract in writing, but by reason of a mistake of fact by one of the parties, not due to his negligence, the contract is different with respect to the subject matter or terms from what was intended, equity will give to such party a remedy by cancellation where the parties can be placed in the status quo." The Dusenburys argued that the mistake at issue concerned the question of whether the house was suitable for year-round living, a question that they felt was one of subjective opinion rather than a factual representation. But the court disagreed, holding that the mistake was one of fact and a material part of the contract. The trial court had found that the home in question was not suitable for year-round living, and that enforcing the contract at issue would be unconscionable. The appellate court agreed, finding that the Cummings had satisfied all requirements of the unilateral mistake doctrine.

First, the mistake related to a material factual feature of the contract. Since the home was located in an area with severe winters, its capability to serve as a year-round residence was quite important to the transaction. Since the record showed that the buyers had made diligent inquiry regarding the home's suitability for winter use, and since the sellers knew of the buyers' interest in this feature, there was no real dispute about whether the year-round capability of the house was material to the contract, and that the buyers thus did not receive what they had bargained for. Second, the court found that the buyers had exercised reasonable care in inquiring into the suitability of the home for winter living by receiving direct assurances from the sellers, who had lived in the house during the winter. Third, it was possible to rescind the contract and place the sellers in status quo. The court held that the Dusenburys' loss of use while the house was occupied by the Cummings was easily compensated by the trial court's award of rent for the time that they were out of possession. The court also rejected the Dusenburys' claim for a refund of the broker commission, as the seller must only be restored to the status quo "insofar as [the other] received any benefit"—here, the buyers received no benefit from the Dusenbury's payment of the commission. As a result of these three findings, the court held that the facts and evidence supported the trial court's award of rescission.

INTERESTING DISCUSSION ISSUES

1. *Unilateral mistake and negligence.* The court quoted the following "rule" from another Illinois decision:

> If by reason of a mistake of fact by one of the parties to a contract not due to his negligence, the contract is different with respect to the subject matter or terms from what was intended, equity will rescind the contract where the parties can be placed in status quo.

Later, the court said:

> Generally, the rule is that the unilateral mistake of one party to a contract may not be relied upon to relieve that party from its obligations under the contract where the party's own negligence and lack of prudence resulted in the mistake.

The lesson is, and should be, that a court will not rescue one party to an agreement from a unilateral mistake that she could have avoided through the exercise of reasonable care. Such a rule is clearly in accordance with economic concepts of contract rule efficiency. But the question of what constitutes such disqualifying "negligence" may lie in the eye of the beholder. Clearly, the Cummings could have engaged a qualified consultant to determine whether the house was in fact suitable for year around occupancy. Was it negligence on their part not to do so? The court wobbled a little on this:

> Although one could argue that the Cummings could have determined for themselves that the house lacked the features necessary for being comfortable in the winter, this argument is somewhat negated by the fact that the record shows they made diligent inquiry into whether it was suitable for winter use. The trial court found that the defendants were aware of plaintiffs' concern in this regard, and that although defendants indicated they had no problems when they inhabited the house, the fact remains that the house, as sold, was not what plaintiffs had bargained for when they purchased the home.

Consider the case of a car buyer who answers an ad in the Sunday paper, responds, test drives the car and buys from a seller who is not a merchant without any third party review. Would it be negligence on the buyer's part not to get a mechanic to survey the car and report? It is fundamental to the answer to this question that the seller not have contributed to the buyer's understanding and that the seller not be aware of any undisclosed problem that the seller should realize would affect the buyer's judgment to proceed with the sale.

2. *Restoration of the status quo.* If the transaction is to unwound, it is logical that any transfers from one party to the other be returned as part of the rescission. It is frequently stated that such a transfer, or the offer of it, is a condition of rescission. Under the earlier common law version of the right of rescission the tender of such a return was a condition precedent to exercising a right of rescission and to bringing suit. The instant court treats the problem of restoration of the parties to their previous position as one of restitutionary justice. The Dusenbury's had paid the real estate broker a commission as part of the sale and purchase. But the court said the Cummings were not

obligated to refund the amount of that commission to the Dusenburys because the payment of that commission provided no benefit to the Cummings. If we assume that the decision in this case is based purely on mistake and not on misrepresentation or active concealment, it is questionable whether the Dusenburys were restored to status quo without reimbursement of that commission.

Quite often, courts find it difficult or impossible to assure a precise restoration of the status quo following a rescission. Understandably, courts seem willing to substitute a pecuniary adjustment where appropriate when literal restoration cannot be accomplished. Thus, the Cummings could not "restore" the months of occupancy of the house they "enjoyed." But the court found a transfer of a reasonable charge for that occupancy in the form of a notional "rent" to be sufficient.

NOTES AND QUESTIONS

1. *Duty to disclose.* Did the sellers fail to disclose that the house was not a year-round house in a manner that creates a voidable contract under Restatement (Second) of Contracts §§ 161(b) and 164? It was disputed whether Mrs. Dusenbury misrepresented that fact to the realtor. But the trial court held for the Cummings on this issue of fact. Assuming there was no misrepresentation, was this a non-disclosure that qualifies under Restatement (Second) of Contracts § 162(b)? Yes, because the Dusenburys knew that this was a material concern for the Cummings and that the Cummings were under a material misunderstanding about the suitability of the house for year around living.

2. *Status quo restoration.* Restatement (Second) of Contracts § 376 states that a party avoiding a contract on grounds including mistake is entitled to restitution for any benefit conferred upon the other party. Restatement (Second) of Contracts § 153 does not mention restitution as a condition of avoidance but the court states such a requirement in cases involving unilateral mistake. Do you see why? The very fact that the court, by rescinding, unravels all commitments made under the contract requires that *both* parties be restored to where they were before the contract was entered into. It is noteworthy that the court refused to order the Cummings to compensate the Dusenburys for the real estate commission the latter paid when the Cummings purchased. The court found that this payment was of no benefit to the Cummings. The court was thus applying the restitutionary standard of relief. Is the other party entitled to restitution as well under all avoidance cases? See Restatement (Second) of Contracts § 384:

(1) Except as stated in Subsection (2), a party will not be granted restitution unless

(a) he returns or offers to return, conditional on restitution, any interest in property that he has received in exchange in substantially as good condition as when it was received by him, or

(b) the court can assure such return in connection with the relief granted.

(2) The requirement stated in Subsection (1) does not apply to property

(a) that was worthless when received or that has been destroyed or lost by the other party or as a result of its own defects,

(b) that either could not from the time of receipt have been returned or has been used or disposed of without knowledge of the grounds for restitution if justice requires that compensation be accepted in its place and the payment of such compensation can be assured, or

(c) as to which the contract apportions the price if that part of the price is not included in the claim for restitution.

3. *Cognitive biases and unilateral mistakes.* Consider situations involving sophisticated repeat players, such as retail merchants offering extended warranties on consumer electronics, and unsophisticated one-shot players, such as consumers purchasing a computer or stereo system. The producer, by virtue of its nearly exclusive access to information about its production processes, materials and components, warranty claims, and failure rates, knows more or less exactly the probability that any given product will fail within a given warranty period. The producer is also aware that consumers lack such information and, because of cognitive biases and bounded rationality, will be unable to determine the value of an extended warranty on the offered goods. See W. David Slawson, Binding Promises 26-34 (1996) (analyzing producers' superior access to information about their products as arguably insurmountable edge in bargaining power). In many contexts, producers make a profit margin of several hundred percent on extended warranties. Given this massive disparity in information and that the producer knows or should know that the consumer is mistaken as to the likelihood of product failure within the warranty or extended warranty period, should the consumer be entitled to rescind such extended warranty agreements on the basis of unilateral mistake? No—the situation does not come within the scope of actionable concealment nor does it go to the basis of the agreement.

CHAPTER 7

CONTRACTS UNENFORCEABLE BY LATER EVENTS: DISCHARGE OF FUTURE DUTIES ABSENT A BREACH

Table of Contents

Introduction to Chapter 7 Coverage

Previous chapters considered grounds for asserting a validly formed and otherwise enforceable contract is void and unenforceable by operation of law (Chapter 5) or voidable and unenforceable by election of one or both of the parties (Chapter 6). Whether void and invalid from the beginning by law or voidable and invalid from the beginning by election, the effect of both doctrines meant the contract was unenforceable ab initio, from the beginning. The remedial response involved restitution designed to restore the parties to their respective positions before the contract was formed. Limited restitution adjustments were explored to balance the equities involved such as minors returning damaged property.

The void and voidable doctrines were developed in response to various problematic defects associated with the formation of the contract. In many cases, the contract involved various degrees of performance by one or both parties. The apparent assent coupled with the performance made it difficult to simply assert a contract of any sort was never formed and simply adopted various mechanisms designed to unwind the defective contractual relationship. Judicial intrusion into the otherwise private contractual relationship was justified because one party asserted the formative defect merited judicial refusal to enforce the literal terms of the contract.

This chapter considers the next chronological doctrinal evolution, a contract validly formed without any of the defects previously explored but yet encountering unexpected various and sundry catastrophes after formation. The mere existence of a validly formed contract coupled with the absence of any formation defects merits special scrutiny. There is nothing wrong with the contract itself except of course that an event occurred after formation without the fault of either party but making full performance by one party literally impossible, highly impracticable, or at the very least more expensive than originally anticipated.

Judicial indifference to such “supervening events” leaves the affected party without a legal excuse for the resulting nonperformance. In turn, nonperformance constitutes a breach entitling the other party to monetary damages explored in Chapter 9. At one extreme, it may seem harsh to simply enforce the literal terms of the contract. But at the other extreme, strict enforcement simply represents a form of judicial indifference to the failure of the parties to specifically consider the effect of supervening events in the contract itself. Should a court superimpose its Solomonic wisdom on the parties? Certainly not where the contract specifically allocates the risk of the occurrence of the supervening event to one of the parties.

When such contracts are silent regarding the effect of such supervening events, a court must determine whether the event merits judicial excuse and, if so, the appropriate remedy. Making the contract invalid *ab initio* might seem suspect as it would deny both parties the value of their intended exchange at least up to the time the event occurred. Consequently, a discharge of future obligations might make more sense with some restitution adjustments if past exchanged performances are unequal. But what justifies the legal excuse if one is to be found? Once again, the rationale is a mistake by the parties as to a basic issue under the agreement.

One justification for judicial excuse might be the supposed intent of the parties. A search for the supposed intent of the parties allocates the risk of the occurrence of such an event to the unaffected party. What is the basis for an implied intent analysis, especially in the unique domain of contractual private ordering? That the parties would have reached such an outcome had they thought of and addressed the problem that developed after execution of the agreement. Is empirical evidence helpful to establish that most contracts specifically considering the effect allocate the risk of occurrence to the unaffected party? Perhaps—such evidence may suggest a relatively standard expectation and outcome in such circumstances. Does that make the implication normative in a world of private ordering? Not necessarily—it can tend to take away the right of the parties to make their own arrangement. Does the implication simply reward the affected party for failing to specifically address the issue in the contract? No—the usual basis for granting relief is that *both* parties overlooked the future event and, had they thought about it, would have provided for a reasonable outcome. If the parties want to change the normative assumption, may they do so in the contract? Absolutely. Another justification might be fairness. But such an implication simply mirrors social mores. Is such an implication justified in private ordering or is it better served in the public law domain? Where there are grounds for concluding that both parties overlooked the possibility of such an event and there is a reasonable solution available, the implication of such a solution is appropriate in private ordering—the volume of cases on these issues indicates that parties are often careless in thinking about events that could arise in the future and derail their basic understanding.

Not surprisingly, contract law begins with the assumption that a contract should be enforced as written by the parties. The ancient *pacta sunt servanda* doctrine (agreements must be kept) begins with just such an assumption. However, a careful reading of history clarifies that contract law has always embraced some form of legal excuse to accommodate supervening events, at least where the contract itself was silent. It is equally true that with the growing sophistication of commercial parties and transactions the basic contours of supervening event excuse law has evolved. Would you expect the doctrine to narrow or expand from Medieval to modern times? We would expect the doctrine to expand with the increasing complexity of modern commercial transactions. Intent-based implications tend to be subjectively oriented and arise from an interpretation of the actual agreement in accordance with the rules discussed in Chapter 4. Fairness and justice-based implications tend to be objectively determined and often take the form of implied-in-law "constructive conditions" discussed in Chapter 8.

A. HISTORICAL DEVELOPMENT OF THE IMPOSSIBILITY DOCTRINE

Unlike civil and cannon law, common law has always embraced a more flexible excuse doctrine. Early cases were sparse but the rationale for the "possible to perform" requirement was that it was absurd for the law to purport to "enforce" a promise literally impossible to perform. Nonetheless, the common law distinguished cases involving promises impossible to perform when made and those becoming impossible to perform by subsequent events. Understandably, the latter category received less favorable treatment. Generally, promises involving supervening impossibility were void only if the impossibility developed through an act of God or a later change in law. An early case, *Paradine v. Jane*, 82 Eng. Rep. 897 (K.B 1647), suggested that the party seeking excuse must provide for the excuse in the contract itself and failure to do so meant that the promise was enforceable:

> [B]ut when the party by his own contract creates a duty or charge upon himself, he is bound to make it good, if he may, notwithstanding any accident by inevitable necessity, because he might have provided against it by his contract. And therefore if the lease covenant to repair a house, though it be burnt by lightening, or thrown down by enemies, yet he ought to repair it.

The fact that the supervening event occurred through no fault of the party unable to perform is legally irrelevant. Excuse must be found in the contract itself for a duty voluntarily assumed.

Notwithstanding the manifest enforceability doctrine expressed in *Paradine,* earlier cases had already embraced the "impossible to perform" doctrine in three important situations: supervening illegality, supervening death or disability, and supervening destruction.

Modern Objective Impossibility Doctrine

Two centuries after *Paradine,* the celebrated English common law case of *Taylor v. Caldwell,* 122 Eng. Rep. 309 (K.B. 1863) reiterated the general doctrine and the exceptions in a case involving supervening destruction. Caldwell rented the Surry Gardens and Music Hall to Taylor for a four-day period so that he could conduct a series of grand concerts. Prior to the scheduled concerts but after Taylor expended sums preparing for the concerts and in reliance on the contract, the music hall was badly damaged by an accidental fire. Caldwell could not deliver occupancy. Taylor sued for various reliance costs but Caldwell defended on the grounds that the music hall was destroyed by fire thereby rendering his performance impossible. Taylor won a trial court verdict on the basis that *Paradine* required strict performance of a contractual duty unless the contract itself absolved Caldwell. Since the contract was silent, Caldwell was liable for the reliance damages. Caldwell appealed and the court reversed affirming the "supervening destruction" exception to the *Paradine* general rule of strict liability. Specifically, the court noted that a positive contractual duty is nonetheless subject to an "implied condition" that the subject matter required for performance must continue to exist at the time of performance. Where the subject matter is destroyed through no fault of either party, the failure to perform is not a breach because legally excused by implication. The court based the "implied condition" on the supposed intent of the parties to intend only the objectively possible. Thus, legal excuse is implied-in-law by way of an "implied condition" unless the contract provides otherwise. The law of "implied conditions," otherwise referred to as "constructive conditions," is fully explored in Chapter 8 but generally a condition is a future event whose occurrence discharges the future duty of performance before it becomes due. Accordingly, a failure to perform that duty is not a breach since the duty fails to become due.

Students should note that the court in *Taylor* followed French civil law authority to reach its conclusion, one which excused Caldwell's duty to perform on the one hand, but left Taylor unreimbursed for the expenses he had incurred in preparing for the concerts. The Restatement (First) of Contracts adopted all three of the earlier excuses: supervening impossibility, illegality, and death or incapacity, as did the Restatement (Second). UCC § 2-615(a) recognized supervening impossibility. The Restatement (First) of Contracts, Restatement (Second) of Contracts, and the UCC do not make any significant changes to common law with regard to strict impossibility. However, slight language changes make clear elemental requirements associated with the doctrine: (i) performance of a duty to render services or transfer goods or property must be literally impossible; (ii) the excused party must not bear the risk of the occurrence of the supervening event as a "basic assumption" of the contract, (iii) the event must have occurred without the fault of the excused party, and (iv) the contract must not have assigned the risk of the event to the excused party. Moreover, the question of constructive conditions is not a fact question for the jury but generally a law matter for the court.

The impossibility and fault issues require little explanation. The risk analysis is slightly more intricate and implicates risk assigned by a court as well as that assigned by the contract itself. The basic assumption of the contract is a "shared risk analysis" assuming the risk assumption is objectively shared by both parties. Generally, this means that the "supervening event" is of the general type most parties assume will not occur even though the contract is silent on the matter. Clearly, supervening illegality, death and destruction fit this pattern. This helps explain why such cases are nearly automatic legal excuse cases at least unless the party specifically assumed the risk in the contract. The basic assumption becomes more problematic when the doctrine expands below to embrace impracticability.

The risk assignment question is more intuitive and simply expresses the notion that the parties may specifically negate the default rule regarding legal excuse for supervening events that make performance impossible.

Modern "Subjective" Impracticability Doctrine

The Restatements (First) and (Second) expanded the concept of impossibility to embrace the "impracticable" as well as the "impossible." The expansion did not merit duty discharge simply because performance, when objectively possible, became more subjectively difficult or expensive. See Restatement (First) of Contracts § 457 (mere unanticipated expense or difficulty not impracticable). Rather, extreme and unreasonable expense and difficulty was required. The expanded impracticability doctrine adds a considerable degree of flexibility and hence complexity. A "near miss" impossibility excuse might now qualify for an impracticability excuse in appropriate cases. The great difficulty lies in appropriate differentiation between performance that becomes "merely" more difficult or expensive and that which becomes "extreme and unreasonable. Restatement (Second) of Contracts § 261, *cmt. d* provides:

> *d. Impracticability.* Events that come within the rule stated in this Section are generally due either to "acts of God" or to acts of third parties. . . . Performance may be impracticable because extreme and unreasonable difficulty, expense, injury, or loss to one of the parties will be involved. . . . However, "impracticability" means more than "impracticality." A mere change in the degree of difficulty or expense . . . unless well beyond the normal range, does not amount to impracticability since it is this sort of risk that a fixed-price contract is intended to cover.

Modern Frustration of Purpose Doctrine.

The concept of unforeseen basic surprise was developed in the 20th century as the "frustration of purpose" doctrine. Here, performance of the contract remains possible, but the basic purpose of the contract as intended by the parties is no longer accomplished by such performance. The classic case is *Krell v. Henry,* 2 Eng. Rep. 740 (K.B. 1903). Krell rented rooms from Henry for the purpose of viewing the coronation procession of Edward VII. The date of that procession was changed.

Krell had made a down payment on the rent but refused to pay the balance. The court found performance of his promise excused but he did not recover the down payment. The rent reserved under the contract was obviously fixed by the parties at a level appropriate only for the special event—the coronation procession. The court determined that the essential purpose of the contract was to view the coronation and therefore the court subjected the promise to pay rent to an implied-in-law "constructive condition." The court justified the constructive condition on the grounds that given the essential and indeed only reason for the contract—rent a room to view the coronation—both parties must have contemplated that if the coronation did not occur the obligation to pay rent would be discharged. Therefore the failure to pay rent was not a breach because the obligation never came due. Although modern law would normally allow a return of the deposit made under restitution theory, Henry abandoned that claim.

The Restatement (Second) § 265 included a frustration doctrine providing that a party's performance duty is discharged when that party's principal purpose for entering the contract is substantially frustrated without fault. The non-occurrence of the event causing the frustration must be a basic assumption of the contract which must not allocate the risk to the party seeking discharge. Under both Restatements, restitution is available to both parties if the considerations exchanged at the time of discharge are not equal.

While UCC § 2-615(a) specifically embraces impracticability, it fails to mention frustration. Since the section refers to legal excuse for a seller, it is tempting to conclude UCC § 2-615 offers no help to a frustrated buyer. However, UCC § 2-615, *cmt. 9* specifically mentions that a buyer may utilize the doctrine as well. Also, UCC § 1-103 adopts common law by reference unless a UCC section specifically displaces common law.

Modern Impracticability and Frustration Risk Analysis.

Both Restatement (Second) of Contracts §§ 261 ("supervening impracticability") and 265 ("supervening frustration") provide two related but independent risk analysis paradigms. Both are designed to determine whether the party whose performance is excused bears the risk of the supervening event. If the party seeking excuse bears the risk, legal excuse and duty discharge is not available. A failure to perform constitutes a breach. Both Restatement (Second) of Contracts §§ 261 ("supervening impracticability") and 265 ("supervening frustration") state the same risk analysis. In both cases, the risk paradigms are captured by specific identical language. First, a party bears the risk of a supervening event if the occurrence of the event was a "basic assumption of the contract." Second, a party bears the risk of a supervening event if the contract "language or circumstances" indicate that party bears the risk. These are two quite different concepts. The first implicates a judicial allocation of the loss to the party seeking excuse whereas the second involves an analysis of whether the parties themselves allocated the risk to the party seeking excuse. Accordingly, the first is a policy and fairness analysis whereas the second searches for the intent of the parties.

It is worth noting the similarity between the supervening event and mistake of fact risk analysis. The mistake risk analysis is captured in Restatement (Second) of Contracts § 154 but in slightly different terms. The mistake risk language is more elaborate but there is little conceptual variation. This leads to a common but somewhat misleading observation that a supervening event is simply a "latent mistake" meaning that the problem could have been avoided by agreement and that the excuse would not be necessary if the parties did not share a common mistake in failing to consider the effect of the event when the contract was formed. The observation is misleading because the remedies associated with mistake implicate rescission of the contract *ab initio* whereas the remedy for supervening event excuse is discharge from the date of the occurrence of the event. The mistake and supervening event rules mostly operate as default rules when the agreement is silent.

The foreseeability of the supervening event at the time of contract will have powerful consequences. Generally, if reasonably foreseeable, the promisor will forfeit the excuse where the agreement itself does not allocate the risk of the foreseeable event to the other party. From one perspective, since nearly every act of god, war or other event has already occurred in history, is it not possible to foresee nearly everything? If so, is the foreseeability test meaningful as an exception or does it swallow the general rule of excuse? To avoid these concerns, some have argued that the test for whether an even was foreseeable ought to be limited to events "so unlikely to occur that reasonable parties see no need explicitly to allocate the risk of its occurrence."

How does the doctrine of conscious ignorance under mistake law differ, if at all, from the doctrine of implied assumption under supervening event law? Restatement (Second) of Contracts § 154, *cmt. c* provides as follows with regard to conscious ignorance:

> Even though the mistaken party did not agree to bear the risk of the mistake, he may have been aware when he made the contract that his knowledge with respect to the facts was limited. If he was not only so aware that his knowledge was limited but undertook to perform in the face of that awareness, he bears the risk of the mistake.

Accordingly, the party "impliedly" assumes the risk of the mistake. In most cases, the assumption is that with minimal costs, the mistaken party could have eliminated the mistake by a reasonable search for the truth. Natural limitations should apply to this doctrine. In many cases based on the economics of the particular transaction, the search will be too time consuming and expensive to fairly and reasonably justify that the mistaken party impliedly assumed the risk by failing to conduct the search or investigation. Does the same doctrine apply to foreseeable contingencies? Some courts have applied a more "subjective" standard with respect to foreseeable contingencies.

Transatlantic Financing Corp. v. United States
CASE BRIEF

This is a 1966 decision of the United States Court of Appeals District of Columbia Circuit. Transatlantic entered into a "voyage charter" with the United States to transport a full ship's cargo of wheat from a United States port to a port in Iran. Transatlantic sued to recover additional freight costs attributable to the fact that the normal sea route was unavailable due to closure of the Suez Canal. The district court denied recovery and this decision was affirmed on appeal.

Egypt "nationalized" the Suez Canal on July 26, 1956 and took over operation of the canal. The contract in question here was entered into in October, 1956 during the international crisis that resulted from the canal's seizure. The charter indicated the end points of the transportation but not the route. The voyage began on October 27, 1956. On October 29 Israel invaded Egypt. On October 31 Great Britain and France invaded the Suez Canal Zone. On November 2 the Egyptian government obstructed the canal with sunken vessels, closing it to traffic. On November 7 a Transatlantic agent contacted the US government requesting instructions on disposition of the cargo and payment of additional compensation for a voyage around the Cape of Good hope. A US government representative demurred but a said that Transatlantic was free to file a claim. The ship changed course and went around the Cape, ultimately delivering its cargo in Iran.

This was a suit under admiralty law. Transatlantic claimed that there was an implied term of the contract that the voyage would be performed by the "usual and customary" route i.e. via Suez. By going around the Cape Transatlantic conferred a benefit on the US for which it should be paid in quantum meruit. Said Judge J. Skelly Wright:

> The doctrine of impossibility of performance has gradually been freed from the earlier fictional and unrealistic strictures of such tests as the "implied term" and the parties' "contemplation.". . . . It is now recognized that "A thing is impossible in legal contemplation when it is not practicable; and a thing is impracticable when it can only be done at an excessive and unreasonable cost.". . . The doctrine ultimately represents the ever-shifting line, drawn by courts hopefully responsive to commercial practices and mores, at which the community's interest in having contracts enforced

> according to their terms is outweighed by the commercial senselessness of requiring performance. When the issue is raised, the court is asked to construct a condition of performance based on the changed circumstances, a process which involves at least three reasonably definable steps. First, a contingency—something unexpected—must have occurred. Second, the risk of the unexpected occurrence must not have been allocated either by agreement or by custom. Finally, occurrence of the contingency must have rendered performance commercially impracticable. Unless the court finds these three requirements satisfied, the plea of impossibility must fail.

He found the first requirement met—the parties could be assumed to have expected performance by the usual and customary route. But, he said, this unexpected development raised rather than resolved the "impossibility" issue which turned additionally on whether the risk of the contingency's occurrence had been allocated and, if not, whether performance by alternative routes was rendered impracticable.

Proof that the risk of a contingency's occurrence had been allocated might be expressed or implied in the contract. Such proof might also be found in the surrounding circumstances, including custom and usage of the trade. The contract did not expressly condition performance on the availability of the canal. Nor were there provisions in the contract from which the court might properly imply that the continued availability of the canal was a condition of performance. In a footnote the court noted that under provisions of the contract the parties "expected the usual and customary route would be used" but in no way conditioned performance upon nonoccurrence of this contingency. The court also found there was nothing in custom or usage of the trade which would support constructing such a condition of performance.

"If anything," the court said, "the circumstances surrounding this contract indicate that the risk of the Canal's closure may be deemed to have been allocated to Transatlantic." It was clear that the canal might become a dangerous area. But foreseeability or even recognition of a risk did not necessarily prove its allocation:

> Parties to a contract are not always able to provide for all the possibilities of which they are aware, sometimes because they cannot agree, often simply because they are too busy. Moreover, that some abnormal risk was contemplated is probative but does not necessarily establish an allocation of the risk of the contingency that actually occurs.... The surrounding circumstances do indicate, however, a willingness by Transatlantic to assume abnormal risks, and this fact should legitimately cause us to judge the impracticability of performance by an alternative route in stricter terms than we would were the contingency unforeseen.

The court then turned to the question of impracticability, noting in a footnote that the issue of impracticability should be an objective determination of whether the promise could be reasonably performed. "Dealers should not be excused because of less than normal capabilities. But if both parties are aware of a dealer's limited capabilities, no objective determination would be complete without taking into account this fact." The goods were not subject to harm because of the longer shipment time. Either party could have insured against the risk:

> If anything, it is more reasonable to expect owner-operators of vessels to insure against the hazards of war. They are in the best position to calculate the cost of performance by alternative routes (and therefore to estimate the amount of insurance required), and are undoubtedly sensitive to international troubles which uniquely affect the demand for and cost of their services. The only factor operating here in appellant's favor is the added expense, allegedly $43,972.00 above and beyond the contract price of $305,842.92, of extending a 10,000-mile voyage by approximately 3,000 miles. While it may be an overstatement to say that increased cost and difficulty of performance never constitute impracticability, to justify relief there must be more of a variation between expected cost and the cost of performing by an available alternative than is present in this case, where the promisor can legitimately be presumed to have accepted some degree of abnormal risk, and where impracticability is urged on the basis of added expense alone.

The court then concluded that performance of this contract was not rendered legally impossible. But interestingly, the court added:

> When performance of a contract is deemed impossible it is a nullity. If the performance rendered has value, recovery in quantum meruit for the entire performance is proper. But here Transatlantic has collected its contract price, and now seeks quantum meruit relief for the additional expense of the trip around the Cape. If the contract is a nullity, Transatlantic's theory of relief should have been quantum meruit for the entire trip, rather than only for the extra expense. Transatlantic attempts to take its profit on the contract, and then force the Government to absorb the cost of the additional voyage. When impracticability without fault occurs, the law seeks an equitable solution, . . . , and quantum meruit is one of its potent devices to achieve this end. There is no interest in casting the entire burden of commercial disaster on one party in order to preserve the other's profit. Apparently the contract price in this case was advantageous enough to deter

appellant from taking a stance on damages consistent with its theory of liability. In any event, there is no basis for relief.

INTERESTING DISCUSSION ISSUES

1. *What explains the court's motivation—"supposed" intent of the parties or abstract fairness?* These two "values" appear to be woven together in this decision. The court's opinion seems to hark back to the mistake of fact standard, conscious ignorance, and the language of Restatement (Second) of Contracts § 154, Comment *c*:

> Even though the mistaken party did not agree to bear the risk of the mistake, he may have been aware when he made the contract that his knowledge with respect to the facts was limited. If he was not only so aware that his knowledge was limited but undertook to perform in the face of that awareness, he bears the risk of the mistake.

The pivotal finding of fact seems to be that, at the precise time of entering into the contract, the safety (and therefore availability) of the Suez Canal was a current lively issue widely known in the world of carriage by sea. This made it likely that a carrier, concerned about cost increases attributable to loss of availability of that route, would have negotiated for specific protection in the contract. Said the court:

> The surrounding circumstances do indicate, however, a willingness by Transatlantic to assume abnormal risks, and this fact should legitimately cause us to judge the impracticability of performance by an alternative route in stricter terms than we would were the contingency unforeseen.

Given the pivotal nature of this statement, the court's result can be attributed to "supposed intent" established objectively. But any such attribution cannot be separated from the court's background evaluation of overall "fairness" of the outcome. The additional costs incurred by Transatlantic were not sufficiently large to lead to a conclusion that "the rise in cost is due to some unforeseen contingency which alters the essential nature of the performance."

In the litigation of cases like the instant one, how important is it that the plaintiff establish a plausible explanation of why no clause allocating the particular risk was included in the contract?

2. *Does the court conflate impossibility with impracticability and, if so, why?* The court treats both in the same way, presumably because of the judicial history of the "impossibility" doctrine. "Impracticability" is treated as an extension of the older doctrine, again turning on the extent to which the supervening event altered the very basis of the

expectation of the parties as to performance, and the fact that this event was explicably outside of the expectations and attentions of the parties at the time of contracting.

3. *Could this case have been argued as one of "frustration" rather than "impracticability?* Was the purpose of the contract the making of a reasonable profit by Transatlantic? We are not told about whether the additional costs of going around the Cape of Good Hope turned what otherwise would have been a profitable contract into an unprofitable one. But we are told that the cost differential was not sufficiently large to take the case outside the reasonable expectations and attention of the parties at the time of contracting. By analogy to the logic of *Sherwood v. Walker* and Rose of Aberlone, the effect of the mistake as to the future was not sufficiently "basic." The frustration of purpose in *Krell* was basic. It is thus clear that there are close similarities in the analysis of mistake of fact, impossibility and impracticability, and frustration. But in Footnote 4, the court noted that the English House of Lords had rejected an argument based on frustration in another Suez Canal case. In Footnote 16, the court noted that "The English regard 'frustration' as substantially identical with "impossibility."

The court made an interesting comment on the way in which Transatlantic formulated its claim:

> When performance of a contract is deemed impossible it is a nullity. . . . If the performance rendered has value, recovery in quantum meruit for the entire performance is proper. But here Transatlantic has collected its contract price, and now seeks quantum meruit relief for the additional expense of the trip around the Cape. If the contract is a nullity, Transatlantic's theory of relief should have been quantum meruit for the entire trip, rather than only for the extra expense.

Does this quotation raise some doubt about the proposition asserted in the introductory notes that while the remedy for mistake of fact is avoidance (retroactively declared nullity) the remedy of impossibility is excuse of the duty of further performance?

4. *The negotiating and drafting challenge.* Students should understand that the negotiation and drafting challenge is the most important concern raised by this case and the associated doctrines. Every "impossibility" case can be described as a failure of negotiation and drafting. Judge Skelly Wright explained that:

> Parties to a contract are not always able to provide for all the possibilities of which they are aware, sometimes because they cannot agree, often simply because they are too busy.

Where a contract has been negotiated and drafted by legal counsel the suggestion that the parties may have been "too busy" to make provision for the supervening event seems to be a "hard sell." It is of the essence of good drafting that the lawyer be able to look into the future and foresee, to the maximum extent possible, future events that might derail the basis of the agreement. See the discussion under Note 4 below of "force majeure" clauses.

NOTES AND QUESTIONS

1. *CISG impracticability.* CISG Art. 79(1) provides that a party is not liable for failure to perform any obligation if the failure was due to an impediment beyond that party's control that could not reasonably be expected to have been taken into account at the time of the contract or to have later avoided. Would this provision have offered Transatlantic more protection? No. The closure of the canal was beyond Transatlantic's control but the added cost was something that it could have been expected to take into account at the time of contracting due to the extreme volatility of the canal situation then. Note the court's statement:

> The surrounding circumstances do indicate, however, a willingness by Transatlantic to assume abnormal risks, and this fact should legitimately cause us to judge the impracticability of performance by an alternative route in stricter terms than we would were the contingency unforeseen.

2. *UCC analysis.* The Court references UCC § 2-615. Is the UCC applicable? No—this was a contract to carry cargo, not for its sale and purchase. If not why would the Court reference the UCC rather than the common law and the Restatement (first) of Contracts? Because of the persuasive value of the UCC and the fact that it has been enacted as legislation (in some form) in every state. Is there a difference concerning impracticability doctrinal analysis and outcome between the common law and the UCC? No—see earlier introductory note.

3. *Three factor test.* The Court adopts a three-factor test to find legal excuse by impracticability: (i) supervening event, (ii) risk not allocated to the party to be excuse by agreement or circumstances, and (iii) performance impracticable even though not impossible. The closing of the Suez Canal after the contract was made is obviously a supervening event. But that occurrence simply triggers the second and third analyses. The carriage contract simply stated the final destination for the goods, but not the route. Transatlantic argued that since the "normal route" from the US to Iran was through the Suez Canal, that route should be an implied term of the contract. How did the Court address this argument? It held that both parties contemplated a route through the canal but availability of this route was not made an express condition of the contract. The Court

determined that the closing of the Suez Canal was reasonably foreseeable. Does that fact alone allocate the risk to the party seeking legal excuse since Transatlantic failed to include the route in the contract? Not necessarily—said the court:

> Foreseeability or even recognition of a risk does not necessarily prove its allocation. . . . Moreover, that some abnormal risk was contemplated is probative but does not necessarily establish an allocation of the risk of the contingency that actually occurs.

What is the effect of supervening events that are foreseeable at the time the contract is formed? They are entitled to probative but not conclusive weight. Must all such events be accounted for in the contract? No—explained the court, "Parties are not always able to provide for all the possibilities of which they are aware. . . ." Finally, the alternate route was obviously not impossible as Transatlantic took that route. Does the fact that the alternative route was available and a possible alternative suggest that it is never impossible and seldom impracticable? No. How did the Court analyze this factor? Said the court:

> While it may be an overstatement to say that increased cost and difficulty of performance never constitute impracticability, to justify relief there must be more of a variation between expected cost and the cost of performing by an available alternative than is present in this case, where the promisor can legitimately be presumed to have accepted some degree of abnormal risk, and where impracticability is urged on the basis of added expense alone.

The court quoted UCC § 2-615, comment 4 in support of this statement to the effect that "Increased cost alone does not excuse performance unless the rise in cost is due to some unforeseen contingency which alters the essential nature of the performance."

4. *Force majeure clause.* Would the presence of a traditional *force majeure* clause have protected Transatlantic in this case? Black's Law Dictionary defines such a clause as follows:

> A contractual provision allocating the risk if performance becomes impossible or impracticable, esp. as a result of an event or effect that the parties could not have anticipated or controlled.

That definition does not explain or define the function of such a clause if triggered. Its function may, depending on the particular wording, excuse delay while the condition continues, discharge any further duty to perform, or apply in some other fashion. Does a *force majeure* clause simply grant a legal excuse or does it also grant a positive remedy for an alternative but more expensive performance? It can do either or both depending on the particular wording. If only the former, what language would you have provided in the contract to protect Transatlantic? A clause might have been included as follows:

> The charge for freight of $305,842.92 is calculated on a sea voyage between the two ports via the Suez Canal. If, for any reason, this route of voyage has to be changed, creating increased costs of transportation, any and all such increased cost (including the carrier's reasonable profit) shall be chargeable to and paid by the cargo owner.

Why do you suppose Transatlantic failed to include such a clause in the contract? Perhaps the contract of carriage was based on a US government invitation to bid and the addition of such a clause to Transatlantic's bid documents could have made its bid nonresponsive and thus it would have been automatically rejected. Do you think the United States would have agreed? Not if some other carrier were willing to undertake the freight contract without the inclusion of such a clause. If not, what does that failure alone and the resulting silence suggest? That the risk of increased cost through altered route was foreseeable and, as a matter of interpretation of the contract, assumed by Transatlantic. Does it preclude recovery for additional compensations? According to the court the answer is "Yes" unless the standard set out in UCC § 2-615 can be invoked, "Increased cost alone does not excuse performance unless the rise in cost is due to some unforeseen contingency which alters the essential nature of the performance."

5. *Impracticability and the availability of insurance.* See text. Could the cost of insurance policies that would have covered the supervening event provide any information regarding whether such an event would have been in the contemplation of the parties? Yes. Alternatively, what if the United States could show that there was a well-developed insurance market for exactly the type of risk actually caused by the supervening event, but that Transatlantic did not purchase such insurance. Would that showing strengthen or weaken Transatlantic's case? It would strengthen its case. What if Transatlantic could show that no insurer would have been willing to insure against the risk of canal closure at any price? This would support the argument that Transatlantic knew of and assumed the risk of canal closure.

6. *Supervening events and law by other means.* See text. In the absence of effective state enforcement mechanisms, how can the parties protect themselves against the risk of supervening events? By appropriate careful and explicit drafting.

B. MODERN IMPOSSIBILITY, IMPRACTICABILITY, AND FRUSTRATION DOCTRINES

Mel Frank Tool & Supply, Inc. v. Di-Chem Co.
CASE BRIEF

This is a 1998 decision of the Iowa Supreme Court. D-Chem ("DC") leased space in a building for "storage and distribution" purposes from Mel Frank Tool ("MFT"). After the lease took effect the city, by ordinance, prohibited the storage of "hazardous materials" in the building because of its lack of fire extinguisher installation and other loss preventive features. DC's business included the storage of hazardous materials and accordingly, DC gave notice of termination of the lease on the grounds that the new ordinance made performance of the lease impossible, thus releasing DC from further liability under the lease. MFT sued for breach of the lease and won in the district court. That decision was affirmed on appeal to the Supreme Court.

The opinion recited the following facts: MFT, prior to conclusion of the lease, new that the business of the lessee would involve storage of chemicals, but no knowledge that such chemicals would be hazardous; DC's business included storage of hazardous chemicals but included storage of other chemicals; the lease required DC to "make no unlawful use of the premises and . . . to comply with all . . . City Ordinances"; the fire chief ordered the removal of all hazardous materials unless and until the building was brought up to code for such uses; MFT decided that the cost of upgrading the building was prohibitive and he declined to do so; DC claimed that the city's position "makes the structure useless to us as a chemical warehouse"; and no representation had been made to DC that the warehouse was suitable for any specific purpose.

The court reviewed the law of impossibility of performance as set out in Restatement (Second) of Contracts. It quoted the following statement, "An extraordinary circumstance may make performance so vitally different from what was reasonably to be expected as to alter the essential nature of that performance." In these circumstances said the court, again quoting from the Restatement, "the court must determine whether justice requires a departure from the general rule that the obligor bear the risk that the contract may become more burdensome or less desirable." Whether such extraordinary circumstances existed was a question of law for the court. Said the court, interpreting the Restatement, "The rationale behind the doctrines of impracticability and frustration is whether the nonoccurrence of the circumstance was a basic assumption on which the contract was made. . . . The parties need not have been conscious of alternatives for them to have had a "basic assumption."

Again citing the Restatement rationale the court said:

> [T]he obligor is relieved of his duty because the contract, having been made on a different "basic assumption," is regarded as not covering the case that has arisen. It is an omitted case, falling within a "gap" in the contract. Ordinarily, the just way to deal with the omitted case is to hold that the obligor's duty is discharged, in the case of changed circumstances, or has never arisen, in the case of existing circumstances, and to shift the risk to the obligee.

The court identified this case as one of frustration of purpose, citing Restatement (Second) of Contracts § 265. For frustration of purpose to be operative three conditions had to be met: the purpose frustrated must be the principal purpose of the contract, that purpose must be substantially frustrated, and the nonoccurrence of the frustrating event must have been a basic assumption of the parties at the time of contracting.

The Supreme Court then summarized applicable law as follows:

> A subsequent governmental regulation like a statute or ordinance may prohibit a tenant from legally using the premises for its originally intended purpose. In these circumstances, the tenant's purpose is substantially frustrated thereby relieving the tenant from any further obligation to pay rent. The tenant is not relieved from the obligation to pay rent if there is a serviceable use still available consistent with the use provision in the lease. The fact that the use is less valuable or less profitable or even unprofitable does not mean the tenant's use has been substantially frustrated.

The court then held that DC had not carried its affirmative burden of proof that its principal purpose for leasing the facility—storing and distributing chemicals—was substantially frustrated by the city's actions. Its business included the storage and distribution of chemicals that were not hazardous and this portion of its business was not precluded by reason of the new ordinance.

DC had argued that provisions of the lease indicated assumption of this risk by the lessor. To the contrary, the court found that the lease provisions cited by DC referred only to the circumstance of substantial loss or destruction of the building by fire.

INTERESTING DISCUSSION ISSUES

1. *The similarity of the requirement that the mistake or oversight go to the basis of the transaction under the doctrines of mistake of fact, impossibility-impracticability, and frustration of purpose. Sherwood v. Walker* enunciated the doctrine that for relief based on mutual mistake of fact the mistake had to be "basic." *Lenawee* did not change that

aspect of the doctrine. Both *Transatlantic* and *Mel Frank* establish a comparable requirement with respect to any supervening event. The merit of this requirement is obvious. All three doctrines, if applied, lead to the disappointment of the expectations of one of the parties who, by assumption, is innocent. Such a disappointment should occur only in the most serious disruption of expectations, and then only when the risk of that disruption was not allocated expressly or impliedly under the contract, and was not caused by the fault of the party seeking relief.

The introductory notes point out that the relief granted for basic mutual mistake is avoidance of the contract with, as required, appropriate restitutionary adjustment. The relief for impossibility, impracticability and frustration, according to the notes, is not avoidance but excuse of any duty of further performance under the contract. Students may have difficulty is seeing this difference and whether there should be such a difference. After all, Judge Skelly Wright said that if there was a remedy in that case for impossibility/impracticability then the result would be a declaration that the contract was a nullity (same result as retroactive avoidance). The real difference, however, is best seen against the facts of *Mel Frank*. Assume that the frustration of purpose was found to be basic. The correct relief would be not avoidance *ab initio* of the lease but rather relief of DC from any further obligation going forward under the lease. Nevertheless, some cases of impossibility-impracticability-frustration can pose challenging problems involving the need of restitution-based relief.

2. *The importance of the burden of proof in cases involving affirmative defenses.* Students need to be reminded that the basic ruling of the court in this case was that the defendant failed to satisfy its burden of proof under the affirmative defense that the contract was vitiated under the doctrine of frustration of purpose. The defendant, then, failed to prove that the storage and distribution of hazardous materials was the basic purpose of the lease as understood by both parties.

NOTES AND QUESTIONS

1. *Supervening impracticability by governmental regulation.* Restatement (Second) of Contracts § 261 provides that a party's duty to perform is discharged when made "impracticable" by a supervening event occurring without fault of the discharged party and whose nonoccurrence was a basic assumption of the contract. Restatement (Second) of Contracts § 264 states a specific instance in which the nonoccurrence of a supervening event was a basic assumption of the contract. Compliance with a change in law or regulation is such a supervening event. Restatement (Second) of Contracts § 264, *cmt. a*

provides: "It is a 'basic assumption on which the contract was made' that the law will not intervene to make performance impracticable when it is due." The fact that it is "possible" for a party to perform if that party breaks the law is irrelevant.

Restatement (Second) of Contracts § 261 clearly provides that performance will not be discharged if the "language or circumstances" indicate that performance is not to be discharged notwithstanding the occurrence of an otherwise qualifying supervening change in governmental regulations or orders. In such a case, the affected party essentially agrees or assumes the risk of foregoing the legal excuse and paying damages for the resulting unexcused breach by failure to perform. Restatement (Second) of Contracts § 264, *cmt. b* makes clear that the governmental regulation may emanate from any level of government and distinctions between "law," "regulation," and "order" are disregarded.

It was clear that the change in the Fire Code occurred after the lease was executed. The lease prohibited any unlawful use of the premises but at the time of the lease storage of hazardous materials was presumably not unlawful Indeed, if Mel Frank made certain changes to the building (sprinkler, exhaust, spill and drainage), the hazardous materials could continue to be stored on the premises. But it is equally clear that the hazardous materials could not be stored after the Fire Code change without alterations. Viewed this way, this issue translates to whether Mel Frank was required by the lease to make the alterations and if not was Di-Chem excused from the lease because it could not continue to store hazardous materials. While the alterations were discussed, no agreement was reached and so Di-Chem vacated, Mel Frank sued for breach of lease, and Di-Chem defended in part asserting legal excuse by impracticability from supervening change in governmental regulations.

Does the Court accept the impracticability doctrine as stated in Restatement (Second) of Contracts §§ 261 and 264? Yes. If so, why did Di-Chem lose? Because the basic purpose of the lease, the storage and distribution of chemicals, was not frustrated—only that portion of the business relating to hazardous materials. Was it clear that a basic assumption of the contract at the time it was formed included the notion that supervening governmental regulation would not prohibit Di-Chem from using the building as for its intended purpose of "storage and distribution?" Yes. Total interference with that business would have frustrated not only the basic but also the total business purpose of the lease as defined in the lease. Is the storage of hazardous materials "storage" within the meaning of the lease language? Yes. Is it relevant that Mel Frank did not know exactly what type of materials were to be stored on the premises provided such storage was legal at the time the lease was executed? Had he known that the chemicals to be stored included hazardous materials, this could have strengthened the argument that storage of such chemicals constituted a basic purpose of the lease. Was the case decided on the basis of Restatement (Second) of Contracts §§ 261 and 264? No—on the basis of § 265, frustration of purpose. Did the change in the Fire Code prevent the property from being used for "storage and distribution?" No—a factor fundamental to the court's disposition of the case.

2. *Supervening frustration.* Assuming for the moment that the change in the Fire Code did not prevent the premises from being used for "storage and distribution" then the Restatement (Second) of Contracts §§ 261 and 264 impracticability legal excuse is not available to Di-Chem. Stated another way, the premises remain available for use in accordance with the terms of the lease. If so, why does the Court and Di-Chem shift analysis to Restatement (Second) of Contracts §§ 265 and discharge by frustration of purpose? The argument is that while performance may continue to be practicable, such performance does not satisfy the basic purpose of the agreement—see the *Krell* case. In *Krell,* performance of the lease remained completely possible—the point was that the basic purpose to be accomplished by the lease, watching Edward VII's coronation procession, was frustrated. Di-Chem now argues its purpose in leasing the premises (to store hazardous materials) has been frustrated by a supervening event (change in the Fire Code). This appears to be quite true and yet Di-Chem once again loses. Why? Because the storage and distribution of hazardous chemicals was only part of its business and not necessarily a basic part of that business, and Di-Chem failed to meet its burden of proof with respect to frustration of a basic element of the arrangement.

Recall the early roots of the frustration doctrine in *Krell v. Henry.* The landlord leased the premises to the tenant for the specific known purpose of viewing the coronation. In this case, was Mel Frank aware that Di-Chem leased the premises primarily to legally store hazardous chemicals? No. Assuming that was Di-Chem's principal or primary purpose, would frustration depend upon Mel Frank's knowledge of the same? Yes.

3. *Lease language.* Di-Chem also argued particular lease language allocated the risk of the supervening change to Mel Frank. The lease clause referenced was set forth under a section titled "Fire and Casualty, Partial Destruction of Premises." Was any portion of the premises affected by fire, casualty or partially destroyed? No.

4. *UCC frustration.* Does UCC § 2-615 cover frustration of purpose or only impracticability? Both—see notes introductory to this section of the book. If the latter, is it possible to make a frustration argument in a case governed by the UCC? Yes. If so, how would you do so? By reliance on the common law and incorporation of that law under the UCC per Article 1-103.

5. *Frustration of purpose and the availability of assignment.* See text and questions. The availability of a third party willing to accept an assignment would not affect the availability of the frustration of purpose defense.

C. DISCHARGE OF DUTY BY ASSENT OR MODIFICATION

The connection between the materials in this section and the those of the preceding section is that they show yet another way how a contract, valid and effective, as originally entered into, can be changed or discharged by a supervening event—in this case discharge by assent or modification. Total rescission of a previous agreement rarely creates any problem. Each party gives up rights under the preceding agreement and thus adequate consideration binding the new bargain.

More common and more problematic are agreements purporting to modify the duties of just one of the parties because of some unforeseen event not anticipated when the original contract was formed. Typically the agreement will contemplate a voluntary assumption of an increased duty of one party to compensate the other party for agreeing to continue to perform notwithstanding the unforeseen event. When a modification occurs, a question may arise regarding whether and when the modification is legally enforceable.

These materials consider the initially enforceable question and in the context of two forms of modified contracts. The first form is referred to as an "executory bilateral accord" that considers the duty discharged in the future but only upon completion or "satisfaction" of the accord agreement. Restatement (Second) 281(1). Until the occurrence of the event of that satisfaction, the referenced duty is not discharged but merely suspended. The obligor's breach of the satisfaction terms entitles the obligee to elect to sue for breach of either the original contract or the executory accord agreement. Restatement (Second) 281(2). This has enormous consequences with regard to the settlement of lawsuits and is amplified in the *Clark* case below. The second form is referred to as a "substituted contract." Restatement (Second) of Contracts § 279. Unlike an executory bilateral accord, a substituted contract contemplates that an obligee accepts the substituted contract (rather than the later satisfaction) in satisfaction of the obligor's duty under the original contract. Restatement (Second) of Contracts § 279(1). If the substituted contract involves the substitution of another party to release the original obligor, the substituted contract results in a "novation." Restatement (Second) of Contracts § 280. Once a contract is characterized as a "substituted contract," the original duty is immediately discharged and upon a later failure of the duty under the substituted contract, the obligee may sue only to enforce the substituted contract duty. Restatement (Second) of Contracts § 279(2). The critical difference between an executory bilateral accord and a substituted contract concerns when the obligor's duty under the original contract is discharged.

Regardless of whether the modified contract is classified as an executory bilateral accord or a substituted contract, the modified contract may not be enforceable *ab initio* unless it is supported by adequate consideration. The answer depends upon whether the matter is governed by common law or the UCC. The common law still clutches to the remnants of the ancient preexisting legal duty rule and thus requires "fresh" consideration for the modified contract. That consideration is normatively found in the bargain for the obligor's modified promised performance. A "different" performance of course could precipitate the obligee voluntarily agreeing to make a new and different promise. Exactly the same performance will not do as it is merely gratuitous. Common law therefore continues to examine the comparative nature of the obligor's original and modified performance obligations in a search for a peppercorn. While a different performance may arise from the ashes of a doubtful original promised performance now subject to an honest dispute regarding its nature and extent, a mere pretense of a bargain will not do. Fortunately, while common law retained the preexisting legal duty rule, it also developed mitigating doctrines. The most important specifically addresses situations under which the common law will enforce a modification of an executory contract notwithstanding the absence of consideration (because of the preexisting legal duty rule). In cases not involving unfair pressure, Restatement (Second) of Contracts § 89(a) provides that a promise modifying an executory duty (not fully performed) is binding notwithstanding the absence of consideration provided the modification is "fair and equitable" in view of circumstances "not anticipated" when the contract was formed.

The UCC rejects entirely the preexisting legal duty rule. UCC § 2-209(a) unabashedly states that an agreement modifying a contract requires "no consideration to be binding."

1. Doctrinal Development

The next three cases consider the modern pre-existing legal duty rule in different contexts. The next section assumes the existence of a valid theory of obligation but explores whether some remnant of the Statute of Frauds nonetheless precludes enforcement.

a. Preexisting Legal Duty Rule

The preexisting legal duty rule has caused considerable tension in contract law. As the original guardian of unjustified "hold up" cases where one party refused to complete performance unless the other party paid more for originally contracted services, the doctrine soon expanded to cover cases where an honest dispute existed regarding the nature of the original services. Modern contract law considers "hold up" cases under the economic duress doctrine discussed in Chapter 6. But what remains of the common law preexisting legal duty rule in other cases? An answer is to be found in the following case which is reflected in Restatement (Second) of Contracts § 89. Some have argued that the common law consideration requirement for modifications should be abandoned (like UCC § 2-209(1)) and that the economic duress doctrine should be used to police abusive behavior involving an unwarranted threat to breach a contract.

Angel v. Murray
CASE BRIEF

This is a 1974 decision of the Supreme Court of Rhode Island. This was a suit by a resident of Newport against Murray, the city's director of finance and Maher, alleging that Maher had been illegally paid $20,000 by Murray and praying for an order that the money be repaid to the city. The city had entered into a five year refuse-collection service contract with Maher beginning in 1964. The contract provided that Maher was to be paid $137,000 per year in return for collecting and removing all combustible and noncombustible waste materials generated within the city. In June of 1967 Maher requested an additional $10,000 per year from the city council because there had been a substantial increase in the cost of collection due to an unexpected and unanticipated increase of 400 new dwelling units. Maher's testimony, which was uncontradicted, indicated the 1964 contract had been predicated on the fact that since 1946 there had been an average increase of 20 to 25 new dwelling units per year. The city council agreed to pay him an additional $10,000 for the year ending on June 30, 1968. Maher made a similar request again in June of 1968 for the same reasons, and the city council again agreed to pay an additional $10,000 for the year ending on June 30, 1969.

The trial judge found that both payments had been made in violation of law and should be refunded. There were two grounds for the trial court decision: one on technical grounds, and the other based on the absence of consideration to support the promise to pay the additional money. Said the Supreme Court, "It appears that he based this portion of the decision upon the rule that Maher had a preexisting duty to collect the refuse generated by the 400 additional units, and thus there was no consideration for the two additional payments."

The Supreme Court held that the technical ground was not justified. Recognizing that the first payment had been made and collected, and thus fully executed at the time of commencement of the suit, the court held that the presence or absence of consideration was "unimportant" (irrelevant).

The court acknowledged that, "It is generally held that a modification of a contract is itself a contract, which is unenforceable unless supported by consideration." The preexisting duty rule is applicable:

> Under this rule an agreement modifying a contract is not supported by consideration if one of the parties to the agreement does or promises to do something that he is legally obligated to do or refrains or promises to refrain from doing something he is not legally privileged to do. . . . Although the preexisting duty rule is followed by most jurisdictions, a small minority of jurisdictions, Massachusetts, for example, find that there is consideration for a promise to perform what one is already legally obligated to do because the new promise is given in place of an action for damages to secure performance. . . . This rule, however, has been widely criticized as an anomaly. . . . The primary purpose of the preexisting duty rule is to prevent what has been referred to as the "hold-up game." . . . [One] example of the "hold-up game" is found in the area of construction contracts. Frequently, a contractor will refuse to complete work under an unprofitable contract unless he is awarded additional compensation. The courts have generally held that a subsequent agreement to award additional compensation is unenforceable if the contractor is only performing work that would have been required of him under the original contract. . . . However, the courts have been reluctant to apply the preexisting duty rule when a party to a contract encounters unanticipated difficulties and the other party, not influenced by coercion or duress, voluntarily agrees to pay additional compensation for work already required to be performed under the contract. For example, the courts have found that the original contract was rescinded, . . . abandoned, . . . or waived.

The court noted Corbin's criticism of the soundness of the preexisting duty rule as a matter of social policy, and described the "modern" trend as enforcing agreements modifying contracts when unexpected and unanticipated difficulties had arisen during course of performance even though there no consideration supporting the modification. The court noted that the UCC Article 2 had dispensed with the requirement of consideration to support a contract amendment. It then quoted as support the forerunner of Restatement (Second) of Contracts § 89 which had been given tentative approval by the time of this decision. The court found that section to state the proper rule and applied it, thus dismissing the suit. This section:

> . . . only enforces a modification if the parties voluntarily agree and if (1) the promise modifying the original contract was made before the contract was fully performed on either side, (2) the underlying

circumstances which prompted the modification were unanticipated by the parties, and (3) the modification is fair and equitable.

The court found the application of that concept appropriate to the facts of the case despite the presence in the contract of the following clause 2(a):

> The Contractor, haring made his proposal after his own examinations and estimates, shall take all responsibility for, and bear, any losses resulting to him in carrying out the contract; and shall assume the defense of, and hold the City, its agents and employees harmless from all suits and claims arising from the use of any invention, patent, or patent rights, material, labor or implement, by or from any act, omission or neglect of, the Contractor, his agents or employees, in carrying out the contract. (Emphasis added).

The court observed that the trial justice had "overlooked the thrust of sec. 2(a) when read in its entirety."

INTERESTING DISCUSSION ISSUES

1. *The preexisting duty rule revisited—or why the common law may still require that a modification of an earlier contract be supported with bargained for consideration.* Corbin proved to be a weighty critic of the English courts' "preexisting legal duty" rule. Karl Llewellyn produced Article 2-209 dispensing with the need of consideration to support the amendment of a contract. The result is the limited modification of the effect of that rule found in Restatement (Second) of Contracts § 89, the application of which is illustrated by the instant case. Some students will hold the opinion that the common law approach should be dropped in favor of the UCC approach. Others will argue that we still need a means of protecting against "hold up" claims.

NOTES AND QUESTIONS

1. *Effect of full performance.* Before exploring the enforceability of an executory contract, the Court notes that the city's first promise to pay and additional $10,000 in June 1967 had been paid. No longer "executory" (performance remaining), the Court noted that ". . . consideration is only a test of the enforceability of executory promises, the presence or absence of consideration for the first payment is unimportant because the city council's agreement to make the first payment was fully executed at the time of the commencement of this action." Chapter 2 explored consideration cases involving payments in a continuing executory contract. In those cases (e.g., *Webb v. McGowin*)

the consideration doctrine was utilized as a shield by the promisor to terminate future payments—not seek a return of past payments also unsupported by consideration. Characteristically, full performance of a promise unsupported by consideration is often referred to as a completed "gift." Another equally compelling theory might be waiver or estoppel. Once the promise is fully performed, the maker waives or is estopped from using the consideration doctrine as a sword to retrieve past payments. These actions are far more rare than attempts to use the lack of consideration as a shield. See Williston on Contracts § 7.37 (4th Ed. 2006). Do you see why lack of consideration is more effective as a shield against a suit to enforce the promise than as a sword to recover payments already made? The doctrine of consideration was developed as a "form" of authenticating that a true agreement had been entered into—see the discussion in Chapter 2. Once the agreement had been fully performed on both sides there was no longer any need for such a 'form" as evidence of intent. The same is true of an executed gift—the property once effectively transferred cannot be recovered based on failure or absence of consideration.

2. *Modified contract status.* The Court notes that a modified contract is a contract itself. If so, what happened to the original contract? The answer depends upon the wording of the modification. One modification may change only a word, a sentence or a paragraph of the original agreement. Another may rescind the original agreement in its entirety, substituting the new revised agreement in place of the original agreement. Does this analogy suggest that the modification involves a simultaneous two-step process: the rescission of the original contract and a substitution of a new modified contract? In the second case but not the first. Exactly what is the significance of the "substituted contract" concept? Where this concept applies, the original contract is extinguished so that no rights or duties etc. are any longer generated by it or remaining under it. Is the importance related to the discharge of duties under the original contract by way of a substitution of the new duty? Yes. See Restatement (Second) of Contracts § 279:

> (1) A substituted contract is a contract that is itself accepted by the obligee in satisfaction of the obligor's existing duty.
> (2) The substituted contract discharges the original duty and breach of the substituted contract by the obligor does not give the obligee a right to enforce the original duty.

3. *Partial payment of a debt.* As the Court notes, the quintessential modern pre-existing legal duty rule concerns enforceability of a creditor's promise to accept less than the full amount of the debt owed in order to induce a lump-sum payment of less than the full amount owed. Is the creditor then precluded from seeking the remaining unpaid balance from the debtor? Not if the rule is applied.

Courts have mitigated the harshness of this application of the rule by finding that any new promise by the debtor, be it ever so small, is sufficient to make the compromise enforceable. Thus a promise by the debtor to pay a week earlier than obligated under the debt contract will support the modification agreement. If the creditor's promise was not supported by consideration, the promise to accept less than the full amount of the debt is not enforceable. Unless the parties contested or disputed the precise amount of the debt, the preexisting legal duty rule negates consideration thereby permitting the creditor to accept the partial payment and sue for the balance. Indeed, the preexisting legal duty rule owes its origins to the partial debt payment context. However, dissatisfaction with the outcome has created exceptions that can nearly eclipse the general rule. For example, nearly any bargained for consideration in the form of a variation of the debtor's obligation to pay a fixed sum of money on a fixed date will do. See text for further detail.

4. *The seamen hold-up case.* See text.

5. *The absence of coercion and consideration.* The Court notes that the trend is to uphold contract modifications voluntarily made even when traditional consideration is absent. Given the preexisting legal duty rule focuses on a lack of consideration as the reason not to enforce the modified promise, is the absence of coercion in the traditional "hold-up game" all that is necessary? No—under Restatement (Second) of Contracts § 89, the modification must be fair and equitable in view of circumstances not anticipated by the parties when the contract was made, or to the extent that justice requires enforcement in view of material change of position in reliance on the promise. The Court adopts the rationale of Restatement (Second) of Contracts § 89 to enforce the city's promise. However, the preexisting legal duty rule is reflected in Restatement (Second) of Contracts § 73. Could the Court have just as easily decided the case under Restatement (Second) of Contracts § 73 by finding a "peppercorn" of consideration in the similar but yet different refuse collection performance obligation? The court could only have reached this result if it found that there was a genuine dispute between the parties as to the meaning and application of the contract, which dispute was compromised under the terms of the modified agreement. Why did the Court determine that the modification was "fair and equitable in view of circumstances not anticipated by the parties when the contract was made" within the meaning of Restatement (Second) of Contracts § 89? So as to preclude the rule from being used to justify "hold up" modifications. Did the Court reverse the trial court because the lower court had applied the wrong law or found the wrong facts? Because the trial court had applied the wrong law and because it had failed to appraise the facts correctly, namely the preexisting legal duty rule without the § 89

qualification. Did not the trial court determine as a factual matter that "these 400 additional units were within the contemplation of the parties when they entered into the contract"? The Supreme Court reversed this finding of fact. If so, why the reversal? Because the trial court finding was not supported by the record reviewed as a whole.

b. Agreed Resolution of Disputes—Accord and Satisfaction

The preexisting legal duty rule discussion above relates mostly to the common law assumption that consideration is lacking when the parties agree to modify an agreement under which an obligor assumes no greater or different burden than imposed under the original contract. However, when a valid dispute (versus improper threat of breach) is introduced into the equation, the consideration analysis shifts.

The determination of the existence of a valid dispute involves some uncertainty. At one extreme, the common law is clear that the surrender of or forebearance to assert an "invalid claim" is not consideration for the promise received in exchange. In both cases, the promisor may avoid the promise as not supported by consideration. Of course, the issue is when a claim is "invalid." Generally, a claim is invalid if there is a valid defense to enforceability. But a claim may be believed to be valid and thus fairly traded by way of bargain and consideration. Early courts applied an objective test of probable validity. The Restatement (First) required that the person surrendering the claim have an "honest and reasonable" belief in the claim's possible validity. This involved both a subjective and an objective element of assessment. The modern trend is to require an honest belief in the possible validity of the claim—objectively determined invalidity may serve as a basis for inferring lack of honesty or good faith. But under Restatement (Second) of Contracts § 74, where a claim is clearly not objectively doubtful, the subjective standard will suffice only where the person asserting the subjective belief can also show that belief honestly existed, thus the requirement that the party prove good faith belief. While it is certainly easier to prove a belief is honest when any objectively reasonable person would also entertain the belief (unlikely since the claim was not objectively doubtful), the subjective good faith standard at least provides the party asserting the belief an opportunity to prove that belief to a jury.

Assuming that the claim satisfies the doubtful or belief test, does the settlement agreement discharge the claim? The answer depends upon whether the parties intend that the settlement arrangement as an "accord and satisfaction" or rather a "substituted contract."

Clark v. Elza
CASE BRIEF

This is a 1979 decision of the Court of Appeals of Maryland. Elza sued Clark as a result of injuries received in a motor accident. Prior to trial the parties entered into an oral agreement to settle the pending lawsuit. Papers were prepared and sent to Elza who refused to sign them saying that he had new evidence of more serious injuries. Clark filed a motion to enforce the settlement. At the trial Elza argued that the settlement was not binding because "it was merely an executory accord, and could only be enforced upon satisfaction." The court observed that if the agreement were a substituted contract, as opposed to an executory accord, then it would be binding. Finding that the intention of the parties was to create an executory accord, the trial judge denied the motion of the defendants to enforce the settlement. The Court of Special Appeals dismissed Clark's appeal on grounds that the ruling on the motion was not appealable at that point in the lawsuit. The Supreme Court granted Clark's petition for review and held that the motion was properly appealable at that point.

The court then dealt with the trial court's ruling that the agreement was an executory accord and not a substitute contract. The court quoted Corbin's definition of an "executory accord":

> The term "accord executory" is and always has been used to mean an agreement for the *future discharge* of an existing claim by a substituted performance. In order for an agreement to fall within this definition, it is the promised performance that is to discharge the existing claim, and not the promise to render such performance. Conversely, all agreements for a future discharge by a substituted performance are accords executory. It makes no difference whether or not the existing claim is liquidated or unliquidated, undisputed or disputed, except as these facts bear upon the sufficiency of the consideration for some promise in the new agreement. It makes no difference whether or not a suit has already been brought to enforce the original claim; or whether that claim arises out of an alleged tort or contract or quasi-contract. . . ." (Emphasis Added)

The court then contrasted the nature and function of a "substituted contract:

> On the other hand, where the parties intend the new agreement itself to constitute a substitute for the prior claim, then this substituted contract immediately discharges the original claim. Under this latter type of arrangement, since the original claim is fully extinguished at the time the agreement is made, recovery may only be had upon the substituted contract.

The distinction between these two types of settlement agreement raises a factual issue of the parties' intent. In case of doubt as to that intent, the court found a presumption applicable that "the parties each intended to surrender their old rights and liabilities only upon performance of the new agreement. In other words, unless there is clear evidence to the contrary, an agreement to discharge a pre-existing claim will be regarded as an executory accord." Thus, on the instant facts, the court agreed with the trial court that the parties here intended an executory accord and not a substitute contract. A release was to be executed upon performance of the settlement contract. Had the parties intended a substitute contract, the underlying tort action would have been extinguished.

The trial court erred, however, in permitting Elza to proceed with the complaint following the making of the executory accord. While it was true that an executory accord does not operate to discharge the previous claim, parties generally intend that the previous action is to be suspended during the period for performance of the accord. As long as the debtor has committed no breach of the accord the creditor should not be allowed to proceed with the action. The court found this view preferable to that enunciated in several earlier cases and consistent with Restatement (First) of Contracts § 417:

> Except as stated in §§ 142, 143 with reference to contracts for the benefit of third persons and as stated in § 418, the following rules are applicable to a contract to accept in the future a stated performance in satisfaction of an existing contractual duty, or a duty to make compensation:
>
> (a) Such a contract does not discharge the duty, but suspends the right to enforce it as long as there has been neither a breach of the contract nor a justification for the creditor in changing his position because of its prospective non-performance.
>
> (b) If such a contract is performed, the previously existing duty is discharged.
>
> (c) If the debtor breaks such a contract the creditor has alternative rights. He can enforce either the original duty or the subsequent contract.
>
> (d) If the creditor breaks such a contract, the debtor's original duty is not discharged. The debtor acquires a right of action for damages for the breach, and if specific enforcement of that contract is practicable, he acquires an alternative right to the specific enforcement thereof. If the contract is enforced specifically, his original duty is discharged.

Thus an executory accord does not discharge the underlying claim until it is performed. Until there is a breach of the accord, or justifiable change of position based on prospective non-performance, or satisfaction of it, the original cause of action is suspended. It was logical to hold that executory accords were enforceable since they are simply a type of bilateral contract. The decision of the trial court was reversed and the case remanded.

In a footnote at the end of the case the court noted that Elza had argued in his brief that the settlement agreement should be avoided on the basis of mutual mistake. For procedural reasons the court declined to review or consider this argument.

INTERESTING DISCUSSION ISSUES

1. *The enforceability of an "executory accord."* It is difficult to understand why earlier courts might have had reservations about enforcing an "executory accord." It is, after all, a bilateral (usually) contract with promises by both parties to be performed in the future, and enforceable like any other executory contract.

2. The *difference between an "executory accord" and a substitute contract.* The difference between these two ways of dealing with a settlement agreement is of obvious importance to the parties to a settlement. Perhaps the most important part of this case is to alert the future draftsperson of a settlement agreement to the need to be explicit: (1) the accord, though executory, is intended to be enforceable while still executory; (2) in the event of breach by the defendant offering the settlement payment, the plaintiff intends explicitly to retain the right to elect to reinstate the lawsuit rather than be restricted to suing for the amount of the agreed settlement.

NOTES AND QUESTIONS

1. *Accord versus substituted performance or substituted contract.* Elza filed a tort suit seeking damages from Clark for negligent physical injury. Thereafter, the parties reached an "oral agreement" to settle the tort lawsuit by Clark paying $9,500. Later Elza refused to sign various release and settlement documents arguing that a subsequent discovery disclosed the injuries were more serious than thought. That explains Elza's motive but is that adequate to breach an oral promise to settle? Not if there was an effective oral agreement to settle the lawsuit. What was the consideration for Elza's promise to settle? Clark's promise to pay $9,500, the agreed amount of the settlement. Assuming consideration existed, why did Elza argue the settlement was an accord and not a substituted contract? A finding that the parties had entered into a substituted contract would have extinguished Elza's tort claim, leaving Elza a remedy only on the substituted contract.

According to Restatement (Second) of Contracts § 281(1) an "accord" is an enforceable bilateral contract itself under which an obligee (Elza) promises to accept a stated performance ($9,500) in satisfaction of the obligor's (Clark) existing tort liability duty. The Court refers to a bilateral accord as an "executory accord." Performance of the accord is the satisfaction of the bilateral promise and discharges the original duty. But until the satisfaction of the bilateral executory accord, the obligor's (Clark's) duty is merely suspended. Only actual satisfaction (payment) according to the terms of the bilateral accord agreement together with execution and delivery of the release "discharges" the obligor's (Clark's) duty under the tort suit. Until discharge, the original duty is simply suspended. Restatement (Second) of Contracts § 281(2). As with any bilateral contract, either party can breach the executory accord. A breach by the obligor (Clark) in the form of a failure to fully satisfy the accord, gives the obligee (Elza) a choice: (i) pursue the original tort suit or (ii) pursue the breach of the accord contract. Compare Restatement (Second) of Contracts § 281(2)(obligor breach with obligee right to pursue either claim) and § 281(3) (obligee breach entitles obligor to seek specific performance of the accord—in this case in the form of a "Motion to Enforce Settlement").

The most natural corollary to "accord and satisfaction" is the concept of a "substituted contract." Restatement (Second) of Contracts § 279(1) defines a "substituted contract" as one that is itself accepted by the obligee (Elza) in satisfaction of the obligor's (Clark) existing duty. Unlike with accord and satisfaction, Elza can only sue for breach of the substituted contract and may no longer pursue the tort claim as it was discharged upon acceptance of the substituted contract.

However, a third alternative exists not well articulated by the Court and perhaps not by Elza's counsel. Restatement (Second) of Contracts § 278(1) considers the effect of an offer of a "unilateral accord." Like any unilateral offer, the offer may be revoked by the offeror at anytime prior to acceptance (satisfaction). In this case, a unilateral offer requires acceptance by performance and thus a contract can only be created by the acceptance. Revocation of the offer prior to performance is not a breach of contract because no contract has yet been concluded. Restatement (Second) of Contracts §§ 50(2) and 53(3).

With these three alternatives in mind, how would you analyze Elza's intent? Do you think Elza intended to create a (i) unilateral accord offer, (ii) bilateral executory accord, or (iii) substituted contract? It is more likely that both parties intended an oral agreement whereby both promised to settle the lawsuit but such settlement was to be contingent on the timely execution of the paper work and the exchange of money for release. Does it make any sense for Elza to argue bilateral executory accord versus substituted contract when the outcome under either is the same if Elza breaches? Under the earlier case law referred to by the supreme court the executory accord would not have been enforceable. By making the accord enforceable this court created new law, following the lead of the Restatement, for the state.

If you represented Elza, which type of settlement arrangement would you suggest? I would recommend against a substituted contract because that version eliminates the lawsuit and leaves Elza only a new suit to be brought for failure to perform the settlement agreement. Since settlements are presumptively compromises by both parties, the substitute contract would hold Elza to the compromise even though he was not assured of payment in hand under the settlement agreement. What factors would lead you to seek a substituted contract over a bilateral executory accord? We cannot think of any so far as Elza is concerned. The accord would give Elza the option of resuming the tort law suit or suing for breach of the settlement agreement—the best of both worlds. While a substitute contract might simplify contested issues of fact, Elza would have that option under the executory accord. Given that a breach of a bilateral executory accord gives your client more options (pursue either the original tort suit or the breach of settlement contract claim), why would you seek a substituted contract? We cannot think of a good reason why Elza would want a substitute contract which perhaps explains the presumption, recited by the court, in favor of an accord and against a substituted contract. Which would you prefer as defense counsel for Clark and why? If the settlement number was attractive, and in my opinion there was substantially higher liability potential over and above the settlement number, I would want to lock that number in by means of a substitute agreement. This would preclude Elza from pursuing the tort action and would limit his claim to enforcement of the settlement agreement at the stipulated number. Assuming Elza prefers an accord rather than a substituted contract, what factors would cause you to advise a unilateral accord rather than a bilateral accord? We cannot think of any—unilateral contracts are usually a "snare and a delusion." Once you determine which arrangement is preferred, how can you assure your client obtains the desired result? By the use of carefully drafted precise language in a signed written agreement.

2. *Mistake law and personal injury settlements.* As acknowledged in footnote 4, Elza 's counsel also argued that even if a valid bilateral executory accord was created, the contract was voidable by reason of mutual mistake. It is quite common for an injured party to seek to avoid an earlier settlement agreement even after settlement proceeds are accepted. Defendant's insurance counsel may often seek a quick settlement after the filing of a claim. The payment of the settlement is always accompanied by the execution of a release regarding any future claims arising out of the insured accident. Plaintiff's injury may not be adequately known or discoverable at the time of the settlement. When later discovered to be far more serious than anticipated, should the release be enforceable to preclude the injured plaintiff from seeking greater and more fair compensation? The "quick settlement" accomplished by an insurance adjuster is often covered by applicable

state law providing for revocation. Where the "quick settlement" follows the commencement of a lawsuit a much more difficult problem arises. Assuming an absence of fraud or misrepresentation, the attempt to revoke the settlement is usually premised on "mutual mistake." Since the release purports to cover claims 'known or unknown" it is hard to establish a basis for any such mutual mistake. The argument has been successful in a few cases where the court was able to conclude that the settlement was predicated on a range of injury and damage, which range and damage proved later to be completely inadequate due to later information.

This topic was discussed in Chapter 6 along with the mistake doctrine.

3. *Novation.* See text.

4. *UCC accord and satisfaction.* It is quite common to offer a check in "full satisfaction" of less than the amount claimed by a UCC creditor. At the very least, the offer of such a check represents an offer of a unilateral accord. If the creditor simply cashes the check, does that act constitute acceptance of the accord offer and thus extinguish the remainder of the claim? Under the discussion above, this would be the normative common law rule, provided at least a valid disputed claim existed and economic duress was not involved. Does the UCC adopt the same notion? In general, yes, but see the comments below. Depending on the size of the creditor, routine checks are cashed without examining the face for qualifying language. Thus, the common law rule might work substantial surprise under the UCC.

UCC § 1-207 specifically addresses the matter. While UCC § 1-207(1) permits the creditor to reserve all rights by so indicating on the check, a 1990 amendment adding UCC § 1-207(2) makes clear that the section does not apply to accord and satisfaction. To clarify matters, UCC § 1-207, *cmt. 3* provides:

> 3. Judicial authority was divided on the issue of whether former Section 1-207 (present subsection (1)) applied to an accord and satisfaction. Typically the cases involved attempts to reach an accord and satisfaction by use of a check tendered in full satisfaction of a claim. Subsection (2) of revised Section 1- 207 resolves this conflict by stating that Section 1-207 does not apply to an accord and satisfaction. Section 3-311 of revised Article 3 governs if an accord and satisfaction is attempted by tender of a negotiable instrument as stated in that section. If Section 3-311 does not apply, the issue of whether an accord and satisfaction has been effected is determined by the law of contract. Whether or not Section 3-311 applies, Section 1-207 has no application to an accord and satisfaction.

Prior to the 1990 amendment, the general rule was that creditors could accept and cash a full satisfaction check without compromising the remainder of their claim by simply making proper notation that, notwithstanding the full satisfaction notation, the creditor was cashing the check with a full reservation of rights. Thus, before 1990, the creditor generally prevailed in the "battle of check notations" because UCC § 1-207 trumped the traditional contrary common law rule of accord and satisfaction.

The effect of the 1990 amendment, clarified by the quoted comment 3, is rather clear. First, UCC § 1-207 does not apply to accord and satisfaction matters. As a result, the common law rule concerning accord and satisfaction once again is controlling in all UCC cases (at least those not involving a negotiable instrument). Importantly, UCC § 3-311 is referenced as controlling the law of negotiable instruments such as checks. Thus, UCC § 1-207 in essence forces resolution of the common law accord and satisfaction rules as applicable to full satisfaction checks to be resolved by UCC § 3-311. That section sets out specific statutory rules for accord and satisfaction cases involving negotiable instruments such as checks. Michael D. Floyd, "How Much Satisfaction Should You Expect From An Accord?" 26 Loy. U. Chi. L. Rev. 1 (1994) and Jay Winston, "The Evolution of Accord and Satisfaction: Common Law; UCC Section 1-207; UCC Section 3-311," 28 New Eng. L. Rev. 189 (1993).

UCC § 3-311(1) provides that the section applies to a person against whom a claim is asserted if that person proves (i) a good faith tender of an instrument to the claimant as full satisfaction of the claim, (ii) the amount of the claim was unliquidated or subject to a bona fide dispute, and (iii) the claimant obtained payment of the instrument. For this purpose, UCC § 3-103(a)(4) defines good faith as "honesty in fact and the observance of reasonable commercial standards of fair dealing." Accordingly, good faith includes both subjective and objective components regarding honesty. In such circumstances, the claim is normally discharged when the check is cashed provided the check notation in full satisfaction was conspicuous. UCC § 3-311(b). An important exception provides discharge does not occur where prior to cashing such a check, an organization claimant sent the debtor a conspicuous statement directing any such checks to be directed to a specific individual and the check was not sent to the designated person. UCC § 3-311(c)(1). Actual knowledge of authorized persons that the check was submitted in full satisfaction may also permit discharge. UCC § 3-311(d).

How do the UCC § 3-311 accord and satisfaction rules compare to the common law accord and satisfaction rules? Are there major differences? If so, what is the point of the differences? The UCC rules applicable to negotiable instruments, subject to certain exceptions, provide the same general effect as the common law. The first exception, found in UCC § 3-311(c) guards against inadvertent cashing of the check through mechanical processing without any personal review of the endorsement. The first method of protection enables the sending of a conspicuous notice to debtors that communications concerning disputed debts must be sent to a particular person, office or place. The debtor's failure to do so will negate the usual accord and satisfaction. The second enables avoidance of the accord through the repayment of the amount of the check within 90 days. Subsection (d) places some restrictions on the protections available under (c). The point of these differences is the dangers of inadvertent accord and satisfaction through modern mechanical processing. The point of these protections is well taken.

c. Dispute Resolution Under Duress

Many argued duress cases arise in the context of modification of contracts. Where one party refuses to perform even if the failure constitutes a breach, the judicial breach remedy available to the other party is slow and often will not allow the nonbreaching party to meet its contractual obligations to others. Accordingly, there is a powerful incentive for a nonbreaching party to amend the contract if only to continue its business relationship under its other contracts. Knowing this, a purported breaching party may be inclined to threaten breach simply to enhance its contractual position. When the parties modify their contract under these often difficult circumstances, the innocent party may later return to the issue and use economic duress to set aside the modification and sue for damages based on the terms of the original contract once the remaining contractual relationships are secure.

Kelsey-Hayes Co. v. Galtaco Redlaw Castings Corp.
CASE BRIEF

This is a 1990 decision of the United States District Court for the Eastern District of Michigan. Plaintiff Kelsey-Hayes ("KH") sued Galtaco Castings ("GC") alleging breach of a three year requirements contract for the purchase by KH of castings to be made by GC. KH also sought a declaratory judgment that it did not have to pay GC's price increases to which it agreed in 1989 (part way through the three year contract). KH asserted that the 1989 modifications to the three year contract were (1) agreed to under duress, (2) unconscionable, (3) demanded by GC in bad faith, and (4) constituted unjust enrichment to GC. GC responded that KH had waived its breach of contract claims and that KH's other claims were without merit. GC counterclaimed for the monies owed under the 1989 modifications and KH moved for leave to file a second amended complaint. GC moved for summary judgment.

The court suggested in Footnote 4 that there appeared to be no merit to KH's claims of unconscionability, bad faith and unjust enrichment, but found the allegations of duress to be relevant. The court found sufficient evidence on the issue of duress to preclude GC's motion for summary judgment—that is to say the pleadings together with associated affidavits "presented enough evidence to allow a reasonable finder of facts to conclude the 1989 agreements were executed under duress."

GC was a sole source provider of castings to KH who incorporated these castings into brake assemblies sold to major automobile manufacturers. By the spring of 1989 GC had been experiencing continued monetary losses for several years. Its board of directors decided to cease production of castings:

> Galtaco recognized that an immediate shut down of its foundry operations would seriously inconvenience its customers, because they would need additional castings before they could cover from other sources. Therefore, Galtaco offered all of its customers, including Kelsey-Hayes, an agreement to keep its foundries operating for "several months" in exchange for price increase of 30 percent effective with shipments of May 15, 1989.
>
> If Galtaco were to have immediately terminated its foundry operations, Kelsey-Hayes concluded that it would not have been able to obtain a sufficient supply of castings from alternative sources for 18-24 weeks. As a result, Kelsey-Hayes determined that declining to accept Galtaco's offer would have the effect of shutting down the assembly plants of two of its major clients, Chrysler and Ford. Kelsey-Hayes was Ford's sole source of certain brake assemblies, and Ford had no significant bank of those parts. Any interruption of the supply of brake assemblies longer than five to ten days would likely have resulted in the halting of Ford production of a vehicle line.

KH accepted this offer at a 30% price increase. KH "did not reserve any rights under the 1987 contract when it accepted Galtaco's offer." Within a month, during which period GC's other customers had found alternative suppliers, GC announced that it needed an additional 30% price increase from KH "to offset the rising fixed costs Galtaco would continue to incur if it were to remain in operation for Kelsey-Hayes' sole benefit." Having not yet found an alternate supplier KH again agreed to the second increase and again did not reserve any rights under the 1987 agreement.

KH paid for 187 shipments on a timely basis but failed to pay for the final 84 shipments (this shortfall approximating the cost of the price increases). KH did not say that it would sue GC but did "strenuously protest" GC's actions.

This suit was governed by Michigan law. Said the court:

> It is true that under Michigan law, entering a superseding, inconsistent agreement covering the same subject matter rescinds an earlier contract and operates as a waiver of any claim for breach of the earlier contract not expressly reserved.... However, a subsequent contract or modification is invalid and therefore does not supersede an earlier contract when the subsequent contract was entered into under duress.... There is sufficient evidence to allow a reasonable finder of the facts to determine that Kelsey-Hayes was under duress when it executed the 1989 agreements.

GC relied on earlier Michigan authority suggesting that, to make a claim of duress, the person must be subjected to threat of an unlawful act in the nature of a tort or crime. The court concluded, "However, the doctrine of duress has been greatly expanded since its common-law origin. Now, a contract is voidable if a party's manifestation of assent is induced by an improper threat by another party that leaves the victim no reasonable alternative," citing, among other authorities, Restatement (Second) of Contracts § 175. In so opining, the court admitted that a survey of Michigan cases involving duress revealed that there had never been a decision that explicitly adopted the modern version of duress, but concluded that the Michigan Supreme Court would rule that economic duress need not stem from an "illegal" threat.

[This prediction was stoutly denied by a more recent federal district court opinion applying Michigan law—*Whirlpool Corp. v. Grigoleit Co.*, 2006 WL 1997402, (W.D.Mich. Jul 13, 2006) Said that court:

> Because this Court's constitutional mandate counsels obedience to Michigan precedent, the Court's duty is to neither divine a rule of Michigan law as its own nor comment on the providence of existing precedent, but to apply Michigan law, without reservation. *Erie R.R.*, 304 U.S. at 78. Therefore, this Court finds that in order to avoid the parties' agreement on a theory of duress, Plaintiff must plead illegality at the hands of Defendant.
>
> In Footnote 4 in that case the court explained:
>
> FN4. Plaintiff relies heavily on Kelsey-Hayes Co. v. Galtaco Redlaw Castings Corp., 749 F.Supp. 794 (E.D. Mich. 1990). In that case, the district court predicted that if the Michigan Supreme Court revisited the issue of economic duress, it would no longer require unlawful coercion to state a cause of action. Id. at 797 n. 5. Given that Kelsey's herald did not prove true, this Court does not regard it as persuasive authority. Furthermore, while a federal court may be called upon to predict Michigan Supreme Court precedent in the

> absence of controlling authority, when Michigan's highest court has expressly considered a particular issue, federal courts are not free to disregard that edict and conclude that it would now change its mind. *Bradley v. Gen. Motors Corp.,* 512 F.2d 602, 604 (6th Cir.1975). Since the Michigan Supreme Court had expressly and repeatedly held that in order to avoid a contractual obligation because of duress, one must allege unlawful coercion, *see, e.g., Norton,* 24 N.W.2d at 135, that rule was controlling and the Kelsey court was constitutionally required to abide by it. See Note 3 in the book.]

The court identified the alleged wrongful acts as follows:

> Kelsey-Hayes has alleged wrongful acts of Galtaco in its complaint and has offered proof of them in affidavits. Specifically, Kelsey-Hayes says Galtaco threatened to breach its contract and go out of business, stopping production and delivery of castings, unless Kelsey-Hayes agreed to significant price hikes. Austin Instrument, Inc. v. Loral Corp., 29 N.Y. 2d 124, 324 N.Y.S. 2d 22, 272 N.E. 2d 533 (1971) (threat by one party to breach contract by not delivering required items is wrongful).

The court next concluded that KH had met a second requirement of the requisite proof—that KH had no reasonable alternative other than acquiescing in GC's demand. Its normal legal remedy of accepting GC's breach of contract and then suing for damages would have been inadequate under the circumstances. KH, the evidence strongly suggested, would not have been able to locate an alternate supplier. As a result its business reputation might have suffered and its major customers might have been forced to shut down automobile production lines.

The court recognized a third requirement for a successful suit based on duress—that the buyer must at least display some protest against the increased prices "putting the seller on notice that the modification is not freely entered into.... While Kelsey-Hayes did not expressly reserve the right to sue under the 1987 contract, a reasonable trier of the facts could determine its protests effectively put Galtaco on notice that the 1989 agreements were agreed to under duress."

The court next addressed GC's argument that the common law doctrine of duress had been subsumed by the UCC's "good faith" test. (See UCC § 2-209), and concluded that, "This contention is frivolous." The "duress" concept was available via UCC § 1-103.

In addition to denying GC's motion for summary judgment the court also granted KH's motion for leave to amend the complaint.

3. *Michigan case law.* See text.

INTERESTING DISCUSSION ISSUES

1. *Are there sound reasons for the "modernization" of "duress" law?* It is quite noteworthy that two federal district courts, both writing in the last twenty years, disagreed sharply on applicable Michigan law dealing with the affirmative defense of "duress." The *Kelsey* court ruled, following Restatement (Second) of Contracts § 175, that if the coercion was "wrongful" then relief under the duress doctrine was available. The *Whirlpool* court (see Note 3 in the book and discussion interpolated in the Case Brief above), likewise applying Michigan law, ruled the coercion must be "illegal." This disagreement highlights the profound effect that application of a "duress" doctrine to commercial transactions can have on the respective rights of the parties. It can override and negate the express undertakings of the parties. "Freedom of contract" theory would suggest a narrow rather than a broad application of such an invasive doctrine. In *Kelsey*, there was no doubt about the fact that Kelsey had expressly agreed to both of the price increases. Kelsey's agreement represented a volitional act taken with knowledge of the consequences. The "duress" doctrine, as discussed in Chapter 6, when sought and applied, results in the avoidance of the agreement ab initio. Such avoidance is based on a bargaining failure. Whether there can be such a bargaining failure turns, under the Restatement, on "wrongful" coercion—posing the conundrum of what is to constitute such "wrongful" behavior. Kelsey's threatened breach of contract was not "illegal"—compare the discussion of the doctrine of "efficient breach" in Chapter 9. Advocates of "efficient breach" argue that a party to any contract should be able to elect whether to perform or default and pay such damages as the wronged party can establish and collect. Thus presumably, advocates of "efficient breach" would side with Galtaco. The problem of "hold up" claims was discussed earlier in this chapter. For some the concept of a "hold up" claim involves one where good faith is lacking on the part of the asserting party. Galtaco's argument addressed this view directly—they acted, they argued, in both subjective and objective good faith.

Restatement (Second) of Contracts § 175(1) provides:

> (1) If a party's manifestation of assent is induced by an improper threat by the other party that leaves the victim no reasonable alternative, the contract is voidable by the victim.

§ 176(2) provides:

> (2) A threat is improper if the resulting exchange is not on fair terms, and
>
> (a) the threatened act would harm the recipient and would not significantly benefit the party making the threat,

(b) the effectiveness of the threat in inducing the manifestation of assent is significantly increased by prior unfair dealing by the party making the threat, or

(c) what is threatened is otherwise a use of power for illegitimate ends.

Comment *e* to this section provides in part:

> *Breach of contract.* A threat by a party to a contract not to perform his contractual duty is not, of itself, improper. Indeed, a modification induced by such a threat may be binding, even in the absence of consideration, if it is fair and equitable in view of unanticipated circumstances. See § 89. The mere fact that the modification induced by the threat fails to meet this test does not mean that the threat is necessarily improper. However, the threat is improper if it amounts to a breach of the duty of good faith and fair dealing imposed by the contract. See § 205. *As under the Uniform Commercial Code, the "extortion of a 'modification' without legitimate commercial reason is ineffective as a violation of the duty of good faith.* . . . The test of 'good faith' between merchants or as against merchants includes 'observance of reasonable commercial standards of fair dealing in the trade' (Section 2-103), and may in some situations require an objectively demonstrable reason for seeking a modification. But such matters as a market shift which makes performance come to involve a loss may provide such a reason even though there is no such unforeseen difficulty as would make out a legal excuse from performance under Sections 2-615 and 2-616." Comment 2 to Uniform Commercial Code § 2-209. However, a threat of non-performance made for some purpose unrelated to the contract, such as to induce the recipient to make an entirely separate contract, is ordinarily improper. See Illustration 9. Furthermore, a threat may be a breach of the duty of good faith and fair dealing under the contract even though the threatened act is not itself a breach of the contract. . . . (Emphasis added.)

Students may wonder whether the facts of *Kelsey* should justify the invocation of the "duress" remedy as enunciated in the Restatement.

NOTES AND QUESTIONS

1. *UCC economic duress.* As discussed in Chapter 6, the common law states explicit provisions regarding duress, including economic duress. Thus, even where a contract satisfies the statute of frauds and is supported by consideration, it may nonetheless be set aside. Restatement (Second) of Contracts § 175(1) provides that a contract is voidable by a victim where the contract was a product of an "improper

threat" leaving the victim no reasonable alternative. Regardless of whether the resulting contract is on fair terms, an "improper threat" includes a threat that is itself a breach of the duty of good faith and fair dealing. Restatement (Second) of Contracts § 176(1)(d).

The UCC does not state a specific duress or economic duress rule. However, UCC § 1-103 incorporates principles of the common law not otherwise specifically displaced, specifically including the law of duress. The seller (Galtaco) argued common law duress did not apply to a UCC case but the Court labeled that argument as "frivolous" and referenced UCC § 1-103.

The Court also rejected Galtaco's argument that since UCC § 2-209(1) specifically governed modifications of contracts and required no consideration, it displaced the common law by specific reference. Galtaco therefore relied upon UCC § 2-209, *cmt. 2*:

> 2. Subsection (1) provides that an agreement modifying a sales contract needs no consideration to be binding.
>
> However, modifications made thereunder must meet the test of good faith imposed by this Act. The effective use of bad faith to escape performance on the original contract terms is barred, and the extortion of a "modification" without legitimate commercial reason is ineffective as a violation of the duty of good faith. Nor can a mere technical consideration support a modification made in bad faith.
>
> The test of "good faith" between merchants or as against merchants includes "observance of reasonable commercial standards of fair dealing in the trade" (Section 2-103), and may in some situations require an objectively demonstrable reason for seeking a modification. But such matters as a market shift which makes performance come to involve a loss may provide such a reason even though there is no such unforeseen difficulty as would make out a legal excuse from performance under Sections 2-615 and 2-616.

Using this language, Galtaco argued the UCC had specifically displaced common law economic duress and substituted a test of "good faith." Ordinarily, Galtaco would prefer that its conduct be judged solely by reference to its own good faith. At the time of this lawsuit, UCC § 1-201(19) defined "good faith" to only require honesty in fact in the conduct or transaction concerned—a subjective test. If this standard were used, Galtaco could argue it acted in good faith by not immediately shutting down the foundry and even extended the deadline another month solely for Kelsey so it would have a supply. However, its heavy losses mandated that it receive a price increase or simply shut down the plant. Thus, Galtaco was not trying to renegotiate just the Kelsey contract in a hold-up game and it believed it acted in utmost good faith.

However, if the common law standard applies, then Kelsey need only establish that it had no reasonable alternative but to agree to the contract increase (no alternative source of brake linings) and that Galtaco's threat to breach without the price increases was a breach of good faith (subjective honest belief) and fair dealing (objectively reasonable practice in industry). Of course, the case was not at a trial stage but the Court holding will establish the issues to be tried since Galtaco's motion for summary judgment was denied.

Do you see any difference between the arguments? Yes. The common law standard, as reflected in Restatement (Second) of Contracts § 175, would have allowed Kelsey a remedy upon a showing that Galtaco's conduct was "wrongful"—that is was based on a threat to commit a breach of contract. Application of the UCC "good faith" standard might have allowed Galtaco to escape upon a showing that it acted in subjective good faith and in accordance with objective commercial standards. In other words, Galtaco might have escaped on the basis that merchants would recognize its problem of insolvency together with its efforts to protect Kelsey from severe losses based on an immediate shut down of foundry production. At trial, assuming that Kelsey had no reasonable alternative, what will decide the outcome of the case? Assuming that Kelsey made an adequate showing of protest at the time of agreeing to the price increases and met the other elements of required proof, the result at trial should follow the allegations of fact in the complaint, affidavits and depositions. How do you think the court or jury should rule given the facts as stated in the case? Again, assuming the satisfaction of the other required elements of proof, the court or jury should find that the threat of breach of contract was "wrongful." As the notes introductory to this section point out, Galtaco could have sought the protection of a bankruptcy court which might have made life tough for Kelsey.

2. *Prior case law.* Galtaco specifically cited and relied upon an Ohio case in *Roth Steel Products v. Sharon Steel Corp.*, 705 F.2d 134 (6th Cir. 1983) to argue that the UCC intended good faith as a test for contractual modifications governed by UCC § 2-201(1). Indeed, *Roth* specifically noted that the ability to modify contracts under the UCC is broader than under common law because of the UCC § 2-209(1) elimination of the consideration requirement. Specifically the court noted that:

> A party's ability to modify an agreement is limited only by Article Two's general obligation of good faith... Official Comment 2, O.R.C. Sec. 1302.12 (U.C.C. Sec. 2-209).... In determining whether a particular modification was obtained in good faith, a court must make two distinct inquiries: whether the party's conduct is consistent with "reasonable commercial standards of fair dealing in the trade," ... and whether the parties were in fact

> motivated to seek modification by an honest desire to compensate for commercial exigencies. . . . The first inquiry is relatively straightforward; the party asserting the modification must demonstrate that his decision to seek modification was the result of a factor, such as increased costs, which would cause an ordinary merchant to seek a modification of the contract. . . . The second inquiry, regarding the subjective honesty of the parties, is less clearly defined. Essentially, this inquiry requires the party asserting the modification to demonstrate that he was, in fact, motivated by a legitimate commercial reason and that such a reason is not offered merely as a pretext. . . .
>
> The second part of the analysis, honesty in fact, is pivotal. The district court found that Sharon "threatened not to sell Roth and Toledo any steel if they refused to pay increased prices after July 1, 1973" and, consequently, that Sharon acted wrongfully. Sharon does not dispute the finding that it threatened to stop selling steel to the plaintiffs. Instead, it asserts that such a finding is merely evidence of bad faith and that it has rebutted any inference of bad faith based on that finding. We agree with this analysis; although coercive conduct is evidence that a modification of a contract is sought in bad faith, that prima facie showing may be effectively rebutted by the party seeking to enforce the modification. . . . [G]ood faith insistence upon a legal right [with coercive effect] which one believes he has usually is not duress, even if it turns out that that party is mistaken and, in fact, has no such right.

At trial, if the Court applies these standards, should Galtaco prevail? Yes, based on a commercially reasonable need to close down its castings production.

3. *Cover and buyers' remedies for seller breach under the UCC.* See text. Given the uncertainty of the economic duress doctrine in Michigan at the time of this case, why do you think that Kelsey-Hayes did not claim damages under the UCC rules governing cover? There is no clear explanation.

4. *Subsequent Michigan case law.* See text.

2. Effect of Writing Restricting Oral Modification

This section considers oral modifications to written contracts. Because the law rules are different, the discussion is organized according whether the common law or UCC Statute of Frauds require the original contract to be in writing. If so, the otherwise enforceable oral modification must also generally be in writing (unless an applicable Statute of Frauds exception applies). The trouble concerns original contracts that are in writing even though the Statute of Frauds did not require the writing.

Problems arise where the original contract was reduced to writing and signed and that contract contained a provision reciting that it could only be amended by a further signed writing and not orally. Such a private "statute of frauds" purports to protect the parties from false oral allegations of amendment. The other side of this argument is that parties should be free to modify their agreement, including the clause requiring signed written amendments. This particular tension has caused more than its fair share of difficulty.

Such restrictive clauses can take either or both of two forms—"no oral modification" ("NOM") and/or "no oral waiver" ("NOW"). The parol evidence rule does not preclude parol evidence of either oral modification or oral waiver. The question is not evidentiary admissibility of modification or waiver but rather the legal effect of the evidence once admitted.

The common law and the UCC differ somewhat on this subject. The common law is antagonistic to such clauses while the UCC generally embraces them.

Contracts "Subject to" the Statute of Frauds

Under the common law, modification of a contract within the Statute of Frauds must also be in writing and signed by the party to be charged. Moreover, except for contracts involving the sale of goods, even a written and signed modification requires an independent enforcement obligation theory such as consideration or reliance. Where the oral modification is not enforceable, restitution "off the contract" remains available to prevent unjust enrichment. Restatement (Second) of Contracts § 375.

Contracts "Not Subject to" the Statute of Frauds

Are oral modifications required to be in writing simply because the parties chose to put the original contract in writing? Clearly, oral modifications to such written contracts are not required to be in writing simply because the original contract was in writing. However, where the original written contract includes a NOM clause (and perhaps a NOW clause as well), the common law and UCC differ on whether a NOM clause is enforceable. Since the base NOM clause is generally not enforceable under common law but generally is enforceable under the UCC, waiver and the NOW clause becomes more important.

Restatement (Second) of Contracts § 283 (with Comment *b*) establishes that a provision in an earlier contract purporting to require modification only by a subsequent writing "does not impair the effectiveness of an oral agreement of rescission." Such a provision does not limit the power of the parties to agree otherwise subsequently. Therefore the subsequent oral modification simply operated as a rescission of the prior agreement followed by a substitution of the new agreement.

The UCC specifically changes the common law and purports to approve NOM clauses by the following language: "[a] signed agreement which excludes modification or rescission except by a signed writing cannot be otherwise modified or rescinded." UCC § 2-209(2). Unfortunately, because of other UCC § 2-209 provisions, the NOM language is neither absolute nor clear.

The general language respecting NOM clauses is subject to the following proviso: "but except as between merchants such a requirement on a form supplied by a merchant must be separately signed by the other party." Accordingly, a NOM clause in an original contract between a merchant and consumer is only binding if the original contract is actually signed by the consumer. Otherwise, a consumer may avoid the operation of the clause. However, as between merchants, the clause is effective if in a controlling form agreement even if that form agreement was not signed by either party. Of course the NOM clause must be a binding part of the agreement between the merchants exchanging forms.

More importantly, UCC §§ 2-209(3)-(4) directly impact the right of a UCC party to insist on strict compliance with an otherwise enforceable UCC § 2-209(2) NOM clause. First, UCC § 2-209(4) provides a subsequent oral rescission or modification may "operate as a waiver" even though the attempt is otherwise precluded by the NOM clause under UCC § 2-209(2) or the Statute of Frauds requirement in UCC § 2-209(3). The latter exemption simply refers to an oral modification of an original agreement required to be in writing. As discussed earlier, when the Statute of Frauds requires the original agreement to be in writing, all later modification must also be in writing. The former exemption simply applies to original agreements in writing even though not required to be so by the Statute of Frauds (arguably a small domain). But in either event, the broad UCC § 2-209(4) exemption provides that the attempt to orally modify the written agreement "can operate as a waiver."

Technically, reliance on a promise of oral modification can be used to invoke promissory estoppel to avoid the Statute of Frauds. But promissory estoppel's poorer "waiver" cousin generally does not require reliance and is not commonly thought to avoid the effect of the public law Statute of Frauds. Unlike promissory estoppel, waiver is a temporary concept normally applicable to private law terms created by the parties rather than public law. Once made, a waiver of a right to strict performance of a promise continues until retracted at which time the duty is reinstated. Thus, unless a "waiver" is coupled with consideration (rare) or promissory estoppel reliance (more common) to make it permanent, the waiving party may reinstate strict compliance with contractual terms for future and continuing performance with reasonable notice to the other party.

The *Wisconsin Knife* case below explores the effectiveness of a NOM clause and its waiver generally under the UCC.

Wisconsin Knife Works v. National Metal Crafters
CASE BRIEF

This is a 1986 decision of the United States Court of Appeals, Seventh Circuit. The majority opinion was written by Judge Posner, and the dissenting opinion by Judge Easterbrook.

The majority opinion:

Wisconsin Knife ("WK") decided to manufacture "spade bits" for sale to its parent, Black & Decker, a large producer of tools including drills. "Spade bits" are made from a chunk of metal called a "spade bit blank." Following negotiations with National Metal Crafters ("NMC") WK sent NMC a series of purchase orders on the back of each of which was printed:

> "acceptance of this order, either by acknowledgment or performance, constitutes an unqualified agreement to the following." A list of "Conditions of Purchase" follows, of which the first is:
>
> No modification of this contract, shall be binding upon Buyer [Wisconsin Knife Works] unless made in writing and signed by Buyer's authorized representative. Buyer shall have the right to make changes in the Order by a notice, in writing, to Seller.

There were six purchase orders in all, each with the identical conditions. National Metal Crafters acknowledged the first two orders (which had been placed on August 21, 1981) by letters that said, "please accept this as our acknowledgment covering the above subject order," followed by a list of delivery dates. The purchase orders had left those dates blank. Wisconsin Knife Works filled them in, after receiving the acknowledgments, with the dates that National Metal Crafters had supplied in the acknowledgments. There were no written acknowledgments of the last four orders (placed several weeks later, on September 10, 1981). Wisconsin Knife Works wrote in the delivery dates that National Metal Crafters orally supplied after receiving purchase orders in which the space for the date of delivery had again been left blank.

Delivery was due in October and November 1981. NMC missed these deadlines. WK did not declare a breach, but issued a new batch of purchase orders (later rescinded). By December 1982 NMC was producing blanks for WK under the original set of purchase orders although well behind the delivery dates in those orders. On January 13, 1983, KW notified NMC that the contract was terminated. By that date only 144,000 of the more than 281,000 blanks ordered had been delivered.

WK sued for breach of contract. NMC replied that the delivery dates provided had not been intended as firm dates, and introduced substantial evidence of WK's acquiescence in an extended delivery schedule—one that NMC was meeting. NMC also filed a counterclaim the resolution of which was not material to the main issues of the case.

The trial judge ruled that a contract had been entered into but left the jury to decide whether the contract had been modified and, if so, whether the modified contract had been broken. The jury found the contract had been modified and not broken, and WK's suit was dismissed. WK appealed.

Judge Posner opined:

> The principal issue is the effect of the provision in the purchase orders that forbids the contract to be modified other than by a writing signed by an authorized representative of the buyer. The theory on which the judge sent the issue of modification to the jury was that the contract could be modified orally or by conduct as well as by a signed writing. National Metal Crafters had presented evidence that Wisconsin Knife Works had accepted late delivery of the spade bit blanks and had cancelled the contract not because of the delays in delivery but because it could not produce spade bits at a price acceptable to Black & Decker.

He quoted UCC § 2-209(2) which provides that:

> . . . [A] signed agreement which excludes modification or rescission except by a signed writing cannot be otherwise modified or rescinded, but except as between merchants such a requirement on a form supplied by the merchant must be separately signed by the other party.

He noted that "One" might reasonably think that any signature should be that of the party to be charged rather than the offeror. But this did not have to be resolved since both parties were "merchants" within the meaning of the Code. A signed written agreement existed containing an express NOM clause and covering all of the purchase orders. NMC prepared and delivered "pert charts" and delivered these to WK showing new target dates for delivery but not purporting to modify the contract. These charts were not signed by WK. He then concluded, "that the clause forbidding modifications other than in writing was valid and applicable and that the jury should not have been allowed to consider whether the contract had been modified in some other way."

But, he added, this may, however, have been harmless error" because of the language of UCC § 2-209(4) which he said "provides that an 'attempt at modification' which does not satisfy a contractual requirement that modifications be in writing nevertheless 'can operate as a waiver.' Although in instructing the jury on modification the judge did not use the word "waiver," maybe he gave the substance of a waiver instruction and maybe therefore the jury found waiver but called it modification." He concluded that the jury instruction could have been understood as one including the possibility of waiver. To determine whether the instruction was in substance an instruction on waiver it was necessary to consider the background of §2-209.

He expressed concern about the possibility of "hold up" claims for modification. The common law, he said, dealt with this problem by refusing to enforce modifications unsupported by fresh consideration:

> But this solution is at once over-inclusive and under-inclusive—the former because most modifications are not coercive and should be enforceable whether or not there is fresh consideration, the latter because, since common law courts inquire only into the existence and not the adequacy of consideration, a requirement of fresh consideration has little bite. B might give A a peppercorn, a kitten, or a robe in exchange for A's agreeing to reduce the contract price, and then the modification would be enforceable and A could no longer sue for the original price.

The drafters of the UCC took a fresh approach by making modifications enforceable even if not supported by consideration (§ 2-209(1)) and looking to the doctrines of duress and bad faith for the main protection against exploitive or opportunistic attempts at modification. But they also allowed the parties to exclude subsequent oral modifications. "National Metal Crafters argues that two subsections later they took back this grant of power by allowing an unwritten modification to operate as a waiver." The common law refused to enforce NOMs on the ground that the parties were always free to agree orally to cancel their contract along with the NOM clause. He suggested that the UCC drafters may have felt the need, having removed the requirement of consideration for a modification, to replace that protection with something else—the power to enforce a NOM:

> An equally important point is that with consideration no longer required for modification, it was natural to give the parties some means of providing a substitute for the cautionary and evidentiary function that the requirement of consideration provides; and the means chosen was to allow them to exclude oral modifications.

If § 209(4) was interpreted so broadly that any oral modification is effective as a waiver, then both subsections (2) and (4) would be superfluous and we would be back in the common law, only without any requirement of consideration. He considered an argument that would distinguish between a modification that substitutes a new term for an old, and a waiver which merely removes an old term. He found this to be a distinction without a difference. Whether called modification or waiver, NMC was seeking to nullify a key term other than by a signed writing. "If it can get away with this merely by testimony about an oral modification, section 2-209(2) becomes very nearly a dead letter."

He found the answer in the language of § 2-209(4) which does not say that an attempted modification is a waiver but rather that it can operate as a waiver. He found that both subsections could be harmonized if an attempted modification is effective as a waiver only if there is reliance. Reliance, he said, was a common substitute for consideration in making promises legally enforceable, "in part because it adds something in the way of credibility to the mere say-so of one party. The main purpose of forbidding oral modifications is to prevent the promisor from fabricating a modification that will let him escape his obligations under the contract; and the danger of successful fabrication is less if the promisor has actually incurred a cost, has relied."

He said that he found support for this view in the secondary literature. He then explained that this interpretation was not inconsistent with § 2-209(5) "which allows a waiver to be withdrawn while the contract is executory, provided there is no 'material change of position in reliance on the waiver.'" The point of that section was that a waiver could be withdrawn unless there had been reliance. This subsection was not limited in its application to modifications invalid under subsections (2) and (3): "it applies, for example, to an express written and signed waiver, provided only that the contract is still executory."

Addressing the basic purpose of the drafters, he said:

> We know that the draftsmen of section 2-209 wanted to make it possible for parties to exclude oral modifications. They did not just want to give "modification" another name—"waiver." Our interpretation gives effect to this purpose. It is also consistent with, though not compelled by, the case law. There are no Wisconsin cases on point.

He found fault with the jury instruction since it contained no reference to reliance, "that is, to the incurring of costs by National Metal Crafters in reasonable reliance on assurances by Wisconsin Knife Works that late delivery would be acceptable." It was therefore necessary to remand the case back to the trial court. He found it unnecessary to discuss other claimed errors at the trial but he did point out that WK's objections to the introduction of parol evidence have no merit once the issue is recast as one of waiver." He then concluded with words likely to ring in the ears of the trial judge on remand:

> Obviously National Metal Crafters has a strong case both that it relied on the waiver of the delivery deadlines and that there was no causal relationship between its late deliveries and the cancellation of the contract. We just are not prepared to say on the record before us that it is such a strong case as not to require submission to a jury. . . .

The minority opinion

Judge Easterbrook dissented holding that there was no basis for reading any requirement of reliance into the provision of UCC § 2-209(4) providing that "attempt at modification" might be a "waiver." He said, "I do not think that detrimental reliance is an essential element of waiver under § 2-209(4). . . . "Waiver" is not a term the UCC defines. At common law "waiver" means an intentional relinquishment of a known right. A person may relinquish a right by engaging in conduct inconsistent with the right or by a verbal or written declaration. I do not know of any branch of the law-common, statutory, or constitutional-in which a renunciation of a legal entitlement is effective only if the other party relies to his detriment. . . . The introduction of a reliance requirement into a body of law from which the doctrine of consideration has been excised is novel."

He then pointed to an arguable inconsistency between the majority view and § 2-209(5):

> Section 2-209(5) states that a person who "has made a waiver affecting an executory portion of the contract may retract the waiver" on reasonable notice " unless the retraction would be unjust in view of a material change of position in reliance on the waiver." Section 2-209 therefore treats "waiver" and "reliance" as different. Under § 2-209(4) a waiver may be effective; under § 2-209(5) a waiver may be effective prospectively only if there was also detrimental reliance.

Subsections (4) and (5) work well together "if waiver means 'intentional relinquishment of a known right' in both."

He then addressed the policy concerns behind the majority's position:

> The majority makes reliance an ingredient of waiver not because the structure of the UCC demands this reading, but because it believes that otherwise the UCC would not deal adequately with the threat of opportunistic conduct. The drafters of the UCC chose to deal with opportunism not through a strict reading of waiver,

> however, but through a statutory requirement of commercial good faith. . . . The modification-only-in-writing clause has nothing to do with opportunism. A person who has his contracting partner over a barrel, and therefore is able to obtain a concession, can get the concession in writing. The writing will be the least of his worries. . . . A modification-only-in-writing clause may permit the parties to strengthen the requirement of commercial good faith against the careless opportunist, but its principal function is to make it easier for business to protect their agreement against casual subsequent remarks and manufactured assertions of alteration. It strengthens the Statute of Frauds. . . . In other words, the UCC made modification-only-in-writing clauses effective for the first time, but the drafters meant to leave loopholes. . . .

The presence or absence of reliance was not important on the facts of this case since "the claim of waiver here is largely based on the course of performance." Here WK waived the delay and then withdrew the waiver in 1983. Thus no problem arose under subsection (5):

> National Metal Crafters has not argued that it had the sort of reliance that would enable it to enforce the executory portion of any modification, and therefore Wisconsin Knife Works was entitled to cancel the contract and walk away in January 1983 free from liability save for goods furnished or expenses incurred in reliance before January 1983. This treatment of § 2-209(5) solves, for the most part, the problem of fabricated claims of modification. "Attempts at modification" generally are not enforceable prospectively-and if there is commercial bad faith (that is, opportunistic conduct), they are not enforceable at all. There is no serious remaining problem to which a reliance element in the definition of waiver is a solution.

He concluded that the jury, although improperly instructed, had found enough to support a judgment discharging NMC from liability.

INTERESTING DISCUSSION ISSUES

1. *Was the drafting of UCC § 2-209 botched (compare § 2-207)?* Both the language and the purpose behind the language used are unclear. See Robert A. Hillman, *"How To Create A Commercial Calamity,"* 68 Ohio St. L. J. 335 (2007). "Section 2-209 illustrates what happens when lawmakers who boldly seek to reform the law cannot bring themselves to carry out their plan or never fully understand the ramifications of what they are doing. Instead they waver. The result is chaos—a commercial calamity." Such a section poses a dilemma to those seeking to give it meaning, and the process of trying to resolve

that dilemma can provide students with an insight into approaches to statutory interpretation.

An early 17th century English case suggested that, to understand a new statutory provision, the reader should, among other things, look to the problem that was intended to be solved by that section. The drafters of this section were unimpressed with the rule of "preexisting legal duty" and apparently considered that a requirement of consideration to support a modification of a contract was wrong. The parties had engaged in a bargained for exchange initially, and should that not be enough? If they wanted to change the original bargain, was not each side both giving something up and getting something new and should not that be sufficient to justify enforcement of the modification agreement?

Then why did the drafters of this section enable parties to the initial contract to include in that initial contract a clause prohibiting subsequent oral modification of that agreement? Under the common law, such a clause was ineffective (absent a Statute of Frauds problem) on the ground that the parties could always modify or rescind by oral agreement any previous agreement whether written or oral. The answer must lie in a desire on the part of the drafters to permit the parties, by appropriate agreement, to limit the risk of "he said, she said" claims of oral amendment, claims that the parol evidence rule was supposed to block when the "he said, she said" occurred prior to the final agreement. Was not such testimony equally suspect where it occurred after conclusion of the agreement as when it occurred before? But if the agreement, by hypothesis, was oral in the first place, what was the additional danger of admitting "he said, she said" oral claims of modification? Whatever the answers to these questions, the drafters did two things: they removed the common law requirement of consideration necessary to support enforceability of a contract modification, and they authorized the parties, by inclusion of an appropriate clause in the initial contract, to prohibit oral modifications. But then they did a third thing—they provided that an attempted modification that failed for lack of a writing "may" be enforceable as a waiver. The key word in the linguistic puzzle, as pointed out by Judge Posner, was "may." The challenge was to determine to what extent the "waiver" language of subsection (4) took back the ability granted under subsection (2) to prohibit future oral amendments, that is to say, give the parties the opportunity to create their own statute of frauds. Where were courts to find the boundaries of the "purpose" in providing a "waiver" to trump the "prohibition of oral modifications" clause? According to Judge Easterbrook, Judge Posner was concerned about limiting "opportunistic" behavior such as modifications forced by "hold up" threats." But this attribution does not mesh precisely with Judge Posner's insistence on finding that there must be reliance on the waiver.

2. *The "he said, she said" problem.* Perhaps the core of the difficulty in UCC § 2-209(4) is the risk of "he said, she said" claims of modification without any further evidentiary confirmation of such claims. Judge Posner imported a requirement of detrimental reliance before an oral waiver would be enforced in the context of a NOM clause. Such detrimental reliance would necessarily be established by objective evidence and not just a "he said, she said" claim otherwise unsupported. Judge Easterbrook challenged this importation suggesting that "waiver" had a clearly understood meaning under the common law and that meaning did not include reliance. Under the common law, a waiver could be operative until withdrawn and could be withdrawn on notice to the other party unless the waiver was supported by consideration or detrimental reliance. Furthermore, he said, § 209(5) clearly distinguished between "waiver" and "reliance"—thus the drafters did not consider these two concepts to be the same thing. But, most interestingly, he said reliance was not an important issue in this case because of the "course of performance" of the parties—a performance that could be objectively determined. Frank A. Rothermel, in "*Role Of Course Of Performance And Confirmatory Memoranda In Determining The Scope, Operation And Effect Of 'No Oral Modification Clauses,"* 48 U. Pitt. L. Rev. 1239 (1987), rejected the court's reliance requirement because "the Code's drafters intended to permit the parties to exclude oral modifications pursuant to a NOM clause," but "also intended to permit the admissibility of oral testimony of the parties' course of performance to show a waiver of the NOM clause." Compare UCC § 2-208.

3. *Rules of statutory construction violated?* A cannon of both statutory and contract interpretation says that a court should try to give effect to all words used and not adopt a construction depriving some words of any effect. Was this rule observed? Did Judge Posner deprive the word "waiver" of its generally accepted common law meaning (there being no special definition in the Code)? Did he ignore the fact that § 209(5) uses both words "waiver" and "reliance" suggesting that the drafters used them with different meanings? Did Judge Easterbrook, in recognizing "waiver" without "reliance" essentially deprive subsection (2) (permitting the use of NOM clauses) of any substantial meaning and application? Perhaps the conundrum of this case illustrates the difficulty of trying to make sense (via canons of interpretation) of that which defies a sensible harmonious overall interpretation. When in doubt, courts often emphasize the importance of ascertaining the purpose of the statute section or the contract clause and trying to find an interpretation that recognizes and gives effect to that interpretation. Judges Posner and Easterbrook seem to have differed primarily over what that purpose may have been.

NOTES AND QUESTIONS

1. *Contract formation and terms.* The buyer Wisconsin Knife mailed six purchase orders to the seller National Metal Crafters. The back of each purchase order stated that "acceptance of this order, either by acknowledgment or performance, constitutes an unqualified agreement to the following" the first of which was a NOM clause. National Metal Crafters responded with signed letters stating "please accept this as our acknowledgment covering the above subject order." Wisconsin Knife used the delivery dates specified in the letters to enter identical dates on its first two purchase orders and those orally supplied on the last four purchase orders. All deliveries were due in October and November 2001. Did the Wisconsin Knife purchase orders constitute an offer? Yes. If so, did the National Metal Crafters letters constitute an acceptance? Yes. If so, on what terms? The terms set out in the purchase order plus the printed terms on the back of the order. Specifically, was the NOM clause part of any contract formed? Yes.

2. *UCC Statute of Frauds.* Assuming a contract was formed by the purchase orders and the letters, did those writings satisfy UCC § 2-201(1)? Yes. Were the purchase orders required to be signed? Yes, by the party to be charged—but subject to the "merchants exception" applicable on these facts. Who was the party "against whom enforcement is sought?" National Metal Crafters. If UCC § 2-201(1) was not satisfied, would UCC § 2-201(2) (merchant's exception) apply? Yes—both were merchants. If not, would UCC § 2-201(3)(b) apply? Not applicable.

3. *Oral modification and consideration.* When the goods were not timely delivered, Wisconsin Knife did not terminate or sue for breach and indeed issued more purchase orders. Deliveries began in December 2002 (more than a year later after the delivered dates in the original six purchase orders) and after it had accepted over 50% of the goods delivered late, Wisconsin Knife terminated the contract in January 2004 and sued for breach. National Metal Crafters argued that the original contract delivery dates were orally and mutually modified to the new dates. Wisconsin Knife then asserted the NOM clause requiring all modifications be in writing. Assuming Wisconsin Knife orally agreed to modify the delivery dates, did National Metal Crafters provide any additional consideration to make that promise enforceable? No. Is additional consideration necessary? No—none required under the terms of § 2-209. If not, is there another applicable theory of obligation such as reliance? Yes. See UCC § 1-103. But the statute dispensed with the common law requirement of consideration while authorizing the use of a NOM clause. As Judge Easterbrook pointed out, the common law "waiver" doctrine does not rely on either

consideration or detrimental reliance except where the issue is subsequent withdrawal of the waiver.

4. *Oral modification and the writing requirement source.* Were the original six purchase order contracts over $500? Yes, presumably. Assuming so, why is the NOM clause relevant? § 2-209(3) says explicitly that "The requirements of the statute of frauds section of this Article (Section 2-201) must be satisfied if the contract as modified is within its provisions," but that statute of frauds requirement is satisfied provided only that the signed writing identifies the quantity of goods sold. Why would UCC § 2-209(3) simply require the modification to be in writing? To be consistent with the basic policy of § 2-201. Does the "waiver" provision of UCC § 2-209(4) apply with equal force to modifications required to be in writing under UCC § 2-209(3) (Statute of Frauds) as well as UCC § 2-209(2) (NOM clauses)? Yes. If so, is the central issue "waiver" within the meaning of UCC § 2-209(4) and not whether the oral modification was required to be in writing by the Statute of Frauds section or the NOM clause section? Yes. Do you think the outcome and policies are the same? The answer depends upon the meaning and elements assigned to the concept of "waiver." Does the UCC statutory treatment of a NOM clause "elevate" it to the public law stature of the Statute of Frauds? No. Of course, the NOM clause does not enjoy such elevated status under the common law.

5. *Actual waiver versus "operate as a waiver."* It appears that Judge Posner distinguishes a true "waiver" from oral modification conduct that can "operate as a waiver." Why does he consider this necessary? Otherwise, in his opinion, subsection (2) authorizing the use of NOMs would be reduced essentially to a nullity. How does he then characterize Wisconsin Knife's oral modification behavior? He does not decide. He says that it will be up to the trial judge upon remand to decide whether or not National Metal Crafters relied to their detriment. But, interestingly, he gratuitously characterized their reliance as follows: "Obviously National Metal Crafters has a strong case both that it relied on the waiver of the delivery deadlines and that there was no causal relationship between its late deliveries and the cancellation of the contract. We just are not prepared to say on the record before us that it is such a strong case as not to require submission to a jury. . . ." Why does Judge Easterbrook disagree with Judge Posner's waiver analysis? First, because "waiver" is not defined in the UCC and does have a generally accepted meaning and operation under the common law, not including any requirement of reliance. Second, because Judge Posner's interpretation of "waiver" as requiring detrimental reliance in addition fails to take account of the fact that in subsection (5) both "waiver" and "reliance" are used, and obviously the two terms are intended under that section to have different meanings and applications. Third, Judge Easterbrook attributes Judge Posner's

position to a policy concern about opportunistic "hold up" modifications, problems which Judge Easterbrook finds addressed under different standards such as duress. What is the relevance of reliance in this case? Judge Posner's closing observation suggests that the answer is very little. That it is likely that the trial court, upon remand, would find the course of performance of the parties' persuasive evidence of their intent and of detrimental reliance. The importance of "reliance" for Judge Posner is that the trial court's jury instruction failed to recognize and incorporate that concept, thus requiring a new trial.

6. *Merchants' proviso exception.* The UCC § 2-209(2) opening clause provides that a signed agreement expressly excluding oral modification or rescission by way of a NOM clause cannot be modified or rescinded except in writing. Do you find this odd? Having removed any requirement of consideration to support the modification, the drafters apparently wished to give the parties an opportunity to create their own private statute of frauds. The concern of the drafters may well have been the risk of otherwise unsubstantiated "he said, she said" claims of subsequent oral modification. The parties that made the contract have legally prohibited themselves from even orally rescinding the entire written agreement? Yes, subject to subsection (4) and waiver. What advice would you offer a client that had signed such an agreement but who orally agreed with the other party to simply forget about the contract? "Get it in a signed writing!" The proviso clause provides that a NOM clause will only be enforceable against a consumer if the consumer signs the original agreement containing the NOM clause. Why is this clause necessary when the introductory clause requires a signed agreement in the first instance? Because of the very limited nature of the UCC statute of frauds provision, requiring only that the signed writing identify the quantity of goods sold. Finally, the merchants' exception to the proviso does not require signature. But how does this fit with the introductory clause that requires a signed agreement? The signature of the party sending the "confirmation" under § 2-201(2) is attributed to the other merchant in the absence of a timely objection. How does Judge Posner interpret the merchants' exception? He said:

> One might think that an agreement to exclude modification except by a signed writing must be signed in any event by the party against whom the requirement is sought to be enforced, that is, by National Metal Crafters, rather than by the party imposing the requirement. But if so the force of the proviso ("but except as between merchants . . .") becomes unclear, for it contemplates that between merchants no separate signature by the party sought to be bound by the requirement is necessary. A possible reconciliation, though not one we need embrace in order to decide this case, is to read the statute to require a separate signing or initialing of the

clause forbidding oral modifications, as well as of the contract in which the clause appears. There was no such signature here; but it doesn't matter; this was a contract "between merchants."

7. *Judicial activism, opportunism, and hindsight.* See text. Is it true that UCC § 2-209 is confusingly drafted? Yes—see the difference between majority and dissenting opinions! As for the remaining questions, they do not change this assessment.

CHAPTER 8

WHEN AN ENFORCERABLE PROMISE BECOMES DUE: BREACH OF PROMISE AND CONDITIONS

Table of Contents

Introduction to Chapter 8 Coverage

The conceptual "breach" of a contract is linked to "any nonperformance" of a duty under a contract when that duty becomes due. As a corollary, full or perfect performance of a contractual duty discharges that duty. Therefore, the function and role of the contract is twofold—to define both the scope and timing of the contractual duties of both parties. Because of this timing analysis, the materials in this chapter are generally organized by subject matters controlling the timing of when a performance is due because until that time, there is no breach analysis. By definition, the failure to perform a duty before that duty is due is not a breach. Consequently, the other party is not entitled to any contractual remedy at that point in the contractual relationship. But one party may signal in advance an intention not to perform, or circumstances may change raising doubt that performance will occur. This first situation is considered under the ancient doctrine of "anticipatory repudiation." Second, every promise of a performance is subject to some type of "condition." The only question is whether the condition arises by operation of law ("constructive conditions") or by the express language and implied conduct of the parties ("express conditions"). Since a condition is defined as an event that must occur before performance becomes due, conditions are extremely powerful contractual concepts. Specifically, performance of a promise subject to a condition cannot become due unless the condition either occurs or is excused. Thus, the nonoccurrence of a condition discharges the promise before it ever becomes due thereby eliminating any possible breach of the promise.

A. ANTICIPATORY REPUDIATION

Generally, a clear repudiation of a duty before it is due discharges the injured party's duty to perform (like a condition discussed in the next section) and creates an immediate claim for total breach and damages at the time of the repudiation. The total breach and damages characteristic alone places enormous tension on what type of words or conduct constitute a legal repudiation. Equivocation alone is inadequate to the task but in marginal cases, and there will always be marginal cases, who should assume the risk of marginal and equivocal repudiation? Even where repudiation is clearly unequivocal, it could be based on the repudiating party's mistaken but good faith belief that their performance is no longer due.

The famous decision in *Hochester v. De la Tour,* dealing with an anticipatory breach of a personal service contract by De la Tour (the employer), established two consequences of the anticipatory repudiation: (i) Hochester's (the employee) duties were immediately discharged and thus he was free to mitigate and find other employment, and (ii) Hochester was free to sue immediately for damages (even though other employment might mitigate the damage claim and would be unknown until after the date performance was due). The decision that the injured party could sue immediately for damages was both criticized and supported. Notwithstanding commanding support, the measurement of damages at the time of anticipatory repudiation remains a complex issue under common law and the UCC.

Following general acceptance of the doctrine, efforts turned toward defining the proper contours of a true repudiation (versus a simple equivocation) and whether an otherwise valid repudiation could be withdrawn. On the latter score, since a repudiation is in fact "not a breach," it can be withdrawn absent detrimental reliance by the injured party. In this sense, unlike a breach which cannot be withdrawn, a repudiation is like a waiver of performance by the repudiating party that can be retracted unless and until the injured party incurs detrimental reliance. The injured party does not "waive" the right to rely on the repudiation even when urging the repudiating party to perform. The CISG principles are similar in effect.

Where the statements or conduct may fall short of an outright repudiation they may nevertheless create substantial uncertainty regarding future performance. Both the Restatement (Second) of Contracts § 251 and the UCC § 2-609 make provision for the affected party to seek adequate assurance that the future performance will indeed be forthcoming. Repudiation can consist of a statement or an act rendering the obligor actually or apparently unable to perform without a breach. The statement or act must be substantial or substantially impair the value of the contract.

A number of difficult cases arise out of a refusal to perform unless certain conditions are first satisfied, conditions that the threatening party is not legally entitled to demand. According to the common law commentary, the statement must be unequivocal and, if so, a mistaken belief regarding a right not to perform, even if asserted in good faith, will not save the statement from being considered a legal repudiation. The objective theory of contracts applies preferring the injured party's reasonable interpretation to the subjective secret intent of the repudiating party.

Truman L. Flatt & Sons Co., Inc. v. Schupf
CASE BRIEF

This is a 1995 decision of the Illinois Appellate Court. In March, 1993, defendant (seller) entered into a contract to sell plaintiff (buyer) a parcel of land for $160,000 subject to an express condition that the contract was to be voidable at the election of the buyer if the city denied the plaintiff's rezoning request for the parcel. On May 21 buyer's attorney sent seller's attorney a letter advising of substantial public opposition to the rezoning request and their decision to withdraw the request for rezoning. The letter also expressed the view that, without rezoning, the property was worth less to the buyer and offered to close at a lower price. The seller's attorney was asked by the letter to check with the client seller. The seller's attorney responded rejecting the offer to sell at a lower price and expressing regret that the zoning change had not been approved. On June 14 the buyer's attorney wrote electing to purchase the property at the price stated in the contract. On July 8 seller's attorney stated the client's position that the buyer's failure to waive the rezoning requirement coupled with a new offer to purchase at a lower price constituted a repudiation effectively voiding the contract.

Buyer sued for specific performance but the trial court granted seller's motion for summary judgment based on the buyer's repudiation of the contract. Buyer appealed arguing that: (1) it did not repudiate the contract; and (2) even if it did repudiate, it retracted that repudiation in a timely manner. The court of appeals granted the appeal and reversed the trial court's grant of summary judgment.

On appeal the buyer argued that the doctrine of anticipatory repudiation requires a clear manifestation of an intent not to perform on the date of performance and that seller had not made such a showing. In considering the issue of repudiation the court cited favorably to both the Restatement and the UCC. Whether anticipatory repudiation occurred was a question of fact and the judgment of the trial court thereon would not be disturbed unless against the manifest weight of evidence. A statement of intention not to perform except on conditions which went beyond the contract would constitute a repudiation. A suggestion for modification of the contract would not, such as a request for a price change. The court disagreed with the seller's argument that the letter and surrounding circumstances implied a threat of nonperformance if the price term was not modified. The court found that the May 21 letter did not constitute a clearly implied threat of nonperformance, but provided only a weak inference of nonperformance. The letter was ambiguous and thus not a clear repudiation.

In any case, the buyer provided a timely retraction of any repudiation. With respect to such a retraction the court cited Restatement (Second) of Contracts § 256 which states that a repudiation is nullified by a retraction where notice of the retraction comes to the attention of the injured party before he materially changes position in reliance on the repudiation or indicates to the other that he considers the repudiation to be final. After reviewing the authorities the court concluded:

> These authorities stand for the proposition that after an anticipatory repudiation, the aggrieved party is entitled to choose to treat the contract as rescinded or terminated, to treat the

> anticipatory repudiation as a breach by bringing suit or otherwise changing its position, or to await the time for performance.

Seller asserted it chose to treat the contract as rescinded but it failed to communicate that intent to buyer. The court rejected seller's argument that the seller could treat the contract as terminated or rescinded without notice or other indication being given to the repudiating party. The court accepted the statement that no such notice would be required in the event of material change of position in reliance on the repudiation. But absent such a change of position notice to the other party was required. Were the law otherwise, there would be no opportunity for an effective retraction.

The court concluded that assuming there had been a repudiation it was retracted before notice or change of position and therefore the retraction was effective. The court did not rule expressly on whether or not there had in fact been a repudiation.

INTERESTING DISCUSSION ISSUES

1. *The devil is in the details of "anticipatory repudiation."* In some cases the facts are plain and involve no equivocation. Where A agrees to sell her home to B and then, instead, sells the home to C, A by her own actions has made it impossible for her to perform her contract with B and has committed an anticipatory repudiation by act or conduct. In other situations, the words or conduct of the obligor may be equivocal—the framing subcontractor tells the general contractor that he may not be able to finish the job. Can the subcontractors' stated doubts about his ability to perform amount to an anticipatory repudiation? According to the opinion in the case above, the repudiation must be clear and not ambiguous and so the dubious subcontractor may not have committed an anticipatory repudiation. Yet another series of fact situations pose a major dilemma under this rubric. These situations involve a statement by the obligor that the obligor will not perform as contracted unless specified conditions are met by the obligee. If these additional conditions involve actions to which the obligor is not entitled under the contract, the obligor's demand for those actions constitutes a repudiation. Consider, for instance, the case of a contractor who agreed to construct a home and was to be paid monthly installments based on progress of the work. If the owner refuses to pay an installment on time is the contractor entitled to treat that failure as a material breach of contract. If the owner says she will not pay unless the contractor redoes a particular part of the work, is the contractor privileged to regard such a refusal together with the attached condition as a repudiation? Evaluating such situations and advising the client appropriately can be a taxing exercise in practice.

NOTES AND QUESTIONS

1. *Paragraph 14 zoning condition.* Paragraph 14 of the contract stated an express condition that the purchase was contingent upon buyer's ability to obtain a zoning change to build an asphalt plant. Whose contractual obligation was the condition designed to protect, the buyer or the seller? It was designed to protect the buyer who apparently wanted the parcel to use for an asphalt plant which could not be done without rezoning. Had the buyer made no attempt to seek a zoning variance would the buyer be entitled to invoke the condition to discharge its purchase obligation? No. Comparable to the common financing contingency attached to a contract to buy a home, there is an implied condition that, where the happening of the contingency is within the control of the party, that party will make a good faith effort to have the contingency satisfied. Assuming that the buyer made reasonable but unsuccessful efforts to obtain the zoning change, may the seller refuse to sell since the condition (zoning change) did not occur? Certainly the buyer could rescind but the condition was inserted for the benefit of the buyer and not the seller. It would seem that the seller should not be able to rely on the failure of the contingency—the buyer should have the election whether or not to proceed with the sale in any event. If not, does this suggest that the buyer cannot rely on a condition in its favor without some effort and that the seller cannot invoke a condition designed to protect the other party? Yes. Is this result consistent with the intent of the parties? Yes—as discussed above. Does the Chapter 7 discussion of "waiver" of a NOM clause apply with equal force to an express condition? Yes, but a condition such as the present one once "waived" is dead whether or not supported by consideration or material reliance. This happens because the buyer has a one time "election" to choose which path to travel. As discussed in the last section of this chapter, an obligor whose duty is subject to an express condition may indeed "waive" the condition thereby promising to perform notwithstanding the nonoccurrence of the condition. Did the buyer's May 21st letter waive the rezoning condition or repudiate the contract? It did neither clearly—the letter was ambiguous in this regard and thus the clear evidence of repudiation was not available. Should the seller be able to waive a condition favoring the buyer? No, such a power could deprive the buyer of the protection negotiated for in the form of the condition. Consider the case of the financing contingency and the result if the seller were able to waive the buyer's financing contingency. The buyer would obligated to buy when the buyer, by assumption, has been unable to get the financing necessary to permit the buyer to close.

2. *Buyer's alleged repudiation.* The seller and trial court argued that the buyer's May 21st letter repudiated the contract (rather than simply waiving the condition). If so, the seller was privileged to

terminate the contract, discharge its duty to sell and sue for any damages (arguably none unless determined by a resale at a lower price and a resale was not in play). The May 21st buyer "repudiation" letter contained at least five statements relevant to the factual repudiation question: (i) the request for zoning change was withdrawn in the face of near certain defeat (condition waiver or repudiation of contract?); (ii) we are still interested in the property but it is not worth as much as currently zoned (negotiation or repudiation?); (iii) in an effort to keep things moving we are offering $142,500 (negotiation or repudiation?); (iv) please check with your clients and advise whether the price adjustment is acceptable (negotiation or repudiation?); and (v) if acceptable we can accelerate the closing and bring matter to a speedy conclusion (negotiation or repudiation?).

Restatement (Second) of Contracts § 250, *cmt. b* makes clear that the nature of the statements must be "sufficiently positive to be reasonably interpreted to mean the party will not or cannot perform." Whose interpretation matters under this standard, the buyer's actual intent or the seller's objective understanding? The seller's objective understanding. Do you think this was a question to be decided as a matter of law (summary judgment) or by a jury (trial)? This, as pointed out by the court, should be a fact question for the jury. Since the facts were not disputed, the question was simply the meaning of those facts, not what actual facts were true.

Under repudiation doctrine, what is the legal effect of proposing a modification to the contract? If it is truly only a proposal or an inquiry, none. Compare the case of the offer followed by an inquiry about different terms. That inquiry is not a counteroffer and thus does not cause the revocation of the offer. Does the mere proposal of a modification repudiate the contract as a *per se* declaration that the proposing party will not perform under the original terms if the proposal is not accepted? No, not without significant different and pointed language making it clear that unless additional terms are met (to which the party is not entitled) that party will not perform. On this account, UCC § 2-610, *cmt. 2* states:

> Under the language of this section, a demand by one or both parties for more than the contract calls for in the way of counter-performance is not itself a repudiation nor does it invalidate a plain expression of desire for future performance. However, when under a fair reading it amounts to a statement of intention not to perform except on conditions which go beyond the contract, it becomes a repudiation.

Did the May 21st letter indicate to a reasonable person that the buyer would not proceed unless the seller agreed to a price reduction? No. The seller concluded that the price reduction offer was an implied threat not to perform unless the seller agreed to the proposal modification. In light of the buyer's request that the seller let the buyer know whether the proposal was satisfactory, was the seller's subjective understanding reasonable? The seller's argument would deprive those words of any meaning and effect. Shouldn't the parties generally have the freedom to propose modifications without committing a repudiation? Yes, of course. Does that result promote the ability of the parties to voluntarily adjust to changes? Yes. Do other doctrines adequately police coerced modifications? See the discussions of duress and unconscionability and the preexisting duty rule in previous chapters.

3. *Seller's response to alleged repudiation.* The closing was not scheduled until June 30. In response to the buyer's May 21st letter suggesting a lower price, the seller responded in a June 9th letter that it was not interested in lowering the price. Insisting on performance under the terms of the contract is certainly not a repudiation. Assuming that the May 21st letter was not a sufficiently clear repudiation, what appears to be the status of the contract after the June 9th letter? The buyer's duty remained subject to the express condition of rezoning. Following the seller's June 9th letter, the buyer immediately responded on June 14th that it was nonetheless prepared to close on June 30th pursuant to the terms of the original contract. Absent a response, the buyer wrote two more letters on June 23rd and July 6th inquiring about the status of the closing. What is the status of the contract on June 30th assuming that buyer did not repudiate the contract? It is enforceable as written except that the rezoning contingency is dropped from the contract.

4. *Retraction before reliance.* Even if the buyer repudiated the contract in its May 21sts letter, the closing was not scheduled until June 30. What is the significance of the seller's June 14th letter stating that the buyer was prepared to proceed to a closing on June 30th under the terms of the contract? This constituted a waiver of the rezoning contingency which, thereafter, was dead as a condition of the contract. Clearly, the buyer waived the zoning change condition at that point. Restatement (Second) of Contracts § 256(1) provides that a repudiation may be retracted provided the retraction occurs before the injured party either (i) materially changes position in reliance on the repudiation or (ii) indicates to the repudiating party that the repudiation is considered final. See also UCC § 2-611. The seller agreed that it had not materially changed its position in reliance on the repudiation. Therefore, retraction was still possible unless the seller communicated to the buyer that the repudiation was final before the retraction. Given the uncertainty of whether a statement constitutes a repudiation, do you expect that an injured party will communicate in all but the clearest cases that it is treating the repudiation as final? Only if that party wants to get out of the contract. What is the purpose

in doing so? Locking in the termination of the contract. The seller is always privileged to rely on the repudiation until it is retracted and notice is not necessary. Of course, relying on a weak repudiation carries the same risk as communicating that the repudiation is final—if the statement was not a repudiation, the injured party will have breached the contract. Does the court make clear that the injured party must communicate that it is treating the repudiation as final? Yes, if that is the injured party's intent but such communication is not necessary where the repudiation becomes final as the result of detrimental reliance and change of position.

5. *Reasonable grounds for assurance.* If an injured party mistakenly treats a statement or conduct as a repudiation and it is later determined no repudiation occurred, then the injured party will breach by failing to perform when its performance comes due. Accordingly, a weak but ineffective repudiation does not discharge the duty of performance of the other party. Restatement (Second) of Contracts § 253(2). Because of the uncertainty surrounding whether a particular statement constitutes an unequivocal repudiation, it may be wise to adopt an intermediate position. First, the injured party could seek clarification whether the other party is repudiating the contract. This gives the other party a chance to clarify or retract. Alternatively, without giving up rights under the so-called repudiation, the injured party could urge the party to perform notwithstanding the repudiation. See Restatement (Second) of Contracts § 257.

Importantly, under Restatement (Second) of Contracts § 251(1) when an injured party has "reasonable grounds" to believe that the obligor will commit a breach, the injured party may "demand adequate assurance" of due performance and suspend performance until such assurance is forthcoming. See also UCC § 2-609(1). See Gregory S. Crespi, *"The Adequate Assurances Doctrine After U.C.C. § 2-609: A Test of the Efficiency of the Common Law,"* 38 Vill. L. Rev. 179 (1993). However, an obligee does not have a unilateral right to demand assurance that the obligor will perform. Restatement (Second) of Contracts § 251, *cmt. a.* The critical inquiry is when "reasonable grounds" exist to trigger the right to seek assurance. Restatement (Second) of Contracts § 251, *cmt c* provides as follows:

> *c. Reasonable grounds for belief.* Whether "reasonable grounds" have arisen for an obligee's belief that there will be a breach must be determined in the light of all the circumstances of the particular case. The grounds for his belief must have arisen after the time when the contract was made and cannot be based on facts known to him at that time. Nor, since the grounds must be reasonable, can they be based on events that occurred after that time but as to which he took the risk when he made the contract. But minor breaches may give reasonable grounds for a belief that there will be

more serious breaches, and the mere failure of the obligee to press a claim for damages for those minor breaches will not preclude him from basing a demand for assurances on them. Compare § 241(d), Comment e to that section, and Comment b to § 242. Even circumstances that do not relate to the particular contract, such as defaults under other contracts, may give reasonable grounds for such a belief. See Comment a to § 252. *Conduct by a party that indicates his doubt as to his willingness or ability to perform but that is* *__not sufficiently positive to amount to a repudiation__* *(see Comment b to § 250), may give reasonable grounds for such a belief.* And events that indicate a party's apparent inability, but do not amount to a repudiation because they are not voluntary acts, may also give reasonable grounds for such a belief. . . . Another important application of the rule occurs when an obligor who is allowed a period of time within which to perform makes an offer of defective performance. It may still be possible for him, if the offer is refused, to make an offer of conforming performance within the period allowed. Nevertheless, the offer of defective performance may give the obligee reasonable grounds to believe that the obligor will commit a breach under this Section. A third important application of the rule occurs when a party becomes insolvent. The effect of insolvency will vary according to the nature of the obligor's duty. If, for example, it is merely to perform personal services, the fact of insolvency alone may not give reasonable grounds to believe that the obligor will commit a breach, but if it is to pay for goods on credit it will. . . . [Emphasis Added]

Assuming that you are seller's counsel, and that your client—after receiving the May 21st letter—has decided to cancel the contract. Realizing that the language of the May 21st letter does not unequivocally repudiate the contract, what correspondence would you recommend to your client. Write to the buyer asking whether or not he is waiving the rezoning contingency. Does the May 21st letter at least represent "reasonable grounds" to "demand adequate assurance" and suspend performance until it was received? Yes. As a policy matter, do you think reasonable grounds to demand assurance should be more flexibly applied than repudiation? Yes. Restatement (Second) of Contracts § 251, *cmt. d* provides that written demand is preferable but not required. Compare UCC § 2-609(1) (demand must be in writing). In all cases, the demand must be made in good faith.

B. CONDITIONAL PROMISES

Historically, the enforcement of the promise of one party to a contract was not contingent on performance of the counterpart promise of the other party. Each promise was "independent" and enforced as such. Lord Mansfield was responsible for the change to viewing mutual promises as dependent rather than independent. Thus, the nonperformance of a return promise became an excuse for nonperformance by the other party. The performance on one side could be impliedly conditioned on performance on the other. But not all promises are mutually dependent. They may be stated as independent in the contract. Thus in a sale of goods on thirty day credit terms, payment for the goods by the buyer is expressly made independent of the promise of the seller to deliver the goods. Other facts may be established in a contract as either express or implied conditions of a duty to perform. Thus, the common c ondition of architect approval before owner duty to pay contractor so operates. Unless the condition of architect approval is satisfied, waived or excused, the owner's duty to pay is not triggered.

A condition is generally a fact that must occur before a promise becomes due. Conditions can be express, implied in fact or implied in law (constructive conditions). Regardless of the nature of the condition, the effect is always the same. The failure of the condition means the other party's performance does not become due making breach legally impossible. Consequently, that duty is also discharged by the failure of the condition to occur. Moreover, the failure of the condition is rarely itself a breach unless the party also promised the event would occur.

The following materials explore the primary methodology driving the creation, operation and effect of express and constructive conditions. In particular, separating the exploration of express and constructive conditions is an analysis of the function of constructive conditions to order the performances of the parties (who must perform first). Since many exchanges are not simultaneous, this important matter considers whether a defect in the first party's performance operates as a condition to discharge the other party's trailing performance obligation.

1. Express Conditions

Express conditions are created by the agreement of the parties, not implied in law by a court. Because the effect of an express condition discharges an obligor's duty to perform the conditioned promise, it is used in order to make clear that the transactions will not occur unless a specified event occurs. Where the language is not clear, judicial interpretation discussed in Chapter 4 must be used. However, because of the enormous effect of conditions, special rules guide the interpretative process.

In cases of doubt, language and circumstances are interpreted to *not create* a condition in order to reduce the obligee's risk of forfeiture, at least if the event is within the obligee's control or the obligee has otherwise assumed the risk. Also, if the event is within the control of the obligee, in cases of doubt language and circumstances are interpreted to create a promise by the obligee that the event will occur rather than a condition of the obligor's duty to perform.

The following case reviews the serious impact and effect of an express condition.

Oppenheimer & Co., Inc. v. Oppenheim, Appel, Dixon & Co.
CASE BRIEF

This is a 1995 decision of the New York Court of Appeals. The parties entered into a letter agreement setting forth certain conditions precedent to the formation and existence of a sublease between them. The agreement provided that there would be no sublease between the parties "unless and until" plaintiff delivered to defendant the prime landlord's written consent to certain " tenant work" on or before a specified deadline. If this condition did not occur, the sublease was to be deemed "null and void." Plaintiff provided only oral notice on the specified date. Plaintiff sued to enforce the agreement to enter into the sublease but was met with the defense that an express condition to that agreement taking effect had not been met—such oral notice was considered not a satisfaction of the condition and the sublease was held void.

The agreement covering the proposed sublease included two conditions. The first was the prime landlord's written confirmation that the defendant was a subtenant reasonably acceptable to the prime landlord. (We can assume that the prime lease required such landlord's consent in the event of a proposed sublease.) While this condition was in fact satisfied, the agreement also provided a requirement that the plaintiff obtain a similar written consent from the prime landlord to "tenant work" proposed to be done by the defendant in order to adapt the premises to its needs. Such consent was to be delivered to the defendant on or before January 30, 1987. If this did not happen, both the agreement and attached sublease were to be "null and void and of no further force and effect" and neither party was to have "any rights against nor obligations to the other."

The parties extended these time deadlines but plaintiff never delivered the prime landlord's written consent to the proposed tenant work on or before the modified deadline of February 25, 1987. Instead, plaintiff's attorney telephoned defendant's attorney on February 25 and informed the defendant that the prime landlord's consent had been secured. On February 26, defendant informed plaintiff's attorney that the letter agreement and sublease were invalid for failure to timely deliver the prime landlord's written consent and that it would not agree to an extension of the time deadline. The prime landlord's written consent was not delivered until March 20, 1987.

Plaintiff sued for breach of contract alleging that the defendant had waived or was estopped by virtue of its conduct from insisting on physical delivery of the written consent. Plaintiff argued that it could have met the deadline, but failed to do so only because defendant, acting in bad faith, induced plaintiff into delaying delivery of the landlord's consent. Plaintiff asserted that the parties had previously extended the agreement's deadlines as a matter of course. It also alleged that it had substantially performed the condition.

The trial court charged the jury with respect to substantial performance and the jury found that the plaintiff had so performed, awarding damages of $1.2 million. The jury also found that the defendant had not waived the February 25 deadline for delivery of the landlord's written consent, and was not equitably estopped from requiring the plaintiff's strict adherence to that deadline.

The defendant moved for judgment notwithstanding the verdict and the trial court granted that motion, ruling as a matter of law that the doctrine of substantial performance had no application to this dispute. The appellate division reversed, restoring the verdict. The Court of Appeals reversed, restoring the trial court's grant of judgment nov.

The court then reviewed relevant principles. "A condition precedent is "an act or event, other than a lapse of time, which, unless the condition is excused, must occur before a duty to perform a promise in the agreement arises," they said. Most conditions precedent describe acts or events which must occur before a party is obliged to perform. Such conditions are to be distinguished from a condition precedent to the formation or existence of a contract. In this later situation no contract arises unless and until the condition occurs. Conditions can be express or implied. Implied or constructive conditions are those "imposed by law to do justice." "Express conditions must be literally performed, whereas constructive conditions, which ordinarily arise from language of promise, are subject to the precept that substantial compliance is sufficient." The court quoted Professor Williston: "Since an express condition . . . depends for its validity on the manifested intention of the parties, it has the same sanctity as the promise itself. . . . Where, however, the law itself has imposed the condition, in absence of or irrespective of the manifested intention of the parties, it can deal with its creation as it pleases, shaping the boundaries of the constructive condition in such a way as to do justice and avoid hardship." Doubtful language will be interpreted as a promise rather than a condition. Interpretation as a means of reducing the risk of forfeiture cannot be employed if "the occurrence of the event as a condition is expressed in unmistakable language." Nevertheless the nonoccurrence of the condition may yet be excused by waiver, breach or forfeiture. The court quoted the Restatement definition of a "forfeiture" as "the denial of compensation that results when the obligee loses [its] right to the agreed exchange after [it] has relied substantially, as by preparation or performance on the expectation of that exchange." See Restatement (Second) of Contracts § 229, comment *b*.

The language in the case at bar unambiguously established an express condition precedent. The court found no basis for applying the doctrine of "substantial performance."

The court found that plaintiff's reliance on *Jacobs & Youngs v. Kent* was misplaced. The court quoted Justice Cardozo's opinion in that case as follows:

> This is not to say that the parties are not free by apt and certain words to effectuate a purpose that performance of every term shall be a condition of recovery. That question is not here. This is merely to say that the law will be slow to impute the purpose, in the silence of the parties, where the significance of the default is grievously out of proportion to the oppression of the forfeiture

The court concluded:

> Freedom of contract prevails in an arm's length transaction between sophisticated parties such as these, and in the absence of countervailing public policy concerns there is no reason to relieve them of the consequences of their bargain.

INTERESTING DISCUSSION ISSUES

1. *Conditions are to be strictly, and not "substantially" performed or satisfied.* As discussed later in this chapter, the common law developed the concept of "substantial performance" to rescue the obligor who performed but somewhat inadequately. The earlier sanction of denying the obligor any remedy against the obligee under the contract produces unduly harsh results. This was particularly true where the shortfall in performance could be compensated adequately by an award of damages. And so, like horseshoes, close will usually permit the obligor to recover under the contract subject to adjustment for the cost of repair or completion of the incomplete work. In this case, the plaintiff argued that "close" constituted substantial satisfaction of the condition of delivery of the written consent of the prime landlord. Oral (but not written) notice was provided on a timely basis. The New York Court of Appeals drew a line in the sand, saying that "close" did not constitute satisfaction of the condition of delivery of the written consent of the prime landlord. Oral notice of consent was not written notice of consent. Students understand the rationale of substantial performance as applied to promises. They have more difficulty in understanding the rationale for refusing to provide a parallel approach to satisfaction of conditions.

Unfortunately, they will not have had much opportunity to see and understand the role and function of conditions in many legal transactions. An example drawn from the closing of a simple buy-sell transaction may help. Suppose the contract is for the sale and purchase of a home and calls for payment with "good funds." The buyer shows up at the closing with a personal check. A call to the buyer's bank establishes that the buyer has funds to cover the check but the seller refuses to close claiming that the requirement of "good funds" has not been met. If the transaction is a more complex commercial transaction, the satisfaction of conditions to closing become more and more important.

NOTES AND QUESTIONS

1. *Condition to contract formation or performance of promise under existing contract.* The operative effect of the condition in the *Oppenheimer* case is unusual. By the terms of the letter agreement, the attached sublease was to be "executed" only upon the satisfaction of certain specified conditions. Restatement (Second) of Contracts § 224 defines a condition as an event that must occur before performance "under a contract" becomes due. Do the various letter agreement terms referred to as "conditions" upon which a sublease will be executed fall within this definition? Yes. Restatement (First) of Contracts § 250 referred to conditions precedent and subsequent. A condition precedent was defined as a fact that must occur before a duty arises. Restatement (First) of Contracts § 250(1). A condition subsequent was defined as a fact that extinguished a duty to make compensation for a breach of a contractual promise. Do the various letter agreement terms referred to as "conditions" upon which a sublease will be executed fall within this definition? Yes.

Restatement (First) of Contracts § 24 defined an offer as a promise "conditional" upon an act, forbearance or return promise being given in exchange. However, Restatement (Second) of Contracts § 24 defines an offer as a manifestation of willingness to enter into a bargain. Comparing the two, it is quite obvious that Restatement (First) of Contracts used the term "condition" more broadly and that the Restatement (Second) of Contracts confined the use of the term "condition" to those events that prevent a duty under an "existing contract" from becoming due. This distinguishing characteristic helps to explain the elimination of the condition precedent and subsequent distinction as well as the use of facts or events that prevent the formation of a contract. Rather, formation requirements are confined to offer and acceptance. See Restatement (Second) of Contracts § 224, *cmt. c*. Viewed in this light, are the letter agreement terms that must be satisfied before the sublease will be executed true conditions? Yes. The parties had a letter agreement in force between them. The attached sublease was to be executed only subject to fulfillment of stated conditions precedent. One difference might be that events that must occur before a contract is formed leave both parties free to retreat from the transaction until the event occurs and a contract is formed. If a contract does not yet exist, does either party have a duty of good faith and fair dealing with respect to the occurrence of a condition within its control? Yes—compare the buyer's obligation with respect to satisfying a financing contingency.

For example, paragraph 1(a) required Oppenheimer to obtain the landlord's written consent that Oppenheim was an acceptable tenant by December 30, 1986. Paragraph 4(c) further required Oppenheimer to obtain and deliver landlord's written consent by January 30, 1987, that Oppenheim's proposed tenant communication improvements were acceptable. Importantly, paragraph 4(d) provided that the sublease would not be executed unless the paragraph 1(a) and 4(c) conditions were "timely satisfied." Did Oppenheimer have a contractual duty to exercise good faith and fair dealing to obtain the landlord's written consents even though these "conditions" were for the most part within Oppenheimer's control? Yes. Could Oppenheim maintain an action for the failure of Oppenheimer to do so? No—failure of a condition cannot be the basis of an action for damages unless there was an associated promise that the condition would be satisfied. Do you see the difference between events that might be fairly attached to the formation of a contract versus those that are attached to promises to become due under an existing contract? Yes—in the pre-contract situation, we have an offer-acceptance analogy—the offer requires a mirror image acceptance and if the condition of acceptance is not met that mirror image is lacking. However, in this case, although the sublease was never executed, the letter agreement appeared to be a valid contract.

2. *Conditioning language.* Forgetting for the moment the somewhat artificial distinction between conditions to contract formation and to performance of promises, examine carefully the express language chosen to create the conditions. Restatement (Second) of Contracts § 226, *cmt. a* provides that an express condition may be created by the parties by any language but it is customary to use words such as "provided that" or "if." Notice that the conditioning language in paragraph 1(a) of the letter agreement used the words "if such written notice of conformation were not obtained" and then coupled that language with a specific consequence of failure that the proposed sublease "shall be deemed null and void and of no further force and effect and neither party shall have any rights against nor obligations to the other." The paragraph 4(c) stated similar language.

What is the theoretical value of including words making clear both the express condition itself as well as the effect of the failure of the condition? Prescribing the effect of failure of the condition reinforces the intent that the requirement is a material condition precedent. Given that the effect of the condition forfeits the affected party's rights to pursue a breach remedy under the contract, courts take a dim view of doubtful conditional language as a form of private ordering "surprise" forfeiture. This accounts for the interpretation preferences construing doubtful language as not creating a condition—to protect a party from a surprise forfeiture of rights for breach of contract. See Restatement (Second) of Contracts § 227, *cmt. b*. Where is the surprise forfeiture when the contract language specifically identifies the consequences of a condition failure? It should not be there, although these words may well be part of boilerplate drafting. Does this create any clues regarding drafting techniques used in connection with the creation of express conditions? Yes—stating both the condition and the intended effect reinforce the message and should reinforce the likelihood that the provision will be given full effect.

3. *Time of essence clauses*. See text.

4. *Strict enforcement of written notice requirements*. Somewhat like the Statute of Frauds, a written notice requirement protects an innocent party from false allegations of oral notice. However, the prior chapter distinguished the effect of technical writing requirements imposed by public law (Statute of Frauds) and those imposed purely by private ordering (NOM clauses). That discussion generally provided that NOM clauses are generally not enforced under common law but are generally enforceable by statute under UCC § 2-209(2). If a NOM clause is generally not enforceable under common law, do you see any principled reason why a clause requiring "written notification" of the satisfaction of a condition should be strictly enforced? No—strict performance can be waived. One reason might include mutual agreement. A NOM clause purports to preclude the parties from mutually agreeing to rescind or modify their agreement. A written notification clause could of course be waived by the party benefiting from the written notice requirement, but absent waiver by that party should the other party be free to unilaterally disregard the written notice requirement? No.

Restatement (Second) of Contracts § 84 specifically addresses waivers of conditions and is discussed in more detail in the last section of this chapter. Generally, Restatement (Second) of Contracts § 84(1)(a) provides that the benefited party (Oppenheim) may "waive" a condition in any form including a writing requirement unless the condition is a material part of the agreed exchange. Restatement (Second) of Contracts § 84, *cmt. d* discusses the materiality requirement:

> *d. Conditions which may be waived*. The rule of subsection (1) applies primarily to conditions which may be thought of as procedural or technical, or to instances in which the non-occurrence of condition is comparatively minor. Examples are conditions which merely relate to the time or manner of the return performance or provide for the giving of notice or the supplying of proofs. . . .

It is reasonably clear that the landlord's approval of the communication system was a material part of the agreed exchange. But it is also reasonably clear that the written notice requirement was more "procedural or technical," particularly when coupled with the actual oral notification. Thus it is reasonably clear that Oppenheim could waive the written notification requirement but perhaps not the landlord consent (the later requiring a theory of obligation such as consideration or estoppel). Although the Court cites a law review article with approval that express conditions must be strictly enforced, the article actually argues that all conditions should be subject to substantial performance to avoid inequitable and harsh results in all but the most extreme cases. See Robert Childress, "Conditions in the Law of Contracts," 45 N.Y.U. L. Rev. 33 (1970).

Was there any evidence in this case that Oppenheim's counsel did not receive timely oral notification of the satisfaction of the landlord's consent? No—on the contrary the oral notice was timely. If not, why does the court adopt a strict formalist approach requiring written notice rather than oral notice? Because the parties intentionally made notice in written form of the essence of their agreement. What was important and material to effectuate the reasonable intent of the parties—the landlord's timely approval and oral notification or timely approval and written notification? The reason for insistence on written notice would be avoidance of the "he said, she said" risk. Separating the form of notification (oral versus written) from the actual nonoccurrence of the conditional event (landlord timely consent) tends to shift the analysis to the materiality of the notice provision versus the condition itself.

Does the opinion suggest that Oppenheim's counsel intentionally "waived" the written notice requirement when Oppenheimer's counsel telephoned on February 25th to communicate the landlord had orally approved the telecommunication system? No. From all that can be gleaned from the opinion Oppenheim counsel merely received the oral notice without comment or objection. The jury found no conduct on that counsel's part that could amount to an estoppel. In fact, following client instructions, Oppenheim counsel wrote a letter the next day on February 26th stating the written notice condition had not occurred and therefore the condition failed.

5. *Lawyer conduct.* Oppenheimer's counsel may have done all that was possible. After all, the lawyer cannot force the landlord to rush a decision, state it in writing, or coerce the other party to an agreed extension. However, lawyer conduct can also fall short of best practices and indeed often cross into malpractice. The *Oppenheimer* opinion relied on two earlier New York cases as precedent to justify strict enforcement of express conditions. The first was *Maxton Builders. v. Lo Gabo*, 502 N.E. 2d 184 (NY 1986). As summarized by the Court, a buyer agreed to purchase a home for $210,000 on the condition that the buyer had a right to cancel the purchase if real estate taxes exceeded $3,500. The buyer made a $21,000 down payment by check. The right

to cancel was required to be in writing and received within three days of the August 3rd contract. The contract did not state that time was of the essence. The next day, the buyer learned that the real estate taxes did indeed exceed $3,500 and so informed their counsel who telephoned the seller's counsel that the condition failed and the sale was cancelled. The seller's counsel assured buyer's counsel that the cancellation was effective and a trailing letter was adequate. The buyer stopped payment on the deposit check. Buyer's attorney immediately followed up with a written confirmation certified letter on August 5th (within three days) but the letter was not actually received by seller's counsel until August 9th or well after the three days. The seller refused to cancel the contract on the grounds that the terms of the receipt of written notice were not satisfied and the court agreed. The house was later resold for the same price but only after a real estate commission (not paid under the first sale). The seller was entitled to recover the $21,000 down payment.

To make matters worse, the frustrated buyer later brought suit against her attorney alleging malpractice for the failure to timely deliver written notice pursuant to the terms of the contract. The buyer argued that her attorney's failure to deliver timely written notice to cancel was malpractice as a matter of law thus seeking summary judgment. The court agreed noting that the buyer's counsel was not entitled to rely on an oral assurance by the seller's counsel that the timely written receipt was waived. See *Logalbo v. Plishkin, Rubano & Baum*, 558 N.Y.S. 2d 185 (1990). Of course, buyer's counsel also brought a third party complaint against the seller's attorney. While beyond the scope of this course, do you think that seller's counsel had authority to waive the requirement on behalf of the client? Not without the client's prior authorization—no such implied or apparent authority. If not, why should the buyer's attorney be able to recover from seller's attorney for an unauthorized waiver? An agent who acts as if authorized or claims to be authorized warrants his authority and is liable for breach of that warranty.

6. *Substantial performance of express conditions.* The Court's traditional response relies upon Restatement (Second) of Contracts § 237, *cmt. d:*

> *d. Substantial performance. . . .* If, however, the parties have made an event a condition of their agreement, there is no mitigating standard of materiality or substantiality applicable to the nonoccurrence of that event. If, therefore, the agreement makes full performance a condition, substantial performance is not sufficient and if relief is to be had under the contract, it must be through excuse of the non-occurrence of the condition to avoid forfeiture.

The Restatement (Second) of Contracts commentary plus the Williston language quoted by the Court exemplify the doctrine of strict performance of express conditions unless the requirement promotes forfeiture thus violating public policy. In the section on constructive conditions, substantial performance of an implied condition at law is adequate. Consequently, the duty of the party receiving less than perfect but nonetheless substantial performance is adequate to satisfy the condition implied in law requiring only substantial and not perfect performance. Do you see any reason why the doctrine of substantial performance applies to constructive conditions implied in law by courts but not to express conditions created by the parties? The doctrine of constructive conditions is a creature of the courts exercising their equitable discretion—"he who seeks equity must do equity"—hence the balancing power of the court. The doctrine of express conditions implements the expressly indicated intention of the parties—the parties are the judges of their own bargain and that bargain should be respected.

7. *Conditions of satisfaction.* See text.

2. Ordering of Performances

A critical function of conditions is to determine whether the parties are to perform simultaneously or rather whether one party must perform first before the other must perform. Purchase and sale of readily available goods illustrate the first and the second involves contracts where the performance of personal services requires time. The parties are always free to expressly order their performances. Express conditions are quite common where performance will require a significant expenditure of time and resources. The provider of time and resources will often require installment payments to help finance the progress of the work rather than waiting until the end of the contract to be compensated. But absent the use of express conditions to determine the order and sequence of performance, the common law provides two primary constructive condition default rules that are implied by law. Constructive ordering conditions are the primary subject of this section.

Constructive Conditions for Simultaneous Exchanges

Where performances can be exchanged simultaneously, they are due simultaneously. In a simultaneous performance exchange, each party's duty to perform is subject to an "implied condition" that the other party actually performs or offers to perform ("tender").

Constructive Condition for Nonsimultaneous Exchanges

Where performances cannot be exchanged simultaneously because one party's performance takes time, the performance requiring time is due first. In a non-simultaneous exchange, the party's performance due second is subject to an "implied condition" that the first party's performance will not be materially defective. In other words, the first party must substantially perform before the other party's performance becomes due. While substantial performance is not perfect performance and thus constitutes a breach of contract entitling the other party to damages, the other party receiving substantial performance must still perform as there is no condition of perfect performance.

El Dorado Hotel Properties, Ltd. v. Mortensen
CASE BRIEF

This is a 1983 decision of the Arizona Court of Appeals. El Dorado entered into a contract (note and deed of trust) to sell property to Mortenson and associates (hereafter "Mortensen," the parties liable on the note). The sale closed on January 22, 1982 at a price of $2,200,000. Mortensen paid a total of $300,000 and gave a note for the balance of $1,900,000. The next payment of $400,000 was due on March 1, 1982. The contract provided for the release of portions of the property by El Dorado to Mortensen as parts of the remaining purchase price were paid.

The promissory note provided that it was to be paid "in installments" as follows: "$400,000 on March 1, 1982 . . . ."

The note also contained a standard acceleration provision that "should default be made in payment of any installment of principal or interest when due the whole sum of principal and interest shall become immediately due at the option of the holder . . . ." The note also contained a statement that it was secured by the deed of trust. The release provision of the contract in issue in the case provided in part as follows:

> Upon payment of the $400,000.00 plus interest payment due on March 1, 1982, the trustors shall be entitled to have released free and clear of the purchase money Deed of Trust given to secure the unpaid balance herein 70,000 square feet of the subject real estate and any easement reasonably necessary for development of the first released parcel and any subsequent releases provided that:
>
> (a) Trustors shall have submitted to Beneficiary a plat of the subject property showing the location of the original release and the location, proposed use, size and order of future parcels to be released. This plat shall be approved by Beneficiary to be

> consonant with the requirements set forth in this paragraph. Such approval shall not be unreasonably withheld.
>
> (b) The parcel to be released shall be a compact parcel, one side of which shall be entirely contiguous to a property boundary of the subject parcel.
>
> (c) The parcel selected shall not unduly harm or be to the detriment of the utilization of the balance of the property.
>
> (d) No portion of any release shall include the golf course, clubhouse or the parking area reasonably necessary for the operation of the clubhouse and golf course. . . .

Mortensen did not secure a loan commitment for funds with which to make the March 1sts payment until late February, when they contacted El Dorado and secured an agreement that if payment was made by noon on March 5 there would be no default. On March 3rd counsel for Mortensen notified counsel for El Dorado that he would be delivering the "release plat" and "deed of release" for the first parcel. El Dorado said they would not consider reviewing the plat—there was not sufficient time to review it—and insisted that payment must be made first. In a letter the following day El Dorado counsel said that if unconditional payment was not made by noon on March 5 he would file a foreclosure action. Mortensen's counsel replied the same day claiming "we are entitled to the release upon payment." Mortensen tendered payment of the $400,000 conditioned on a deed of release and the payment was refused.

The trial court entered summary judgment for El Dorado holding that the release provision of the contract did not contemplate simultaneous performance by the parties (i.e. that payment by Mortensen was due first and delivery of the deed of release later). Said the trial court:

> Where the performance of one party requires a period of time, (e.g. examination and verification of the release provision) and the performance of the other party does not, (the $400,000.00 payment) their performances cannot be simultaneous. Since one of the parties must perform first, he must forego the security that a requirement of simultaneous performance affords against disappointment of his expectation of an exchange of performances, and he must bear the burden of financing the other party before the latter has performed (See Comment E, Section 234, Restatement of Contracts 2d.)

The court of appeals reversed, holding that the terms of the contract, properly construed, did require simultaneous performance and that as a consequence Mortensen was not in breach. The trial court's reliance on the Restatement comment was misplaced—the court should have applied Restatement (Second) of Contracts § 234(1) namely:

> (1) Where all or part of the performances to be exchanged under an exchange of promises can be rendered simultaneously, they are to that extent due simultaneously, unless the language or the circumstances indicate the contrary.

Said the court;

> The fact situation which is most applicable here is found in comment (b) which states, in part, that where a time is fixed for the performance of one of the parties (the payment of $400,000.00 on March 1) and no time is fixed for the other (the approval and delivery of the release) simultaneous performance is possible and will be required unless the language or the circumstances indicate the contrary.

Whether the release plat was tendered in time to permit review and exchange on March 5 was a material disputed fact precluding summary judgment.

Not only did the trial court err in its utilization of the Restatement, it also erred in holding, as a matter of law, that the provision "upon payment" meant "after payment." The payment and release could be exchanged simultaneously if the release information was provided in sufficient time.

INTERESTING DISCUSSION ISSUES

1. *Understanding the timing of a duty to perform and drafting the contract accordingly. El Dorado* can be seen as a clinical case—as a failure of the parties to foresee and plan explicitly for the relative order of performances under the contract. Many contracts involve simultaneous performance on both sides. Others do not. Consider the case of a sale of merchandise by a manufacturer to a buyer. The manufacturer would clearly prefer to be paid first and manufacture and deliver afterwards. If the contract so provides, the manufacturer is so entitled but the buyer carries the credit risk. If the manufacturer defaults, the buyer is at best an unsecured creditor—an unhappy situation. The buyer may say, in effect, "I will pay for the goods but only after delivery and a satisfactory inspection." If the contract so provides, well and good, but now the manufacturer has the credit risk. The relative timing of the respective performances is often of major importance. Parties, not advised by effective legal counsel, may not address these issues carefully and precisely, leading to someone's disappointed expectations. The work of the drafting lawyer can be critically important.

NOTES AND QUESTIONS

1. *Failure of language.* It is clear from the brief facts that the seller expected that the buyer would first make payment and the deed would be released after payment was received or, at the earliest, simultaneously if the buyer release request was submitted well in advance for review and approval. Assuming this to be the case, how would you rephrase the language of the contract to make certain that result occurred? Insert a requirement that the requested "release plat" be furnished for review by the seller not less than fourteen days before the date scheduled for exchange of money and deed. Do you think language governing the submission and review time would be helpful? Yes—see the last comment.

2. *Trial court rule and holding.* The trial court opinion is somewhat confusing. First, the court correctly states that the payment of money (buyer) does not require time. Second, the court correctly states that examination and verification of the release (seller) does require time. The court then proceeds to quote the Restatement (Second) of Contracts § 234(2) nonsimultaneous exchange default rule. That rule requires the party whose performance requires time must occur first (seller). But the court determined the seller should prevail as a matter of law even though it failed to perform first or perform at all. How do you reconcile the facts, rule and decision? The trial court's opinion considered the payment and the delivery of the release deed uncoupled transactions. This would make no commercial sense since, in all likelihood, the buyer would need to finance the purchase and would be unable to do so using the parcel as security unless the deed to the parcel was exchanged at least contemporaneously with the payment of the money. Notwithstanding the reference to the default rule regarding nonsimultaneous exchanges, does the trial court decide the matter in favor of the seller because the express "upon payment" language of the contract required the buyer to perform first? That was apparently one of the bases for the trial court ruling. This case is a classic illustration of defective drafting. The respective order of performance of promises must be addressed with great care and reflect the commercial needs of both parties.

3. *Appellate court rule and holding.* The Appellate Court opinion correctly notes that Restatement (Second) of Contracts § 234 prefers a simultaneous exchange default rule in order to avoid the problem referred to by the trial court. If the party whose performance takes time is required to perform first, that party must proceed without a guarantee of trailing performance by the other party. To avoid that risk, whenever possible, Restatement (Second) of Contracts § 234 prefers that all exchanges be simultaneous if possible. Restatement (Second) of Contracts § 234, *cmt. b* provides:

> *b. When simultaneous performance possible under agreement....* Cases in which simultaneous performance is possible under the terms of the contract can be grouped into five categories: (1) where the same time is fixed for the performance of each party; (2) where a time is fixed for the performance of one of the parties and no time is fixed for the other; (3) where no time is fixed for the performance of either party; (4) where the same period is fixed within which each party is to perform; (5) where different periods are fixed within which each party is to perform. The requirement of simultaneous performance applies to the first four categories. The requirement does not apply to the fifth category, even if simultaneous performance is possible, because in fixing different periods for performance the parties must have contemplated the possibility of performance at different times under their agreement.

Based on this language, where an agreement specifies matters each party must accomplish to perform, the only time the nonsimultaneous rule applies is when the parties specify a different time for each performance. In this case, the parties did not specify a different time for each performance and therefore the fifth rule does not apply. Accordingly, this is a case governed by the simultaneous exchange rule. As a result, the tender of payment of money will trigger the corresponding obligation to tender the deed release (provided of course adequate time for review was provided and the record implicated adequate time was given). If so, the tender of the money would trigger the breach for failure to tender the deed release. See Restatement (Second) of Contracts § 238. According to the appellate court, since the parties discussed timing, the nonsimultaneous default rule did not apply and is not preferred. Do you agree? Yes, for the financing reasons explained under Note 2 above. At least the appellate court disagrees with the trial court conclusion that the words "upon payment" meant that the default rules did not apply and the buyer was required to perform first by express language.

3. Constructive Conditions

Rules of "substantial performance" were developed to protect plaintiffs who had almost but not quite completed performance. Constructive conditions are not created by the parties but rather are implied in law to fulfill both the reasonable but unexpressed intent of the parties as well as to promote fairness in the enforcement of otherwise unconditional promises. Restatement (Second) of Contracts § 226. While courts imply constructive conditions in many circumstances such as to discharge a duty by reason of a supervening event (see *Taylor v. Caldwell* case in Chapter 7) and to determine the sequence of related contractual performance obligations (see

Restatement (Second) of Contracts § 234), this section discusses the most common and ancient of all constructive conditions—the doctrine of substantial performance.

The doctrine of substantial performance essentially considers the effect of less than perfect performance by the first party required to perform on the second party's obligation to perform. Where the first party does not substantially perform, a material breach occurs. If the breach is material, and no cure is forthcoming, the injured party has two options. The injured party may cancel the contract and sue for total breach because substantial performance is a condition of the second party's performance obligation. Alternatively, the injured party may continue with the contract and sue for partial breach. Where the breach is not material, the injured party must continue the contract and may not cancel but nonetheless retains the right to sue for partial breach.

While some have criticized the substantial performance rule because it requires the injured party to continue the contract and their own performance while retaining the right for damages for partial breach, it has nonetheless become a mainstay of domestic and international common law. Importantly, even when a breach is material, the other party's performance duty is not discharged, it is merely suspended. Only when the material breach is not cured is the duty discharged.

Both the concepts of the materiality of the breach and the proper duration of the cure period justifying cancellation and discharge are imbued with uncertainty.

Jacob & Youngs v. Kent
CASE BRIEF

This is a celebrated 1921 decision of the New York Court of Appeals written by Justice Cardozo. The plaintiff, a builder, built a country residence for the defendant. The contract specified that:

> All wrought-iron pipe must be well galvanized, lap welded pipe of the grade known as "standard pipe" of Reading manufacture.

After the building was finished the defendant discovered that some of the pipe used was the product of other factories than Reading. The owner's architect then directed the builder to do the work anew, which would have required demolition of a substantial part of the work previously done at great expense. The builder did not redo the work but instead asked the architect for a certificate of completion. When this request was denied the builder sued for the unpaid balance under the contract of $3,483.46.

The court concluded first, that the omission of the prescribed brand of pipe was neither fraudulent nor willful. It was the result of oversight and inattention of the builder's subcontractor. The defendant's architect inspected the pipe as delivered to the site but failed to notice the discrepancy. At the trial the builder offered to show that the pipe used was of the same quality but this offer was refused, the evidence excluded, and a verdict directed for the defendant. The appellate division reversed and granted a new trial. The Court of Appeals affirmed. Said Cardozo:

> We think the evidence, if admitted, would have supplied some basis for the inference that the defect was insignificant in its relation to the project. The courts never say that one who makes a contract fills the measure of his duty by less than full performance. They do say, however, that an omission, both trivial and innocent, will sometimes be atoned for by allowance of the resulting damage, and will not always be the breach of a condition to be followed by a forfeiture. . . . From the conclusion that promises may not be treated as dependent to the extent of their uttermost minutiae without a sacrifice of justice, the progress is a short one to the conclusion that they may not be so treated without a perversion of intention. Intention not otherwise revealed may be presumed to hold in contemplation the reasonable and probable. If something else is in view, it must not be left to implication. There will be no assumption of a purpose to visit venial faults with oppressive retribution. . . . Those who think more of symmetry and logic in the development of legal rules than of practical adaptation to the attainment of a just result will be troubled by a classification where the lines of division are so wavering and blurred.

Nowhere would change be tolerated if it was so determinant or pervasive as in any real or substantial measure to frustrate the purpose of the contract. The question was one of degree to be answered by the triers of fact, and if the inferences were certain, by the judges of the law. The parties could, of course, by the use of appropriate words make performance of every term a condition of recovery. But such relief would not be available for the willful transgressor. In the circumstances, the appropriate measure of damage would be the difference in value which here would be either nominal or nothing. The ordinary measure for failure to perform a building contract would be the cost of replacement of the defective work but not where the cost of completion is grossly and unfairly out of proportion to the good to be obtained. In this situation the appropriate measure was the difference in value. He concluded:

> The rule that gives a remedy in cases of substantial performance with compensation for defects of trivial or inappreciable importance

> has been developed by the courts as an instrument of justice. The measure of the allowance must be shaped to the same end.

Justice McLaughlin dissented:

> I dissent. The plaintiff did not perform its contract. Its failure to do so was either intentional or due to gross neglect which, under the uncontradicted facts, amounted to the same thing, nor did it make any proof of the cost of compliance, where compliance was possible. . . . The question of substantial performance of a contract of the character of the one under consideration depends in no small degree upon the good faith of the contractor. If the plaintiff had intended to, and had, complied with the terms of the contract except as to minor omissions, due to inadvertence, then he might be allowed to recover the contract price, less the amount necessary to fully compensate the defendant for damages caused by such omissions. . . . But that is not this case. . . . Defendant contracted for pipe made by the Reading Manufacturing Company. What his reason was for requiring this kind of pipe is of no importance. . . . He agreed to pay only upon condition that the pipe installed were made by that company and he ought not to be compelled to pay unless that condition be performed. . . . The rule, therefore, of substantial performance, with damages for unsubstantial omissions, has no application.

This was a 4-3 decision.

INTERESTING DISCUSSION ISSUES

1. *The critical importance of the doctrine of "substantial performance" of a promise.* This doctrine reflects an element of basic fairness—if the shortfall in performance can be remedied by a compensatory award of damages, it may not be fair to preclude the obligor from suing for the agreed upon price subject to the compensatory award. To the extent that the obligor has conferred a benefit on the obligee, the obligor may have a remedy in restitution but that remedy is based not on the contract price but on the objective value of the benefit actually conferred. Where the doctrine of substantial performance is available, the obligor is entitled to the contract price, and not just the objective value of the benefit conferred, subject to a compensatory award of damages. This is frequently the equitable result. As the introductory note points out, this doctrine brings with it substantial uncertainty in its application.

NOTES AND QUESTIONS

1. *Fastidious adherence to idiosyncratic preference?* Why would Kent insist on Reading pipe? We cannot guess. Would not any pipe suffice? Not necessarily—Kent might have a subjective preference for Reading pipe. Or he might be a shareholder in the Reading Pipe company with a special interest in getting pipe made by that company. We have no idea what the reason for his specification was. As Judge Cardozo observed even though the evidence was excluded Jacob & Youngs ". . . . tried to show that the brands installed, though made by other manufacturers, were the same in quality, in appearance, in market value, and in cost as the brand stated in the contract—that they were, indeed, the same thing, though manufactured in another place." Assuming the pipe to be of equal quality why would Kent insist on replacement at great and significant cost? We cannot tell. For the rest see the text of this Note.

2. *Express or constructive condition?* The construction contract in question specifically provided that "[a]ll wrought-iron pipe must be well galvanized, lap welded pipe of the grade known as 'standard pipe' of Reading manufacture." Judge Cardozo did not interpret this language as creating an express condition: "This is not to say that the parties are not free by apt and certain words to effectuate a purpose that performance of every term shall be a condition of recovery. That question is not here." What prevented Cardozo from determining the language was not an express condition? The harshness of the result otherwise (forfeiture). If the language regarding the use of Reading pipe was not an express condition, then it amounted to no more than doubtful conditional language construed as a "promise" to use such pipe. Restatement (Second) of Contracts § 227(2)(a). The distinction is important. As noted in the *Oppenheimer* case and trailing notes, express conditions require strict performance whereas constructive conditions may be satisfied by substantial performance. Substantial but imperfect performance remains a breach subjecting the breaching party to damages but does not operate as a failed condition to discharge the injured party's obligation to perform. Accordingly, the injured party must still perform but may recover damages for the less than perfect performance.

3. *Damage measure.* Judge Cardozo determined that the proper measure of damages was "not the cost of replacement, which would be great, but the difference in value, which would be either nominal or nothing." The measure of damages is the subject of the Chapter 9. However, Restatement (Second) of Contracts § 347 generally provides the injured party has a right to "loss in value" monetary damages based on an "expectancy interest" measured by the difference between the value of what was promised versus what was actually received.

Under this standard, what is the difference in value between the promised house (with Reading pipe) and the house as is (with Cohoes pipe)? None. Restatement (Second) of Contracts § 348(2) provides a special alternative rule specifically applicable to cases involving a breach "in defective or unfinished construction." Where the loss in value is not proven with sufficient certainty, the injured party may instead recover monetary damages based on the (i) diminution in the market price of the property caused by the defect, (ii) the reasonable cost of completing performance, or (iii) the reasonable cost of remedying the defects. However, the cost to remedy measure is only available where the "cost is not clearly disproportionate to the probable loss in value."

Where performance is defective (as in *Jacob & Youngs*) rather than incomplete, proof of loss in value with reasonable certainty is usually not feasible. As a result, the normative recovery is the cost to "remedy the defect." The remedial recovery will usually be greater than loss in value but the small resulting windfall is usually preferred to the more serious risk of undercompensation from loss in value. Restatement (Second) of Contracts § 348, *cmt. c.* However, in many cases a large portion of the cost to remedy will involve a significant cost to undo what was improperly done. In those cases, the cost to remedy the defects will be disproportionately large compared to the minute loss in value measure and results in a forfeiture of sorts to the breaching party. In such cases, the injured party is not likely to actually make the improvements because the great cost will result in such a small value increase in value. Accordingly, in such cases, the loss in value measure will be preferred.

Do you think this case involved just such a situation? Yes—tearing out much of the construction work already done in completion of the house would have been gross waste compared to any possible difference in value based on which pipe was used. If the loss in value is nominal and it costs $50,000 to tear up the walls and the home to substitute the Reading pipe, do you think the homeowner would pocket the $50,000 or spend it on the home even though it does not increase the value of the home? The average homeowner would pocket the money and use it otherwise thus indicating that the money was in fact a "windfall." Restatement (Second) of Contracts § 348(2) was based on Restatement (First) of Contracts § 346(1)(a)(i) which provided that the cost to remedy did not involve "unreasonable economic waste." The economic waste doctrine was rejected in Restatement (Second) of Contracts § 348(2) because it is presumed such expenditures will not be made and thus result in a windfall to the injured party who pockets the damages. Does this question depend in part upon whether the property involved is the injured party's personal residence? This issue is explored in more detail in Chapter 9.

4. *Substantial performance versus material breach.* An uncured material breach discharges the other party's duty to perform. Restatement (Second) of Contracts § 225(2). The Restatement does not utilize the phrase "substantial performance" developed by Judge Cardozo in *Jacob & Youngs.* However, material breach is the antithesis of substantial performance. While Restatement (Second) of Contracts § 241 lists various competing factors to make this determination, one is nonetheless left with a considerable degree of uncertainty as to exactly when and how performance crosses the line to fall short of substantial performance and thus become a material breach. But the factors are more a "list of ingredients than a recipe" and thus truly provide little practical guidance to this quite important question (the consequence of a material breach is the concomitant discharge of the performance duty of the other party). One suggestion advocates applying these factors with a particular policy focus in mind:

> This Article proposes a new perspective on material breach. It argues that materiality is best understood in terms of the specific purpose of the cancellation remedy that material breach entails. That [cancellation] remedy is designed to secure and enhance the likelihood that *future* duties will be properly performed. It does so by enabling the victim of a breach to acquire elsewhere the performance (or its economic equivalent) of the future duties that were to have been rendered by the other party. A breach should be considered material only when, given the particular facts of the case at hand, the victim needs that ability. Although this perspective does not eliminate doubt or uncertainty, it has the advantage of a simple and internally coherent theory. It remains for the courts to exercise judgment, but by using the approach proposed by this Article the courts are aided by a clear view of the questions they must answer. Eric G. Andersen, "A New Look At Material Breach In The Law of Contracts," 21 U. C. Davis L. Rev. 1073, 1077 (1988).

Utilizing this standard, is there any value in *Jacob & Youngs* in awarding Kent the right to cancel the contract in addition to an award of monetary damages? It is highly unlikely that Kent would have used any recover to tear down, replace the pipe and rebuild. Hence Andersen's approach would lead to the same result reached by Justice Cardozo. Would this ever occur once performance is completed? Yes, if destruction of the misbuilt house was the only way to give the plaintiff the performance the plaintiff was entitled to expect. If not, then is *Jacob & Youngs* truly about the right to cancel the contract or the proper measure of damages? Not necessarily. Why then the discussion of substantial performance at all? Because, as Justice Cardozo pointed out, the parties can make precise adherence to specific terms a condition of payment and either willfulness or fraud will remove grounds for a finding of substantial performance. See also Amy B. Cohen, *"Reviving Jacob & Youngs, Inc. v. Kent: Material Breach Doctrine Reconsidered,"* 42 Vill. L. Rev. 65 (1997).

5. *UCC perfect tender rule.* See text.

6. *CISG approach.* See text.

7. *Willful transgressor.* Judge Cardozo opines that the doctrine of substantial performance will not protect a willful transgressor: "The willful transgressor must accept the penalty of his transgression." What do you think he means? The doctrine of substantial performance, being essentially equitable in nature, will not be available to help someone who does not merit such help—the willful or the fraudulent wrongdoer. Does willfulness increase the damage measure or simply allow cancellation as a material breach? Motive is generally irrelevant in determination of contract damages. Thus the answer, usually, is that willfulness will result in a finding of material and not immaterial breach. Restatement (Second) of Contracts § 241(e) also suggests a similar point in its multi-factor analysis to determine whether a breach is material by referencing "the extent to which the behavior of the party failing to perform or to offer to perform comports with standards of good faith and fair dealing." Restatement (Second) of Contracts § 241, *cmt f* explains:

> *f. Absence of good faith or fair dealing.* A party's adherence to standards of good faith and fair dealing (§ 205) will not prevent his failure to perform a duty from amounting to a breach (§ 236(2)). Nor will his adherence to such standards necessarily prevent his failure from having the effect of the non-occurrence of a condition (§ 237; cf. § 238). The extent to which the behavior of the party failing to perform or to offer to perform comports with standards of good faith and fair dealing is, however, a significant circumstance in determining whether the failure is material (Subsection (e)). In giving weight to this factor courts have often used such less precise terms as "willful." Adherence to the standards stated in Subsection (e) is not conclusive, since other circumstances may cause a failure to be material in spite of such adherence. Nor is non-adherence conclusive, and other circumstances may cause a failure not to be material in spite of such non-adherence.

To some degree, the requirement of good faith imports the moral requirement of subjective honesty and belief in conduct. Do you think that the law should require good faith only as purely economic and analytical reasoning of business risks? No. A generalized requirement of good faith is suggested by both the Restatement (Second) and the UCC. Putting such good faith together with a Posner theory of "efficient breach" can prove challenging. See Eric G. Andersen, *"Three Degrees of Promising,"* 2003 B.Y.U. L. Rev. 829 (2003) and Caroline N. Brown, *"Teaching Good Faith,"* 44 St. Louis U. L. J. 1377 (2000).

8. *Dependent and independent promises.* Judge Cardozo refers to minor deviations of contractual duties as constructive conditions as similar to dependent promises: "The distinction is akin to that between dependent and independent promises, or between promises and conditions. . . . Some promises are so plainly independent that they can never by fair construction be conditions of one another. . . . Others are so plainly dependent that they must always be conditions. Others, though dependent and thus conditions when there is departure in point of substance, will be viewed as independent and collateral when the departure is insignificant." Clearly conditions are far broader than mere promises and include any fact specified by the parties that must occur before performance is due. On what basis did Judge Cardozo create the constructive condition of substantial performance? Intent implied from what rational parties would most likely expect and intend. Was it the presumed intent of the parties, justice or both? Both. What do you think he means by the following reference: "Considerations partly of justice and partly of presumable intention are to tell us whether this or that promise shall be placed in one class or in another."? As he pointed out, a standard of objective fairness will give way to the clearly expressed intention of the parties otherwise.

9. *Total and partial breach.* See text.

10. *Divisible contracts.* See text.

4. Excuse, Waiver and Other Relief From Effect of Conditions

There are a number of important exceptions all designed to mitigate the harshness of all forms of express and constructive conditions (although these principles have little effect on the doctrine of substantial performance, itself a mitigating doctrine). In all cases, some behavior or equitable principle overrides the nonoccurrence of the condition and its normal consequence of discharging the other party's performance obligation. In each case, when the nonoccurrence of the condition is excused, the correlative duty will become due. Stated another way, the excuse of the condition converts the conditional duty to an unconditional duty.

Doctrine of Good Faith

The parties must exercise good faith and fair dealing (i) to refrain from preventing or hindering the occurrence of the condition (doctrine of prevention), and (ii) to take affirmative steps to cause its occurrence at least when the occurrence is within that party's control.

Doctrine of Waiver

Another important exception is the doctrine of waiver. The party who benefits from the nonoccurrence of the condition may waive its effect in most cases. As a general rule, it is easier to waive constructive conditions since waiver of material express conditions is prohibited.

Doctrine of Forfeiture

Courts may also excuse conditions that would cause an unconscionable forfeiture. Even though both unconscionability and the excuse to avoid forfeiture doctrine limit the freedom of the parties to contract, they are applied at different moments in time. Unconscionability is determined at the time the contract is formed, whereas courts analyze whether to excuse conditions to avoid a forfeiture at the time of the occurrence of the condition. Curiously, as with waiver of express conditions, the condition excuse by reason of disproportionate forfeiture can only occur where the condition was not a material part of the exchange. Forfeiture excuse cases are inextricably tied to equitable balancing of the reasonable expectations of the parties.

Holiday Inns of America, Inc. v. Knight
CASE BRIEF

This is a 1969 decision of the California Supreme Court written by Chief Justice Traynor. Plaintiffs entered into an option contract with defendant giving them the option to purchase a parcel of land for a stated price. The parcel was next to land the plaintiffs were developing at considerable cost and the reason for the option was to allow the plaintiffs to secure the beneficial increase in value of the option parcel attributable to the development next door. The option contract provided for an initial payment of $10,000 and four additional payments each of $10,000 to be paid to the grantors of the option on July 1sts of each of the four succeeding years. The option agreement contained the following cancellation provision:

> [I]t is mutually understood that failure to make payment on or before the prescribed date will automatically cancel this option without further notice.

Prior to the time for the second payment the parties amended the agreement to require that the payments be received by an escrow agent by July 1. The initial payment and the next two annual payments were made on time. In 1966 when the third installment payment was due the plaintiffs mailed a check for $10,000 to the defendant dated June 30, 1966. Defendant received the check on July 2 and returned it to the plaintiffs who then made several additional attempts to tender the $10,000 payment, all of which were rejected by the defendant who argued that the option contract had been terminated.

Plaintiffs sought a declaratory judgment that the option contract was in effect, arguing that the payment was made when the check was mailed on June 30 and, in the alternative, that the trial court should relieve them from forfeiture based on the following California statutory provision:

> Whenever, by the terms of an obligation, a party thereto incurs a forfeiture, or a loss in the nature of a forfeiture, by reason of his failure to comply with its provisions, he may be relieved therefrom, upon making full compensation to the other party, except in case of a grossly negligent, willful, or fraudulent breach of duty.

The trial court entered summary judgment for the defendant.

The California Supreme Court decided the issue on the basis of the forfeiture provision without considering plaintiff's other arguments, and stated the issue as, "whether the right to exercise the option in the future was forfeited by a failure to pay the consideration for that right precisely on time." Plaintiffs, said the court, were not seeking to extend the period during which the option could be exercised. The sole issue therefore was whether there would be a loss in the nature of a forfeiture suffered by the plaintiffs if the option contract were terminated. The court held on the facts that termination would cause such a forfeiture:

> With the passage of time, plaintiffs have paid more and more for the right to renew, and it is this right that would be forfeited by requiring payment strictly on time. At the time the forfeiture was declared, plaintiffs had paid a substantial part of the $30,000 for the right to exercise the option during the last two years. Thus, they have not received what they bargained for and they have lost more than the benefit of their bargain. In short, they will suffer a forfeiture of that part of the $30,000 attributable to the right to exercise the option during the last two years.

The court noted that at all times the plaintiffs had remained willing and able to continue performance of the contract and had acted in good faith. Defendant had not suffered any injury justifying termination of the contract and none of his reasonable expectations had been defeated. The trial court judgment was reversed and that court was ordered to enter summary judgment for the plaintiffs.

INTERESTING DISCUSSION ISSUES

1. *When does the doctrine of strict performance of a condition produce an inequitable result?* This case illustrates just such a situation. Excuse of a condition on the grounds of forfeiture is not a common outcome. In the case above it was clear to the court that the defendants received the substantial benefit of performance they had contracted for despite the very minor failure to satisfy the condition precisely. Does this case subvert the doctrine of the *Oppenheimer* case that satisfaction of conditions is not a case of horse shoes? The comparison and contrast of the decision in these two cases provides for interesting discussion. Students need to understand that relief from strict satisfaction of a condition is granted only infrequently, and then only where, as in *Holiday Inns,* the obligee received the substantial benefit of the performance contracted for. Relief for forfeiture is clearly an "equitable" doctrine and subject to the many rules derived from chancery practice.

NOTES AND QUESTIONS

1. *Mailbox rule.* See text.

2. *Holiday Inn forfeiture.* What did Judge Traynor decide that Holiday Inn forfeited? The value of the $30,000 in payments previously paid when part of the reason for those payments was to keep the option open for a period of five years. Did the refusal of the seller to accept the late payment cause any forfeiture of the land already developed by Holiday Inn? No—it had no effect on the other adjoining land that the plaintiffs were developing. Did the failure of the seller cause Holiday Inn to lose the undisputed value of the adjacent land caused by its adjacent development? No. Or did Judge Traynor simply determine that Holiday Inn would forfeit the $30,000 expended in 1963, 1964, and 1965? Yes –that they would forfeit the benefit they had contracted for and substantially paid for with those payments.

3. *Disproportionate forfeiture.* Assuming Holiday Inn would forfeit the $30,000, how material to the seller was the condition that payment must be received by July 1 of each year? The record apparently contained no evidence that a short delay would inconvenience the defendant or impair the value of the performance sought under the contract by the defendant. Did Holiday Inn seek to extend the deadline for exercising the option to purchase the land for approximately $200,000 beyond April 1, 1968? No. The court turns a square corner on the distinction between accepting the late payment and extending the time period of the option. Given that the only purpose of the option was to allocate the increase in value of the land caused by the adjacent

development, do you see why the seller would argue the July 1 deadline was a valid time of essence clause? Yes—the defendant's behavior appears to have been arbitrary and "opportunistic", designed to allow the defendant to pick up the increased value of the parcel attributable to the developments next door. Had Holiday Inn attempted to extend the April 1, 1968, deadline in a similar manner do you think it would have been successful? No.

4. *Purpose of option.* The purpose of the option and the $10,000 annual payment was to allow Holiday Inn to retain the right to speculate on the value of the adjacent property. Given the great increase in value of that land, do you think Holiday Inn would intentionally risk loss of that value by making a payment one day late? No. Since the payment was only one day late and the eventual option exercise date of April 1, 1968 was not extended, how would you compare and evaluate the respective forfeitures of the two parties? There was no proportionality between the two situations. The defendant had contracted to give the plaintiffs the option of acquiring the benefit and lost nothing (except perhaps interest for a day) when payment was tendered one day late.

5. *California statutory law.* The case relies on a California statute similar to the language in Restatement (Second) of Contracts § 229. If the common law applied, would you expect a different outcome? No—the California statute was interpreted in accordance with the common law.

CHAPTER 9

REMEDIES FOR BREACH OF CONTRACT

Table of Contents

Introduction to Chapter 9 Coverage

Chapter 8 explored a breach of contract defined as any non-performance of a promise when due. Restatement (Second) of Contracts § 235(2). The effect of express and implied conditions determined when a promise became due and anticipatory repudiation explored breach before a promise became due. This chapter assumes a breach has occurred and therefore considers the important remedial effects to both the breaching and injured parties.

The common law history of remedies for breach of contract was damages, enhanced, where money damages were inadequate, by equitable injunctive relief. The bulk of this chapter deals with the calculation, measure and limitations on monetary damages, followed by a review of the constraints applicable to injunctive relief.

Fuller and Perdue described three forms of monetary damage recovery: where the plaintiff has conferred some value on the defendant in reliance on the defendant's promise leading to a disgorging of the value received—the "restitution" interest; where the plaintiff has changed position in reliance on the defendant's promise leading to restoration of the plaintiff's position prior to the reliance—the "reliance" interest; and where the plaintiff seeks to recover the value of the expectancy created by the promise—the "expectation" interest. They considered that these three types of situation were arranged in descending order in terms of the cogency of the need for providing a remedy. Why, they asked, should a promise which has not been relied on ever be enforced at all? Modern contract law has embraced all three forms of remedy, the "expectancy" remedy however, being the leader—see Restatement (Second) of Contracts §§ 344, 347.

Any breach will give rise to a claim for damages, even nominal, where no other damages are proven under the applicable limitations.

American jurisprudence does not award attorney fees to the victor. Considering the risks and costs and litigation, do you suspect that any measure of contract damages will place the injured party in the same position as if the contract had been fully performed? No. While the award of damages may be structured to give the plaintiff her full benefit of the bargain, the "American rule," whereby each side of a lawsuit pays their own legal fees, means that the plaintiff's "expectancy" recovery ends up being reduced usually by the litigation costs of obtaining that recovery. In short, the plaintiff who is forced to litigate will not realize that full "expectancy." Do you imagine that contract litigation damages always fail to restore the injured party to status quo? Yes—see the preceding sentence. Given this inadequacy principle, how do you view a court order of specific performance to compel performance in accordance with the terms of the contract? This is said to be the common approach of European courts which use the "civil law" system. In America, courts view the difficulties of such an approach, combined with the judicial time and energy that could be consumed in supervising such injunctive orders, compelling. Perhaps more significantly, this is not the path of the common law as it evolved in England, was adopted in the states in this country, and has continued to date.

A. ELECTION OF CONTRACT BREACH REMEDIES

Breach can produce multiple remedy opportunities. Must the injured party choose one at the peril of losing one of the other remedies more easily available? Or may the injured party plead these measures in the alternative such that a loss on one count does not automatically eliminate a loss on the others? The usual rule now permits the plaintiff to plead multiple inconsistent theories of possible recovery and elect prior to entry of judgment. Of course the rules preclude the plaintiff from multiple recoveries on different theories.

B. ELECTION TO SEEK RESCISSION AND RESTITUTION DAMAGES OFF THE CONTRACT

Restitution theory has been explored in previous chapters. This chapter focuses only on restitution connected to breach of contract. The discussion that follows assumes that the injured party elects to treat the uncured material breach as a total breach and cancels or otherwise terminates the contractual relationship. Confronted with a total breach by the breaching party the injured party may seek a forward-looking remedy involving expectancy damages. In this case, the continuing existence and validity of the contract is a necessary predicate of any award of damages. In the alternative, the plaintiff may elect to pursue the retrospective remedy based on the plaintiff's election to rescind the contract and recover restitutionary damages.

The Losing Contract and Effect of Contract Price

As explored more fully below, the goal of expectancy damages is to place the injured party in as good a position as if had the contract been performed. A necessary corollary is that the award may not place the injured party in a better position than would have occurred had there been no breach. Generally, the contract operates as a practical upper limit on damages recovery except where the breaching party commits an uncured material breach before the injured party has fully performed and the injured party seeks restitution off the contract. Scholars are divided on the question whether the contract should provide a ceiling on recovery in this latter case. The next case poses and deals with the answer to that question.

United States v. Algernon Blair, Inc.
CASE BRIEF

This is a 1973 decision of the United States Circuit Court of Appeals for the Fourth Circuit. Algernon Blair, Inc. (Blair) contracted with the federal government to build a naval hospital in South Carolina. Blair subcontracted with Coastal Steel Contractors (Coastal) to perform certain steel erection tasks for the project. Coastal began using its own cranes for the steel erection, but Blair refused to pay for the crane rental; after completing twenty-eight percent of the subcontract, Coastal terminated its performance because of Blair's refusal to pay for crane rental. Coastal filed suit against Blair under the Miller Act, and the district court found that Blair's refusal to pay for crane rental justified Coastal's termination of performance; this issue was not appealed. The court found that the amount due for Coastal's performance to that point, less money already paid, was approximately $37,000; it also found that Coastal would have lost over $37,000 if it had completed performance of the subcontract. The court thus denied any recovery to Coastal, holding that any amount due Coastal must be offset by any loss that Coastal would have incurred by complete performance. Coastal appealed, claiming that it was entitled to recover in quantum meruit.

The court of appeals agreed with Coastal, and cited opinions from the Second and Tenth Circuits stating, respectively, that a party may claim as damages the reasonable value of his performance, and that the right to seek recovery under quantum meruit in a Miller Act case is clear. In the current case, Coastal, at its own expense, provided Blair with use of equipment and labor; Blair retained the benefits without paying for them. Commentators have argued that such "restitution interest" cases actually support twice as strong a claim to judicial intervention as a mere reliance interest because of an unjust enrichment paired with an unjust loss.

The court stated that the measure for recovery for quantum meruit is the reasonable value of the performance, undiminished by any loss that would have been incurred by complete performance. While the contract price may be evidence of reasonable value of the services, it does not measure the value of the performance to limit recovery. Rather, the standard for measuring the reasonable value of the services rendered is the amount for which the services could have been purchased from one in the plaintiff's position at the time and place the services were rendered.

The court held that quantum meruit was the proper measure of damages, and remanded for determination of the amount to be awarded Coastal.

INTERESTING DISCUSSION ISSUES

1. *Should contract damages be a cap on restitution damages when the plaintiff elects restitution-based relief rather than expectancy or reliance damages?* The pros and cons of such a cap are discussed in the introductory notes. This issue is one of some controversy but, happily, seems to arise only rarely. Coastal conferred a benefit on Blair and thus should qualify for unjust enrichment relief unless the absence of any recoverable contract damages should serve as a cap on any such restitutionary recovery. Some argue that although the damages rules would have precluded Coastal from recovering either expectancy or reliance damages here, the two theories are distinct and should not be confused—restitution should be available whenever a benefit has been conferred under circumstances indicating that the benefit was not intended or received as a gift.

NOTES AND QUESTIONS

1. *The "Miller Act" and government contracts.* See text.

2. *Availability of the losing contract restitution remedy.* The general contractor Algernon Blair argued that the construction contract with the subcontractor Coastal Steel required Coastal to pay for its own crane. After completing approximately 28% of the contract with no Algernon crane reimbursement, Coastal determined to stop work and sue Algernon who hired another subcontractor to complete the project. Why did Coastal not breach the contract when it stopped work after completing only 28%? Coastal treated Algernon's failure to pay for crane reimbursement as a material uncured breach of the contract. Coastal was found justified by the court in so treating the reimbursement failure. Coastal then elected to rescind the contract and sue for its restitution based remedy. What legal rule permitted this behavior while foreclosing a suit by Algernon against Coastal? See the explanation in the preceding sentence.

Once Algernon committed an uncured material breach, Coastal had an option to elect to continue the contract, complete its own performance and sue Algernon for partial breach of contract. If Coastal had fully performed the contract what would it have been entitled to recover? The value of its expectancy interest which would have been a negative number. See Restatement (Second) of Contracts § 373(2). The remaining option was to terminate or cancel the contract with Algernon. At that point, Coastal once again had two options. First, it could sue on the contract for total breach damages. Alternatively, since the contract was terminated it could sue for restitution. Obviously, it elected to sue for restitution. Why do you think it did so? Because the restitution-based remedy number was $37,000 whereas the expectancy value number was a negative. Are any of these various three "elections" (terminate or not, sue on the contract, sue off the contract), precluded by the election of remedies provisions? See Restatement (Second) of Contracts § 378. Not unless they are inconsistent and the defendant changes her position in reliance on the "manifestation."

Algernon alleged the $37,000 restitution recovery was excessive because Coastal had made a poor contract by grossly underestimating its true expenses. Assuming that to be true, is the contract price a limitation on Coastal's recovery? Not according to the decision on these facts and Restatement (Second) of Contracts. See Restatement § 373(1).

3. *Restitution measure.* Once Coastal determined to sue for restitution, how is that to be measured and what is the function and role of the contract itself in that determination? The measure of Coastal's recovery is the market value of the benefit conferred on Algernon. The trial court determined that even though Algernon owed $37,000 on the contract, it was entitled to reduce that amount by any amount it could prove Coastal would lose by completing performance. This is certainly the rule in an expectancy recovery. See Restatement (Second) of Contracts § 347(c) (recovery reduced by any loss avoided by not having to perform). That topic is explored further under expectancy recovery. The appellate court reversed noting that "recovery is undiminished by any loss which would have been incurred by complete performance."

The Court cites Restatement (First) of Contracts § 347(1) (for the total breach of a contract, the injured party can get judgment for the reasonable value of a performance rendered by him, measured as of the time it was rendered) to allow Coastal to recover the market value of the services to Algernon Blair rather than the contractual price. Restatement (Second) of Contracts § 373(1) also provides that the injured party is entitled to restitution for any benefit conferred on the other party. However, the measurement of the restitution interest is now contained in Restatement (Second) of Contracts § 371 that provides the restitution interest may be measured, as required by justice, either by (a) the reasonable value received by the breaching party determined by reference to the actual or hypothetical cost to obtain replacement services from another person in the position of the injured party, or (b) the value of the increase in the breaching party's interest. Would the outcome in this case be any different using Restatement (Second) of Contracts § 371(a)? No. Did Algernon complete the project using another subcontractor? Yes. Would the cost to complete not be the measurement standard? No—that would be the standard only if Algernon was suing, based on a breach by Coastal, for the cost of obtaining a substitute performance. Does Algernon have to pay twice? No. First, Algernon must pay the replacement subcontractor. Must it also pay Coastal, the party injured by the breach? Yes—the measurements are different. Is that fair and if so what justifies this result? Algernon received the benefit conferred and to that extent did not have to pay the second contractor for that same work. Had Coastal breached the contract, Algernon would have hired another subcontractor to complete the project but unless the cost to complete was greater than the remaining unpaid cost in the original contract, Algernon would simply have paid the full contract price but to two different parties. How and why is this situation so radically different? One case involves Algernon not committing a breach, the other posits such a breach. How would you decide the "justice" limitation specifically stated in Restatement (Second) of Contracts § 371? Whether the plaintiff herself was in breach or not could make a difference. Do you think a restatement section must state a "justice" requirement in order for a court to reach a just result? No. If not, why do some restatement sections specifically mention justice while others are silent? In those sections specifically mentioning "justice" the purpose is to alert a court to the fact that it has a discretion. As noted by the scholarly debate earlier, scholars are divided on whether Coastal should be able to recover the market value of its services or rather should be limited by the contract price.

4. *Breaching plaintiff and restitution.* Although not addressed by *Algernon Blair,* restitution is available to a breaching party as well as the injured party. See Restatement (Second) of Contracts § 374. Typically, this will occur in situations where a buyer makes a deposit on a purchase contract but is unable to complete the purchase. The injured seller is of course entitled to damages but if the deposit exceeds those damages, the breaching purchaser is entitled to a return of the excess and may bring a suit to enforce. The same rule existed under Restatement (First) § 357(1). Importantly, Restatement (First) of Contracts § 357(1)(a) required that the breach not be deliberate or willful. However, Restatement (Second) of Contracts § 374 blackletter omits the willful breach limitation as does the intervening UCC § 2-718(2) enacted after the Restatement (First) of Contracts but before the Restatement (Second) of Contracts. However, the commentary somewhat retains the concept:

> *b. Measurement of benefit.* If the party in breach seeks restitution of money that he has paid, no problem arises in measuring the benefit to the other party. See Illustration 1. If, however, he seeks to recover a sum of money that represents the benefit of services rendered to the other party, measurement of the benefit is more difficult. Since the party seeking restitution is responsible for posing the problem of measurement of benefit, doubts will be resolved against him and his recovery will not exceed the less generous of the two measures stated in § 370, that of the other party's increase in wealth. See Illustration 3. If no value can be put

on this, he cannot recover. See Illustration 5. Although the contract price is evidence of the benefit, it is not conclusive. However, in no case will the party in breach be allowed to recover more than a ratable portion of the total contract price where such a portion can be determined.

A party who intentionally furnishes services or builds a building that is materially different from what he promised is properly regarded as having acted officiously and not in part performance of his promise and will be denied recovery on that ground even if his performance was of some benefit to the other party. This is not the case, however, if the other party has accepted or agreed to accept the substitute performance. See §§ 278, 279.

The elimination of the blackletter willful breach limitation represents a deliberate policy shift. The two competing policies include comparing the overcompensation to the injured party in one case (favored by Restatement (First) of Contracts)) with rewarding deliberate breaching behavior (favored by Restatement (Second) of Contracts)). The inclusion of a recovery measure in both cases was precipitated by an early important article recognizing that most cases refused to penalize the breaching party by rewarding the injured party with overcompensation. See Arthur L. Corbin, *"The Right of a Defaulting Vendee to the Restitution of Installments Paid,"* 40 Yale L. J. 1013 (1931). See also Comment, *"Defaulting Vendee Relieved From Forfeiture,"* 2 Stan. L. Rev. 235 (1949). Such a shift may reflect a more general acceptance among scholars, lawyers, and judges that breachers of contract are not necessarily wrongdoers. "Rules of contract law are not rules of punishment; the contract breacher is not an outlaw. His restitution interest deserves protection to the extent that it does not subvert the legitimate interests of the party aggrieved by the breach." Joseph M. Perillo, *"Restitution in the Second Restatement of Contracts,"* 81 Colum. L. Rev. 37, 50 (1981).

Accepting the doctrine for the moment as the rule, should the parties be able to expressly alter the rule in the contract itself? Yes—freedom of contract should prevail here. Is the rule a default rule or a mandatory rule that in all cases disfavors overcompensation of the injured party to discouraging deliberate and willful breaching behavior? The rule is a default rule which the parties can override. Can overcompensation in such cases be related to punitive damages? Perhaps—but if a court determines that the contract provision is operating as a "penalty" it can ignore the provision—see the discussion of "penalty" damages later in this chapter. See Restatement (Second) of Contracts § 355. Should an intentional and deliberate breach of a contract constitute a tort? Not unless the conduct involved is otherwise tortious.

5. *Willful breach doctrines as a quasi-punitive remedy.* As noted above, American contract law is generally unconcerned with the fault of the breaching party. Nonetheless, courts react in many cases to the willfulness of a breach by either conscious or unconscious bias against the breaching party, or by application of several doctrines expressly dealing with willfulness. Judge Cardozo's discussion in dicta in *Jacob & Youngs v. Kent*—analyzed in Chapter 8—suggests that the decision whether to apply a cost-of-completion or a difference-in-value measure of damages depends upon the willfulness of the breach. Courts also relax the degree of certainty required to prove the amount of damages in cases of willful breach. See William S. Dodge, "The Case for Punitive Damages in Contracts," 48 Duke L.J. 629, 689 & n. 328 (1999). Do you think that such exceptions to the general rule that courts will not inquire into the wrongfulness or fault involved in a breach reflect a hidden agenda by courts to punish "wrongful" breaches of contract? "Punish" may be the wrong word—just allocation of responsibility and measurement of the loss may be more appropriate.

C. ELECTION TO SEEK DAMAGES ON THE CONTRACT

While often controversial and sometimes questioned, the expectancy remedy has become the clear norm for modern contract damage purposes. Also, as explored earlier in this chapter, injunctive relief may also be available when monetary damages are inadequate.

1. The Expectancy Interest

The object of the expectancy interest is to protect the injured party's interest in having the "benefit of the bargain"—to place that party in "as good a position" (but no better) than would have occurred had the contract been fully performed as promised by the breaching party.

Subject to limitations to be explored later in this chapter, the injured party's measure of the expectancy interest for total breach (see Restatement (Second) of Contracts § 347) involves the following four factors:

- "Loss in value" caused by the breaching party's failure or deficiency; [Element 1]
- Plus any "other loss" caused by the breach, including incidental and consequential losses; [Element 2]
- Less any "cost avoided" by not having to perform; [Element 3] and
- Less any "loss avoided" by not having to perform [Element 4].

The first two elements are applicable to partial as well as total breach. Elements 3 and 4 are normally only associated with a total breach.

Element 1(A). Loss in Value Component

Where the defective performance is a partial breach, the calculation of "value" is normally equal to the difference between the value that the performance would have had if there had been no breach and the value of such performance as was actually rendered. The loss in value formulation requires proof of the "market value" of the promise in order to compare that value to the value established by the contract. "Market value", an imprecise if not elusive concept, implies an objective determination rather than a subjective one, and often leads to difficult issues of proof.

Element 1(B). *Cost Alternative to Loss in Value Component.*

Cost of repair or replacement is frequently used to measure loss in value, and appears to be the preferred measure under Restatement (Second) of Contracts § 348(2). The injured party can still recover the "loss in value" measure where neither repair nor replacement is done. But under this section cost of repair or replacement will not be allowed where such cost is clearly disproportionate to the probable loss in value. In this situation, the loss in value becomes the only available measure.

Element 2. *Plus Other Loss Recovery.*

Damages under this heading will normally be incidental and/or consequential. Incidental losses typically occur after the breach and include additional costs incurred by the injured party to avoid further losses. Consequential losses represent losses to the injured party's property or to persons. Damages conceptually adopt one of two primary forms. First, "general" or "direct" damages flow from the "ordinary course of events" normatively expected to result from a breach. See, e.g., UCC 2-714(1) (damages for any nonconformity of tender the loss resulting in the "ordinary course of events" from the seller's breach). Second, "consequential" or "special" damages are those that do not flow from the ordinary course of events but that result from the general or particular needs and requirements of the injured party that the breaching party had reason to know. The "had reason to know" language implies a generally accepted objective standard and rejects a more restrictive "tacit agreement" standard that would require the breaching party to specifically contemplate the damage and thus specifically assume the risk. The single most important class of consequential damages includes profits lost by the injured party on other or collateral contracts as a result of the breach of the contract between the breaching and injured party. Lost profits on the primary contract between the breaching and injured party are general or direct damages because they are usually expected and foreseeable as an ordinary result of a breach.

Element 3. *Less Costs Avoided.*

In cases involving total breach where the injured party terminates the contract, the injured party will save the cost of any further performance. Given that the avoidance limitation discussed below most often requires the injured party to terminate its performance, further costs will normally be avoided. The costs so avoided are subtracted from the "loss in value" determined as above.

Element 4. *Less Losses Avoided.*

Also in cases involving total breach where the injured party terminates the contract, the injured party might avoid some losses by salvaging and redirecting some of the resources otherwise to be devoted to completing performance on the terminated contract. For example, a wrongfully discharged employee will normally seek other employment using the services freed up by the employer's breach.

In the next case, consider the expectancy interest and its market formulation in the context of the court's jury instruction. Did that instruction adequately convey to the jury the required elements of proof? No—hence the remand for a new trial. How was market value of the promise to be determined? In the Supreme Court decision the jury was instructed to determine the value of a good hand to Hawkins and subtract the value of the hand Hawkins ended up with.

Hawkins v. McGee
CASE BRIEF

Plaintiff Hawkins had sustained severe burns on his hand by virtue of contact with an electrical wire. In order to convince Hawkins to undergo a skin graft that would attempt to repair the scar tissue on his hand using skin from his chest, Defendant Dr. McGee told Hawkins, "I will guarantee to make the hand a hundred per cent perfect hand or a hundred per cent good hand." But when Dr. McGee's surgery did not result in "a hundred per cent perfect hand or a hundred per cent good hand," Hawkins sued McGee for breach of contract.

While the court held that the parties clearly understood Dr. McGee's statement that Hawkins would only be in the hospital for "three or four days, not over four" as an expression of opinion, it did take up the issue of whether Dr. McGee's words regarding Hawkins's hand "could possibly have the meaning imputed to them by [Hawkins]," who took the words as a warranty. In light of the fact that Dr. McGee "repeatedly solicited" from Hawkins's father the opportunity to perform the operation (McGee wished to "experiment on skin grafting"), the court held that the jury could have reasonably accepted Hawkins's assertion that McGee's words were an inducement for the granting of Hawkins's consent. The question of promise (warranty) had thus been properly submitted to the jury.

The court also held that the trial court's instruction regarding damages was erroneous because it permitted the jury to consider: (1) pain and suffering from the operation; and (2) positive effects of the operation on Hawkins's hand. The court held that the instructions were improper because damages were to be determined in light of the contract, putting the plaintiff in as good of a position as he would have been had the defendant fulfilled the contract. Damages were not to be determined in light of the parties' standing before entering the contract. The court described the present case as analogous to one in which a machine is built for a certain purpose and warranted to do certain work. In such case, the measure of damages is the difference in value between the machine as promised and the machine as delivered, as well as other incidental damages. Here, the damages owed Hawkins were the difference between the perfect hand that was promised him and the hand that he now possessed. Hawkins's suffering did not measure that difference in value, and examining the improvement of his hand from its previous state was the exact opposite way to determine his damages.

Finally, the court held that the trial court properly denied defendant McGee's proposed jury instructions. The court held that it would have been misleading to instruct the jury that (1) the only question to be answered was whether the plaintiff and defendant had a special contract to produce a perfect hand; or (2) in order to find McGee liable, both McGee and Hawkins must have understood that McGee guaranteed a perfect hand. The court also rejected an instruction that would have mitigated damages unless the jury determined that the damage could not be repaired with further surgery (McGee had refused to perform such surgery).

INTERESTING DISCUSSION ISSUES

1. *How would counsel establish the value of a 100% good hand?* While this case recites a classic formulation of the benefit of the bargain or "expectancy" measure of damages, it leaves students wondering how either of the two required calculations under that formula would be either proven or judged by a jury. What is the worth of a 100% good hand? On what basis did the trial judge rule, as reported in the Supreme Court opinion, "The court denied the motion upon the first three grounds, but found that the damages were excessive, and made an order that the verdict be set aside, unless the plaintiff elected to remit all in excess of $500"? For some suggestions on these issues see Notes 3 and 9 below.

NOTES AND QUESTIONS

1. *Promissory language.* Dr. McGee told Hawkins and his father that Hawkins would be in the hospital "Three or four days, not over four." The court said that clearly this statement was not language of promise but rather a statement of an opinion. On the other hand, the words, "I will guarantee to make the hand a hundred per cent perfect hand or a hundred per cent good hand" did create a promise, giving rise to an action for damages when the promise was not fulfilled. Dr. McGee's lawyer argued that these words should be interpreted in the light of the rule of objective interpretation. No reasonable person would understand these words as anything more than a strong statement of opinion and not promise. Are you persuaded that the difference the court saw between these two statements was "clear"? No, but it would be within the province of the finder of fact (jury) to draw such a distinction, and within the province of the court to respect such a jury finding. If so, why? See the previous sentence.

The question of whether the guarantee was a promise or not was judged first as a matter of law for the court. Thus, before the jury could be involved, the court had to rule that it was possible that a reasonable person could understand the words as a promise. Once this preliminary issue of law for the court was resolved, then it was the function of the jury to determine whether, in fact, the words could reasonably be understood by Hawkins to be a promise. Courts often distinguish between expressions of intent to make a prediction or express an opinion, neither of which constitutes a promise, and an assurance as to a future event. Do you think the distinction helpful to properly exclude some language from becoming promissory? Yes. Is the distinction between commitment and prediction clear? No—subject to determination by the finder of fact. See the discussion of the *King* case in Chapter 2. See Restatement (Second) of Contracts §2, *cmt. f*.

2. *Total breach versus partial breach.* Assuming that a contract existed and it was breached, do you consider the breach partial or total? The breach was total in that the shortfall in performance went to the basis of what Hawkins was promised compared to what he received. How do you make this determination and what is the relevance? The making of this determination was covered in Chapter 8 above. Had the breach been partial, Dr. McGee might have been entitled to an opportunity to cure the damage by further surgery. Are there future losses or costs to be avoided by Hawkins as a result of the breach and Hawkins' not having to perform his side of the contract? No. What were Hawkins' obligations under the contract? To rest and recover. Did he fully perform? Yes. If so, does the partial and total breach distinction have any meaning to this particular case? See the discussion above. Hawkins treated the breach as total.

3. *Expectancy interest loss in value measure.* Having determined the case was contractual and not tort based, the primary measure of damages was designed to protect the expectancy interest. The first component of the expectancy interest is the loss in value measure that requires comparing the market value of the promise to the market value of what was actually received. These two market values are then compared to determine the difference or loss in value. What were the relative market values of the promised perfect hand and the hand following the surgery? The values to a person with Hawkins' background and work capability. Did the jury instruction properly prepare the jury to determine this difficult matter? No. What proof of market values were provided by the parties? The court opinion does not disclose an answer to this question. What proof would you present? The recovery tables for Workman's Compensation might apply by analogy. We would rather use an expert and get that expert to calculate the percentage impairment in Hawkins' future ability to work and then calculate the true present worth of that delta of lost future wages.

The Supreme Court also determined it was improper for the trial court to instruct the jury to consider any worsening of the hand as a result of the surgery. Do you understand this instruction? Yes—a comparison of the relative worsening of the hand would involve comparing the hand after the burn and before surgery with the hand after surgery. Doing the calculation this way would preclude any "expectation" value of a 100% good hand. The proper calculation would compare the value of a 100% good hand with the value of the hand he ended up with. Was the trial court instruction consistent with the expectancy interest formulation in Restatement (Second) of Contracts § 347? No. Did Hawkins expect any pain and suffering or at least the severity actually incurred? Apparently yes. If not, is this calculus appropriate under the "loss in value" determination or is it "any other loss" caused by the breach? Additional pain objectively unanticipated would be further "loss in value." See Restatement (Second) of Contracts § 347(c).

4. *The machine analogy.* The Court stated that "[a]uthority for any specific rule of damages in cases of this kind seems to be lacking, but, when tested by general principle and by analogy, it appears that the foregoing instruction was erroneous." The opinion then referred by analogy to the measure of damages available for breach of a warranty as to the performance of a machine. Do you find this analogy helpful? Superficially, the comparison of a machine to a human being seems inappropriate. But to the extent that the machine case illustrates the measure comparison to be used, it is helpful. If not why not? See the last sentence. Is the analogy cited simply to illustrate that the measure of loss in value is the difference in value between what was promised and what was received? Yes. Or is the analogy meant to suggest

something more such as equating personal injury cases with damage to physical equipment? No. If the latter, is the analogy helpful? No.

5. *Adequacy of proper expectancy interest.* Assuming that the expectancy interest and its loss in value measure can be properly applied, will the expectancy monetary recovery place Hawkins in the same position as if the contract had been properly performed? No. The recovery will be no more than an approximation of future earnings and personal comfort loss. The unequivocal answer is almost always never and it has less to do with the measurement of the recovery than the risk and costs of litigation. Unless the contract specifies otherwise, American common law requires that each party bear its own litigation expense, win or lose. If an injured party is insured, the insurance company will normally be required to sue or defend but only with regard to the insurable elements. Normally, this includes medical bills but seldom is a plaintiff insured against personal injury. Moreover, once medical bills are paid, the insurance company is subrogated (by contract or equity) to the insured's claim and thus its expenses normally are subtracted first from any recovery. This means that the legal risk and litigation cost of even a victorious plaintiff must be paid by the plaintiff. As a consequence, given the enormous costs of litigation, regardless of whether the attorney is retained on a fixed fee or contingent fee basis, the plaintiff will simply never be made whole. This aspect of American jurisprudence has led some commentators to suggest specific performance ought to be the normative remedy, even though the legal expense of achieving that order will also not compensate the plaintiff. See Melvin A. Eisenberg, *"Actual and Virtual Specific Performance, The Theory of Efficient Breach, And the Indifference Principle in Contract Law,"* 93 Cal. L. Rev. 975, 977 (2005) and Stewart Macaulay, "The Reliance Interest and the World Outside the Law Schools' Doors," 1991 Wisc. L. Rev. 247 (1991).

The international rule is normatively otherwise. In most foreign common law and civil law jurisdictions, the losing party bears the expense of the prevailing party's litigation costs. See John Gotanda, "Awarding Costs and Attorneys' Fees in International Commercial Transactions," 21 Mich. J. Int'l Law 1 (1999). These costs must be reasonably foreseeable. See CISG Art. 74 and UNIDROIT Art. 7.4.4 but this condition is normally satisfied, even in American and foreign contracts. See e.g., *Zapata Hermanos Sucesores, S.A. v. Hearthside Baking Co.,* 2001 WL 1000927 (N.D. Ill. 2001).

Which rule do you prefer? Abstractly, the "loser pays" rule is attractive—providing an incentive to settle rather than litigate. A "loser pays" rule is thought in America to be inconsistent with contingent fee litigation and contingent fee litigation in this country is regarded as frequently the only key to the courtroom available to the plaintiff. In England, where the dominant rule used to be "loser pays," that rule has lost much of its applicability due to the number of plaintiff suits now subsidized by the English government. The rationale? The government could not be thought of as bringing a lawsuit that would be improvident and for which costs should be taxed against it! Which rule do you think most clearly and fairly advances the interests of the injured party? Given the importance of contingent fee litigation in this country, a case can be made for the current American practice. Does the American rule discourage or encourage litigation? It encourages litigation by failing to "punish" improvident or "losing" litigation. If it discourages litigation, why is America so comparatively litigious? It encourages rather than discourages litigation. Does the attorney fee rule work in some magical tandem with contingent fees? See the discussion above. Do you think contingent fee cases dominate the landscape in foreign jurisdictions? No.

6. *Expectancy interest versus reliance interest.* Reconsider three protected interests, especially comparing the expectancy and reliance interests. Do you think the reliance interest is a preferred measure to the expectancy measure in a contract case involving personal injury? No. If so, how would you measure the reliance damages? By measuring the difference in value for the plaintiff before and after the injury. How would the reliance interest measure differ from the expectancy interest measure? The reliance interest would not give Hawkins the present value of his lost future earning capacity, it would merely attempt to restore the status quo. Do you think either measure deterred McGee from fulfilling his promise? No. See Melvin A. Eisenberg, *"Actual and Virtual Specific Performance, the Theory of Efficient Breach, and the Indifference Principle in Contract Law,"* 93 Cal. L. Rev. 975 (2005) preferring expectancy interest:

> If a promisor was only liable for the promisee's costs—that is, if a promisor faced a remedial regime that only implemented the cost principle—the full value of a contract to the promisee would not enter into a purely self-interested calculation by the promisor, and promisors might therefore take too few precautions and breach too often." *Id.* at 980.

Was the trial court jury instruction more suited to a reliance measure or an expectancy measure? A reliance measure. Diagram the elements of a proper jury charge in both cases and determine how the trial court and appellate court instruction language fit both paradigms. The Supreme Court's instruction implements the expectancy paradigm.

7. *Emotional disturbance damages.* See text.

8. *Foreseeability limitation on damages.* As discussed later in this chapter, a plaintiff's recovery of contract damages is limited by three

factors: foreseeability, certainty, and avoidability. Does the quotation by the Supreme Court from the *Davis* case, "The only losses that can be said fairly to come within the terms of a contract are such as the parties must have had in mind when the contract was made, or such as they either knew or ought to have known would probably result from a failure to comply with its terms," relate to the foreseeability of damages, or to the expectancy of the parties? It relates to foreseeability which is a limitation on expectancy. Does this quotation suggest that the justification for an award of damages is to be found by interpreting what the parties would or might have provided by way of damages had they thought about it? Perhaps. Is this a throwback to the "will theory" of contracts? Perhaps, but it is commonly regarded as a sound statement today. It is a paraphrase of the holding of *Hadley v. Baxendale*—presented later in this chapter.

9. *Certainty limitation on damages.* Can a jury determine the value to Hawkins of a perfect hand with certainty? No. Then do you think the jury could fairly determine the value to Hawkins of his hand in its condition as of the date of the trial? No. The best a jury could do in both cases is indulge in an approximation guess. But well advised plaintiff's counsel would have used expert testimony to quantify the delta of future lost wage earnings. It is worth noting that, while in some senses it is both impossible and distasteful to attempt to value the loss suffered by Hawkins, there exist numerous actuarial sources from which it is possible to approximate the dollar value of a lost limb or body part, physical injury, or loss of life. Indeed, tort law routinely engages in such a personal calculus.

10. *Case aftermath.* The complaint included two counts, the first for negligence and the second for breach of contract. The negligence count was dismissed at trial. On the breach of contract count Hawkins was awarded a $3,000 jury verdict but the trial court determined the damages were excessive beyond $500. The appellate opinion then reversed that finding and ordered a new trial. McGee ultimately settled the case for $1,400 and then brought suit against his malpractice insurance company seeking reimbursement for the settlement plus attorney fees and other costs. In *McGee v. United States Fidelity & Guarantee Co.*, 53 F.2d 953 (1st Cir. 1931), it was noted that McGee's insurance policy provided : "The assured shall not voluntarily assume any liability . . ." Both the federal district court and the First Circuit found that Dr. McGee's malpractice insurance policy did not cover contractual liability, the basis of the settlement. Does the fact that the court found no prima facie case of negligence proven change your view with respect to contractual liability? No. Hawkins pleaded two counts, the first for malpractice, the second for breach of promise (warranty). Dismissal of the first count was unrelated to the suit for breach of promise. The jury apparently concluded that Dr. McGee did not operate

negligently (medical malpractice) but did fail to perform the promise of producing a 100% good hand.

American Standard, Inc. v. Schectman
CASE BRIEF

This is a 1981 decision of the Illinois Supreme Court. American Standard entered into a contract with Schectman under which Schectman was to remove old machinery and walls to a depth of one foot below grade and regrade the surface. Schectman failed to perform as promised. The jury found that cost of completion of the work to bring the property up to the standard contracted for was $90,000. Schectman appealed arguing that the trial court should have instructed the jury that the measure of damages to be applied was the diminution in value of the property attributable to the unfinished work. Schectman offered proof that American had sold the property for only $3,000 less than market value if the work had been completed, and thus the jury award would be a windfall for American. The trial court rejected that offer and entered judgment based on the jury verdict. The Supreme Court affirmed, holding that the proper measure of damage in this case was cost of completion and not diminution in value.

The Supreme Court said the general rule of damages for breach of a construction contract was recovery of those damages "which are the direct, natural and immediate consequence of the breach and which can reasonably be said to have been in the contemplation of the parties when the contract was made." In the case of defective or incomplete performance the reasonable cost of replacement or completion was the applicable measure. By way of exception, "When, however, there has been a substantial performance of the contract made in good faith but defects exist, the correction of which would result in economic waste, courts have measured the damages as the difference between the value of the property as constructed and the value if performance had been properly completed." The court cited the *Jacobs & Youngs, Inc.* decision as authority in support. There the breach was unintentional, the consequences of the omission trivial, and the cost of replacing the pipe grievously out of proportion to the significance of the default. The court referred to the Restatement concept of "unreasonable economic waste" as underlying this exception. The court referred to the Minnesota Supreme Court decision in *Groves v. John Wunder Co.,* where a contractor who had promised to restore the surface of a gravel pit failed to perform and claimed that damages for nonperformance should be limited to diminution in value. The Minnesota Supreme Court allowed recovery of the full cost of completion, an amount far in excess of any diminution in value of the land attributable to the failure to perform. The court said that the "economic waste" referred to by the Restatement generally entailed defects in construction which were irremediable or which could not be repaired without substantial tearing down of the structure. Where the breach was only incidental to the main purpose of the contract and completion would be disproportionately costly, the value measure would be used. For this proposition the court cited the *Peevyhouse v. Garland Coal & Min. Co.* case, suggesting (a highly debatable suggestion) that the main objective of the contract in that case was the mining of coal and the promise to restore the surface of the land was only incidental.

To obtain the benefit of the doctrine of substantial performance, as laid down in the *Jacob & Youngs* case, the breach must be unintentional and the performance must have been substantial. Here, the grading and removal of debris were not incidental to the main purpose. "Defendant's completed performance would not have involved undoing what in good faith was done improperly but only doing what was promised and left undone." Schectman did not attempt in good faith to finish the job. His default was neither unintentional nor trivial.

INTERESTING DISCUSSION ISSUES

1. *The puzzling language of Restatement (Second) of Contracts* § 348(2). The case law is replete with situations where damages for defective or incomplete construction have been measured by the cost of redoing or remedying the defective or incomplete work. Cost of completion is often described as an obvious and straightforward application of the "expectancy" principle. This Restatement section, however, seems to raise not just one but two questions. The provision states:

> (2) If a breach results in defective or unfinished construction and the loss in value to the injured party is not proved with sufficient certainty, he may recover damages based on.
>
> (a) the diminution in the market price of the property caused by the breach, or
>
> (b) the reasonable cost of completing performance or of remedying the defects if that cost is not clearly disproportionate to the probable loss in value to him.

The introductory words appear to suggest a hierarchy of measures of which "loss in value" is primary. Only if such loss in value is not proved with sufficient certainty do we proceed further. This suggested hierarchy is at odds with the case law. The language of subsection (b) raises the "economic waste" or "clearly disproportionate" issue made so famous in the *Peevyhouse* case—see Notes 2 and 4 below, and dealt with in the instant case.

The words "probable loss in value to him" raise yet another ambiguity—is such loss to be evaluated subjectively or objectively—see the notes to Problem 5-1 below.

NOTES AND QUESTIONS

1. *Economic waste standard.* The case references the "economic waste" doctrine as a policy directive for judicial selection of diminution in value or cost to repair. See Restatement (First) of Contracts § 346 which was titled "Damages For Breach Of A Construction Contract." In essence, Restatement (First) of Contracts § 346(1)(a)(i)-(ii) articulated that the injured party in a case of total breach was entitled to the reasonable cost to correct or complete unless that cost involved "unreasonable economic waste." If so, the diminution (loss) in value rule applied. Restatement (First) of Contracts § 346, *cmt. b* provided:

> b. The purpose of money damages is to put the injured party in as good a position as that in which full performance would have put him; but this does not mean that he is to be put in the same specific physical position. Satisfaction for his harm is made either by giving him a sum of money sufficient to produce the physical product contracted for or by giving him the exchange value that that product would have had if it had been constructed. In very many cases it makes little difference whether the measure of recovery is based upon the value of the promised product as a whole or upon the cost of producing and constructing it piecemeal. There are numerous cases, however, in which the value of the finished product is much less than the cost of producing it after the breach has occurred. Sometimes defects in a completed structure cannot be physically remedied without tearing down and rebuilding, at a cost that would be imprudent and unreasonable. The law does not require damages to be measured by a method requiring such economic waste. If no such waste is involved, the cost of remedying the defect is the amount awarded as compensation for failure to render the promised performance.

Restatement (Second) of Contracts § 348(2)(b) governs defective or unfinished construction cases but does not adopt the "economic waste" language standard noted above. Rather, it provides that the reasonable cost to complete or repair is to be utilized unless that cost is "clearly disproportionate" to the probable loss (diminution) in value to him. Restatement (Second) of Contracts § 348, *cmt. c* provides:

> c. *Incomplete or defective performance.* If the contract is one for construction, including repair or similar performance affecting the condition of property, and the work is not finished, the injured party will usually find it easier to prove what it would cost to have the work completed by another contractor than to prove the difference between the values to him of the finished and the unfinished performance. Since the cost to complete is usually less

than the loss in value to him, he is limited by the rule on avoidability to damages based on cost to complete. See § 350(1). If he has actually had the work completed, damages will be based on his expenditures if he comes within the rule stated in § 350(2).

Sometimes, especially if the performance is defective as distinguished from incomplete, it may not be possible to prove the loss in value to the injured party with reasonable certainty. In that case he can usually recover damages based on the cost to remedy the defects. Even if this gives him a recovery somewhat in excess of the loss in value to him, it is better that he receive a small windfall than that he be under-compensated by being limited to the resulting diminution in the market price of his property.

Sometimes, however, such a large part of the cost to remedy the defects consists of the cost to undo what has been improperly done that the cost to remedy the defects will be clearly disproportionate to the probable loss in value to the injured party. Damages based on the cost to remedy the defects would then give the injured party a recovery greatly in excess of the loss in value to him and result in a substantial windfall. *Such an award will not be made. It is sometimes said that the award would involve "economic waste," but this is a misleading expression since an injured party will not, even if awarded an excessive amount of damages, usually pay to have the defects remedied if to do so will cost him more than the resulting increase in value to him.* If an award based on the cost to remedy the defects would clearly be excessive and the injured party does not prove the actual loss in value to him, damages will be based instead on the difference between the market price that the property would have had without the defects and the market price of the property with the defects. This diminution in market price is the least possible loss in value to the injured party, since he could always sell the property on the market even if it had no special value to him. [Emphasis Added].

In other contexts, the phrase "disproportionate" usually implies a comparison of the benefit to one party versus the cost to the other but is not limited to situations involving what may be thought of as "economic waste." The latter phrase implies no value to anyone. However, particularly where the defective construction involves an item of intrinsic value to the injured party, such as a personal residence, is completion or repair without economic value to the homeowner? No. See discussion in "Interesting Discussion Issues" above. Even Judge Cardozo suggested in *Jacob & Youngs* that he would have decided otherwise if either (i) the conditional language requiring the use of Reading pipe had been expressed as a condition rather than merely as a promise; or (ii) the breach (using Cohoes rather than Reading pipe) was willful or intentional. In the latter case, justice does not favor saving the breaching party the money even if the repair expenditure does not proportionately increase the value of the project.

In the context of this case, is "economic waste" the same analysis as "clearly disproportionate?" Yes—see discussion in "Interesting Discussion Issues" above. Since the language of Restatement (Second) of Contracts § 348(2)(b) focuses on the probable loss to "him" (the injured party), does that focus introduce a measure of subjectivity? Arguably yes—see discussion in "Interesting Discussion Issues" above.

2. *The Peevyhouse case.* See text.

3. *Public law intervention for private ordering failures.* See text.

4. *The Groves case.* Groves owned land with sizeable sand and gravel deposits. He entered into a seven-year lease granting the right to process and remove sand and gravel. Like the *Peevyhouse* lease, the *Groves* lease required the lessee to restore the land to its original condition at the end of the lease. As matters developed, the restoration required the lessee to remove and store nearly 300,000 cubic yards of "overburden" at the beginning of the lease and then use this material as top cover to restore the property. The lessee willfully refused to comply with the restoration term. The lessee argued that the approximate $60,0000 restoration cost only increased value of the land by approximately $12,160 and therefore was excused under the "economic waste" standard. The trial court agreed and awarded the owner only the lesser diminution in value. On appeal, the Minnesota Supreme Court reversed and awarded the cost to repair and replace. The court argued the "economic waste" limitation on the repair cost only applied to destruction of physical structures. Rather, the 1939 opinion relied more heavily on the "willful" behavior of the lessee following the earlier *Jacob & Youngs* standard announced in 1921 by Judge Cardozo as one of the exceptions to the doctrine of substantial performance. See Richard Posner, *Economic Analysis of Law* § 4.8 5th ed. 1998). Do you think that the lessee's behavior in *Peevyhouse* was willful? Absolutely! What is the difference between willful noncompliance and bad faith, an implied term discussed in Chapter 4? Restatement (Second) of Contracts § 205 provides that "Every contract imposes upon each party a duty of good faith and fair dealing in its performance and its enforcement." UCC § 1-201 defines "good faith" as "honesty in fact and the observance of reasonable commercial standards of fair dealing." Willful noncompliance is simply the intentional (but not necessarily "bad faith") failure to perform a promise.

5. *Bad faith and the doctrine of efficient breach.* The concept of "efficient breach" has roots in early 20th century common law and Oliver Wendell Holmes, Jr.'s observation that monetary damages for

contract breach are to be compensatory, not punitive, and thus "every person has a legal right 'to break his contract if he chooses' thereby electing to pay damages rather than perform." See, Oliver Wendell Holmes, Jr., The Common Law 236 (1881) and Grant Gilmore, The Death of Contract 16 (1974). In general, the "efficient breach" theory is supported by economic theory in redirecting resources to a superior use. But not every scholar is a huge fan:

> {The "efficient breach" theory] holds that if a promisor would gain more from breaching the contract, even after payment of expectation damages, than the promise would lose, breach is efficient and for that reason should be encouraged. . . . In its most significant application, the theory of efficient breach does nothing to promote efficiency. On the contrary, if widely adopted the theory would promote inefficiency. Melvin A. Eisenberg, *"Actual and Virtual Specific Performance, the Theory of Efficient Breach, and the Indifference Principle in Contract Law,"* 93 Cal. L. Rev. 975, 977-8 (2005).

See also David W. Barnes, *"The Anatomy of Contract Damages and Efficient Breach Theory,"* 6 S. Cal. Interdisc. L. J. 397 (1998), Richard Craswell, *"Contract Remedies, Renegotiation, and the Theory of Efficient Breach,"* 61 So. Cal. L. Rev. 629 (1988), and Joseph M. Perillo, *"Misreading Oliver Wendell Holmes on Efficient Breach and Tortious Interference,"* 68 Fordham L. Rev. 1085 (2000).

Chapter 4 explores in more detail the implied covenant of good faith. But bad faith is the antithesis of good faith and involves a deliberate intent to frustrate the purposes of the contract. Do you think a theory of efficient breach is conceptually consistent with good faith or do you think an intentional breach of a contract is *per se* proof of bad faith? The answer depends upon the meaning assigned to "good faith." If that meaning is "absence of deception or trickery" then an intentional breach is not *per se* proof of bad faith. If the latter, what damages should the court award? The available remedy will depend upon the court's ruling as to whether there was or was not substantial performance and whether the breach was or was not material and uncured. Damages, as such, are not assessed simply for the "bad faith" component but rather for the actual breach. Finally, courts are frequently sensitive to the degree of certainty of proof required for recovery of lost profits based on the wrongfulness of the breaching party's behavior. In short, while motive is frequently said to be irrelevant in cases of breach of contract, motive does nevertheless become significant in a variety of different contexts. See e.g. Christopher W. Frost, "Reconsidering the Reliance Interest," 44 St. Louis U. L. J. 1361, 1372 (2000).

6. *Efficient breach controversy.* As discussed above, the "efficient breach" concept is controversial. Holmes' early observation that the motive of the contract breaker is irrelevant has been controversial. Under efficient breach theory, a contract breaker intentionally breaches the contract because the breaching party can devote its resources more profitably to other contracts. Thus, the contract breaker can make more profit from the redirection of the contract resources than the damages incurred on the breach. The breach is thus said to be "efficient" from the perspective of the breaching party and the injured party receives expectancy interest damages and is thus placed in the same position as if the contract had been performed. Indeed, both parties are better off for the breach: the injured party receives expectancy interest damages, and the breaching party receives the excess over those damages.

Critical to this question is whether the motive of the contract breaker plays a role in measuring damages. One approach might be to award the contract breaker's breach "profit" to the injured party. Of course, that places the injured party in a better position than performance but allocates the windfall to the innocent party rather than rewarding an intentional breach. See e.g. Daniel Friedman, *"The Efficient Breach Fallacy,"* 18 J. Leg. Stud. 1 (1989) and Ian R. Macneil, *"Efficient Breaches of Contract: Circles in the Sky,"* 68 Va. L. Rev. 947 (1982). Cases involving efficient breach are rare because the injured party receives adequate compensation and seldom learns of the breaching party's efficiency profit. For an example, see *Handicapped Children's Education Board v. Lukaszewski*, 332 N.W.2d 774 (1983). In *Lukaszewski*, a teacher was hired at $10,760 annual salary, but before the school year began she repudiated the school contract and accepted a higher paying job closer to home due in part to health concerns. The new position paid $13,000. The school sued and won an award for $1,026, the additional amount necessary to hire her replacement over and above her original $10,760 salary. In sum, the teacher netted $1,214 after the breach and paying breach damages because of the higher pay at the other position. She was therefore better off by the breach, and the school was no worse off. Should the school have also been entitled to her $1,214 windfall, or should the breaching teacher be entitled to retain that amount? The teacher should be entitled to retain the $1,214—the chain of causation is broken, negating any claim by the school for that sum. But see the draft § 39 below for a contrary view. That issue was not presented or discussed in the case.

The current draft of Restatement (Third) of Restitution and Unjust Enrichment § 39 provides:

> § 39. Profit Derived From Opportunistic Breach.
> (1) If a breach of contract is both material and opportunistic, the injured promisee has a claim in restitution to the profit realized by the defaulting promisor as a result of the breach. Liability in

restitution with disgorgement of profit is an alternative to liability for contract damages measured by injury to the promisee.

(2) A breach is "opportunistic" if

(a) the breach is deliberate;

(b) the breach is profitable by the test of subsection (3); and

(c) the promisee's right to recover damages for the breach affords inadequate protection to the promisee's contractual entitlement. In determining the adequacy of damages for this purpose,

(i) damages are ordinarily an adequate remedy if they can be used to acquire a full equivalent to the promised performance in a substitute transaction; and

(ii) damages are ordinarily an inadequate remedy if they cannot be used to acquire a full equivalent to the promised performance in a substitute transaction.

(3) A breach is "profitable" when it results in gains to the defaulting promisor (net of potential liability in damages) greater than the promisor would have realized from performance of the contract. Profits from breach include saved expenditure and consequential gains that the defaulting promisor would not have realized but for the breach. The amount of such profits must be proved with reasonable certainty.

(4) Disgorgement by the rule of this Section will be denied

(a) if the parties' agreement authorizes the promisor to choose between performance of the contract and a remedial alternative such as payment of liquidated damages; or

(b) to the extent that disgorgement would result in an inappropriate windfall to the promisee, or would otherwise be inequitable in a particular case.

The concept is obviously controversial and the restitution reversal of the efficient breach will no doubt continue to precipitate considerable debate. Indeed, at the 2005 ALI proceedings, the Reporter made the following observation:

> § 39 on restitution for opportunistic breach of contract is something of an innovation. The innovation consists in the attempt to state a general rule; it is not an attempt to dictate outcomes that have never been thought of before. The Illustrations are all based on real cases; they are not recommendations for how we think life ought to be organized. The general rule has not been stated either this way or any other way, to my knowledge. It does not appear in the Second Restatement of Contracts, and it is not easy to decide how to write it. For these reasons and others, § 39 was the most difficult to prepare and is perhaps the most open to criticism of all the material in the draft.

7. *The ethics of willful breach—an empirical analysis.* While courts and commentators often seem to treat the business world as filled with hard-nosed bargainers and coldhearted, calculating business people, in reality there are serious ethical and reputational consequences for a willful breach. In one empirical survey of the reactions of business people to a willful breach, for example, 105 respondents out of 168 total stated that deliberately breaching a contract because a better deal can be found elsewhere is unethical. See David Baumer & Patricia Marschall, *"Willful Breach of Contract for the Sale of Goods: Can the Bane of Business Be an Economic Bonanza?,"* 65 Temple L. Rev. 159, 165 (1992). Ninety-six of the respondents stated that they would "almost always" or "always" withhold future business from a party who willfully breached a valid contract, although only 68 respondents stated that they would inform associates of such bad faith conduct. See id. at 166. Finally, 88 of the respondents stated that they would more likely file suit in cases of deliberate breach. See id. If this survey accurately reflects the general attitudes of business people toward willful or deliberate breaches, how would this affect a party's determination of whether to willfully breach a contract? It should provide food for thought and deter many deliberate breaches because of the social and commercial consequences. Are there some types of businesses that are more sensitive to, or more insulated from, such reactions to willful breach? Yes—for instance, those where the parties are not known to each other are more insulated, as in a stock exchange routed sale and purchase of securities.

Optional Problem 9-1

George had always wanted to build his own "dream" house. After working very hard for twenty years, he had been able to put aside funds to buy a premium unique lake frontage lot and build his dream house there. He purchased such a lot for $1,000,000. He retained an architect to draw up detailed plans and specifications for a 6,000 square foot house to be constructed on that lot. After calling for competitive bids, he entered into a contract with Fudd Construction to build the house for the price of $2,000,000 all in accordance with the plans and specifications. After Fudd had finished the framing, put the roof on and was installing doors and windows, George discovered a problem. The plans had indicated a room on the ground floor, overlooking the lake, and large enough (30x24 feet) to provide comfortably for the location of a full size billiard table and appropriate comfortable chairs. George now discovered that Fudd had made a mistake in locating walls and, instead of a room with 30x24 foot dimensions, this room was only 16x24 feet—a size which would not permit the installation of a full size billiard table. George called for a halt to further construction and insisted that Fudd rebuild the house in strict accordance with the plans, including the 30x24 foot room. Fudd complained that to do so would cost $100,000 extra because of the tear-down and reconstruction involved. When Fudd refused to fix the problem George sued. George testified about his "dream" house and his special love for the game of billiards. Without his billiard room, he said, the house would no longer meet his "dream." Fudd retained an acknowledged real estate expert who testified that the house, built as Fudd was building it, would be worth exactly the same amount on the market as one containing the billiard room. The real estate expert concluded that Fudd's mistake would make no difference to the intrinsic market value of the house and property after the construction was finished. As judge how would you rule? What reasons would you give for your ruling?

Answer:

This problem poses the question of whether the comparison between "cost of completion" and "loss in value" should involve value to the plaintiff subjectively or value objectively. Restatement (Second) of Contracts § 347 Comment b favors subjective value and provides:

> *b. Loss in value.* The first element that must be estimated in attempting to fix a sum that will fairly represent the expectation interest is the loss in the value to the injured party of the other party's performance that is caused by the failure of, or deficiency in, that performance. If no performance is rendered, the loss in value caused by the breach is equal to the value that the performance would have had to the injured party. See Illustrations 1 and 2. If defective or partial performance is rendered, the loss in value caused by the breach is equal to the difference between the value that the performance would have had if there had been no breach and the value of such performance as was actually rendered. In principle, this requires a determination of the values of those performances to the injured party himself and not their values to some hypothetical reasonable person or on some market. See Restatement, Second, Torts § 911. They therefore depend on his own particular circumstances or those of his enterprise, unless consideration of these circumstances is precluded by the limitation of foreseeability (§ 351). Where the injured party's expected advantage consists largely or exclusively of the realization of profit, it may be possible to express this loss in value in terms of money with some assurance. In other situations, however, this is not possible and compensation for lost value may be precluded by the limitation of certainty. See § 352. In order to facilitate the estimation of loss with sufficient certainty to award damages, the injured party is sometimes given a choice between alternative bases of calculating his loss in value. The most important of these are stated in § 348. See also §§ 349 and 373.

2. The Reliance Interest Alternative

In the next section, various limitations on the recovery of monetary damages are explored including the requirements that (i) the breaching party could reasonably foresee the claimed breach damages at the time the contract was formed; (ii) the injured party took reasonable efforts to mitigate any post-breach increase in the amount of claimed damages relating to the breach; and (iii) the injured party must be able to prove the amount of damages with reasonable certainty. As will be seen in the discussion relating to the certainty limitation, "lost profits" damages on the contract are often the most elusive because proof of such damages implicates difficult problems of income and expense forecasts of future events. Lost profits are recoverable under the "loss in value" category discussed in the previous section.

This section explores the important question regarding the implications associated with the injured party's inability to prove expectancy interest damages with reasonable certainty but actual costs in reliance on the contract have been incurred. These costs are ordinarily far easier to prove simply by showing receipts for the cost. The reliance interest provides an alternative to the expectancy interest recovery, allowing the injured party to recover damages based on the reliance interest, including expenditures made in preparation for performance. An important limitation provides that the reliance interest alternative recovery may be reduced by any loss that the breaching party can prove with reasonable certainty the injured party would have suffered had the contract been fully performed. Where such proof is possible by the breaching party, the net effect is that the reliance remedy is limited to the contract price.

Walser v. Toyota Motor Sales, U.S.A., Inc.
CASE BRIEF

This is a 1994 decision of the United States Court of Appeals for the Eighth Circuit. Walser (and McLaughlin) negotiated with Toyota for a new Lexus franchise in the Twin Cities. Toyota's process involved three steps, the submission of an application by the would-be dealer, the signing of a letter of intent (usually with further conditions to be satisfied); and the mutual signing of a final agreement. The form of application stated clearly that any contract would abide the execution of the final dealership agreement.

In April 1988 Hagg, Toyota's regional manager, contacted Walser and found them interested in pursuing a Lexus dealership. Walser submitted an application. Walser's initial proposals were rejected but negotiations continued. Unknown to Toyota, Walser was also negotiating to buy a Mazda and BMW dealership in St. Paul. Toyota was not satisfied with the property proposed as the site for the new dealership. Walser negotiated to buy an additional parcel of land and Walser's father reached a "handshake" deal for that land. Walser reported this progress but failed to disclose that Walser's father was the proposed buyer.

On October 24, Walser called Hagg to inquire whether a letter of intent would be forthcoming. Hagg told Walser that although the letter of intent was not yet executed, things looked positive, the deal was done, and only one more signature was needed, and finalizing the deal was basically a rubber stamp. Later that day Walser's father signed a purchase agreement for the new parcel of land.

In December the letter of intent was formally approved by Lexus management. Hagg called Walser, congratulated him and said "you're our dealer" and that the letter would be coming by mail. Later that day Hagg was told that, based on new financial information, the letter of intent would be put on hold. Hagg called Walser, told him the letter of intent had not been approved, and requested further financial information.

On January 3, 1990, Walser's father closed on the purchase of the parcel of land. In February Hagg informed Walser that Lexus would not be issuing the letter of intent. On March 7 Walser filed a seven count complaint. Among the counts were one for breach of contract, another for promissory estoppel, and a third for fraud. The case went to trial on the contract, estoppel and fraud claims. The jury found for Lexus on the breach of contract and fraud claims but found for Walser on the estoppel claim. Walser had claimed $7.6 million for lost profits. Instead, the jury returned a verdict for $232,131 out-of-pocket expenses under the promissory estoppel claim. The trial judge had instructed the jury to limit damages under that claim to reliance out-of-pocket expenses. The trial court denied Walser's request for specific performance, motion for judgment as a matter of law on the contract claim, and a disputed amount of post-judgment interest (Walser had refused to accept a check from Toyota because it was claimed to be 89 cents short). Walser appealed.

The primary issues on appeal were the trial court's instruction that damages under the estoppel claim were to be limited to out-of-pocket expenses, and the claim for specific performance. The Eighth Circuit affirmed the trial court's rulings.

The court found that Minnesota law was applicable in this diversity suit and that Minnesota had adopted the doctrine of promissory estoppel as set out in Restatement (Second) of Contracts § 90. The pivotal words of that section in question were "The remedy granted for breach may be limited as justice requires." A comment to that section indicated that relief could be limited to restitution or reliance damages. Minnesota decisions had indicated that relief could be limited to reliance damages, namely out-of-pocket expenses. The court found the ability to limit recovery to such reliance damages was discretionary with the trial court, and that the trial court committed no abuse of discretion on the present facts in so limiting recovery. The court mentioned the following factors as supporting the trial court's exercise of discretion: the grant of the dealership was far from certain (Walser having financial challenges); the negotiations broke down at a preliminary stage; the promise on which they relied did not guarantee they would get the dealership as there were other conditions that would have to be satisfied; the period of reliance was very brief (only a couple of days); and Walser did not demonstrate any opportunity they lost by virtue of relying on the Toyota promise. In footnote #3 the court cited an illustration provided in connection with § 90 summarizing the decision of the Wisconsin Supreme Court in *Hoffman*. Like this case, that was a decision involving incomplete negotiations for a lease agreement coupled with detrimental reliance on promises made in the course of negotiating an agreement that was never finalized.

Walser next claimed that the trial court erred in calculating out-of-pockets as the "difference between the actual value of the property and the price paid for it." It claimed "that they should have been allowed to "recoup" at least the full amount of the "unamortized capital investments" they made in attempting to obtain the dealership. They claim the full value of their investment totals more than $1,000,000 including the $676,864 they paid for the land and the various expenses in maintaining it." The court rejected this argument holding that the recoverable amount was the delta measured by the difference between actual value and the amount paid for the property.

The court ruled that a grant of specific performance was discretionary with the trial court and that no abuse of discretion was shown. The trial court had ruled that the award of damages provided adequate relief in the circumstances. The 89 cents issue did not merit discussion—*de minimis not curat lex.* Walser was not entitled to judgment as a matter of law on their contract claim—the letter of intent was not a contract. The initial application specified very clearly that there would be no dealership contract until the final dealership agreement was formed, and the parties never agreed otherwise (i.e. this provision was never modified by further agreement). The court then found no violation under Minnesota franchise law regarding termination of a franchise agreement since no such agreement had ever been formed.

INTERESTING DISCUSSION ISSUES

1. *The conundrum—when can a promise made in the course of negotiation of a contract be the basis of a remedy in damages?* By hypothesis, both parties to a negotiation know that the intended objective is a mutually concluded and accepted contract. When, and if so why, can a promise made in the course of such negotiations be the basis of damages when both sides know that a contract, yet to be

finalized, is intended as the source of rights and duties between them? In the instant case, the paperwork made it crystal clear that there was to be no dealership contract unless and until such a contract had been concluded and signed by both parties. But nevertheless, the detrimental reliance found in this case was an assertion by the Lexis agent that a contract acceptable to Lexus would be forthcoming. The court refused any remedy based on breach of contract but allowed the detrimental reliance claim. Students should be referred back to a similar issue covered in *Pops' Cones* in Chapter 3. Clearly, promises justifiably inducing reliance can made in the course of negotiations and prior to the conclusion of any formal contract as anticipated. Students will then ask why the remedy for such reliance is anything other than rights based on a concluded contract. The court's opinion in the above case is instructive on why the reliance remedy should not be extended to or confused with what would have been the breach of contract remedy had the contract actually been concluded.

NOTES AND QUESTIONS

1. *Specific performance denied.* The Court denied the plaintiff's claim requesting that Toyota be required by court order to award the Lexus dealership, What was the Court's reasoning? The court ruled that a grant of injunctive relief was discretionary with the trial court and that there was no evidence of abuse of discretion by the trial court in this case. The trial court had held that damages were a sufficient remedy on the present facts. Would it have made any difference if the relief had been requested before trial rather than at the end of the trial? No. See Restatement (Second) of Contracts § 359(a).

2. *Promissory estoppel claim.* The Court mentions that the plaintiff filed three original claims: one for breach of contract, one for the tort of fraud, and one for promissory estoppel. Is promissory estoppel an independent cause of action or merely a basis for enforcing a promise not supported by consideration? It is both. Promissory estoppel is usually relied on where there is no bargained for promise exchange involved. But it can also be a basis for enforcing a promise not supported by consideration. Is such a claim nonetheless still a breach of contract claim or does the absence of consideration transform the claim into something else? The answer depends upon the reader's definition of a "contract" claim. The basis for enforcement, however, is not a promise constituting part of a bargained for exchange, but rather detrimental reliance on a promise not so bargained for. If not a breach of contract, is it a tort-based claim? No, but the remedy is analogous–restoration of the prior status quo. Do you think the promissory estoppel "claim" was merely another theory of obligation seeking essentially a breach of contract award for monetary damages? Walser so treated it and based their main argument on appeal on such an

approach. They lost. If so, does that explain why the plaintiff sought expectancy interest damages for the promissory estoppel claim? Yes, but they lost. Does this case help to explain why a contract claim should first and foremost be based upon traditional notions of consideration where promissory estoppel justice limitations on damages do not exist? Yes—students need to realize the substantial difference in potential remedies between a claim based on breach of contract and one based on detrimental reliance. Walser understood this dichotomy, suing both for breach of an alleged contract and for detrimental reliance. They lost before the jury on the contract claim. Identify and articulate the justice elements that the Court used to deny expectancy interest damages and rather limit to reliance damages.

The court mentioned the following factors as supporting the trial court's exercise of discretion: the grant of the dealership was far from certain (Walser having financial challenges); the negotiations broke down at a preliminary stage; the promise on which they relied did not guarantee they would get the dealership as there were other conditions that would have to be satisfied; the period of reliance was very brief (only a couple of days); and Walser did not demonstrate any opportunity they lost by virtue of relying on the Toyota promise. In footnote #3 the court cited an illustration provided in connection with Restatement (Second) of Contracts § 90 summarizing the decision of the Wisconsin Supreme Court in *Hoffman*. Like this case, that was a decision involving incomplete negotiations for a lease agreement coupled with detrimental reliance on promises made in the course of negotiating an agreement that was never finalized.

3. *Promissory estoppel reliance and contract reliance compared.* Assume that this was a traditional breach of contract claim not based on promissory estoppel. Further assume that the plaintiff could not prove with reasonable certainty the future lost profits on the Lexus dealership (quite likely as a new business). See Restatement (Second) of Contracts § 352. That would mean that the plaintiff could still seek reliance damages on the breach of contract action? Yes. See Restatement (Second) of Contracts § 349. How would those reliance damages be calculated? Precisely as reliance damages were calculated in this case. How were the reliance damages calculated in this case? Out-of-pocket expense being the difference between the price paid for the parcel of land in reliance on Toyota's assurance and its market value. Is there a difference in the calculation of reliance damages under a breach of contract claim based on promissory estoppel and one based on consideration? Not necessarily, but students should remember the cautionary words of § 90 that "The remedy granted for breach may be limited as justice requires." Does the "justice limitation" language in Restatement (Second) of Contracts § 90 relate to a limitation on reliance interest damages or expectancy interest damages? Reliance damages—§ 90 makes it plain that the basis of

recovery under that section is action induced by a promise i.e. reliance. Many of the Restatement (Second) of Contracts § 90 illustrations do not provide for expectancy damages creating the impression that the "justice limitation" is indeed intended as a general restriction relegating promissory estoppel to reliance damages. See text for the balance of the content of this note.

4. *The many weaknesses of reliance damages in remedying breach of contract.* See text.

3. Limitations on the Expectancy and Reliance Interests

Both the expectancy and reliance interests are subject to three important limitations. The first, and arguably most important limitation, is the foreseeability standard. The second limitation concerns mitigation avoidance of damages. Once breach occurs, and particularly where the breach is total and the injured party terminates the contract, the injured party must adopt reasonable measures to avoid incurring any further loss that would increase the damage claim against the breaching party. Finally, the certainty limitation permits the injured party to recover only for damages that can be proven with reasonable certainty.

a. Foreseeability Limitation

This is an 1854 decision of the Court of Exchequer of England. This limitation has a particularly important impact on the measurement and recovery of "other losses." Its genesis is the *Hadley* case that follows. Prior to this 1854 decision of the Court of Exchequer in England, assessment of damages had been left to jury determination with few if any guiding rules or limitations. Under that decision, regarded as good law today under Restatement (Second) of Contracts, damages are not recoverable for loss that the breaching party did not have reason to foresee as a probable result of the breach at the time the contract was formed. Foreseeability is tested at the time of entering into the contract and on an objective basis. Damages that flow naturally and in the ordinary course of events from a breach are deemed *per se* foreseeable. These damages are frequently referred to as "general" or "direct" damages. Other damages, not flowing from the ordinary course of events are recoverable only if foreseeable and are usually described as "consequential" or "special." Recovery of consequential damages is also subject to limitation based on "disproportionate forfeiture." See Restatement (Second) of Contracts § 351

Hadley v. Baxendale
CASE BRIEF

Plaintiffs conducted a milling business at Gloucester. On May 11, their mill was stopped because of a broken crank shaft. Plaintiffs discovered the fracture on May 12 and determined that they would need to send the broken shaft to the maker in Greenwich to serve as a template for a new shaft. On May 13, plaintiffs sent a servant to the office of the defendants, a carrier called Pickford & Co., in order to have the shaft sent to Greenwich. Plaintiffs' servant told the Pickford clerk "that the mill was stopped, and that the shaft must be sent immediately." The clerk responded that, if the shaft went out before noon on any day, it would arrive in Greenwich the next day. On May 14, plaintiffs brought the shaft to Pickford before noon and paid the carriage fee to send the shaft to Greenwich; plaintiffs' agent stressed to the clerk that, if necessary, a special notation should be entered to hasten delivery of the shaft. Through some manner of neglect on the defendant's part, the delivery to Greenwich was delayed, and plaintiffs did not receive their new shaft until several days after they should have received it. The delay resulted in extra down time for the mill and cost the plaintiffs profits that they otherwise would have realized. Plaintiffs sued defendant, seeking recovery of L.300 in profits and other costs that were lost while the mill was inoperative; defendants objected that the damages were too remote, and thus defendants could not be liable for the damages. The jury found for plaintiffs, but awarded only L.50. Plaintiffs moved for a new trial on the ground that the jury had not received proper instructions.

The court agreed that plaintiffs ought to receive a new trial, and laid out the rule that was to govern that trial: "Where two parties have made a contract which one of them has broken, the damages which the other party ought to receive in respect of such breach of contract should be such as may fairly and reasonably be considered either arising naturally, i.e., according to the usual course of things, from such a breach of contract itself ("Hadley I"), or such as may reasonably be supposed to have been in the contemplation of both parties, at the time they made the contract, as the probable result of the breach of it ("Hadley II)." The court stated that if the special circumstances under which a contract was made were communicated by plaintiffs to the defendants, the damages resulting from such a breach would be the amount of injury that would flow from breach under those special circumstances. But if the circumstances were not known to both parties, the parties could only be held liable for injuries that they could reasonably have foreseen as a result of the breach, as the parties may have conducted themselves differently with the benefit of knowledge of the special circumstances.

Here, Baron Alderson found that the only circumstances communicated to the delivery company were that the plaintiffs were millers, and that the shaft to be delivered was a broken shaft from that mill. He held that these circumstances were insufficient to show that the mill would be altogether halted by the unreasonable delay in delivery of the broken shaft, as it would have been reasonable for the carrier to believe that the mill could well have been in possession of a back-up shaft, and thus operation of the mill would not have been endangered by tardy delivery of the shaft. Since plaintiffs did not explain to the defendants the special circumstances under which they were making this agreement, Baron Alderson held that the trial judge ought to have instructed the jury that they should not take the loss of profits into consideration at all in estimating plaintiffs' damages.

INTERESTING DISCUSSION ISSUES

1. *Did the Court of Exchequer follow its own rule as announced?* The question of what the plaintiff's clerk said to the defendant's clerk is covered first in the reporter's notes introductory to the court's decision. Those notes recited that "The plaintiff's servant told the clerk that the mill was stopped, and that the shaft must be sent immediately...." And that "the defendants' clerk was told that a special entry, if required, should be made to hasten its delivery." Baron Alderson, on the other hand, said, "we find that the only circumstances here communicated by the plaintiffs to the defendants at the time the contract was made, were, that the article to be carried was the broken shaft of a mill, and that the plaintiffs were the millers of that mill." Was the reporter's note in error or did the court willfully or otherwise overlook the facts established at trial? The reader could be forgiven for concluding that the key issue involved in this case was one of fact that should have been left to the jury and not treated as a matter of law. It has been suggested that this decision resulted not only in a jury instruction guide but also in a directive to trial judges to keep some questions away from the jury. Clearly, this case was a groundbreaking assertion by the court of specific control over jury verdicts in contracts damages cases.

2. *How did the court deal with the business risk inherent in the facts of the case?* Given our present day assumptions about allocation of business risks, it seems almost preposterous to posit the presence or absence of substantial liability depending on what one low level employee said to another low level employee. Why should Baxendale's (Baxendale was the Pickford company's managing director) liability depend upon the words and actions of a low level clerk in the company's employ? Apparently, counsel for Hadley was concerned about the possibility of the court finding that Baxendale was not liable for the clerk's knowledge and acceptance of the order and shifted the primary argument from breach of contract to breach of the common carrier's traditional duty to carry goods safely and deliver them within

a reasonable time (Count I that was dismissed at trial). The posting of notices limiting liability had developed as a practice but, at the time of this case, there was considerable doubt whether, under the common law, a "common carrier" could limit liability by the posting of such a notice. This issue would have been of the greatest importance to Pickfords and other "common carriers." Richard Danzig, in *"Hadley v. Baxendale: A Study in the Industrialization of the Law,"* 4 J. of Legal Studies 249, 267 (1975) suggested potential bias and conflict of interest on the court: "Baron Martin (one of the three judges who heard the case on appeal) had represented Pickford & Co. before ascending to the bench, and Baron Parke's brother had been the managing director of the company before Baxendale."

The implicit assumption of Baron Alderson's rule is that the carrier, when put on notice of the shipper's needs and the financial implications of those needs, can decide whether to accept the shipping contract or not (a decision probably not then permitted to the carrier under the old common law duties of a "common carrier"), and alternatively, arrive at a reasonable estimate in advance of the value of the risk being assumed, permitting the calculation of an appropriate excess charge. In many situations, the person invited to assume the risk can be alerted to the presence of increased risk but may have little ability to predict with any degree of certainty the actual economic cost of that risk assumed. This inability to predict with accuracy provides a partial explanation of the strong aversion of business people to assume the risk of consequential damages and their strong insistence on the inclusion of terms in the contract excluding any and all liability for consequential damages. See, for instance, the processes used by the U.S. Postal Service, FedEx, UPS and others to limit risk in the event of loss of the article or delay in delivery.

The rule in this case has been described as a "default" rule. That is to say, the rule will be applicable unless the parties otherwise provide in their contract. The well advised seller will thus try to include a standard clause negating liability for consequential damage. UCC §2-207 thus poses a potential trap for sellers. If the conflicting clauses of buyer and seller are "knocked out" and the "gap-fillers" fall in, §§2-714 and -715 leave the seller exposed to liability for consequential damages. Well advised sellers, however, do not limit their contract forms to excluding liability for consequential damages. To the extent permitted by §2-719 they limit liability otherwise arising under Hadley I to repair or replacement.

NOTES AND QUESTIONS

1. *Legal archaeology revisited.* See text.

2. *A tale of two rules in Hadley I & II.* See text.

3. *Applicability to expectancy and reliance interests damages.* See text.

4. *The justice limitation applied to lost profits.* Restatement (Second) of Contracts § 351(3) provides that even if a damages are foreseeable, a court may eliminate recovery for lost profits and confine the recovery to lesser reliance damages when justice requires such a result in order to avoid disproportionate forfeiture. Ordinarily, courts view disproportionate forfeiture as an unjust penalty and are hesitant to assess damages in such a case. The justice concept carries this notion forward. Restatement (Second) of Contracts § 351, *cmt. f* explains:

> *f. Other limitations on damages.* It is not always in the interest of justice to require the party in breach to pay damages for all of the foreseeable loss that he has caused. There are unusual instances in which it appears from the circumstances either that the parties assumed that one of them would not bear the risk of a particular loss or that, although there was no such assumption, it would be unjust to put the risk on that party. One such circumstance is an extreme disproportion between the loss and the price charged by the party whose liability for that loss is in question. The fact that the price is relatively small suggests that it was not intended to cover the risk of such liability. Another such circumstance is an informality of dealing, including the absence of a detailed written contract, which indicates that there was no careful attempt to allocate all of the risks. The fact that the parties did not attempt to delineate with precision all of the risks justifies a court in attempting to allocate them fairly. The limitations dealt with in this Section are more likely to be imposed in connection with contracts that do not arise in a commercial setting. Typical examples of limitations imposed on damages under this discretionary power involve the denial of recovery for loss of profits and the restriction of damages to loss incurred in reliance on the contract. Sometimes these limits are covertly imposed, by means of an especially demanding requirement of foreseeability or of certainty. The rule stated in this Section recognizes that what is done in such cases is the imposition of a limitation in the interests of justice.

Does *Hadley I* still leave considerable scope for a jury to decide the quantum of damage recoverable under an instruction on that rule? Yes. The scope of the category of damages that arise "naturally" and in the "ordinary course of things" is anything but clear and takes on meaning only as applied by the finder of fact to the facts of the particular case. *Hadley II* announces three distinct predicates for recovery: first, the damages must reasonably have been supposed to have been in the contemplation of both parties (courts now generally say contemplation of the defendant); second, at the time of contracting; and third, they must have contemplated such damage as the probable result of the breach. Finally, do these predicates restrict or expand the measure of damage recovery? The *Hadley II* additional standards can operate to significantly restrict the measure of recoverable damages. See Melvin A. Eisenberg, *"The Principle of Hadley v. Baxendale,"* 80 Cal. L. Rev. 563 (1992); Larry T. Garvin, *"Disproportionality and the Law of Consequential Damages: Default Theory and Cognitive Reality,"* 59 Ohio St. L. J. 339 (1998); and William b. Harvey, *"Discretionary Justice Under the Restatement (Second) of Contracts,"* 67 Cornell L. Rev. 666 (1982).

5. *Organizational liability from information directed to regular employees.* The *Hadley II* standard requires that liability attaches for consequential damages only when the breaching party "had reason to know" of special circumstances beyond the ordinary course of events. Restatement (Second) of Contracts § 351(2)(b). Importantly, the parol evidence rule does not preclude admission of evidence to establish that the breaching party had reason to know of special circumstances. Restatement (Second) of Contracts § 351(2)(b), *cmt. b.* However, when the breaching party involves an organization such as Microsoft, to whom must the injured party communicate the information regarding the special circumstances in order to charge the organization with the requisite *Hadley II* knowledge? See the discussion of this issue under "Interesting Discussion Issues" above.

Restatement (Second) of Contracts § 351(2)(b) merely requires "reason to know" rather than actual knowledge. Therefore, proper notice to an agent of an organization will likely suffice. Restatement (Second) of Agency § 268 provides that notice to an agent (e.g., employee) is notice to the principal (e.g., employee) provided the agent had actual or apparent authority to receive the notice. Actual authority is determined by manifestations from the principal directly to the agent but apparent authority is determined by manifestations from the principal to the third party as, for example, by placing the agent in a particular position. Compare, Restatement (Second) of Agency §§ 26 (actual authority) and 27 (apparent authority).

6. *The rejected tacit agreement test.* See text.

7. *CISG consequential damages* See text.

8. *UCC version of general and consequential damages and foreseeability.* See text.

Florafax International, Inc. v. GTE Market Resources, Inc.
CASE BRIEF

This is a 1997 decision of the Supreme Court of Oklahoma. Florafax entered into a contract with GTE whereby GTE was to provide telecommunications and/or telemarketing services for Florafax. Florafax claimed damages for lost profits under a collateral contract with a third party which was cancelled when GTE breached its contract with Florafax. The plaintiff was a "flowers-by-wire" company acting as a clearinghouse to allow the placement and receipt of orders between florists throughout the United States and internationally. Florafax maintained a list of members and a directory. Florafax assisted the transaction by collecting money from the florist taking the order and guaranteeing payment to the florist delivering the flowers. Florafax also solicited agreements with third party clients that advertised the sale of floral products by various methods. Florafax facilitated the placing and satisfaction of orders on behalf of such third parties. Bellerose Floral had contracted with Florafax as such a third party whereby Florafax would accept direct consumer orders on behalf of Bellerose.

GTE provided a call-answering center and transmitted orders by telephone or computer for fulfillment. Its contract with Florafax was to run for a three year period. It contained a termination clause for cause and recited that "GTE agrees to pay Florafax consequential damages and lost profits on the business lost." The court found that GTE knew specifically when it signed the contract with Florafax that Bellerose was considering turning over a portion of its inbound and outbound business to Florafax and that Bellerose was Florafax's largest customer. GTE's performance in the first half of 1990 was not up to the standard required by its contract and GTE admitted that it no longer wanted the contract because GTE was making no money under the pricing scheme provided in the contract. GTE had attempted unsuccessfully to negotiate for a pricing increase. Evidence established that GTE intentionally failed to perform its duties under the contract adequately by failing to provide adequate staffing at its call answering center. As a result Bellerose cancelled its contract with Florafax under a 60 day termination clause. Bellerose's president testified, however, that he had expected a long term relationship with Florafax but pulled out because of GTE's poor performance. The court found that such poor performance was the direct cause of Bellerose's termination of the contract.

As a result of GTE's breach Florafax, in addition to losing profits under the Bellerose contract, also incurred costs associated with taking steps necessary to set up its own call answering service to perform the duties GTE was supposed to perform. In addition to proof of such incidental costs, to support its claim for lost profits Florafax presented economic projections through an expert witness as to how much profit

Florafax would have made from the Bellerose contract. Its expert estimated the Bellerose loss at $1,921,028 for a period extending out three years—i.e. for the time remaining under the GTE contract when Bellerose cancelled. GTE's expert estimated a loss of $294,044.

The jury awarded Florafax $750,000 in lost profits under the Bellerose contract and $820,000 as costs associated with setting up or expanding a call center.

The key issue on appeal was the claim for lost profits. GTE disputed the award of lost profits on three bases: that Florafax had not established such a loss with sufficient certainty; that such lost profits were not within the contemplation of the parties at the time of entry into the contract; and that any such recoverable profits must be limited to a sixty day period following Bellerose's cancellation because "profits beyond this time must be deemed too remote, speculative or uncertain, and Florafax could not be said to be reasonably assured of any profits from its relationship with Bellerose for any longer period, given the Florafax/Bellerose contract clause allowing either Florafax or Bellerose the right to terminate that contract upon sixty (60) days notice." The court found each of these three arguments to be without merit.

Said the court, if properly proven, lost profits under such a collateral contract are recoverable under Oklahoma law. GTE's view that such profits were inherently too remote, speculative and unforeseeable was mistaken. Loss of profit is recoverable:

> (1) if the loss is within the contemplation of the parties at the time the contract was made, (2) if the loss flows directly or proximately from the breach—i.e. if the loss can be said to have been caused by the breach—and (3) if the loss is capable of reasonably accurate measurement or estimate.

The recovery of lost profits often reflects the fulfillment of the plaintiff's expectancy interest. What is or is not in the contemplation of the parties at the time of contracting is a question of fact. Here GTE had within its contemplation at the time of contracting the potential of profits from Florafax's association with Bellerose. A clause in the contract expressly reflected the parties' contemplation. Thus lost profits under the Bellerose contract were recoverable.

GTE had also argued that any such lost profits should be limited to a 60 day period since Bellerose had a right under the contract to cancel on 60 days' notice. It relied on an earlier decision implementing an Oklahoma statutory provision to the effect that "no person can recover a greater amount in damages for the breach of an obligation, than he could have gained by the full performance thereof on both sides...." [I.e. the "as good as but not better than" rule.] The court found the present facts to present a quite different situation. Florafax argued that it was GTE's breach that caused Bellerose to exercise its power of termination of the contract. But for that breach Bellerose would have continued the relationship on a long term basis. GTE had no such similar right of termination on 60 days' notice. On the contrary, Florafax was guaranteed performance by GTE for a two year period. Application of the rule from the earlier case would improperly allow GTE "to benefit from a cancellation right it had no ability to exercise."

The court next held that Florafax had proven its lost profit damages with reasonable certainty. This issue was also one of fact to be decided by the jury. There was competent evidence in the record to sustain the jury finding in this case. It was not necessary that such lost profits be established with absolute certainty—only reasonable certainty was required:

> In essence, what a plaintiff must show for the recovery of lost profits is sufficient certainty that reasonable minds might believe from a preponderance of the evidence that such damages were actually suffered. . . . Once it is made to clearly appear that loss of business profits has been suffered by virtue of the breach, it is proper to let the jury decide what the loss is from the best evidence the nature of the case admits. . . . When a breach of a contractual obligation with resulting damages has been established, although the amount of damages may not be based on mere speculation, conjecture and surmise alone, the mere uncertainty as to the exact amount of damages will not preclude the right of recovery. . . . It is sufficient if the evidence shows the extent of damage by just and reasonable inference.

The required showing of causation, that the lost profits were the result of GTE's breach, had been met.

Evidence also established that Bellerose's business expanded substantially after termination of the contract. There was thus evidence tending to show that the level of sales for Florafax would in all probability have increased substantially had its contract with Bellerose continued. It was proper to consider this post-breach evidence in arriving at a reasonable estimate of the loss. The $750,000 awarded by the jury was within the range of estimates of the expert witnesses.

The court did not consider the issue of Florafax's costs incurred in attempting to create its own call center—leaving the trial court's judgment in favor of Florafax on those costs in place.

INTERESTING DISCUSSION ISSUES

1. *Lost profits under a collateral contract.* In considering whether or not lost profit damages should be categorized as direct or consequential it will be important for the student to ask whether the profits claimed to be lost are profits under the contract sued on or are profits under a separate contract with a third party. Many mistakenly believe that "lost profits" signal consequential damages. Not only is

such a belief frequently erroneous, but similar reasoning may mislead a party into thinking that a clause disclaiming liability for consequential damages protects against a lost profits claim. Consider the case of a manufacturer who enters into a distribution contract with a middleman and then fails to deliver product in accordance with the contract. The middleman can be expected to sue for, among other things, lost profits arguing that lost profits under such a contract are Hadley I damages. Why would the middleman enter into such a contract unless a primary object was the making of a profit on resale—causing the lost profits damages to accrue naturally and in the ordinary course as a result of such a breach.

2. *Costs incurred incidental to an effort to mitigate damages.* Florafax's costs incurred in developing its own call center in order to replace and replicate the system on which GTE had defaulted illustrate a different category of "other losses." So-called "mitigation damages" are covered in the next question. It is worth noting that the Oklahoma Supreme Court wasted no effort in affirming the jury's assessment of such costs as recoverable damages.

3. *The plaintiff's burden of proof to establish damages with reasonable certainty.* While this is the subject of a separate later section of this chapter, this case presents two interesting issues with respect to the relative degree of certainty of proof that is required. First, a claim for lost profits necessarily results in a guessing game. How do we know that Florafax would have made a profit if GTE had performed, a profit that it lost when GTE failed to perform? If we can be relatively sure that Florafax would have made a profit, how can we determine how much of a profit the company would have made? We can concede at the outset that Florafax could not prove with any great precision exactly how much profit it would have made. But this court makes the point that precise and exact quantification is not required. Were this not the case, few awards would achieve providing the true expectancy anticipated by the plaintiff. Students should be encouraged to reflect on two things: first, how Florafax presented its case on lost profits damages; second, what uncertainties clearly continued notwithstanding that proof. From time to time we point out to students the strategic necessity of plaintiff's counsel retaining an expert witness or witnesses as part of attempting to make the required proof. In this case it is clear that the plaintiff's expert testimony was crucial in persuading the court not only that damage had been suffered but that the offered quantification of that damage was sufficiently accurate to be acceptable as proof. Students may wonder whether the defendant's opposing expert was less persuasive. Plaintiff's expert, in putting together an explanation of profits lost, had to specify a period of time over which the loss should be calculated. He then had to specify whether straight line profits should be assumed or, rather, whether it

should be assumed that Florafax's profits would have ramped up over the two years of the GTE contract as Bellerose's profits had done. Plaintiff's expert testified to a ramp up of profits and, apparently, the jury bought that presentation to some extent, although not altogether. A critical difference between the plaintiff and the defendant was whether lost profit damages should be cut off after sixty days since Bellerose had an unfettered right to terminate the contract for any reason on sixty days' notice. An earlier Oklahoma case had held precisely that in such a situation, lost profits for the sixty days was the maximum recoverable. Florafax counsel had to persuade the jury that, had GTE not breached, the relationship with Bellerose would have continued at least for the two year period for which lost profits damages were claimed. Defense counsel would have argued, "We will never know!" Students need to notice that the court concluded: first, that there was evidence in the record that could have led the jury to conclude that the relationship would have continued for at least the two year period; second, that the issue was one of fact so that the jury's verdict in this regard could not be overturned since there was reasonable supporting evidence in the record.

4. *The importance of winning at the trial level.* Students are apt to conclude that what happens on appeal is far more important than what happened at the trial level. This case provides a good opportunity to point out, as in the *King* case (first case in the book), just how important that outcome at trial may be. Here, the supreme court decision on several issues relating to both the recovery of, and the measure of, damages turned on the findings of the jury and the fact that there was evidence in the record that could reasonably support such findings.

NOTES AND QUESTIONS

1. *Breach of contract identification.* This case depends upon identifying and understanding the difference between two separate contracts. The first contract was between Florafax and GTE. On that contract, Florafax sought to recover damages for a GTE uncured material total breach. What damages were directly or generally caused by the breach of the GTE contract? First, Florafax incurred the additional costs of trying to establish its own call center, minimizing the loss caused by GTE's failure to provide an adequate call center. Second, Florafax lost the profits it would have received under the Bellerose contract had Bellerose not cancelled that contract with Florafax. Were those damages foreseeable? Yes—expressly so provided for under the contract between Florafax and GTE—also established by evidence as expressly foreseen at time of contracting. Florafax argued that since GTE's breach of contract with Florafax also caused Bellerose to terminate its contract with Florafax, damages should include losses

Florafax suffered as a result of the termination of its contract with Bellerose. If Florafax had sought lost profits on its contract with GTE, would such damages be general or consequential? The damages under the contract sued on and not under a collateral contract would be presumptively general (Hadley I). Since Florafax also sought damages for lost profits it would have made in its contract with Bellerose had GTE not breached, are those damages general or consequential? Consequential. Do you see why damage characterization makes a difference? First, it determines whether or not the plaintiff has a burden to prove reasonable foreseeability or not. Second, it may be critical in deciding whether a common clause barring "consequential damages" is applicable or not. Do you understand why lost profits on the contract breached by the defendant are not (generally) subject to the foreseeability standard? Where the nature of the contract and the parties to it indicate that the purpose of the contract was to make a profit, the loss of that profit is something expectable in the ordinary course as naturally resulting from the breach. Only lost profits on so-called "collateral contracts" (those other than the breached contract between the plaintiff and defendant) are subject to the foreseeability standard. Do you understand why? Actually, both direct and consequential damages are subject to a notional test of "foreseeability." In the case of direct damages, that foreseeability factor is presumed or inferred from the very nature of the transaction and the parties to it. In the case of consequential damages, the foreseeability must be proven by the plaintiff. Such proof is foundational to any such recovery and the reason is basic fairness. Consequential loss can be very large and should not be recoverable unless it was priced in the contract. Whether or not it was so priced is resolved by what the defendant knew or should have known about attendant risk at the time of entry into the contract.

2. *Consequential damage assumption clause.* The Florafax-GTE contract contained a consequential damage clause (Clause 20) specifically making GTE aware that its breach could cause Florafax to suffer "tremendous damage to its business" and therefore GTE specifically agreed to pay Florafax for its resulting "consequential damages and lost profits on the business lost." Was this clause necessary to make GTE responsible for consequential damages? No. Evidence of GTE's awareness of the risk at time of contract would have sufficed, but such a clause helps remove a potential "he said, she said" issue from the trial. If not, is this clause as written necessary to make GTE liable for damages for lost profits on the Bellerose contract? No—same reason. Exactly what kind of knowledge of "special circumstances" is required under the *Hadley II* standard? "Had reason to know." That comment also provides in part:

> *a. Requirement of foreseeability.* A contracting party is generally expected to take account of those risks that are foreseeable at the time he makes the contract. He is not, however, liable in the event of breach for loss that he did not at the time of contracting have reason to foresee as a probable result of such a breach. The mere circumstance that some loss was foreseeable, or even that some loss of the same general kind was foreseeable, will not suffice if the loss that actually occurred was not foreseeable. It is enough, however, that the loss was foreseeable as a probable, as distinguished from a necessary, result of his breach. Furthermore, the party in breach need not have made a "tacit agreement" to be liable for the loss. Nor must he have had the loss in mind when making the contract, for the test is an objective one based on what he had reason to foresee. There is no requirement of foreseeability with respect to the injured party. . . .

Restatement (Second) of Contracts § 351(2)(b), *cmt b* provides that "[i]n the case of a written agreement, foreseeability is sometimes established by the use of recitals in the agreement itself." If you drafted the contract on behalf of Florafax, how would you modify Clause 20? The clause in the contract provided:

> 20. Termination
>
> a. Termination for cause. Any non-defaulting party shall have the right to terminate this agreement at any date not less than forty-five (45) days after an event of default occurs and so long as it continues. In the event GTE ceases to perform its duties hereunder after a notice of termination is given or otherwise, Florafax may suffer tremendous damage to its business. GTE agrees to pay Florafax consequential damages and lost profits on the business lost.

The clause could have been improved by reciting Florafax's intent to enter into third party contracts such as the contract with Bellerose, the profit potential under such contracts, and the fact that GTE failure to perform could impact such profits.

3. *Consequential damage elimination.* The Restatement (Second) of Contracts is silent with regard to contract provisions that attempt to reduce or eliminate a particular remedy. Thus, such a clause would be tested under other contractual doctrines such as public policy and unconscionability. However, the UCC is quite specific regarding the elimination of remedies. UCC § 2-719(3) specifically permits a contract for the sale of goods to limit or exclude consequential damages. However, a clause limiting (or eliminating) consequential damages arising from personal injury is *prima facie* unconscionable. Such clauses are presumptively valid however where personal injury is not

involved. Given this restriction, do think that common law contractual waivers of liability for personal injuries due to negligence should be enforceable or should they also be *prima facie* unconscionable? Yes, but the law in many states is to the contrary. See Restatement (Second) of Contracts § 195 and compare that section with § 208. Is there a policy reason justifying freedom of contract not involving the sale of goods that does not apply to negligent services causing personal physical injury? Yes—reasonable assumption of risk. Consider, for instance, the person who wishes to do a parachute jump. The company refuses to take the customer up or allow the jump without a release of personal liability. § 195 suggests that the signature of a release of liability for negligence in such a situation is presumptively valid. The justification for enforcement of such clauses is that, but for . . ., the customer would be denied the desired opportunity. Risk allocation in such a situation should be tolerated as long as there is fair disclosure and no abuse of bargaining power. Generally, common law waivers of liability for personal injuries arising from mere negligence are enforceable. See e.g. *Sharon v. City of Newton*, 769 N.E. 2d 738 (MA 2002) (father capable of waiver school liability for negligent personal injuries suffered by his daughter).

4. *Parol evidence to establish foreseeability.* If Clause 20 was perfectly drafted, why was testimonial evidence necessary to prove that GTE knew (or should have known) about the Bellerose contract? Such evidence should not have been mandatory but was probably offered on a "belt and suspenders" basis. Clearly the court regarded the specific evidence of foreseen lost profit as important. If you represented GTE, would you object to the admission of such evidence by Florafax on the grounds that it violated the parol evidence rule? You could object but the objection would be overruled. See the introductory notes prior to this case. If so, would you likely be successful in preventing Florafax from admitting testimonial evidence to the jury for the purpose of establishing whether GTE knew or should have known about the collateral contract with Bellerose? No—the parol evidence rule is not applicable. Does the parol evidence rule apply? No. If so, would a merger clause help to exclude such evidence? No. See Restatement (Second) of Contracts § 351(2)(b), *cmt b* to the effect that "[t]he parol evidence rule (§ 213) does not, however, preclude the use of negotiations prior to the making of the contract to show for this purpose circumstances that were then known to a party." Can you explain why Restatement (Second) of Contracts § 213 does not preclude parol evidence for this purpose? To allow the parol evidence rule to preclude such evidence would emasculate the very basis of the rule with respect to circumstances under which consequential damages can be recovered. What is the relevance of Restatement (Second) of Contracts § 214(e)? Presumably, the exclusion of the parol evidence rule is explained as "other remedy" under that subsection.

5. *Non-economic losses as consequential or incidental damages.* See text.

6. *The effectiveness of contract mechanisms to deter willful breach.* The consequential damages clause in the GTE-Florafax contract is one mechanism by which contracting parties may attempt to make willful breach more expensive, and thus attempt to deter such breaches during contract performance. Other mechanisms include clauses requiring posting of a bond or other security that will be forfeited upon nonperformance, liquidated damages clauses that specify the amount of damages for which a breaching party will be liable (discussed below), clauses awarding attorney fees and other legal costs to the nonbreaching party, and most favored customer clauses that give discounts or other benefits to regular, trusted trading partners. See David Baumer & Patricia Marschall, *"Willful Breach of Contract for the Sale of Goods: Can the Bane of Business Be an Economic Bonanza?,"* 65 Temple L. Rev. 159, 170-71 (1992). One empirical survey of 168 businesses in North Carolina reported that while attorney fees provisions were the most commonly used protective mechanism among respondents, perceived bond requirements and liquidated damages clauses were perceived as more effective at deterring breach. Why would parties be reluctant to include such terms if they more effectively deter willful breaches? The problem may lie in negotiating room—one side might like to include a string of such clauses but the other side might not be willing to go along. From a different perspective, one side might be unwilling to ask for such clauses because of the air of distrust of the other party such a request might well convey. From yet a different perspective, parties frequently negotiate contracts with rosy expectations that performance will match exactly the original expectations of the parties. That attitude during negotiations tends to lead the parties to avoid including provisions covering the "what ifs." Lawyers, rather than clients, tend to think of including such clauses. Importantly, none of these clauses were deemed universally effective. What factors would cause a party to decide to breach even in the face of such clauses? Frequently, the main reason is simple inability to perform the promise as made. Here, however, it appears that GTE could have chosen to perform albeit without making any profit. Why GTE would choose not to perform under the present facts is something of a puzzle. Without knowing the numbers, it is easy to guess that GTE's pain would have been less if it had performed, taking into account the cost of the litigation, the judgment, and the adverse publicity it probably received in the market place.

b. Mitigation Limitation

Restatement (Second) of Contracts § 347(d) provides that an injured party's loss in value (including lost profits) damages must be reduced by any other cost or loss avoided by not having to perform. The costs and losses avoided are most often referred to as "mitigation of damages" to imply that the failure to mitigate has negative consequences. As implied by Restatement (Second) of Contracts § 347, the injured party is expected to undertake reasonable steps to avoid increasing the breaching party's loss following a breach. Failure to take such mitigating steps breaks the chain of causation and diminishes any damages recovery by the amount that, with reasonable effort, might have been saved. The plaintiff has not promised to mitigate and does not commit a breach of contract by failing to mitigate. Instead, the failure to mitigate is used as a shield. The burden of proving both the opportunity to mitigate and the fact that efforts to mitigate would have been successful is on the defendant. Restatement (Second) of Contracts § 350(1) therefore simply states that damages are not recoverable for any loss that the injured party could have avoided without undue risk, burden or humiliation. Such avoidance can occur in the form of expenses which the plaintiff would have had to incur had she been obliged to perform the contract fully (expense avoided), or in the form of a new opportunity for profit created as a result of discharge of the plaintiff's obligation under the contract. A builder, for example, who contracted to build a house but was excused by the owner's uncured material breach may be able to make a profit by building another house, an opportunity that would not have been possible had the contractor been obliged to build the first house.

Rockingham County v. Luten Bridge Co.
CASE BRIEF

This is a 1929 decision of the United States Circuit Court of Appeals for the Fourth Circuit. On January 7, 1924, the Board of Commissioners of Rockingham County voted to award to plaintiff Luten Bridge Co. (Luten) a contract to build a bridge. Three of the five county commissioners favored building the bridge, while two commissioners opposed the idea. The debate generated such a large amount of emotion that on February 11, 1924, W. K. Pruitt, one of the commissioners who voted in favor of the bridge, sent his resignation to the county clerk, who accepted and noted the resignation that same day. Later that day, Pruitt reconsidered his decision, and called the clerk to rescind his resignation. The clerk ignored the attempted withdrawal and the next day appointed W. W. Hampton as a member of the board to succeed Pruitt. After his resignation, Pruitt attended no further meetings of the board, and took no further action as a commissioner. Similarly, Pratt and McCollum, the other two commissioners who had voted in favor of the bridge contract also attended no further meetings. Hampton, on the other hand, met regularly with the two remaining members of the board, Martin and Barber, and attended to the business of the county.

On February 21, during a regular meeting of the board, the three unanimously adopted a resolution declaring that the contract for the bridge was not legal and valid, and directing the clerk of the board to notify Luten that the board refused to recognize the contract as valid, and that Luten should halt work on the bridge. The clerk so notified Luten. The resolution also rescinded approval of the construction of a hard-surfaced road, of which the bridge was to be the connecting link. On March 3, the board passed another resolution, directing the clerk to notify Luten that any work done on the bridge would be at Luten's own risk and hazard, and that even if the board were mistaken as to the validity of the construction contract, they did not desire to build a bridge, and would contest payment for the bridge if constructed. The clerk again sent notice of the resolution to Luten. On April 7, the board passed a resolution stating that the board had been informed that one of its members had been privately insisting that the bridge be built, but that the board repudiated this action and gave notice that it would not be recognized. At a September meeting, the board passed another resolution that it would not pay for any bills presented by Luten or anyone connected with the bridge. At that time, little work had been done on the bridge (only $1900 in labor and materials had been expended); nonetheless, in spite of the county's repudiation of the contract, Luten continued with the bridge construction. On November 24, 1924, Luten instituted an action against Rockingham County and its board of commissioners, alleging that the county owed Luten over $18,000 for work that had been done in building the bridge up to November 3, 1924. At trial, the court ordered a directed verdict in favor of Luten for the full amount of damages claimed. Rockingham County appealed.

The court held that, after the board had given notice that it did not wish to proceed with the contract, Luten could not proceed to build the bridge and recover the contract price. After Luten had received notice of the breach, it owed a duty not to increase the damages resulting from that breach. Luten's only remedy at that point was to treat the contract as broken and sue for the recovery of such damages as it may have sustained, such as lost profits. While the court noted that a contrary view existed under English law, the court stated that such a view was at odds with the American rule that a plaintiff cannot hold a defendant liable for damages which need not have been incurred. The court supported that view with a wide variety of citations. And in the cases that Luten cited, the court found that the legal principles were not on point with the case at hand, and none of the cases supported the argument that Luten owed no duty not to increase the breach damages.

The court held that, since Luten was given due notice that the County did not want the bridge built, the proper measure of Luten's damages was an amount sufficient to compensate it for labor and materials expended and expense incurred in the part performance of the contract before repudiation, plus the profit that Luten would have realized if the contract had been completed.

INTERESTING DISCUSSION ISSUES

1. *To what damages was Luten entitled?* Students have no difficulty with the notion that Luten was entitled to the profit it would have made in constructing the bridge—its "loss in value." The perennially difficult proposition which so many students have trouble with is that, in addition to lost profits, Luten was entitled to recover its "sunk costs" as part of its "loss in value." Here, the county's breach of contract was a repudiation (not anticipatory since construction had been begun before the time of repudiation). At this point Luten had a duty not to incur further costs that could otherwise be avoided. But if Luten's only recovery were net profit, and not "sunk costs," Luten's profit would be eroded by every dollar of expense actually incurred up to the time of repudiation.

2. *How should lost profits be calculated?* One way of doing the necessary calculation would be to start with the contract price and then subtract from that price all expense Luten was able to avoid following the repudiation. Thus, all materials used in construction, all labor costs to date of repudiation, and all overhead items that were not apportionable or cancelable, are costs that are not to be deducted from the contract price. The cost of materials contracted for but not used would be a deductible expense to the extent they could not be used on another job or returned to the supplier. The cost of wages contracted for but not used prior to repudiation would not be deducted to the extent not savable. Suppose that the contractor, at the time of repudiation, had a contractual liability to give her carpenters two weeks' notice before termination. The cost of that two weeks of labor would not be a deductible expense unless the carpenters could be immediately fully used on a different contract without any loss. These savings, to the extent possible, would be costs avoided. To the extent that the defendant might be able to show that the contractor, as a result of the repudiation, was able to take on other profitable work that the contractor could not have handled but for the repudiation, any profit allocable to the substituted work would constitute "loss avoided." While it is unlikely in such a case that the contractor would have a claim for consequential damages, any such claim would come under the heading of "other losses." To the extent that the contractor incurred expense in trying to mitigate any loss involved, such additional

mitigation costs would also be recoverable. Such costs are often referred to as "incidental" expenses.

3. *Why do you suppose the Luten Bridge Company continued with the work after being told the county would not pay for the work?* The law relating to a duty to mitigate did not start with this case but, in the United States, developed earlier—see the court's cited cases. Was it just stubbornness that led Luten to continue work and essentially finish the bridge? Or was there some other reason? The political background of the case suggests that, at least for a period of months after the letter purporting to repudiate, there was reasonable doubt as to whether the appointment of the replacement commissioner was either legal or effective. Consequently there was reasonable doubt as to whether the board of commissioners had legally repudiated the contract—whether the notice of repudiation was validly and legally voted on and adopted as the action of the commission. Could Luten have argued that it continued with the building because of such reasonable doubt? What would have happened if, several months after the letter of repudiation, a reconstituted board had sent Luten another letter instructing that the "repudiating letter" was null and void and without effect—and asking how the work on the bridge was progressing? It is interesting that counsel for Luten apparently advanced no such argument.

NOTES AND QUESTIONS

1. *Famous case.* See text.

2. *Legal archaeology revisited.* Judge John Parker's famous opinion and case may have been more about politics than the duty to mitigate, the doctrine for which it became famous:

> *Rockingham County v. Luten Bridge Co.* is now a staple in most contracts casebooks. The popular story goes as follows: Rockingham County entered into a contract with the Luten Bridge Company to build a bridge over the Dan River. Shortly after work commenced, the county repudiated the contract. Nonetheless, the Luten Bridge Company continued with its construction project and sued the county for the entire bill. Judge John J. Parker, the long-time Chief Judge of the Fourth Circuit, ruled in the famous 1929 opinion that the county was liable only for the costs up until the time of breach, a sum of approximately $1,900, plus the anticipated profit, and not for the entire bill that was closer to $18,000. The case is used to illustrate the "duty to mitigate," whereby a party to a contract against whom a breach has occurred is obligated to mitigate the damages resulting from that breach.

> A closer look at the case reveals that the underlying dispute was more about the legitimacy of local government. The dispute emerged when angry taxpayers charged the county commissioners with pursuing a corrupt agenda on behalf of the industrialist who sponsored their political campaigns. But the conflict also revealed traditional tensions between the county's farmers and its mercantile mill owners and constituted a microcosm of the larger political conflict—endemic throughout North Carolina and the South—over investing in public improvements to promote industrialization. Judge Parker's opinion was an effort to arm county governments with the powers necessary to facilitate industrialization and secure good governance. The duty to mitigate damages was merely an afterthought. Barak Richman, Jordi Weinstock & Jason Mehta, *"A Bridge, A Tax Revolt, and the Struggle to Industrialize: The Story and Legacy of Rockingham County v. Luten Bridge Co.,* " 84 N. C. L. Rev. 1841 (2006).

Judge John Parker, the architect and author of the opinion, was a respected jurist also caught up in the politically charged atmosphere surrounding the case. See Peter G. Fish, *"Crossing Judge Parkers' Luten Bridge: Partisan Politics, Economic Visions, and Government Reform in Retrospect: A Comment to Professor Richman,"* 84 N. C. L. Rev. 1913 (2006).

3. *American and English jurisprudence.* As Judge Parker fairly admits, the rule as to mitigation at the time was otherwise in England. He cites s contrary view by Lord Cockburn in *Frost v. Knight,* 7 L. R. Exch. 111 (1872). Why do you think Judge Parker chose a different path given the early heavy reliance of American common law on English common law? He saw the repudiation as starting a break in the chain of causation—leading to the conclusion that any loss of expenditure beyond that point was no longer causally related to the county's breach. English cases had struggled with what the courts saw as a choice for the plaintiff—to treat the repudiation as a partial and not a total breach, allowing the plaintiff the option of continuing to perform. See John V. Orth, *"A Bridge, A Tax Revolt, and the Struggle to Industrialize: A Comment,"* 84 N. C. L. Rev. 1927 (2006).

4. *Who owns the bridge?* Assuming that Luten Bridge (from Tennessee) found it more problematic and expensive to tear down the bridge after the case, what happens to the bridge and how does the case account for the future development? While the bridge was not then in use does it have any value whatsoever to the County? What if three years later the County builds roads to and from the bridge and the route serves a valuable public function? Did the County receive a bridge it did not currently want but might use in the future nearly free?

After the tumult of the 1920s, the Fishing Creek Bridge sat quietly over the Dan River during the 1930s, unencumbered by traffic and alone in the woods. Occasionally the remote bridge played host to picnics and parties attended by young people from the area, including some elegant dinners and dances. Through the following decades, the absurdity of the Fishing Creek Bridge's existence became part of Rockingham County folklore and soon "Mebane's Bridge" also became known as "Mebane's Folly." All the while, there were questions about who owned the bridge. If Rockingham County never paid for the bridge (assuming Spray Water Power and Land did, in fact, make the ultimate payment to the Luten Bridge Co.), some suggested that the county might not own the bridge, and so it might not collect property taxes from the actual owner. In 1935 any question as to the ownership of the bridge was answered when the North Carolina State Department of Transportation assumed ownership of the bridge and finally connected the bridge to dirt roads leading to Spray and Leaksville.

In a last-gasp effort to reclaim their losses on the Fishing Creek Bridge, the Luten Bridge Company instituted another lawsuit in 1936, this time against the state highway commission for $9,800. At the time, the company stated that "the bridge cost $44,000.00 and that only $34,200.00 had been paid, with $9,200.00 of it coming from the county and $25,000.00 from the Spray Water Power and Land Company." The suit was thrown out after the Luten Bridge Company failed to appear at a scheduled court date. The company does not appear in any further public records in Rockingham County.

In 1968, the State Department of Transportation finally paved a road on both sides of the bridge. Dismissing the span's actual name, the Fishing Creek Bridge, the new street signs read "Mebane Bridge Road." And what might be the bridge's final chapter arrived in the fall of 2003, when the famous bridge was permanently closed to traffic. The single-lane bridge still crosses high above the Dan River and remains available for pedestrians, and it now ingloriously supports a sewage pipe leading to Eden's water treatment facility. There have been threats that North Carolina's Department of Transportation might decide to demolish the bridge, but that sewage pipe might just save the bridge from destruction. However long it remains above the Dan River, Mebane's Bridge will serve as a monument to industrial ambition, cronyism, a countryside in transition, Judge Parker's most famous opinion, and one of the most bizarre and heated moments in Rockingham County's history. Barak Richman, Jordi Weinstock & Jason Mehta, *"A Bridge, A Tax Revolt, and the Struggle to Industrialize: The Story and Legacy of Rockingham County v. Luten Bridge Co.,* "84 N. C. L. Rev. 1841, 1907-1908 (2006).

Parker v. Twentieth Century Fox-Film Corp.
CASE BRIEF

This is a 1970 decision of the California Supreme Court. "Parker" was in fact the celebrated actress Shirley MacLaine. Under a contract dated August 6, 1965, plaintiff Parker was to play the lead role in defendant Twentieth Century Fox's ("Fox") motion picture, *Bloomer Girl*. The contract guaranteed Parker a minimum compensation of $750,000, to be paid out weekly over 14 weeks, beginning on May 23, 1966. Before May 1966, Fox decided not to produce the picture, and by letter dated April 4, 1966 notified Parker of the decision and that it would not "comply with our obligations to you under" the written contract. Rather, for the purpose of "avoiding any damage" to Parker, Fox offered to employ Parker as the leading actress in another film entitled *Big Country, Big Man*; compensation was to be identical, as were 31 of 34 contractual provisions of the original contract. But while *Bloomer Girl* was to have been a musical production filmed in California, *Big Country, Big Man* would be a dramatic "western-type" movie that was to be filmed in Australia. Fox allowed Parker one week to accept; she refused and the offer lapsed. Parker then filed suit to recover the agreed guaranteed compensation. Parker's first cause of action was for money due under the contract, while the second cause was for damages resulting from Fox's breach of the contract. Fox admitted the existence and validity of the contract, Parker's compliance with all terms, and the fact that it breached and anticipatorily repudiated the contract. But Fox denied that any recovery was due to Parker under either cause of action because of her failure to mitigate the damages by her unreasonable refusal of the leading role in *Big Country, Big Man*. The trial court granted Parker's motion for summary judgment and awarded her $750,000 plus interest. Fox appealed.

The court stated the general rule that recovery by a wrongfully discharged employee is the amount of salary agreed upon for the period of service, less the amount which the employer affirmatively proves that the employee has earned or with reasonable effort might have earned from other employment. But before projected earnings may be applied in mitigation, the employer must show that the other employment was substantially similar to that of which the employee has been deprived. An employee's rejection of or failure to seek different or inferior employment may not be used to mitigate damages. In this case, the only issue that Fox raised was whether Parker's refusal of the role in *Big Country, Big Man* could be used in mitigation of damages. But Fox did not cite, nor did the court find, any precedent to indicate that reasonableness was to be used to determine if a wrongfully discharged employee's option to reject different or inferior employment would be charged against her in mitigation of damages. As such, the court held that Parker's refusal of the role in *Big Country, Big Man* could not be applied against her in mitigation of damages because the offer was both different and inferior, compared to the original offer of the lead in *Bloomer Girl*. The court stated that the styles of the two movies, the different shooting locations, and the elimination of Parker's director and screenplay approval rights from *Bloomer Girl* all demonstrated that Fox's back-up offer was both different from, and inferior to, the original employment agreed upon. As such, Parker was excused from attempting to mitigate damages, and the trial court's ruling was upheld.

DISSENT (Sullivan, C.J.) Acting Chief Judge Sullivan found that the basic question in this case was whether or not Parker acted reasonably in rejecting Fox's offer of alternate employment, an answer that was dependent upon whether Fox's offer of replacement work was of a different or inferior kind, compared to the originally offered work. Judge Sullivan stated that such a question was properly regarded as a factual issue that the trial court should not have determined on motion for summary judgment.

Judge Sullivan stated that it has never been the law that the mere existence of differences between two jobs in the same field is sufficient, as a matter of law, to excuse a wrongfully discharged employee from accepting the other in order to mitigate damages. Judge Sullivan also stated that the court's analysis of the differences between the two films merely constituted a statement of the differences, and not an analysis of whether such differences were substantive enough to permit Parker to be excused from mitigation. Rather, both the trial court and court of appeals misused judicial notice and failed to show why the differences between the two films were so substantial that the second film constituted employment different or inferior, such that Parker could refuse it without repercussions.

INTERESTING DISCUSSION ISSUES

1. *Does the test of "inferior or different" pose an issue of fact?* The wrongfully discharged employee does not commit a breach of promise by not seeking to mitigate. That failure simply breaks the chain of causation between the breach of wrongful termination and the damage. That failure merely becomes an impediment to recovery of damages, usually only a partial impediment. Cases of wrongful discharge often pose difficult counseling challenges for the lawyer counseling the discharged employee. Suppose that the employee was serving as chief executive officer of the company when she was wrongfully terminated. Suppose further, that she was quickly offered a vice presidency at a lower salary by another company. Should she have to accept the lower paying job, seeking to recover only the pay difference between the two positions? Assuming that the issue is one of fact, what advice should

the lawyer give her client? Assuming further that she rejects the offered position, what evidence will her counsel present at the trial? An expert witness testifying that job titles are significant and that moving from chief executive officer to vice president would be seen in the trade as a demotion likely to adversely impact her future employment prospects would be helpful.

NOTES AND QUESTIONS

1. *Famous actress.* The Court noted the case involved a famous actress but did not name her. In fact, that actress was Shirley MacLaine. Approximately one year before this case, Shirley MacLaine had co-starred as an nun with an unsavory past with actor Clint Eastwood in a western set in Mexico. Universal released that motion picture titled "Two Mules for Sister Sara." Consequently, MacLaine was certainly not philosophically opposed to western movies with unfavorable portrayal of women and set in a foreign country. Victor P. Goldberg, *"Bloomer Girl Revisited or How to Frame an Unmade Picture,"* 1998 Wis. L. Rev. 1051, 1052.

2. *Pay-or-play provision and breach theory.* See text.

3. *MacLaine's acclaim as an actress.* See text.

4. *Law and feminism.* See text.

5. *Mitigation burden of proof.* This case is traditionally used to illustrate a wrongfully discharged employee's duty to mitigate after termination of employment. Of course, an at-will employee seldom has a breach of contract action. Most employment breach contracts extend beyond one year, are in written form to satisfy the Statute of Frauds, and involve an exploration of the wrongfully discharged employee's responsibilities to seek other gainful employment for the remainder of the employment period.

Restatement (Second) of Contracts § 350(1) essentially provides that an injured party cannot recover for a loss that could have been reasonably avoided without undue, risk, burden or humiliation. Fox argues the entire loss could have been avoided had MacLaine simply accepted their offer of further employment at the same salary. California law is similar to other state laws on this topic. A wrongfully discharged employee must exercise reasonable efforts to locate other employment. The failure to do so means that the employee's damages are the salary for the remainder of the employment period reduced by the amount that such reasonable efforts would have produced.

Importantly, the burden of proof on mitigation is on the employer. The employee does not have to prove that he or she properly mitigated. The employer must prove the employee failed to properly mitigate and the reasonable amount that would have been available from the alternative employment. See Restatement (Second) of Contracts § 350, *cmt. c* and *Boehm v. American Broadcasting Co.,* 929 F. 2d 482 (9th Cir. 1991).

The Court considers various factors controlling on the similarity question: location of job performance, type of acting role, hours or employment, status and title. Do you consider the employer able to meet this difficult burden? Obviously, meeting this burden is a difficult task. Should an employee be required to accept a comparable job at a lower salary or with a different title, recovering only the difference between the two salaries? As the dissent in the above case points out, the issue should be one of fact to be determined by the trier of fact. The dissent challenged the majority's position here that, as a matter of law, the employment offered in the second film was inferior and different from that in *Bloomer Girl.* Neither majority nor dissent dwell on the administrative differences between the two contracts, the second taking away Parker's discretion to approve certain actions taken by Fox.

6. *Effect of employer's offer to reemploy.* In *Ford Motor Co. v. E.E.O.C.,* 458 U.S. 219 (1982), the Supreme Court determined that an employer's unconditional offer to reemploy a wrongfully discharged employee in a new position terminates its liability for further Title VII damages if the employee refuses to accept the offer without justification. However, the offered position must be either the same job or one that is "substantially similar." See also Boehm v. American Broadcasting Co., 929 F. 2d 482 (9th Cir. 1991). It can be argued strongly that such reemployment could, under some circumstances, amount to "humiliation," a condition the Restatement says the employee is not obligated to accept.

7. *Substantially similar employment.* See text.

Optional Problem 9-2

Lisa is a nationally-known performance artist dedicated to showing the oppression of the working class through personal experience. To further this ambition, she took a job as a fry cook at Burger Chef, a fast food restaurant. To promote retention, Burger Chef contracted with Lisa to employ her for a period of 1 year at a wage of $7.50 per hour. Two months later, Burger Chef fired Lisa in breach of the employment contract. The next day, representatives from Fry Queen, a competing fast food chain, offered Lisa employment as a cashier at a restaurant located adjacent to her old Burger Chef job at $7.25 per hour. Lisa rejected the offer because she believed Fry Queen employment would not satisfy her artistic vision and devoted the next 10 months to developing a performance art routine centered upon her experiences as a Burger Chef fry cook. At the end of the year, Lisa sued Burger Chef for her back pay for the last 10 months for breach of the employment contract. What relief is the court most likely to award and why?

Answer:

This problem raises the issue of whether the "inferior or different" standard should be applied objectively or subjectively taking into account the discharged employee's personal reasons for accepting the original employment. The issue should be one of fact, raising the counseling question of what evidence plaintiff's counsel should introduce at the trial. The fact that the work of the offered job—a cashier's position compared to a fry cook—may not make the offer inferior or different since the pay was the same for both positions. On the facts of the Problem however, Lisa had a particular motive and reason for accepting the Burger Chef position in the first place. If a subjective test approach is to be taken, should Lisa have to show that Burger Chef was aware of her subjective purpose at the time she was hired? Should a "reasonably foreseeable" test be used even though the issue is not one of breach of promise but only failure to mitigate? Or can an analogy be drawn to the cases on cost of completion compared to loss in value? Comment *e* to Restatement (Second) of Contracts § 350 says in part:

> *e. What is a "substitute."* Whether an available alternative transaction is a suitable substitute depends on all the circumstances, including the similarity of the performance and the times and places that they would be rendered. If discrepancies between the transactions can be adequately compensated for in damages, the alternative transaction is regarded as a substitute and such damages are awarded.

The second sentence of this comment could provide some support for Lisa's argument that the other job does not provide a suitable alternative transaction. But the issue should be one of fact for a jury and not one of law justifying summary judgment for Burger Chef.

c. Certainty Limitation

Remember the handling of the "certainty" issue in *Florafax.* This requirement follows logically from the requirement of a chain of causation connecting damage to the breach. If the damage is not proven with sufficient certainty, the demonstration of required causal connection fails. The phrase "reasonable certainty" is vague. Comment *a* to § 352 provides a little further information and refinement of content. First, greater certainty of proof may be required in a breach of contract case than in a tort case. But as discussed above, courts may resolve doubts against the breaching party, especially where the breach was willful.

While the certainty limitation applies equally to both reliance and expectancy damages, it is more likely that a nonbreaching party will be able to prove reliance costs and incidental damages than lost profits. In some cases, where the contract takes place in the context of a well-developed and active market for contract goods or services, the market provides a good indication of the amount of damages caused by a breach of contract. In many cases, however, a well-developed market for the goods or services that can provide accurate price information from which to determine damages caused by the breach does not exist. New businesses, without established histories of similar contracts, often experience difficulty in proving lost profits with reasonable certainty.

A-S Development, Inc. v. W.R. Grace Land Corporation
CASE BRIEF

This is a 1982 decision of the United States District Court for New Jersey. In 1974, A.S. Development, Inc. ("A.S.") decided to terminate its real estate activities and to sell all of its substantial real estate holdings across the United States to W.R. Grace Land Corporation ("Grace"). The parties agreed to the terms of this transfer on June 30, 1974. Through no fault of either party, one of the parcels in the transaction, Channel Club Tower ("CCT"), which was under construction, became involved in a dispute regarding its electrical power supply. As a result, the parties agreed to remove CCT from the main agreement, and made it subject to a supplemental agreement with its own specific conditions and contingencies that was also dated June 30, 1974. Under the agreement, the sale price of CCT was to be the book value of CCT as of the close of business on the day prior to closing.

On March 12, 1975, A.S. advised Grace that the book value was approximately $9.6 million, as certified by accountants Arthur Young & Co. Grace refused to close on CCT on March 13, 1975, and A.S. was forced to sell the individual apartment units to retail buyers. Due to a slow market, the units took almost five years to sell out; the cash receipts from the sales amounted to over $13.8 million by June 1980. Grace contended that the sale receipts or the 1975 real estate tax assessment of nearly $11.2 million were indisputable evidence of the property's value and should be used to conclude that A.S. suffered no damages from Grace's breach. But A.S. argued that the monthly sales receipts were merely an attempt to mitigate damages, and presented evidence that it suffered the loss of the $9.6 million sale price for nearly five years, and that this lost time had a monetary value. A.S. advanced three methodologies to reflect the damages that it sustained:

(1) the involuntary loan theory; (2) the alternative capital receipts; and (3) the alternative sales price. Under the involuntary loan theory, A.S. would treat the breach as though they had issued a loan in the amount of the closing price to Grace, under conditions similar to those provided Grace by its actual lender for the purchase. Treating the monthly sales receipts as Grace's payments toward interest and principal, A.S. showed that Grace would owe it over $5.8 million as of December 31, 1981. Under the alternative capital receipts theory, A.S. presented expert testimony regarding the fact that, if A.S. had the benefit of the sales price on March 13, 1975, investment of those funds would have resulted in a return of nearly $7.6 million more than Grace received by selling the units individually over five years. Under the alternative sales price theory, A.S. provided expert testimony to show that, if all sales receipts from 1975 to 1980 were converted into 1975 dollars by means of present value calculations, the damages as of March 13, 1975 would be over $2.6 million; applying 16% annual interest (based largely on the bond market) to the amount, the damages as of December 31, 1981 were over $7.8 million. Weighting the three theories from least subjective to most subjective (greatest reliance on No. 1, least reliance on No. 2), A.S. projected a figure of $6 million as necessary to make it whole because of the breach. Grace objected to these methodologies as illogical theories with no precedent in law, and as attempts to create damages where none existed. But the court rejected this argument and went on to evaluate A.S.'s proffered theories.

Before determining a methodology to employ, the court examined the shortcomings of each of A.S.'s recovery methodologies. The court first stated that the involuntary loan theory relied on assumptions that were disputable (e.g., interest rate, repayment schedule), and was overly harsh in that damages continued to grow even after the project was completely sold out. The court also held that the theory placed A.S. in a highly favorable position of a commercial mortgagee with a fail-safe mortgage despite the fact that A.S. might not have found such a desirable investment with the sale price that it ought to have received from Grace. With regard to the alternative capital receipts theory, the court stated that the theory did not necessarily reflect real estate rates of interest, and A.S. did not show any investments that it contemplated that would have resulted in the specified rate of return. Finally, the court stated that the alternative sales price theory was less satisfying than the involuntary loan theory because it relied on interest rates in the bond market without any connection of how such rates applied to the current situation. In its final analysis, the court decided that the involuntary loan theory provided the fairest means by which to determine compensation to A.S., and fashioned a recovery based on this scheme.

The general rule for measuring damages for the sale or purchase of real estate is that damages are assessed as the difference between the contract price and market value at the time of the breach. While Grace urged the use of this metric to show that A.S. had not suffered any damages (market value exceeded the contract price), the court stated that this methodology did not address the unique injuries that A.S. suffered due to the loss of the use of a large sum of money for an extended period of time. The court noted that delay in receiving compensation is an element of determining damages, and thus the time-value of money was a legitimate aspect of calculating compensation because it helped to put the injured party in the position that it should have occupied if performance had been rendered as promised. While this case involved a difficult calculation of damages, the court noted that difficulty or lack of certainty does not preclude the award of damages to a successful party. In fact, doubts are generally to be resolved against the party in breach, who has forced the other party to seek compensation for the injury sustained.

The court rejected an assertion on the part of Grace that the New Jersey prejudgment interest rule ought to limit the interest rate that could be used in determining A.S.'s damages. While the rule was intended to ensure that a winning party is made whole by receiving full benefit of lost use of money, the court ruled that it was inapplicable here. The question in this case was whether an award for damages in a contract case could be fashioned in reliance on the time-value of money when plaintiff has received the full contract price as the result of its efforts to mitigate damages. The court held that such an award theory must be available. As a result, the court found that A.S. was entitled to damages in an amount to be calculated on the involuntary loan theory (with an interest rate 2% above prime, simple not compound interest) through the date that the judgment was entered, as well as post-judgment interest to be calculated at 12% simple interest.

INTERESTING DISCUSSION ISSUES

1. *Interest as a recoverable item of damages.* Where payment of money under a contract obligation to do so is made late, interest on the overdue payment seems to be a logical element of damages. Money clearly has a "time value." Thus many contracts, familiar in our commercial market, provide expressly for the payment of interest at a prescribed rate in the event of late payment. Credit card contracts provide a common example. Where the missed payment was of a sum certain, the logic of recovering interest seems irrefutable. In such a situation, most states have either a statute or a court rule providing for the collection of interest at a prescribed rate as part of a suit to recover damages for nonpayment. Where the missed payment is, however, not for a sum certain but rather for a sum of an amount unknown until verdict or judgment, a more complex problem arises. Take the case of an insured's claim against its insurer under a products liability policy coverage. It frequently takes years for a lawsuit against the insurer to mature to verdict or judgment. Should the insurer owe in addition to

the amount of the verdict a sum of interest calculated on the basis of the "time value" of the verdict measured from the date of the claim until payment? Factoring interest into the amount recoverable makes sense logically. The insurer has had the use of the insured's money from the time payment of that money first became due. That period is frequently a number of years. But insurers argue, as Grace did in the instant case, that the local state or court rule provided for the recovery of "prejudgment" interest only in the case of a claim for a sum certain. This statute or court rule is often asserted to preempt the recovery of interest in any case other that the sum certain—an assertion that is not a logical dictate. Where the contract provides explicitly for the recovery of interest, the problem does not arise. Where this is not the case, difficult issues, in addition to the "prejudgment interest" argument, arise—what rate of interest should be recoverable and should this interest be calculated as simple or compound, and at what intervals? The above case is one of a small number dealing with the recovery of interest as damages under a contract which failed to provide expressly for late payment.

NOTES AND QUESTIONS

1. *Reasonable certainty versus mathematical certainty.* The certainty limitation on damages does not require that the damages be ascertainable with mathematical certainty. Indeed, as the *A-S Development* opinion indicates, even the best models and calculations of the parties' experts will involve, to some extent, guesses and speculations. Remember these issues in *Florafax.* How does the court resolve the question of how to justify the application of one model over another? Using fairness, assumed foreseeability, and chain of causation analysis. For instance, A-S's second theory involved use of the rate of return on equity accomplished by its parent company (A-S was a wholly owned subsidiary). That rate of return on equity was based on investments having nothing to do with land and land developments and was thus a figure far removed by way of analogy from the particular facts of the case. Likewise, does the court's eventual adoption of the involuntary loan theory at 2% over the prime rate (versus the 4% over prime rate measure proposed by plaintiff's expert) appear particularly reasoned and justifiable, or does the court appear to pull this number out of thin air? Rather clearly the latter! No clear reason was articulated for the choice of either rate, just as no clear reason was articulated for the choice of rest periods to be used in interest calculation, and even more significantly, for the choice between simple and compound interest. But it was clear to the judge that A-S had been deprived of the use of a substantial sum of money for a period of years and that the use of some interest factor was appropriate. The final determination was thus an approximation. Also, note the wide range of possible damages given by the different models proposed by

the plaintiff's expert. Why wouldn't such widely varying results indicate that damages were not reasonably ascertainable? Perhaps the plaintiff's expert was attempting to establish both a floor and a ceiling rate. It is highly unusual for an expert to offer a range of views leading to different end calculations. But if a plaintiff can plead inconsistent causes of action, an expert ought to be able to offer alternative theories—recognizing however, the danger of weakening the effect of such testimony by introducing alternative and competing models.

2. *Prejudgment interest on a "sum certain"?* How did the judge deal with "prejudgment" interest on a sum which, at the time of suit, was "uncertain"? In this case, prejudgment interest dates from the time the action is filed until judgment. Interest from the date of breach to the time the action is filed can only be recovered as damages. In adopting the primary theory offered, the judge created a "sum certain" by assuming a loan by A-S in the amount of the total purchase price, reduced by payments from time to time treated as both payments of interest and reduction of principal as the units were sold individually. Would the plaintiff have recovered a true "expectancy" measure of damages without the inclusion of interest? Clearly no. Is the outcome suggested by Restatement (Second) of Contracts § 354 based on the relative uncertainty involved in calculating interest on a sum that remains unliquidated until entry of judgment? § 354 provides:

> (1) If the breach consists of a failure to pay a definite sum in money or to render a performance with fixed or ascertainable monetary value, interest is recoverable from the time for performance on the amount due less all deductions to which the party in breach is entitled.
> (2) In any other case, such interest may be allowed as justice requires on the amount that would have been just compensation had it been paid when performance was due.

The words "as justice requires" provide a good deal of leeway. The opposition to allowing prejudgment interest on a "sum uncertain" is said to have been based on the unfairness of holding the defendant to the payment of a sum that the defendant had no opportunity to satisfy by a payment into court after the filing of the complaint or any time thereafter prior to verdict and judgment.

3. *Certainty and valuation in complex transactions.* As noted above, complex transactions such as large-scale real property sales, corporate mergers and acquisitions, and many financial transactions present extraordinarily difficult issues with respect to valuation and determining damages with reasonable certainty. See, e.g., Keith Sharfman, *"Contractual Valuation Mechanisms and Corporate Law,"* 2 Va. L. & Bus. Rev. 53, 57-63 (2007) (" Legal valuation is thus less about

searching for the truth than about choosing one plausible value from a range of plausible alternatives."). In such cases, there is no single valuation rule for determining the amount of damages caused by a breach of contract. See Jay W. Eisenhofer & John L. Reed, *"Valuation Litigation,"* 22 Del. J. Corp. L. 37, 88-94 (1997) ("With regard to the actual valuation [of a target corporation], there is no methodology that is legally correct per se, but the method employed should be generally accepted in the financial community."). Consequently, while expert testimony is necessary to introduce a particular model for calculating damages with reasonable certainty into evidence, the lawyer's role in crafting a good narrative justifying adoption of one damages model and rejection of others is paramount. Based upon your reading of the case above, how could counsel for W.R. Grace Land Corp. have better countered A-S Development's arguments regarding damages models? Grace did argue that the second model, based on return on investment, was logically unconnected in any way with Grace's breach—the chain of causation was missing. Grace argued that the third method was "off the wall." The first method, Grace argued, put A-S in the position of a preferred mortgage lender having the loan fully secured by the property in question. This was a financially superior position to that in which A-S would have found itself had payment in full been made at the time of closing as promised under the contract. A-S was thus being placed in a position "better than" it would have enjoyed had Grace fully performed—thus a violation of the basic expectancy rule—"as good as but not better than . . . ." Grace's best argument, and one that was in all probability made, was that the very fact that three alternative models were offered by plaintiff's expert witness indicated the basic uncertainty involved—an uncertainty that precluded recovery. This argument lost because it was clear to the judge that A-S had truly suffered a loss of interest, a loss that needed to be compensated if only on the basis of a rough approximation, and an approximation that the judge deliberately downgraded by choosing simple rather than compound interest and a rate only 2% above the then prevailing prime rate of interest. If damages do not include interest, is the contract breaker encouraged to slow recovery and judgment?

4. *Prejudgment interest, liquidation of claims, and ascertainability.* Historically, courts opposed allowing the award of interest because they were opposed, it is said, to the concept of interest itself. See e.g. Patrick C. Diamond, *"The Minnesota Prejudgment Interest Amendment: An Analysis of the Counter-Offer Provision,"* 69 Minn. L. Rev. 1401, 1403 (1985). More recently, the law in many states changed, either by statute, court rule or decision, permitting the recovery of interest if the claim was for a definite sum or one of ascertainable fixed value. So-called unliquidated claims, in many states, are supposedly not entitled to bear interest until converted into a judgment of the court. Restatement (Second) of Contracts § 354(1)

appears to perpetuate this result. Demonstrably, this result fails to recognize the time value of money as applied to unliquidated claims, the apparent justification being that until the obligation is quantified by judgment, the defendant would not know how much to pay so as to avoid the interest cost. Moreover, would an award of pre-judgment interest adequately compensate injured promisees who were forced into bankruptcy as a result of the breach? Perhaps—would depend upon the facts of the particular case. See Royce de R. Barondes, *"Rejecting the Marie Antoinette Paradigm of Prejudgment Interest,"* 43 Brandeis L. J. 1 (2004).

5. *The lost chance doctrine of allegatory contracts.* See text.

6. *Certainty as a limitation under the CISG.* See text.

D. EQUITABLE ALTERNATIVES WHEN MONETARY DAMAGES ARE INADEQUATE

1. Inadequate Monetary Remedy

As detailed in earlier chapters the growth of the common law produced a separation between the Kings and Queens courts (royal courts) and the court of Chancery. The exclusive remedy in the royal courts was an award of damages. In Chancery (equity) courts however the relief granted was not damages but injunctive. The defendant was summoned before the chancellor and then ordered to do or refrain from doing something. Equity law developed in several ways that contrasted with the common law of the royal courts. First the form of the relief available, second the fact that the granting of any such relief was always discretionary with the court, and third that the burden of proof was "clear and convincing" rather than "a preponderance" of the evidence. That discretion was exercised only where a monetary award would not do justice and then only where the court was able to supervise (enforce) the injunctive relief on a practicable basis. The granting of injunctive relief today relates back directly to the equity practice in courts of Chancery and is subject to all of the rules that were developed in Chancery practice, including certain defenses not available in the royal courts. Since the chancellor sat alone and without a jury, and since we inherited the English common law as it existed in 1791 including the absence of a jury in chancery court proceedings, that is the situation today despite the right to a jury trial as set forth in the Seventh Amendment.

The threshold question then, in equity is whether a remedy of damages will provide adequate relief. Factors affecting the adequacy of damages in a particular case include the difficulty of proving damages with reasonable certainty, the difficulty of procuring a substitute performance, or the likelihood that a damages award would be uncollectable. Sales of an interest in realty are, for reasons of history, presumed to require enforcement by injunction. Sales of interests in personal property presumptively do not. The UCC however, expands situations in which a court may award specific performance in favor of a nonbreaching buyer. A court will never order affirmative specific performance of a contract of employment, but sometimes, as explained in *Lumley v. Wagner,* the second case to follow, a court will impose a negative injunction requiring the defendant to refrain from doing something.

The text raises several questions about whether a system of freer availability of injunctive relief would improve the present course of justice. These questions are answered in the materials following the next case.

Sedmark v. Charlie's Chevrolet, Inc.
CASE BRIEF

This is a 1981 decision of the Missouri Court of Appeals, Eastern District, Division Four. The Sedmarks sued to enforce a claimed oral agreement with Charlie's Chevrolet to sell them a special Corvette, one of a limited number of 6,000, manufactured to commemorate the selection of the Corvette as the Pace Car for the Indy 500. Charlie breached by refusing to honor the alleged oral contract. The trial court granted the Sedmarks specific performance, directing Charlie's to make the car available for delivery. Charlie's offered three defenses: (1) the existence of an oral contract is not supported by the credible evidence; (2) if an oral contract exists, it is unenforceable because of the Statute of Frauds; and (3) specific performance is an improper remedy because the Sedmarks did not show their legal remedies were inadequate. The court of appeals affirmed the grant of specific performance finding each of Charlie's three arguments to be unpersuasive. The court found adequate evidence to support an oral agreement to buy and sell the car for approximately $15,000 based on the manufacturer's suggested retail price. Charlie's argument that no price was ever agreed upon was rejected—the manufacturer's list price, including changes as requested, was sufficiently descriptive of an agreed price. The Sedmarks had requested specific modifications to the Corvette and the car Charlie's received contained those modifications. The court found the Statute of Frauds requirement satisfied by the payment and receipt of a deposit for $500 as a down payment on the car. Charlie's had made a fanciful argument that the Sedmark's check for $500 was to give them an opportunity to bid on the car—the court rejected this argument. The Sedmarks had agreed in January that Charlie's could keep the car in its showroom until after the Indy 500 had run.

The car arrived in April and the Sedmarks were notified but told they could not buy—only participate by bidding. The Sedmarks sued.

Charlie's last argument was that the Sedmarks had failed to prove that an award of damages would not suffice. The court cited the UCC standard, set out in § 2-716, authorizing a court to grant specific performance "where the goods are unique or in other proper circumstances." The court found that these words were intended to encourage a more liberal attitude towards the grant of specific performance. The court agreed that since 6,000 of these Pace Car Corvettes had been manufactured the car was not unique but that, nevertheless the circumstances justified the grant of specific performance. Concluded the court:

> However, as the record reflects, this is limited production. In addition, only one of these cars was available to each dealer, and only a limited number of these were equipped with the specific options ordered by plaintiffs. Charlie's had not received a car like the Pace Car in the previous two years. The sticker price for the car was $14,284.21. Yet Charlie's received offers from individuals in Hawaii and Florida to buy the Pace Car for $24,000.00 and $28,000.00 respectively. As sensibly inferred by the trial court, the location and size of these offers demonstrated this limited edition was in short supply and great demand. We agree, with the trial court. This case was a "proper circumstance" for ordering specific performance.

INTERESTING DISCUSSION ISSUES

1. *The UCC authorization of specific performance is found intended to liberalize the grant of specific performance.* The central issue of this case was whether or not the trial court should have exercised its discretion to award specific performance as the appropriate remedy for Charlie's repudiation and breach of contract. Charlie's argued that an award of damages would have been sufficient and that therefore the first requirement of proof for injunctive relief had not been met. The court impliedly accepted the argument that such a car could have been purchased on the open market at a significantly higher price and that the car was not unique. What then, were the factors involved in this case that justified the injunctive relief? Apparently the court was persuaded that an award of damages would not readily enable the Sedmarks to make a substitute purchase without significant additional cost, personal effort and time. Significant inconvenience and difficulty as well as increased cost were factors identified by the court. Translated, this decision of the court significantly relaxes the proof required to justify the grant of specific performance against a breaching seller. There was clearly a strong showing of willful breach together with seriously dissembling behavior

on Charlie's part. Could this case lead to a lessening of the showing required under the common law to obtain injunctive relief? Perhaps. Students should note that the injunction granted was easily supervised and enforced.

NOTES AND QUESTIONS

1. *"Unique or in other proper circumstances."* Historically, specific performance was available as a remedy for breach of a contract for the sale of goods usually only where the goods were truly unique, such as "heirlooms or priceless works of art." See UCC § 2-716 *cmt.* 2. UCC § 2-716 significantly expands the situations in which a nonbreaching plaintiff may be awarded specific performance by specifying that such relief is appropriate not just for unique goods, but also in other circumstances. See Harold Greenberg, *"Specific Performance Under Section 2-716 of the Uniform Commercial Code: 'A More Liberal Attitude' in the 'Grand Style',"* 17 New Eng. L. Rev. 321 (1982); Wendy C. Lowengrub, Note, *"Unique or Ubiquitous: Art Prints and the Uniform Commercial Code,"* 72 Ind. L.J. 595, 611-12 (1997). Was the car in Sedmak "unique" in any sense? No, and the court admitted this. There were 6,000 such cars manufactured and thus available on the market at a price. Or was this case one of "other proper circumstances"? Yes it was. Would specific performance still be appropriate if the Sedmarks had merely ordered a car without specifying additional options? Yes, if the evidence clearly established an oral contract including a promise to deliver by Charlie's.

2. *Comparing the UCC "unique or in other proper circumstances" to the common law "no adequate remedy at law" standard for awarding specific performance.* Compare the UCC standard applied in Sedmak to the common-law standard that generally requires that the plaintiff may obtain the equitable relief of specific performance only where there is "no adequate remedy at law." The quintessential remedy at law is an award of damages, and consequently equity will step in only where damages cannot compensate the nonbreaching party for the loss caused by the breach. If this were a common-law case, could the Sedmarks have shown that they had no adequate remedy at law? The answer would depend on the judge's discretion. The strongest argument to be made against injunctive relief is that an award of damages, if large enough, would have enabled the Sedmarks to get a substitute vehicle—although finding one with the additions they had requested might have complicated accomplishing such a transaction. The fact that Charlie's behaved willfully and, apparently deceptively affected the decision to exercise the discretion. The UCC change in the applicable standard could lead judges in common law cases to be more willing to consider injunctive relief.

3. *Bargaining power and specific performance.* Does the court's order that Charlie's Chevrolet must deliver the corvette to the Sedmarks necessarily mean that the Sedmarks will take the car, or could the parties still negotiate a different outcome? They could still negotiate a different outcome. Why do you think that Charlie's Chevrolet decided to refuse to deliver the car to the Sedmarks? Greed—they discovered that there was a special market out there which, but for their contract, might have let them sell the car at twice the manufacturer's list price. At the time of Charlie's initial refusal to deliver the car, what could the Sedmarks have done to induce Charlie's Chevrolet to deliver the car? They could have offered the "market price" which Charlie suggested by inviting them to "bid." Obviously they did not respond to Charlie's invitation. After the order of specific performance, what could Charlie's Chevrolet do to convince the Sedmarks not to take delivery of the car? Charlie's could have offered them a cash incentive (amount to be negotiated) to cancel their contract. In light of your answers above, how did the order of specific performance shift the relative bargaining power of the parties? Clearly, the grant of specific performance gave the Sedmarks a trump card, completely changing the landscape of any post-award negotiation. See Richard A. Posner, *Economic Analysis of Law* 131-132 (6th ed. 2003).

4. *Replevin of goods.* See text.

5. *Specific performance of contracts for the sale of an interest in real property.* Because of the unique characteristics of land as the source of political and economic power in medieval England, contracts for the sale of an interest in real property have historically been presumably enforceable by an award of specific performance. See Lawrence M. Friedman, *Contract Law in America: A Social and Economic Case Study* 131 (1965). In the United States, this presumption continued in force despite that land no longer carried with it the attendant political and class privileges that existed in England. See id. Nonetheless in many circumstances involving contracts for the sale of an interest in real property, the uniqueness of the interest becomes so tenuous that the presumption should no longer apply. In *Centex Holmes Corp. v. Boag*, 320 A.2d 194 (N.J. Super. 1974), for example, the Boags contracted to purchase a condominium unit in the plaintiff's housing project. When the Boags breached their contract, the plaintiff sought specific performance. The court held that specific performance was not appropriate:

> Here the subject matter of the real estate transaction— a condominium apartment unit— has no unique quality but is one of hundreds of virtually identical units being offered by a developer for sale to the public. The units are sold by means of sample, in this case model apartments, in much the same manner as items of

> personal property are sold in the market place. The sales prices for the units are fixed in accordance with a schedule filed by Centex as part and the only variance as between apartments having the same floor plan (of which six plans are available) is the floor level or the building location within the project. In actuality, the condominium apartment units, regardless of their realty label, share the same characteristics as personal property. Id.

See also *Van Wagner Advertising Corp. v. S & M Enterprises*, 492 N.E.2d 756 (NY 1986) (refusing to order specific performance for allegedly "unique" billboard location lease contract). Do you think that the presumption in favor of ordering specific performance of contracts for the sale of an interest in real property should continue to be eroded? Yes—the controlling general principle should be whether or not an award of damages will provide adequate relief. It should not matter whether or not the subject matter of the contract is land or personal property. See Jonathan Levy, *"Against Supercompensation: A Proposed Limitation on the Land Buyer's Right to Elect Between Damages and Specific Performance as a Remedy for Breach of Contract,"* 35 Loy. U. Chi. L.J. 555 (2004); Jason S. Kirwan, Note, *"Appraising a Presumption: A Modern Look at the Doctrine of Specific Performance in Real Estate Contracts,"* 47 Wm. & Mary L. Rev. 697 (2005). Or is there something unique and special about real property that justifies the continued presumption? There should be no general presumption to that effect, but the particular facts of a land transaction could justify injunctive relief just as in other cases.

6. *Contracting for or prohibiting specific performance as a remedy.* See text.

7. *Certainty of damages versus certainty of terms.* Restatement (Second) of Contracts § 362 provides that a court may not order specific performance or negative injunctive relief "unless the terms of the contract are sufficiently certain to provide a basis for an appropriate order." The comments further note that there may be cases in which the terms of a contract will permit a court to determine damages with reasonable certainty, but that are not certain enough to guide a court in ordering injunctive relief. See Restatement (Second) of Contracts § 362 *cmt. a.* How is that possible? There may be an open question as to how the promise should be performed. If the terms of the contract are sufficiently definite to permit a court to determine with reasonable certainty the damages arising out of the parties' obligations, how could those same terms not be sufficiently definite to permit a court to order specific performance of those terms? Where the contract provides a range of ways in which the defendant could perform. It is more likely however, that a court would base a refusal to grant injunctive relief on

"discretion" (tied to comparative fairness) or on difficulty of court supervision of the proposed affirmative order.

8. *The indifference principle and specific performance.* Ideally, remedies for breach of contract should provide exactly the amount and type of relief that a nonbreaching party is indifferent to whether the other party breaches or performs the contract. See Melvin A. Eisenberg, *"Actual and Virtual Specific Performance, the Theory of Efficient Breach, and the Indifference Principle in Contract Law,"* 93 Cal. L. Rev. 975, 979 (2005). But litigation costs and damages limitations generally cause damages remedies to undercompensate injured plaintiffs, meaning that most plaintiffs probably would rather have received performance than damages. Would a rule permitting the nonbreaching party an election between the remedies of specific performance or damages come closer to fulfilling the goal of the indifference principle? No. Why or why not? Specific performance is and should be a "discretionary" remedy, given the number of types of case in which a court simply will not enter an affirmative order—e.g. personal services. See Ronen Avraham & Zhiyon Liu, *"Incomplete Contracts with Asymmetric Information: Exclusive Versus Optional Remedies,"* 8 Am. L. & Econ. Rev. 523 (2006).

9. *Comparative law perspective on specific performance.* See text.

2. Personal Service Contracts

Lumley v. Wagner
CASE BRIEF

This is an 1852 decision of the English Court of Chancery. Johanna Wagner contracted to sing at Her Majesty's Theatre for a certain number of nights (for a three month period) and also contracted that she would not sing elsewhere during that period. The court admitted lack of authority to compel Johanna to perform at Her Majesty's Theatre but added, "but she has no cause of complaint if I compel her to abstain from the commission of an act which she has bound herself not to do, and thus possibly cause her to fulfill her engagement. . . . The effect, too, of the injunction in restraining J. Wagner from singing elsewhere may, in the event of an action being brought against her by the Plaintiff, prevent any such amount of vindictive damages being given against her as a jury might probably be inclined to give if she had carried her talents and exercised them at the rival theatre; the injunction may also, as I have said, tend to the fulfillment of her engagement; though, in continuing the injunction, I disclaim doing indirectly what I cannot do directly. . . ."

INTERESTING DISCUSSION ISSUES

1. *Injunctive relief will not be granted where it would involve affirmatively ordering the defendant to fulfill a personal service contract.* The court acknowledged that it could not and would not affirmatively order Johanna Wagner to sing. Such an order would be totally impractical from several different perspectives, just one of those being the judicial time and effort that would be required to supervise an affirmative order. The most important reason for refusing an order of specific performance in such circumstances is that "You can lead a horse to water but cannot compel it to drink!"

2. *But a negative injunction may sometimes work.* Lord St. Leonards did agree, however, to enter a negative injunction restraining Johanna Wagner from singing anywhere else during the contracted for three month period. Students need to understand the practical difference between the grant of a negative injunction versus an affirmative injunction in these circumstances. Students may be confused by the judge's apparent reliance on Johanna's promise not to sing elsewhere during the three month period—and conclude that the negative injunction should only be available where there is such an express negative promise in the contract. A closer reading of the case suggests that the judge would have granted the negative injunction with or without her express negative promise. Later cases made it clear that an express promise in a contract is properly interpreted to preclude the promisor from doing anything which would preclude the possibility of the promisor performing as contracted. In other words, the express promise will often imply a promise not do anything inconsistent with the performance of that promise.

3. *Judicial economy and the negative injunction.* Another practical dimension of the trial judge's exercise of discretion whether or not to grant injunctive relief is the time, effort and practicability of judicial oversight involved. The students can see this dimension of discretion if they think of a judge trying to supervise the grant of an affirmative injunction to proceed with the construction of a building.

NOTES AND QUESTIONS

1. *Contracts for personal service or supervision will not be enforced.* The commentary to Restatement (Second) of Contracts § 367 proposes that an order of specific performance in the personal services context is unworkable for two reasons. First, an affirmative injunction requires supervision and enforcement by the court, and courts are reluctant to attempt to evaluate whether the employee has complied with the injunction. See id. *cmt. a.* Second, an employer may enforce an order of specific performance against a recalcitrant employee by

moving for an order of contempt against the employee. A court may fine or imprison the employee who resists such a contempt order, raising the spectre of state-enforced slavery and involuntary servitude. See id. Which of these propositions is more compelling in this case? Both—but the thought of a judge trying to supervise an affirmative order that Johanna sing is amusing.

2. *Effectiveness of negative injunctions in enforcing employment agreements.* What did Lumley really win in this case? Lumley effectively prevented Johanna Wagner from singing for a competitor. Frustrating her planed "jumping of ship" may have provided some encouragement to her to fulfill her promise to Lumley. The court clearly hoped that the grant of the injunction would "tend to the fulfillment of [Wagner's] engagement," but explicitly disclaimed any ability to monitor Wagner's performance under the contract if she returned to her engagement with Lumley. What would happen if Wagner returned to Lumley's employment but provided services that, while within the letter of the employment agreement, fell below the parties' original expectations? If the shortfall in performance amounted to a breach of contract Lumley would have a claim for damages. At that point, Lumley would face a difficult choice—continue to employ the technically performing Wagner (and suffer possible business and reputational losses as customers became dissatisfied) or terminate Wagner and face a possible suit for breach of contract. See Geoffrey Christopher Rapp, *"Affirmative Injunctions in Athletic Employment Contracts: Rethinking the Place of the Lumley Rule in American Sports Law,"* 16 Marq. Sports L. Rev. 261, 270-71 (2006). What incentives would Wagner have to avoid such conduct? The risk of a lawsuit and its attendant costs and publicity and the risk of damage to her public reputation. Could Lumley structure the contract to protect himself against such substandard performance? He might want the right to terminate her employment (with or without cause) if, in his judgment, her performance was deficient. Or he could consider a contract payment scheme whereby what Johanna received related proportionally to the attendance at her performances.

3. *Negative injunctions and involuntary servitude.* To what extent does the negative injunction in this case practically equate to an actual order that Wagner specifically perform her obligations under the contract? It does not, and the judge was quick to point that out. The order did not force Johanna to sing at Her Majesty's Theatre. Do you agree with Lord St. Leonards' argument that his order would not result in forcing Johanna Wagner to perform at Her Majesty's Theatre? Yes. What other options did she have for earning a livelihood under this order? Certainly not singing somewhere else. Intriguingly, the 1852 *Lumley v. Wagner* decision coincided with increasing political tension

in the United States over slavery that ultimately culminated in the U.S. Civil War.

4. *The* Lumley *rule and gender bias.* See text.

5. *Should such a negative injunction be granted in the context of employment contracts and a covenant not to compete?* See text.

E. REMEDIES SPECIFIED OR MODIFIED BY CONTRACT

The common law rules regarding the expectancy, reliance, and restitution interests and the foreseeability, avoidability, and certainty limitations provide base level default rules that govern where the parties' contract is silent. But, as with virtually all other aspects of their relationship, parties may decide to opt out of that system of default rules in favor of their own private ordering. This section deals with situations in which parties specified through contract types, measures, or the availability of particular remedies for breach of contract. First, parties may attempt to specify ex ante the measure and method of calculation of damages that a court shall apply in the event of breach. Such "liquidated damages" clauses are generally enforceable under modern law, provided that they reasonably approximate possible damages caused by a breach of contract. Where the parties failed to reasonably approximate or predict their possible damages, however, courts will likely invalidate clauses specifying remedies as "penalty clauses."

Second, instead of specifying a particular measure of damages, the parties may also attempt to modify or exclude damages for certain types of injury, such as consequential damages or damages for personal injury. In some cases, such modifications and exclusions may have the effect of denying the injured party any possibility of relief.

1. Remedies Specified by Contract

Parties may attempt to specify at the time of contract formation terms governing the amount of damages for which the breaching party shall be liable. Contract terms providing for unreasonably large liquidated damages are unenforceable penalties. The touchstone of liquidated damages analysis is the reasonableness of the parties' attempt to estimate their damages, at the time of contract and the time of breach. The reasonableness standard is satisfied if the parties' estimate at the time of contracting is reasonable but does not approximate the actual loss, or if the liquidated damages clause approximates the actual loss even though it does not reflect other losses that might have been anticipated. Importantly, however, under UCC § 2-718(1), some courts have interpreted the "reasonable in light of the anticipated or actual harm caused by the breach" element to require the parties' estimates of anticipated harm at the time of drafting to approximate the actual harm suffered at the time of breach. The second prong is potentially more problematic. The injury that the parties attempt to resolve ex ante through the liquidated damages clause must be difficult to prove with reasonable certainty. Many commentators have argued that courts should enforce all liquidated damages provisions.

Bd. of Co. Comm. of Adams Co. v. City & Co. of Denver
CASE BRIEF

This is a 2001 decision of the Colorado Court of Appeals. Defendant, the city and county of Denver (Denver) entered into an Intergovernmental Agreement (IGA) with plaintiffs, Board of County Commissioners of Adams County, City of Aurora, City of Brighton, City of Commerce City, and City of Thornton (collectively, Adams) on April 21, 1988. At the outset of negotiations, Denver needed a new airport, but did not have enough land to build one. Plaintiffs originally sought a multijurisdictional airport, in which they would share some of the authority with Denver, but Denver insisted on retaining sole ownership and control of the airport. In response, Adams sought to negotiate an agreement that would address its primary concern regarding the impact of airport noise on its cities. Under the IGA, Denver promised to operate Denver International Airport (DIA) within maximum noise levels called noise exposure performance standards (NEPS), and agreed that if those noise levels were exceeded and not cured as provided under the IGA, Denver would compensate Adams with noise mitigation payments.

Noise problems followed shortly after DIA opened in 1995. After noise violations were not cured in the second year, Adams brought suit in accordance with the IGA. Adams moved for summary judgment on the grounds that the noise mitigation payment provision of the IGA was an alternative performance or guarantee of performance provision. In the alternative, Adams argued that the payments were valid and enforceable liquidated damages. Denver moved for summary judgment on the ground that the provision was a liquidated damages clause, but unenforceable as a penalty. The trial court held that the provision was a liquidated damages provision, but that issues of fact existed as to whether it was enforceable. After a bench trial, the court awarded Adams $4 million in damages and over $1.3 million in prejudgment interest; Denver appealed and Adams cross-appealed.

The court held that the trial court did not err in finding the noise mitigation payment provision to be an enforceable liquidated damages clause. Unless a contract reveals on its face that the stipulated payment is so disproportionate to any possible loss as to constitute a penalty, evaluation of such provisions is properly a question for the fact finder. To properly determine that a liquidated damages clause is valid and enforceable, the court stated that a fact finder must find: (1) at the time the contract was created, anticipated damages for breach were difficult to ascertain; (2) the parties mutually intended to liquidate damages in advance; and (3) the amount of liquidated damages, when viewed as of the time of contract creation, was a reasonable estimate of the potential actual damages that breach would cause.

The court held that Denver bore the burden of proving that the provision was an unenforceable penalty, and that the trial court had properly determined that the provision was not facially disproportionate to potential damages. Further, the court found that the trial court properly considered the three elements above in holding that the provision was enforceable. First, the trial court found that the fifty- to one hundred-year duration of the IGA made it particularly difficult to project future population, land use, and damages, and also noted that Denver's own expert agreed with the difficulty in predicting damages.

Second, the trial court properly interpreted the plain language of the IGA and the parties' actions as demonstrating that the parties intended to liquidate damages in advance. Evidence showed that the IGA was intensely negotiated over three years, and both parties were represented by sophisticated business people. Moreover, the IGA was "replete with language identifying the parties' shared understanding of the critical importance of noise exposure levels and compliance with the NEPS provisions" and there was substantial evidence that the language surrounding the provisions had been carefully considered and negotiated to ensure that it would stand as a valid liquidated damages provision. The court did not accept Denver's assertions that officials from both sides had variously referred to the payments as fines or penalties, stating that remarks made outside the scope of the original negotiations do not function to negate the parties' intent at the time they entered the agreement.

Third, the trial court properly held that the liquidated damages, at the time of the creation of the contract, were a reasonable estimate of actual breach damages. The parties agreed that the NEPS were established to protect not only areas in the immediate vicinity, but also areas well beyond the grid points. And both parties' negotiators testified that, in negotiating the IGA, the parties assumed that Adams would be harmed if the NEPS provisions were violated. Adams's negotiator added that the parties negotiated the liquidated damages value with an understanding of the difficulty in predicting actual damages, and only arrived at the final value after extensive negotiations. In upholding the reasonableness of the estimate, the court also rejected Denver's argument that the fixed amount for all Class II violations made that amount akin to a penalty, holding that Denver had again failed to show that the number was disproportionate to actual harm that the parties anticipated. Finally, since the evidence at trial amply demonstrated the parties' difficulty in establishing the amount of loss at the time of creation of the IGA, the court properly allowed Adams great latitude in showing that the payment amount was in fact a reasonable estimate of damages.

Beyond Denver's arguments against the liquidated damages term, the court also rejected Denver's arguments that Adams failed to prove any actual damages. The court noted that Denver's argument was largely mooted by the fact that Colorado law did not require actual damages to support enforcement of a liquidated damages provision, but focused instead on whether the liquidated damages provision itself was valid and enforceable. Nonetheless, the court held that the trial court had found actual injury to Adams, in that noise levels from NEPS violations constituted a quadrupling of the projected noise energy levels, and far exceeded the ambient noise levels of the affected cities. In closing, the court also rejected Denver's claim that prejudgment interest violated the IGA, holding that Colorado courts have broadly construed a party's right to recover under the state's prejudgment interest statute. All aspects of the judgment were affirmed.

INTERESTING DISCUSSION ISSUES

1. *The value of negotiating a "liquidated damages" provision.* The assumed purpose of a liquidated damages provision is the mooting of a need in subsequent litigation to prove the amount of actual damage, thus potentially avoiding issues of relative certainty of damages proof, and saving substantial additional litigation expense. The plaintiff who prevails on an early summary judgment motion receives the real benefit of such drafting. If the judge refuses such a motion, the real value of the clause may be lost. For this reason, the cases and writers dealing with the UCC provision, and making relevant the amount of actual damage suffered after the breach, undermine the whole value of the concept of "liquidating damages."

2. *The public policy behind the concept of "penalty" damages.* The striking of a damages clause found to be a "penalty" constitutes an unusual interference by a court with the patent mutual agreement of the parties. Why is public policy offended by such a clause found to be a "penalty"? Other doctrines are available to try to protect the unwary who is duped or coerced into agreeing to a contract with such a clause. Why, then, does the court step in to rewrite the contract that the parties in fact made by striking a damages clause found to be a "penalty"? Why don't they step in to adjust any other contract provision found to be "unfair"? The only sure answer is that this is the way the common law grew—an historical explanation going back to English practice. Comment *a* to Restatement (Second) of Contracts § 356 provides in part, "The central objective behind the system of contract remedies is compensatory, not punitive. Punishment of a promisor for

having broken his promise has no justification on either economic or other grounds and a term providing such a penalty is unenforceable on grounds of public policy." See Note 4 below.

3. *"Blunderbuss" drafting.* See Note 3 below.

NOTES AND QUESTIONS

1. *Is the classification of a clause as a "penalty" a question of law or fact?* This court appears to rule that the issue of penalty or not is one of law if the effect of the clause as a penalty is capable of determination on the face of the document: if not, the issue is one of fact. Does this approach make sense? Yes. What evidence would be introduced to establish that the "liquidated damages" clause was a reasonable approximation of foreseeable damage and that quantification of any such damages would (from the perspective of the parties at the time of reaching agreement) be difficult in the event of breach? First, the terms of the contract itself, including recitals and preambles describing the purposes of the parties, the damages contemplated, and the difficulty of quantification of those damages. Second, the negotiating history of the clause—this played a central role in the above case. Clearly, this parol testimony raises the familiar "he said, she said" problem. This case provides a learning opportunity for the potential draftsperson—showing the value of including a "purpose" clause in the contract together with recitals of the negotiating history and rationale for inclusion of the damages provision. It also shows the risk of using the "p" word. Don't describe your damages provision as a penalty! But there is one classic case where the contract used the exact word "penalty" to describe the damage clause but, on the facts, the court held the clause to be, in fact, a liquidated damages provision and not a "legal" penalty. Needless to say, the clause in that case was not drafted by a lawyer.

2. *Intent of the parties to liquidate damages in advance.* The *Adams County* court applies a three-prong test for assessing the validity of the liquidated damages clause: "(1) at the time the contract was entered into, the anticipated damages in case of breach were difficult to ascertain; (2) the parties mutually intended to liquidate them in advance; and (3) the amount of liquidated damages, when viewed as of the time the contract was made, was a reasonable estimate of the potential actual damages the breach would cause." How does this standard compare to the elements of the Restatement (Second) of Contracts § 356 test? Is there room in the § 356 test for an intent element? § 356 provides:

> (1) Damages for breach by either party may be liquidated in the agreement but only at an amount that is reasonable in the light of

> the anticipated or actual loss caused by the breach and the difficulties of proof of loss. A term fixing unreasonably large liquidated damages is unenforceable on grounds of public policy as a penalty.
> (2) A term in a bond providing for an amount of money as a penalty for non-occurrence of the condition of the bond is unenforceable on grounds of public policy to the extent that the amount exceeds the loss caused by such non-occurrence.

Yes—to be found in the reasonableness of the anticipated or actual loss. Comment *c* to that section provides in part, "Neither the parties' actual intention as to its validity nor their characterization of the term as one for liquidated damages or a penalty is significant in determining whether the term is valid." Thus, the intention of the parties in foreseeing difficulty in proof of damage, and their intent in negotiating a reasonable approximation of that damage, is relevant. But their intention that the clause be either a "penalty" or not a "penalty" is not controlling—the question is one of effect of the clause.

3. *Labeling and disguising liquidated damages and penalty clauses.* Merely labeling a clause as "liquidated damages," a "penalty," or even a discount for early performance will not control a court's analysis of whether the clause in fact represents liquidated damages or is an impermissible penalty. The comments to § 356 expressly provide that the parties' characterization has no significance in the liquidated damages/penalty clause analysis. "Although the parties may in good faith contract for alternative performance and fix discounts or valuations, a court will look to the substance of the agreement to determine whether this is the case or whether the parties have attempted to disguise a provision for a penalty that is unenforceable under this Section." Restatement (Second) of Contracts § 356 *cmt. d.* How did the *Adams County* court deal with the parties' characterization of the liquidated damages clause? The court found the clause to be characterized as a liquidated damages clause. Denver argued that in press releases and other similar public comments they had called the clause a "penalty." The court was not persuaded by Denver's argument. While the parties' characterization of the clause is not determinative, is it possible that the parties' choice of contract language may nonetheless guide the court's analysis regarding the reasonableness of the liquidated damages clause and the difficulty of proving losses in the event of breach? Yes.

4. *The danger of "blunderbuss" drafting.* The City of Denver argued that the court should not enforce the liquidated damages clause because it specified a single lump sum liability—$500,000—for a variety of different types and levels of breach. Suppose that a builder and an owner contract for $1,000 in liquidated damages in the event of

any breach of their building contract. The common law standard requires that the liquidated damages reasonably approximate the anticipated or actual damages and that the damages be difficult to prove. Why would such a lump sum liquidated damages award potentially violate that standard? As a matter of logic, the clause applies to a series of breaches each obviously posing a different amount of actual damage. Thus the choice of one global amount to cover disparate potential breaches necessarily fails, as a matter of logic, to constitute a reasonable approximation of potential damage. Which element of the common law standard would such a clause violate? The requirement that the amount fixed in the clause be a reasonable approximation of potential damage. See the preceding discussion.

5. *Liquidated damages and freedom of contract.* What, if anything, justifies the common law and UCC § 2-718 suspicion toward liquidated damages clauses? An assumption that a "penalty" is necessarily unfair because it provides not compensation but rather punishment. Continuing this assumption, if the clause is in fact a penalty it must have been included as a result of some failure in the bargaining process. Is the judicial hostility to penalty clauses merely a holdover from ossified historical resistance to such contract terms? Yes, in part. Or is it based upon jealously regarding private parties attempting to encroach upon the damages-setting functions of the courts? This seems to be a questionable interpretation. Alternatively, do liquidated damages rules represent state paternalism and a lack of trust in the capacity of contracting parties to assess and consent to the damages they are willing to pay at the time of contract formation? Paternalism seems closer to the mark, leaving a problem of explaining why paternalism surfaces in this particular one place and not in the many other cases of unfair provisions. See the discussion under "Interesting Discussion Issues" #2 above. See Anthony T. Kronman, *"Paternalism and the Law of Contracts,"* 92 Yale L.J. 763, 776-77 (1983).

6. *Liquidated damages and unconscionability.* Assume that courts are concerned with liquidated damages clauses because of the potential unfairness of penalties and the fact that contracting parties may not sufficiently appreciate the risks associated with such clauses. If that is the case, would the unconscionability doctrine be a better tool for regulating and policing such clauses? Yes. See Larry A. DiMatteo, *"A Theory of Efficient Penalty: Eliminating the Law of Liquidated Damages,"* 38 Am. Bus. L.J. 633, 655-57 (2001). Why or why not? Unconscionability would be a better tool because it would discriminate between the case where the clause was imposed as a result of abuse of power from one where the parties truly agreed to it as part of an arms length bargained for exchange. Hence the argument by a number of authors that liquidated damages clauses should be enforced as written.

7. *The "no actual damages" defense.* The City of Denver argued unsuccessfully that the court should invalidate the liquidated damages clause because the county suffered no actual damages. While the *Adams County* court rejected this argument, a number of other courts have held that even if a liquidated damages clause reasonably estimates anticipated damages at the time of contracting, equity prohibits enforcement of such clauses if the nonbreaching party did not suffer any actual loss. See, e.g., Susan V. Ferris, *"Liquidated Damages Recovery Under the Restatement (Second) of Contracts,"* 67 Cornell L. Rev. 862, 866-67 (1982). The commentary to § 356 supports this rule: "If, to take an extreme case, it is clear that no loss at all has occurred, a provision fixing a substantial sum as damages is unenforceable." Restatement (Second) of Contracts § 356 *cmt. b.* Does this rule make sense? No. It frustrates the basic purpose of a liquidated damages clause—namely, to simplify and avoid issues of proof at trial. See "Interesting Discussion Issues" #1 above. Alternatively, should courts apply this rule only in situations where the absence of actual damages was not foreseeable as a consequence of breach? No—for the same reasons. Opening up such a fact issue at trial destroys the value of a liquidated damages clause.

8. *Should the presence of a "liquidated damages" clause in the contract preclude a grant of specific performance?* The terms of the contract themselves may affect the availability of equitable relief. Consider, for example, the implications of a valid liquidated damages clause. To be valid, the clause must be a reasonable approximation of the parties' damages at the time of execution and the time of breach or trial but still be uncertain. Such a term then provides a schizophrenic implication with respect to the propriety of equitable relief. On the one hand, the mere existence of the liquidated damages clause impliedly represents an agreement by the parties that the liquidated money damages will compensate in the event of a breach. On the other hand, the requirements necessary for the validity of the liquidated damages clause are similar to the arguments necessary to show the unavailability of equitable relief. E. Allan Farnsworth suggested that a liquidated damages term by itself should not preclude a claim for equitable relief, but a contract provision prohibiting equitable relief should bar an order of specific performance, providing the parties clearly demonstrate that intent. See E. Allan Farnsworth, *Contracts* § 12.6 (4th ed. 2004) ("Nor does a provision for liquidated damages preclude the grant of specific performance or injunction instead of or in addition to the award of such damages, though a clear provision to the contrary will be given effect.") and 25 Samuel Williston & Richard A. Lord, *A Treatise on the Law of Contracts* § 67:9 (4th ed. 2002). Restatement (Second) of Contracts § 361, perhaps not surprisingly, supports Farnsworth's position. Do you agree or disagree with

Farnsworth's argument? We disagree that the presence of a liquidated damages clause should not bar an order of specific performance. Surely, as a matter of logic, the inclusion of such a clause is an admission against interest that damages will provide an adequate remedy. But a clause purporting to exclude injunctive relief should be given effect because, once again, the inclusion of such a clause constitutes a mutual admission against interest that damages will be a sufficient and adequate remedy. Or should the parties' agreement to a valid liquidated damages clause be deemed conclusive proof that damages would adequately compensate the parties in the event of breach? Yes—see the discussion above.

9. *Liquidated damages and penalties in Chinese contract law.* Article 114 of the 1999 Contract Law for the People's Republic of China provides that parties may contract for penalties for breach of contract:

> The parties may stipulate that in case of breach of contract by either party a certain amount of penalty shall be paid to the other party according to the seriousness of the breach, and may also stipulate the method for calculating the sum of compensation for losses caused by the breach of contract. If the stipulated penalty for breach of contract is lower than the loss caused by the breach, the party concerned may apply to a people's court or an arbitration institution for an increase. If the stipulated penalty for breach of contract is excessively higher than the loss caused by the breach, the party concerned may apply to a people's court or an arbitration institution for an appropriate reduction. If the parties agree upon a penalty for the breach of contract by a delayed fulfillment, the breaching party shall, after paying the penalty for breach of contract, discharge the debts notwithstanding.

To what extent, if at all, does this approach differ from the common law or UCC rules discussed above? Totally, in that it requires a post breach review of damages and adjustment up or down of any "liquidated damages" amount depending on the post-breach facts. This approach negates the inherent value of including a liquidated damages clause in the first place.

2. Remedies Modified by Contract

Personal Injury.

As a general rule, parties may agree by contract to act with respect to one another in a manner that would be tortious in the absence of such a contract. Likewise, the parties may also contract to limit their liability to one another for negligence in the course of their contractual relationship. Consequently, to some extent, the parties may subordinate tort principles to contract through their voluntary agreements. Restatement (Second) of Contracts § 195(1) provides that parties may not contract to limit or exclude liability for intentional or reckless torts, reflecting a long line of decisions to that effect. Subsection (2) of that section extends this public policy limitation for personal injuries caused by negligence to providers of certain classes of contracts.

Terms designed to restrict or eliminate otherwise available common law remedies for breach of contract can take a variety of forms. They may start by negating the existence of a particular promise-based duty (exclude warranties express or implied); they may expressly allocate any particular risk to one party or the other; they may impose a dollar cap on any liability; they may define a specific dollar amount as the sole and exclusive remedy for breach (liquidated damages); they may require the aggrieved party to indemnify or hold the breaching party harmless; or they may prescribe an exclusive remedy for breach, negligent or otherwise, such as repair or replacement. They may also contain a "forum selection" clause or an arbitration clause. The law of "unconscionability" (discussed in Chapters 3 and 5) restricts the enforceability of remedies limitations that unfairly deprive the injured party of a remedy but has been slow and somewhat erratic in its development.

As you read the following case, consider the relationship between the doctrine of unconscionability and the standards relating to contract clauses excluding or limiting liability. Why do parties include such terms in their contracts? Because, for example, the provider of a service would refuse to provide such a service in the absence of an appropriate agreement and release of liability for negligence. Consider, for instance, the company that offers to provide a parachute jump. Is a contract term that provides the injured party no meaningful relief for breach or personal injury enforceable? Yes, subject to abuse of power or unreasonable surprise. Is it possible for even a dickered liability limitation to produce substantive unfairness that renders the clause unconscionable? Perhaps—consider the case of a negligent injury settlement (injuries both known and unknown) and after acquired information that the personal injuries were much more severe than understood at the time of settlement.

Schrier v. Beltway Alarm Company
CASE BRIEF

This is a 1987 decision of the Court of Special Appeals of Maryland. In September 1977, Mr. Schrier, on behalf of Veteran's Liquors, entered into an Alarm Protection Agreement with Beltway Alarm Co. (Beltway) for the installation and maintenance of an alarm system. Schrier agreed to pay a $287 installation fee and $49.50 per month for a three-year service contract. In November 1980, the parties entered into a second contract that called for monthly payments of $65.86 for continued maintenance of the system. Both contracts contained a provision (paragraph 8) that limited Beltway's liability in the event of loss or damage due to breach of the contract or negligence on Beltway's part. On August 31, 1981, Schrier was shot and wounded during a hold-up of his liquor store. Schrier claimed that he activated two alarm buttons during the robbery, before he was shot. Schrier later sued Beltway for negligence, breach of contract, and breach of warranty, alleging that Beltway delayed fourteen minutes in notifying the police department of the alarm, and but for that delay, Schrier would not have been injured. The trial court upheld a $250 limitation of liability provision in the parties' contract and granted summary judgment for Beltway for claims in excess of that amount. Schrier appealed, claiming that (1) the limitation of liability provision was an invalid liquidated damages clause; (2) the limitation of liability clause was void as a matter of public policy; (3) he had a cause of action in negligence; and (4) he was not bound by the liquidated damages provision of the contract. The court of appeals rejected all four theories.

The court began by noting that, for the purposes of this case, there was no real distinction between a liquidated damages clause, a limited liability clause, and an exculpatory clause, and that courts had uniformly upheld such clauses. Though the court disagreed with Schrier's characterization of paragraph 8 as a liquidated damages clause, it chose to address the underlying argument because it presented an issue of first impression in Maryland. The court first noted that it had previously upheld the enforceability of an exculpatory clause similar to the clause in this case, noting that there was no disparity in bargaining power between the parties and that the effect of the clause on the public at large was "nil." The court also noted that the enforceability of liquidated damages clauses was well-settled in Maryland, provided that such clauses did not provide for an amount that was grossly excessive and out of proportion to the damages that might reasonably have been expected to result from a breach. The court held that, since the limitation of liability provision was inserted because of the parties' inability to determine in advance the amount of damages that might result from a breach, the provision could not be invalidated as a penalty.

The court also held that the provision in dispute was a limitation of liability provision, and not liquidated damages. The purpose of the clause was to limit Beltway's liability to no more than $250, and thus, unlike a true liquidated damages clause, the clause in question (1) still required that damages resulting from the breach must be proved; and (2) allowed for variable liability up to the stated maximum. Since the clause was not liquidated damages, the court held that it was thus immaterial whether the limitation of liability was a reasonable estimate of probable damages that would result from a breach because the provision at hand functioned merely to cap the liability of Beltway.

The court also rejected Schrier's argument that the clause at issue was unconscionable. It held that the Maryland Legislature had not created any law that prohibited limitation of liability clauses except as between landlords and their tenants. Since the parties here were businesses dealing at arm's length, there was no reason to force upon Beltway the responsibility to insure its customers against harm from robberies. Other courts had held similarly, stating that it would likely be impossible for anyone to prove that an alarm would actually have prevented a crime, and thus it would be impossible to prove that the failure of an alarm caused any damage. The court concluded that the limitation of liability provision was a "commercially sensible agreement" that the court would not rewrite in order to compel Beltway to act as an insurer.

The court next rejected Schrier's claim that the limitation clause was invalid as a "transaction affected with a public interest." Under the court's opinion in *Winterstein v. Wilcom*, a transaction involved an invalid exculpatory provision if it exhibited some or all of the following characteristics: (1) it concerned a business generally suitable for public regulation; (2) party seeking exculpation performs a service of great importance to public; (3) party holds himself out as willing to perform the service to any member of the public who seeks it; (4) party invoking exculpation has decisive advantage in bargaining strength due to essential nature of service; (5) party confronts the public with a standardized adhesion contract, and provides no means by which purchaser may obtain additional protection; and (6) as a result of transaction, person or property of purchaser is placed under control of seller. With respect to these claims, the court held that: (1) there is essentially no regulation of the burglar alarm business; (2) and (4) burglar alarms are not an essential service, and are only one of many options that a store owner may use to secure his store; (5) contract was not one of adhesion, and Beltway provided an opportunity for customers to purchase additional coverage at reasonable prices; and (6) there is no evidence that Schrier was under the control of Beltway in any meaningful way. Since the case at hand failed almost every facet of the *Winterstein* test, the court held that a contract for installation and maintenance of a burglar alarm does not "affect the public interest," and the limitation of liability clause was therefore valid.

Regarding Schrier's claim of a cause of action in negligence, the court held that the issue was controlled by the parties' contract because the limitation of liability clause explicitly covered loss resulting from negligence. The court stated that its discussion upholding the limitation of liability in parts I and II of the opinion applied with equal force to the issue of negligence.

Finally, the court dismissed Schrier's claim that he, as an individual, was not a party to the contract, which was solely between

Veteran's Liquors and Beltway. Since Schrier admitted to being the principal shareholder of the privately held company, and that he had executed the agreement on behalf of Veteran's, the court held that, "functionally and effectively, [Schrier is] 'Veteran's Liquors,' and [is] individually bound by the terms of the contract."

INTERESTING DISCUSSION ISSUES

1. *Contract trumps tort.* Students, typically, have difficulty in seeing why the terms of the contract should prevent a suit in tort for negligence. It is important for them to recognize that exclusion of liability for negligence may be an important consideration in fixing the price to be charged for any particular product or service. This was the commercially relevant point of the limitation clause in this case.

2. *Policy behind permitting contracting out of negligence.* Here, freedom of contract again comes to the fore. Provided there is no abuse of power or deception as to the terms of the transaction, competent parties should be free to allocate risk under the terms of their contract. Thus, a contractor, doing remodeling work on the owner's house, should be free to allocate under the terms of the contract the risk of loss by fire on the owner and the owner's insurer. It is commercially useful for the parties to be able to allocate risk by contract. There is no reason why such risk should not be capable of allocation by other means such as the limitation of liability clause used in *Schrier*. In some contexts, such as those of the *Winterstein* case cited in the opinion, the service or opportunity would not be made available to the customer without the obtaining of a release from liability in advance. In other contexts, the cost to be charged for the service or goods would be fixed far differently but for the contractual waiver of liability for negligence. The negation of risk may be just as important in determining the pricing point as limiting any liability for such risk. As the court pointed out in this case, the contract as written made perfectly good business sense as an arms length transaction between the parties.

3. *"No real distinction . . . between a liquidated damages clause, a limited liability clause, and an exculpatory clause."* This can be a misleading statement. The court itself points out that a "liquidated damages" clause functions in a way designed to avoid the need for proof of actual damage at trial. Such a clause "fixes" the amount of damages that are to be recovered in the event of breach. The clause used in the contract here was a "limitation of liability" clause. The effect of such a clause, as the court pointed out, is not to relieve the plaintiff of a duty to prove actual damage but rather to limit the dollar amount of such damage that the plaintiff may be able to recover regardless of actual damage proved. Under this kind of clause the plaintiff still has to prove actual damage but the amount of such damage that may be recovered

is capped. An "exculpatory" clause is different yet again. This kind of a clause does not focus on the scope and extent of damages—it focuses instead on removal of any duty of care in the circumstances. Thus, an exculpatory clause will, ordinarily, recite the fact that the customer or client waives or relinquishes in advance any claim that might arise out of the transaction based on the defendant's negligence. Consider the case of a company providing sky-diving or bungee-jumping opportunities. The provider of service wants to negate any liability at all for ordinary negligence, that is to say negate the otherwise applicable duty of care. Clauses of this sort are more apt to raise an issue of public policy—see Restatement (Second) of Contracts § 195(2)(b). Contracting out of the duty of care can lead to careless behavior harmful to the general public interest. While the court does not add to the list of ways of avoiding liability, another relatively common way of allocating risk under a contract is a "hold harmless" or "indemnification" clause.

4. *Unconscionability.* One of Schrier's claims was that the provision limiting liability was unconscionable. In some cases courts have refused to enforce clauses negating duty of care or limiting liability for negligence on the basis of unconscionability—covered earlier in Chapter 3. In these cases plaintiffs must generally show an abuse of power on the other side and a marked unfairness in the result.

NOTES AND QUESTIONS

1. *Limiting liability by negating the duty of care that would otherwise underlie negligent conduct.* As discussed in Chapter 4, contracting parties generally may agree to limit or exclude warranties as a means of avoiding liability. See, e.g., UCC § 2-316. A sale "as is, where is," excludes all warranties and leaves little room for, or need of, a liability limitation clause. Did the alarm company exclude any duty of care? No. Instead they placed a cap on damages liability. What is the meaning of the contract term providing, "that the Company makes no guarantee or warranty including any implied warranty of merchantability or fitness that the system or service supplied will avert or prevent occurrences or the consequences therefrom which the system or service is intended to detect or prevent; . . ."? This clause excludes a promise relevant to the quality of service the system will supply. It negates any promise that the system "will avert or prevent occurrences or the consequences therefrom" but it does not, by these words, exclude liability for negligence. The difference lies in descriptive promises of what the system will do compared to negligent operation of the system as it is.

2. *The difference between a liquidated damages clause, a limited liability clause, and an exculpatory clause.* See "Interesting Discussion

Issues" #3 above. The court used the following quotation, "[T]here is no real distinction for present purposes between a liquidated damages clause, a limited [liability] clause and an exculpatory clause." Do you agree? No, see #3 above. If you do not agree, what are the differences between these three methods of fixing or limiting liability? See #3 above. Should public policy apply in the same way to all three, or differently to one or more? See #3 above.

3. *A "low-ball" liquidated damages clause.* Liquidated damages clause cases normally deal with situations in which the liquidated damages far exceed (at least in the defendant's estimate) the amount of actual damages. Can a liquidated damages provision be challenged because it fixes an unduly low, rather than high, amount? Yes—the standard for justifying such a clause requires that it be a reasonable approximation. Does an unduly low liquidated damages amount satisfy the "reasonable approximation" element of the test for distinguishing liquidated damages from penalties? No. In sale of goods cases, UCC § 2-718(1) provides that "A term fixing unreasonably large liquidated damages is void as a penalty," but contains no comparable provision for clauses fixing damages at an unreasonably low amount. The comment to this section suggests, however, that such clauses may be unconscionable. See UCC § 2-718 *cmt. 1.* See also Debora L. Threedy, *"Liquidated And Limited Damages And The Revision Of Article 2: An Opportunity To Rethink The U.C.C.s Treatment of Agreed Remedies,"* 27 Idaho L. Rev. 427, 452-57 (1990/1991). But UCC § 2-719 may permit the parties to achieve the same results by limiting or eliminating liability for breach. See Roy R. Anderson, *"Liquidated Damages Under The Uniform Commercial Code,"* 41 Sw. L. J. 1083, 1106 (1988). Is it possible to reconcile these two sections? No, other than by referring to the separate evolution of the two provisions.

4. *Distinguishing between personal and economic injuries.* Should courts apply different public policy considerations to the enforceability of exculpatory clauses in cases of personal injury versus economic injury? Yes. The consequences of economic injury are usually personal to the parties involved. The consequences of personal injury are more likely to affect directly the public interest—at least the public interest that desires rules creating incentives to avoid personal injury. As noted above, the Restatement (Third) of Tort: Products Liability § 1 provides that a seller or distributor of a defective product is liable for personal or property injuries caused by the defect. UCC § 2-719(3) accords with this principle by expressly defining limitations of liability for personal injury in the case of consumer goods (but not commercial goods) as presumptively unconscionable. Notably, the court in this case, dealing with common law principles, refused to treat personal injury as a category of harm protected against the effect of an exculpatory clause. Do you agree or disagree with this rule? The *Schrier* rule is appropriate

if confined to cases of reasonable risk allocation. The rule ceases to be advisable in cases involving abuse of power and unfair results.

5. *The difference between a cap on liability and an exculpatory clause.* See "Interesting Discussion Issues" #3 above. Functionally, a cap on liability simply establishes a ceiling on damages beyond which, if the provision is enforceable, an award cannot go. The plaintiff is not relieved of responsibility for proving liability, but having proven liability cannot go beyond the cap. Can you see why a liquidated damages clause will be thrown out if not based on a reasonable approximation of the potential harm, while there is apparently no such predicate of enforceability for a damages cap? No, the public policy restriction on "penalty" damages is anomalous. An exculpatory clause, if enforceable, precludes the plaintiff from establishing liability—it has an effect similar to the extinction of the duty necessarily underlying the charge of negligence.

6. *Bargaining power and exculpation clauses.* Generally, bargaining power appears as an explicit element in only a few contract doctrines, including unconscionability, public policy, and the enforceability of certain potentially adhesive contract terms such as forum selection clauses and exculpatory clauses. See Daniel D. Barnhizer, *"Inequality of Bargaining Power,"* 76 U. Colo. L. Rev. 139, 144-50 (2005). What about the bargaining power relationship in the exculpation clause context justifies such explicit scrutiny? The opportunities for abuse of power, lack of notice, surprise and unfairness are great, as they are in the case of hold harmless provisions. See James F. Hogg, *"Consumer Beware: The Varied Application of Unconscionability Doctrine to Exculpation and Indemnification Clauses in Michigan, Minnesota, and Washington,"* 2006 Mich. St. L. Rev. 1011 (2006).

7. *Public interest and exculpatory clauses.* The plaintiff in *Schrier* argued that the court should invalidate the exculpatory clause because the burglary alarm business was "affected with a public interest." How does the court distinguish between such transactions and other, presumably non-public businesses? The distinction goes back to early English common law when courts held that neither innkeepers nor common carriers could contract out of liability for negligence. See Hogg, *supra* Note 6 at 1016, 17:

> In the United States, some courts extended the innkeeper and common carrier exceptions to hospitals, doctors, public utilities, public warehousemen, and those involved in extra-hazardous activities. Thus, in *Tunkl v. Regents of University of California*, the California Supreme Court held that a release from liability for future negligence as a condition for admission to a charitable

> research hospital was ineffective. While this decision involved the interpretation of a California statute, the court addressed the broader issue of exculpatory clauses affecting the public interest, noting that "[t]he view that the exculpatory contract is valid only if the public interest is not involved represents the majority holding in the United States." When explaining the meaning of "public interest," the court identified six characteristics of a transaction concerned with such an interest. First, "[i]t concerns a business generally thought suitable for public regulation. The party seeking exculpation is engaged in performing a service of great importance to the public" and is "willing to perform this service for any member of the public who seeks it." This party is also the "party invoking exculpation" and "possesses a decisive advantage of bargaining strength." Such party uses a "standardized adhesion contract of exculpation," and "the person or property of the [person involved] is placed under the control of the seller, subject to the risk of carelessness by the seller or his agents." Of special interest, the court associated the standard invoked with that of the historical relationship between innkeepers and their guests.

Why should the validity of the exculpatory clause depend on whether the contract deals with a subject matter in the public interest (admission to a charitable hospital for instance) or simply a private deal between two parties? There seems to be no persuasive explanation other than the historical. The Restatement (Second) of Contracts deals with this issue in § 195 while it deals with "unconscionability" generally in § 208.

8. *Nondisclaimable warranties and statutory preclusion of exculpatory clauses.* The case comments on the fact that the state legislature had precluded landlord exculpation in landlord and tenant leases, and other jurisdictions impose a mandatory, nondisclaimable warranty of habitability into residential lease contracts. See Anthony T. Kronman, *"Paternalism and the Law of Contracts,"* 92 Yale L.J. 763, 766-774 (1983). And some jurisdictions also impose nondisclaimable tort liability upon landlords who fail to take reasonable measures to protect their tenants from criminal acts by third parties. See William K. Jones, *"Private Revision of Public Standards: Exculpatory Agreements in Leases,"* 63 N.Y.U. L. Rev. 717, 738-45 (1988) and Corey Mostafa, Comment, *"The Implied Warranty of Habitability, Foreseeability, and Landlord Liability for Third-Party Criminal Acts against Tenants"*, 54 UCLA L. Rev. 971, 991-92 (2007). Likewise, UCC § 2-719(2) provides that "[l]imitation of consequential damages for injury to the person in the case of consumer goods is prima facie unconscionable . . . ." What factors would justify making warranties and liability for certain injuries nondisclaimable in some situations but

not others? Presumably, standard fact patterns where the risks of abuse of power, surprise and unfairness are most likely to occur.

Economic Injury and Failure of Essential Purpose.

Karl Llewellyn and the other authors of UCC Article 2 developed an elaborate framework into which the issues of the existence or non-existence of express or implied warranties were placed, together with the provision of or limitation on remedies for breach. This framework was discussed in Chapter 4. In cases involving the sale of goods these provisions have a powerful impact on shaping liability for breach and thus damages. UCC §§ 2-312-316(1)-(3) deal with the inclusion or exclusion of the implied warranties themselves. § 2-316(4) on the other hand, deals with the limitation of remedies for breach of any such warranties, citing the methodology found in UCC § 2-718 on liquidation or limitation of damages, and UCC § 2-719 on contractual modification of remedies. Clearly, § 2-719 contemplates that the parties may not wholly eliminate all remedies for breach through their exclusions or modifications. Comment 1 provides, for instance, that "If the parties intend to conclude a contract for sale within this Article they must accept the legal consequence that there be at least a fair quantum of remedy for breach of the obligations or duties outlined in the contract." Courts have split regarding whether a proven failure of essential purpose also renders an exclusion of consequential damages unenforceable, with some invalidating a consequential damages clause that fails of its essential purpose and others denying relief unless the consequential damages clause is also unconscionable. Finally, § 2-719(3) provides that consequential damages may be limited or excluded unless the limitation or exclusion is "unconscionable." Such a limitation for damages for injury to the person in the case of consumer goods is prima facie unconscionable, but the parties may limit damages for "commercial" losses. UCC § 2-719(3) is thus roughly compatible with the tort law principle of strict liability where a manufacturer or seller of a dangerous product is accountable for personal, but not economic, injury without proof of negligence. The "economic loss" doctrine is founded on the assumption and expectation that commercial entities can effectively negotiate contracts and warranties that allocate the risks of product failure.

Cayuga Harvester, Inc. v. Allis-Chalmers Corporation
CASE BRIEF

This is a 1983 decision of the Supreme Court, Appellate Division, of New York. Plaintiff Cayuga Harvester, Inc. (Cayuga) purchased an N-7 harvesting machine manufactured by defendant Allis-Chalmers Corporation (Allis) from defendant R.C. Church & Sons, Inc. (Church), a farm equipment dealer. Cayuga alleged that the machine did not operate or function properly and that it suffered numerous failures and breakdowns that prevented Cayuga from making a timely and effective harvest of its 1981 corn crop. In its complaint, Cayuga sought damages of $10 million, including consequential damages and loss of profits under ten causes of action: (1) and (2) against Allis and Church for breach of express warranties; (3) and (4) against Church alone for breach of an implied warranty of merchantability and an implied warranty of fitness for a particular purpose; (5) against Allis and Church for fraud; (6) against Allis alone for strict products liability; (7) against Allis alone for negligence in design, manufacture, repair, and promotion of the N-7 combine; (8) against Church alone for negligence in delivery, testing, assembly, inspection, and repair of the combine; (9) against the Cayuga's lender and Church for a judgment declaring that Cayuga had no obligation to them by reason of its purchase of the combine; and (10) against the lender and Church for a return of Cayuga's down payment. The trial court granted the defendants' motions for summary judgment with respect to claims (1), (2), (5), (6), (7), and (8) and dismissed the actions in their entirety; Cayuga appealed.

In addressing Cayuga's appeal, the court broke out the various issues as follows:

> The issues considered concerning various sections of the Uniform Commercial Code are as follows:
>
> I.A. whether the limited repair and replacement warranty failed of its essential purpose (§ 2-719, subd. 2);
> B. if so, whether, despite the failure, the consequential damages exclusion remains in effect; and
> C. whether the clause excluding consequential damages is unconscionable (§§ 2-719, subd. 3; 2-302, subds. 1, 2).
>
> The following questions, not related to the Code and pertaining to tort causes of action, are also examined:
>
> II. Whether in the cause of action for fraud, the buyer may recover consequential damages including damage to its crops and loss of profits or whether such damages are excluded . . . and whether the allegations in the fraud cause of action are of the nature that would support an award of punitive damages; and
> III. Whether in the causes of action for negligence and strict products liability, the buyer may recover for the destruction of its corn crop allegedly resulting from the defective machine or whether such damages are an economic loss for which recovery is precluded . . . .

I. In the purchase order for the combine, Allis gave an express warranty limited to the repair or replacement of defective parts. The trial court held that the exclusion of consequential damages in that warranty operated as an absolute bar to Cayuga's express warranty claims, and thus never reached the issues that the court addressed regarding the alleged failure of the essential purpose of the repair and replacement warranty under UCC § 2-719(2).

I.A. The appellate division held that, in order to establish the failure of a limited remedy under § 2-719(2), it is not necessary to show that the warrantor's conduct in failing to effect repairs was willfully dilatory or even negligent. Rather, the section was to apply whenever an exclusive remedy, which may have appeared fair and reasonable at the inception of the contract, as a result of later circumstances operates to deprive a party of a substantial benefit of the bargain. The court also held that a delay in supplying the remedy could just as effectively deny the purchaser the product he expected as could the total inability to repair. As such, the court held that the question at issue was whether Cayuga had made a prima facie showing that the limited remedy failed of its essential purpose. Since Cayuga presented evidence that the combine suffered over 100 mechanical failures over the space of eight months, and Cayuga was thus unable to harvest its corn crop, the court held that Cayuga had made such a prima facie showing, and if it could prove that allegation at trial, it would be free to pursue any UCC remedy as though the limited remedy clause did not exist. The court held that the trial court's grant of summary judgment for claims (1) and (2) should be reversed.

I.B. The court next addressed the question of whether the consequential damage exclusion in the purchase order agreement would survive a finding that the limited repair and replacement warranty in that paragraph of the agreement had failed of its essential purpose. Though authorities were in conflict on the issue, the court adopted Allis's argument that the two provisions were independent and unrelated. There was no wording in the agreement to indicate that the provisions were interrelated, or that a failure to repair or replace would invalidate the consequential damages exclusion; rather, the two clauses stood on their own and could be given effect without regard to one another. If the court had adopted Cayuga's argument that the two clauses were linked, it would have left Allis in the position where a failure to effectively repair or replace would have exposed Allis to damages many times the value of the combine, something that Allis would not possibly have intended.

Moreover, the court found that nothing in the UCC ruled out the construction that it adopted. Rather, UCC § 2-719 provides that parties are free to shape remedies to their particular requirements, and the comment thereto specifically recognizes the validity of clauses excluding consequential damages, so long as they do not operate in an unconscionable manner. The court also noted that the Third Circuit, in addressing this issue, had noted that the UCC tests a limited remedy of repair and a consequential damages exclusion by different standards. In examining jurisdictions that adopted an opposite view of the matter, the court found that, since there was no claim that Allis had acted dilatorily or in bad faith, none of those jurisdictions' leading decisions were inconsistent with the court's holding. As a result, the court held that the order granting summary judgment on the claims (1) and (2) should be modified to a grant of partial summary judgment dismissing only those elements of the claims that sought consequential damages. The court further held that claims (1) and (2) against Church must both be dismissed, as there was no express warranty binding the dealer, and because the agreement explicitly stated that the dealer had no power to make oral express warranties.

I.C. With regard to Cayuga's claim that the limited remedies were unconscionable, the court stated that a plaintiff generally must show an absence of meaningful choice on the part of one of the parties together with contract terms that are unreasonably favorable to the other party. The court also noted that courts have rarely found unconscionability in commercial transactions. Here, in light of the nature of Cayuga's business as a large commercial grower, the size of the transaction involved, the fact that Cayuga had other sources from which it could have procured equipment, the experience of its president, and his familiarity with damage exclusion causes, the court held that the trial court had properly found that Cayuga was not put in a bargaining position where it lacked a meaningful choice. As such, the court upheld the trial court's determination that the damage exclusion clauses were not unconscionable.

II. In regard to Cayuga's fraud claims, the court held that the trial court had improperly classified Cayuga's losses as being "benefit of the bargain" damages, rather than an "actual pecuniary loss." Under New York law, fraud damages are limited to indemnity for the actual loss sustained by the plaintiff (*Reno v. Bull*); the injury in a fraud action is the inducement to make a contract that the plaintiff would not otherwise have made, and thus damages for the benefit of the bargain cannot be recovered. The court held that the damages that Cayuga sought were not precluded by the *Reno v. Bull* rule because it sought damages for the corn crop that it had lost, not the profit that it would have realized if it had received the full benefit of the bargain that it sought. Since the loss of the crop was a direct consequence of the alleged fraud, the court held that Cayuga's direct pecuniary loss from any fraud on the defendants' part could be recovered. But the court held that punitive damages could not be recovered because they were only available in cases where the "wrong complained of is morally culpable, or is actuated by evil and reprehensible motives," which was not the case here.

III. Finally, the court addressed Cayuga claims (6), (7), and (8), which were based on strict products liability and negligence. It stated that the law in New York was settled that, if the loss of Cayuga's crops and consequential damages resulting therefrom were economic damages, plaintiff could not recover. The reason for this bar was explained by Justice Traynor in *Seely v. White Motor Co.*, where he said that a manufacturer can properly be held liable for physical injuries caused by defects by requiring his goods to match a standard of safety defined in terms of conditions that create unreasonable risks of harm. But a manufacturer cannot be properly held liable for the level of performance of his products in the consumer's business unless the manufacturer agreed that the product was designed to meet the consumer's demands. As a result, the court held that the trial court properly granted summary judgment dismissing claims (6), (7), and (8).

INTERESTING DISCUSSION ISSUES

1. *UCC Article 2 departures from the common law.* The implied warranties of merchantability and fitness for a particular purpose are a novel change from the common law. The provisions of UCC § 2-719 authorizing limitation of remedies for breach, while not inconsistent with common law tradition, introduce specific standards not found in the common law—the authorization of restriction of remedies to repair or replacement (if worded properly) and the exclusion of consequential damages unless unconscionable. The presumption of unconscionability in the case of personal injury is novel, as is the concept of "failure of essential purpose," one of the key issues in the case above. From one perspective, the UCC gives with one hand and takes away with the other. The implied warranties, if applicable, may give a cause of action while the limitation of remedies cuts down the relief available for breach of promise including the implied warranties.

Consequential damages are anathema to manufacturers and sellers—because of the difficulty of establishing a pricing point for the goods that would cover the risk of losses largely unpredictable to the seller. Consequential damages are thus commonly excluded. To assure compliance with the requirements of the UCC, clauses limiting or excluding liability are routinely printed in larger type, or different color or are otherwise made "conspicuous." The question raised in this case of whether the express limitation of consequential damages failed with the "failure of essential purpose" of the contract prescribed sole remedy of repair or replacement was important. The draftsperson should take note of the desirability of negating consequential damages in a clause separate from that providing for a limited remedy of repair or replacement. As pointed out earlier in this chapter an exclusion of consequential damages may not be effective to exclude lost profits under the contract breached as compared and contrasted with lost profits under a "collateral" contract.

2. *The tort law concept of "economic loss."* As the introductory notes before this case point out, tort law does not provide a remedy for "economic" (as contrasted with personal injury) loss under either a theory of negligence or strict liability. The reasons are best explained by Justice Traynor in the *Seeley* case cited in those notes. The recovery of economic loss then, becomes an issue solely of contract law and breach of promise.

NOTES AND QUESTIONS

1. *"Failure of essential purpose."* Allis-Chalmers provided a warranty limited to repair or replacement. This warranty was stated expressly to be the exclusive available warranty. Why did the district court below dismiss Cayuga's claims based on express warranty? Presumably on the ground that the contract itself prescribed an express and exclusive remedy for breach of warranty, namely repair or replacement. Did these claims not raise a material question of fact? Presumptively yes. Did they necessarily involve consequential as opposed to direct damage? Again, presumptively no. What kind of a showing did Cayuga make with respect to the alleged failure of essential purpose? They showed evidence of more than 100 machine breakdowns rendering it totally ineffective for bringing in the harvest. Did the appellate court decide that there had been a failure? Yes. If such a failure is proven to have happened, what remedies then become available to the plaintiff? Once the restrictive remedy is struck from the contract the remedies express and implied under the UCC become available such as direct damages, incidental damages and (unless effectively excluded) consequential damages. Where the gap-fillers of the UCC become available, can these remedies ever not "leave at least a fair quantum" of remedy? No but . . . They will always achieve a fair quantum of remedy unless the exclusion of consequential damages precludes the availability of such a fair quantum.

2. *Was the exclusion of consequential damages affected by the failure of essential purpose of the express warranties?* Cayuga's argument that the exclusion of consequential damages was a part of and dependent upon the express warranties and therefore failed with the express warranties was rejected by the appellate court. Do you agree? Yes—see the discussion under "Interesting Discussion Issues" above with respect to the seller's selection of a fair and effective price point for the goods sold. Under what circumstances might an exclusion of consequential damages preclude the leaving of "at least a fair quantum" of remedy? Depending on the facts of the particular case the only damage might be consequential and thus the exclusion of consequential damages might leave the plaintiff with no fair quantum of remedy.

3. *Was the exclusion of consequential damages accomplished in accordance with the requirements of UCC § 2-316? If so, how could such an exclusion be "unconscionable"?* What reasoning persuaded the appellate court that the exclusion of consequential damages was not unconscionable? Applying a basic concept of "freedom of contract," the court pointed out that the exclusion of consequential damages was express, expected and understood by parties both of whom were experienced in transactions of this sort. There was no abuse of power, surprise or great unfairness involved. Who had the burden of proof of unconscionability? Cayuga, the plaintiff seeking to have the clause excluding liability for consequential damages struck. The topic of "unconscionability" is covered more fully in Chapter 6.

4. *Unconscionability and the (unconscious) judicial bias against small businesses.* The court, in assessing Cayuga Harvester's unconscionability claims, rejects those claims in part because it determined that Cayuga Harvester had equal bargaining power compared to Allis-Chalmers and/or the dealer, R.C. Church & Sons. What factors did the court consider in making this determination? The business experience of the Cayuga manager and his ability to shop for the required machine at other sellers than Allis-Chalmers. The court asserts that "In cases involving transactions of a commercial nature, courts have rarely found unconscionability, and it has been held that 'when businessmen contract in a commercial setting, a presumption of conscionability arises.'" While the court seems to focus on the status of the parties, are there any situational factors surrounding the making of the agreement that arguably demonstrate an absence of meaningful choice, inability to negotiate, or other procedural or substantive factors that could support a finding of unconscionability? It may be a safe assumption that the form of contract employed by other sellers of such equipment carried a similar if not identical description of available relief and exclusion of any other relief. It may also be assumed that such clauses were and are "nonnegotiable." The "freedom to shop elsewhere" explanation of the court may, therefore, constitute thin ice for the court. On the other hand, finding the limitation of consequential damages provision to be unconscionable could have draconian consequences for the manufacturer and seller—consequences not considered in the fixing of the pricing point for the goods. For an extensive and detailed analysis of the judicial bias against small businesses in the context of bargaining power determinations, see Blake D. Morant, *"The Quest for Bargains in an Age of Contractual Formalism: Strategic Initiatives for Small Businesses,"* 7 J. Small & Emerging Bus. L. 233 (2003).

5. *The fraud allegation.* The court quoted the rule in *Reno v. Bull* to the effect that Cayuga, under the tort law of fraud, would be entitled

to what it had lost, not what it might have gained. Lost profits were not recoverable in tort since the measure of damages is retrospective and not prospective (as in contract). Cayuga claimed for the loss of its crops. How would those crops be valued? Presumably the cost of planting and growing as contrasted with the price at which the crop might have been sold (lost profit). Does the court suggest that the applicable value would be that in the market and, if so, would not market value include profit? Yes, thus introducing a real conundrum which the court did not explicate.

6. *Strict liability, negligence and the economic loss rule.* The court applies the "economic loss" rule to prohibit Cayuga Harvester from recovering its purely economic losses caused by the allegedly defective Allis Chalmers product under either a strict liability or negligence theory. What is the justification for this rule? See "Interesting Discussion Issues" #2 above and Justice Traynor's explanation in the *Seeley* case. Economic loss will ordinarily be experienced by one of the parties to the contract and such loss should be regulated by the terms of the bargain the parties negotiated and not trumped by a later assertion of negligent breach of contract. Do you agree that strict liability should apply to personal or "other" property damage but not to "economic loss"? Yes. See the discussion under "Interesting Discussion Issues" above. What distinguishes economic losses from personal injuries or property losses? In the case of personal injury the state has a primary interest in providing sanctions making the use of care a predictable outcome. Assume, for example, that Allis-Chalmers' harvester had exploded and the resulting fire burned all of Cayuga Harvester's crops—would such losses be recoverable under the economic loss rule as personal injury or property damage? Yes, but Jones *infra* argues to the contrary based on economic efficiency. See William K. Jones, *"Product Defects Causing Commercial Loss: The Ascendancy of Contract over Tort,"* 44 U. Miami L. Rev. 731, 731-32 (1990). Likewise, how would courts have responded to attempts by Allis-Chalmers to insulate itself from liability for such an explosion through an exclusionary clause in the contract? A number of courts would preclude any such insulation but Jones argues they should not. See id. If the exclusion of strict liability and negligence was accomplished by provisions of the contract, was there privity between Cayuga and Allis-Chalmers? This court, like those of many other states, have taken to assuming such privity between the manufacturer and the customer. In the present case the contract, as presented and signed, ran directly between the manufacturer and the customer. This is why the contract claims against the seller, Church, were dismissed.

F. UCC BUYER AND SELLER REMEDIES

In contrast to the relatively general approach toward party remedies under the common law, the UCC explicitly provides for different remedies depending upon whether the seller or the buyer breaches the contract and the circumstances of that breach. The remedies available to the buyer and seller vary with the different types of breaches, and the UCC provides non-breaching buyers and sellers with several options regarding their form of remedy. In general, however, UCC remedies provisions give both parties the option to terminate the contract and sue for money damages or to engage in "self-help" remedies such as demands for adequate assurances of performance, "cover," "cure," revocation of acceptance, and resale.

1. Buyer's Remedies

A seller can breach a contract for the sale of goods by anticipatory repudiation, non-delivery of goods, or delivery of non-conforming goods. We emphasize that the purpose of this section is not to provide a detailed exegesis on the law of sale of goods, but rather to present some important provisions of the UCC Article 2 which contrast to some extent with common law precedents.

a. Delivery of Non-conforming Goods—The "Perfect Tender Rule" Versus Damages For Loss in Value

At common law, as discussed in Chapter 8, a performance that fails to conform constitutes either a substantial performance—which gives the nonbreaching party a right to sue for damages but not to cancel the contract and terminate its own performance—or a material breach—which gives the nonbreaching party a right to terminate its performance, cancel the contract, and sue for damages for the breach. In contrast, the UCC requires that the seller's performance under a sale of goods contract must perfectly conform to the terms of the contract and, with important exceptions, gives the buyer a right to reject the goods for even minor nonconformities. In rejecting goods under the UCC perfect tender doctrine, the buyer has a duty to specify the particular defect or defects justifying the rejection, and thereafter may not rely on other unstated defects to justify rejection or establish breach.

The timing of the delivery and rejection of nonconforming goods determines the rights of the seller to cure the nonconformity, depending on whether the time for performance has expired and whether the seller reasonably believed any goods delivered would be acceptable under the contract. A seller who delivers nonconforming goods before performance is due has an absolute right to attempt to cure the defect before the time for performance expires. If the time for performance has passed, a seller has a conditional right to cure the defect, provided that the seller "had reasonable grounds to believe" the performance would be acceptable, "with or without a money allowance."

After acceptance of nonconforming goods a buyer has two options. First, even at that late date, a buyer may revoke acceptance of the delivery within a reasonable time after discovery of the non-conformity if the "non-conformity substantially impairs its value to him." But this option is only available if the buyer either reasonably assumed the seller would cure the non-conformity (and the seller actually has failed to cure), or if the buyer only discovered the defect after delivery and the defect was difficult to discern or the buyer relied upon the seller's assurances.

After the buyer notifies the seller of rejection or revocation of acceptance of nonconforming goods, the seller must give instructions regarding disposition of such goods within a reasonable time. Alternatively, the buyer may keep the goods and sue for damages for the difference between the value of the goods as promised and the value of the goods as delivered, together with incidental and consequential damages.

b. Buyer Monetary Damages for Seller Breach

If the seller repudiates or fails to deliver, or if the buyer rightfully rejects or revokes acceptance of any nonconforming delivery, UCC § 2-711 lists several options for remedying the seller's breach. First, the buyer may "cover"—that is, make a substitute purchase of comparable goods on the market and sue the buyer for the difference between the cost of cover and the market price. Second, absent cover the buyer may sue for damages based upon the difference between the market price and the contract price or, in the case of nonconforming goods, the difference between the value of the goods as promised and the value received. Third, in proper cases the buyer may obtain specific performance or replevin of the goods. Finally, a buyer in possession or control of properly rejected, nonconforming goods may resell them and offset the proceeds of resale against the buyer's damages. As discussed above, the parties may vary these default remedies through a liquidated damages clause. This section deals primarily with the first two options available to the nonbreaching buyer. The buyer may seek incidental and consequential damages, as discussed previously in this chapter, but the buyer may not recover consequential damages that it could have reasonably prevented "by cover or otherwise."

Despite clarifying the buyer's right to damages based upon the cost of cover, § 2-712 provides only ambiguous guidance regarding how the court will assess the buyer's exercise of that right. As illustrated by the following case, terms such as "good faith," "without unreasonable delay," "reasonable purchase," and even "goods in substitution" may support a challenge to the buyer's attempts to approximate the performance promised by the seller.

Dangerfield v. Markel
CASE BRIEF

This is a 1979 decision of the Supreme Court of North Dakota. In a contract dated June 13, 1972, defendant Markel contracted to sell 25,000 cwt. of chipping potatoes to plaintiff Dangerfield during the 1972-73 shipping season. Markel allegedly breached the contract by failing to deliver 15,055 cwt. during the contract period, and Dangerfield was allegedly forced to buy potatoes on the open market to fulfill a contract with potato processors. As a result of the alleged breach, Dangerfield claimed to have suffered severe financial hardship, shortage of capital, damaged business reputation, loss of business, and reduced business growth. Dangerfield prayed for general damages of \$56,310 and consequential damages of \$101,745, less a set-off of \$3,840.68 withheld by Dangerfield from payments due to Markel for potatoes delivered. Markel counterclaimed for the \$3,840.68 that Markel withheld, and for additional damages allegedly suffered as a result of the buyer's alleged breach of contract. The trial court found for Dangerfield; Markel appealed.

The court stated that the primary issue on appeal was whether or not the trial court made an erroneous award of damages to the buyer, Dangerfield, under the UCC. The trial court essentially found that Markel was entitled to damages under UCC § 2-712 for the amount expended by the buyer to purchase the 15,055 cwt. of potatoes that were due under the contract. The trial court determined that Dangerfield completed his "cover" of the contract on March 21, 1973, thirty-eight days after the date of breach. Dangerfield's purchases averaged \$4.41 per cwt. during the first half of the period, and \$5.41 per cwt. during the second half, with many purchases as high as \$6.00 per cwt. Markel argued that, under §§ 2-711 and 2-712, thirty-eight days did not constitute cover "without unreasonable delay" in a rapidly rising market; as such, he claimed that damages should have been calculated under § 2-713 (difference between market price at time of breach and contract price, plus incidental damages). Markel argued that, since the average market price at the time of breach was \$4.00 per cwt., the proper damages under § 2-713 would be \$15,894.66 less than the court awarded Dangerfield for cover damages. Dangerfield responded that, due to the perishable nature of the product involved, the cover period was not unreasonable under § 2-712.

The court held that, under § 2-712, the test of proper cover is whether, at the time and place, the buyer acted reasonably and in good faith. Hindsight regarding the cheapest or most effective cover is immaterial. Here, evidence from trial showed that Dangerfield could not cover the balance of the contract at the date of breach because no seller would commit more than one or two loads at a time because of the rising market. Despite his efforts, Dangerfield was unable to secure potatoes in February for delivery in May. The trial court agreed that Dangerfield acted reasonably, especially in light of the fact that the contract was originally intended to consist of deliveries over a period of months. The court held that, since Markel did not meet his burden of showing that cover was improperly obtained or that the trial court's findings were clearly erroneous, the trial court's award of cover damages was affirmed.

With respect to Dangerfield's claim for consequential damages of greater than $100,000 due to "severe financial hardship, shortage of capital, damaged business reputation, loss of business, and lessened business growth," the court simply quoted the trial court's decision regarding his failure to prove the damages. In this case, Dangerfield was merely entitled to recover for the additional costs incurred in covering for Markel's breach. The trial court held that Markel was not a guarantor of Dangerfield's standing as a potato broker, and in any event, Markel's breach did not put Dangerfield out of business or materially impede his operations during that shipping season. Since Dangerfield cited no authority that would allow consequential damages for a party in his circumstances, the court held that the trial court was correct in its holding.

INTERESTING DISCUSSION ISSUES

1. *Illustrating the process of "cover" and commercially reasonable behavior.* This case is helpful in getting students to deal with how cover in fact works, including the incidental costs of cover which are separately recoverable. The decision emphasizes that acts of, or attempts at, cover are to be judged by what was commercially reasonable to the buyer at the time and not by hindsight.

NOTES AND QUESTIONS

1. *The reasonableness of buyer's "cover" purchases.* In a rapidly rising market, do you think that Dangerfield (the buyer) made reasonable and prudent efforts to cover? Yes, he did the best he could when sellers would commit to only one or two loads at a time. Could he have bought more potatoes than he did at the earlier lower prices? According to the court opinion, no. What was the significance of the fact that the underlying contract called for deliveries of potatoes in a series of installments? It appears from the opinion that he could not deal with a shipment of the entire order at one time and hence the original contract was for delivery in installments, suggesting that cover in matching installments would have been appropriate.

2. *What would Dangerfield have recovered as damages under UCC § 2-713?* The difference between contract and market price at the time of breach. The market price of potatoes at the time of breach was much lower than some of the prices he paid in "covering." Markel argued that Dangerfield should be required to take his remedy under § 2-713 and not § 2-712. Do you see any reason why Markel's argument should be successful? No. If his argument were successful the intended value of cover as an alternative remedy would be negated.

3. *Would a buyer faced with a seller's breach ordinarily select "cover" under § 2-712 as a preferred remedy?* Assuming that the buyer wants to and can accomplish a substitute purchase, "cover" will be the applicable remedy. Suppose, contrary to the facts in the case above, the market price of potatoes falls after the date of the seller's breach and the buyer can buy potatoes at a price below that stated in the contract. May the buyer claim §2-713 damages, and simply not treat his post-breach purchases as "cover"? Yes. The remedies are stated as alternatives at the election of the buyer. Suppose that buyer finds it to her advantage not to cover and not to acquire substitute potatoes. In this situation, should buyer still be able to recover §2-713 damages based on the difference between the contract price and market price at the time of breach? Yes, as explained above. Should her failure to cover break the "chain of causation" of buyer's loss? According to the statute, no. Suppose the only goods available meet the purposes of the goods contracted for but have additional, and therefore, more expensive features. Should the buyer be able to treat such purchase of "better" goods as "cover" if that was the only choice available? Yes. Cover, in this situation, matches what the actual damages would have been.

4. *Recovery of "incidental" damages.* What "incidental" damages do you think that Dangerfield should have been able to recover? The costs he incurred in finding an alternative supplier. Why is it necessary to recognize a class of damages separate from the cost of cover? The costs of cover would not include such out-of-pocket expenses as telephone calls or travel, of costs of paying an agent to find an alternative supplier. Are such damages "direct" damages under the principle of *Hadley I*? Yes. Are "cover" damages also "direct" damages or must they be proven to be reasonably foreseeable by the seller at the time of entering into the contract? Cover damages are direct since they are precisely the kind of damage that can be expected to flow from a breach of this kind of contract.

5. *Recovery of "consequential" damages.* What was the nature of the "consequential" damages that Dangerfield sought to recover? According to the court, "The buyer contends that as a result of the seller's breach, he suffered consequential damages in the amount of $101,675 due to his severe financial hardship, shortage of capital,

damaged business reputation, loss of business, and lessened business growth." Should he have been able to recover these damages? Since theses are all "consequential" damages, they would have to have been reasonably foreseeable. These claimed losses were attributable to Dangerfield's lack of sufficient capital and the "squeeze" placed on his capital resources by having to pay for the cover potatoes even though he had already paid Markel and at that point was not able to recover his earlier payment from Markel. A plaintiff who decides to "cover" may well have to pay up front to purchase a substitute product from a different seller in addition to any amounts already paid to the breaching seller. How would this affect the financial situation of a buyer like Dangerfield? He got "squeezed." Should such financial strain be a basis of recovery, assuming it is proven with adequate certainty? The first question would be whether such loss was reasonably foreseeable by Markel at the time of contracting. What difficulties would a court likely encounter attempting to determine damages resulting from "financial strain" caused by a seller's breach? Insufficient certainty of proof would be an additional likely basis for denying recovery.

6. *Buyer's damages under the CISG.* See text.

2. Seller's Remedies—UCC § 2-708 and the "Lost Volume Seller" Rule

The UCC limits the remedies available to a seller, compared to those available to a buyer, in several important respects. Most notably, there is no provision for a nonbreaching seller to obtain either specific performance or consequential damages. The specific performance limitation makes intuitive sense, given that the buyer's obligations under sale of goods contracts generally are limited to the payment of money—the breach of such payment obligations may easily be remedied by money damages. The justification for limiting seller recovery of consequential damages is less obvious. While the result is clear in cases involving suit for price, the denial of consequential damages in other situations raises, on occasion, significant obstacles in the way of sellers recovering their true "expectancy" measure of damages. In seeking to limit these obstacles, courts have given a generous interpretation to what can be claimed as "incidental" damages. Outside of these limitations, UCC § 2-703 lists six options for seller remedies for a buyer's anticipatory repudiation or breach of contract for the sale of goods, including:

- Withholding delivery of goods;
- Stopping delivery by bailee intermediaries;
- Reselling or salvaging the goods and recovering damages based upon the difference between the resale price and the contract

price, plus incidental damages, minus expenses saved because of the breach (UCC §§ 2-704 & 2-706);
- Recovering damages for non-acceptance, including lost profits and overhead (UCC § 2-708);
- Maintaining an action for the contract price if the buyer has accepted or the seller cannot resell the goods (UCC § 2-709); or
- Cancel the contract.

As the following case illustrates, the parties may further alter these default rules through liquidated damages and limitation of liability provisions.

UCC § 2-709 permits the nonbreaching seller to maintain an "action for the price" against a buyer that fails to pay the price as it becomes due. In such cases, the seller can sue for that price plus incidental damages as provided for in UCC § 2-710. An action for price under UCC § 2-709 is only available in explicitly defined circumstances: (1) the goods have been accepted by the buyer, (2) conforming goods have been lost or damaged after the risk of loss passed to the buyer, or (3) having "identified" goods to the contract the seller is unable to resell after "reasonable" efforts at a "reasonable" price or the circumstances "reasonably" indicate that such an effort will be unavailing. Contrary to student expectations, an action for price is not the usual remedy.

Where the buyer has rejected the goods, however, the seller may not maintain an action for price where the buyer has rejected the goods, even where such rejection is wrongful. In such situations, the seller has two options. First, the nonbreaching seller may resell or contract to resell the rejected goods pursuant to § 2-706. Provided the seller makes such a resale in good faith and in a commercially reasonable manner, the seller may sue for the difference between the contract price and the proceeds of resale, plus any incidental costs, less any expenses saved as a consequence of the breach.

Second, and alternatively, the seller may sue for lost profits under § 2-708. In general, the measure of seller lost profit damages is based upon "the difference between the market price at the time and place for tender and the unpaid contract price," plus incidental damages, less expenses saved in consequence of the breach. But as § 2-708(2) acknowledges, in many situations this measure will not fully compensate the seller, and in that case the nonbreaching seller may claim damages based upon "the profit (including reasonable overhead) which the seller would have made from full performance by the buyer" plus incidental damages and "due allowance for costs reasonably incurred and due credit for payments or proceeds of resale." This provision has become the primary mechanism under the UCC for determining seller damages.

Section 2-708(1)—recovery of the difference between market and contract price—generally compensates the seller for the buyer's breach only where there is a market for the goods. Many sale of goods situations are not amenable to the remedy of resale and recovery of the difference between contract price and proceeds of the resale plus incidentals. Yet another type of potentially undercompensated seller is the maker of goods which are not complete at the time of breach, leaving the seller with a challenge—whether to finish the goods, thus putting more time, effort and expense, into the ultimate cost of the goods resold, or to sell the materials, as they stand, for scrap. Frequently, such goods will be "special order" with no ready market for the completed product. In such situations, the seller faces a choice between finishing manufacture of the goods and reselling the completed product, or ceasing production and selling the incomplete product as scrap. Although Article 2 does not expressly address this problem, UCC § 1-103 incorporates common law standards that are not displaced by other UCC provisions, and thus courts may analyze the seller's actions under the more general common law duty to mitigate.

In resolving the problem of undercompensation in such cases, Section 2-708(2) creates the "lost volume seller" rule. The lost volume seller rule applies only in limited circumstances. The seller must show that is had a sufficient supply of goods that it could have additionally performed the second sales contract, and that it would have successfully solicited the ultimate purchaser, even if the original buyer had not breached its contract. Nonetheless, the lost volume seller rule often appears to give sellers a windfall in terms of a double recovery of otherwise mitigated lost profits and has been heavily criticized. But courts have followed the "lost profits" approach with enthusiasm, and this subsection has been described as the seller's "pearly gates."

R. E. Davis Chemical Corp. v. Diasonics, Inc.
CASE BRIEF

This is a 1987 decision of the Seventh Circuit Court of Appeals. R.E. Davis Chemical Corp. (Davis) was an Illinois corporation; Diasonics, Inc. was a California corporation that manufactured and sold medical diagnostic equipment. On February 23, 1984, Davis entered into a written contract with Diasonics to purchase equipment; Davis paid Diasonics a $300,000 deposit on February 29. Before its purchase contract with Diasonics, Davis had contracted with Dr. Glen Dobbin and Dr. Galdino Valvassori to establish a medical facility where the Diasonics equipment would be used. Dobbin and Valvassori subsequently breached their agreement with Davis, which caused Davis to breach its agreement with Diasonics, as it refused to take delivery of the equipment or pay the balance due under the agreement. Diasonics later sold the equipment to a third party for the same price at which it was to be sold to Davis.

Davis sued Diasonics, demanding restitution of its $300,000 down payment under UCC § 2-718(2). Diasonics counterclaimed. It did not deny that Davis was entitled to recover nearly all of its deposit under § 2-718(2)(b). But Diasonics argued that it was entitled to an offset under § 2-718(3), and as a "lost volume seller," it was entitled to recover its lost profit on the contract under § 2-708(2). Diasonics also filed a third-party complaint against Dobbin and Valvassori, alleging that they tortiously interfered with its contract with Davis; the court dismissed that complaint for failure to state a claim. The court also entered summary judgment for Davis and held that lost volume sellers were not entitled to recover damages under § 2-708(2), but were limited to recovering the difference between the resale price and contract price along with incidental damages under § 2-706(1). The court awarded Davis $322,656, which represented Davis's down payment plus prejudgment interest, less Diasonics' incidental damages. Diasonics appealed the damages holding and the dismissal of its third-party complaint.

With respect to the district court's damages holding, the court stated that no Illinois court had ever addressed whether a lost volume seller's damages were limited under § 2-706. As such, the court was bound to decide the issue as it believed the Illinois Supreme Court would decide the issue. Noting that other states had unanimously adopted the position that a lost volume seller could recover its lost profits under § 2-708(2), the court held that the Illinois Supreme Court would likely follow those cases.

The court noted that, under § 2-718(3)(a), Davis's right to restitution was qualified to the extent that Diasonics could establish a right to recover damages under any other provision of UCC Article 2. While the court noted that the UCC did not provide much guidance in choosing between remedies, the district court had read the UCC to state that a seller could only recover under § 2-708 when neither § 2-706 nor § 2-709 applied. The court found this reading to be problematic in that it created a hierarchy of remedies that was not supported by the UCC itself. But while the court held that Diasonics was free to proceed under § 2-708, it held that Diasonics was not automatically entitled to its lost profit because § 2-708 provided for two alternate measures of damages. Section 2-708(2) provides for the lost profit measure that Diasonics sought, but only when the damages under § 2-708(1)—damages equal to the excess of contract price over market price—are inadequate to put the seller in as good of a position as full performance would have done.

To determine whether Diasonics met the criteria of § 2-708(2), the court first defined the term "lost volume seller." While other courts had defined the term as one that has a predictable and finite number of customers and that has the capacity to either sell to all new buyers or to make one additional sale represented by the resale after the breach. Thus, a lost volume seller would have made the sale in question whether or not the breach had occurred, and thus the difference between contract and market price would not make the lost volume seller whole. But the court added to that definition the condition that not only must the seller be able to produce the breached units in addition to its actual volume, but it also must have been profitable for the seller to produce both units. The court held that, on remand, Diasonics would need to show (1) that it had the capacity to produce the breached unit in addition to the unit resold; and (2) that it would have been profitable to Diasonics to sell both such units. Finally, to properly apply § 2-708, the court felt that it needed to address the fact that § 2-708(2) required that proceeds from resale be credited against the amount of damages, which would generally leave a lost volume seller with only nominal damages. As a result, the court adopted the position of a majority of courts, which have held that the language only applies to proceeds realized from the resale of uncompleted goods from scrap, a reading inapplicable to this case. The court reversed the grant of summary judgment in favor of Davis and remanded with instructions to calculate Diasonics' damages under § 2-708(2) if Diasonics could carry the burdens listed above.

With regard to Diasonics' third-party complaint, the court held that a complaint should not be dismissed under Rule 12(b)(6) for failure to state a claim upon which relief may be granted unless it appeared that the plaintiff could not likely prove any facts to support his claim. The elements of the tort of interference with contractual relations under Illinois law were: (1) valid contract; (2) defendant's knowledge of the contract; (3) defendant's intentional and malicious inducement of the breach of contract; (4) breach caused by wrongful conduct; and (5) resultant damage to the plaintiff. The court held that, since Diasonics had not alleged that the doctors intended to induce Davis to breach its contract, the district court had properly dismissed Diasonics' third-party complaint.

INTERESTING DISCUSSION ISSUES

1. *The case of the "lost volume seller."* The facts of the *Neri* case (see notes introductory to this case) illustrated the sometime problem of a seller in obtaining a full "expectancy" recovery. Neri contracted to purchase a boat from a retail seller. After the seller received the boat Neri repudiated. The seller later sold the boat to another buyer at the same price. From a common law perspective this was a simple illustration of mitigation of loss. But the lost volume rule under § 2-708(2) appears to depart radically from the common law. The New York Court of Appeals allowed the boat seller to keep the profit on the resale while recovering the lost profit from Neri. The reasoning was that if Neri had performed the seller would have made the profit from both sales. Interestingly, the UCC "lost volume seller" approach has

since been applied to a common law situation—see *Jetz Service Co., Inc. v. Salina Properties,* 19 Kan.App.2d 144, 865 P.2d 1051 (1993).

2. *UCC § 2-708(2) as another drafting challenge.* That section provides:

> (2) If the measure of damages provided in subsection (1) is inadequate to put the seller in as good a position as performance would have done then the measure of damages is the profit (including reasonable overhead) which the seller would have made from full performance by the buyer, together with any incidental damages provided in this article (section 336.2-710), due allowance for costs reasonably incurred and due credit for payments or proceeds of resale.

The "due credit" language would preclude recovery under a *Neri* situation. Courts have elected to ignore the application of these words to such a situation.

NOTES AND QUESTIONS

1. *Subsequent proceedings.* See text.

2. *The role and function of UCC § 2-718.* See text.

3. *Should § 2-706 be the primary or exclusive remedy?* The trial court held that Diasonic's recovery was required to be calculated under § 2-706—contract price minus proceeds of sale. As a result, that decision limited Diasonic's recovery to incidental damages since the machine had been resold at the same price as established in the Davis contract. How does the court resolve the potential inconsistency between the remedy granted under § 2-706 and that granted under § 2-708? The court found that Comment 1 to § 2-703, which catalogued the remedies available to a seller, stated that these "remedies are essentially cumulative in nature" and that "whether the pursuit of one remedy bars another depends entirely on the facts of the individual case." The court also found that courts of jurisdictions other than Illinois had not limited a seller to recovery under § 2-706 but had permitted the recovery of "lost volume seller" profits under § 2-708(2). It decided to follow the decisions of those other jurisdictions. How much weight should be accorded Comment 1 to § 2-704 which describes § 2-706 as the aggrieved seller's primary remedy? This and other courts attached no weight to this statement. See Footnote 2 to the case above. Some commentators, primarily those who consider the recovery of "lost profits" under the latter section unduly generous, criticize the court's construction of this potential inconsistency. But as the *R.E. Davis*

opinion states, courts have generally granted plaintiffs discretion to choose between the two measures of remedy.

4. *When does § 2-708(1) provide the appropriate remedy?* See text.

5. *"Due credit for . . . proceeds of resale."* The opinion in the case above intentionally ignores these words of UCC § 2-708(2) (enacted as a statutory provision). Do you think the court construed these words correctly? See "Interesting Discussion Issues" #2 above. The court decided to give these words no effect in the case of a "lost volume seller" because to give them effect would preclude that seller from a true expectancy recovery. Courts must read the words and terms of a statute (or a contract) in the context of the whole work. Moreover, courts should also prefer interpretations of statutes and contracts that avoid, as much as possible, depriving words or clauses of any effect. Finally, the words or terms of a statute (or contract) should be interpreted in the light of the proven purpose of the parties. See, for instance, James F. Hogg, *"The International Court: Rules of Treaty Interpretation II,"* 44 Minn. L. Rev. 5, 49-66 (1959-60). Critics of the "lost volume" approach have argued that the "due credit" words were included precisely to cover the case of incomplete goods sold as scrap and should not be ignored. Do you agree? No—applying these words would deprive the seller of a true expectancy recovery. The "lost volume" approach has been said to be inconsistent with the common law and UCC concept of duty to mitigate. Do you agree? Yes, but see Note 8 below and the *Jetz* case which applied the UCC approach to a common law situation. How should the "lost volume" seller be treated under the common law? The same way as treated under the UCC.

6. *The tortious interference issue.* See text.

7. *Are "lost profits" under UCC § 2-708(2) "direct" or "consequential?* Did the court above treat the "lost profits" as direct (*Hadley I*) or consequential (*Hadley II*) damages? Direct, Hadley I. Do you agree with the court's treatment of this issue? Yes.

8. *The "lost volume" seller under the common law.* See text and "Interesting Discussion Issues" 1 above.

9. *The "lost volume" seller under the CISG.* See text.

CHAPTER 10

RIGHTS AND DUTIES OF PERSONS NOT ACTUAL PARTIES TO THE CONTRACT

Table of Contents

Teaching Note

We have kept this chapter short and heavily text based. In our experience Contract professors usually run out of time before they get to the topics of third party beneficiaries and assignment. In view of that common experience, this chapter has been written in a form which can either be assigned for student reading without class discussion or made available to students for reading when the time comes for them to prepare for a bar exam. It can, of course, be used for in-class discussion. As a result, the professor who intends to cover these subjects is advised to read the full text in the book rather than the abbreviated summary that follows.

Introduction to Chapter 10 Coverage

The term "party" to a contract literally means a person who forms a contract. While one person cannot form a contract without another person, more than two persons may form a contract. Most contracts are formed between two individuals each referred to as a "party" to that contract. The term "person" includes individuals but is much broader. Accordingly, a contract may include organizations as parties.

Previous chapters focused nearly exclusively on the rights and duties of the parties to the contract itself to each other. The original parties to the contract are said to be in a relationship referred to as "privity in contract." As explored below, the concept of privity originally developed to allow the parties to the contract to sue each other but to prevent other persons—collectively referred to as "third parties"—from doing so. This chapter briefly explores the previously unchartered terrain concerning the extent to which such third parties may become engaged in the performance and enforcement of the contract. The first section considers the rights of so-called "third party beneficiaries" to enforce the terms of a promise against one of the actual contracting parties. Importantly, third party beneficiary status is created, if at all, at the time the actual parties to the contract form the contract. Once the third party beneficiary's rights become vested, the original contracting parties remain free to amend the contract but the amendment is not effective against the third party beneficiary without its consent.

The second section considers the power of one or both of the actual contracting parties to "assign" or transfer the right of some performance right due them under the contract. This section also considers the power of one or both of the actual contracting parties to delegate performance due the other party. In an assignment of a right, the assignor disappears and the assignee literally steps into the shoes of the assignor who disappears from the contract. In this sense, an assignment should be thought of as a transfer of a property interest. A delegation of duty is different. Even if a proper delegation occurs, the delegator remains contractually liable for any performance breach by the delegatee.

A. THIRD-PARTY BENEFICIARIES

Third party beneficiary doctrine determines who, other than the actual parties to the contract, has the right and therefore the standing to enforce those contractual obligations. In deciding whether a third party beneficiary has standing to sue on the contract, generally the relationship between the third party and the promisee will be examined to see whether the promisee sought the promise primarily for the commercial or altruistic benefit of the third party. The recognition of third party standing to sue is of relatively recent origin. At least until the early part of the 20th century, American common law was clearly antagonistic to third party beneficiary status on grounds that the rights of such parties were beyond contractual imagination, the third party beneficiary stranger to the contract had no equivalent or mutual obligation to match the asserted right, and lacked privity because not a party to the contract. A sea change began with the *Lawrence v. Fox*, 20 N.Y. 268 (1859) decision where the facts were found as follows:

> . . . the evidence established that "one Holly, in November, 1857, at the request of the defendant, loaned and advanced to him $300, stating at the time that he owed that sum to the plaintiff for money borrowed of him, and had agreed to pay it to him the then next day; that the defendant in consideration thereof, at the time of receiving the money, promised to pay it to the plaintiff the then next day.

This then, was the archetypal illustration of the "creditor beneficiary" model where one party, for bargained for consideration, agreed to discharge the debt of the promisee to a third party. In this situation the third party was found entitled to sue directly even though the promisee could have sued the promisor, achieving the same ultimate result but in a roundabout way. Williston thought the doctrine a narrow exception rather than the rule—compare "meeting of the minds" analytic theory. Williston modified his early theory later on. His early theory fails to reflect practical notions inherent in modern objective contract theory. In many cases, the third party beneficiary is the only party existing or sufficiently interested in the outcome to seek enforcement of the promise.

Williston's view (and that of the Restatement (First)) was, however, heavily influenced by a 1918 decision of the New York Court of Appeals, *Seaver v. Ransom,* extending the earlier *Lawrence* rule to a donee third party beneficiary. That case recognized the right of a donee third party beneficiary to bring an action against the estate of a decedent promisor to enforce a promise made for her benefit. A wife, on her death bed, instructed her husband, a judge, about the terms she wanted prepared in her will. The husband prepared a version but she was not satisfied with the draft, saying that she wanted her house to go to her niece. She was concerned she would not live long enough to sign a redrafted will and so she signed the original on the basis of her husband's promise that he would make the gift to the niece good out of his estate. When he died having failed to do so, the niece sued successfully to enforce the husband's promise to his wife, thus providing the archetypal illustration of the donee third party beneficiary.

1. Restatement Positions Compared

The Restatement (First) adopted the bifurcation between creditor beneficiaries and donee beneficiaries. The creditor beneficiary was the dominant beneficiary status, that of the donee beneficiary being residual. The critical and determinative test was the intent of the promisee to benefit the third party at the time the contract was formed. Once a creditor or donee beneficiary relationship has been found to exist, the promisor's promise may be enforced either by the original promisor or the third party beneficiary. Full and complete performance by the promisor discharges the duty to perform to both the promisee and the third party, and the promisor retains all the contract defenses otherwise available under the contract against the promisee as well as against the third party beneficiary. Creation of third party beneficiary status requires neither knowledge nor the assent of the third party beneficiary. Unless the contract otherwise provides, the parties to the contract may amend the contract but such an amendment is not effective against the donee beneficiary. In the case of a creditor beneficiary, the amendment is effective until the creditor beneficiary either brings suit upon or materially changes position in reliance on the promise.

The Restatement (Second) rejected the rigid two category approach of the Restatement (First). Instead it substituted a more flexible "intent to benefit" test, reflecting the intent of both parties and not just the promisee. The Restatement (Second) of Contracts § 310 eliminates the dual vesting rules inherent in Restatement (First) of Contracts § 142 (donee beneficiary) and Restatement (First) of Contracts § 143 (creditor beneficiary). Under those rules, a donee beneficiary's rights vested immediately when the contract was formed but a creditor beneficiary's rights did not vest at contract formation but only later upon bringing suit or incurring a material change in position. Restatement (Second) of Contracts § 310 rejects the donee beneficiary immediate vesting rule in favor of a reliance rule resembling the creditor beneficiary.

2. The Problem of Incidental Beneficiaries and Government Contracts

The range of interested parties expands nearly exponentially when government contracts are considered. The very purpose of most government contracts is dominated by some public purpose to benefit the members of the governmental unit being served. Do all the members of the public with a residual interest in the performance of the government contract have standing to enforce a breach or is enforcement restricted to the governmental party itself? These questions were answered in slightly different ways by the two restatements. In all cases, competing policies exist. The third party beneficiary law is conceptually justice based often allowing a third party to sue for enforcement when the original cannot or chooses not do so. Of course, it may well be that a private cause of action will be created by a specific state or federal statute. In those cases, the action is direct and under the statute and not derivative under the contract as a third party beneficiary. Finally, in some cases statutes may also create administrative remedies.

Both restatements exclude a category of beneficiary referred to as "incidental." Restatement (First) of Contracts § 147 provides that an "incidental beneficiary" acquires by virtue of the promise no right against the promisor or the promisee. An incidental beneficiary is defined as a residual category including all third parties deriving some benefit from a contract but not classified as either creditor or donee beneficiaries.

The definitional requirements regarding third party beneficiaries of government or public contracts have not shifted radically from the Restatement (First) of Contracts to the Restatement (Second) of Contracts. Obviously, any beneficiary of a government or public contract that is not regarded as either a creditor or donee beneficiary under the Restatement (First) of Contracts or an intended beneficiary under the Restatement (Second) of Contracts becomes an incidental beneficiary without any right to enforce the contract.

Martinez v. Socoma Companies, Inc.
CASE BRIEF

This is a 1974 4-3 decision of the California Supreme Court. Plaintiffs brought this class action on behalf of themselves and other disadvantaged unemployed persons, alleging that defendants failed to perform contracts with the United States government under which defendants agreed to provide job training and at least one year of employment to certain numbers of such persons. They claimed that they and other such persons were third party beneficiaries of the contracts and were thus entitled to damages for defendants' nonperformance. The complaint was dismissed on the ground that the plaintiffs lacked standing to sue as third party beneficiaries. The Supreme Court affirmed this dismissal, finding that the benefits to be derived from the defendants' performance were clearly intended not as gifts to such persons but as a means of executing the public purposes stated in the contracts and the underlying statute. The plaintiffs were thus only incidental beneficiaries.

The complaint named three companies and eleven individual defendants. The three companies had entered into contracts with the federal Secretary of Labor implementing a 1972 act of Congress designed to benefit residents of areas with unusually high concentrations of low income persons and chronic unemployment. The Labor Department designated the East Los Angeles neighborhood as a "special impact area" and made federal funds available for contracts with local private industry for the benefit of the hard-core unemployed residents of East Los Angeles. The Secretary then entered into contracts with each of the three corporate defendants under which each agreed to lease and renovate designated property, establish a manufacturing facility, train and employ in such a facility for a period of at least 12 months, at minimum wage rates a specific number of East Los Angeles residents certified as disadvantaged by the government.

Plaintiffs were allegedly members of a class of no more than 2,107 East Los Angeles residents who were certified as disadvantaged and were qualified for employment under the contracts. One of the eleven causes of action sought damages calculated on the basis of twelve months' wages at minimum rates and $1,000 for loss of training for each of the jobs the defendant contracted to provide. Each cause of action alleged that the "express purpose of the (Government) in entering into (each) contract was to benefit (the) certified disadvantaged hard-core unemployed residents of East Los Angeles (for whom defendants promised to provide training and jobs) and none other, and those residents are thus the express third party beneficiaries of (each) contract."

Plaintiffs contended that they were third party beneficiaries under a California statute that provided, "A contract, made expressly for the benefit of a third person, may be enforced by him at any time before the parties thereto rescind it." American law, the court said, generally classifies persons having enforceable rights under contracts to which they are not parties as either creditor beneficiaries or donee beneficiaries.

Said the court:

> A person cannot be a creditor beneficiary unless the promisor's performance of the contract will discharge some form of legal duty owed to the beneficiary by the promisee. . . . Clearly the Government (the promisee) at no time bore any legal duty toward

plaintiffs to provide the benefits set forth in the contracts and plaintiffs do not claim to be creditor beneficiaries.

The court described a donee beneficiary as follows:

> A person is a donee beneficiary only if the promisee's contractual intent is either to make a gift to him or to confer on him a right against the promisor. . . . If the promisee intends to make a gift, the donee beneficiary can recover if such donative intent must have been understood by the promisor from the nature of the contract and the circumstances accompanying its execution. . . . This rule does not aid plaintiffs, however, because, as will be seen, no intention to make a gift can be imputed to the Government as promisee.

The court considered that the fact that a government program conferred benefits upon individuals who were not required to render contractual consideration in return did not necessarily imply that the benefits were intended as gifts. Such benefits were provided not simply as gifts to the recipients but as a means of accomplishing a larger public purpose. This furtherance of public purpose was in the nature of the consideration to the government, displacing any government intent to furnish the benefits as gifts. The court quoted Restatement (First) of Contracts § 133(1)(a) with approval:

> (1) Where performance of a promise in a contract will benefit a person other than the promisee, that person is, except as stated in Subsection (3):
>
> (a) a donee beneficiary if it appears from the terms of the promise in view of the accompanying circumstances that the purpose of the promisee in obtaining the promise of all or part of the performance thereof is to make a gift to the beneficiary or to confer upon him a right against the promisor to some performance neither due nor supposed or asserted to be due from the promisee to the beneficiary;

While the government could deliberately implement a public purpose expressly conferring such individual rights, such an intent could not be inferred simply from the fact that the third persons were intended to enjoy the benefits. The present contract manifested no intention that the defendants pay damages for nonperformance. It contained a dispute provision with administrative remedies in favor of the government against the defendants and included what the court called a "liquidated damages" provision obligating the contractor to refund all amounts received from the government, with interest in the event of failure to perform. This provision, concluded the court, indicated an absence of contractual intent to impose direct liability in favor of the plaintiffs. "To allow plaintiffs' claim would nullify the limited liability for which defendants bargained and which the Government may well have held out as an inducement in negotiating the contracts." In a footnote, quoted in part, the court noted:

> Comment A of a section 145 of the Tentative Drafts of the Restatement Second of Contracts points out that these factors—retention of administrative control and limitation of contractor's liability—make third party suits against the contractor inappropriate. . . .

The true intention of the government was not to benefit individuals as such but to utilize the training and employment of disadvantaged persons as a means of improving the East Los Angeles neighborhood. The fact that plaintiffs were in a position to benefit more directly than certain other members of the public from performance of the contract did not alter their status as incidental beneficiaries.

Dismissal of the class action was affirmed.

Justice Burke wrote the dissenting opinion concurred in by two other members of the court. He concluded that the certified hard-core unemployed of East Los Angeles were the express, not incidental beneficiaries of the contracts in question and therefore had standing to enforce those contracts. It was no objection to an action by the third party that the contracting party (here the government) could also sue on the contract for the same breach. All that the California statutory section required was that the contract be "made expressly for the benefit of a third person." He concluded that the plaintiffs were express beneficiaries of the contract. The majority erred in concluding that the intended beneficiaries were the community. The intent was to benefit both the community and the individual impoverished persons in such communities. As on the facts of this case, one of the usual characteristics of a third party beneficiary contract was that performance was to be rendered directly to the beneficiary.

The fact that the government might also bring an action for the same breach did not bar the third party beneficiary from enforcing his rights.

The question was one of interpretation. On this issue he said:

> The majority contend that the inclusion of liquidated damages clauses in each of the contracts limits defendants' financial risks and was intended to preclude the assertion of third party claims. (p. 590.) Yet, these clauses simply provide for various refunds of monies advanced by the government in the event of a default. These so-called "liquidated damages" clauses nowhere purport to limit damages to the specified refunds. Nothing in the contracts

limits the right of the government or, more importantly, plaintiffs' class, to seek additional relief.

INTERESTING DISCUSSION ISSUES

1. *The rising importance of third party beneficiary issues under government contracts.* Creditor beneficiary situations are uncommon in practice. Donee beneficiary situations also appear to be limited in number. Third party beneficiary doctrine might languish as relatively insignificant in the total scheme of contract law but for the emergence and growth of cases where intended beneficiaries of government contracts claim standing to sue and right to recover damages. It is noteworthy that the decision above was reached on a 4-3 vote. The majority emphasized the fact that the contract provided remedies available directly to the government in the event of nonperformance by the contracting defendant companies. It is a challenge to figure out how damages would have been calculated and worked out had the decision been 4-3 the other way. Would the damages claimed by the class action plaintiffs have been foreseeable by the defendant companies at the time they entered into the contracts? Would such damages have been, in effect, cumulative with the repayment obligations they owed the government? The wording of the Restatement (Second) of Contracts § 313(2), including the words "consequential damages," is troubling:

> (2) In particular, a promisor who contracts with a government or governmental agency to do an act for or render a service to the public is not subject to contractual liability to a member of the public for consequential damages resulting from performance or failure to perform unless
>
> (a) the terms of the promise provide for such liability; or
>
> (b) the promisee is subject to liability to the member of the public for the damages and a direct action against the promisor is consistent with the terms of the contract and with the policy of the law authorizing the contract and prescribing remedies for its breach.

NOTES AND QUESTIONS

1. *Intent-to-benefit test.* Would the adoption of the "intent" standard of Restatement (Second) of Contracts change the result in the case? No. Both majority and minority purport to have their opinions turn on "intent."

2. *Scholarly commentary.* The majority opinion has been criticized by scholars but remains the law in California. See Ernest M. Jones, *"Legal Protection Of Third Party Beneficiaries: On Opening Courthouse Doors,"* 46 U. Cinn. L. Rev. 313 (1977). Mostly, the criticism is directed

at the finding regarding the promisor's intent. Under this interpretation, a finding of shared intentions that the beneficiaries receive the benefit of promisor's performances would be reasonable. This notion is based on the understanding that there is general agreement beneficiaries of government contracts should to be protected when promisor and promisee share intentions to provide such protection. Do you agree? Yes—so do both the majority and minority opinions—they diverge on the issue of evidence of such intent. See also Note, *"Martinez v. Socoma Companies: Problems In Determining Contract Beneficiaries' Rights,"* 27 Hastings L. J. 137 (1976).

3. *Implied right of private suit under statute.* One of the most famous situations where the United States Supreme Court has found an implied right of private action under a federal statute is § 10 of the Securities and Exchange Act, 1934. Robert S. Adelson in *"Third Party Beneficiary And Implied Right Of Action Analysis: The Fiction Of Governmental Intent,"* 94 Yale L.J. 875 (1985) compared the implied right of action under a statute with the implied right of a third party beneficiary under a public contract authorized by statute. Do you agree with the following comparative analysis?

> Plaintiffs benefited by a federal contract have two claims if the contract is breached. First, they can assert a private right of action based on the statute authorizing the contract. The Supreme Court's increasingly restrictive view of implied rights of action makes the success of this claim unlikely. Second, they can assert standing as third party beneficiaries of the contract. In recent years the number of third party claims arising from welfare-related public contracts has grown significantly. Yet courts have improperly conflated the third party beneficiary and implied right of action analyses by failing to distinguish congressional from administrative agency intent, and, as a result, have denied third party beneficiary standing in cases in which it is a conceptually distinct alternative to implied right of action standing. . . . In suits in which third parties assert rights based on government contracts, many courts focus only on intent to benefit, while other courts, more faithful to section 313 (or section 145 of the First Restatement), search for an intent to grant standing to enforce the benefit. This inconsistency, however, obscures neither the analytic similarity of third party beneficiary and implied right of action analysis nor their judicial conflation. . . . Implied right of action and third party beneficiary analyses are not the same. They implicate different levels of governmental intent. A closer judicial examination of the role of agency intent will restore the independence of third party standing to sue on public contracts. Robert S. Adelson, *"Third Party Beneficiary And Implied Right Of*

Action Analysis: The Fiction Of Governmental Intent," 94 Yale L. J. 875, 879-880. 894 (1985). Yes.

4. *The UCC and Third Party Beneficiary Status.* See text.

5. *CISG third party beneficiary rules.* See text.

B. ASSIGNMENT AND DELEGATION

Like third party beneficiary status, a third party does not become a "party" to the contract simply by virtue of an assignment of a right ("assignee") or a delegation of a duty ("delegatee"). Technically, a third party simply acquires rights or duties under the original contract and the assigning ("assignor") or delegating ("delegator") party remains a party to the contract. One exception exists. When the other party to the contract consents to release a delegating party and substitute the other party, the delegating party is no longer a party and the substituted party becomes a true party to the contract. A contract must have at least two parties and each party has both a duty to perform ("obligor") to the other party ("obligee") and a correlative right to the performance of the other party. The right to performance under the contract may be separately assigned and the duty to perform may be separately delegated. While courts tend to respect the intent of the parties when rights are assigned separately from a delegation of duties, it is also possible to "assign" or "transfer" the entire contract. When this occurs, the transfer is at once both an assignment and a delegation. Especially in such cases, the term "transfer" is often used rather than "assignment" because the latter implies a voluntary assignment whereas the term transfer is broader.

Unlike third party beneficiary law, a person not a party to the original contract generally obtains rights and duties under that contract by assignment or delegation after the contract is formed, not at the time the contract is formed. The law generally favors delegation and certainly assignment provided the assignment or delegation does not have a material negative effect upon the other party to the contract.

1. Assignment of Contract Rights

The term "assignment" has a non-intuitive aspect. By definition, when a right is effectively assigned, the assignor's right to enforce the right against the obligor is extinguished. At the same time, the assignee acquires the right to the obligor's performance. As a result, the obligor's duty is switched from the assignor to the assignee and without consent of the obligor. Of course, this alteration might come as an unwelcome surprise to the obligor who anticipated dealing with the original contract party but now must render performance to perhaps an unknown and unwelcome assignee. Notwithstanding the "rights" substitution, technically the assignee does not become a party to the contract. Indeed, the assignor remains a party to the contract with contract duties continuing to the other party. Upon breach, the assignor is subject to suit but the assignee is not.

As in the case of the obligor under a third party beneficiary contract, the obligor usually retains all defenses against the assignor. By way of exception, the assignee takes free of any modification of the contracting parties that arises after notice of the assignment.

Herzog v. Irace
CASE BRIEF

This is a 1991 decision of the Supreme Court of Maine. Gary Jones was injured in a motor cycle accident. He retained Irace and Lowry ("Irace") to represent him and bring a law suit to recover damages for his injury. Subsequently he injured his shoulder twice more, unrelated to the original accident. Dr. Herzog examined his shoulder and recommended surgery. Jones was unable to pay for that surgery but Dr. Herzog agreed to operate in return for an "assignment of benefits" in connection with his pending lawsuit. The paper signed by Jones provided:

> I, Gary Jones, request that payment be made directly from settlement of a claim currently pending for an unrelated incident, to John Herzog, D.O., for treatment of a shoulder injury which occurred at a different time.

Dr. Herzog notified Irace and Lowry that Jones had signed an "assignment of benefits" from the motorcycle personal injury action to cover the cost of surgery on his shoulder and was informed by an employee of Irace and Lowry that the assignment was sufficient to allow the firm to pay Dr. Herzog's bills at the conclusion of the case. Dr. Herzog performed the surgery and continued to treat Jones for approximately one year. In May, 1989, Jones received a $20,000 settlement in the personal injury action. He then instructed Irace not to distribute any funds to Dr. Herzog indicating that he would make the payments himself. Irace informed Dr. Herzog that Jones had revoked his permission to have them pay Dr. Herzog. Irace then issued a check to Jones for $10,027 and disbursed the remaining funds to Jones' other creditors. Jones sent a check to Dr. Herzog but it was dishonored and Dr. Herzog was never paid. He sued Irace seeking to enforce the "assignment of benefits." The trial court found there was a valid and effective assignment of the settlement proceeds enforceable against Irace. Irace appealed.

The supreme court first determined that under applicable Maine law, "We review the District Court's findings of fact based on stipulated facts and documentary evidence only for clear error."

The court stated and applied the following rules relating to assignments. The assignment must be absolute and the assignor must not retain any control over the right assigned or any power of revocation. An assignment is effective without any action by the obligor. Once the obligor has notice of the assignment, the fund is impressed with a trust for the benefit of the assignee. "After receiving notice of the assignment, the obligor cannot lawfully pay the amount assigned either to the assignor or to his other creditors and if the obligor does make such a payment, he does so at his peril because the assignee may enforce his rights against the obligor directly."

The right to settlement proceeds involved in this case was a freely assignable right. "Ordinary rights, including future rights, are freely assignable unless the assignment would materially change the duty of the obligor, materially increase the burden or risk imposed upon the obligor by his contract, impair the obligor's chance of obtaining return performance, or materially reduce the value of the return performance to the obligor, and unless the law restricts the assignability of the specific right involved." A right may be assigned in part as well as completely. The court concluded, "Given that Irace and Lowry do not dispute that they had ample notice of the assignment, the court's finding on the validity of the assignment is fully supported by the evidence and will not be disturbed on appeal."

The court then addressed Irace's claim "that the assignment, if enforceable against them, would interfere with their ethical obligation to honor their client's instruction in disbursing funds." The court disagreed, holding that a client has the power to assign his right to funds held by his attorney.

INTERESTING DISCUSSION ISSUES

1. *The troublesome ability of an assignment to affect the rights and duties of the obligor without consent of that obligor.* Many rights under a contract are rights to payment. Assignment of such rights is routine in many important commercial transactions and the presumption that such rights are freely assignable as an interest in property is well recognized. Following notice of the assignment to the obligor, payment by the obligor to the assignor no longer discharges the financial obligation—it amounts to payment to the wrong person. This case illustrates the ease with which the obligor may fail to appreciate a communication as sufficient notice of an assignment. The court in the above case paid little attention to whether Irace had adequate warning that the writing in question was a formal written assignment and not merely authorization to disperse funds to someone other than the client.

NOTES AND QUESTIONS

1. *Mode of assignment.* The *Herzog* court properly noted that the question of whether Jones made a valid legal assignment of his interest in the settlement proceeds involves interpretation of his purported intent. The particular intent required is to transfer his rights to the assigned amount permanently and without further action on his part. Restatement (Second) of Contracts § 324. The *Herzog* court phrased this intent in the reverse but similar manner—an intent to permanently relinquish the right. The particular words chosen by the assignor need not be formal such as "permanently assign and relinquish" and indeed need not even be in writing. Restatement (Second) of Contracts § 324. However, where other law requires the contract itself to be in writing (e.g., land under common law or goods under the UCC), an equal dignity rule would require the assignment itself to be in writing. See Restatement (Second) of Contracts § 324, cmt. *b*. Unless the assignment language is chosen and written by a lawyer, the language is likely to be ambiguous on the question of intent to permanently relinquish. As a result, the court must utilize the rules of interpretation discussed in Chapter 4 to ascertain the assignor's intent. As reflected in the *Herzog* case, the matter of whether an "assignment" has occurred in the first instance is of primary importance. A notice of a "purported assignment" is of no consequence as to the obligor (law firm) unless Jones made a valid assignment in the first instance. Do you agree that Jones intended to make an assignment of his payment right to Dr. Herzog? Yes, although the language of the assignment was ambiguous. It was apparently not Jones' intent that the whole settlement amount be paid to Dr. Herzog—presumably only enough to pay off Dr. Herzog's bill. The word "request" did not necessarily signal an immediate and complete transfer of the right. The clause could have been interpreted as only an authorization to Irace to pay funds belonging to Jones to Dr. Herzog. If not, what would be Dr. Herzog's remaining remedies? If the words used had been held not to constitute an assignment, Dr. Herzog would have been remitted to a claim against Jones for the value of his services rendered. The record suggests that such a claim would have ended up as a "dry well."

2. *Subrogation versus assignment.* See text.

3. *Attorney professional responsibility and ethical issues.* Lawyers' obligations to clients flow from essentially three sources: professional standards, law in general, and governing principles of ethics and morality. See Nathan M. Crystal, *An Introduction to Professional Responsibility* (Aspen Law & Business 1998). Nearly all states regulate the practice of law in that state and the regulations are interpreted and

enforced by the highest court in the state. Under the authority to regulate, courts issue rules of professional responsibility. Each state could of course simply write their own rules and standards but given the similar nature of the practice of law from state to state, most states adopt some form of standard rules promulgated by the American Bar Association. Several iterations have occurred over the years. In 1908, the ABA released the Canons of Ethics which were amended from time-to-time. In 1969, the ABA released the Model Code of Professional Responsibility. In 1983, the ABA released the Model Rules of Professional Conduct ("MRPC"). The MRPC were amended fourteen times between 1983 and 2000. In 2002 the MRPC were again amended to adopt several amendments arising from an Ethics 2000 Commission comprehensive review of the MRPC. Thus, the rules are intended to be a model and in a constant state of flux. State adoption of the MRPC in various stages varies from state to state.

When adopted by a particular state, the MRPC bear the state name such as in the *Herzog* case referring to the Maine Bar Rules. In Minnesota, the rules are referred to as the Minnesota Rules of Profession Conduct. Like the Restatement (Second) of Contracts, the MRPC adopt blackletter rules supported by comments. The comments are intended only as interpretative guides. Most states have adopted some version of the MRPC and many have varied some of the rules to some extent. State rules can usually be obtained from the website of the state supreme court and the MRPC can be obtained from the ABA website.

When a lawyer receives funds on behalf of a client regardless of the source, MRPC 1.15(a) requires the lawyer to hold that property separate from the lawyer's own property. MRPC 1.15(c) requires that a lawyer deposit into a trust account legal fees paid by the client in advance. Virtually every state now participates in the ABA Interest On Lawyers Trust Accounts ("IOLTA") program which requires that all such trust accounts be interest bearing and that the interest is not paid by or to the lawyer or the client and is not taxable to either. Rather the interest is used for public purposes to promote justice.

MRPC 1.15(d)(e) provides that if the lawyer trust account has funds over which third parties have or claim liens that are disputed, the lawyer must keep the property separate. Once separated, the lawyer assists in the resolution of the dispute and then promptly disperses the funds.

The attorney in *Herzog* argued that even an otherwise valid assignment by the client would violate rules of professional responsibility by requiring the lawyer to act adversely to the client's interest. The *Herzog* court dismissed this argument since the funds belonged to the client, the client was free to assign those funds and honoring that assignment was not an ethical violation. Did the court properly address the lawyer's concern? Perhaps. The court might have asked whether the words of the "assignment of benefits" clause were objectively clear to Irace as effecting an outright assignment. Whether the words used were intended as an assignment or not should be answered objectively from the point of view of the obligor, Irace. Did the client change his mind and direct his attorney not to make the payment to the physician? Yes—but the assignment, in the view of the court, was already complete and not rescindable. In any case, there had been detrimental reliance on it. Why would the client do so? As a guess, the client decided not to pay Dr. Herzog but do something else with the settlement money. If the client disputes the assignment and therefore the lawyer's right or obligation to pay the physician, how does the MRPC require the attorney to act with regard to the funds? Section 1.15 provides:

> (b) Upon receiving funds or other property in which a client or third person has an interest, a lawyer shall promptly notify the client or third person. Except as stated in this rule or otherwise permitted by law or by agreement with the client, a lawyer shall promptly deliver to the client or third person any funds or other property that the client or third person is entitled to receive and, upon request by the client or third person, shall promptly render a full accounting regarding such property.

According to the official comments, the rationale for this rule is that the lawyer should recognize the creditor's property interest in the funds in the lawyer's possession. One comment observes that a lawyer should hold property of others with "the care required of a professional fiduciary" and that all "property of clients or third persons" should be kept separate from the lawyer's property.

This court held that the client had the right to assign the proceeds and that Irace had to respect that right and its exercise by Jones. See Charles M. Cork, *"A Lawyer's Ethical Obligations When the Client's Creditors Claim A Share of the Tort Settlement Proceeds,"* 39 Tort Trial & Ins. Prac. L. J. 121 (2003); Sylvia Stevens, *"The 'PUSHMI-PULLYU' Resolving Third-Party Claims To Client Funds,"* 60 -SEP Or. St. B. Bull. 25 (2000). An interesting hypothetical question could be posed: what if Irace's contingent fee reduced the proceeds to an amount less than that owed to Dr. Herzog—would Irace have priority over Dr. Herzog in collecting the full contingent fee?

4. *Assignment of malpractice lawsuits and public policy.* See text.

5. *Partial assignments.* See text.

2. Delegation of Contract Duties

As discussed in the prior section, the determination of whether a right may be assigned is determined by focusing upon whether the assignment has a material effect on the other party to the contract or the obligor. Similarly, the determination of whether a duty may be delegated is determined by focusing upon whether the delegation has a material effect on the other party to the contract or the obligee. However, because the performance of a duty is much more likely to materially effect the obligee, delegation is both more restricted by default rule and contract language precluding delegation is more highly regarded.

Under the default rule, a contractual duty may be delegated to another without the consent of the obligee unless contrary to public policy or the terms of the agreement preclude delegation. An interest will not be delegable generally only when the contract involves (i) personal services of a particular individual (and not a company or business entity) or (ii) when the contract requires the exercise of personal skill or discretion.

3. Assignment of an Entire Contract

In the purchase and sale of businesses, contracts become amalgamated with all other assets. All transfer together unless language in specific contracts effectively precludes that particular transfer. Language may manifest intent to assign or transfer the entire contract rather than simply assign rights or delegate duties independently. In such cases, the assignment or transfer of the contract constitutes both an assignment of the rights and a delegation of the duties. What is the effect in a change in ownership and control of one of the parties? Does the mere fact that one of the contract business entities is owned by a different party have any impact on the transfer of the contract—even assuming the same parties will continue to perform as before the change in ownership? These questions are answered in the case that follows.

Sally Beauty Co. v. Nexxus Products Co.
CASE BRIEF

This is a 1986 decision of the United States Seventh Circuit Court of Appeal. Best Barber entered into a contract with Nexxus whereby Best Barber would be the exclusive distributor of Nexxus hair care products to barbers and hair stylists in Texas. Best Barber, the majority found, impliedly promised to use its best efforts in marketing Nexxus products. Best was subsequently acquired by Sally Beauty in a stock purchase transaction—Best was merged into Sally Beauty. Nexxus then refused to perform further and purported to cancel the agreement on the ground that Sally Beauty was a wholly owned subsidiary of Alberto-Culver, a direct competitor of Nexxus' in hair care products. Sally Beauty brought a suit for breach of contract but

Nexxus' motion for summary judgment was granted by the trial court on the basis that Best's duties under the contract were personal services which could not be assigned (delegated?). The Seventh Circuit held that the trial court erred in its ruling since the question of whether or not the contract involved personal services was a question of fact that could not be resolved on a motion for summary judgment. The Seventh Circuit, however, affirmed the resultant grant of summary judgment but on a different ground, namely that under the UCC § 210 the contract could not be assigned (transferred?) to the wholly owned subsidiary of a direct competitor. Judge Posner dissented on the ground that Alberto-Culver sold many different hair products manufactured by different companies each in competition with the others and therefore it could not be presumed that Nexxus' interests would be harmed by the sale. He suggested that Nexxus should have asked Sally Beauty for appropriate assurances that Sally Beauty would use their "best efforts" to market Nexxus products.

Sally Beauty argued unsuccessfully that the contract was freely assignable because (1) it was between two corporations, not two individuals, and (2) the character of the performance would not be altered by the substitution of Sally Beauty for Best. The successful performance of the contract, it urged, was in no way dependent upon any particular personality, individual skill or confidential relationship. The trial court ruled that the contract was of a personal nature such that it was not assignable without Nexxus' consent.

The Seventh Circuit held that Texas uses a dominant factor test in deciding whether a contract is for the sale of goods or services. It concluded that the distributorship agreement here involved was dominantly a contract for the sale of goods (majority state court view) and thus the UCC was applicable. The Code, said the majority, recognizes both delegation of performance and assignability as normal and permissible incidents of a contract for the sale of goods except where the delegated performance would be unsatisfactory to the obligee. The majority quoted UCC § 2-210(1), "A party may perform his duty through a delegate unless otherwise agreed to or unless the other party has a substantial interest in having his original promisor perform or control the acts required by the contract." While the trial court had said that Alberto-Culver's direct competition raised serious questions about Sally Beauty's ability to perform the distribution agreement in the same manner as Best, the majority held that Sally Beauty's position as a wholly-owned subsidiary of Alberto-Culver was sufficient to bar the delegation of Best's duties under the agreement. The policy behind this limitation, they said, was concern with preserving the bargain the obligee had struck. The risk of an unfavorable outcome was not one which the law could force Nexxus to take.

Judge Posner dissented. He described the majority view as "judicial intuition" about what businessmen consider reasonable. He noted that there had been no trial on the issue of Sally Beauty furnishing "best efforts." The majority's interpretation of UCC § 2-210 he said, "Does not leap out of the language of the provisions [of the UCC] or of the contract; so one would expect, but does not find, a canvass of the relevant case law." The general rule, he said, was that a change of corporate form, including a merger, did not in and of itself affect contractual rights and obligations. He noted that Alberto-Culver distributed hair care supplies made by many different companies which, so far as appeared, competed with Alberto-Culver as vigorously as Nexxus did. He concluded that it was not very likely that the acquisition of Best could hurt Nexxus—that there was no real conflict in fact.

INTERESTING DISCUSSION ISSUES

1. *The sale and purchase of a business, due diligence and review of the seller's contracts.* Lawyers who do mergers, acquisitions and sales of businesses are familiar with the obligations of the buyer to do a "due diligence" review of the seller's contracts, among other things. The problem in the above case would not necessarily "jump out" at the due diligence reviewer as one likely to cause difficulties after the sale or merger. Had the buyer's lawyer in the instant case "caught" the issue, the buyer, Sally Beauty, might have concluded that the sale and merger should go forward anyway—a buyer's business judgment. The lawyer, however, does not want to be caught having failed to flag and advise the buyer of the potential problem of nonassignability of the contract. It is trite black letter law that a personal services contract cannot be delegated and therefore cannot be effectively "transferred." This case illustrates the grey area of law—the boundaries of such personal service contracts. One of the teachings of this case is the need for careful review and assessment of the seller's contracts for problems of this sort.

NOTES AND QUESTIONS

1. *Transfer versus assignment.* The contract in this case was transferred by operation of law under Texas corporate merger law. Once the shareholders of both corporations approve a plan of merger, all the assets and liabilities of the target corporation transfer by operation of law to the surviving corporation on the effective date specified in the plan of merger. Should it matter that the transfer occurred as a matter of law rather than by way of a "voluntary" assignment of the entire but isolated contract? No—the question is one of impact on performance contracted for by the obligee. If the delegation is not prohibited by the contract itself, what test does the common law apply to determine whether the delegation is effective? Whether the performance contracted for by the obligee would be

adversely affected by the delegation. Although the court disproved of the delegation could the rights have been assigned separately from the delegation of duties? Yes. The rights would have been to payment for the Nexxus products sold and rights to payment are usually assignable.

2. *Terms prohibiting delegation.* The contract in *Sally Beauty* did not include language prohibiting a delegation of duties. If it had included such language would the court have reached a different conclusion? For the majority, the conclusion in this context would have been *a fortiori*.

3. *Posner dissent.* Judge Posner makes a compelling argument that at least on this record it is unclear that the delegation will have a material negative impact on Nexxus. In so doing he attempts to analyze the essence of the Nexxus' argument—that the company that acquired Sally Beauty is a competitor. Judge Posner concludes they have very little in common in the competitive market place because of how and where the products are sold. Is that the only test? No—the issue was whether Nexxus' products would, under the circumstances following the merger, receive the "best efforts" of the Alberto-Culver subsidiary. Regardless of where marketed, does Alberto-Culver sell substitute products similar to Nexxus? Yes. For an interesting analysis of Judge Posner's dissenting opinions in general (including *Sally Beauty*), see Robert F. Blomquist, *"Dissent, Posner-Style: Judge Richard A. Posner's First Decade of Dissenting Opinions: 1981-1991—Toward An Aesthetics of Judicial Dissenting Style,"* 69 Mo. L. Rev. 73 (2004).